Student Supplement to accompany

Principles of
Corporate Finance

Tenth Edition

With Select Material from

Solutions Manual
Tenth Edition

Prepared by
George Geis
University of Virginia

and

Study Guide
Tenth Edition

Prepared by
V. Sivarama Krishnan
University of Central Oklahoma

for Principles of Corporate Finance
Tenth Edition

Richard A. Brealey
London Business School

Stewart C. Myers
Massachusetts Institute of Technology

Franklin Allen
University of Pennsylvania

 **Learning Solutions**

Boston   Burr Ridge, IL   Dubuque, IA   New York   San Francisco   St. Louis
Bangkok   Bogotá   Caracas   Lisbon   London   Madrid
Mexico City   Milan   New Delhi   Seoul   Singapore   Sydney   Taipei   Toronto

The McGraw·Hill Companies

Student Supplement to accompany Principles of Corporate Finance, Tenth Edition

This book is a McGraw-Hill Learning Solutions textbook and contains select material from the following sources:
Solutions Manual for Principles of Corporate Finance, Tenth Edition prepared by George Geis. Copyright © 2011, 2008, 2006, 2003, 2000, 1996, 1991, 1988, 1984, 1981 by The McGraw-Hill Companies, Inc.
Study Guide for Principles of Corporate Finance, Tenth Edition prepared by V. Sivarama Krishnan. Copyright © 2011, 2008, 2006, 2003, 2000, 1996, 1991, 1988, 1984, 1981 by The McGraw-Hill Companies, Inc.
Reprinted with permission of the publisher. Many custom published texts are modified versions or adaptations of our best-selling textbooks. Some adaptations are printed in black and white to keep prices at a minimum, while others are in color.

2 3 4 5 6 7 8 9 0   DIG DIG   12 11 10

ISBN-13: 978-0-07-747335-8
ISBN-10: 0-07-747335-3

Learning Solutions Representative: Nikki Schmitt
Production Editor: Jessica Portz
Cover Design: Aivo Kivi
Printer/Binder: Digital Impressions

Solutions Manual

for

Principles of
Corporate Finance

Tenth Edition

TABLE OF CONTENTS

CHAPTER 1
Goals and Governance of the Firm

Answers to Problem Sets

1. a. real

    b. executive airplanes

    c. brand names

    d. financial

    e. bonds

    f. investment

    g. capital budgeting

    h. financing

2. c, d, e, and g are real assets. Others are financial.

3. a. Financial assets, such as stocks or bank loans, are claims held by investors. Corporations sell financial assets to raise the cash to invest in real assets such as plant and equipment. Some real assets are intangible.

    b. Capital budgeting means investment in real assets. Financing means raising the cash for this investment.

    c. The shares of public corporations are traded on stock exchanges and can be purchased by a wide range of investors. The shares of closely held corporations are not traded and are not generally available to investors.

    d. Unlimited liability: investors are responsible for all the firm's debts. A sole proprietor has unlimited liability. Investors in corporations have limited liability. They can lose their investment, but no more.

    e. A corporation is a separate legal "person" with unlimited life. Its owners hold shares in the business. A partnership is a limited-life agreement to establish and run a business.

4.   c, d.

5.   b, c.

6.   Separation of ownership and management typically leads to agency problems, where managers prefer to consume private perks or make other decisions for their private benefit – rather than maximize shareholder wealth.

7.   a.   Assuming that the encabulator market is risky, an 8% expected return on the F&H encabulator investments may be inferior to a 4% return on U.S. government securities.

     b.   Unless their financial assets are as safe as U.S. government securities, their cost of capital would be higher. The CFO could consider what the expected return is on assets with similar risk.

8.   Shareholders will only vote for (a) maximize shareholder wealth. Shareholders can modify their pattern of consumption through borrowing and lending, match risk preferences, and hopefully balance their own checkbooks (or hire a qualified professional to help them with these tasks).

9.   If the investment increases the firm's wealth, it will increase the value of the firm's shares. Ms. Espinoza could then sell some or all of these more valuable shares in order to provide for her retirement income.

10. As the Putnam example illustrates, the firm's value typically falls by significantly more than the amount of any fines and settlements. The firm's reputation suffers in a financial scandal, and this can have a much larger effect than the fines levied. Investors may also wonder whether all of the misdeeds have been contained.

11. Managers would act in shareholders' interests because they have a legal duty to act in their interests. Managers may also receive compensation, either bonuses or stock and option payouts whose value is tied (roughly) to firm performance. Managers may fear personal reputational damage that would result from not acting in shareholders' interests. And managers can be fired by the board of directors, which in turn is elected by shareholders. If managers still fail to act in shareholders' interests, shareholders may sell their shares, lowering the stock price, and potentially creating the possibility of a takeover, which can again lead to changes in the board of directors and senior management.

12. Managers that are insulated from takeovers may be more prone to agency problems and therefore more likely to act in their own interests rather than in shareholders'. If a firm instituted a new takeover defense, we might expect to see the value of its shares decline as agency problems increase and less shareholder value maximization occurs. The counterargument is that defensive measures allow managers to negotiate for a higher purchase price in the face of a takeover bid – to the benefit of shareholder value.

Appendix Questions:

1. Both would still invest in their friend's business. A invests and receives $121,000 for his investment at the end of the year (which is greater than the $120,000 it would receive from lending at 20%). G also invests, but borrows against the $121,000 payment, and thus receives $100,833 today.

2. a. He could consume up to $200,000 now (foregoing all future consumption) or up to $216,000 next year (200,000*1.08, foregoing all consumption this year). To choose the same consumption (C) in both years, C = (200,000 – C) × 1.08 or
C = $103,846.

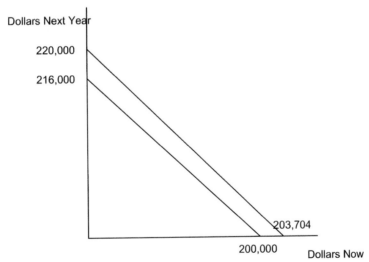

b. He should invest all of his wealth to earn $220,000 next year. If he consumes all this year, he can now have a total of $203,703.7 (200,000 × 1.10/1.08) this year or $220,000 next year. If he consumes C this year, the amount available for next year's consumption is (203,703.7 – C) x 1.08. To get equal consumption in both years, set the amount consumed today equal to the amount next year:
C = (203,703.7 – C) × 1.08
C = $105,769.2

CHAPTER 2
How to Calculate Present Values

Answers to Problem Sets

1. If the discount factor is .507, then $.507 * 1.12^6 = \$1$

2. $125/139 = .899$

3. $PV = 374/(1.09)^9 = 172.20$

4. $PV = 432/1.15 + 137/(1.15^2) + 797/(1.15^3) = 376 + 104 + 524 = \$1,003$

5. $FV = 100 * 1.15^8 = \$305.90$

6. $NPV = -1,548 + 138/.09 = -14.67$ (cost today plus the present value of the perpetuity)

7. $PV = 4/(.14 - .04) = \$40$

8. a. $PV = 1/.10 = \$10$

   b. Since the perpetuity will be worth $10 in year 7, and since that is roughly double the present value, the approximate PV equals $5.
   $PV = (1 / .10)/(1.10)^7 = 10/2 = \$5$ (approximately)

   c. A perpetuity paying $1 starting now would be worth $10, whereas a perpetuity starting in year 8 would be worth roughly $5. The difference between these cash flows is therefore approximately $5. $PV = 10 - 5 = \$5$ (approximately)

   d. $PV = C/(r - g) = 10,000/(.10 - .05) = \$200,000.$

9. a. $PV = 10{,}000/(1.05^5) = \$7{,}835.26$ (assuming the cost of the car does not appreciate over those five years).

    b. You need to set aside (12,000 × 6-year annuity factor) = 12,000 × 4.623 = $55,476.

    c. At the end of 6 years you would have $1.08^6 \times (60{,}476 - 55{,}476) = \$7{,}934$.

10. a. $FV = 1{,}000e^{.12 \times 5} = 1{,}000e^{.6} = \$1{,}822.12$.

    b. $PV = 5e^{-.12 \times 8} = 5e^{-.96} = \$1.914$ million

    c. $PV = C \left(1/r - 1/re^{rt}\right) = 2{,}000(1/.12 - 1/.12e^{.12 \times 15}) = \$13{,}912$

11. a. $FV = 10{,}000{,}000 \times (1.06)^4 = 12{,}624{,}770$

    b. $FV = 10{,}000{,}000 \times (1 + .06/12)^{(4 \times 12)} = 12{,}704{,}892$

    c. $FV = 10{,}000{,}000 \times e^{(4 \times .06)} = 12{,}712{,}492$

12. a. $PV = \$100/1.01^{10} = \$90.53$

        $PV = \$100/1.13^{10} = \$29.46$

        $PV = \$100/1.25^{15} = \$3.52$

        $PV = \$100/1.12 + \$100/1.12^2 + \$100/1.12^3 = \$240.18$

13. a. $DF_1 = \dfrac{1}{1+r_1} = 0.905 \Rightarrow r_1 = 0.1050 = 10.50\%$

    b. $DF_2 = \dfrac{1}{(1+r_2)^2} = \dfrac{1}{(1.105)^2} = 0.819$

    c. $AF_2 = DF_1 + DF_2 = 0.905 + 0.819 = 1.724$

    d. PV of an annuity = $C \times$ [Annuity factor at r% for t years]

Here:

$24.65 = $10 \times [AF_3]$

$AF_3 = 2.465$

e. $AF_3 = DF_1 + DF_2 + DF_3 = AF_2 + DF_3$

$2.465 = 1.724 + DF_3$

$DF_3 = 0.741$

14. The present value of the 10-year stream of cash inflows is:

$$PV = \$170{,}000 \times \left[\frac{1}{0.14} - \frac{1}{0.14 \times (1.14)^{10}}\right] = \$886{,}739.66$$

Thus:

$$NPV = -\$800{,}000 + \$886{,}739.66 = +\$86{,}739.66$$

At the end of five years, the factory's value will be the present value of the five remaining $170,000 cash flows:

$$PV = \$170{,}000 \times \left[\frac{1}{0.14} - \frac{1}{0.14 \times (1.14)^{5}}\right] = \$583{,}623.76$$

15.

$$NPV = \sum_{t=0}^{10} \frac{C_t}{(1.12)^t} = -\$380{,}000 + \frac{\$50{,}000}{1.12} + \frac{\$57{,}000}{1.12^2} + \frac{\$75{,}000}{1.12^3} + \frac{\$80{,}000}{1.12^4} + \frac{\$85{,}000}{1.12^5}$$

$$+ \frac{\$92{,}000}{1.12^6} + \frac{\$92{,}000}{1.12^7} + \frac{\$80{,}000}{1.12^8} + \frac{\$68{,}000}{1.12^9} + \frac{\$50{,}000}{1.12^{10}} = \$23{,}696.15$$

16. a. Let S_t = salary in year t

$$PV = \sum_{t=1}^{30} \frac{40{,}000 \, (1.05)^{t-1}}{(1.08)^t}$$

$$= 40{,}000 \times \left[\frac{1}{(.08-.05)} - \frac{(1.05)^{30}}{(.08-.05) \times (1.08)^{30}}\right] = \$760{,}662.53$$

b.   PV(salary) × 0.05 = $38,033.13

Future value = $38,018.96 × $(1.08)^{30}$ = $382,714.30

c.

$$PV = C \times \left[\frac{1}{r} - \frac{1}{r \times (1+r)^t} \right]$$

$$\$382,714.30 = C \times \left[\frac{1}{0.08} - \frac{1}{0.08 \times (1.08)^{20}} \right]$$

$$C = \$382,714.30 \Bigg/ \left[\frac{1}{0.08} - \frac{1}{0.08 \times (1.08)^{20}} \right] = \$38,980.30$$

17.

Period		Present Value
0		−400,000.00
1	+100,000/1.12 =	+ 89,285.71
2	+200,000/1.12^2 =	+159,438.78
3	+300,000/1.12^3 =	+213,534.07
	Total = NPV =	$62,258.56

18.   We can break this down into several different cash flows, such that the sum of these separate cash flows is the total cash flow. Then, the sum of the present values of the separate cash flows is the present value of the entire project. (All dollar figures are in millions.)

- Cost of the ship is $8 million

  PV = −$8 million

- Revenue is $5 million per year, operating expenses are $4 million. Thus, operating cash flow is $1 million per year for 15 years.

  $$PV = \$1\,\text{million} \times \left[\frac{1}{0.08} - \frac{1}{0.08 \times (1.08)^{15}} \right] = \$8.559\ \text{million}$$

- Major refits cost $2 million each, and will occur at times t = 5 and t = 10.

  PV = (−$2 million)/$1.08^5$ + (−$2 million)/$1.08^{10}$ = −$2.288 million

- Sale for scrap brings in revenue of $1.5 million at t = 15.

  PV = $1.5 million/$1.08^{15}$ = $0.473 million

Adding these present values gives the present value of the entire project:

NPV = –$8 million + $8.559 million – $2.288 million + $0.473 million
NPV = –$1.256 million

19.   a.   PV = $100,000

      b.   PV = $180,000/$1.12^5$ = $102,136.83

      c.   PV = $11,400/0.12 = $95,000

      d. $PV = \$19,000 \times \left[\dfrac{1}{0.12} - \dfrac{1}{0.12 \times (1.12)^{10}} \right] = \$107,354.24$

      e.   PV = $6,500/(0.12 – 0.05) = $92,857.14

Prize (d) is the most valuable because it has the highest present value.

20.   Mr. Basset is buying a security worth $20,000 now. That is its present value. The unknown is the annual payment. Using the present value of an annuity formula, we have:

$$PV = C \times \left[\frac{1}{r} - \frac{1}{r \times (1+r)^t} \right]$$

$$\$20,000 = C \times \left[\frac{1}{0.08} - \frac{1}{0.08 \times (1.08)^{12}} \right]$$

$$C = \$20,000 \Bigg/ \left[\frac{1}{0.08} - \frac{1}{0.08 \times (1.08)^{12}} \right] = \$2,653.90$$

21.   Assume the Zhangs will put aside the same amount each year. One approach to solving this problem is to find the present value of the cost of the boat and then equate that to the present value of the money saved. From this equation, we can solve for the amount to be put aside each year.

$$PV(boat) = \$20,000/(1.10)^5 = \$12,418$$

$$PV(savings) = \text{Annual savings} \times \left[\frac{1}{0.10} - \frac{1}{0.10 \times (1.10)^5} \right]$$

Because PV(savings) must equal PV(boat):

$$\text{Annual savings} \times \left[\frac{1}{0.10} - \frac{1}{0.10 \times (1.10)^5} \right] = \$12,418$$

$$\text{Annual savings} = \$12,418 \Big/ \left[\frac{1}{0.10} - \frac{1}{0.10 \times (1.10)^5} \right] = \$3,276$$

Another approach is to use the future value of an annuity formula:

$$\text{Annual savings} \times \left[\frac{(1+.10)^5 - 1}{.10} \right] = \$20,000$$

$$\text{Annual savings} = \$3,276$$

22. The fact that Kangaroo Autos is offering "free credit" tells us what the cash payments are; it does not change the fact that money has time value. A 10% annual rate of interest is equivalent to a monthly rate of 0.83%:

$$r_{monthly} = r_{annual}/12 = 0.10/12 = 0.0083 = 0.83\%$$

The present value of the payments to Kangaroo Autos is:

$$\$1,000 + \$300 \times \left[\frac{1}{0.0083} - \frac{1}{0.0083 \times (1.0083)^{30}} \right] = \$8,938$$

A car from Turtle Motors costs \$9,000 cash. Therefore, Kangaroo Autos offers the better deal, i.e., the lower present value of cost.

23. The NPVs are:

$$\text{at } 5\% \Rightarrow NPV = -\$170,000 - \frac{\$100,000}{1.05} + \frac{\$320,000}{(1.05)^2} = \$25,011$$

$$\text{at } 10\% \Rightarrow NPV = -\$170,000 - \frac{\$100,000}{1.10} + \frac{320,000}{(1.10)^2} = \$3,554$$

$$\text{at } 15\% \Rightarrow NPV = -\$170,000 - \frac{\$100,000}{1.15} + \frac{320,000}{(1.15)^2} = -\$14,991$$

The figure below shows that the project has zero NPV at about 11%.

As a check, NPV at 11% is:

$$NPV = -\$170,000 - \frac{\$100,000}{1.11} + \frac{320,000}{(1.11)^2} = -\$371$$

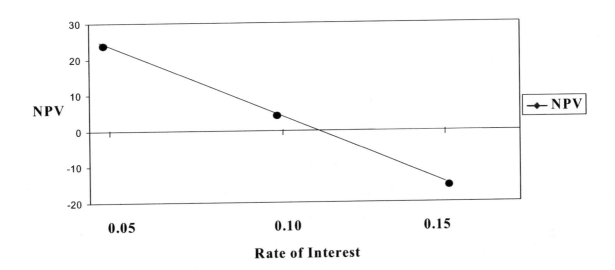

24. a. This is the usual perpetuity, and hence:

$$PV = \frac{C}{r} = \frac{\$100}{0.07} = \$1,428.57$$

   b. This is worth the PV of stream (a) *plus* the immediate payment of $100:

$$PV = \$100 + \$1,428.57 = \$1,528.57$$

   c. The continuously compounded equivalent to a 7% annually compounded rate is approximately 6.77%, because:

$$e^{0.0677} = 1.0700$$

Thus:

$$PV = \frac{C}{r} = \frac{\$100}{0.0677} = \$1,477.10$$

Note that the pattern of payments in part (b) is more valuable than the pattern of payments in part (c). It is preferable to receive cash flows at the start of every year than to spread the receipt of cash evenly over the year; with the former pattern of payment, you receive the cash more quickly.

25. a. PV = $1 billion/0.08 = $12.5 billion

b. PV = $1 billion/(0.08 – 0.04) = $25.0 billion

c. $PV = \$1 \text{ billion} \times \left[\dfrac{1}{0.08} - \dfrac{1}{0.08 \times (1.08)^{20}} \right] = \$9.818 \text{ billion}$

d. The continuously compounded equivalent to an 8% annually compounded rate is approximately 7.7% , because:

$$e^{0.0770} = 1.0800$$

Thus:

$$PV = \$1 \text{ billion} \times \left[\frac{1}{0.077} - \frac{1}{0.077 \times e^{(0.077)(20)}} \right] = \$10.203 \text{ billion}$$

This result is greater than the answer in Part (c) because the endowment is now earning interest during the entire year.

26. With annual compounding: FV = $100 × (1.15)^{20} = $1,636.65

With continuous compounding: FV = $100 × $e^{(0.15 \times 20)}$ = $2,008.55

27. One way to approach this problem is to solve for the present value of:
(1) $100 per year for 10 years, and
(2) $100 per year in perpetuity, with the first cash flow at year 11.
If this is a fair deal, these present values must be equal, and thus we can solve for the interest rate (r).
The present value of $100 per year for 10 years is:

$$PV = \$100 \times \left[\frac{1}{r} - \frac{1}{(r) \times (1+r)^{10}} \right]$$

The present value, as of year 10, of $100 per year forever, with the first payment in year 11, is: $PV_{10} = \$100/r$

At t = 0, the present value of PV_{10} is:

$$PV = \left[\frac{1}{(1+r)^{10}} \right] \times \left[\frac{\$100}{r} \right]$$

Equating these two expressions for present value, we have:

$$\$100 \times \left[\frac{1}{r} - \frac{1}{(r) \times (1+r)^{10}} \right] = \left[\frac{1}{(1+r)^{10}} \right] \times \left[\frac{\$100}{r} \right]$$

Using trial and error or algebraic solution, we find that r = 7.18%.

28. Assume the amount invested is one dollar.
    Let A represent the investment at 12%, compounded annually.
    Let B represent the investment at 11.7%, compounded semiannually.
    Let C represent the investment at 11.5%, compounded continuously.

    After one year:

    $FV_A = \$1 \times (1 + 0.12)^1 \quad = \$1.1200$

    $FV_B = \$1 \times (1 + 0.0585)^2 \quad = \$1.1204$

    $FV_C = \$1 \times e^{(0.115 \times 1)} \quad = \$1.1219$

    After five years:

    $FV_A = \$1 \times (1 + 0.12)^5 \quad = \$1.7623$

    $FV_B = \$1 \times (1 + 0.0585)^{10} \quad = \$1.7657$

    $FV_C = \$1 \times e^{(0.115 \times 5)} \quad = \$1.7771$

    After twenty years:

    $FV_A = \$1 \times (1 + 0.12)^{20} \quad = \$9.6463$

    $FV_B = \$1 \times (1 + 0.0585)^{40} \quad = \$9.7193$

    $FV_C = \$1 \times e^{(0.115 \times 20)} \quad = \$9.9742$

    The preferred investment is C.

29. Because the cash flows occur every six months, we first need to calculate the equivalent semi-annual rate. Thus, $1.08 = (1 + r/2)^2$ => r = 7.85 semi-annually compounded APR. Therefore the rate for six months is 7.85/2 or 3.925%:

    $$PV = \$100,000 + \$100,000 \times \left[\frac{1}{0.03925} - \frac{1}{0.03925 \times (1.03925)^9} \right] = \$846,081$$

30. a. Each installment is: $9,420,713/19 = $495,827

    $$PV = \$495,827 \times \left[\frac{1}{0.08} - \frac{1}{0.08 \times (1.08)^{19}} \right] = \$4,761,724$$

b. If ERC is willing to pay \$4.2 million, then:

$$\$4,200,000 = \$495,827 \times \left[\frac{1}{r} - \frac{1}{r \times (1+r)^{19}} \right]$$

Using Excel or a financial calculator, we find that r = 9.81%.

31. a. $$PV = \$70,000 \times \left[\frac{1}{0.08} - \frac{1}{0.08 \times (1.08)^8} \right] = \$402,264.73$$

b.

Year	Beginning-of-Year Balance	Year-end Interest on Balance	Total Year-end Payment	Amortization of Loan	End-of-Year Balance
1	402,264.73	32,181.18	70,000.00	37,818.82	364,445.91
2	364,445.91	29,155.67	70,000.00	40,844.33	323,601.58
3	323,601.58	25,888.13	70,000.00	44,111.87	279,489.71
4	279,489.71	22,359.18	70,000.00	47,640.82	231,848.88
5	231,848.88	18,547.91	70,000.00	51,452.09	180,396.79
6	180,396.79	14,431.74	70,000.00	55,568.26	124,828.54
7	124,828.54	9,986.28	70,000.00	60,013.72	64,814.82
8	64,814.82	5,185.19	70,000.00	64,814.81	0.01

32. This is an annuity problem with the present value of the annuity equal to \$2 million (as of your retirement date), and the interest rate equal to 8% with 15 time periods. Thus, your annual level of expenditure (C) is determined as follows:

$$PV = C \times \left[\frac{1}{r} - \frac{1}{r \times (1+r)^t} \right]$$

$$\$2,000,000 = C \times \left[\frac{1}{0.08} - \frac{1}{0.08 \times (1.08)^{15}} \right]$$

$$C = \$2,000,000 \Big/ \left[\frac{1}{0.08} - \frac{1}{0.08 \times (1.08)^{15}} \right] = \$233,659$$

With an inflation rate of 4% per year, we will still accumulate \$2 million as of our retirement date. However, because we want to spend a constant amount per year in real terms (R, constant for all t), the nominal amount (C_t) must increase each year. For each year t: $R = C_t /(1 + \text{inflation rate})^t$

Therefore:

PV [all C_t] = PV [all $R \times (1 + \text{inflation rate})^t$] = \$2,000,000

$$R \times \left[\frac{(1+0.04)^1}{(1+0.08)^1} + \frac{(1+0.04)^2}{(1+0.08)^2} + \ldots + \frac{(1+0.04)^{15}}{(1+0.08)^{15}} \right] = \$2,000,000$$

$R \times [0.9630 + 0.9273 + \ldots + 0.5677] = \$2,000,000$

$R \times 11.2390 = \$2,000,000$

$R = \$177,952$

Alternatively, consider that the real rate is $\frac{(1+0.08)}{(1+0.04)} - 1 = .03846$. Then, redoing the steps above using the real rate gives a real cash flow equal to:

$$C = \$2,000,000 \Big/ \left[\frac{1}{0.03846} - \frac{1}{0.03846 \times (1.03846)^{15}} \right] = \$177,952$$

Thus C_1 = (\$177,952 × 1.04) = \$185,070, C_2 = \$192,473, etc.

33. a. $$PV = \$50,000 \times \left[\frac{1}{0.055} - \frac{1}{0.055 \times (1.055)^{12}} \right] = \$430,925.89$$

   b. The annually compounded rate is 5.5%, so the semiannual rate is:

   $(1.055)^{(1/2)} - 1 = 0.0271 = 2.71\%$

   Since the payments now arrive six months earlier than previously:

   PV = \$430,925.89 × 1.0271 = \$442,603.98

34. In three years, the balance in the mutual fund will be:

   FV = \$1,000,000 × $(1.035)^3$ = \$1,108,718

   The monthly shortfall will be: \$15,000 – (\$7,500 + \$1,500) = \$6,000

   Annual withdrawals from the mutual fund will be: \$6,000 × 12 = \$72,000

   Assume the first annual withdrawal occurs three years from today, when the balance in the mutual fund will be \$1,108,718. Treating the withdrawals as an annuity due, we solve for t as follows:

   $$PV = C \times \left[\frac{1}{r} - \frac{1}{r \times (1+r)^t} \right] \times (1+r)$$

$$\$1{,}108{,}718 = \$72{,}000 \times \left[\frac{1}{0.035} - \frac{1}{0.035 \times (1.035)^t} \right] \times 1.035$$

Using Excel or a financial calculator, we find that t = 22.5 years.

35.   a.   PV = 2/.12 = \$16.667 million

b. $PV = \$2 \times \left[\dfrac{1}{0.12} - \dfrac{1}{0.12 \times (1.12)^{20}} \right] = \$14.939 \text{ million}$

c.   PV = 2/(.12 − .03) = \$22.222 million

d. $PV = \$2 \times \left[\dfrac{1}{(0.12 - .03)} - \dfrac{1.03^{20}}{(0.12 - .03) \times (1.12)^{20}} \right] = \$18.061 \text{ million}$

36.   a.   Using the Rule of 72, the time for money to double at 12% is 72/12, or 6 years. More precisely, if x is the number of years for money to double, then:

$(1.12)^x = 2$

Using logarithms, we find:

x (ln 1.12) = ln 2

x = 6.12 years

b.   With continuous compounding for interest rate r and time period x:

$e^{rx} = 2$

Taking the natural logarithm of each side:

r x = ln(2) = 0.693

Thus, if r is expressed as a percent, then x (the time for money to double) is: x = 69.3/(interest rate, in percent).

37.   Spreadsheet exercise.

38.   a.   This calls for the growing perpetuity formula with a negative growth rate (g = −0.04):

$$PV = \frac{\$2 \text{ million}}{0.10 - (-0.04)} = \frac{\$2 \text{ million}}{0.14} = \$14.29 \text{ million}$$

b. The pipeline's value at year 20 (i.e., at t = 20), assuming its cash flows last forever, is:

$$PV_{20} = \frac{C_{21}}{r - g} = \frac{C_1(1+g)^{20}}{r - g}$$

With C_1 = $2 million, g = –0.04, and r = 0.10:

$$PV_{20} = \frac{(\$2\ \text{million}) \times (1-0.04)^{20}}{0.14} = \frac{\$0.884\ \text{million}}{0.14} = \$6.314\ \text{million}$$

Next, we convert this amount to PV today, and subtract it from the answer to Part (a):

$$PV = \$14.29\ \text{million} - \frac{\$6.314\ \text{million}}{(1.10)^{20}} = \$13.35\ \text{million}$$

Answers to Problem Sets

1. a. Does not change.

  b. Price falls.

  c. Yield rises.

2. a. If the coupon rate is higher than the yield, then investors must be expecting a decline in the capital value of the bond over its remaining life. Thus, the bond's price must be greater than its face value.

  b. Conversely, if the yield is greater than the coupon, the price will be below face value and it will rise over the remaining life of the bond.

3. The yield over 6 months is $3.965/2 = 1.79825\%$.
Therefore, PV $= 3/1.0179825 + 3/1.0179825^2 + ... + 103/1.0179825^{34} = 130.37$

4. Yields to maturity are about 4.3% for the 2% coupon, 4.2% for the 4% coupon, and 3.9% for the 8% coupon. The 8% bond had the shortest duration (7.65 years), the 2% bond the longest (9.07 years).

5. a. Fall (e.g., 1-year 10% bond is worth 110/1.1 5 100 if r 5 10% and is worth $110/1.15 = 95.65$ if r = 15%).

  b. Less (e.g., See 5a).

  c. Less (e.g., with r = 5%, 1-year 10% bond is worth $110/1.05 = 104.76$).

  d. Higher (e.g., if r = 10%, 1-year 10% bond is worth $110/1.1 = 100$, while 1-year 8% bond is worth $108/1.1 = 98.18$).

  e. No, low-coupon bonds have longer durations (unless there is only one period to maturity) and are therefore more volatile (e.g., if r falls from 10% to 5%, the value of a 2-year 10% bond rises from 100 to 109.3 (a rise of 9.3%). The value of a 2-year 5% bond rises from 91.3 to 100 (a rise of 9.5%).

6.   a.   Spot interest rates. Yield to maturity is a complicated average of the separate spot rates of interest.

       b.   Bond prices. The bond price is determined by the bond's cash flows and the spot rates of interest. Once you know the bond price and the bond's cash flows, it is possible to calculate the yield to maturity.

7.   a.   4%

       b.   PV = $1,075.44

8.   a. $PV = \dfrac{50}{1+r_1} + \dfrac{1,050}{(1+r_2)^2}$

       b. $PV = \dfrac{50}{1+y} + \dfrac{1,050}{(1+y)^2}$

       c.   Less (it is between the 1-year and 2-year spot rates).

9.   a. $r_1 = 100/99.423 - 1 = .58\%$; $r_2 = (100/97.546)^{.5} - 1 = 1.25\%$; $r_3 = (100/94.510)^{.33} - .1 = 1.90\%$; $r_4 = (100/90.524)^{.25} - 1 = 2.52\%$.

       b.   Upward-sloping.

       c.   Lower (the yield on the bond is a complicated average of the separate spot rates).

10.   a.   Price today is 108.425; price after 1 year is 106.930.

       b.   Return = (106.930 1 8)/108.425 − 1 = .06, or 6%.

       c.   If a bond's yield to maturity is unchanged, the return to the bondholder is equal to the yield.

11.   a.   False. Duration depends on the coupon as well as the maturity.

       b.   False. Given the yield to maturity, volatility is proportional to duration.

c. True. A lower coupon rate means longer duration and therefore higher volatility.

d. False. A higher interest rate reduces the relative present value of (distant) principal repayments.

12.

	Year	C_t	PV(C_t)	Proportion of Total Value	Proportion × Time
Security A	1	40	37.04	.359	.359
	2	40	34.29	.333	.666
	3	40	31.75	.308	.924
		V =	103.08	1.0	Duration = 1.949 years
Security B	1	20	18.52	.141	.141
	2	20	17.15	.131	.262
	3	120	95.26	.728	2.184
		V =	130.93	1.0	Duration = 2.587 years
Security C	1	10	9.26	.088	.088
	2	10	8.57	.082	.164
	3	110	87.32	.830	2.490
		V =	105.15	1.0	Duration = 2.742 years

Volatilities: A, 1.80; B, 2.40; C, 2.49.

13. 7.01% (the extra return that you earn for investing for two years rather than one is $1.06^2/1.05 - 1 = .0701$).

14. a. Real rate $= 1.10/1.05 - 1 = .0476$, or 4.76%

b. The real rate does not change. The nominal rate increases to $1.0476 \times 1.07 - 1 = .1209$, or 12.9%.

15. With annual coupon payments:

$$PV = 5 \times \left[\frac{1}{0.06} - \frac{1}{0.06 \times (1.06)^{10}} \right] + \frac{100}{(1.06)^{10}} = €92.64$$

16. a.

$$PV = 275 \times \left[\frac{1}{0.026} - \frac{1}{0.026 \times (1.026)^{20}} \right] + \frac{10,000}{(1.026)^{20}} = \$10,231.64$$

b.

Interest rate	PV of Interest	PV of Face value	PV of Bond
1.0%	$5,221.54	$9,050.63	$14,272.17
2.0%	4,962.53	8,195.44	13,157.97
3.0%	4,721.38	7,424.70	12,146.08
4.0%	4,496.64	6,729.71	11,226.36
5.0%	4,287.02	6,102.71	10,389.73
6.0%	4,091.31	5,536.76	9,628.06
7.0%	3,908.41	5,025.66	8,934.07
8.0%	3,737.34	4,563.87	8,301.21
9.0%	3,577.18	4,146.43	7,723.61
10.0%	3,427.11	3,768.89	7,196.00
11.0%	3,286.36	3,427.29	6,713.64
12.0%	3,154.23	3,118.05	6,272.28
13.0%	3,030.09	2,837.97	5,868.06
14.0%	2,913.35	2,584.19	5,497.54
15.0%	2,803.49	2,354.13	5,157.62

17. Purchase price for a 6-year government bond with 5 percent annual coupon:

$$PV = 50 \times \left[\frac{1}{0.03} - \frac{1}{0.03 \times (1.03)^6}\right] + \frac{1,000}{(1.03)^6} = \$1,108.34$$

Price one year later (yield = 3%):

$$PV = 50 \times \left[\frac{1}{0.03} - \frac{1}{0.03 \times (1.03)^5}\right] + \frac{1,000}{(1.03)^5} = \$1,091.59$$

Rate of return = [$50 + ($1,091.59 − $1,108.34)]/$1,108.34 = 3.00%

Price one year later (yield = 2%):

$$PV = 50 \times \left[\frac{1}{0.02} - \frac{1}{0.02 \times (1.02)^5}\right] + \frac{1,000}{(1.02)^5} = \$1,141.40$$

Rate of return = [$50 + ($1,141.40 − $1,108.34)]/$1,108.34 = 7.49%

18. The key here is to find a combination of these two bonds (i.e., a portfolio of bonds) that has a cash flow only at t = 6. Then, knowing the price of the portfolio and the cash flow at t = 6, we can calculate the 6-year spot rate.

We begin by specifying the cash flows of each bond and using these and their yields to calculate their current prices:

Investment	Yield	C_1	...	C_5	C_6	Price
6% bond	12%	60	...	60	1,060	$753.32
10% bond	8%	100	...	100	1,100	$1,092.46

From the cash flows in years one through five, we can see that buying two 6% bonds produces the same annual payments as buying 1.2 of the 10% bonds. To see the value of a cash flow only in year six, consider the portfolio of two 6% bonds minus 1.2 10% bonds. This portfolio costs:

$$(\$753.32 \times 2) - (1.2 \times \$1{,}092.46) = \$195.68$$

The cash flow for this portfolio is equal to zero for years one through five and, for year 6, is equal to:

$$(1{,}060 \times 2) - (1.2 \times 1{,}100) = \$800$$

Thus:

$$\$195.68 \times (1 + r_6)^6 = 800$$

$$r_6 = 0.2645 = 26.45\%$$

19. Downward sloping. This is because high coupon bonds provide a greater proportion of their cash flows in the early years. In essence, a high coupon bond is a 'shorter' bond than a low coupon bond of the same maturity.

20. a.

Year	Discount Factor	Forward Rate
1	$1/1.05 = 0.952$	
2	$1/(1.054)^2 = 0.900$	$(1.054^2/1.05) - 1 = 0.0580 = 5.80\%$
3	$1/(1.057)^3 = 0.847$	$(1.057^3/1.054^2) - 1 = 0.0630 = 6.30\%$
4	$1/(1.059)^4 = 0.795$	$(1.059^4/1.057^3) - 1 = 0.0650 = 6.50\%$
5	$1/(1.060)^5 = 0.747$	$(1.060^5/1.059^4) - 1 = 0.0640 = 6.40\%$

b.　i.　5%, two-year note:

$$PV = \frac{\$50}{1.05} + \frac{\$1050}{(1.054)^2} = \$992.79$$

ii.　5%, five-year bond:

$$PV = \frac{\$50}{1.05} + \frac{\$50}{(1.054)^2} + \frac{\$50}{(1.057)^3} + \frac{\$50}{(1.059)^4} + \frac{\$1050}{(1.060)^5} = \$959.34$$

iii.　10%, five-year bond:

$$PV = \frac{\$100}{1.05} + \frac{\$100}{(1.054)^2} + \frac{\$100}{(1.057)^3} + \frac{\$100}{(1.059)^4} + \frac{\$1100}{(1.060)^5} = \$1{,}171.43$$

c. First, we calculate the yield for each of the two bonds. For the 5% bond, this means solving for r in the following equation:

$$\$959.34 = \frac{\$50}{1+r} + \frac{\$50}{(1+r)^2} + \frac{\$50}{(1+r)^3} + \frac{\$50}{(1+r)^4} + \frac{\$1050}{(1+r)^5}$$

r = 0.05964 = 5.964%

For the 10% bond:

$$\$1171.43 = \frac{\$100}{1+r} + \frac{\$100}{(1+r)^2} + \frac{\$100}{(1+r)^3} + \frac{\$100}{(1+r)^4} + \frac{\$1100}{(1+r)^5}$$

r = 0.05937 = 5.937%

The yield depends upon both the coupon payment and the spot rate at the time of the coupon payment. The 10% bond has a slightly greater proportion of its total payments coming earlier, when interest rates are low, than does the 5% bond. Thus, the yield of the 10% bond is slightly lower.

d. The yield to maturity on a five-year zero coupon bond is the five-year spot rate, here 6.00%.

e. First, we find the price of the five-year annuity, assuming that the annual payment is $1:

$$PV = \frac{1}{1.05} + \frac{1}{(1.054)^2} + \frac{1}{(1.057)^3} + \frac{1}{(1.059)^4} + \frac{1}{(1.060)^5} = \$4.2417$$

Now we find the yield to maturity for this annuity:

$$4.2417 = \frac{1}{1+r} + \frac{1}{(1+r)^2} + \frac{1}{(1+r)^3} + \frac{1}{(1+r)^4} + \frac{1}{(1+r)^5}$$

r = 0.05745 = 5.745%

f. The yield on the five-year note lies between the yield on a five-year zero-coupon bond and the yield on a 5-year annuity because the cash flows of the Treasury bond lie between the cash flows of these other two financial instruments during a period of rising interest rates. That is, the annuity has fixed, equal payments, the zero-coupon bond has one payment at the end, and the bond's payments are a combination of these.

21. Assuming we are calculating the durations as of February 2009, the strip's duration equals

$$Duration = \frac{6 \times 88.745}{88.745} = 6$$, and the modified duration equals 6/1.02 = 5.88. At a

semi-annual yield of 1.5%, the price of the 6-year strips equals 91.424, and at a semi-annual yield of 2.5%, the price of the strips equals 86.151. The difference in the prices, 5.273 is 5.94% of the price of the strips. This is close to the 5.88 duration, and the difference is due to the first-order approximation of the price change provided by duration.

To calculate the duration for the 4% bonds, consider the following table similar to Table 3.3:

Year	0.5	1	1.5	2	2.5	3	3.5	4	4.5	5	5.5	6
Cash Payment	2	2	2	2	2	2	2	2	2	2	2	102
PV at 2% ytm	1.980	1.961	1.941	1.922	1.903	1.884	1.865	1.847	1.829	1.811	1.793	90.520
fraction value	0.018	0.018	0.017	0.017	0.017	0.017	0.017	0.017	0.016	0.016	0.016	0.814
year x fraction of value	0.009	0.018	0.026	0.035	0.043	0.051	0.059	0.066	0.074	0.081	0.089	4.882

Total PV = 111.26, and the duration = 5.432. The modified duration equals 5.432/1.02 = 5.325.

The price of the 4% coupon bond at 1.5% and 2.5% equals 114.294 and 108.310, respectively. This price difference, 5.984, is 5.38% of the original price, which is very close to the 5.33 duration.

22.   Table 3.3 can be flipped and recalculated as follows:

Date	Year	Cash Payment	Discount Factor at 2%	PV	Fraction of Total Value	Year times Fraction of Value
Aug-09	0.5	5.63	0.990148	5.57	3.66%	0.02
Feb-10	1.0000	5.63	0.980	5.51	3.63%	0.04
Aug-10	1.5000	5.63	0.971	5.46	3.59%	0.05
Feb-11	2.0000	5.63	0.961	5.41	3.55%	0.07
Aug-11	2.5000	5.63	0.952	5.35	3.52%	0.09
Feb-12	3.0000	5.63	0.942	5.30	3.48%	0.10
Aug-12	3.5000	5.63	0.933	5.25	3.45%	0.12
Feb-13	4.0000	5.63	0.924	5.20	3.42%	0.14
Aug-13	4.5000	5.63	0.915	5.15	3.38%	0.15
Feb-14	5.0000	5.63	0.906	5.09	3.35%	0.17
Aug-14	5.5000	5.63	0.897	5.04	3.32%	0.18
Feb-15	6.0000	105.63	0.888	93.79	61.65%	3.70
TOTAL				152.13	100.00%	4.83

a. Decreasing the coupon payments to 8% of face boosts duration to 5.05:

Date	Year	Cash Payment	Discount Factor at 2%	PV	Fraction of Total Value		Year times Fraction of Value
Aug-09	0.5	4.00	0.990148	3.96	2.96%		0.01
Feb-10	1.0000	4.00	0.980	3.92	2.93%		0.03
Aug-10	1.5000	4.00	0.971	3.88	2.90%		0.04
Feb-11	2.0000	4.00	0.961	3.84	2.87%		0.06
Aug-11	2.5000	4.00	0.952	3.81	2.84%		0.07
Feb-12	3.0000	4.00	0.942	3.77	2.82%		0.08
Aug-12	3.5000	4.00	0.933	3.73	2.79%		0.10
Feb-13	4.0000	4.00	0.924	3.70	2.76%		0.11
Aug-13	4.5000	4.00	0.915	3.66	2.73%		0.12
Feb-14	5.0000	4.00	0.906	3.62	2.71%		0.14
Aug-14	5.5000	4.00	0.897	3.59	2.68%		0.15
Feb-15	6.0000	104.00	0.888	92.35	69.00%		4.14
TOTAL				133.83	100.00%		5.05

This makes sense as we are now receiving smaller payments early in the life of the bond.

b. Increasing the yield to 6% reduces duration to 4.70:

Date	Year	Cash Payment	Discount Factor at 2%	PV	Fraction of Total Value		Year times Fraction of Value
Aug-09	0.5	5.63	0.971	5.46	4.31%		0.02
Feb-10	1.0000	5.63	0.943	5.31	4.19%		0.04
Aug-10	1.5000	5.63	0.916	5.15	4.07%		0.06
Feb-11	2.0000	5.63	0.890	5.01	3.95%		0.08
Aug-11	2.5000	5.63	0.864	4.86	3.84%		0.10
Feb-12	3.0000	5.63	0.840	4.72	3.73%		0.11
Aug-12	3.5000	5.63	0.816	4.59	3.62%		0.13
Feb-13	4.0000	5.63	0.792	4.46	3.52%		0.14
Aug-13	4.5000	5.63	0.769	4.33	3.42%		0.15
Feb-14	5.0000	5.63	0.747	4.20	3.32%		0.17
Aug-14	5.5000	5.63	0.726	4.08	3.22%		0.18
Feb-15	6.0000	105.63	0.705	74.46	58.80%		3.53
TOTAL				126.63	100.00%		4.70

Payments at the end of the bonds life are discounted more heavily, resulting in a greater fraction of total value being paid early.

23. The duration of a perpetual bond is: $[(1 + \text{yield})/\text{yield}]$
The duration of a perpetual bond with a yield of 5% is:

$$D_5 = 1.05/0.05 = 21 \text{ years}$$

The duration of a perpetual bond yielding 10% is:

$$D_{10} = 1.10/0.10 = 11 \text{ years}$$

Because the duration of a zero-coupon bond is equal to its maturity, the 15-year zero-coupon bond has a duration of 15 years.

Thus, comparing the 5% perpetual bond and the zero-coupon bond, the 5% perpetual bond has the longer duration. Comparing the 10% perpetual bond and the 15 year zero, the zero has a longer duration.

24. Answers will differ. Generally, we would expect yield changes to have the greatest impact on long-maturity and low coupon bonds.

25. The calculations are shown in the table below:

	1	2	3	4	Bond Price (PV)	YTM (%)
Spot rates	4.60%	4.40%	4.20%	4%		
Discount factors	0.9560	0.9175	0.8839	0.8548		
Bond A (8% coupon):						
Payment (Ct)	80	1080				
PV(Ct)	76.48	990.88			1067.37	4.407%
Bond B (11% coupon):						
Payment (Ct)	110	110	1110			
PV(Ct)	105.16	100.92	981.11		1187.20	4.226%
Bond C (6% coupon):						
Payment (Ct)	60	60	60	1060		
PV(Ct)	57.36	55.05	53.03	906.09	1071.54	4.028%
Bond D (strip):						
Payment (Ct)	0	0	0	1000		
PV(Ct)				854.80	854.80	4.00%

26. We will borrow $1000 at a five year loan rate of 2.5% and buy a 4-year strip paying 4%. We may not know what interest rates we will earn on the last year (4→5) but our $1000 will come due and we put it in under our mattress earning 0% if necessary to pay off the loan.

   Let's turn to present value calculations: As shown above, the cost of the strip is $854.80. We will receive proceeds from the 2.5% loan = 1000 / (1.025)^5 = $883.90. Pocket the difference of $29.10, smile, and repeat.

   The minimum sensible value would set the discount factors used in year 5 equal to that of year 4, which would assume a 0% interest rate from year 4 to 5. We can solve for the interest rate where $1/(1+r)^5 = 0.8548$, which is roughly 3.19%

27. a. If the expectations theory of term structure is right, then we can determine the expected future one year spot rate (at t=3) as follows: investing $100 in a 3-year instrument at 4.2% gives us 100 * (1+.042)^3 = 113.136. Investing $100 in a 4-year instrument at 4.0% gives us 100 * (1+.04)^4 = 116.986. This reveals a one year spot rate from year 3 to 4 of (116.98 – 113.136) / 113.136 = 3.4%

   b. If investing in long-term bonds carries additional risks, then the risk equivalent one year spot rate in year three would be even less (reflecting the fact that some risk premium must be built into this 3.4% spot rate).

28. a. Your nominal return will be $1.08^2 - 1 = 16.64\%$ over the two years. Your real return is (1.08/1.03) × (1.08/1.05) – 1 = 7.85%

   b. With the TIPS, the real return will remain at 8% per year, or 16.64% over two years. The nominal return on the TIPS will equal (1.08 × 1.03) × (1.08 × 1.05) – 1 = 26.15%.

29. The bond price at a 5.41% yield is:

$$PV = 100 \times \left[\frac{1}{0.0541} - \frac{1}{0.0541 \times (1.0541)^5} \right] + \frac{1,000}{(1.0541)^5} = \$1,196.49$$

If the yield increases to 8.47%, the price would decline to:

$$PV = 100 \times \left[\frac{1}{0.0847} - \frac{1}{0.0847 \times (1.0847)^5} \right] + \frac{1,000}{(1.0847)^5} = \$1,060.34$$

30. Spreadsheet problem; answers will vary.

31. Arbitrage opportunities can be identified by finding situations where the implied forward rates or spot rates are different.

We begin with the shortest-term bond, Bond G, which has a two-year maturity. Since G is a zero-coupon bond, we determine the two-year spot rate directly by finding the yield for Bond G. The yield is 9.5 percent, so the implied two-year spot rate (r_2) is 9.5 percent. Using the same approach for Bond A, we find that the three-year spot rate (r_3) is 10.0 percent.

Next we use Bonds B and D to find the four-year spot rate. The following position in these bonds provides a cash payoff only in year four: a long position in two of Bond B and a short position in Bond D. Cash flows for this position are:

$$[(-2 \times \$842.30) + \$980.57] = -\$704.03 \text{ today}$$
$$[(2 \times \$50) - \$100] = \$0 \text{ in years 1, 2 and 3}$$
$$[(2 \times \$1050) - \$1100] = \$1000 \text{ in year 4}$$

We determine the four-year spot rate from this position as follows:

$$\$704.03 = \frac{\$1000}{(1 + r_4)^4}$$

$$r_4 = 0.0917 = 9.17\%$$

Next, we use r_2, r_3 and r_4 with one of the four-year coupon bonds to determine r_1. For Bond C:

$$\$1,065.28 = \frac{\$120}{1+r_1} + \frac{\$120}{(1.095)^2} + \frac{\$120}{(1.100)^3} + \frac{\$1120}{(1.0917)^4} = \frac{\$120}{1+r_1} + \$978.74$$

$$r_1 = 0.3867 = 38.67\%$$

Now, in order to determine whether arbitrage opportunities exist, we use these spot rates to value the remaining two four-year bonds. This produces the following results: for Bond B, the present value is $854.55, and for Bond D, the present value is $1,005.07. Since neither of these values equals the current market price of the respective bonds, arbitrage opportunities exist. Similarly, the spot rates derived above produce the following values for the three-year bonds: $1,074.22 for Bond E and $912.77 for Bond F.

32. We begin with the definition of duration as applied to a bond with yield r and an annual payment of C in perpetuity

$$DUR = \frac{\dfrac{1C}{1+r} + \dfrac{2C}{(1+r)^2} + \dfrac{3C}{(1+r)^3} + \cdots + \dfrac{tC}{(1+r)^t} + \cdots}{\dfrac{C}{1+r} + \dfrac{C}{(1+r)^2} + \dfrac{C}{(1+r)^3} + \cdots + \dfrac{C}{(1+r)^t} + \cdots}$$

We first simplify by dividing both the numerator and the denominator by C:

$$DUR = \frac{\dfrac{1}{(1+r)} + \dfrac{2}{(1+r)^2} + \dfrac{3}{(1+r)^3} + \cdots + \dfrac{t}{(1+r)^t} + \cdots}{\dfrac{1}{1+r} + \dfrac{1}{(1+r)^2} + \dfrac{1}{(1+r)^3} + \cdots + \dfrac{1}{(1+r)^t} + \cdots}$$

The denominator is the present value of a perpetuity of $1 per year, which is equal to (1/r). To simplify the numerator, we first denote the numerator S and then divide S by (1 + r):

$$\frac{S}{(1+r)} = \frac{1}{(1+r)^2} + \frac{2}{(1+r)^3} + \frac{3}{(1+r)^4} + \cdots + \frac{t}{(1+r)^{t+1}} + \cdots$$

Note that this new quantity [S/(1 + r)] is equal to the square of denominator in the duration formula above, that is:

$$\frac{S}{(1+r)} = \left(\frac{1}{1+r} + \frac{1}{(1+r)^2} + \frac{1}{(1+r)^3} + \cdots + \frac{1}{(1+r)^t} + \cdots \right)^2$$

Therefore:

$$\frac{S}{(1+r)} = \left(\frac{1}{r} \right)^2 \Rightarrow S = \frac{1+r}{r^2}$$

Thus, for a perpetual bond paying C dollars per year:

$$DUR = \frac{1+r}{r^2} \times \frac{1}{(1/r)} = \frac{1+r}{r}$$

33.   We begin with the definition of duration as applied to a common stock with yield r and dividends that grow at a constant rate g in perpetuity:

$$DUR = \frac{\dfrac{1C(1+g)}{1+r} + \dfrac{2C(1+g)^2}{(1+r)^2} + \dfrac{3C(1+g)^3}{(1+r)^3} + \cdots + \dfrac{tC(1+g)^t}{(1+r)^t} + \cdots}{\dfrac{C(1+g)}{1+r} + \dfrac{C(1+g)^2}{(1+r)^2} + \dfrac{C(1+g)^3}{(1+r)^3} + \cdots + \dfrac{C(1+g)^t}{(1+r)^t} + \cdots}$$

We first simplify by dividing each term by [C(1 + g)]:

$$DUR = \frac{\dfrac{1}{1+r} + \dfrac{2(1+g)}{(1+r)^2} + \dfrac{3(1+g)^2}{(1+r)^3} + \cdots + \dfrac{t(1+g)^{t-1}}{(1+r)^t} + \cdots}{\dfrac{1}{1+r} + \dfrac{1+g}{(1+r)^2} + \dfrac{(1+g)^2}{(1+r)^3} + \cdots + \dfrac{(1+g)^{t-1}}{(1+r)^t} + \cdots}$$

The denominator is the present value of a growing perpetuity of $1 per year, which is equal to [1/(r − g)]. To simplify the numerator, we first denote the numerator S and then divide S by (1 + r):

$$\frac{S}{(1+r)} = \frac{1}{(1+r)^2} + \frac{2(1+g)}{(1+r)^3} + \frac{3(1+g)^2}{(1+r)^4} + \cdots + \frac{t(1+g)^{t-2}}{(1+r)^{t+1}} + \cdots$$

Note that this new quantity [S/(1 + r)] is equal to the square of denominator in the duration formula above, that is:

$$\frac{S}{(1+r)} = \left(\frac{1}{1+r} + \frac{1+g}{(1+r)^2} + \frac{(1+g)^2}{(1+r)^3} + \cdots + \frac{(1+g)^{t-1}}{(1+r)^t} + \cdots\right)^2$$

Therefore:

$$\frac{S}{(1+r)} = \left(\frac{1}{r-g}\right)^2 \Rightarrow S = \frac{1+r}{(r-g)^2}$$

Thus, for a perpetual bond paying C dollars per year:

$$DUR = \frac{1+r}{(r-g)^2} \times \frac{1}{[1/(r-g)]} = \frac{1+r}{r-g}$$

34. a. We make use of the one-year Treasury bill information in order to determine the one-year spot rate as follows:

$$\$93.46 = \frac{\$100}{1+r_1}$$

$r_1 = 0.0700 = 7.00\%$

The following position provides a cash payoff only in year two:

a long position in twenty-five two-year bonds and a short position in one one-year Treasury bill. Cash flows for this position are:

[(−25 × $94.92) + (1 × $93.46)] = −$2,279.54 today
[(25 × $4) − (1 × $100)] = $0 in year 1
(25 × $104) = $2,600 in year 2

We determine the two-year spot rate from this position as follows:

$$\$2,279.54 = \frac{\$2,600}{(1+r_2)^2}$$

$r_2 = 0.0680 = 6.80\%$

The forward rate f_2 is computed as follows:

$$f_2 = [(1.0680)^2/1.0700] - 1 = 0.0660 = 6.60\%$$

The following position provides a cash payoff only in year three:

a long position in the three-year bond and a short position equal to (8/104) times a package consisting of a one-year Treasury bill and a two-year bond. Cash flows for this position are:

$$[(-1 \times \$103.64) + (8/104) \times (\$93.46 + \$94.92)] = -\$89.15 \text{ today}$$
$$[(1 \times \$8) - (8/104) \times (\$100 + \$4)] = \$0 \text{ in year 1}$$
$$[(1 \times \$8) - (8/104) \times \$104] = \$0 \text{ in year 2}$$
$$1 \times \$108 = \$108 \text{ in year 3}$$

We determine the three-year spot rate from this position as follows:

$$\$89.15 = \frac{\$108}{(1+r_3)^3}$$

$$r_3 = 0.0660 = 6.60\%$$

The forward rate f_3 is computed as follows:

$$f_3 = [(1.0660)^3/(1.0680)^2] - 1 = 0.0620 = 6.20\%$$

b. We make use of the spot and forward rates to calculate the price of the 4 percent coupon bond:

$$P = \frac{40}{(1.07)} + \frac{40}{(1.07)(1.066)} + \frac{1040}{(1.07)(1.066)(1.062)} = \$931.01$$

The actual price of the bond ($950) is significantly greater than the price deduced using the spot and forward rates embedded in the prices of the other bonds ($931.01). Hence, a profit opportunity exists. In order to take advantage of this opportunity, one should sell the 4 percent coupon bond short and purchase the 8 percent coupon bond.

35. a. Bond D allows us to calculate the four year spot rate by solving for the YTM using the 841.78 price of Bond D:

$$\$841.78 = \frac{\$0}{1+r} + \frac{\$0}{(1+r)^2} + \frac{\$0}{(1+r)^3} + \frac{\$1000}{(1+r)^4}$$

$$r_4 = 4.4\%$$

We can then set up the following three equations using the prices of bonds A, B, and C:

$$\text{Using bond A: } \$1075.82 = \frac{\$80}{1+r1} + \frac{\$1080}{(1+r2)^2}$$

$$\text{Using bond B: } \$1189.10 = \frac{\$110}{1+r1} + \frac{\$110}{(1+r2)^2} + \frac{\$1110}{(1+r3)^3}$$

$$\text{Using bond C: } \$1058.76 = \frac{\$60}{1+r1} + \frac{\$60}{(1+r2)^2} + \frac{\$60}{(1+r3)^3} + \frac{\$1060}{(1+r4)^4}$$

We know r4 = 4.4% so we can substitute that into the last equation. Now we have three equations and three unknowns and can solve this with variable substitution or linear programming to get r1 = 3.5%, r2 = 4%; r3 = 4.2%; r4 = 4.4%

b.   We will want to invest in the underpriced C and borrow money at the current spot market rates to construct an offsetting position. For example, we might borrow $60 at the 1 year rate of 3.5%, 60 at the 2 year rate of 4%, 60 at the 3 year rate of 4.2% and 1060 at the 4 year rate of 4.4%. Of course the PV amount we will receive on these loans is $1058.76. Now we purchase the discounted bond C at $1040, use the proceeds of this bond to repay our loans as they come due. We can pocket the difference of $18.76, smile, and repeat.

CHAPTER 4
The Value of Common Stocks

Answers to Problem Sets

1. a.   True

    b.   True

2. Investors who buy stocks may get their return from capital gains as well as dividends. But the future stock price always depends on subsequent dividends. There is no inconsistency.

3. $P_0 = (5 + 110)/1.08 = \$106.48$.

4. $r = 5/40 = .125$.

5. $P_0 = 10/(.08 - .05) = \$333.33$.

6. By year 5, earnings will grow to $18.23 per share. Forecasted price per share at year 4 is $18.23/.08 = \$227.91$.

$$P_0 = \frac{10}{1.08} + \frac{10.50}{(1.08)^2} + \frac{11.03}{(1.08)^3} + \frac{11.58}{(1.08)^4}$$
$$+ \frac{227.91}{(1.08)^4} = 203.05$$

7. $15/.08 + PVGO = 333.33$; therefore PVGO = $145.83.

8. Z's forecasted dividends and prices grow as follows:

	Year 1	Year 2	Year 3
Dividend	10	10.50	11.03
Price	350	367.50	385.88

Calculate the expected rates of return:

From year 0 to 1: $\dfrac{10+(350-333.33)}{333.33}=.08$

From year 1 to 2: $\dfrac{10.50+(367.50-350)}{350}=.08$

From year 2 to 3: $\dfrac{11.03+(385.88-367.50)}{367.50}=.08$

Double expects 8% in each of the first 2 years. Triple expects 8% in each of the first 3 years.

9. a.   False

    b.   True

10. PVGO = 0, and EPS_1 equals the average future earnings the firm could generate under no-growth policy.

11. Free cash flow is the amount of cash thrown off by a business after all investments necessary for growth. In our simple examples, free cash flow equals operating cash flow minus capital expenditure. Free cash flow can be negative if investments are large.

12. The value at the end of a forecast period. Horizon value can be estimated using the constant-growth DCF formula or by using price–earnings or market–book ratios for similar companies.

13. If PVGO = 0 at the horizon date H, horizon value = earnings forecasted for $H +$ 1 divided by r.

14. Newspaper exercise, answers will vary.

15.

	Expected Future Values		Present Values		
Horizon Period (H)	Dividend (DIV$_t$)	Price (P$_t$)	Cumulative Dividends	Future Price	Total
0		100.00		100.00	100.00
1	10.00	105.00	8.70	91.30	100.00
2	10.50	110.25	16.64	83.36	100.00
3	11.03	115.76	23.88	76.12	100.00
4	11.58	121.55	30.50	69.50	100.00
10	15.51	162.89	59.74	40.26	100.00
20	25.27	265.33	83.79	16.21	100.00
50	109.21	1,146.74	98.94	1.06	100.00
100	1,252.39	13,150.13	99.99	0.01	100.00

<u>Assumptions</u>
1. Dividends increase at 5% per year compounded.
2. Capitalization rate is 15%.

16. $$P_A = \frac{DIV_1}{r} = \frac{\$10}{0.10} = \$100.00$$

$$P_B = \frac{DIV_1}{r-g} = \frac{\$5}{0.10-0.04} = \$83.33$$

$$P_C = \frac{DIV_1}{1.10^1} + \frac{DIV_2}{1.10^2} + \frac{DIV_3}{1.10^3} + \frac{DIV_4}{1.10^4} + \frac{DIV_5}{1.10^5} + \frac{DIV_6}{1.10^6} + \left(\frac{DIV_7}{0.10} \times \frac{1}{1.10^6}\right)$$

$$P_C = \frac{5.00}{1.10^1} + \frac{6.00}{1.10^2} + \frac{7.20}{1.10^3} + \frac{8.64}{1.10^4} + \frac{10.37}{1.10^5} + \frac{12.44}{1.10^6} + \left(\frac{12.44}{0.10} \times \frac{1}{1.10^6}\right) = \$104.50$$

At a capitalization rate of 10%, Stock C is the most valuable.

For a capitalization rate of 7%, the calculations are similar.

The results are:

P$_A$ = $142.86
P$_B$ = $166.67
P$_C$ = $156.48

Therefore, Stock B is the most valuable.

17. a. $$P_0 = DIV_0 + \frac{DIV_1}{r-g} = \$1.35 + \frac{\$1.35 \times 1.0275}{0.095 - 0.0275} = \$21.90$$

b. First, compute the real discount rate as follows:

$$(1 + r_{nominal}) = (1 + r_{real}) \times (1 + \text{inflation rate})$$

$$1.095 = (1 + r_{real}) \times 1.0275$$

$$(1 + r_{real}) = (1.095/1.0275) - 1 = .0657 = 6.57\%$$

In real terms, g = 0. Therefore:

$$P_0 = DIV_0 + \frac{DIV_1}{r-g} = \$1.35 + \frac{\$1.35}{0.0657} = \$21.90$$

18. a.   Plowback ratio = 1 − payout ratio = 1.0 − 0.5 = 0.5

Dividend growth rate = g= Plowback ratio × ROE = 0.5 × 0.14 = 0.07

Next, compute EPS_0 as follows:

ROE = EPS_0 /Book equity per share

$0.14 = EPS_0 /\$50 \Rightarrow EPS_0 = \$7.00$

Therefore: DIV_0 = payout ratio × EPS_0 = 0.5 × \$7.00 = \$3.50

EPS and dividends for subsequent years are:

Year	EPS	DIV
0	\$7.00	\$7.00 × 0.5 = \$3.50
1	\$7.00 × 1.07 = \$7.4900	\$7.4900 × 0.5 = \$3.50 × 1.07 = \$3.7450
2	\$7.00 × 1.07^2 = \$8.0143	\$8.0143 × 0.5 = \$3.50 × 1.07^2 = \$4.0072
3	\$7.00 × 1.07^3 = \$8.5753	\$8.5753 × 0.5 = \$3.50 × 1.07^3 = \$4.2877
4	\$7.00 × 1.07^4 = \$9.1756	\$9.1756 × 0.5 = \$3.50 × 1.07^4 = \$4.5878
5	\$7.00 × 1.07^4 × 1.023 = \$9.3866	\$9.3866 × 0.5 = \$3.50 × 1.07^4 × 1.023 = \$4.6933

EPS and dividends for year 5 and subsequent years grow at 2.3% per year, as indicated by the following calculation:

Dividend growth rate = g = Plowback ratio × ROE = (1 − 0.08) × 0.115 = 0.023

b. $$P_0 = \frac{DIV_1}{1.115^1} + \frac{DIV_2}{1.115^2} + \frac{DIV_3}{1.115^3} + \frac{DIV_4}{1.115^4} + \left(\frac{DIV_5}{0.115} \times \frac{1}{1.115^4} \right)$$

$$= \frac{3.745}{1.115^1} + \frac{4.007}{1.115^2} + \frac{4.288}{1.115^3} + \frac{4.588}{1.115^4} + \left(\frac{4.693}{0.115 - 0.023} \times \frac{1}{1.10^4} \right) = \$45.65$$

The last term in the above calculation is dependent on the payout ratio and the growth rate after year 4.

19. a. $$r = \frac{DIV_1}{P_0} + g = \frac{8.5}{200} + 0.075 = 0.1175 = 11.75\%$$

b.   g = Plowback ratio × ROE = (1 − 0.5) × 0.12 = 0.06 = 6.0%

The stated payout ratio and ROE are inconsistent with the security analysts' forecasts. With g = 6.0% (and assuming r remains at 11.75%) then:

$$P_0 = \frac{DIV_1}{r-g} = \frac{8.5}{0.1175 - 0.06} = 147.83 \text{ pesos}$$

20.   The security analyst's forecast is wrong because it assumes a perpetual constant growth rate of 15% when, in fact, growth will continue for two years at this rate and then there will be no further growth in EPS or dividends. The value of the company's stock is the present value of the expected dividend of $2.30 to be paid in 2020 plus the present value of the perpetuity of $2.65 beginning in 2021. Therefore, the actual expected rate of return is the solution for r in the following equation:

$$\$21.75 = \frac{\$2.30}{1+r} + \frac{\$2.65}{r(1+r)}$$

Solving algebraically (using the quadratic formula) or by trial and error, we find that: r = 0.1201 = 12.01%

21.   a.   <u>An Incorrect Application</u>. Hotshot Semiconductor's earnings and dividends have grown by 30 percent per year since the firm's founding ten years ago. Current stock price is $100, and next year's dividend is projected at $1.25. Thus:

$$r = \frac{DIV_1}{P_0} + g = \frac{1.25}{100} + 0.30 = 0.3125 = 31.25\%$$

This is *wrong* because the formula assumes perpetual growth; it is not possible for Hotshot to grow at 30 percent per year forever.

<u>A Correct Application</u>. The formula might be correctly applied to the Old Faithful Railroad, which has been growing at a steady 5 percent rate for decades. Its EPS_1 = $10, DIV_1 = $5, and P_0 = $100. Thus:

$$r = \frac{DIV_1}{P_0} + g = \frac{5}{100} + 0.05 = 0.10 = 10.0\%$$

Even here, you should be careful not to blindly project past growth into the future. If Old Faithful hauls coal, an energy crisis could turn it into a growth stock.

b.   <u>An Incorrect Application</u>. Hotshot has current earnings of $5.00 per share. Thus:

$$r = \frac{EPS_1}{P_0} = \frac{5}{100} = 0.05 = 5.0\%$$

This is too low to be realistic. The reason P_0 is so high relative to earnings is not that r is low, but rather that Hotshot is endowed with valuable growth opportunities. Suppose PVGO = \$60:

$$P_0 = \frac{EPS_1}{r} + PVGO$$

$$100 = \frac{5}{r} + 60$$

Therefore, r = 12.5%

<u>A Correct Application</u>. Unfortunately, Old Faithful has run out of valuable growth opportunities. Since PVGO = 0:

$$P_0 = \frac{EPS_1}{r} + PVGO$$

$$100 = \frac{10}{r} + 0$$

Therefore, r = 10.0%

22.   Share price $= \frac{EPS_1}{r} + \frac{NPV}{r-g}$

Therefore:

$$P_\alpha = \frac{EPS_{\alpha 1}}{r_\alpha} + \frac{NPV_\alpha}{(r_\alpha - 0.15)}$$

$$P_\beta = \frac{EPS_{\beta 1}}{r_\beta} + \frac{NPV_\beta}{(r_\beta - 0.08)}$$

The statement in the question implies the following:

$$\frac{NPV_\beta}{(r_\beta - 0.08)} \bigg/ \left(\frac{EPS_{\beta 1}}{r_\beta} + \frac{NPV_\beta}{(r_\beta - 0.08)} \right) > \frac{NPV_\alpha}{(r_\alpha - 0.15)} \bigg/ \left(\frac{EPS_{\alpha 1}}{r_\alpha} + \frac{NPV_\alpha}{(r_\alpha - 0.15)} \right)$$

Rearranging, we have:

$$\frac{NPV_\alpha}{(r_\alpha - 0.15)} \times \frac{r_\alpha}{EPS_{\alpha 1}} < \frac{NPV_\beta}{(r_\beta - 0.08)} \times \frac{r_\beta}{EPS_{\beta 1}}$$

a. $NPV_\alpha < NPV_\beta$, everything else equal.

b. $(r_\alpha - 0.15) > (r_\beta - 0.08)$, everything else equal.

c. $\dfrac{NPV_\alpha}{(r_\alpha - 0.15)} < \dfrac{NPV_\beta}{(r_\beta - 0.08)}$, everything else equal.

d. $\dfrac{r_\alpha}{EPS_{\alpha 1}} < \dfrac{r_\beta}{EPS_{\beta 1}}$, everything else equal.

23. a. Growth-Tech's stock price should be:

$$P = \dfrac{\$0.50}{(1.12)} + \dfrac{\$0.60}{(1.12)^2} + \dfrac{\$1.15}{(1.12)^3} + \left(\dfrac{1}{(1.12)^3} \times \dfrac{\$1.24}{(0.12 - 0.08)} \right) = \$23.81$$

b. The horizon value contributes:

$$PV(P_H) = \dfrac{1}{(1.12)^3} \times \dfrac{\$1.24}{(0.12 - 0.08)} = \$22.07$$

c. Without PVGO, P_3 would equal earnings for year 4 capitalized at 12 percent:

$$\dfrac{\$2.49}{0.12} = \$20.75$$

Therefore: PVGO = $31.00 – $20.75 = $10.25

d. The PVGO of $10.25 is lost at year 3. Therefore, the current stock price of $23.81 will decrease by:

$$\dfrac{\$10.25}{(1.12)^3} = \$7.30$$

The new stock price will be: $23.81 – $7.30 = $16.51

24. a. Here we can apply the standard growing perpetuity formula with $DIV_1 = \$4$, $g = 0.04$ and $P_0 = \$100$:

$$r = \dfrac{DIV_1}{P_0} + g = \dfrac{\$4}{\$100} + 0.04 = 0.08 = 8.0\%$$

The $4 dividend is 60 percent of earnings. Thus:

EPS$_1$ = 4/0.6 = $6.67

Also:

$$P_0 = \dfrac{EPS_1}{r} + PVGO$$

$$\$100 = \frac{\$6.67}{0.08} + PVGO$$

$$PVGO = \$16.63$$

b. DIV_1 will decrease to: $0.20 \times 6.67 = \$1.33$

However, by plowing back 80 percent of earnings, CSI will grow by 8 percent per year for five years. Thus:

Year	1	2	3	4	5	6	7, 8 . . .
DIV_t	1.33	1.44	1.55	1.68	1.81	5.88	Continued growth at
EPS_t	6.67	7.20	7.78	8.40	9.07	9.80	4 percent

Note that DIV_6 increases sharply as the firm switches back to a 60 percent payout policy. Forecasted stock price in year 5 is:

$$P_5 = \frac{DIV_6}{r-g} = \frac{5.88}{0.08 - 0.04} = \$147$$

Therefore, CSI's stock price will increase to:

$$P_0 = \frac{1.33}{1.08} + \frac{1.44}{1.08^2} + \frac{1.55}{1.08^3} + \frac{1.68}{1.08^4} + \frac{1.81 + 147}{1.08^5} = \$106.21$$

25. a. First, we use the following Excel spreadsheet to compute net income (or dividends) for 2009 through 2013:

	2009	2010	2011	2012	2013
Production (million barrels)	1.8000	1.6740	1.5568	1.4478	1.3465
Price of oil/barrel	65	60	55	50	52.5
Costs/barrel	25	25	25	25	25
Revenue	117,000,000	100,440,000	85,625,100	72,392,130	70,690,915
Expenses	45,000,000	41,850,000	38,920,500	36,196,065	33,662,340
Net Income (= Dividends)	72,000,000	58,590,000	46,704,600	36,196,065	37,028,574

Next, we compute the present value of the dividends to be paid in 2010, 2011 and 2012:

$$P_0 = \frac{58,590,000}{1.09} + \frac{46,704,600}{1.09^2} + \frac{36,196,065}{1.09^3} = \$121,012,624$$

The present value of dividends to be paid in 2013 and subsequent years can be computed by recognizing that both revenues and expenses can be treated as growing perpetuities. Since production will decrease 7% per year while costs per barrel remain constant, the growth rate of expenses is: -7.0%

To compute the growth rate of revenues, we use the fact that production decreases 7% per year while the price of oil increases 5% per year, so that the growth rate of revenues is:

$$[1.05 \times (1 - 0.07)] - 1 = -0.0235 = -2.35\%$$

Therefore, the present value (in 2012) of revenues beginning in 2013 is:

$$PV_{2012} = \frac{70,690,915}{0.09 - (-0.0235)} = \$622,827,445$$

Similarly, the present value (in 2012) of expenses beginning in 2013 is:

$$PV_{2012} = \frac{33,662,340}{0.09 - (-0.07)} = \$210,389,625$$

Subtracting these present values gives the present value (in 2012) of net income, and then discounting back three years to 2009, we find that the present value of dividends paid in 2013 and subsequent years is: $318,477,671

The total value of the company is:

$$\$121,012,624 + \$318,477,671 = \$439,490,295$$

Since there are 7,000,000 shares outstanding, the present value per share is:

$$\$439,490,295 / 7,000,000 = \$62.78$$

b. $EPS_{2009} = \$72,000,000/7,000,000 = \$10.29$

$EPS/P = \$10.29/\$62.78 = 0.164$

26.   [Note: In this problem, the long-term growth rate, in year 9 and all later years, should be 8%.]

The free cash flow for years 1 through 10 is computed in the following table:

	Year									
	1	2	3	4	5	6	7	8	9	10
Asset value	10.00	12.00	14.40	17.28	20.74	23.12	25.66	28.36	30.63	33.08
Earnings	1.20	1.44	1.73	2.07	2.49	2.77	3.08	3.40	3.68	3.97
Investment	2.00	2.40	2.88	3.46	2.38	2.54	2.69	2.27	2.45	2.65
Free cash flow	−0.80	−0.96	−1.15	−1.38	0.10	0.23	0.38	1.13	1.23	1.32
Earnings growth from previous period	20.0%	20.0%	20.0%	20.0%	20.0%	11.5%	11.0%	10.5%	8.0%	8.0%

Computing the present value of the free cash flows, following the approach from Section 4.5, we find that the present value of the free cash flows occurring in years 1 through 7 is:

$$PV = \frac{-0.80}{1.10^1} + \frac{-0.96}{1.10^2} + \frac{-1.15}{1.10^3} + \frac{-1.38}{1.10^4} + \frac{0.10}{1.10^5} + \frac{0.23}{1.10^6} + \frac{0.38}{1.10^7} = -\$2.94$$

The present value of the growing perpetuity that begins in year 8 is:

$$PV = \left(\frac{1}{(1.10)^7} \times \frac{1.1343}{(0.10 - 0.08)} \right) = \$29.10$$

Therefore, the present value of the business is:

-$2.94 + $29.10 = $26.16 million

27. From the equation given in the problem, it follows that:

$$\frac{P_0}{BVPS} = \frac{ROE \times (1-b)}{r - (b \times ROE)} = \frac{1-b}{(r / ROE) - b}$$

Consider three cases:

$$ROE < r \Rightarrow (P_0/BVPS) < 1$$

$$ROE = r \Rightarrow (P_0/BVPS) = 1$$

$$ROE > r \Rightarrow (P_0/BVPS) > 1$$

Thus, as ROE increases, the price-to-book ratio also increases, and, when ROE = r, price-to-book equals one.

28. Assume the portfolio value given, $100 million, is the value as of the end of the first year. Then, assuming constant growth, the value of the contract is given by the first payment (0.5 percent of portfolio value) divided by (r − g). Also:

r = dividend yield + growth rate

Hence:

r − growth rate = dividend yield = 0.05 = 5.0%

Thus, the value of the contract, V, is:

$$V = \frac{0.005 \times \$100 \text{ million}}{0.05} = \$10 \text{ million}$$

For stocks with a 4 percent yield:

r − growth rate = dividend yield = 0.04 = 4.0%

Thus, the value of the contract, V, is:

$$V = \frac{0.005 \times \$100 \text{ million}}{0.04} = \$12.5 \text{ million}$$

29. If existing stockholders buy newly issued shares to cover the $3.6 million financing requirement, then the value of Concatco equals the discounted value of the cash flows (as computed in Section 4.5): $18.8 million. Since the existing stockholders own 1 million shares, the value per share is $18.80.

Now suppose instead that the $3.6 million comes from new investors, who buy shares each year at a fair price. Since the new investors buy shares at a fair price, the value of the existing stockholders' shares must remain at $18.8 million. Since existing stockholders expect to earn 10% on their investment, the expected value of their shares in year 6 is:

$$\$18.8 \text{ million} \times (1.10)^6 = \$33.39 \text{ million}$$

The total value of the firm in year 6 is:

$$\$1.59 \text{ million} / (0.10 - 0.06) = \$39.75 \text{ million}$$

Compensation to new stockholders in year 6 is:

$$\$39.75 \text{ million} - \$33.39 \text{ million} = \$6.36 \text{ million}$$

Since existing stockholders own 1 million shares, then in year 6, new stockholders will own:

$$(\$6.36 \text{ million} / \$33.39 \text{ million}) \times 1,000,000 = 190,300 \text{ shares}$$

Share price in year 6 equals:

$$\$39.75 \text{ million} / 1.1903 \text{ million} = \$33.39$$

CHAPTER 5
Net Present Value and Other Investment Criteria

Answers to Problem Sets

1. a.   A = 3 years, B = 2 years, C = 3 years

    b.   B

    c.   A, B, and C

    d.   B and C (NPV$_B$ = $3,378; NPV$_C$ = $2,405)

    e.   True

    f.   It will accept no negative-NPV projects but will turn down some with positive NPVs. A project can have positive NPV if all future cash flows are considered but still do not meet the stated cutoff period.

2. Given the cash flows C$_0$, C$_1$, . . . , C$_T$, IRR is defined by:

$$NPV = C_0 + \frac{C_1}{1 + IRR} + \frac{C_2}{(1 + IRR)^2}$$
$$+ \cdots + \frac{C_T}{(1 + IRR)^T} = 0$$

It is calculated by trial and error, by financial calculators, or by spreadsheet programs.

3. a. $15,750; $4,250; $0

    b.   100%

4. No (you are effectively "borrowing" at a rate of interest higher than the opportunity cost of capital).

5. a.   Two

    b.   −50% and +50%

    c.   Yes, NPV = +14.6.

6. The incremental flows from investing in Alpha rather than Beta are –200,000; +110,000; and 121,000. The IRR on the incremental cash flow is 10% (i.e., –200 + 110/1.10 + 121/1.10^2 = 0). The IRR on Beta exceeds the cost of capital and so does the IRR on the incremental investment in Alpha. Choose Alpha.

7. 1, 2, 4, and 6

8. a. $NPV_A = -\$1000 + \dfrac{\$1000}{(1.10)} = -\$90.91$

   $NPV_B = -\$2000 + \dfrac{\$1000}{(1.10)} + \dfrac{\$1000}{(1.10)^2} + \dfrac{\$4000}{(1.10)^3} + \dfrac{\$1000}{(1.10)^4} + \dfrac{\$1000}{(1.10)^5} = +\$4,044.73$

   $NPV_C = -\$3000 + \dfrac{\$1000}{(1.10)} + \dfrac{\$1000}{(1.10)^2} + \dfrac{\$1000}{(1.10)^4} + \dfrac{\$1000}{(1.10)^5} = +\$39.47$

   b. Payback$_A$ = 1 year
   Payback$_B$ = 2 years
   Payback$_C$ = 4 years

   c. A and B

   d. $PV_A = \dfrac{\$1000}{(1.10)^1} = \$909.09$

   The present value of the cash inflows for Project A never recovers the initial outlay for the project, which is always the case for a negative NPV project.

   The present values of the cash inflows for Project B are shown in the third row of the table below, and the cumulative net present values are shown in the fourth row:

C_0	C_1	C_2	C_3	C_4	C_5
–2,000.00	+1,000.00	+1,000.00	+4,000.00	+1,000.0	+1,000.00
–2,000.00	909.09	826.45	3,005.26	683.01	620.92
	–1,090.91	–264.46	2,740.80	3,423.81	4,044.73

   Since the cumulative NPV turns positive between year two and year three, the discounted payback period is:

   $$2 + \dfrac{264.46}{3,005.26} = 2.09 \text{ years}$$

   The present values of the cash inflows for Project C are shown in the third row of the table below, and the cumulative net present values are shown in the fourth row:

C_0	C_1	C_2	C_3	C_4	C_5
–3,000.00	+1,000.00	+1,000.00	0.00	+1,000.0	+1,000.0
–3,000.00	909.09	826.45	0.00	683.01	620.92
	–2,090.91	–1,264.46	–1,264.46	–581.45	39.47

Since the cumulative NPV turns positive between year four and year five, the discounted payback period is:

$$4 + \frac{581.45}{620.92} = 4.94 \text{ years}$$

e. Using the discounted payback period rule with a cutoff of three years, the firm would accept only Project B.

9. a. When using the IRR rule, the firm must still compare the IRR with the opportunity cost of capital. Thus, even with the IRR method, one must specify the appropriate discount rate.

b. Risky cash flows should be discounted at a higher rate than the rate used to discount less risky cash flows. Using the payback rule is equivalent to using the NPV rule with a zero discount rate for cash flows before the payback period and an infinite discount rate for cash flows thereafter.

10.

	r = –17.44%	0.00%	10.00%	15.00%	20.00%	25.00%	45.27%
Year 0	–3,000.00	–3,000.00	–3,000.00	–3,000.00	–3,000.00	–3,000.00	–3,000.00
Year 1	3,500.00	4,239.34	3,500.00	3,181.82	3,043.48	2,916.67	2,800.00	2,409.31
Year 2	4,000.00	5,868.41	4,000.00	3,305.79	3,024.57	2,777.78	2,560.00	1,895.43
Year 3	–4,000.00	–7,108.06	–4,000.00	–3,005.26	–2,630.06	–2,314.81	–2,048.00	–1,304.76
	PV =	–0.31	500.00	482.35	437.99	379.64	312.00	–0.02

The two IRRs for this project are (approximately): –17.44% and 45.27% Between these two discount rates, the NPV is positive.

11. a. The figure on the next page was drawn from the following points:

	Discount Rate		
	0%	10%	20%
NPV_A	+20.00	+4.13	–8.33
NPV_B	+40.00	+5.18	–18.98

b. From the graph, we can estimate the IRR of each project from the point where its line crosses the horizontal axis:

$IRR_A = 13.1\%$ and $IRR_B = 11.9\%$

c.   The company should accept Project A if its NPV is positive and higher than that of Project B; that is, the company should accept Project A if the discount rate is greater than 10.7% (the intersection of NPV_A and NPV_B on the graph below) and less than 13.1%.

d.   The cash flows for (B – A) are:

$$C_0 = \quad \$\ 0$$
$$C_1 = \quad -\$60$$
$$C_2 = \quad -\$60$$
$$C_3 = \quad +\$140$$

Therefore:

	Discount Rate		
	0%	10%	20%
NPV_{B-A}	+20.00	+1.05	−10.65

IRR_{B-A} = 10.7%

The company should accept Project A if the discount rate is greater than 10.7% and less than 13.1%. As shown in the graph, for these discount rates, the IRR for the incremental investment is less than the opportunity cost of capital.

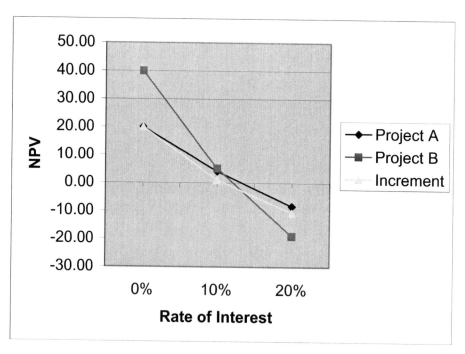

12. a.   Because Project A requires a larger capital outlay, it is possible that Project A has both a lower IRR and a higher NPV than Project B. (In fact, NPV_A is greater than NPV_B for all discount rates less than 10 percent.) Because the goal is to maximize shareholder wealth, NPV is the correct criterion.

b. To use the IRR criterion for mutually exclusive projects, calculate the IRR for the incremental cash flows:

	C_0	C_1	C_2	IRR
A – B	–200	+110	+121	10%

Because the IRR for the incremental cash flows exceeds the cost of capital, the additional investment in A is worthwhile.

c. $$NPV_A = -\$400 + \frac{\$250}{1.09} + \frac{\$300}{(1.09)^2} = \$81.86$$

$$NPV_B = -\$200 + \frac{\$140}{1.09} + \frac{\$179}{(1.09)^2} = \$79.10$$

13. Use incremental analysis:

	C_1	C_2	C_3
Current arrangement	–250,000	–250,000	+650,000
Extra shift	–550,000	+650,000	0
Incremental flows	–300,000	+900,000	–650,000

The IRRs for the incremental flows are (approximately): 21.13% *and* 78.87%
If the cost of capital is between these rates, Titanic should work the extra shift.

14. a. $$PI_D = \frac{-10,000 + \dfrac{20,000}{1.10}}{-(-10,000)} = \frac{8,182}{10,000} = 0.82$$

$$PI_E = \frac{-20,000 + \dfrac{35,000}{1.10}}{-(-20,000)} = \frac{11,818}{20,000} = 0.59$$

b. Each project has a Profitability Index greater than zero, and so both are acceptable projects. In order to choose between these projects, we must use incremental analysis. For the incremental cash flows:

$$PI_{E-D} = \frac{-10,000 + \dfrac{15,000}{1.10}}{-(-10,000)} = \frac{3,636}{10,000} = 0.36$$

The increment is thus an acceptable project, and so the larger project should be accepted, i.e., accept Project E. (Note that, in this case, the better project has the lower profitability index.)

15. Using the fact that Profitability Index = (Net Present Value/Investment), we find:

Project	Profitability Index
1	0.22
2	−0.02
3	0.17
4	0.14
5	0.07
6	0.18
7	0.12

Thus, given the budget of $1 million, the best the company can do is to accept Projects 1, 3, 4, and 6.

If the company accepted *all* positive NPV projects, the market value (compared to the market value under the budget limitation) would increase by the NPV of Project 5 plus the NPV of Project 7: $7,000 + $48,000 = $55,000
Thus, the budget limit costs the company $55,000 in terms of its market value.

16. The IRR is the discount rate which, when applied to a project's cash flows, yields NPV = 0. Thus, it does not represent an opportunity cost. However, if each project's cash flows could be invested at that project's IRR, then the NPV of each project would be zero because the IRR would then be the opportunity cost of capital for each project. The discount rate used in an NPV calculation is the opportunity cost of capital. Therefore, it is true that the NPV rule does assume that cash flows are reinvested at the opportunity cost of capital.

17. a.

$C_0 = -3{,}000$ $C_0 = -3{,}000$
$C_1 = +3{,}500$ $C_1 = +3{,}500$
$C_2 = +4{,}000$ $C_2 + PV(C_3) = +4{,}000 - 3{,}571.43 = 428.57$
$C_3 = -4{,}000$ MIRR = 27.84%

b. $$xC_1 + \frac{xC_2}{1.12} = -\frac{C_3}{1.12^2}$$

$$(1.12^2)(xC_1) + (1.12)(xC_2) = -C_3$$

$$(x)[(1.12^2)(C_1) + (1.12C_2)] = -C_3$$

$$x = \frac{-C_3}{(1.12^2)(C_1) + (1.12C_2)}$$

$$x = \frac{4{,}000}{(1.12^2)(3{,}500) + (1.12)(4{,}000)} = 0.45$$

$$C_0 + \frac{(1-x)C_1}{(1+IRR)} + \frac{(1-x)C_2}{(1+IRR)^2} = 0$$

$$-3,000 + \frac{(1-0.45)(3,500)}{(1+IRR)} + \frac{(1-0.45)(4,000)}{(1+IRR)^2} = 0$$

Now, find MIRR using either trial and error or the IRR function (on a financial calculator or Excel). We find that MIRR = 23.53%.

It is not clear that either of these modified IRRs is at all meaningful. Rather, these calculations seem to highlight the fact that MIRR really has no economic meaning.

18. Maximize: $NPV = 6,700x_W + 9,000x_X + 0x_Y - 1,500x_Z$

  subject to: $10,000x_W + 0x_X + 10,000x_Y + 15,000x_Z \leq 20,000$

  $10,000x_W + 20,000x_X - 5,000x_Y - 5,000x_Z \leq 20,000$

  $0x_W - 5,000x_X - 5,000x_Y - 4,000x_Z \leq 20,000$

  $0 \leq x_W \leq 1$

  $0 \leq x_X \leq 1$

  $0 \leq x_Z \leq 1$

Using Excel Spreadsheet Add-in Linear Programming Module:

  Optimized NPV = $13,450

  with $x_W = 1$; $x_X = 0.75$; $x_Y = 1$ and $x_Z = 0$

If financing available at t = 0 is $21,000:

  Optimized NPV = $13,500

  with $x_W = 1$; $x_X = (23/30)$; $x_Y = 1$ and $x_Z = (2/30)$

Here, the shadow price for the constraint at t = 0 is $50, the increase in NPV for a $1,000 increase in financing available at t = 0.

In this case, the program viewed x_Z as a viable choice even though the NPV of Project Z is negative. The reason for this result is that Project Z provides a positive cash flow in periods 1 and 2.

If the financing available at t = 1 is $21,000:

  Optimized NPV = $13,900

  with $x_W = 1$; $x_X = 0.8$; $x_Y = 1$ and $x_Z = 0$

Hence, the shadow price of an additional $1,000 in t =1 financing is $450.

CHAPTER 6
Making Investment Decisions with the Net Present Value Rule

Answers to Problem Sets

1. a, b, d, g, h.

2. Real cash flow = 100,000/1.04 = $96,154; real discount rate = 1.08/1.04 – 1 = .03846

$$PV = \frac{96,154}{1.03846} = \$92,593$$

3. a. False

   b. False

   c. False

   d. False

4. The longer the recovery period, the less the -present value of depreciation tax shields. This is true regardless of the discount rate. If r = .10, then 35% of the 5-year schedule's PV is .271. The same calculation for the 7-year schedule yields .252.

5.

	2010	2011	2012	2013	2014
Working capital	50,000	230,000	305,000	250,000	0
Cash flows	+50,000	+180,00	+75,000	–55,000	–250,000

6. Comparing present values can be misleading when projects have different economic lives and the projects are part of an ongoing business. For example, a machine that costs $100,000 per year to buy and lasts 5 years is not necessarily more expensive than a machine that costs $75,000 per year to buy but lasts only 3 years. Calculating the machines' equivalent annual costs allows an unbiased comparison.

7. PV cost = 1.5 + .2 X 14.09 = $4.319 million. Equivalent annual cost = 4.319/14.09 = .306, or $306,000.

8. a. NPV_A = $100,000; NPV_B = $180,000

   b. Equivalent cash flow of A = 100,000/1.736 5 $57,604; equivalent cash flow of B = 180,000/2.487 = $72,376

   c. Machine B.

9. Replace at end of 5 years ($80,000 > $72,376).

10. See the table below. We begin with the cash flows given in the text, Table 6.6, line 8, and utilize the following relationship from Chapter 3:

   Real cash flow = nominal cash flow/(1 + inflation rate)^t

   Here, the nominal rate is 20%, the expected inflation rate is 10%, and the real rate is given by the following:

   $$(1 + r_{nominal}) = (1 + r_{real}) \times (1 + \text{inflation rate})$$
   $$1.20 = (1 + r_{real}) \times (1.10)$$
   $$r_{real} = 0.0909 = 9.09\%$$

   As can be seen in the table, the NPV is unchanged (to within a rounding error).

	Year 0	Year 1	Year 2	Year 3	Year 4	Year 5	Year 6	Year 7
Net Cash Flows (Nominal)	−12,600	−1,484	2,947	6,323	10,534	9,985	5,757	3,269
Net Cash Flows (Real)	−12,600	−1,349	2,436	4,751	7,195	6,200	3,250	1,678

   NPV of Real Cash Flows (at 9.09%) = $3,804

11. The following spreadsheet calculates a NPV of −$147,510 (in nominal terms):

Nominal Calculation

				YEAR			
	0	1	2	3	4	5
Capital Investment	500,000					
Accumulated Depreciation		100,000	200,000	300,000	400,000	500,000
Year-End Book Value	500,000	400,000	300,000	200,000	100,000	0
Working capital	40,000	44,000	48,400	53,240	58,564	0
Total Book Value	540,000	444,000	348,400	253,240	158,564	0

	0	1	2	3	4	5
Revenues		200,000	220,000	242,000	266,200	292,820
Costs		100,000	110,000	121,000	133,100	146,410
Depreciation		100,000	100,000	100,000	100,000	100,000
Pretax Profit		0	10,000	21,000	33,100	46,410
Taxes at 35%		0	3,500	7,350	11,585	16,244
Profit after tax		0	6,500	13,650	21,515	30,167
Revenues		200,000	220,000	242,000	266,200	292,820
Costs		100,000	110,000	121,000	133,100	146,410
Tax on operations		0	3,500	7,350	11,585	16,244
Cash Flow from Operations		100,000	106,500	113,650	121,515	130,167
Change in working capital	−40,000	−4,000	−4,400	−4,840	−5,324	58,564
Capital Investment	−500,000					
Net Cash Flows	−540,000	96,000	102,100	108,810	116,191	188,731
Discount Factor @ 15%	1.000	0.870	0.756	0.658	0.572	0.497
Present Value	−540,000	83,478	77,202	71,544	66,433	93,832
NPV	−147,510					

Since the nominal rate is 15% and the expected inflation rate is 10%, the real rate is given by the following:

$$(1 + r_{nominal}) = (1 + r_{real}) \times (1 + \text{inflation rate})$$
$$1.15 = (1 + r_{real}) \times (1.10)$$
$$r_{real} = 0.04545 = 4.545\%$$

Adjusting the cash flows to real dollars and using this real rate gives us the same result for NPV (with a slight rounding error).

		YEAR				
	0	1	2	3	4	5
Net Cash Flows (Nominal)	−540,000	96,000	102,100	108,810	116,191	188,731
Adjustment Factor for Real CF	1	0.909	0.826	0.751	0.683	0.621
Net Cash Flows (Real)	−540,000	87,273	84,380	81,751	79,360	117,187
Discount Factor @ 4.545%	1.000	0.957	0.915	0.875	0.837	0.801
Present Value	−540,000	83,479	77,203	71,545	66,434	93,834
NPV	−147,505					

12. No, this is not the correct procedure. The opportunity cost of the land is its value in its best use, so Mr. North should consider the $45,000 value of the land as an outlay in his NPV analysis of the funeral home.

13. Investment in net working capital arises as a forecasting issue only because accrual accounting recognizes sales when made, not when cash is received (and costs when incurred, not when cash payment is made). If cash flow forecasts recognize the exact timing of the cash flows, then there is no need to also include investment in net working capital.

14. If the $50,000 is expensed at the end of year 1, the value of the tax shield is:

$$\frac{0.35 \times \$50,000}{1.05} = \$16,667$$

If the $50,000 expenditure is capitalized and then depreciated using a five-year MACRS depreciation schedule, the value of the tax shield is:

$$[0.35 \times \$50,000] \times \left(\frac{0.20}{1.05} + \frac{0.32}{1.05^2} + \frac{0.192}{1.05^3} + \frac{0.1152}{1.05^4} + \frac{0.1152}{1.05^5} + \frac{0.0576}{1.05^6} \right) = \$15,306$$

If the cost can be expensed, then the tax shield is larger, so that the after-tax cost is smaller.

15. Note: This answer assumes that the $3 million initial research costs are sunk and excludes this from the NPV calculation. It also assumes that working capital needs begin to accrue in year 0. The following spreadsheet calculates a project NPV of –$465,000.

Figures in 000's

				YEAR			
	0	1	2	3	4	5
Capital Investment	6,000					–500
Accumulated Depreciation		1,200	2,400	3,600	4,800	6,000
Year-End Book Value	6,000	4,800	3,600	2,400	1,200	0
Working capital	200	240	400	400	240	0
Total Book Value	6,200	5,040	4,000	2,800	1,440	0
Unit Sales		500	600	1,000	1,000	600
Revenues		2,000	2,400	4,000	4,000	2,400
Costs		750	900	1,500	1,500	900
Depreciation		1,200	1,200	1,200	1,200	1,200

Pretax Profit (includes salage in yr 5)		50	300	1,300	1,300	800
Taxes at 35%		18	105	455	455	280
Profit after tax		33	195	845	845	520
Revenues		2,000	2,400	4,000	4,000	2,400
Costs		750	900	1,500	1,500	900
Tax on operations		18	105	455	455	280
Cash Flow from Operations		1,233	1,395	2,045	2,045	1,220
Change in working capital	−200	−40	−160	0	160	240
Capital Investment	−6,000					
Net Cash Flows	−6,200	1,193	1,235	2,045	2,205	1,460
Discount Factor @ 12%	1.000	0.893	0.797	0.712	0.636	0.567
Present Value	−6,200	1,065	985	1,456	1,401	828
NPV	−465					

16. a. $$NPV_A = -\$100,000 + \sum_{t=1}^{5} \frac{\$26,000}{1.08^t} = \$3,810$$

NPV_B = −Investment + PV(after-tax cash flow) + PV(depreciation tax shield)

$$NPV_B = -\$100,000 + \sum_{t=1}^{5} \frac{\$26,000 \times (1-0.35)}{1.08^t} +$$

$$[0.35 \times \$100,000] \times \left[\frac{0.20}{1.08} + \frac{0.32}{1.08^2} + \frac{0.192}{1.08^3} + \frac{0.1152}{1.08^4} + \frac{0.1152}{1.08^5} + \frac{0.0576}{1.08^6} \right]$$

NPV_B = −$4,127

Another, perhaps more intuitive, way to do the Company B analysis is to first calculate the cash flows at each point in time, and then compute the present value of these cash flows:

	t = 0	t = 1	t = 2	t = 3	t = 4	t = 5	t = 6
Investment	100,000						
Cash Inflow		26,000	26,000	26,000	26,000	26,000	
Depreciation		20,000	32,000	19,200	11,520	11,520	5,760
Taxable Income		6,000	−6,000	6,800	14,480	14,480	−5,760
Tax (at 35%)		2,100	−2,100	2,380	5,068	5,068	−2,016
Cash Flow	−100,000	23,900	28,100	23,620	20,932	20,932	2,016
NPV (at 8%) = −$4,127							

b. $IRR_A = 9.43\%$

$IRR_B = 6.39\%$

Effective tax rate $= 1 - \dfrac{0.0639}{0.0943} = 0.322 = 32.2\%$

17. a.

TABLE 6.5 Tax payments on IM&C's guano project ($thousands)									
No. of years depreciation	7								
Tax rate (percent)	35								
					Period				
	0	1	2	3	4	5	6	7	
MACRS %		14.29	24.49	17.49	12.49	8.93	8.92	13.38	
Tax depreciation		1,429	2,449	1,749	1,249	893	892	1,338	
(MACRS% x depreciable investment)									
1. Sales	0	523	12,887	32,610	48,901	35,834	19,717	0	
2. Cost of goods sold	0	837	7,729	19,552	29,345	21,492	11,830	0	
3. Other costs	4,000	2,200	1,210	1,331	1,464	1,611	1,772	0	
4. Tax depreciation	0	1,429	2,449	1,749	1,249	893	892	1,338	
5. Pretax profits	−4,000	−3,943	1,499	9,978	16,843	11,838	5,223	611	
6. Tax	−1,400	−1,380	525	3,492	5,895	4,143	1,828	214	

TABLE 6.6 IM&C's guano project – revised cash flow analysis with MACRS depreciation ($thousands)								
					Period			
	0	1	2	3	4	5	6	7
1. Sales	0	523	12,887	32,610	48,901	35,834	19,717	0
2. Cost of goods sold	0	837	7,729	19,552	29,345	21,492	11,830	0
3. Other costs	4,000	2,200	1,210	1,331	1,464	1,611	1,772	0
4. Tax	−1,400	−1,380	525	3,492	5,895	4,143	1,828	214
5. Cash flow from operations	−2,600	−1,134	3,423	8,235	12,197	8,588	4,287	−214
6. Change in working capital		−550	−739	−1,972	−1,629	1,307	1,581	2,002
7. Capital investment and disposal	−10,000	0	0	0	0	0	0	1,949
8. Net cash flow (5+6+7)	−12,600	−1,684	2,684	6,263	10,568	9,895	5,868	3,737
9. Present value	−12,600	−1,403	1,864	3,624	5,096	3,977	1,965	1,043
Net present value =	3,566							
Cost of capital (percent)	20							

b.

	TABLE 6.1 IM&C's guano project – projections ($thousands) reflecting inflation and straight line depreciation								
						Period			
		0	**1**	**2**	**3**	**4**	**5**	**6**	**7**
1.	Capital investment	15,000							−1,949
2.	Accumulated depn.		2,417	4,833	7,250	9,667	12,083	14,500	0
3.	Year-end book value	15,000	12,583	10,167	7,750	5,333	2,917	500	0
4.	Working capital		550	1,289	3,261	4,890	3,583	2,002	0
5.	Total book value (3 + 4)		13,133	11,456	11,011	10,223	6,500	2,502	0
6.	Sales		523	12,887	32,610	48,901	35,834	19,717	
7.	Cost of goods sold		837	7,729	19,552	29,345	21,492	11,830	
8.	Other costs	4,000	2,200	1,210	1,331	1,464	1,611	1,772	
9.	Depreciation		2,417	2,417	2,417	2,417	2,417	2,417	0
10.	Pretax profit	−4,000	−4,931	1,531	9,310	15,675	10,314	3,698	1,449
11.	Tax	−1,400	−1,726	536	3,259	5,486	3,610	1,294	507
12.	Profit after tax (10 − 11)	−2,600	−3,205	995	6,052	10,189	6,704	2,404	942
	Notes:								
	No. of years depreciation				6				
	Assumed salvage value in depreciation calculation				500				
	Tax rate (percent)				35				

	TABLE 6.2 IM&C's guano project – initial cash flow analysis with straight-line depreciation ($thousands)								
						Period			
		0	**1**	**2**	**3**	**4**	**5**	**6**	**7**
1.	Sales	0	523	12,887	32,610	48,901	35,834	19,717	0
2.	Cost of goods sold	0	837	7,729	19,552	29,345	21,492	11,830	0
3.	Other costs	4,000	2,200	1,210	1,331	1,464	1,611	1,772	0
4.	Tax	−1,400	−1,726	536	3,259	5,486	3,610	1,294	507
5.	Cash flow from operations	−2,600	−788	3,412	8,468	12,606	9,121	4,821	−507
6.	Change in working capital		−550	−739	−1,972	−1,629	1,307	1,581	2,002
7.	Capital investment and disposal	−15,000	0	0	0	0	0	0	1,949
8.	Net cash flow (5+6+7)	−17,600	−1,338	2,673	6,496	10,977	10,428	6,402	3,444
9.	Present value	−17,600	−1,206	2,169	4,750	7,231	6,189	3,423	1,659
	Net present value =	6,614							
	Cost of capital (percent)	11							

c.

						Period			

TABLE 6.1 IM&C's guano project – projections ($thousands) reflecting inflation and straight line depreciation

		0	1	2	3	4	5	6	7
1.	Capital investment	15,000							– 1,949
2.	Accumulated depn.		2,417	4,833	7,250	9,667	12,083	14,500	0
3.	Year–end book value	15,000	12,583	10,167	7,750	5,333	2,917	500	0
4.	Working capital		605	1,418	3,587	5,379	3,941	2,202	0
5.	Total book value (3 + 4)		13,188	11,585	11,337	10,712	6,858	2,702	0
6.	Sales		575	14,176	35,871	53,791	39,417	21,689	
7.	Cost of goods sold		921	8,502	21,507	32,280	23,641	13,013	
8.	Other costs	4,000	2,200	1,210	1,331	1,464	1,611	1,772	
9.	Depreciation		2,417	2,417	2,417	2,417	2,417	2,417	0
10.	Pretax profit	−4,000	−4,962	2,047	10,616	17,631	11,749	4,487	1,449
11.	Tax	−1,400	−1,737	716	3,716	6,171	4,112	1,570	507
12.	Profit after tax (10 – 11)	−2,600	−3,225	1,331	6,900	11,460	7,637	2,917	942
	Notes:								
	No. of years depreciation				6				
	Assumed salvage value in depreciation calculation				500				
	Tax rate (percent)				35				

TABLE 6.2 IM&C's guano project – initial cash flow analysis with straight-line depreciation ($thousands)

						Period			

		0	1	2	3	4	5	6	7
1.	Sales	0	575	14,176	35,871	53,791	39,417	21,689	0
2.	Cost of goods sold	0	921	8,502	21,507	32,280	23,641	13,013	0
3.	Other costs	4,000	2,200	1,210	1,331	1,464	1,611	1,772	0
4.	Tax	−1,400	−1,737	716	3,716	6,171	4,112	1,570	507
5.	Cash flow from operations	−2,600	−809	3,747	9,317	13,877	10,053	5,333	−507
6.	Change in working capital		−605	−813	−2,169	−1,792	1,438	1,739	2,202
7.	Capital investment and disposal	−15,000	0	0	0	0	0	0	1,949
8.	Net cash flow (5+6+7)	−17,600	−1,414	2,934	7,148	12,085	11,491	7,072	3,644
9.	Present value	−17,600	−1,274	2,382	5,227	7,961	6,819	3,781	1,755
	Net present value =	9,051							
	Cost of capital (percent)	11							

18.　Assume the following:

a.　The firm will manufacture widgets for at least 10 years.

b.　There will be no inflation or technological change.

c.　The 15% cost of capital is appropriate for all cash flows and is a real, after-tax rate of return.

d.　All operating cash flows occur at the end of the year.

e.　We cannot ignore incremental working capital costs and recovery

Note: Since purchasing the lids can be considered a one-year 'project,' the two projects have a common chain life of 10 years.

Compute NPV for each project as follows:

$$NPV(\text{purchase}) = -\sum_{t=1}^{10} \frac{(\$2 \times 200{,}000) \times (1 - 0.35)}{1.15^t} = -\$1{,}304{,}880$$

$$NPV(\text{make}) = -\$150{,}000 - \$30{,}000 - \sum_{t=1}^{10} \frac{(\$1.50 \times 200{,}000) \times (1 - 0.35)}{1.15^t}$$

$$+ \left[0.35 \times \$150{,}000\right] \times \left[\frac{0.1429}{1.15^1} + \frac{0.2449}{1.15^2} + \frac{0.1749}{1.15^3} + \frac{0.1249}{1.15^4} + \right.$$

$$\left. \frac{0.0893}{1.15^5} + \frac{0.0893}{1.15^6} + \frac{0.0893}{1.15^7} + \frac{0.0445}{1.15^8} \right] + \frac{\$30{,}000}{1.15^{10}} = -\$1{,}118{,}328$$

Thus, the widget manufacturer should make the lids.

19.　a.　*Capital Expenditure*
1.　If the spare warehouse space will be used now or in the future, then the project should be credited with these benefits.
2.　Charge opportunity cost of the land and building.
3.　The salvage value at the end of the project should be included.
Research and Development
1.　Research and development is a sunk cost.
Working Capital
1.　Will additional inventories be required as volume increases?
2.　Recovery of inventories at the end of the project should be included.
3.　Is additional working capital required due to changes in receivables, payables, etc.?
Revenue
1.　Revenue forecasts assume prices (and quantities) will be unaffected by competition, a common and critical mistake.

Operating Costs
1.   Are percentage labor costs unaffected by increase in volume in the early years?
2.   Wages generally increase faster than inflation. Does Reliable expect continuing productivity gains to offset this?

Overhead
1.   Is "overhead" truly incremental?

Depreciation
1.   Depreciation is not a cash flow, but the ACRS deprecation does affect tax payments.
2.   ACRS depreciation is fixed in nominal terms. The real value of the depreciation tax shield is reduced by inflation.

Interest
1.   It is bad practice to deduct interest charges (or other payments to security holders). Value the project as if it is all equity-financed.

Tax
1.   See comments on ACRS depreciation and interest.
2.   If Reliable has profits on its remaining business, the tax loss should not be carried forward.

Net Cash Flow
1.   See comments on ACRS depreciation and interest.
2.   Discount rate should reflect project characteristics; in general, it is *not* equivalent to the company's borrowing rate.

b.   1.   Potential use of warehouse.
     2.   Opportunity cost of building.
     3.   Other working capital items.
     4.   More realistic forecasts of revenues and costs.
     5.   Company's ability to use tax shields.
     6.   Opportunity cost of capital.

c.   The table on the next page shows a sample NPV analysis for the project. The analysis is based on the following assumptions:
     1.   *Inflation*: 10% per year.
     2.   *Capital Expenditure:* $8 million for machinery; $5 million for market value of factory; $2.4 million for warehouse extension (we assume that it is eventually needed or that electric motor project and surplus capacity cannot be used in the interim). We assume salvage value of $3 million in real terms less tax at 35%.
     3.   *Working Capital*: We assume inventory in year t is 9.1% of expected revenues in year (t + 1). We also assume that receivables *less* payables, in year t, is equal to 5% of revenues in year t.
     4.   *Depreciation Tax Shield*: Based on 35% tax rate and 5-year ACRS class. This is a simplifying and probably inaccurate assumption; i.e., not all the investment would fall in the 5-year class. Also, the

factory is currently owned by the company and may already be partially depreciated. We assume the company can use tax shields as they arise.

5. *Revenues*: Sales of 2,000 motors in 2010, 4,000 motors in 2011, and 10,000 motors thereafter. The unit price is assumed to decline from $4,000 (real) to $2,850 when competition enters in 2012. The latter is the figure at which new entrants' investment in the project would have NPV = 0.
6. *Operating Costs*: We assume direct labor costs decline progressively from $2,500 per unit in 2010, to $2,250 in 2011 and to $2,000 in real terms in 2012 and after.
7. *Other Costs*: We assume true incremental costs are 10% of revenue.
8. *Tax:* 35% of revenue less costs.
9. *Opportunity Cost of Capital*: Assumed 20%.

	2009	2010	2011	2012	2013	2014
Capital Expenditure	−15,400					
Changes in Working Capital						
Inventories	−801	−961	−1,690	−345	380	−418
Receivables − Payables		−440	−528	−929	−190	−209
Depreciation Tax Shield		1,078	1,725	1,035	621	621
Revenues		8,800	19,360	37,934	41,727	45,900
Operating Costs		−5,500	−10,890	−26,620	−29,282	−32,210
Other costs		−880	−1,936	−3,793	−4,173	−4,590
Tax		−847	−2,287	−2,632	−2,895	−3,185
Net Cash Flow	−16,201	1,250	3,754	4,650	5,428	5,909

	2015	2016	2017	2018	2019	2030
Capital Expenditure					5,058	
Changes in Working Capital						
Inventories	−459	−505	−556	−612	6,727	
Receivables − Payables	−229	−252	−278	−306	−336	3,696
Depreciation Tax Shield	310					
Revenues	50,489	55,538	61,092	67,202	73,922	
Operating Costs	−35,431	−38,974	−42,872	−47,159	−51,875	
Other costs	−5,049	−5,554	−6,109	−6,720	−7,392	
Tax	−3,503	−3,854	−4,239	−4,663	−5,129	
Net Cash Flow	6,128	6,399	7,038	7,742	20,975	3,696

NPV (at 20%) = $5,991

20. The table below shows the real cash flows. The NPV is computed using the real rate, which is computed as follows:

$$(1 + r_{nominal}) = (1 + r_{real}) \times (1 + \text{inflation rate})$$
$$1.09 = (1 + r_{real}) \times (1.03)$$
$$r_{real} = 0.0583 = 5.83\%$$

	t = 0	t = 1	t = 2	t = 3	t = 4	t = 5	t = 6	t = 7	t = 8
Investment	−35,000.0								15,000.0
Savings		8,580.0	8,580.0	8,580.0	8,580.0	8,580.0	8,580.0	8,580.0	8,580.0
Insurance		−1,200.0	−1,200.0	−1,200.0	−1,200.0	−1,200.0	−1,200.0	−1,200.0	−1,200.0
Fuel		1,053.0	1,053.0	1,053.0	1,053.0	1,053.0	1,053.0	1,053.0	1,053.0
Net Cash Flow	−35,000.0	8,433.0	8,433.0	8,433.0	8,433.0	8,433.0	8,433.0	8,433.0	23,433.0

NPV (at 5.83%) = $27,254.2

21. All numbers are in thousands:

	t = 0	t = 1	t = 2	t = 3	t = 4	t = 5	t = 6	t = 7	t = 8
Sales		4,200.0	4,410.0	4,630.5	4,862.0	5,105.1	5,360.4	5,628.4	5,909.8
Manufacturing Costs		3,780.0	3,969.0	4,167.5	4,375.8	4,594.6	4,824.4	5,065.6	5,318.8
Depreciation		120.0	120.0	120.0	120.0	120.0	120.0	120.0	120.0
Rent		100.0	104.0	108.2	112.5	117.0	121.7	126.5	131.6
Earnings Before Taxes		200.0	217.0	234.8	253.7	273.5	294.3	316.3	339.4
Taxes		70.0	76.0	82.2	88.8	95.7	103.0	110.7	118.8
Cash Flow – Operations		250.0	261.1	272.6	284.9	297.8	311.3	325.6	340.6
Working Capital	350.0	420.0	441.0	463.1	486.2	510.5	536.0	562.8	0.0
Increase in W.C.	350.0	70.0	21.0	22.1	23.1	24.3	25.5	26.8	−562.8
Initial Investment	1,200.0								
Sale of Plant									400.0
Tax on Sale									56.0
Net Cash Flow	−1,550.0	180.0	240.1	250.5	261.8	273.5	285.8	298.8	1,247.4

NPV(at 12%) = $85.8

22. We can use the following spreadsheet to calculate a NPV of 6.352 billion RMB for the Ambassador China project. This calculation uses the following assumptions:

1. Calculations are done on a nominal basis, converting the salvage value estimate from a real to a nominal value (638) using the 5% inflation estimate; Salvage = book value so no taxes are incurred on salvage.

2. Depreciation is calculated at 4000 − 638 (salvage) / 5 = 672.4 per year

3. Cars sales occur in year 1 (there is some ambiguity here as the problem state it takes a year for the plant to become operational but also that sales will occur in the first year).

4. The tax shield in year 0 can be used to offset profits from other operations.

5. No working capital costs (this is unrealistic, but no figures are given)

RMB; figures in millions				YEAR		
	0	1	2	3	4	5
Capital Investment	4,000					−638
Accumulated Depreciation		672	1,345	2,017	2,689	3,362
Year-End Book Value	4,000	3,328	2,655	1,983	1,311	638
Unit Sales		0.10	0.10	0.10	0.10	0.10
Price / unit (growing 4%)		65,000	67,600	70,304	73,116	76,041
Raw Material Cost / Unit (growing 3%)		18,000	18,540	19,096	19,669	20,259
Revenues		6,500	6,760	7,030	7,312	7,604
Raw Material Costs		1,800	1,854	1,910	1,967	2,026
Labor Costs (growing 7%)		1,100	1,177	1,259	1,348	1,442
Land costs (prepaid)	300	300	300	300	300	
Depreciation		672.4	672.4	672.4	672.4	672.4
Pretax Profit	−300	2,628	2,757	2,889	3,025	3,464
Taxes at 25%	−75	657	689	722	756	866
Profit after tax	−225	1,971	2,067	2,167	2,269	2,598
Revenues		6,500	6,760	7,030	7,312	7,604
Cash costs	300	3,200	3,331	3,469	3,614	3,468
Tax on operations		657	689	722	756	866
Cash Flow from Operations	−300	2,643	2,740	2,839	2,941	3,270
Capital Investment	−4,000					638
Net Cash Flows	−4,300	2,643	2,740	2,839	2,941	3,908
Discount Factor @ 12%	1.000	0.893	0.797	0.712	0.636	0.567
Present Value	−4,300	2,360	2,184	2,021	1,869	2,218
NPV	6,352					

23.   [Note: Section 6.2 provides several different calculations of pre-tax profit and taxes, based on different assumptions; the solution below is based on Table 6.6 in the text.]

See the table below. With full usage of the tax losses, the NPV of the tax payments is $4,779. With tax losses carried forward, the NPV of the tax payments is $5,741. Thus, with tax losses carried forward, the project's NPV decreases by $962, so that the value to the company of using the deductions immediately is $962.

	t = 0	t = 1	t = 2	t = 3	t = 4	t = 5	t = 6	t = 7
Pretax Profit	–4,000	–4,514	748	9,807	16,940	11,579	5,539	1,949
Full usage of tax losses immediately (Table 7.6)	–1,400	–1,580	262	3,432	5,929	4,053	1,939	682
NPV (at 20%) = $4,779								
Tax loss carry-forward	0	0	0	714	5,929	4,053	1,939	682
NPV (at 20%) = $5,741								

24. In order to solve this problem, we calculate the equivalent annual cost for each of the two alternatives. (All cash flows are in thousands.)

Alternative 1 – Sell the new machine: If we sell the new machine, we receive the cash flow from the sale, pay taxes on the gain, and pay the costs associated with keeping the old machine. The present value of this alternative is:

$$PV_1 = 50 - [0.35(50 - 0)] - 20 - \frac{30}{1.12} - \frac{30}{1.12^2} - \frac{30}{1.12^3} - \frac{30}{1.12^4} - \frac{30}{1.12^5}$$
$$+ \frac{5}{1.12^5} - \frac{0.35\,(5 - 0)}{1.12^5} = -\$93.80$$

The equivalent annual cost for the five-year period is computed as follows:

$PV_1 = EAC_1 \times$ [annuity factor, 5 time periods, 12%]

–93.80 = $EAC_1 \times$ [3.605]

EAC_1 = –26.02, or an equivalent annual cost of $26,020

Alternative 2 – Sell the old machine: If we sell the old machine, we receive the cash flow from the sale, pay taxes on the gain, and pay the costs associated with keeping the new machine. The present value of this alternative is:

$$PV_2 = 25 - [0.35(25 - 0)] - \frac{20}{1.12} - \frac{20}{1.12^2} - \frac{20}{1.12^3} - \frac{20}{1.12^4} - \frac{20}{1.12^5}$$
$$- \frac{20}{1.12^5} - \frac{30}{1.12^6} - \frac{30}{1.12^7} - \frac{30}{1.12^8} - \frac{30}{1.12^9} - \frac{30}{1.12^{10}}$$
$$+ \frac{5}{1.12^{10}} - \frac{0.35\,(5 - 0)}{1.12^{10}} = -\$127.51$$

The equivalent annual cost for the ten-year period is computed as follows:

$PV_2 = EAC_2 \times$ [annuity factor, 10 time periods, 12%]

–127.51 = $EAC_2 \times$ [5.650]

EAC_2 = –22.57, or an equivalent annual cost of $22,570

Thus, the least expensive alternative is to sell the old machine because this alternative has the lowest equivalent annual cost.

One key assumption underlying this result is that, whenever the machines have to be replaced, the replacement will be a machine that is as efficient to operate as the new machine being replaced.

25. Assuming that the light bulb purchases occur at year 0 (for use during the following year or years), the cost structure and PV of each option is

YEAR

	0	1	2	3	4	5	6	7	8	9	PV @ 5%
Low Energy	3.50	1.60	1.60	1.60	1.60	1.60	1.60	1.60	1.60	1.60	14.87
Conventional	0.50	6.60									6.79

The equivalent annual cost for the low energy bulb is computed as follows:

$$PV_{LE} = EAC_{LE} \times [\text{annuity factor, 9 time periods, 5\%}]$$

$$14.87 = EAC_{LE} \times [7.108]$$

$EAC_{LE} = \$2.09$, which is much cheaper than the \$6.79 cost of using a conventional light bulb for the year.

26. The current copiers have net cost cash flows as follows:

Year	Before-Tax Cash Flow	After-Tax Cash Flow	Net Cash Flow
1	–2,000	$(-2,000 \times .65) + (.35 \times .0893 \times 20,000)$	–674.9
2	–2,000	$(-2,000 \times .65) + (.35 \times .0892 \times 20,000)$	–675.6
3	–8,000	$(-8,000 \times .65) + (.35 \times .0893 \times 20,000)$	–4,574.9
4	–8,000	$(-8,000 \times .65) + (.35 \times .0445 \times 20,000)$	–4,888.5
5	–8,000	$(-8,000 \times .65)$	–5,200.0
6	–8,000	$(-8,000 \times .65)$	–5,200.0

These cash flows have a present value, discounted at 7%, of –$15,857. Using the annuity factor for 6 time periods at 7% (4.767), we find an equivalent annual cost of $3,326. Therefore, the copiers should be replaced only when the equivalent annual cost of the replacements is less than $3,326.

When purchased, the new copiers will have net cost cash flows as follows:

Year	Before-Tax Cash Flow	After-Tax Cash Flow	Net Cash Flow
0	–25,000	–25,000	–25,000.0
1	–1,000	$(-1,000 \times .65) + (.35 \times .1429 \times 25,000)$	600.4
2	–1,000	$(-1,000 \times .65) + (.35 \times .2449 \times 25,000)$	1,492.9
3	–1,000	$(-1,000 \times .65) + (.35 \times .1749 \times 25,000)$	880.4
4	–1,000	$(-1,000 \times .65) + (.35 \times .1249 \times 25,000)$	442.9

5	−1,000	$(-1,000 \times .65) + (.35 \times .0893 \times 25,000)$	131.4
6	−1,000	$(-1,000 \times .65) + (.35 \times .0892 \times 25,000)$	130.5
7	−1,000	$(-1,000 \times .65) + (.35 \times .0893 \times 25,000)$	131.4
8	−1,000	$(-1,000 \times .65) + (.35 \times .0445 \times 25,000)$	−260.6

These cash flows have a present value, discounted at 7%, of −$21,967. The decision to replace must also take into account the resale value of the machine, as well as the associated tax on the resulting gain (or loss).

Consider three cases:

a. The book (depreciated) value of the existing copiers is now $6,248. If the existing copiers are replaced now, then the present value of the cash flows is:

$$-21,967 + 8,000 - [0.35 \times (8,000 - 6,248)] = -\$14,580$$

Using the annuity factor for 8 time periods at 7% (5.971), we find that the equivalent annual cost is $2,442.

b. Two years from now, the book (depreciated) value of the existing copiers will be $2,678. If the existing copiers are replaced two years from now, then the present value of the cash flows is:

$$(-674.9/1.07^1) + (-675.6/1.07^2) + (-21,967/1.07^2) +$$

$$\{3,500 - [0.35 \times (3,500 - 2,678)]\}/1.07^2 = -\$17,602$$

Using the annuity factor for 10 time periods at 7% (7.024), we find that the equivalent annual cost is $2,506.

c. Six years from now, both the book value and the resale value of the existing copiers will be zero. If the existing copiers are replaced six years from now, then the present value of the cash flows is:

$$-15,857 + (-21,967/1.07^6) = -\$30,495$$

Using the annuity factor for 14 time periods at 7% (8.745), we find that the equivalent annual cost is $3,487.

The copiers should be replaced immediately.

27. a.

	Year 1	Year 2	Year 3	Year 4	Year 5	Year 6	Year 7	Year 8	Year 9	Year 10	Year 11
MACRS Percent	10.00%	18.00%	14.40%	11.52%	9.22%	7.37%	6.55%	6.55%	6.56%	6.55%	3.29%
MACRS Depr.	40.00	72.00	57.60	46.08	36.88	29.48	26.20	26.20	26.24	26.20	13.16
Tax Shield	15.60	28.08	22.46	17.97	14.38	11.50	10.22	10.22	10.23	10.22	5.13
Present Value (at 7%) = $114.57 million											

The equivalent annual cost of the depreciation tax shield is computed by dividing the present value of the tax shield by the annuity factor for 25 years at 7%:

Equivalent annual cost = $114.57 million/11.654 = $9.83 million

The equivalent annual cost of the capital investment is:

$34.3 million – $9.83 million = $24.47 million

b.   The extra cost per gallon (after tax) is:

$24.47 million/900 million gallons = $0.0272 per gallon

The pre-tax charge = $0.0272/0.65 = $0.0418 per gallon

28.   a. $$PV_A = 40,000 + \frac{10,000}{1.06} + \frac{10,000}{1.06^2} + \frac{10,000}{1.06^3}$$

PV_A = $66,730 (Note that this is a cost.)

$$PV_B = 50,000 + \frac{8,000}{1.06} + \frac{8,000}{1.06^2} + \frac{8,000}{1.06^3} + \frac{8,000}{1.06^4}$$

PV_B = $77,721 (Note that this is a cost.)

Equivalent annual cost (EAC) is found by:

PV_A = EAC_A × [annuity factor, 6%, 3 time periods]

66,730 = EAC_A × 2.673

EAC_A = $24,964 per year rental

PV_B = EAC_B × [annuity factor, 6%, 4 time periods]

77,721 = EAC_B × 3.465

EAC_B = $22,430 per year rental

b.   Annual rental is $24,964 for Machine A and $22,430 for Machine B. Borstal should buy Machine B.

c.   The payments would increase by 8% per year. For example, for Machine A, rent for the first year would be $24,964; rent for the second year would be ($24,964 × 1.08) = $26,961; etc.

29.   Because the cost of a new machine now decreases by 10% per year, the rent on such a machine also decreases by 10% per year. Therefore:

$$PV_A = 40,000 + \frac{9,000}{1.06} + \frac{8,100}{1.06^2} + \frac{7,290}{1.06^3}$$

$PV_A = \$61,820$ (Note that this is a cost.)

$$PV_B = 50,000 + \frac{7,200}{1.06} + \frac{6,480}{1.06^2} + \frac{5,832}{1.06^3} + \frac{5,249}{1.06^4}$$

$PV_B = \$71,614$ (Note that this is a cost.)

Equivalent annual cost (EAC) is found as follows:

$PV_A = EAC_A \times$ [annuity factor, 6%, 3 time periods]

$61,820 = EAC_A \times 2.673$

$EAC_A = \$23,128$, a reduction of 7.35%

$PV_B = EAC_B \times$ [annuity factor, 6%, 4 time periods]

$71,614 = EAC_B \times 3.465$

$EAC_B = \$20,668$, a reduction of 7.86%

30. With a 6-year life, the equivalent annual cost (at 8%) of a new jet is:

$\$1,100,000/4.623 = \$237,941$

If the jet is replaced at the end of year 3 rather than year 4, the company will incur an incremental cost of $237,941 in year 4. The present value of this cost is:

$\$237,941/1.08^4 = \$174,894$

The present value of the savings is: $\displaystyle\sum_{t=1}^{3} \frac{80,000}{1.08^t} = \$206,168$

The president should allow wider use of the present jet because the present value of the savings is greater than the present value of the cost.

31. a.

	Year 0	Year 1	Year 2	Year 3	Year 4	Year 5	Year 6	Year 7
Pre-Tax Flows	–14,000	–3,064	3,209	9,755	16,463	14,038	7,696	3,951

IRR = 33.5%

	Year 0	Year 1	Year 2	Year 3	Year 4	Year 5	Year 6	Year 7
Post-Tax Flows	–12,600	–1,630	2,381	6,205	10,685	10,136	6,110	3,444

IRR = 26.8%

Effective Tax Rate = 20.0%

b. If the depreciation rate is accelerated, this has no effect on the pretax IRR, but it increases the after-tax IRR. Therefore, the numerator decreases and the effective tax rate decreases.

If the inflation rate increases, we would expect pretax cash flows to increase at the inflation rate, while after-tax cash flows increase at a slower rate. After-tax cash flows increase at a slower rate than the inflation rate because depreciation expense does not increase with inflation. Therefore, the numerator of T_E becomes proportionately larger than the denominator and the effective tax rate increases.

c.
$$T_E = \frac{\dfrac{C}{I(1-T_c)} - \dfrac{C(1-T_c)}{I(1-T_c)}}{\dfrac{C}{I(1-T_c)}} = \left[\frac{C}{I(1-T_c)} - \frac{C}{I}\right]\left[\frac{I(1-T_c)}{C}\right] = 1-(1-T_c) = T_c$$

Hence, if the up-front investment is deductible for tax purposes, then the effective tax rate is equal to the statutory tax rate.

32.　a.　With a real rate of 6% and an inflation rate of 5%, the nominal rate, r, is determined as follows:

$$(1 + r) = (1 + 0.06) \times (1 + 0.05)$$

$$r = 0.113 = 11.3\%$$

For a three-year annuity at 11.3%, the annuity factor is: 2.4310
For a two-year annuity, the annuity factor is: 1.7057

For a three-year annuity with a present value of $28.37, the nominal annuity is: ($28.37/2.4310) = $11.67

For a two-year annuity with a present value of $21.00, the nominal annuity is: ($21.00/1.7057) = $12.31

These nominal annuities are not realistic estimates of equivalent annual costs because the appropriate rental cost (i.e., the equivalent annual cost) must take into account the effects of inflation.

　　b.　With a real rate of 6% and an inflation rate of 25%, the nominal rate, r, is determined as follows:

$$(1 + r) = (1 + 0.06) \times (1 + 0.25)$$

$$r = 0.325 = 32.5\%$$

For a three-year annuity at 32.5%, the annuity factor is: 1.7542
For a two-year annuity, the annuity factor is: 1.3243

For a three-year annuity with a present value of $28.37, the nominal annuity is: ($28.37/1.7542) = $16.17
For a two-year annuity with a present value of $21.00, the nominal annuity is: ($21.00/1.3243) = $15.86

With an inflation rate of 5%, Machine A has the lower nominal annual cost ($11.67 compared to $12.31). With inflation at 25%, Machine B has the lower nominal annual cost ($15.86 compared to $16.17). Thus it is clear that inflation has a significant impact on the calculation of equivalent annual cost, and hence, the warning in the text to do these calculations in real terms. The rankings change because, at the higher inflation rate, the machine with the longer life (here, Machine A) is affected more.

33. a. The spreadsheet on the next two pages indicates that the NPV for the Mid-American wind farm investment is: –$87,271,675
By eliminating the tax in the spreadsheet, we find that the NPV is still negative: –$7,692,376
NPV becomes positive with a tax subsidy of approximately 3.5%.

    b. Using the same spreadsheet, we can show that a capacity factor of 30% reduces NPV to: –$138,249,182

ESTIMATED NPV OF MIDAMERICAN ENERGY'S WINDFARM PROJECT IN THE ABSENCE OF ANY TAX BREAKS

PROJECT DATA

Capacity (megawatts)	360.5
Load factor	35%
Year 1 electricity price $/mWh	55.00
Year 1 maintenance & other costs ($)	18,900,000
Inflation	3.00%
Total capital cost ($)	386,000,000
MACRS years	20
Cost of capital	12.0%

Year	0	1	2	3	4	5	6
Capital cost	386,000,000						
Revenues		60,791,115	62,614,848	64,493,294	66,428,093	68,420,936	70,473,564
Maintenance & other costs		18,900,000	19,467,000	20,051,010	20,652,540	21,272,117	21,910,280
MACRS depreciation		14,475,000	27,869,200	25,784,800	23,854,800	22,040,600	20,380,800
Pretax profit		27,416,115	15,278,648	18,657,484	21,920,752	25,108,219	28,182,484
Tax		9,595,640	5,347,527	6,530,119	7,672,263	8,787,877	9,863,869
Cash flow	−386,000,000	32,295,475	37,800,321	37,912,165	38,103,289	38,360,942	38,699,414
PV	−386,000,000	28,835,245	30,134,185	26,985,130	24,215,329	21,767,029	19,606,328
NPV	−87,271,675						
MACRS depreciation (%)		3.75	7.22	6.68	6.18	5.71	5.28

Year	7	8	9	10	11	12	13	14
Capital cost								
Revenues	72,587,770	74,765,404	77,008,366	79,318,617	81,698,175	84,149,120	86,673,594	89,273,802
Maintenance & other costs	22,567,588	23,244,616	23,941,955	24,660,213	25,400,020	26,162,020	26,946,881	27,755,287
MACRS depreciation	18,875,400	17,447,200	17,215,600	17,215,600	17,215,600	17,215,600	17,215,600	17,215,600
Pretax profit	31,144,782	34,073,588	35,850,811	37,442,803	39,082,556	40,771,500	42,511,113	44,302,915
Tax	10,900,674	11,925,756	12,547,784	13,104,981	13,678,894	14,270,025	14,878,890	15,506,020
Cash flow	39,119,508	39,595,032	40,518,627	41,553,422	42,619,261	43,717,075	44,847,824	46,012,495
PV	17,695,679	15,991,769	14,611,423	13,379,090	12,252,019	11,221,084	10,277,964	9,415,068
NPV								
MACRS depreciation (%)	4.89	4.52	4.46	4.46	4.46	4.46	4.46	4.46

Year	15	16	17	18	19	20	21
Capital cost							
Revenues	91,952,016	94,710,576	97,551,894	100,478,450	103,492,804	106,597,588	0
Maintenance & other costs	28,587,946	29,445,584	30,328,952	31,238,820	32,175,985	33,141,264	0
MACRS depreciation	17,215,600	17,215,600	17,215,600	17,215,600	17,215,600	17,215,600	8,607,800
Pretax profit	46,148,470	48,049,392	50,007,342	52,024,030	54,101,219	56,240,724	-8,607,800
Tax	16,151,965	16,817,287	17,502,570	18,208,411	18,935,427	19,684,253	-3,012,730
Cash flow	47,212,106	48,447,705	49,720,372	51,031,220	52,381,392	53,772,070	3,012,730
PV	8,625,475	7,902,870	7,241,491	6,636,079	6,081,835	5,574,377	278,857
NPV							
MACRS depreciation (%)	4.46	4.46	4.46	4.46	4.46	4.46	2.23

CHAPTER 7
Introduction to Risk and Return

Answers to Problem Sets

1. Expected payoff is $100 and expected return is zero. Variance is 20,000 (% squared) and standard deviation is 141%.

2. a. Standard deviation = 19.3%

    b. Average real return = –2.2%

3. Ms. Sauros had a slightly higher average return (14.6% vs. 14.4% for the market). However, the fund also had a higher standard deviation (13.6% vs. 9.4% for the market).

4. a. False

    b. True

    c. False

    d. False

    e. False

    f. True

    g. True

    h. False

5. d

6.

$x_1^2 \sigma_1^2$	$x_1 x_2 \sigma_{12}$	$x_1 x_3 \sigma_{13}$
$x_1 x_2 \sigma_{12}$	$x_2^2 \sigma_2^2$	$x_2 x_3 \sigma_{23}$
$x_1 x_3 \sigma_{13}$	$x_2 x_3 \sigma_{23}$	$x_3^2 \sigma_3^2$

7.   a.   26%

     b.   zero

     c.   .75

     d.   Less than 1.0 (the portfolio's risk is the same as the market, but some of this risk is unique risk).

8.   1.3 (Diversification does not affect market risk.)

9.   A, 1.0; B, 2.0; C, 1.5; D, 0; E, 21.0

10. Recall from Chapter 4 that:

$$(1 + r_{nominal}) = (1 + r_{real}) \times (1 + \text{inflation rate})$$

Therefore:

$$r_{real} = [(1 + r_{nominal})/(1 + \text{inflation rate})] - 1$$

a.   The real return on the stock market in each year was:

1929:	−14.7%
1930:	−23.7%
1931:	−38.0%
1932:	0.5%
1933:	56.5%

b.   From the results for Part (a), the average real return was: −3.89%

c.   The risk premium for each year was:

1929:	−19.3%
1930:	−30.7%
1931:	−45.0%
1932:	−10.9%
1933:	57.0%

d.   From the results for Part (c), the average risk premium was: −9.78%

e.   The standard deviation (σ) of the risk premium is calculated as follows:

$$\sigma^2 = \left(\frac{1}{5-1}\right) \times [(-0.193-(-0.0978))^2 + (-0.307-(-0.0978))^2 + (-0.450-(-0.0978))^2$$

$$+ (-0.109-(-0.0978))^2 + (0.570-(-0.0978))^2] = 0.155739$$

$$\sigma = \sqrt{0.155739} = 0.394637 = 39.46\%$$

11.   a.   A long-term United States government bond is always absolutely safe in terms of the dollars received. However, the price of the bond fluctuates as interest rates change and the rate at which coupon payments received can be invested also changes as interest rates change. And, of course, the payments are all in nominal dollars, so inflation risk must also be considered.

      b.   It is true that stocks offer higher long-run rates of return than do bonds, but it is also true that stocks have a higher standard deviation of return. So, which investment is preferable depends on the amount of risk one is willing to tolerate. This is a complicated issue and depends on numerous factors, one of which is the investment time horizon. If the investor has a short time horizon, then stocks are generally not preferred.

      c.   Unfortunately, 10 years is not generally considered a sufficient amount of time for estimating average rates of return. Thus, using a 10-year average is likely to be misleading.

12.   The risk to Hippique shareholders depends on the market risk, or beta, of the investment in the black stallion. The information given in the problem suggests that the horse has very high unique risk, but we have no information regarding the horse's market risk. So, the best estimate is that this horse has a market risk about equal to that of other racehorses, and thus this investment is not a particularly risky one for Hippique shareholders.

13.   In the context of a well-diversified portfolio, the only risk characteristic of a single security that matters is the security's contribution to the overall portfolio risk. This contribution is measured by beta. Lonesome Gulch is the safer investment for a diversified investor because its beta (+0.10) is lower than the beta of Amalgamated Copper (+0.66). For a diversified investor, the standard deviations are irrelevant.

14. $x_I = 0.60$ $\sigma_I = 0.10$
        $x_J = 0.40$ $\sigma_J = 0.20$

      a. $\rho_{IJ} = 1$

$$\sigma_p^2 = [x_I^2\sigma_I^2 + x_J^2\sigma_J^2 + 2(x_I x_J \rho_{IJ}\sigma_I\sigma_J)]$$

$$= [(0.60)^2(0.10)^2 + (0.40)^2(0.20)^2 + 2(0.60)(0.40)(1)(0.10)(0.20)] = 0.0196$$

b. $\rho_{IJ} = 0.50$

$$\sigma_p^2 = [x_I^2\sigma_I^2 + x_J^2\sigma_J^2 + 2(x_I x_J \rho_{IJ}\sigma_I\sigma_J)]$$

$$= [(0.60)^2(0.10)^2 + (0.40)^2(0.20)^2 + 2(0.60)(0.40)(0.50)(0.10)(0.20)] = 0.0148$$

c. $\rho_{ij} = 0$

$$\sigma_p^2 = [x_I^2\sigma_I^2 + x_J^2\sigma_J^2 + 2(x_I x_J \rho_{IJ}\sigma_I\sigma_J)]$$

$$= [(0.60)^2(0.10)^2 + (0.40)^2(0.20)^2 + 2(0.60)(0.40)(0)(0.10)(0.20)] = 0.0100$$

15. a. Refer to Figure 7.13 in the text. With 100 securities, the box is 100 by 100. The variance terms are the diagonal terms, and thus there are 100 variance terms. The rest are the covariance terms. Because the box has (100 times 100) terms altogether, the number of covariance terms is:

$$100^2 - 100 = 9{,}900$$

Half of these terms (i.e., 4,950) are different.

b. Once again, it is easiest to think of this in terms of Figure 7.13. With 50 stocks, all with the same standard deviation (0.30), the same weight in the portfolio (0.02), and all pairs having the same correlation coefficient (0.40), the portfolio variance is:

$$\sigma^2 = 50(0.02)^2(0.30)^2 + [(50)^2 - 50](0.02)^2(0.40)(0.30)^2 = 0.03708$$

$$\sigma = 0.193 = 19.3\%$$

c. For a fully diversified portfolio, portfolio variance equals the average covariance:

$$\sigma^2 = (0.30)(0.30)(0.40) = 0.036$$

$$\sigma = 0.190 = 19.0\%$$

16. a. Refer to Figure 7.13 in the text. For each different portfolio, the relative weight of each share is [one divided by the number of shares (n) in the portfolio], the standard deviation of each share is 0.40, and the correlation between pairs is 0.30. Thus, for each portfolio, the diagonal terms are the same, and the off-diagonal terms are the same. There are n diagonal terms and $(n^2 - n)$ off-diagonal terms. In general, we have:

$$\text{Variance} = n(1/n)^2(0.4)^2 + (n^2 - n)(1/n)^2(0.3)(0.4)(0.4)$$

For one share: Variance = $1(1)^2(0.4)^2 + 0 = 0.160000$

For two shares: Variance = $2(0.5)^2(0.4)^2 + 2(0.5)^2(0.3)(0.4)(0.4) = 0.104000$

The results are summarized in the second and third columns of the table below.

b.   (Graphs are on the next page.) The underlying market risk that can not be diversified away is the second term in the formula for variance above:

$$\text{Underlying market risk} = (n^2 - n)(1/n)^2(0.3)(0.4)(0.4)$$

As n increases, $[(n^2 - n)(1/n)^2] = [(n - 1)/n]$ becomes close to 1, so that the underlying market risk is: $[(0.3)(0.4)(0.4)] = 0.048$

c.   This is the same as Part (a), except that all of the off-diagonal terms are now equal to zero. The results are summarized in the fourth and fifth columns of the table below.

No. of Shares	(Part a) Variance	(Part a) Standard Deviation	(Part c) Variance	(Part c) Standard Deviation
1	.160000	.400	.160000	.400
2	.104000	.322	.080000	.283
3	.085333	.292	.053333	.231
4	.076000	.276	.040000	.200
5	.070400	.265	.032000	.179
6	.066667	.258	.026667	.163
7	.064000	.253	.022857	.151
8	.062000	.249	.020000	.141
9	.060444	.246	.017778	.133
10	.059200	.243	.016000	.126

Graphs for Part (a):

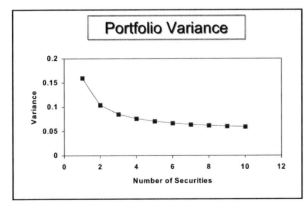

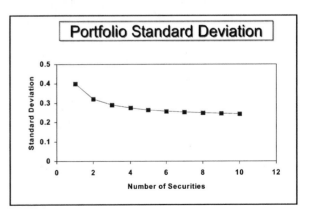

Graphs for Part (c):

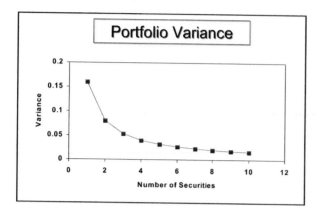

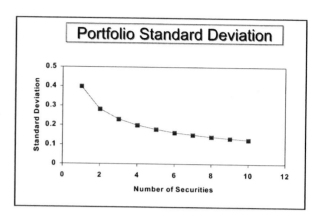

17. The table below uses the format of Figure 7.13 in the text in order to calculate the portfolio variance. The portfolio variance is the sum of all the entries in the matrix. Portfolio variance equals: 0.036643555

	BP	Canadian	Deutsche	Fiat	Heineken	LVMH	Nestle	Tata
BP	0.000770063	0.000157516	0.000232961	0.000247669	0.000222902	0.00021645	0.00008547	0.000134241
Canadian	0.000157516	0.000892516	0.000468888	0.000413283	0.000275261	0.000264095	0.00009777	0.000642313
Deutsche	0.000232961	0.000468888	0.00133225	0.001205321	0.000629488	0.00069277	0.00034429	0.001334075
Fiat	0.000247669	0.000413283	0.001205321	0.001991391	0.000695815	0.00074256	0.00040374	0.001271255
Heineken	0.000222902	0.000275261	0.000629488	0.000695815	0.000558141	0.00039312	0.00023194	0.000634922
LVMH	0.00021645	0.000264095	0.00069277	0.00074256	0.00039312	0.000676	0.00026026	0.0008385
Nestle	0.00008547	9.77659E-05	0.000344286	0.00040374	0.000231938	0.00026026	0.000370563	0.000444916
Tata	0.000134241	0.000642313	0.001334075	0.001271255	0.000634922	0.0008385	0.000444916	0.002889063

18. "Safest" means lowest risk; in a portfolio context, this means lowest variance of return. Half of the portfolio is invested in Canadian Pacific stock, and half of the portfolio must be invested in one of the other securities listed. Thus, we calculate the portfolio variance for seven different portfolios to see which is the lowest. The safest attainable portfolio is comprised of Canadian Pacific and Nestle.

	Variance
BP	0.03164176
Deutsche	0.05060067
Fiat	0.059367565
Heineken	0.032018845
LVMH	0.03354729
Nestle	0.02333776
Tata	0.08105925

19.   a.   In general, we expect a stock's price to change by an amount equal to (beta × change in the market). Beta equal to –0.25 implies that, if the market rises by an extra 5%, the expected change in the stock's rate of return is –1.25%. If the market declines an extra 5%, then the expected change is +1.25%.

      b.   "Safest" implies lowest risk. Assuming the well-diversified portfolio is invested in typical securities, the portfolio beta is approximately one. The largest reduction in beta is achieved by investing the $20,000 in a stock with a negative beta. Answer (iii) is correct.

20.   Expected portfolio return $= x_A \, E[R_A] + x_B \, E[R_B] = 12\% = 0.12$

      Let $x_B = (1 - x_A)$

      $x_A \, (0.10) + (1 - x_A) \, (0.15) = 0.12 \Rightarrow x_A = 0.60$ and $x_B = 1 - x_A = 0.40$

      Portfolio variance $= x_A^2 \, \sigma_A^2 + x_B^2 \, \sigma_B^2 + 2(x_A \, x_B \, \rho_{AB} \, \sigma_A \, \sigma_B)$

$$= (0.60^2)(20^2) + (0.40^2)(40^2) + 2(0.60)(0.40)(0.50)(20)(40) = 592$$

      Standard deviation $= \sigma = \sqrt{592} = 24.33\%$

21.   a.   In general:

$$\text{Portfolio variance} = \sigma_P^2 = x_1^2 \sigma_1^2 + x_2^2 \sigma_2^2 + 2 x_1 x_2 \rho_{12} \sigma_1 \sigma_2$$

      Thus:

$$\sigma_P^2 = (0.5^2)(30.9^2) + (0.5^2)(17.2^2) + 2(0.5)(0.5)(0.31)(30.9)(17.2)$$

$$\sigma_P^2 = 395.942$$

      Standard deviation $= \sigma_P = 19.88\%$

      b.   We can think of this in terms of Figure 7.13 in the text, with three securities. One of these securities, T-bills, has zero risk and, hence, zero standard deviation. Thus:

$$\sigma_P^2 = (1/3)^2(30.9^2) + (1/3)^2(17.2^2) + 2(1/3)(1/3)(0.31)(30.9)(17.2)$$

$$\sigma_P^2 = 175.574$$

      Standard deviation $= \sigma_P = 13.25\%$

      Another way to think of this portfolio is that it is comprised of one-third T-Bills and two-thirds a portfolio which is half Dell and half McDonalds. Because the risk of T-bills is zero, the portfolio standard deviation is two-thirds of the standard deviation computed in Part (a) above:

      Standard deviation $= (2/3)(19.88) = 13.25\%$

c. With 50% margin, the investor invests twice as much money in the portfolio as he had to begin with. Thus, the risk is twice that found in Part (a) when the investor is investing only his own money:

Standard deviation = $2 \times 19.88\% = 39.76\%$

d. With 100 stocks, the portfolio is well diversified, and hence the portfolio standard deviation depends almost entirely on the average covariance of the securities in the portfolio (measured by beta) and on the standard deviation of the market portfolio. Thus, for a portfolio made up of 100 stocks, each with beta = 1.41, the portfolio standard deviation is approximately: $1.41 \times 15\% = 21.15\%$
For stocks like McDonalds, it is: $0.77 \times 15\% = 11.55\%$

22. For a two-security portfolio, the formula for portfolio risk is:

Portfolio variance = $x_1^2\sigma_1^2 + x_2^2\sigma_2^2 + 2x_1x_2\rho_{12}\sigma_1\sigma_2$

If security one is Treasury bills and security two is the market portfolio, then σ_1 is zero, σ_2 is 20%. Therefore:

Portfolio variance = $x_2^2\sigma_2^2 = x_2^2(0.20)^2$

Standard deviation = $0.20x_2$

Portfolio expected return = $x_1(0.06) + x_2(0.06 + 0.85)$

Portfolio expected return = $0.06x_1 + 0.145x_2$

Portfolio	X_1	X_2	Expected Return	Standard Deviation
1	1.0	0.0	0.060	0.000
2	0.8	0.2	0.077	0.040
3	0.6	0.4	0.094	0.080
4	0.4	0.6	0.111	0.120
5	0.2	0.8	0.128	0.160
6	0.0	1.0	0.145	0.200

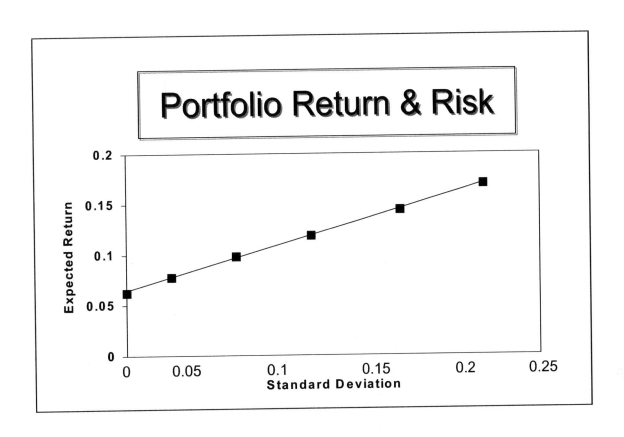

23. The matrix below displays the variance for each of the eight stocks along the diagonal and each of the covariances in the off-diagonal cells:

	BP	Canadian	Deutsche	Fiat	Heineken	LVMH	Nestle	Tata
BP	0.04928	0.01008	0.01491	0.01585	0.01427	0.01385	0.00547	0.00859
Canadian	0.01008	0.05712	0.03001	0.02645	0.01762	0.01690	0.00626	0.04111
Deutsche	0.01491	0.00030	0.08526	0.07714	0.04029	0.04434	0.02203	0.08538
Fiat	0.00016	0.00026	0.00077	0.12745	0.04453	0.04752	0.02584	0.08136
Heineken	0.00014	0.00018	0.00040	0.00045	0.03572	0.02516	0.01484	0.04064
LVMH	0.00014	0.00017	0.00044	0.00048	0.00025	0.04326	0.01666	0.05366
Nestle	0.00005	0.00006	0.00022	0.00026	0.00015	0.00017	0.02372	0.02847
Tata	0.00009	0.00041	0.00085	0.00081	0.00041	0.00054	0.00028	0.18490

The covariance of BP with the market portfolio ($\sigma_{BP, Market}$) is the mean of the eight respective covariances between BP and each of the eight stocks in the portfolio. (The covariance of BP with itself is the variance of BP.) Therefore, $\sigma_{BP, Market}$ is equal to the average of the eight covariances in the first row or, equivalently, the average of the eight covariances in the first column. Beta for BP is equal to the covariance divided by the market variance, which we calculated at 0.03664 in problem 17. The covariances and betas are displayed in the table below:

	Covariance	Mkt Var	Beta
BP	0.01654	0.03664	0.45133
Canadian	0.02569	0.03664	0.70116
Deutsche	0.04621	0.03664	1.26098
Fiat	0.04099	0.03664	1.11854
Heineken	0.01469	0.03664	0.40091
LVMH	0.01438	0.03664	0.39251
Nestle	0.00664	0.03664	0.18114
Tata	0.02354	0.03664	0.64231

CHAPTER 8
Portfolio Theory and the Capital Asset Pricing Model

Answers to Problem Sets

1.   a.   7%

   b.   27% with perfect positive correlation; 1% with perfect negative correlation; 19.1% with no correlation

   c.   See Figure 1 below

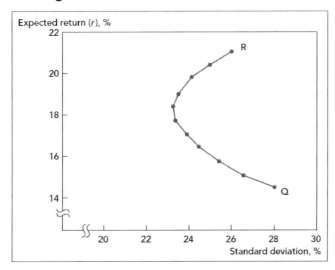

FIGURE 1

   d.   No, measure risk by beta, not by standard deviation.

2.   a.   Portfolio A (higher expected return, same risk)

   b.   Cannot say (depends on investor's attitude -toward risk)

   c.   Portfolio F (lower risk, same -expected return).

3.   Sharpe ratio = 7.1/20.2 = .351

4.   a.   Figure 8.13b: Diversification reduces risk (e.g., a mixture of portfolios A and B would have less risk than the average of A and B).

   b.   Those along line AB in Figure 9.13a.

c.   See Figure 2 below

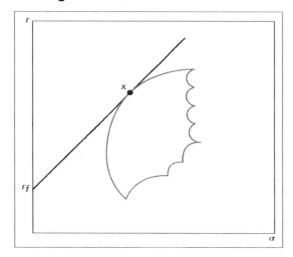

FIGURE 2

5.   a.   See Figure 3 below

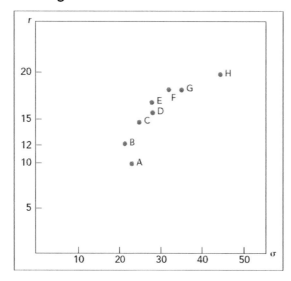

FIGURE 3

b.   A, D, G

c.   F

d.   15% in C

e.   Put 25/32 of your money in F and lend 7/32 at 12%: Expected return = 7/32 × 12 + 25/32 × 18 = 16.7%; standard deviation = 7/32 × 0 + (25/32) × 32 = 25%. If you could borrow without limit, you would achieve as high an expected return as you'd like, with correspondingly high risk, of course.

6. a. $4 + (1.41 \times 6) = 12.5\%$

    b. Amazon: $4 + (2.16 \times 6) = 17.0\%$

    c. Campbell Soup: $4 + (.30 \times 6) = 5.8\%$

    d. Lower. If interest rate is 4%, $r = 4 + (1.75 \times 6) = 14.5\%$; if rate = 6%, $r = 6 + (1.75 \times 4) = 13.0\%$

    e. Higher. If interest rate is 4%, $r = 4 + (.55 \times 6) = 7.3\%$; if rate = 6%, $r = 6 + (.55 \times 4) 5 8.2\%$

7. a. True

    b. False (it offers twice the market risk premium)

    c. False

8. a. 7%

    b. $7 + 1(5) + 1(-1) + 1(2) = 13\%$

    c. $7 + 0(5) + 2(-1) + 0(2) = 5\%$

    d. $7 + 1(5) + (-1.5)(-1) + 1(2) = 15.5\%$.

9. a. False – investors demand higher expected rates of return on stocks with more nondiversifiable risk.

    b. False – a security with a beta of zero will offer the risk-free rate of return.

    c. False – the beta will be: $(1/3 \times 0) + (2/3 \times 1) = 0.67$

    d. True

    e. True

10. In the following solution, security one is Campbell Soup and security two is Boeing. Then:

    $r_1 = 0.031 \qquad \sigma_1 = 0.158$

    $r_2 = 0.095 \qquad \sigma_2 = 0.237$

Further, we know that for a two-security portfolio:

$$r_p = x_1 r_1 + x_2 r_2$$

$$\sigma_p^2 = x_1^2 \sigma_1^2 + 2 x_1 x_2 \sigma_1 \sigma_2 \rho_{12} + x_2^2 \sigma_2^2$$

Therefore, we have the following results:

x_1	x_2	r_p	σ_π when $\rho = 0$	σ_π when $\rho = 0.5$
1	0	3.10%	0.02496	0.02496
0.9	0.1	3.74%	0.02078	0.02415
0.8	0.2	4.38%	0.01822	0.02422
0.7	0.3	5.02%	0.01729	0.02515
0.6	0.4	5.66%	0.01797	0.02696
0.5	0.5	6.30%	0.02028	0.02964
0.4	0.6	6.94%	0.02422	0.03320
0.3	0.7	7.58%	0.02977	0.03763
0.2	0.8	8.22%	0.03695	0.04294
0.1	0.9	8.86%	0.04575	0.04912
0	1	9.50%	0.05617	0.05617

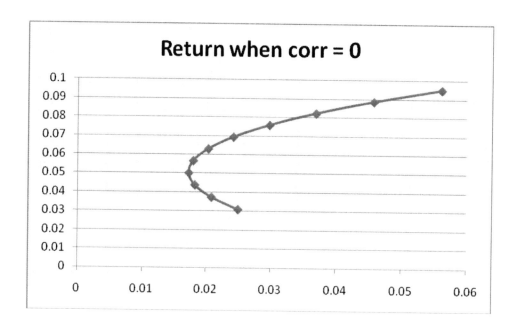

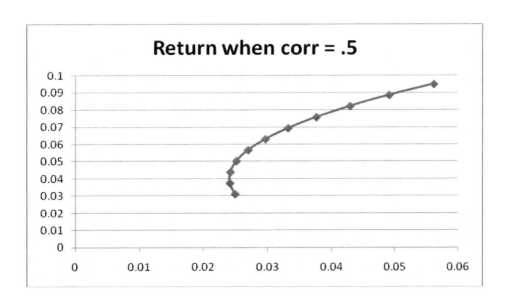

Return when corr = .5

11. a.

Portfolio	r	σ
1	10.0%	5.1%
2	9.0	4.6
3	11.0	6.4

b.   See the figure below. The set of portfolios is represented by the curved line. The five points are the three portfolios from Part (a) plus the following two portfolios: one consists of 100% invested in X and the other consists of 100% invested in Y.

c.   See the figure below. The best opportunities lie along the straight line. From the diagram, the optimal portfolio of risky assets is portfolio 1, and so Mr. Harrywitz should invest 50 percent in X and 50 percent in Y.

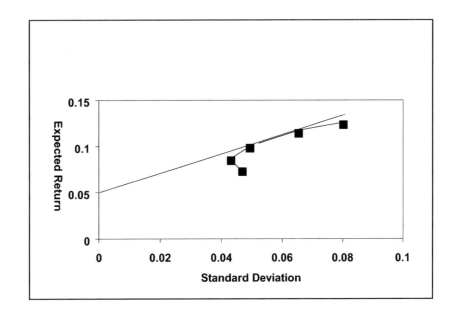

12. a. Expected return = $(0.6 \times 15) + (0.4 \times 20) = 17\%$

Variance = $(0.6^2 \times 20^2) + (0.4^2 \times 22^2) + 2(0.6)(0.4)(0.5)(20)(22) = 327.04$

Standard deviation = $327.04^{(1/2)} = 18.08\%$

b. Correlation coefficient = 0 $\Rightarrow$ Standard deviation = 14.88%

Correlation coefficient = –0.5 $\Rightarrow$ Standard deviation = 10.76%

c. His portfolio is better. The portfolio has a higher expected return *and* a lower standard deviation.

13. a.

	2003	2004	2005	2006	2007	Average	SD	Sharpe Ratio
Sauros	39.1	11.0	2.6	18.0	2.3	14.6	15.2	0.77
S&P500	31.6	12.5	6.4	15.8	5.6	14.4	10.5	1.09
Risk Free	1.01	1.37	3.15	4.73	4.36	2.9	1.7	

On these numbers she seems to perform worse than the market

b. We can calculate the Beta of her investment as follows (see Table 7.7):

						TOTAL
Deviation from Average mkt return	17.2	–1.9	–8.0	1.4	–8.8	
Deviation from Average Sauros return	24.5	–3.6	–12.0	3.4	–12.3	
Squared Deviation from Average market return	296.5	3.5	63.7	2.0	77.1	442.8
Product of Deviations from Average returns	421.9	6.8	95.8	4.8	108.0	637.2
Market variance	88.6					
Covariance	127.4					
Beta	1.4					

To construct a portfolio with a beta of 1.4, we will borrow .4 at the risk free rate and invest this in the market portfolio. This gives us annual returns as follows:

	2003	2004	2005	2006	2007	Average
1.4 times market	44.2	17.5	9.0	22.1	7.8	20.1
less 0.4 time rf	−0.4	−0.5	−1.3	−1.9	−1.7	−1.2
net return	43.84	16.95	7.70	20.23	6.10	19.0

The Sauros portfolio does not generate sufficient returns to compensate for its risk.

14.   a.   The Beta of the first portfolio is 0.714 and offers an average return of 5.9%

	Beta	Expected Return
Disney	0.960	7.700
Exxon Mobil	0.550	4.700
weighted (40,60)	0.714	5.900
Amazon	2.160	22.800
Campbells	0.300	3.100
weighted (14.5, 85.5)	0.570	5.858

   b.   We can devise a superior portfolio with a blend of 85.5% Campbell's Soup and 14.5% Amazon.

   c.

	Beta	Expected Return
Amazon	2.160	22.800
Dell	1.410	13.400
weighted (40,60)	1.710	17.160
Ford	1.750	19.000
Campbell Soup	0.300	3.100
weighted (89, 11)	1.591	17.251

15.   a.

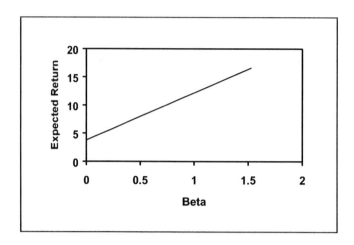

b.   Market risk premium = $r_m - r_f$ = 0.12 − 0.04 = 0.08 = 8.0%

c.   Use the security market line:

$r = r_f + \beta(r_m - r_f)$

$r = 0.04 + [1.5 \times (0.12 - 0.04)] = 0.16 = 16.0\%$

d.   For any investment, we can find the opportunity cost of capital using the security market line. With $\beta = 0.8$, the opportunity cost of capital is:

$r = r_f + \beta(r_m - r_f)$

$r = 0.04 + [0.8 \times (0.12 - 0.04)] = 0.104 = 10.4\%$

The opportunity cost of capital is 10.4% and the investment is expected to earn 9.8%. Therefore, the investment has a negative NPV.

e.   Again, we use the security market line:

$r = r_f + \beta(r_m - r_f)$

$0.112 = 0.04 + \beta(0.12 - 0.04) \Rightarrow \beta = 0.9$

16.   a.   Percival's current portfolio provides an expected return of 9% with an annual standard deviation of 10%. First we find the portfolio weights for a combination of Treasury bills (security 1: standard deviation = 0%) and the index fund (security 2: standard deviation = 16%) such that portfolio standard deviation is 10%. In general, for a two security portfolio:

$\sigma_P^2 = x_1^2\sigma_1^2 + 2x_1x_2\sigma_1\sigma_2\rho_{12} + x_2^2\sigma_2^2$

$(0.10)^2 = 0 + 0 + x_2^2(0.16)^2$

$x_2 = 0.625 \Rightarrow x_1 = 0.375$

Further:

$$r_p = x_1r_1 + x_2r_2$$

$$r_p = (0.375 \times 0.06) + (0.625 \times 0.14) = 0.11 = 11.0\%$$

Therefore, he can improve his expected rate of return without changing the risk of his portfolio.

b.   With equal amounts in the corporate bond portfolio (security 1) and the index fund (security 2), the expected return is:

$$r_p = x_1r_1 + x_2r_2$$

$$r_p = (0.5 \times 0.09) + (0.5 \times 0.14) = 0.115 = 11.5\%$$

$$\sigma_P^2 = x_1^2\sigma_1^2 + 2x_1x_2\sigma_1\sigma_2\rho_{12} + x_2^2\sigma_2^2$$

$$\sigma_P^2 = (0.5)^2(0.10)^2 + 2(0.5)(0.5)(0.10)(0.16)(0.10) + (0.5)^2(0.16)^2$$

$$\sigma_P^2 = 0.0097$$

$$\sigma_P = 0.985 = 9.85\%$$

Therefore, he can do even better by investing equal amounts in the corporate bond portfolio and the index fund. His expected return increases to 11.5% and the standard deviation of his portfolio decreases to 9.85%.

17.   First calculate the required rate of return (assuming the expansion assets bear the same level of risk as historical assets):

$$r = r_f + \beta(r_m - r_f)$$

$$r = 0.04 + [1.4 \times (0.12 - 0.04)] = 0.152 = 15.2\%$$

The use this to discount future cash flows; NPV = –25.29

Year	Cash Flow	Discount factor	PV
0	−100	1	−100.00
1	15	0.868	13.02
2	15	0.754	11.30
3	15	0.654	9.81
4	15	0.568	8.52
5	15	0.493	7.39
6	15	0.428	6.42
7	15	0.371	5.57
8	15	0.322	4.84
9	15	0.280	4.20
10	15	0.243	3.64
NPV			−25.29

18.　a.　True. By definition, the factors represent macro-economic risks that cannot be eliminated by diversification.

　　b.　False. The APT does not specify the factors.

　　c.　True. Different researchers have proposed and empirically investigated different factors, but there is no widely accepted theory as to what these factors should be.

　　d.　True. To be useful, we must be able to estimate the relevant parameters. If this is impossible, for whatever reason, the model itself will be of theoretical interest only.

19.　Stock P: $r = 5\% + (1.0 \times 6.4\%) + [(-2.0) \times (-0.6\%)] + [(-0.2) \times 5.1\%] = 11.58\%$

Stock P^2: $r = 5\% + (1.2 \times 6.4\%) + [0 \times (-0.6\%)] + (0.3 \times 5.1\%) = 14.21\%$

Stock P^3: $r = 5\% + (0.3 \times 6.4\%) + [0.5 \times (-0.6\%)] + (1.0 \times 5.1\%) = 11.72\%$

20.　a.　Factor risk exposures:

b_1(Market) $= [(1/3) \times 1.0] + [(1/3) \times 1.2] + [(1/3) \times 0.3] = 0.83$

b_2(Interest rate) $= [(1/3) \times (-2.0)] + [(1/3) \times 0] + [(1/3) \times 0.5] = -0.50$

b_3(Yield spread) $= [(1/3) \times (-0.2)] + [(1/3) \times 0.3] + [(1/3) \times 1.0] = 0.37$

　　b.　$r_P = 5\% + (0.83 \times 6.4\%) + [(-0.50) \times (-0.6\%)] + [0.37 \times 5.1\%] = 12.50\%$

21.　$r_{Boeing} = 0.2\% + (0.66 \times 7\%) + (01.19 \times 3.6\%) + (-0.76 \times 5.2\%) = 5.152\%$

$R_{J\&J} = 0.2\% + (0.54 \times 7\%) + (-0.58 \times 3.6\%) + (0.19 \times 5.2\%) = 2.88\%$

$R_{Dow} = 0.2\% + (1.05 \times 7\%) + (-0.15 \times 3.6\%) + (0.77 \times 5.2\%) = 11.014\%$

$r_{Msft} = 0.2\% + (0.91 \times 7\%) + (-0.04 \times 3.6\%) + (-0.4 \times 5.2\%) = 4.346\%$

22.　In general, for a two-security portfolio:

$$\sigma_p{}^2 = x_1{}^2\sigma_1{}^2 + 2x_1x_2\sigma_1\sigma_2\rho_{12} + x_2{}^2\sigma_2{}^2$$

and:

$$x_1 + x_2 = 1$$

Substituting for x_2 in terms of x_1 and rearranging:

$$\sigma_p{}^2 = \sigma_1{}^2x_1{}^2 + 2\sigma_1\sigma_2\rho_{12}(x_1 - x_1{}^2) + \sigma_2{}^2(1 - x_1)^2$$

Taking the derivative of σ_p^2 with respect to x_1, setting the derivative equal to zero and rearranging:

$$x_1(\sigma_1^2 - 2\sigma_1\sigma_2\rho_{12} + \sigma_2^2) + (\sigma_1\sigma_2\rho_{12} - \sigma_2^2) = 0$$

Let Campbell Soup be security one ($\sigma_1 = 0.158$) and Boeing be security two ($\sigma_2 = 0.237$). Substituting these numbers, along with $\rho_{12} = 0.18$, we have:

$$x_1 = 0.731$$

Therefore:

$$x_2 = 0.269$$

23.   a.   The ratio (expected risk premium/standard deviation) for each of the four portfolios is as follows:

Portfolio A: $(22.8 - 10.0)/50.9 = 0.251$

Portfolio B: $(10.5 - 10.0)/16.0 = 0.031$

Portfolio C: $(4.2 - 10.0)/8.8 = -0.659$

Therefore, an investor should hold Portfolio A.

b.   The beta for Amazon relative to Portfolio A is identical.

c.   If the interest rate is 5%, then Portfolio C becomes the optimal portfolio, as indicated by the following calculations:

Portfolio A: $(22.8 - 5.0)/50.9 = 0.35$

Portfolio B: $(10.5 - 5.0)/16.0 = 0.344$

Portfolio C: $(4.2 - 5.0)/8.8 = -0.091$

The results do not change.

24.   Let r_x be the risk premium on investment X, let x_x be the portfolio weight of X (and similarly for Investments Y and Z, respectively).

a. $r_x = (1.75 \times 0.04) + (0.25 \times 0.08) = 0.09 = 9.0\%$

$r_y = [(-1.00) \times 0.04] + (2.00 \times 0.08) = 0.12 = 12.0\%$

$r_z = (2.00 \times 0.04) + (1.00 \times 0.08) = 0.16 = 16.0\%$

b.   This portfolio has the following portfolio weights:

$$x_x = 200/(200 + 50 - 150) = 2.0$$

$$x_y = 50/(200 + 50 - 150) = 0.5$$

$$x_z = -150/(200 + 50 - 150) = -1.5$$

The portfolio's sensitivities to the factors are:

Factor 1: $(2.0 \times 1.75) + [0.5 \times (-1.00)] - (1.5 \times 2.00) = 0$

Factor 2: $(2.0 \times 0.25) + (0.5 \times 2.00) - (1.5 \times 1.00) = 0$

Because the sensitivities are both zero, the expected risk premium is zero.

c. This portfolio has the following portfolio weights:

$$x_x = 80/(80 + 60 - 40) = 0.8$$
$$x_y = 60/(80 + 60 - 40) = 0.6$$
$$x_z = -40/(80 + 60 - 40) = -0.4$$

The sensitivities of this portfolio to the factors are:

Factor 1: $(0.8 \times 1.75) + [0.6 \times (-1.00)] - (0.4 \times 2.00) = 0$

Factor 2: $(0.8 \times 0.25) + (0.6 \times 2.00) - (0.4 \times 1.00) = 1.0$

The expected risk premium for this portfolio is equal to the expected risk premium for the second factor, or 8 percent.

d. This portfolio has the following portfolio weights:

$$x_x = 160/(160 + 20 - 80) = 1.6$$
$$x_y = 20/(160 + 20 - 80) = 0.2$$
$$x_z = -80/(160 + 20 - 80) = -0.8$$

The sensitivities of this portfolio to the factors are:

Factor 1: $(1.6 \times 1.75) + [0.2 \times (-1.00)] - (0.8 \times 2.00) = 1.0$

Factor 2: $(1.6 \times 0.25) + (0.2 \times 2.00) - (0.8 \times 1.00) = 0$

The expected risk premium for this portfolio is equal to the expected risk premium for the first factor, or 4 percent.

e. The sensitivity requirement can be expressed as:

Factor 1: $(x_x)(1.75) + (x_y)(-1.00) + (x_z)(2.00) = 0.5$

In addition, we know that:

$$x_x + x_y + x_z = 1$$

With two linear equations in three variables, there is an infinite number of solutions. Two of these are:

1. $x_x = 0$ $x_y = 0.5$ $x_z = 0.5$

2. $x_x = 6/11$ $x_y = 5/11$ $x_z = 0$

The risk premiums for these two funds are:

$r_1 = 0 \times [(1.75 \times 0.04) + (0.25 \times 0.08)]$

$\quad + (0.5) \times [(-1.00 \times 0.04) + (2.00 \times 0.08)]$

$\quad + (0.5) \times [(2.00 \times 0.04) + (1.00 \times 0.08)] = 0.14 = 14.0\%$

$r_2 = (6/11) \times [(1.75 \times 0.04) + (0.25 \times 0.08)]$

$\quad + (5/11) \times [(-1.00 \times 0.04) + (2.00 \times 0.08)]$

$\quad + 0 \times [(2.00 \times 0.04) + (1.00 \times 0.08)] = 0.104 = 10.4\%$

These risk premiums differ because, while each fund has a sensitivity of 0.5 to factor 1, they differ in their sensitivities to factor 2.

f. Because the sensitivities to the two factors are the same as in Part (b), one portfolio with zero sensitivity to each factor is given by:

$\quad\quad x_x = 2.0 \quad\quad x_y = 0.5 \quad\quad x_z = -1.5$

The risk premium for this portfolio is:

$\quad\quad (2.0 \times 0.08) + (0.5 \times 0.14) - (1.5 \times 0.16) = -0.01$

Because this is an example of a portfolio with zero sensitivity to each factor and a nonzero risk premium, it is clear that the Arbitrage Pricing Theory does not hold in this case.

A portfolio with a positive risk premium is:

$\quad\quad x_x = -2.0 \quad\quad x_y = -0.5 \quad\quad x_z = 1.5$

CHAPTER 9
Risk and the Cost of Capital

Answers to Problem Sets

1. Overestimate

2. Company cost of capital = $10 \times .4 + (10 + .5 \times 8) \times .6 = 12.4\%$
   After-tax WACC = $(1 - .35) \times 10 \times .4 + (10 + .5 \times 8) \times .6 = 11.0\%$

3. .297, or 29.7% of variation was due to market movements; .703 or 70.3% of the variation was diversifiable. Diversifiable risk shows up in the scatter about the fitted line. The standard error of the estimated beta was unusually high at .436. If you said that the true beta was $2 \times .436 = .872$ either side of your estimate, you would have a 95% chance of being right.

4. a. The expected return on debt. If the debt has very low default risk, this is close to its yield to maturity.

   b. The expected return on equity.

   c. A weighted average of the cost of equity and the after-tax cost of debt, where the weights are the relative market values of the firm's debt and equity.

   d. The change in the return of the stock for each additional 1% change in the market return.

   e. The change in the return on a portfolio of all the firm's securities (debt and equity) for each additional 1% change in the market return.

   f. A company specializing in one activity that is similar to that of a division of a more diversified company.

   g. A certain cash flow occurring at time t with the same present value as an uncertain cash flow at time t.

5. Beta of assets = $.5 \times .15 + .5 \times 1.25 = .7$

6. A diversifiable risk has no affect on the risk of a well-diversified portfolio and therefore no affect on the project's beta. If a risk is diversifiable it does not change the cost of capital for the project. However, any possibility of bad outcomes does need to be factored in when calculating expected cash flows.

7. Suppose that the expected cash flow in Year 1 is 100, but the project proposer provides an estimate of 100 × 115/108 = 106.5. Discounting this figure at 15% gives the same result as discounting the true expected cash flow at 8%. Adjusting the discount rate, therefore, works for the first cash flow but it does not do so for later cash flows (e.g., discounting a 2-year cash flow of 106.5 by 15% is *not* equivalent to discounting a 2-year flow of 100 by 8%).

8. a. A (higher fixed cost)

   b. C (more cyclical revenues).

9. a. False

   b. False

   c. True

10. a. $$PV = \frac{110}{1 + r_f + \beta(r_m - r_f)} + \frac{121}{[1 + r_f + \beta(r_m + r_f)]^2}$$

   $$= \frac{110}{1.10} + \frac{121}{1.10^2} = \$200$$

   b. $CEQ_1/1.05 = 110/1.10$, $CEQ_1 = \$105$; $CEQ_2/1.05^2 = 121/1.10^2$, $CEQ_2 = \$110.25$.

   c. $Ratio_1 = 105/110 = .95$; $Ratio_2 = 110.25/121 = .91$.

11. a. $r_{equity} = r_f + \beta \times (r_m - r_f) = 0.04 + (1.5 \times 0.06) = 0.13 = 13\%$

   b. $$r_{assets} = \frac{D}{V} r_{debt} + \frac{E}{V} r_{equity} = \left(\frac{\$4 \text{million}}{\$10 \text{million}} \times 0.04 \right) + \left(\frac{\$6 \text{million}}{\$10 \text{million}} \times 0.13 \right)$$

   $r_{assets} = 0.094 = 9.4\%$

   c. The cost of capital depends on the risk of the project being evaluated. If the risk of the project is similar to the risk of the other assets of the company, then the appropriate rate of return is the company cost of capital. Here, the appropriate discount rate is 9.4%.

   d. $r_{equity} = r_f + \beta \times (r_m - r_f) = 0.04 + (1.2 \times 0.06) = 0.112 = 11.2\%$

$$r_{assets} = \frac{D}{V}r_{debt} + \frac{E}{V}r_{equity} = \left(\frac{\$4\text{million}}{\$10\text{million}} \times 0.04\right) + \left(\frac{\$6\text{million}}{\$10\text{million}} \times 0.112\right)$$

$r_{assets} = 0.0832 = 8.32\%$

12. a.

$$\beta_{assets} = \left(\beta_{debt} \times \frac{D}{V}\right) + \left(\beta_{preferred} \times \frac{P}{V}\right) + \left(\beta_{common} \times \frac{C}{V}\right) =$$

$$\left(0 \times \frac{\$100\text{million}}{\$439\text{million}}\right) + \left(0.20 \times \frac{\$40\text{million}}{\$439\text{million}}\right) \times \left(1.20 \times \frac{\$299\text{million}}{\$439\text{million}}\right) = 0.836$$

b. $r = r_f + \beta \times (r_m - r_f) = 0.05 + (0.836 \times 0.06) = 0.10016 = 10.016\%$

13. a. The R^2 value for Toronto Dominion was 0.25, which means that 25% of total risk comes from movements in the market (i.e., market risk). Therefore, 75% of total risk is unique risk.

The R^2 value for Canadian Pacific was 0.30, which means that 30% of total risk comes from movements in the market (i.e., market risk). Therefore, 70% of total risk is unique risk.

b. The variance of Toronto Dominion is: $(25)^2 = 625$

Market risk for Toronto Dominion: $0.25 \times 625 = 156.25$

Unique risk for Alcan: $0.75 \times 625 = 468.75$

c. The t-statistic for β_{CP} is: $1.04/0.20 = 5.20$

This is significant at the 1% level, so that the confidence level is 99%.

d. $r_{TD} = r_f + \beta_{TD} \times (r_m - r_f) = 0.05 + [0.82 \times (0.12 - 0.05)] = 0.1074 = 10.74\%$

e. $r_{TD} = r_f + \beta_{TD} \times (r_m - r_f) = 0.05 + [0.82 \times (0 - 0.05)] = 0.0090 = 0.90\%$

14. The total market value of outstanding debt is $300,000. The cost of debt capital is 8 percent. For the common stock, the outstanding market value is: $50 \times 10,000 = \$500,000$. The cost of equity capital is 15 percent. Thus, Lorelei's weighted-average cost of capital is:

$$r_{assets} = \left(\frac{300,000}{300,000 + 500,000}\right) \times 0.08 + \left(\frac{500,000}{300,000 + 500,000}\right) \times 0.15$$

$r_{assets} = 0.124 = 12.4\%$

15. a. $r_{BN} = r_f + \beta_{BN} \times (r_m - r_f) = 0.05 + (01.01 \times 0.07) = 0.1207 = 12.07\%$

   $r_{IND} = r_f + \beta_{IND} \times (r_m - r_f) = 0.05 + (01.24 \times 0.07) = 0.1368 = 13.68\%$

   b. No, we can not be confident that Burlington's true beta is not the industry average. The difference between β_{BN} and β_{IND} (0.23) is less than two times the standard error ($2 \times 0.19 = 0.38$), so we cannot reject the hypothesis that $\beta_{BN} = \beta_{IND}$ with 95% confidence.

   c. Burlington's beta might be different from the industry beta for a variety of reasons. For example, Burlington's business might be more cyclical than is the case for the typical firm in the industry. Or Burlington might have more fixed operating costs, so that operating leverage is higher. Another possibility is that Burlington has more debt than is typical for the industry so that it has higher financial leverage.

16. Financial analysts or investors working with portfolios of firms may use industry betas. To calculate an industry beta we would construct a series of industry portfolio investments and evaluate how the returns generated by this portfolio relate to historical market movements.

17. We should use the market value of the stock, not the book value shown on the annual report. This gives us an equity value of 500,000 shares times $18 = $9 million. So Binomial Tree Farm has a debt/value ratio of 5/14 = 0.36 and an equity /value ratio of 9/14 = 0.64.

18. a. If you agree to the fixed price contract, operating leverage increases. Changes in revenue result in greater than proportionate changes in profit. If all costs are variable, then changes in revenue result in proportionate changes in profit. Business risk, measured by β_{assets}, also increases as a result of the fixed price contract. If fixed costs equal zero, then: $\beta_{assets} = \beta_{revenue}$. However, as PV(fixed cost) increases, β_{assets} increases.

   b. With the fixed price contract:

   PV(assets) = PV(revenue) – PV(fixed cost) – PV(variable cost)

   $$PV(assets) = \frac{\$20 million}{0.09} - (\$10 million \times annuity\ factor\ 6\%, 10 years) - \frac{\$10 million}{(0.09) \times (1.09)^9}$$

   PV(assets) = $97,462,710

   Without the fixed price contract:

   PV(assets) = PV(revenue) – PV(variable cost)

$$PV(\text{assets}) = \frac{\$20\text{million}}{0.09} - \frac{\$10\text{million}}{0.09}$$

PV(assets) = $111,111,111

19.   a.   The threat of a coup d'état means that the *expected* cash flow is less than $250,000. The threat could also increase the discount rate, but only if it increases market risk.

      b.   The expected cash flow is: $(0.25 \times 0) + (0.75 \times 250{,}000) = \$187{,}500$

           Assuming that the cash flow is about as risky as the rest of the company's business:

           $$PV = \$187{,}500/1.12 = \$167{,}411$$

20.   a.   Expected daily production =

           $$(0.2 \times 0) + 0.8 \times [(0.4 \times 1{,}000) + (0.6 \times 5{,}000)] = 2{,}720 \text{ barrels}$$

           Expected annual cash revenues = $2{,}720 \times 365 \times \$15 = \$49{,}640{,}000$

      b.   The possibility of a dry hole is a diversifiable risk and should not affect the discount rate. This possibility should affect forecasted cash flows, however. See Part (a).

21.   a.   Using the Security Market Line, we find the cost of capital:

           $$r = 0.07 + [1.5 \times (0.16 - 0.07)] = 0.205 = 20.5\%$$

           Therefore:

           $$PV = \frac{40}{1.205} + \frac{60}{1.205^2} + \frac{50}{1.205^3} = 103.09$$

      b. $CEQ_1 = 40 \times (1.07/1.205) = 35.52$
           $CEQ_2 = 60 \times (1.07/1.205)^2 = 47.31$
           $CEQ_3 = 50 \times (1.07/1.205)^3 = 35.01$

      c. $a_1 = 35.52/40 = 0.8880$
           $a_2 = 47.31/60 = 0.7885$
           $a_3 = 35.01/50 = 0.7002$

      d.   Using a constant risk-adjusted discount rate is equivalent to assuming that a_t decreases at a constant compounded rate.

22. At t = 2, there are two possible values for the project's NPV:

$$NPV_2 \text{ (if test is not successful)} = 0$$

$$NPV_2 \text{ (if test is successful)} = -5,000,000 + \frac{700,000}{0.12} = \$833,333$$

Therefore, at t = 0:

$$NPV_0 = -500,000 + \frac{(0.40 \times 0) + (0.60 \times 833,333)}{1.40^2} = -\$244,898$$

23. It is correct that, for a high beta project, you should discount *all* cash flows at a high rate. Thus, the higher the risk of the cash outflows, the less you should worry about them because, the higher the discount rate, the closer the present value of these cash flows is to zero. This result does make sense. It is better to have a series of payments that are high when the market is booming and low when it is slumping (i.e., a high beta) than the reverse.

The beta of an investment is independent of the sign of the cash flows. If an investment has a high beta for anyone paying out the cash flows, it must have a high beta for anyone receiving them. If the sign of the cash flows affected the discount rate, each asset would have one value for the buyer and one for the seller, which is clearly an impossible situation.

24. a. Since the risk of a dry hole is unlikely to be market-related, we can use the same discount rate as for producing wells. Thus, using the Security Market Line:

$$r_{nominal} = 0.06 + (0.9 \times 0.08) = 0.132 = 13.2\%$$

We know that:

$$(1 + r_{nominal}) = (1 + r_{real}) \times (1 + r_{inflation})$$

Therefore:

$$r_{real} = \frac{1.132}{1.04} - 1 = 0.0885 = 8.85\%$$

b.
$$NPV_1 = -10\,million + \sum_{t=1}^{10} \frac{3\,million}{1.2885^t} = -10\,million + [(3\,million) \times (3.1914)]$$

$$NPV_1 = -\$425,800$$

$$NPV_2 = -10\,million + \sum_{t=1}^{15} \frac{2\,million}{1.2885^t} = -10\,million + [(2\,million) \times (3.3888)]$$

$$NPV_2 = -\$3,222,300$$

c.   Expected income from Well 1: [(0.2 × 0) + (0.8 × 3 million)] = \$2.4 million

Expected income from Well 2: [(0.2 × 0) + (0.8 × 2 million)] = \$1.6 million

Discounting at 8.85 percent gives:

$$NPV_1 = -10\,\text{million} + \sum_{t=1}^{10} \frac{2.4\text{million}}{1.0885^t} = -10\,\text{million} + [(2.4\text{million}) \times (6.4602)]$$

$$NPV_1 = \$5,504,600$$

$$NPV_2 = -10\,\text{million} + \sum_{t=1}^{15} \frac{1.6\text{million}}{1.0885^t} = -10\,\text{million} + [(1.6\text{million}) \times (8.1326)]$$

$$NPV_2 = \$3,012,100$$

d.   For Well 1, one can certainly find a discount rate (and hence a "fudge factor") that, when applied to cash flows of \$3 million per year for 10 years, will yield the correct NPV of \$5,504,600. Similarly, for Well 2, one can find the appropriate discount rate. However, these two "fudge factors" will be different. Specifically, Well 2 will have a smaller "fudge factor" because its cash flows are more distant. With more distant cash flows, a smaller addition to the discount rate has a larger impact on present value.

CHAPTER 10
Project Analysis

Answers to Problem Sets

1. a.   False

    b.   True

    c.   True

2. a.   Cash-flow forecasts overstated.

    b.   One project proposal may be ranked below another simply because cash flows are based on different forecasts.

    c.   Project proposals may not consider strategic -alternatives.

3. a.   Analysis of how project profitability and NPV change if different assumptions are made about sales, cost, and other key variables.

    b.   Project NPV is recalculated by changing several inputs to new, but consistent, values.

    c.   Determines the level of future sales at which project profitability or NPV equals zero.

    d.   An extension of sensitivity analysis that explores all possible outcomes and weights each by its probability.

    e.   A graphical technique for displaying possible future events and decisions taken in response to those events.

    f.   Option to modify a project at a future date.

    g.   The additional present value created by the -option to bail out of a project, and recover part of the initial investment, if the project performs poorly.

    h.   The additional present value created by the -option to invest more and expand output, if a project performs well.

4. a. False

   b. True

   c. True

   d. True

   e. False

   f. True

5. a. Describe how project cash flow depends on the underlying variables.

   b. Specify probability distributions for forecast -errors for these cash flows.

   c. Draw from the probability distributions to -simulate the cash flows.

6. a. True

   b. True

   c. False

   d. False

7. Adding a fudge factor to the discount rate pushes project analysts to submit more optimistic forecasts.

8. We assume that the idea for a new obfuscator machine originates with a plant manager in the Deconstruction Division. (Keep in mind however that, in addition to bottom-up proposals, such as the obfuscator machine proposal, top-down proposals also originate with divisional managers and senior management.) Other steps in the capital budgeting process include the following:

   - Many large firms begin the process with forecasts of economic variables, such as inflation and GDP growth, as well as variables of particular interest to the industry, such as prices of raw materials and industry sales projections.
   - The plant manager, often in consultation with the division manager, prepares the proposal in the form of an appropriation request; the appropriation request typically includes an explanation of the need for the expenditure, detailed forecasts, discounted cash flow analysis and other supporting detail such as sensitivity analysis.

- Depending on the size of the investment, the appropriation request is reviewed and approved by the divisional manager, senior management or, in the case of major expenditures, the board of directors.
- The forecast expenditure is included as part of the annual capital budget, which is approved by top management and the board of directors.
- Major cost over-runs typically require a supplementary appropriation request, which includes an explanation of the reason why the additional expenditure was not anticipated.
- When the machine is finally up and running, most firms conduct a postaudit to identify problems and to assess forecast accuracy; the main purpose of the postaudit is to improve the process in the future.

9. a.

$$NPV_F = -\$9,000 + \frac{\$6,000 \times (1-0.08)}{1.10} + \frac{\$5,000 \times (1-0.08)}{(1.10)^2} + \frac{\$4,000 \times (1-0.08)}{(1.10)^3}$$

$$= \$2,584.67$$

$$NPV_G = -\$9,000 + \frac{\$1,800 \times (1-0.08)}{0.10} = \$7,560$$

b. $$NPV_F = -\$9,000 + \frac{\$6,000}{1.18} + \frac{\$5,000}{(1.18)^2} + \frac{\$4,000}{(1.18)^3} = \$2,110.19$$

$$NPV_G = -\$9,000 + \frac{\$1,800}{0.18} = \$1,000$$

c. The 18% discount rate would give an approximation to the correct NPVs for projects with all (or most) of the inflows in the first year.

The present value of $1 to be received one year from now, discounted at 18% is: $0.8475

The present value of $1 × (1 – 0.08) (that is, $0.92) to be received one year from now, discounted at 10% is: $0.8364

The former calculation overstates the correct answer by approximately 1.3%. However, for cash flows five or ten years in to the future, discounting by 18% understates the correct present value by approximately 23% and 46%, respectively. The error increases substantially because the incorrect factor (i.e., 1.18) is compounded, causing the denominator of the present value calculation to be greatly overstated so that the present value is greatly understated.

10.

	Year 0	Years 1-10
Investment	¥15 B	
1. Revenue		¥44.000 B
2. Variable Cost		39.600 B
3. Fixed Cost		2.000 B
4. Depreciation		1.500 B
5. Pre-tax Profit		¥0.900 B
6. Tax @ 50%		0.450 B
7. Net Operating Profit		¥0.450 B
8. Operating Cash Flow		¥1.950 B

$$NPV = -¥15B + \sum_{t=1}^{10} \frac{¥1.950B}{1.10^t} = -¥3.02B$$

11. The spreadsheets show the following results:

	NPV		
	Pessimistic	Expected	Optimistic
Market Size	−1.17	3.43	8.04
Market Share	−10.39	3.43	17.26
Unit Price	−19.61	3.43	11.11
Unit Variable Cost	−11.93	3.43	11.11
Fixed Cost	−2.71	3.43	9.58

The principal uncertainties are market share, unit price, and unit variable cost.

12. a.

	Year 0	Years 1-10
Investment	¥30 B	
1. Revenue		¥37.500 B
2. Variable Cost		26.000
3. Fixed Cost		3.000
4. Depreciation		3.000
5. Pre-tax Profit (1-2-3-4)		¥5.500
6. Tax		2.750
7. Net Operating Profit (5-6)		¥2.750
8. Operating Cash Flow (4+7)		5.750
	NPV =	+ ¥5.33 B

b.

	Inflows		Outflows					
Unit Sales (000's)	Revenues Yrs 1-10	Investment Yr 0	V. Costs Yr 1-10	F. Cost Yr 1-10	Taxes Yr 1-10	PV Inflows	PV Outflows	NPV
0	0.00	30.00	0.00	3.00	–3.00	0.00	–30.00	–30.00
100	37.50	30.00	26.00	3.00	2.75	230.42	–225.09	5.33
200	75.00	30.00	52.00	3.00	8.50	460.84	–420.18	40.66

Note that the break-even point can be found algebraically as follows:

$$\text{NPV} = -\text{Investment} + [(\text{PVA}_{10/10\%}) \times (t \times \text{Depreciation})] +$$
$$[\text{Quantity} \times (\text{Price} - \text{V.Cost}) - \text{F.Cost}] \times (1 - t) \times (\text{PVA}_{10/10\%})$$

Set NPV equal to zero and solve for Q:

$$Q = \frac{I - (\text{PVA}_{10/10\%} \times D \times t)}{(\text{PVA}_{10/10\%}) \times (P - V) \times (1 - t)} + \frac{F}{P - V}$$

$$= \frac{30{,}000{,}000{,}000 - 9{,}216{,}850{,}659}{6.144567 \times (375{,}000 - 260{,}000) \times 0.50} + \frac{3{,}000{,}000{,}000}{375{,}000 - 260{,}000}$$

$$= \frac{20{,}783{,}149{,}341}{353{,}313} + \frac{3{,}000{,}000{,}000}{115{,}000} = 58{,}824 + 26{,}087 = 84{,}911$$

Proof:

1.	Revenue	¥31.84 B
2.	Variable Cost	22.08
3.	Fixed Cost	3.00
4.	Depreciation	3.00
5.	Pre-tax Profit	¥3.76 B
6.	Tax	1.88
7.	Net Profit	¥1.88
8.	Operating Cash Flow	¥4.88

$$\text{NPV} = \sum_{t=1}^{10} \frac{4.88}{(1.10)^t} - 30 = 29.99 - 30 = -0.01$$
(difference due to rounding)

Break-Even

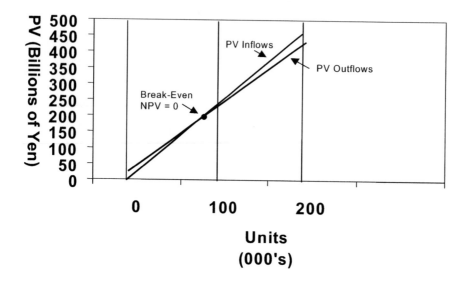

c. The break-even point is the point where the present value of the cash flows, including the opportunity cost of capital, yields a zero NPV.

d. To find the level of costs at which the project would earn zero profit, write the equation for net profit, set net profit equal to zero, and solve for variable costs:

$$\text{Net Profit} = (R - VC - FC - D) \times (1 - t)$$
$$0 = (37.5 - VC - 3.0 - 1.5) \times 0.50$$
$$VC = 33.0$$

This will yield zero profit.

Next, find the level of costs at which the project would have zero NPV. Using the data in Table 11.1, the equivalent annual cash flow yielding a zero NPV would be:

$$¥15 \text{ B}/PVA_{10/10\%} = ¥2.4412 \text{ B}$$

If we rewrite the cash flow equation and solve for the variable cost:

$$NCF = [(R - VC - FC - D) \times (1 - t)] + D$$
$$2.4412 = [(37.5 - VC - 3.0 - 1.5) \times 0.50] + 1.5$$
$$VC = 31.12$$

This will yield NPV = 0, assuming the tax credits can be used elsewhere in the company.

e.   DOL = 1 + (fixed costs / profit)

Fixed costs rise 1.5 due to additional depreciation of the 15 billion yen investment. Profits increase by 0.4 reflecting the lower variable costs.

This gives us a DOL = 1 + ((3 + 1.5 + 1.5) / 3.4) = 2.76

13.   If Rustic replaces now rather than in one year, several things happen:
   i.   It incurs the equivalent annual cost of the $9 million capital investment.
   ii.   It reduces manufacturing costs.

For example, for the "Expected" case, analyzing "Sales" we have (all dollar figures in millions):

   i.   The economic life of the new machine is expected to be 10 years, so the equivalent annual cost of the new machine is:

$9/5.6502 = $1.59

   ii.   The reduction in manufacturing costs is:

$0.5 \times \$4 = \$2.00$

Thus, the equivalent annual cost savings is:

−$1.59 + $2.00 = $0.41

Continuing the analysis for the other cases, we find:

	Equivalent Annual Cost Savings (Millions)		
	Pessimistic	Expected	Optimistic
Sales	0.01	0.41	1.21
Manufacturing Cost	-0.59	0.41	0.91
Economic Life	0.03	0.41	0.60

14. $\text{DOL} = 1 + \dfrac{\text{fixed cost} + \text{depreciation}}{\text{operating profit}}$

Operating profits are unchanged in all scenarios, as we have just shifted the nature of the costs.

With $33 million in variable costs, $\text{DOL} = 1 + \dfrac{(0+1.5)}{3.0} = 1.5$

With $33 million in fixed costs, $\text{DOL} = 1 + \dfrac{(33+1.5)}{3.0} = 12.5$

15. a. Operating leverage = $\dfrac{\text{\% change in operating income}}{\text{\% change in sales}}$

For a 1% increase in sales, from 100,000 units to 101,000 units:

Operating leverage = $\dfrac{0.075/3}{0.375/37.5} = 2.50$

b. Operating leverage = $1 + \dfrac{\text{fixed cost + depreciation}}{\text{operating profit}}$

$= 1 + \dfrac{(3.0 + 1.5)}{3.0} = 2.5$

c. Operating leverage = $\dfrac{\text{\% change in operating income}}{\text{\% change in sales}}$

For a 1% increase in sales, from 200,000 units to 202,000 units:

Operating leverage = $\dfrac{(10.65 - 10.5)/10.5}{(75.75 - 75)/75} = 1.43$

16.

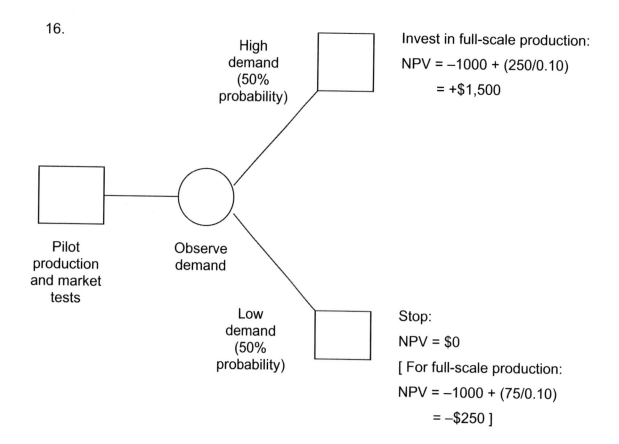

High demand (50% probability)

Invest in full-scale production:
NPV = −1000 + (250/0.10)
= +$1,500

Pilot production and market tests

Observe demand

Low demand (50% probability)

Stop:
NPV = $0
[For full-scale production:
NPV = −1000 + (75/0.10)
= −$250]

17. Problem requires use of Excel program; answers will vary.

18. a. Timing option

    b. Expansion option

    c. Abandonment option

    d. Production option

19. Working from right to left, the following spreadsheet calculates a weighted average NPV of 119 at the start of Phase 3 trials.

Weighted NPV	Prob. of outcome	NPV with abandonment	Resulting NPV with 130 investment; r = 9.6%	Phase III results	PV if successful	Probability of Phase III success
39	5%	781	781	Blockbuster	1500	80%
59	20%	295	295	Above average	700	80%
21	40%	52	52	Average	300	80%
0	25%	0	-69	Below Average	100	80%
0	10%	0	-106	Dog	40	80%
119						

We can calculate the NPV at the initial investment decision as follows:

$$NPV = -18 + .44 \times \frac{119}{(1.096)^2} = \$25.6 \text{ million}$$

So the investment remains positive.

20. Working from right to left, the following spreadsheet shows that the weighted average NPV at the start of the Phase 3 trials increases to $146 million with the higher upside PV.

Weighted NPV	Prob. of outcome	NPV with abandonment	Resulting NPV with 130 investment; r = 9.6%	Phase III results	PV if successful	Probability of Phase III success
119	25%	478	478	Upside	1000	80%
26	50%	52	52	Most likely	300	80%
0	25%	0	-69	downside	100	80%
146						

We can calculate the NPV at the initial investment decision as follows:

$$NPV = -38 + .44 \times \frac{146}{(1.096)^2} = \$15.3 \text{ million}$$

The project is still positive but NPV has fallen, showing that the extra $20 million investment is not worthwhile. Decreasing the probability of phase III success to 75% results in the following calculations:

Weighted NPV	Prob. of outcome	NPV with abandonment	Resulting NPV with 130 investment; r = 9.6%	Phase III results	PV if successful	Probability of Phase III success
110	25%	440	440	Upside	1000	75%
20	50%	41	41	Most likely	300	75%
0	25%	0	-73	downside	100	75%
130						

$$NPV = -38 + .44 \times \frac{130}{(1.096)^2} = \$9.75 \text{ million}$$

So the R&D proposal is still not worthwhile.

21.

a.

Decision Tree

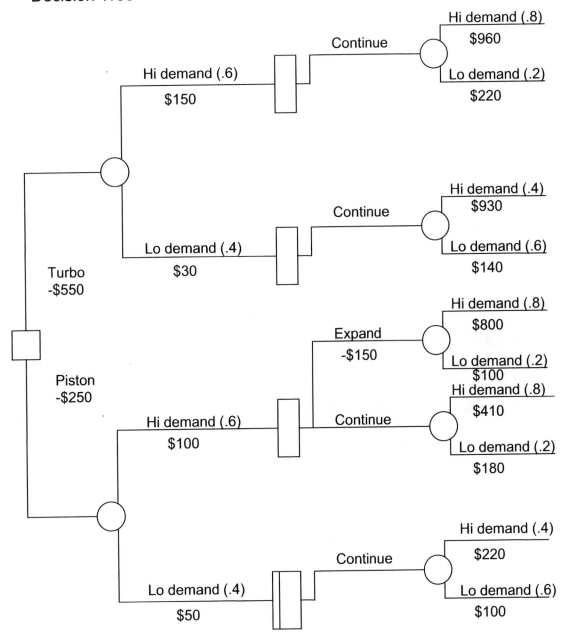

b. Analyze the decision tree by working backwards. If we purchase the piston plane and demand is high:

- The NPV at t = 1 of the 'Expand' branch is:

$$-150 + \frac{(0.8 \times 800) + (0.2 \times 100)}{1.10} = \$450$$

- The NPV at t = 1 of the 'Continue' branch is:

$$\frac{(0.8 \times 410) + (0.2 \times 180)}{1.10} = \$331$$

Thus, if we purchase the piston plane and demand is high, we should expand further at t = 1. This branch has the highest NPV.

c. Continuing the analysis, if we purchase the piston plane and demand is low:

- The NPV of the 'Continue' branch is:

$$\frac{(0.4 \times 220) + (0.6 \times 100)}{1.10} = \$135$$

- We can now use these results to calculate the NPV of the 'Piston' branch at t = 0:

$$-250 + \frac{(0.6) \times (100 + 451) + (0.4) \times (50 + 135)}{1.10} = \$117$$

- Similarly for the 'Turbo' branch, if demand is high, the expected cash flow at t = 1 is:

$$(0.8 \times 960) + (0.2 \times 220) = \$812$$

- If demand is low, the expected cash flow is:

$$(0.4 \times 930) + (0.6 \times 140) = \$456$$

- So, for the 'Turbo' branch, the combined NPV is:

$$NPV = -550 + \frac{(0.6 \times 150) + (0.4 \times 30)}{(1.10)} + \frac{(0.6 \times 812) + (0.4 \times 456)}{(1.10)^2} = \$96$$

Therefore, the company should buy the Piston-engine plane today.

d. To determine the value of the option to expand, we first compute the NPV without the option to expand:

$$NPV = -250 + \frac{(0.6 \times 100) + (0.4 \times 50)}{(1.10)} +$$

$$\frac{(0.6)[(0.8 \times 410) + (0.2 \times 180)] + (0.4)[(0.4 \times 220) + (0.6 \times 100)]}{(1.10)^2} = \$52$$

Therefore, the value of the option to expand is: $117 – $52 = $65

22. Problem requires use of Crystal Ball software simulation; answers will vary.

CHAPTER 11
Investment, Strategy, and Economic Rents

Answers to Problem Sets

1. a.   False

    b.   True

    c.   True

    d.   False

2. $15

3. First consider whether renting the building and opening the Taco Palace is positive NPV. Then consider whether to buy (instead of renting) based on your optimistic view of local real estate.

4. a.   .1 X 3,450/1.005 = $343.3 million

    b.   The expected rate of return is $r_f + \beta(r_m - r_f) = .005 + 1.2(.08 - .005) =$ .095 or 9.5%. The expected price is $3,433 X 1.095 = $3,135. The certainty equivalent price is $3,450.

5. The second-hand market value of older planes falls by enough to make up for their higher fuel consumption. Also, the older planes are used on routes where fuel efficiency is relatively less important.

6. The 757 must be a zero-NPV investment for the marginal user. Unless Boeing can charge different prices to different users (which is precluded with a secondary market), Delta will earn economic rents if the 757 is particularly well suited to Delta's routes (and competition does not force Delta to pass the cost savings through to customers in the form of lower fares). Thus, the decision focuses on the issue of whether the plane is worth more in Delta's hands than in the hands of the marginal user.

    a.   With a good secondary market and information on past changes in aircraft prices, it becomes somewhat more feasible to ignore cash flows beyond the first few years and to substitute the expected residual value of the plane.

b. Past aircraft prices may be used to estimate systematic risk (see Chapter 8).

c. The existence of a secondary market makes it more important to take note of the abandonment option.

7. The key question is: Will Gamma Airlines be able to earn economic rents on the Akron-Yellowknife route? The necessary steps include:

   a. Forecasting costs, including the cost of building and maintaining terminal facilities, all necessary training, advertising, equipment, etc.

   b. Forecasting revenues, which includes a detailed market demand analysis (what types of travelers are expected and what prices can be charged) as well as an analysis of the competition (if Gamma is successful, how quickly would competition spring up?).

   c. Calculating the net present value.

   The leasing market comes into play because it tells Gamma Airlines the opportunity cost of the planes, a critical component of costs.

   If the Akron-Yellowknife project is attractive and growth occurs at the Ulan Bator hub, Gamma Airlines should simply lease additional aircraft.

8. The price of $650 per ounce represents the discounted value of expected future gold prices. Hence, the present value of 1 million ounces produced 8 years from now should be: 650×1 million = $650 million

9. Interstate rail lines can be expected to generate economic rents when they have excess capacity that allows them to accommodate increased demand at low cost. For example, an economic expansion accompanied by high fuel costs would result in economic rents for interstate rail lines. Trucking companies have the flexibility to expand capacity relatively quickly, but high fuel costs could tend to limit the ability of trucking companies to compete effectively with interstate rail lines that are relatively more fuel efficient.

10. First, consider the sequence of events:

   - At $t = 0$, the investment of $25,000,000 is made.
   - At $t = 1$, production begins, so the first year of revenue and expenses is recorded at $t = 2$.
   - At $t = 6$, the patent expires and competition may enter. Since it takes one year to achieve full production, competition is not a factor until $t = 7$. (This assumes the competition does not begin construction until the patent expires.)

- After t = 7, full competition will exist and thus any new entrant into the market for BGs will earn the 9% cost of capital.

Next, calculate the cash flows:

- At t = 0: −$25,000,000
- At t = 1: $0
- At t = 2, 3, 4, 5, 6: Sale of 200,000 units at $100 each, with costs of $65 each, yearly cash flow = $7,000,000.
- After t = 6, the NPV of new investment must be zero. Hence, to find the selling price per unit (P) solve the following for P:

$$0 = -25,000,000 + \frac{200,000 \times (P - 65)}{1.09^2} + \cdots + \frac{200,000 \times (P - 65)}{1.09^{12}}$$

Solving, we find P = $85.02 so that, for years t = 7 through t = 12, the yearly cash flow will be: [200,000 × ($85.02 - $65)] = $4,004,000.

Finally, the net present value (in millions):

$$NPV = -25 + \frac{7}{1.09^2} + \frac{7}{1.09^3} + \cdots + \frac{7}{1.09^6} + \frac{4.004}{1.09^7} + \cdots + \frac{4.004}{1.09^{12}}$$

NPV = $10.69 or $10,690,000

11. The selling price after t = 6 now changes because the required investment is:

$$\$25,000,000 \times (1 - 0.03)^5 = \$21,468,351$$

After t = 5, the NPV of new investment must be zero, and hence the selling price per unit (P) is found by solving the following equation for P:

$$0 = -21,468,351 + \frac{200,000 \times (P - 65)}{1.09^2} + \cdots + \frac{200,000 \times (P - 65)}{1.09^{12}}$$

P = $82.19

Thus, for years t = 7 through t = 12, the yearly cash flow will be:

200,000 × ($82.19 - $65) = $3,438,000

Finally, the net present value (in millions) is:

$$NPV = -25 + \frac{7}{1.09^2} + \frac{7}{1.09^3} + \cdots + \frac{7}{1.09^6} + \frac{3.438}{1.09^7} + \cdots + \frac{3.438}{1.09^{12}}$$

NPV = $9.18 or $9,180,000

12. a. See the table below. The net present value is negative, so management should not proceed with the Polyzone project.

	t = 0	t = 1	t = 2	t = 3	t = 4	t = 5 – 10
Investment	100					
Production	0	0	40	80	80	80
Spread	1.20	1.20	1.20	1.20	1.20	0.95
Net Revenues	0	0	48	96	96	76
Prod. Costs	0	0	30	30	30	30
Transport	0	0	4	8	8	8
Other Costs	0	20	20	20	20	20
Cash Flow	−100	−20	−6	38	38	18

NPV (at 8%) = −$4.40

b. See the table below. The net present value is $40.40 million, and so the project is acceptable.

	t = 0	t = 1	t = 2	t = 3	t = 4	t = 5 – 10
Investment	100					
Production	0	40	80	80	80	80
Spread	1.20	1.20	1.20	1.20	1.10	0.95
Net Revenues	0	48	96	96	88	76
Prod. Costs	0	30	30	30	30	30
Transport	0	4	8	8	8	8
Other Costs	0	20	20	20	20	20
Cash Flow	−100	−6	38	38	30	18

NPV (at 8%) = $40.40

c. See the table below. The net present value is $18.64 million, and so the project is acceptable. However, the assumption that the technological advance will elude the competition for ten years seems questionable.

	t = 0	t = 1	t = 2	t − 3	t = 4	t = 5 – 10
Investment	100					
Production	0	0	40	80	80	80
Spread	1.20	1.20	1.20	1.20	1.10	0.95
Net Revenues	0	0	48	96	88	76
Prod. Costs	0	0	25	25	25	25
Transport	0	0	4	8	8	8
Other Costs	0	20	20	20	20	20
Cash Flow	−100	−20	−1	43	35	23

NPV (at 8%) = $18.64

13. There are four components that contribute to this project's NPV:

- The initial investment of $100,000.
- The depreciation tax shield. Depreciation expense is $20,000 per year for five years and is valued at the nominal rate of interest because it applies to nominal cash flows, i.e., earnings.
- The after-tax value of the increase in silver yield. Like gold, silver has low convenience yield and storage cost. (You can verify this by checking that the difference between the futures price and the spot price is approximately the interest saving from buying the futures contract.) We conclude, therefore, that the PV of silver delivered (with certainty) in the future is approximately today's spot price, and so there is no need to forecast the price of silver and then discount.
- The cost of operating the equipment. This cost is $80,000 per year for ten years and is valued at the real company cost of capital because we do not assume any future increase in cost due to inflation. We are concerned only with the after-tax cost.

$$NPV = -100,000 + \sum_{t=1}^{5} \frac{0.35 \times 20,000}{1.06^t} + (1 - 0.35) \times (10 \times 5,000 \times 20)$$

$$-\sum_{t=1}^{10} \frac{(1 - 0.35) \times 80,000}{1.08^t} = \$230,562$$

14. Assume we can ignore dividends paid on the stock market index. On June 30, 2011, each ticket must sell for $100 because this date marks the base period for the return calculation. At this price, investment in a ticket will offer the same return as investment in the index. On January 1, 2011, you know that each ticket will be worth $100 in 6 months. Therefore, on January 1, 2011, a ticket will be worth:

$100/(1.10)^{1/2} = \$95.35$

The price will be the same for a ticket based on the Dow Jones Industrial Average.

15. If available for immediate occupancy, the building would be worth $1 million. But because it will take the company one year to clear it out, the company will incur $200,000 in clean-up costs and will lose $80,000 net rent. Assume both rent *and* costs are spread evenly throughout the year. Thus (all dollar amounts are in thousands):

PV = 1,000 − PV(200 + 80) = 1,000 − (280 × 0.962) = 731

Since the selling price at each date is the present value of forecasted rents, the only effect of postponing the sale to year 2 is to postpone the sales commission. The commission is currently (0.05 × 1,000) = 50 and grows in line with property value. To estimate the growth rate of value, we can use the constant-growth model:

$$PV = 1{,}000 = 80/(0.08 - g) \text{ so that } g = 0\%$$

Thus, the commission in year 2 is: (50×1.00^2) and:

$$PV \text{ (commission)} = 50 \times (1.00^2/1.08^2) = 43$$

The value of the warehouse, net of the sales commission, is:

$$731 - 43 = 688 \text{ or } \$688{,}000$$

16.   a.   The NPV of such plants is likely to be zero, because the industry is competitive and, after two years, no company will enjoy any technical advantages. The PV of each of these new plants would be $100,000 because the NPV is zero and the cost is $100,000.

      b.   The PV of revenue from such a plant is:

$$[100{,}000 \text{ tons} \times (\text{Price} - 0.85)]/0.10 = 100{,}000$$

Therefore, the price of polysyllabic acid will be $0.95 per ton.

      c.   At $t = 2$, the PV of the existing plant will be:

$$[100{,}000 \text{ tons} \times (0.95 - 0.90)]/0.10 = \$50{,}000$$

Therefore, the existing plant would be scrapped at $t = 2$ as long as scrap value at that time exceeds $50,000.

      d.   No. Book value is irrelevant. NPV of the existing plant is negative after year 2.

      e.   Yes. Sunk costs are irrelevant. NPV of the existing plant is negative after year 2.

      f.   Phlogiston's project causes temporary excess capacity. Therefore, the price for the next two years must be such that the existing plant's owners will be indifferent between scrapping now and scrapping at the end of year 2. This allows us to solve for price in years 1 and 2.

Today's scrap value is $60,000. Also, today's scrap value is equal to the present value of future cash flows. Therefore:

$$\frac{100{,}000 \times (\text{Price} - 0.90)}{1.10} + \frac{100{,}000 \times (\text{Price} - 0.90)}{1.10^2} + \frac{57{,}900}{1.10^2} = 60{,}000$$

Solving, we find that the price is $0.97 per ton. Knowing this, we can calculate the PV of Phlogiston's new plant:

$$PV = 100{,}000 \times \left[\frac{0.97 - 0.85}{1.10} + \frac{0.97 - 0.85}{1.10^2} + \frac{0.95 - 0.85}{0.10 \times 1.10^2} \right] = \$103{,}471$$

17. Aircraft will be deployed in a manner that will minimize costs. This means that each aircraft will be used on the route for which it has the greatest comparative advantage. Thus, for example, for Part (a) of this problem, it is clear that Route X will be served with five A's and five B's, and that Route Y will be served with five B's and five C's. The remaining C-type aircraft will be scrapped.

The maximum price that anyone would pay for an aircraft is the present value of the total additional costs that would be incurred if that aircraft were withdrawn from service. Using the annuity factor for 5 time periods at 10 percent, we find the PV of the operating costs (all numbers are in millions):

Type	X	Y
A	5.7	5.7
B	9.5	7.6
C	17.1	13.3

Again, consider Part (a). The cost of using an A-type aircraft on Route X (Cost = Price of A + 5.7) must be equal to the cost of using a B-type aircraft on Route X (Cost = Price of B + 9.5). Also, the cost of using a B-type aircraft on Route Y (Price of B + 7.6) equals the cost of using a C-type on Route Y (Price of C + 13.3). Further, because five C-type aircraft are scrapped, the price of a C-type aircraft must be $1.0, the scrap value. Therefore, solving first for the price of B and then for the price of A, we find that the price of an A-type is $10.5 and the price of a B-type is $6.7. Using this approach, we have the following solutions:

		Usage		Aircraft Value (in millions)		
	X	Y	Scrap	A	B	C
a.	5A+5B	5B+5C	5C	$10.5	$6.7	$1.0
b.	10A	10B	10C	10.5	6.7	1.0
c.	10A	5A+5B	5B+10C	2.9	1.0	1.0
d.	10A	10A	10B+10C	2.9	1.0	1.0

18. a. $$\text{PV of 1-year-old plant} = \frac{43.33}{1.20} + \frac{58.33}{1.20^2} = \$76.62$$

$$\text{PV of 2-year-old plant} = \frac{58.33}{1.20} = \$48.61$$

b. Given that the industry is competitive, the investment in a new plant to produce bucolic acid must yield a zero NPV. First, we solve for the revenues (R) at which a new plant has zero NPV.

		0	1	2	3
1.	Initial investment	−100			
2.	Revenues net of tax		0.6R	0.6R	0.6R
3.	Operating costs net of tax		−30	−30	−30
4.	Depreciation tax shield		+40		
5.	Salvage value net of tax				+15

Therefore:

$$NPV = -100 + \frac{(0.6R - 30 + 40)}{1.20} + \frac{(0.6R - 30)}{1.20^2} + \frac{(0.6R - 30 + 15)}{1.20^3} = 0$$

$$0 = -100 + 1.264R - 21.181$$

$$R = \$95.87$$

We can now use the new revenue to re-compute the present values from Part (a) above. (Recall that existing plants must use the original tax depreciation schedule.)

$$PV \text{ of } 1 - \text{year} - \text{old plant} = \frac{40.93}{1.20} + \frac{55.93}{1.20^2} = \$72.95$$

$$PV \text{ of } 2 - \text{year} - \text{old plant} = \frac{55.93}{1.20} = \$46.61$$

c. Existing 2-year-old plants have a net-of-tax salvage value of:

$$50 - [(0.4) \times (50.0 - 33.3)] = \$43.33$$

d. Solve again for revenues at which the new plant has zero NPV:

		0	1	2	3
1.	Initial investment	-100			
2.	Revenues		+R	+R	+R
3.	Operating costs		-50	-50	-50
4.	Salvage value				+25

$$NPV = -100 + \frac{(R - 50)}{1.20} + \frac{(R - 50)}{1.20^2} + \frac{(R - 50 + 25)}{1.20^3} = 0$$

$$0 = -100 + 2.106R - 90.856$$

$$R = \$91$$

With revenues of $91:

$$PV \text{ of } 1 - \text{year} - \text{old plant} = \frac{41}{1.20} + \frac{66}{1.20^2} = \$80$$

$$PV \text{ of } 2 - \text{year} - \text{old plant} = \frac{66}{1.20} = \$55$$

CHAPTER 12
Agency Problems, Compensation, and Performance Measurement

Answers to Problem Sets

1. a.   True

    b.   True

    c.   False

    d.   True

2. a.   Agency costs: value lost when managers do not act to maximize value. This includes costs of monitoring and control.

    b.   Private benefits: perks or other advantages enjoyed by managers.

    c.   Empire building: investing for size, not NPV.

    d.   Free-rider problem: when one shareholder, or group of shareholders, acts to monitor and control management, all shareholders benefit.

    e.   Entrenching investment: managers choose or design investment projects that increase the managers' value to the firm.

    f.   Delegated monitoring: monitoring on behalf of principals. For example, the board of directors monitors management performance on behalf of stockholders.

3. Monitoring is costly and encounters diminishing returns. Also, completely effective monitoring would require perfect information.

4. a.   Dollar amount

    b.   EVA = Income earned – (cost of capital × investment)

    c.   They are essentially the same

    d.   EVA makes the cost of capital visible to managers. Compensation based on EVA encourages them to dispose of unnecessary assets and to forego investment unless it earns more than the cost of capital

    e.   Yes.

5. ROI = 1.6/20 = .08 or 8%. Net return = 8 – 11.5 = –3.5%. EVA = 1.6 – (.115 × 20) = –$.7 million. EVA is negative.

6. Cash flow, economic, less, greater.

7. Not usually by creative accounting, but by reducing or delaying discretionary advertising, maintenance, R&D, or other expenses.

8. The typical compensation and incentive plans for top management include salary plus profit sharing and stock options. This is usually done to align as closely as possible the interests of the manager with the interests of the shareholders. These managers are usually responsible for corporate strategy and policies that can directly affect the future of the entire firm.

   Plant and divisional managers are usually paid a fixed salary plus a bonus based on accounting measures of performance. This is done because they are directly responsible for day-to-day performance and this valuation method provides an absolute standard of performance, as opposed to a standard that is relative to shareholder expectations. Further, it allows for the evaluation of junior managers who are only responsible for a small segment of the total corporate operation.

9. a. When paid a fixed salary without incentives to act in shareholders' best interest, managers often act sub-optimally.
      1. They may reduce their efforts to find and implement projects that add value.
      2. They may extract benefits-in-kind from the corporation in the form of a more lavish office, tickets to social events, overspending on expense accounts, etc.
      3. They may expand the size of the operation just for the prestige of running a larger company.
      4. They may choose second-best investments in order to reward existing employees, rather than the alternative that requires outside personnel but has a higher NPV.
      5. In order to maintain their comfortable jobs, managers may invest in safer rather than riskier projects.

   b. Tying the manager's compensation to EVA attempts to ensure that assets are deployed efficiently and that earned returns exceed the cost of capital. Hence, actions taken by the manager to shirk the duty of maximizing shareholder wealth generally result in a return that does not exceed the minimum required rate of return (cost of capital). The more the manager works in the interests of shareholders, the greater the EVA.

10. Shareholders are ultimately responsible for monitoring of top management of public U.S. corporations. However, unless there is a dominant shareholder (or a few major shareholders), monitoring is generally delegated to the board of directors elected by the shareholders. The board of directors of a large public company also retains an independent accounting firm to audit the company's financial statements. In addition, lenders often monitor the company's management in order to protect lenders' interests in the loans they have extended; in the process, monitoring by lenders can also protect stockholders' interests.

11. Since management effort is not observable, management compensation must in practice rely on results. The major problem introduced by rewarding results rather than effort is the fact that, in the corporate setting, results are a consequence of numerous factors, including the manger's efforts. It is generally very difficult, if not impossible, to precisely identify the extent to which a manager's efforts contributed to a particular outcome. Therefore, it is difficult to create the kinds of incentives that are most likely to reward the manager for her contribution, and therefore appropriately motivate the manager.

12. a. If a firm announces the hiring of a new manager who is expected to increase the firm's value, this information should be immediately reflected in the stock price. If the manager then performs as expected, there should not be much change in the share price since this performance has already been incorporated in the stock value.

   b. This could potentially be a very serious problem since the manager could lose money for reasons out of her control. One solution might be to index the price changes and then compare the actual raw material price paid with the indexed value. Another alternative would be to compare the performance with the performance of competitive firms.

   c. It is not necessarily an advantage to have a compensation scheme tied to stock returns. For example, in addition to the problem of expectations discussed in Part (a), there are numerous factors outside the manager's control, such as federal monetary policy or new environmental regulations. However, the stock price does tend to increase or decrease depending on whether the firm does or does not exceed the required cost of capital. To this extent, it is a measure of performance.

13. The issue to consider is which plan creates the most appropriate incentive structure in terms of aligning the CEO's motivations and compensation with those of the shareholders. In this regard, both plans have advantages and disadvantages. With stock-option package (a), the CEO will be compensated if the price of Androscoggin stock increases, regardless of whether the increase is a result of the CEO's actions or a consequence of a situation which is beyond the CEO's control (such as an increase in copper prices). On the other hand, with package (b), the CEO would be compensated if his actions lead to the result that Androscoggin stock outperforms the portfolio of copper-mining company shares; however, the Androscoggin CEO could also be rewarded if the CEOs of the other copper-mining companies performed poorly leading to the result that Androscoggin stock performs better than the lackluster average generated by the CEOs of the other companies.

14. a. EVA = Income earned – (Cost of capital × Investment)

    = \$8.03m – (0.09 × \$55.40m) = \$3.04m

    b. EVA = \$8.03m – (0.09 × \$95m) = –\$0.52m

    The market value of the assets should be used to capture the true opportunity cost of capital.

15. EVA = Income earned – (Cost of capital × Investment)

    = \$1.2m – [0.15 × (\$4m + \$2m + \$8m)] = \$1.2m – \$2.1m = –\$0.9m

16. a. False. The biases rarely wash out. For example, steady state income may not be much affected by investments in R & D but book asset value is understated. Thus, book profitability is too high, even in the steady state.

    b. True. All biases in book profitability can be traced to accounting rules governing which assets are put on the balance sheet and the choice of book depreciation schedules.

17.

	Period		
	1	2	3
Net cash flow	0.00	78.55	78.55
PV at start of year	100.00	120.00	65.45
PV at end of year	120.00	65.45	0.00
Change in value during year	+20.00	–54.55	–65.45
Expected economic income	+20.00	+24.00	+13.10

18. The year-by-year book and economic profitability and rates of return are calculated in the table below. (We assume straight-line depreciation, $10 per year for years one through ten.)

Because a plant lasts for 10 years, 'steady state' for a mature company implies that we are operating ten plants, and every year we close one and begin construction on another. The total book income is $76.0, which is the same as the sum of the Book Income figures from the table (i.e., the sum of −$30.0, −$22.0, $16.0, etc.). Similarly, the total book investment is $550. Thus, the steady state book rate of return for a mature company producing Polyzone is: (76.0/550) = 13.82%. Note that this is considerably different from the economic rate of return, which is 8%.

	0	1	2	3	4	5
Investment	100.00					
Depreciation		10.00	10.00	10.00	10.00	10.00
Book Value – End of Year		90.00	80.00	70.00	60.00	50.00
Net Revenue	0.00	0.00	38.00	76.00	76.00	76.00
Production Costs	0.00	0.00	30.00	30.00	30.00	30.00
Transport & Other	0.00	20.00	20.00	20.00	20.00	20.00
Book Income		−30.00	−22.00	16.00	16.00	16.00
Book Rate of Return		−30.00%	−24.44%	20.00%	22.86%	26.67%
Cash Flow	−100.00	−20.00	−12.00	26.00	26.00	26.00
PV Start of Year		99.29	127.23	149.41	135.37	120.19
PV End of Year		127.23	149.41	135.37	120.19	103.81
Change in PV		27.94	22.18	−14.05	−15.17	−16.38
Economic Depreciation		−27.94	−22.18	14.05	15.17	16.38
Economic Income		7.94	10.18	11.95	10.83	9.62
Economic Rate of Return		8.00%	8.00%	8.00%	8.00%	8.00%

	6	7	8	9	10
Investment					
Depreciation	10.00	10.00	10.00	10.00	10.00
Book Value – End of Year	40.00	30.00	20.00	10.00	0.00
Net Revenue	76.00	76.00	76.00	76.00	76.00
Production Costs	30.00	30.00	30.00	30.00	30.00
Transport & Other	20.00	20.00	20.00	20.00	20.00
Book Income	16.00	16.00	16.00	16.00	16.00
Book Rate of Return	32.00%	40.00%	53.33%	80.00%	160.00%
Cash Flow	26.00	26.00	26.00	26.00	26.00
PV Start of Year	103.81	86.12	67.00	46.36	24.07
PV End of Year	86.12	67.00	46.36	24.07	0.00
Change in PV	−17.70	−19.11	−20.64	−22.29	−24.07
Economic Depreciation	17.70	19.11	20.64	22.29	24.07
Economic Income	8.30	6.89	5.36	3.71	1.93
Economic Rate of Return	8.00%	8.00%	8.00%	8.00%	8.00%

19. a. See table below. Straight-line depreciation would be $166.80 per year. Hence, economic depreciation in this case is accelerated, relative to straight-line depreciation.

b. The true rate of return is found by dividing economic income by the start-of-period present value. As stated in the text, this will always be 10%. The book ROI is calculated in Panel B (using straight-line depreciation).

A. Forecasted Book Income and ROI

	Year					
	1	2	3	4	5	6
Cash Flow	298.00	298.00	298.00	138.00	138.00	140.00
BV at start of year	1000.81	834.01	667.21	500.41	333.61	166.81
BV at end of year	834.01	667.21	500.41	333.61	166.81	0.01
Book depreciation	166.80	166.80	166.80	166.80	166.80	166.80
Book income	131.20	131.20	131.20	−28.80	−28.80	−26.80
Book ROI	0.1311	0.1573	0.1966	−0.0576	−0.0863	−0.1607
EVA	31.12	47.80	64.48	−78.84	−62.16	−43.48

B. Forecasted Economic Income and Rate of Return

	Year					
	1	2	3	4	5	6
Cash Flow	298.00	298.00	298.00	138.00	138.00	140.00
BV at start of year	1000.05	802.06	584.26	344.69	241.16	127.27
BV at end of year	802.06	584.26	344.69	241.16	125.27	0.00
Book depreciation	197.99	217.79	239.57	103.53	113.88	127.27
Book income	100.01	80.21	58.43	34.47	24.12	12.73
Book ROI	0.1000	0.1000	0.1000	0.1000	0.1000	0.1000
EVA	0.00	0.00	0.00	0.00	0.00	0.00

20. For a 10% expansion in book investment, ROI for Nodhead is given in the table below. When the steady-state growth rate is exactly equal to the economic rate of return (i.e., 10%), the economic rate of return and book ROI are the same.

Book Income for Assets Put in Place During Year	1	2	3	4	5	6
1	−66.80	33.20	83.20	131.20	131.20	131.20
2		−73.48	36.52	91.52	144.32	144.32
3			−80.83	40.17	100.67	158.75
4				−88.91	44.19	110.74
5					−97.80	48.61
6						−107.58
Total Book Inc:	−66.80	−40.28	38.89	173.98	322.58	486.04

Book Value for Assets Put in Place During Year	1	2	3	4	5	6
1	1000.81	834.01	667.21	500.41	333.61	166.81
2		1100.89	917.41	733.93	550.45	366.97
3			1210.98	1009.15	807.32	605.50
4				1332.08	1110.07	888.06
5					1465.29	1221.07
6						1611.81
Total BV:	1000.81	1934.90	2795.60	3575.57	4266.74	4860.22
Book ROI:	−0.067	−0.021	0.014	0.049	0.076	0.1000*

*This is the steady state rate of return.

21.

	Year 1	Year 2	Year 3
Cash Flow	5.20	4.80	4.40
PV at start of year	12	8	4
PV at end of year	8	4	0
Change in PV	−4	−4	−4
Economic depreciation	4	4	4
Economic income	1.20	0.80	0.40
Economic rate of return	0.10	0.10	0.10
Book depreciation	4	4	4
Book income	1.20	0.80	0.40
Book rate of return	0.10	0.10	0.10

22. a. See table on next page. Note that economic depreciation is simply the change in market value, while book depreciation (per year) is:

$$[19.69 - (0.2 \times 19.69)]/15 = 1.05$$

Thus, economic depreciation is accelerated in this case, relative to book depreciation.

b. See table on next page. Note that the book rate of return exceeds the true rate in only the first year.

c. Because the economic return from investing in one airplane is 10% each year, the economic return from investing in a fixed number per year is also 10% each year. In order to calculate the book return, assume that we invest in one new airplane each year (the number of airplanes does not matter, just so long as it is the same each year). Then, book income will be (3.67 – 1.05) = 2.62 from the airplane in its first year, (3.00 – 1.95) = 1.95 from the airplane in its second year, etc., for a total book income of 15.21. Book value is calculated similarly: 19.69 for the airplane just purchased, 18.64 for the airplane that is one year old, etc., for a total book value of 185.09. Thus, the steady-state book rate of return is 8.22%, which understates the true (economic) rate of return (10%).

	Year							
	1	2	3	4	5	6	7	8
Market value	19.69	17.99	16.79	15.78	14.89	14.09	13.36	12.68
Economic depreciation		1.70	1.20	1.01	0.89	0.80	0.73	0.68
Cash flow		3.67	3.00	2.69	2.47	2.29	2.14	2.02
Economic income		1.97	1.80	1.68	1.58	1.49	1.41	1.34
Economic return		10.0%	10.0%	10.0%	10.0%	10.0%	10.0%	10.0%
Book value	19.69	18.64	17.59	16.54	15.49	14.44	13.39	12.34
Book depreciation		1.05	1.05	1.05	1.05	1.05	1.05	1.05
Book income		2.62	1.95	1.64	1.42	1.24	1.09	0.97
Book return		13.3%	10.5%	9.3%	8.6%	8.0%	7.5%	7.2%

	Year							
	9	10	11	12	13	14	15	16
Market value	12.05	11.46	10.91	10.39	9.91	9.44	9.01	8.59
Economic depreciation	0.63	0.59	0.55	0.52	0.48	0.47	0.43	0.42
Cash flow	1.90	1.80	1.70	1.61	1.52	1.46	1.37	1.32
Economic income	1.27	1.21	1.15	1.09	1.04	0.99	0.94	0.90
Economic return	10.0%	10.0%	10.0%	10.0%	10.0%	10.0%	10.0%	10.0%
Book value	11.29	10.24	9.19	8.14	7.09	6.04	4.99	3.94
Book depreciation	1.05	1.05	1.05	1.05	1.05	1.05	1.05	1.05
Book income	0.85	0.75	0.65	0.56	0.47	0.41	0.32	0.27
Book return	6.9%	6.6%	6.3%	6.1%	5.8%	5.8%	5.3%	5.4%

CHAPTER 13
Efficient Markets and Behavioral Finance

Answers to Problem Sets

1. c

2. Weak, semistrong, strong, strong, weak.

3. a. False

    b. False

    c. True

    d. False

    e. False

    f. True

4. a. False

    b. False

    c. True

    d. False

5. $6 - (-.2 + 1.45 \times 5) = -1.05\%$.

6. a. True

    b. False

    c. True

    d. True

7. Decrease. The stock price already reflects an expected 25% increase. The 20% increase conveys bad news relative to expectations.

8. a. An investor should not buy or sell shares based on apparent trends or cycles in returns.

    b. A CFO should not speculate on changes in interest rates or foreign exchange rates. There is no reason to think that the CFO has superior information.

    c. A financial manager evaluating the creditworthiness of a large customer could check the customer's stock price and the yield on its debt. A falling stock price or a high yield could indicate trouble ahead.

    d. Don't assume that accounting choices that increase or decrease earnings will have any effect on stock price.

    e. The company should not seek diversification just to reduce risk. Investors can diversify on their own.

    f. Stock issues do not depress price if investors believe the issuer has no private information.

9. a. Evidence that two securities with identical cash flows (e.g. Royal Dutch Shell and Shell Transport & Trading) can sell at different prices.

    b. Small-cap stocks and high book-to-market stocks appear to have given above-average returns for their level of risk.

    c. IPOs provide relatively low returns after their first few days of trading.

    d. Stocks of firms that announce unexpectedly good earnings perform well over the coming months.

    In each case there appear to have been opportunities for earning superior profits.

10. a. An individual *can* do crazy things, but still not affect the efficiency of markets. The price of the asset in an efficient market is a consensus price as well as a marginal price. A nutty person can give assets away for free or offer to pay twice the market value. However, when the person's supply of assets or money runs out, the price will adjust back to its prior level (assuming there is no new, relevant information released by his action). If you are lucky enough to know such a person, you *will* receive a positive gain at the nutty investor's expense. You had better not count on

this happening very often, though. Fortunately, an efficient market protects crazy investors in cases less extreme than the above. Even if they trade in the market in an "irrational" manner, they can be assured of getting a fair price since the price reflects all information.

b. Yes, and how many people have dropped a bundle? Or, more to the point, how many people have made a bundle only to lose it later? People can be lucky and some people can be very lucky; efficient markets do not preclude this possibility.

c. Investor psychology is a slippery concept, more often than not used to explain price movements that the individual invoking it cannot personally explain. Even if it exists, is there any way to make money from it? If investor psychology drives up the price one day, will it do so the next day also? Or will the price drop to a 'true' level? Almost no one can tell you beforehand what 'investor psychology' will do. Theories based on it have no content.

d. What good is a stable value when you can't buy or sell at that value because new conditions or information have developed which make the stable price obsolete? It is the market price, the price at which you can buy or sell today, which determines value.

11. a. There is risk in almost everything you do in daily life. You could lose your job or your spouse, or suffer damage to your house from a storm. That doesn't necessarily mean you should quit your job, get a divorce, or sell your house. If we accept that our world is risky, then we must accept that asset values fluctuate as new information emerges. Moreover, if capital markets are functioning properly, then stock price changes will follow a random walk. The random walk of values is the *result* of rational investors coping with an uncertain world.

b. To make the example clearer, assume that everyone believes in the same chart. What happens when the chart shows a downward movement? Are investors going to be willing to hold the stock when it has an expected loss? Of course not. They start selling, and the price will decline until the stock is expected to give a positive return. The trend will 'self-destruct.'

c. Random-walk theory as applied to efficient markets means that fluctuations from the *expected* outcome are random. Suppose there is an 80 percent chance of rain tomorrow (because it rained today). Then the local umbrella store's stock price will respond *today* to the prospect of high sales tomorrow. The store's *sales* will not follow a random walk, but its stock price will, because each day the stock price reflects all that investors know about future weather and future sales.

12. One of the ways to think about market inefficiency is that it implies there is easy money to be made. The following appear to suggest market inefficiency:
     (b) strong form
     (d) weak form
     (f) semi-strong form

13. The estimates are first substituted in the market model. Then the result from this expected return equation is subtracted from the actual return for the month to obtain the abnormal return.

     Abnormal return (Intel) = Actual return − [(−0.57) + (1.08 × Market return)]

     Abnormal return (Conagra) = Actual return − [(−0.46) + (0.65 × Market return)]

14. The efficient market hypothesis does not imply that portfolio selection should be done with a pin. The manager still has three important jobs to do. First, she must make sure that the portfolio is well diversified. It should be noted that a large number of stocks is not enough to ensure diversification. Second, she must make sure that the risk of the diversified portfolio is appropriate for the manager's clients. Third, she might want to tailor the portfolio to take advantage of special tax laws for pension funds. These laws may make it possible to increase the expected return of the portfolio without increasing risk.

15. They are both under the illusion that markets are predictable and they are wasting their time trying to guess the market's direction. Remember the first lesson of market efficiency: Markets have no memory. The decision as to when to issue stock should be made without reference to 'market cycles.'

16. The efficient-market hypothesis says that there is no easy way to make money. Thus, when such an opportunity seems to present itself, we should be very skeptical. For example:

     •   In the case of short-versus long-term rates, and borrowing short-term versus long-term, there are different risks involved. For example, suppose that we need the money long-term but we borrow short-term. When the short-term note is due, we must somehow refinance. However; this may not be possible, or may be possible only at a very high interest rate.

     •   In the case of Japanese versus United States interest rates, there is the risk that the Japanese yen – U.S. dollar exchange rate will change during the period of time for which we have borrowed.

17.	This does present some evidence against the efficient capital market hypothesis. One key to market efficiency is the high level of competition among participants in the market. For small stocks, the level of competition is relatively low because major market participants (e.g., mutual funds and pension funds) are biased toward holding the securities of larger, well-known companies. Thus, it is plausible that the market for small stocks is fundamentally different from the market for larger stocks and, hence, that the small-firm effect is simply a reflection of market inefficiency.

But there are at least two alternative possibilities. First, this difference might just be coincidental. In statistical inference, we never prove an affirmative fact. The best we can do is to accept or reject a specified hypothesis with a given degree of confidence. Thus, no matter what the outcome of a statistical test, there is always a possibility, however slight, that the small-firm effect is simply the result of statistical chance.

Second, firms with small market capitalization may contain some type of additional risk that is not measured in the studies. Given the information available and the number of participants, it is hard to believe that any securities market in the U.S is not very efficient. Thus, the most likely explanation for the small-firm effect is that the model used to estimate expected returns is incorrect, and that there is some as-yet-unidentified risk factor.

18.	There are several ways to approach this problem, but all (when done correctly!) should give approximately the same answer. We have chosen to use the regression analysis function of an electronic spreadsheet program to calculate the alpha and beta for each security. The regressions are in the following form:

Security return = alpha + (beta × market return) + error term

The results are:

	Alpha	Beta
Executive Cheese	0.803	0.956
Paddington Beer	−0.834	0.730

The abnormal return for Executive Cheese in February 2007 was:

$-2.1 - [0.803 + 0.956 \times (-7.7)] = 4.31\%$

For Paddington Beer, the abnormal return was:

$-9.4 - [-0.834 + 0.73 \times (-7.7)] = -2.95\%$

Thus, the average abnormal return of the two stocks during the month of the earnings announcement was −0.68%.

19. The market is most likely efficient. The government of Kuwait is not likely to have non-public information about the BP shares. Goldman Sachs is providing an intermediary service for which they should be remunerated. Stocks are bought by investors at (higher) ask prices and sold at (lower) bid prices. The spread between the two ($0.11) is revenue for the broker. In the U.S., at that time, a bid-ask spread of 1/8 ($0.125) was not uncommon. The 'profit' of $15 million reflects the size of the order more than any mispricing.

20. Any time there is a separation of ownership and control, it is possible that the resulting agency costs will lead to market distortions. Many people hire others (explicitly or implicitly) to manage their money, and these managers may not have the same incentives to push for the best price. Over large markets, we might expect many of these distortions to have less impact, but some imperfections may remain.

    As described in the text, one example of this is mortgage securitization market. Because banks were paid a fee for packaging the securities and did not retain the risks of ownership, they may not have pushed for adequate underwriting. This may have lead to easy credit terms and a housing market bubble.

21. Opinion question; answers will vary. Some of the blame may indeed rest with borrowers who held overly-optimistic views of housing market appreciation and of their ability to repay mortgages. Similarly, purchasers of mortgage backed securities may have unwisely believed that these instruments offered an adequate return. Alternative explanations include inaccurate ratings, agency cost problems (where loan originators lacked incentives to underwrite the loans effectively, the purchase activity and implicit government backing of Fannie Mae and Freddie Mac, and other information asymmetry problems.

22. a. The probability that mutual fund × achieved superior performance in any one year is 0.50. The probability that mutual fund × achieved superior performance in each of the past ten years is:

    $$0.5^{10} = 0.00097656$$

   b. The probability that, out of 10,000 mutual funds, none of them obtained ten successive years of superior performance is:

    $$(1 - 0.00097656)^{10,000} = 0.00005712$$

    Therefore, the probability that at least one of the 10,000 mutual funds obtained ten successive years of superior performance is:

    $$1 - 0.00005712 = 0.99994288$$

23. It is difficult to define ex ante rules for identifying bubbles where prices differ from some measure of intrinsic value. Research in this area focuses on excessive liquidity, inflationary pressures, a rigorous analysis of "underlying fundamentals," and other factors that may cause prices to exceed intrinsic value (whatever that means). But since we expect prices to move in a random walk—and since this random walk might sometimes move rapidly upwards—the process of identifying bubbles is vexing.

CHAPTER 14
An Overview of Corporate Financing

Answers to Problem Sets

1.   a.   False

     b.   True

     c.   True

2.   a.   40,000/.50 = 80,000 shares

     b.   78,000 shares

     c.   2,000 shares are held as Treasury stock

     d.   20,000 shares

     e.   See table below

     f.   See table below

	(e)	(f)
Common stock	$ 45,000	$40,000
Additional paid-in capital	25,000	10,000
Retained earnings	30,000	30,000
Common equity	100,000	80,000
Treasury stock	5,000	30,000
Net common equity	$ 95,000	$50,000

3.   a.   80 votes

     b.   10 X 80 = 800 votes.

4.   a.   subordinated

     b.   floating rate

c.   convertible

d.   warrant

e.   common stock; preferred stock.

5.   a.   False

     b.   True

     c.   False

6.   a.   Par value is $0.05 per share, which is computed as follows:

          $443 million/8,863 million shares

     b.   The shares were sold at an average price of:

          [$443 million + $70,283 million]/8,863 million shares = $7.98

     c.   The company has repurchased:

          8,863 million − 6,746 million = 2,117 million shares

     d.   Average repurchase price:

          $57,391 million/2,117 million shares = $27.11 per share.

     e.   The value of the net common equity is:

          $443 million + $70,283 million + $44,148 million − $57,391 million

          = $57,483 million

7.   a.   The day after the founding of Inbox:

Common shares ($0.10 par value)	$ 50,000
Additional paid-in capital	1,950,000
Retained earnings	0
Treasury shares	0
Net common equity	$2,000,000

     b.   After 2 years of operation:

Common shares ($0.10 par value)	$ 50,000
Additional paid-in capital	1,950,000
Retained earnings	120,000
Treasury shares	0
Net common equity	$2,120,000

c. After 3 years of operation:

Common shares ($0.10 par value)	$ 150,000
Additional paid-in capital	6,850,000
Retained earnings	370,000
Treasury shares	0
Net common equity	$7,370,000

8. a.

Common shares ($1.00 par value)	$1,008
Additional paid-in capital	5,444
Retained earnings	16,250
Treasury shares	(14,015)
Net common equity	$8,687

b.

Common shares ($1.00 par value)	$1,008
Additional paid-in capital	5,444
Retained earnings	16,250
Treasury shares	(14,715)
Net common equity	$7,987

9. One would expect that the voting shares have a higher price because they have an added benefit/responsibility that has value.

10. a.

Gross profits	$ 760,000
Interest	100,000
EBT	$ 660,000
Tax (at 35%)	231,000
Funds available to common shareholders	$ 429,000

b.

Gross profits (EBT)	$ 760,000
Tax (at 35%)	266,000
Net income	$ 494,000
Preferred dividend	80,000
Funds available to common shareholders	$ 414,000

11.   Internet exercise; answers will vary.

12.   a.   Less valuable

      b.   More valuable

      c.   More valuable

      d.   Less valuable

13.   Answers may differ. Some key events of the financial crisis through the end of
      2008 include:

June 2007:   Bear Stearns pledges $3.2 billion to aid one of its ailing hedge funds
Sept. 2007: Northern Rock receives emergency funding from the Bank of England
Oct. 2007:   Citigroup begins a string of writedowns based on mortgage losses
Dec. 2007:   Fed establishes Term Auction Facility lines
Jan. 2008:   Ratings agencies threaten to downgrade Ambac and MBIA (major bond
             issuers)
Feb. 2008:   Economic stimulus package signed into law
Mar. 2008:   JPMorgan purchases Bear Stearns with support from the Fed
Mar. 2008:   SEC proposes ban on naked short selling
July 2008:   FDIC takes over IndyMac Bank
Sept. 2008: Lehman forced into bankruptcy
             B of A purchases Merrill Lynch
             10 banks create $70 billion liquidity fund
             AIG debt downgraded
             RMC money market fund "breaks the buck"
             Treasury bailout plan voted down in the House
Oct. 2008:   9 large banks agree to capital injection from Treasury
             Revised bailout plan passes in House
             Consumer confidence hits lowest point on record

The NY Fed has an excellent timeline of events at:
www.ny.frb.org/research/global_economy/Crisis_Timeline.pdf

14.   Answers will differ. Some purported causes of the financial crisis include:

      •   Long periods of very low interest rates leading to easy credit conditions
      •   High leverage ratios
      •   The bursting of the US housing market bubble
      •   High rates of default on subprime mortgages
      •   Massive losses on investments in mortgage backed securities

- Opaque derivative markets and amplified losses through credit default swaps
- High rates of unemployment and job losses

15. a. For majority voting, you must own or otherwise control the votes of a simple majority of the shares outstanding, i.e., one-half of the shares outstanding plus one. Here, with 200,000 shares outstanding, you must control the votes of 100,001 shares.

b. With cumulative voting, the directors are elected in order of the total number of votes each receives. With 200,000 shares outstanding and five directors to be elected, there will be a total of 1,000,000 votes cast. To ensure you can elect at least one director, you must ensure that someone else can elect at most four directors. That is, you must have enough votes so that, even if the others split their votes evenly among five other candidates, the number of votes your candidate gets would be higher by one.

Let x be the number of votes controlled by you, so that others control (1,000,000 − x) votes. To elect one director:

$$x = \frac{1,000,000 - x}{5} + 1$$

Solving, we find x = 166,666.8 votes, or 33,333.4 shares. Because there are no fractional shares, we need 33,334 shares.

CHAPTER 15
How Corporations Issue Securities

Answers to Problem Sets

1. a. Further sale of an already publicly traded stock

   b. U.S. bond issue by foreign corporation

   c. Bond issue by industrial company

   d. Bond issue by large industrial company.

2. a. B

   b. A

   c. D

   d. C

3. a. Financing of start-up companies.

   b. Underwriters gather non-binding indications of demand for a new issue.

   c. The difference between the price at which the underwriter buys the security from the company and re-sells it to investors.

   d. Description of a security offering filed with the SEC.

   e. Winning bidders for a new issue tend to overpay.

4. a. A large issue

   b. A bond issue

   c. Subsequent issue of stock

   d. A small private placement of bonds.

5. a. False

    b. False

    c. True

6. a. Net proceeds of public issue = 10,000,000 - 150,000 - 80,000 = $9,770,000; net proceeds of private placement = $9,970,000.

    b. PV of extra interest on private placement =

    $$\sum_{t=1}^{10} \frac{.005 \times 10,000,000}{1.085^t} = \$328,000$$

    i.e., extra cost of higher interest on private placement more than outweighs saving in issue costs.

    N.b. We ignore taxes.

    c. Private placement debt can be custom-tailored and the terms more easily renegotiated.

7. a. Number of new shares, 50,000

    b. Amount of new investment, $500,000

    c. Total value of company after issue, $4,500,000

    d. Total number of shares after issue, 150,000

    e. Stock price after issue, $4,500,000/150,000 = $30

    f. The opportunity to buy one share is worth $20.

8. a. Zero-stage financing represents the savings and personal loans the company's principals raise to start a firm. First-stage and second-stage financing comes from funds provided by others (often venture capitalists) to supplement the founders' investment.

    b. Carried interest is the name for the investment profits paid to a private equity or venture capitalist partnership.

c. A rights issue is a sale of additional securities to existing investors; it can be contrasted with an at large issuance (which is made to all interested investors).

d. A road show is a presentation about the firm given to potential investors in order to gauge their reactions to a stock issue and to estimate the demand for the new shares.

e. A best efforts offer is an underwriter's promise to sell as much as possible of a security issue.

f. A qualified institutional buyer is a large financial institution which, under SEC Rule 144A, is allowed to trade unregistered securities with other qualified institutional buyers.

g. Blue-sky laws are state laws governing the sale of securities within the state.

h. A greenshoe option in an underwriting agreement gives the underwriter the option to increase the number of shares the underwriter buys from the issuing company.

9. a. Management's willingness to invest in Marvin's equity was a credible signal because the management team stood to lose everything if the new venture failed, and thus they signaled their seriousness. By accepting only part of the venture capital that would be needed, management was increasing its own risk and reducing that of First Meriam. This decision would be costly and foolish if Marvin's management team lacked confidence that the project would get past the first stage.

b. Marvin's management agreed not to accept lavish salaries. The cost of management perks comes out of the shareholders' pockets. In Marvin's case, the managers *are* the shareholders.

10. If he is bidding on under-priced stocks, he will receive only a portion of the shares he applies for. If he bids on under-subscribed stocks, he will receive his full allotment of shares, which no one else is willing to buy. Hence, on average, the stocks may be under-priced but once the weighting of all stocks is considered, it may not be profitable.

11. There are several possible reasons why the issue costs for debt are lower than those of equity, among them:
   • The cost of complying with government regulations may be lower for debt.

- The risk of the security is less for debt and hence the price is less volatile. This decreases the probability that the issue will be mis-priced and therefore decreases the underwriter's risk.

12. a. Inelastic demand implies that a large price reduction is needed in order to sell additional shares. This would be the case only if investors believe that a stock has no close substitutes (i.e., they value the stock for its unique properties).

    b. Price pressure may be inconsistent with market efficiency. It implies that the stock price falls when new stock is issued and subsequently recovers.

    c. If a company's stock is undervalued, managers will be reluctant to sell new stock, even if it means foregoing a good investment opportunity. The converse is true if the stock is overvalued. Investors know this and, therefore, mark down the price when companies issue stock. (Of course, managers of a company with undervalued stock become even more reluctant to issue stock because their actions can be misinterpreted.)

    If (b) is the reason for the price fall, there should be a subsequent price recovery. If (a) is the reason, we would not expect a price recovery, but the fall should be greater for large issues. If (c) is the reason, the price fall will depend only on issue size (assuming the information is correlated with issue size).

13. a. Example: Before issue, there are 100 shares outstanding at $10 per share. The company sells 20 shares for cash at $5 per share. Company value increases by: (20 x $5) = $100. Thus, after issue, each share is worth:

$$\frac{(100 \times \$10) + \$100}{100 + 20} = \frac{\$1,100}{120} = \$9.17$$

Note that new shareholders gain: $20 \times \$4.17 = \$83$

Old shareholders lose: $100 \times \$0.83 = \$83$

    b. Example: Before issue, there are 100 shares outstanding at $10 per share. The company makes a rights issue of 20 shares at $5 per share. Each right is worth:

$$\text{Value of right} = \frac{(\text{rights on price}) - (\text{issue price})}{N + 1} = \frac{10 - 5}{6} = \$0.83$$

The new share price is $9.17. If a shareholder sells his right, he receives $0.83 cash and the value of each share declines by: $10 - $9.17 = $0.83 The shareholder's total wealth is unaffected.

14. a. €5 × (10,000,000/4) = €12.5 million

   b. Value of right $= \dfrac{(\text{rights on price}) - (\text{issue price})}{N+1} = \dfrac{6-5}{4+1} = €0.20$

   c. Stock price $= \dfrac{(10,000,000 \times 6) + 12,500,000}{10,000,000 + 2,500,000} = €5.80$

   A stockholder who previously owned four shares had stocks with a value of: (4 × €6) = €24. This stockholder has now paid €5 for a fifth share so that the total value is: (€24 + €5) = €29. This stockholder now owns five shares with a value of: (5 × €5.80) = €29, so that she is no better or worse off than she was before.

   d. The share price would have to fall to the issue price per share, or €5 per share. Firm value would then be: 10 million × €5 = €50 million

15. €12,500,000/€4 = 3,125,000 shares

   10,000,000/3,125,000 = 3.20 rights per share

   Value of right $= \dfrac{(\text{rights on price}) - (\text{issue price})}{N+1} = \dfrac{6-4}{3.2+1} = €0.48$

   Stock price $= \dfrac{(10,000,000 \times 6) + 12,500,000}{10,000,000 + 3,125,000} = €5.52$

   A stockholder who previously owned 3.2 shares had stocks with a value of: (3.2 × €6) = €19.20. This stockholder has now paid €4 for an additional share, so that the total value is: (€19.20 + €4) = €23.20. This stockholder now owns 4.2 shares with a value of: (4.2 × €5.52) = €23.18 (difference due to rounding).

16. Before the general cash offer, the value of the firm's equity is:
   10,000,000 × €6 = €60,000,000
   New financing raised (from Practice Question 16) is €12,500,000
   Total equity after general cash offer = €60,000,000 + €12,500,000 = €72,500,000
   Total new shares = €12,500,000/€4 = 3,125,000
   Total shares after general cash offer = 10,000,000 + 3,125,000 = 13,125,000
   Price per share after general cash offer = €72,500,000/13,125,000 = €5.5238
   Existing shareholders have lost = €6.00 – €5.5238 = €0.4762 per share
   Total loss for existing shareholders = €0.4762 × 10,000,000 = €4,762,000
   New shareholders have gained = €5.5238 – €4.00 = €1.5238 per share

Total gain for new shareholders = €1.5238 × 3,125,000 = €4,761,875

Except for rounding error, we see that the gain for the new shareholders comes at the expense of the existing shareholders.

17. a. 135,000 shares

    b. 500,000 shares in the primary offering; 400,000 shares in the secondary offering

    c. $25 or 31%; this seems higher than the average underpricing of IPOs

    d.

Underwriting cost	$5.04 million
Administrative cost	$0.82 million
Underpricing	$22.5 million
TOTAL	$28.36 million

18. Some possible reasons for cost differences:
    a. Large issues have lower proportionate costs.
    b. Debt issues have lower costs than equity issues.
    c. Initial public offerings involve more risk for underwriters than issues of seasoned stock. Underwriters demand higher spreads in compensation.

19. a. Venture capital companies prefer to advance money in stages because this approach provides an incentive for management to reach the next stage, and it allows First Meriam to check at each stage whether the project continues to have a positive NPV. Marvin is happy because it signals their confidence. With hindsight, First Meriam loses because it has to pay more for the shares at each stage.

    b. The problem with this arrangement would be that, while Marvin would have an incentive to ensure that the option was exercised, it would not have the incentive to maximize the price at which it sells the new shares.

    c. The right of first refusal could make sense if First Meriam was making a large up-front investment that it needed to be able to recapture in its subsequent investments. In practice, Marvin is likely to get the best deal from First Meriam.

20. In a uniform-price auction, all successful bidders pay the same price. In a discriminatory auction, each successful bidder pays a price equal to his own bid. A uniform-price auction provides for the pooling of information from bidders and reduces the winner's curse.

21. Pisa Construction's return on investment is 8%, whereas investors require a 10% rate of return. Pisa proposes a scenario in which 2,000 shares of common stock are issued at $40 per share, and the proceeds ($80,000) are then invested at 8%. Assuming that the 8% return is received in the form of a perpetuity, then the NPV for this scenario is computed as follows:

$$-\$80,000 + (0.08 \times \$80,000)/0.10 = -\$16,000$$

Share price would decline as a result of this project, not because the company sells shares for less than book value, but rather due to the fact that the NPV is negative.

Note that, if investors know price will decline as a consequence of Pisa's undertaking a negative NPV investment, Pisa will not be able to sell shares at $40 per share. Rather, after the announcement of the project, the share price will decline to:

$$(\$400,000 - \$16,000)/10,000 = \$38.40$$

Therefore, Pisa will have to issue: $80,000/$38.40 = 2,083 new shares
One can show that, if the proceeds of the stock issue are invested at 10%, then share price remains unchanged.

CHAPTER 16
Payout Policy

Answers to Problem Sets

1. a. A1, B5; A2, B4; A3, B3; A4, B1; A5, B2

    b. On August 12, the ex-dividend date

    c. $(.35 \times 4)/52 = .027$, or 2.7%

    d. $(.35 \times 4)/4.56 = .31$, or 3.1%

    e. The price would fall to $52/1.10 = \$41.27$

2. a. False. The dividend depends on past dividends and current and forecasted earnings.

    b. True. Dividend changes convey information to investors.

    c. False. Dividends are "smoothed." Managers rarely increase regular dividends temporarily. They may pay a special dividend, however.

    d. False. Dividends are rarely cut when repurchases are being made.

3. a. Reinvest $1,000 \times \$.50 = \$500$ in the stock. If the ex-dividend price is $150 – $2.50, this should involve the purchase of 500/147.50, or about 3.shares.

    b. Sell shares worth $1,000 \times \$3 = \$3,000$. If the ex-dividend price is $200 – $5, this should involve the sale of 3,000/195, or about 15 shares.

4. Reduce repurchases by $10 million or issue new shares for $10 million.

5. a. Company value is unchanged at $5,000 \times 140 = \$700,000$. Share price stays at $140.

    b. The discount rate $r = (DIV_1/P_0) + g = (20/140) + .05 = .193$. The price at which shares are repurchased in year 1 is $140 \times (1 + r) = 140 \times 1.193 = \$167$. Therefore the firm repurchases $50,000/167 = 299$ shares. Total dividend payments in year 1 fall to $5,000 \times 10 = \$50,000$, which is equivalent to 50,000/(5000 – 299) = $10.64 a share. Similarly, in year 2 the firm repurchases 281 shares at $186.52 and the dividend per share increases by 11.7% to $11.88. In each subsequent year, total dividends increase by 5%, the number of shares declines by 6% and, therefore, dividends per share increase by 11.7%. The constant growth model gives PV share = 10.64/ (.193 – .117) = $140.

6. a. $127.25.

    b. Nothing; the stock price will stay at $130. 846,154 shares will be repurchased.

    c. The with-dividend price stays at $130. Ex dividend it drops to $124.50; 883,534 shares will be issued.

7. Current tax law (assuming gains tax cannot be deferred): All investors should be indifferent except the corporation which prefers Hi. Zero tax on capital gains: As under the current tax law except that individuals now prefer Lo. (Note: corporations and security dealers treat capital gains as income).

8. Newspaper exercise; answers will vary depending on the stock chosen.

9. a. Distributes a relatively low proportion of current earnings to offset fluctuations in operational cash flow; lower P/E ratio.

    b. Distributes a relatively high proportion of current earnings since the decline is unexpected; higher P/E ratio.

    c. Distributes a relatively low proportion of current earnings in order to offset anticipated declines in earnings; lower P/E ratio.

    d. Distributes a relatively low proportion of current earnings in order to fund expected growth; higher P/E ratio.

10. Note: The first printing of the book contains an error, please refer to the last sentence of the problem. It should read, "After that, the total amount paid out each year will be as previously forecasted, that is, $1.05 million in year 2 and increasing by 5% in each subsequent year." The solutions below reflect the corrected value.

    a. At = 0 each share is worth $20. This value is based on the expected stream of dividends: $1 at t = 1, and increasing by 5% in each subsequent year. Thus, we can find the appropriate discount rate for this company as follows:

$$P_0 = \frac{DIV_1}{r - g}$$

$$\$20 = \frac{1}{r - 0.05} \quad \Rightarrow \quad r = 0.10 = 10.0\%$$

Beginning at t = 2, each share in the company will enjoy a perpetual stream of growing dividends: $1.05 at t = 2, and increasing by 5% in each subsequent year. Thus, the total value of the shares at t = 1 (after the t = 1 dividend is paid and after N new shares have been issued) is given by:

$$V_1 = \frac{\$1.05\,\text{million}}{0.10 - 0.05} = \$21\,\text{million}$$

If P_1 is the price per share at t = 1, then:

$$V_1 = P_1 \times (1{,}000{,}000 + N) = \$21{,}000{,}000$$

and:

$$P_1 \times N = \$1{,}000{,}000$$

From the first equation:

$$(1{,}000{,}000 \times P_1) + (N \times P_1) = \$21{,}000{,}000$$

Substituting from the second equation:

$$(1{,}000{,}000 \times P_1) + \$1{,}000{,}000 = \$21{,}000{,}000$$

so that P_1 = $20.00

b.   With P_1 equal to $20 the firm will need to sell 50,000 new shares to raise $1,000,000.

c.   The expected dividends paid at t = 2 are $1,050,000, increasing by 5% in each subsequent year. With 1,050,000 shares outstanding, dividends per share are: $1 at t = 2, increasing by 5% in each subsequent year. Thus, total dividends paid to old shareholders are: $1,000,000 at t = 2, increasing by 5% in each subsequent year.

d.   For the current shareholders:

$$PV(t = 0) = \frac{\$2{,}000{,}000}{1.10} + \frac{\$1{,}000{,}000}{(0.10 - 0.05) \times (1.10)} = \$20{,}000{,}000$$

11. From Question 10, the fair issue price is $20 per share. If these shares are instead issued at $10 per share, then the new shareholders are getting a bargain, i.e., the new shareholders win and the old shareholders lose.

   As pointed out in the text, any increase in cash dividend must be offset by a stock issue if the firm's investment and borrowing policies are to be held constant. If this stock issue cannot be made at a fair price, then shareholders are clearly not indifferent to dividend policy.

12. The risk stems from the decision to not invest, and it is not a result of the form of financing. If an investor consumes the dividend instead of re-investing the dividend in the company's stock, she is also 'selling' a part of her stake in the company. In this scenario, she will suffer an equal opportunity loss if the stock price subsequently rises sharply.

13. If the company does not pay a dividend:

Cash	0	0	Debt
Existing fixed assets	4,500	5,500 + NPV	Equity
New project	1,000 + NPV		
	$5,500 + NPV	$5,500 + NPV	

   If the company pays a $1,000 dividend:

Cash	0	0	Debt
Existing fixed assets	4,500	1,000	Value of new stock
New project	1,000 + NPV	4,500 + NPV	Value of original stock
	$5,500 + NPV	$5,500 + NPV	

   Because the new stockholders receive stock worth $1,000, the value of the original stock declines by $1,000, which exactly offsets the dividends.

14. One problem with this analysis is that it assumes the company's net profit remains constant even though the asset base of the company shrinks by 20%. That is, in order to raise the cash necessary to repurchase the shares, the company must sell assets. If the assets sold are representative of the company as a whole, we would expect net profit to decrease by 20% so that earnings per share and the P/E ratio remain the same. After the repurchase, the company will look like this next year:

Net profit:	$8	million
Number of shares:	0.8	million
Earnings per share:	$10	
Price-earnings ratio:	20	
Share price:	$200	

15. a. If we ignore taxes and there is no information conveyed by the repurchase when the repurchase program is announced, then share price will remain at $80.

b. The regular dividend has been $4 per share, and so the company has $400,000 cash on hand. Since the share price is $80, the company will repurchase 5,000 shares.

c. Total asset value (before each dividend payment or stock repurchase) remains at $8,000,000. These assets earn $400,000 per year, under either policy.

Old Policy: The annual dividend is $4, which never changes, so the stock price (immediately prior to the dividend payment) will be $80 in all years.

New Policy: Every year, $400,000 is available for share repurchase. As noted above, 5,000 shares will be repurchased at t = 0. At t = 1, immediately prior to the repurchase, there will be 95,000 shares outstanding. These shares will be worth $8,000,000, or $84.21 per share. With $400,000 available to repurchase shares, the total number of shares repurchased will be 4,750. Using this reasoning, we can generate the following table:

Time	Shares Outstanding	Share Price	Shares Repurchased
t = 0	100,000	$80.00	5,000
t = 1	95,000	$84.21	4,750
t = 2	90,250	$88.64	4,513
t = 3	85,737	$93.31	4,287

Note that the stock price is increasing by 5.26% each year. This is consistent with the rate of return to the shareholders under the old policy, whereby every year assets worth $7,600,000 (the asset value immediately after the dividend) earn $400,000, or a return of 5.26%.

16. If markets are efficient, then a share repurchase is a zero-NPV investment. Suppose that the trade-off is between an investment in real assets or a share repurchase. Obviously, the shareholders would prefer a share repurchase to a negative-NPV project. The quoted statement seems to imply that firms have only negative-NPV projects available.

Another possible interpretation is that managers have inside information indicating that the firm's stock price is too low. In this case, share repurchase is detrimental to those stockholders who sell and beneficial to those who do not. There might also be tax benefits to conducting share repurchases versus issuing dividends. Putting these issues aside it is difficult to see how this could be beneficial to the firm.

17. a. This statement implicitly equates the cost of equity capital with the stock's dividend yield. If this were true, companies that pay no dividend would have a zero cost of equity capital, which is clearly not correct.

b. One way to think of retained earnings is that, from an economic standpoint, the company earns money on behalf of the shareholders, who then immediately re-invest the earnings in the company. Thus, retained earnings do not represent free capital. Retained earnings carry the full cost of equity capital (although issue costs associated with raising new equity capital are avoided).

c. If the tax on capital gains is less than that on dividends, the conclusion of this statement is correct; i.e., a stock repurchase is always preferred over dividends. This conclusion, however, is strictly because of taxes. Earnings per share is irrelevant.

18. a. Because this is a regular dividend, the announcement is not news to the stock market. Hence, the stock price will adjust only when the stock begins to trade without the dividend and, thus, the stock price will fall on the ex-dividend date.

b. With no taxes, the stock price will fall by the amount of the dividend, here $1.

c. With taxes on dividends but no taxes on capital gains, investors will require the same after-tax return from two comparable companies, one of which pays a dividend, the other, a capital gain of the same magnitude. The stock price will thus fall by the amount of the after-tax dividend, here: $1 \times (1 - 0.30) = \$0.70$.

d. If dealers are taxed equally on capital gains and dividends, then they should not demand any extra return for holding stocks that pay dividends. Thus, if shareholders are able to freely trade securities around the time of the dividend payment, there should be no tax effects associated with dividends.

19. a. If you own 100 shares at $100 per share, then your wealth is $10,000. After the dividend payment, each share will be worth $99 and your total wealth will be the same: 100 shares at $99 per share plus $100 in dividends, or $10,000.

b. You yawn. With no taxes, it does not matter how the company transfers wealth to the shareholders; that is, you are indifferent between a dividend and a share repurchase program. In either case, your total wealth will remain at $10,000.

20. *After-tax Return on Share A*: At t = 1, a shareholder in company A will receive a dividend of $10, which is subject to taxes of 30%. Therefore, the after-tax gain is $7. Since the initial investment is $100, the after-tax rate of return is 7%.

After-tax Return on Share B: If an investor sells share B after 2 years, the price will be: $(100 \times 1.10^2) = \$121$. The capital gain of $21 is taxed at the 30% rate, and so the after-tax gain is $14.70. On an initial investment of $100, over a 2-year time period, this is an after-tax annual rate of return of 7.10%.

If an investor sells share B after 10 years, the price will be: $(100 \times 1.10^{10}) = \$259.37$. The capital gain of $159.37 is taxed at the 30% rate, and so the after-tax gain is $111.56. On an initial investment of $100, over a 10-year time period, this is an after-tax annual rate of return of 7.78%.

21. a. (i) The tax-free investor should buy on the with-dividend date because the dividend is worth $1 and the price decrease is only $0.90.

        (ii) The dividend is worth only $0.60 to the taxable investor who is subject to a 40% marginal tax rate. Therefore, this investor should buy on the ex-dividend date.

      [Actually, the taxable investor's problem is a little more complicated. By buying at the ex-dividend price, this investor increases the capital gain that is eventually reported upon the sale of the asset. At most, however, this will cost: $(0.16 \times 0.90) = \$0.14$
This is not enough to offset the tax on the dividend.]

    b. The marginal investor, by definition, must be indifferent between buying with-dividend or ex-dividend. If we let T represent the marginal tax rate on dividends, then the marginal tax rate on capital gains is (0.4T). In order for the net extra return from buying with-dividend (instead of ex-dividend) to be zero:

–Extra investment + After-tax dividend + Reduction in capital gains tax = 0

Therefore, per dollar of dividend:

$$-0.85 + [(1 - T) \times 1.00] + [0.4T \times 0.85] = 0$$
$$T = 0.227 = 22.7\%$$

    c. We would expect the high-payout stocks to show the largest decline per dollar of dividends paid because these stocks should be held by investors in low, or perhaps even zero, marginal tax brackets.

    d. Some investors (e.g., pension funds and security dealers) are indifferent between $1 of dividends and $1 of capital gains. These investors should be prepared to buy any amount of stock with-dividend as long as the fall-off in price is fractionally less than the dividend. Elton and Gruber's result suggests that there must be some impediment to such tax arbitrage (e.g., transactions costs or IRS restrictions). But, in that case, it is difficult to interpret their result as indicative of marginal tax rates.

e.   The tax advantage to capital gains has been reduced. If investors are now indifferent between dividends and capital gains, we would expect that the payment of a $1 dividend would result in a $1 decrease in price.

22.   Even if the middle-of-the-road party is correct about the supply of dividends, we still do not know why investors wanted the dividends they got. So, it is difficult to be sure about the effect of the tax change. If there is some non-tax advantage to dividends that offsets the apparent tax disadvantage, then we would expect investors to demand more dividends after the government reduces the tax rate on dividends. If the apparent tax disadvantage were irrelevant because there were too many loopholes in the tax system, then the reduction in the tax rate on dividends would not affect the demand for dividends. In any case, the middle-of-the-roaders would argue that once companies adjusted the supply of dividends to the new equilibrium, dividend policy would again become irrelevant.

23.   Reducing the amount of earnings retained each year will, of course, reduce the growth rate of dividends. Also, the firm will have to issue new shares each year in order to finance company growth. Under the original dividend policy, we expect next year's stock price to be: ($50 × 1.08) = $54. If N is the number of shares previously outstanding, the value of the company at $t = 1$ is (54N).

Under the new policy, n new shares will be issued at $t = 1$ to make up for the reduction in retained earnings resulting from the new policy. This decrease is: ($4 − $2) = $2 per original share, or an aggregate reduction of 2N. If P_1 is the price of the common stock at $t = 1$ under the new policy, then:

$$2N = nP_1$$

Also, because the total value of the company is unchanged:

$$54N = (N + n)P_1$$

Solving, we find that $P_1 = \$52$.

If g is the expected growth rate under the new policy and P_0 the price at $t = 0$, we have:

$$52 = (1 + g)P_0$$

and:

$$P_0 = \frac{4}{0.12 - g}$$

Substituting the second equation above for P_0 in the first equation and then solving, we find that $g = 4\%$ and $P_0 = \$50$, so that the current stock price is unchanged.

24. Assume that all taxpayers pay a 20% tax on dividend income and 10% tax on capital gains. Firm A pays no dividends but investors expect the price of Firm A stock to increase from $40 to $50 per share. Firm B pays a dividend of $5 per share and investors expect the price of Firm B stock to be $45 next year. Results for Firm A are:

Before-tax rate of return	$10/$40 = 25.00%
Tax on dividend at 20%	$0.00
Tax on capital gains at 10%	$0.10 \times \$10.00 = \$1.00$
Total after-tax income (dividends plus capital gains less taxes)	$0 + $10 – $1 = $9.00
After-tax rate of return	$9/$40 = 22.50%

The price of Firm B stock today must adjust so as to provide an after-tax return equal to that of Firm A. Let × equal the current price of Firm B stock. Then, for Firm B:

Next year's price	$45.00
Dividend	$5.00
Today's stock price	X
Capital gain	$45 – X
Before-tax rate of return	[$5 + ($45 – X)]/X
Tax on dividend at 20%	$0.20 \times \$5.00 = \$1.00$
Tax on capital gains at 10%	$0.10 \times (\$45 - X)$
Total after-tax income (dividends plus capital gains less taxes)	[$5 + ($45 – X)] – [$1 + 0.10 × ($45 – X)]

The price of Firm B stock adjusts so that the after-tax rate of return for Firm B is equal to 22.5%, the after-tax rate of return for Firm A. To find today's price for Firm A stock, solve the following for X:

$$\frac{[\$5 + (\$45 - X)] - \{\$1 + [0.10 \times (\$45 - X)]\}}{X} = 0.225 \Rightarrow X = \$39.56$$

25. It is true that researchers have been consistent in finding a positive association between price-earnings multiples and payout ratios. But simple tests like this one do not isolate the effects of dividend policy, so the evidence is not convincing.

Suppose that King Coal Company, which customarily distributes half its earnings, suffers a strike that cuts earnings in half. The setback is regarded as temporary, however, so management maintains the normal dividend. The payout ratio for that year turns out to be 100 percent, not 50 percent.

The temporary earnings drop also affects King Coal's price-earnings ratio. The stock price may drop because of this year's disappointing earnings, but it does not drop to one-half its pre-strike value. Investors recognize the strike as temporary, and the ratio of price to this year's earnings increases. Thus, King Coal's labor troubles create both a high payout ratio and a high price-earnings ratio. In other words, they create a spurious association between dividend policy and market value. The same thing happens whenever a firm encounters temporary good fortune, or whenever reported earnings underestimate or overestimate the true long-run earnings on which both dividends and stock prices are based.

A second source of error is omission of other factors affecting both the firm's dividend policy and its market valuation. For example, we know that firms seek to maintain stable dividend rates. Companies whose prospects are uncertain therefore tend to be conservative in their dividend policies. Investors are also likely to be concerned about such uncertainty, so that the stocks of such companies are likely to sell at low multiples. Again, the result is an association between the price of the stock and the payout ratio, but it stems from the common association with risk and not from a market preference for dividends.

Another reason that earnings multiples may be different for high-payout and low-payout stocks is that the two groups may have different growth prospects. Suppose, as has sometimes been suggested, that management is careless in the use of retained earnings but exercises appropriately stringent criteria when spending external funds. Under such circumstances, investors would be correct to value stocks of high-payout firms more highly. But the reason would be that the companies have different investment policies. It would not reflect a preference for high dividends as such, and no company could achieve a lasting improvement in its market value simply by increasing its payout ratio.

26.   a.   The marginal investors are the institutions.

   b.   Price of low-payout stock: $P_0 = \dfrac{\$20}{0.12} = \$166.67$

   Price of medium-payout stock: $P_0 = \dfrac{\$10}{0.12} = \$83.33$

   Price of high-payout stock: $P_0 = \dfrac{\$30}{0.12} = \$250.00$

c. For institutions, after-tax return is 12% for each type of stock.

For individuals, after-tax returns are:

For low-payout stock: $$\frac{(0.50\times\$5)+(0.85\times\$15)}{\$166.67}=9.15\%$$

For medium-payout stock: $$\frac{(0.50\times\$5)+(0.85\times\$5)}{\$83.33}=8.10\%$$

For high-payout stock: $$\frac{(0.50\times\$30)+(0.85\times\$0)}{\$250.00}=6.00\%$$

For corporations, after-tax returns are:

For low-payout stock: $$\frac{(0.95\times\$5)+(0.65\times\$15)}{\$166.67}=8.70\%$$

For medium-payout stock: $$\frac{(0.95\times\$5)+(0.65\times\$5)}{\$83.33}=9.60\%$$

For high-payout stock: $$\frac{(0.95\times\$30)+(0.65\times\$0)}{\$250.00}=11.40\%$$

d.

	Low Payout	Medium Payout	High Payout
Individuals	$80 billion		
Corporations			$10 billion
Institutions	$20 billion	$50 billion	$110 billion

16-11

CHAPTER 17
Does Debt Policy Matter?

Answers to Problem Sets

1.

Note the market value of Copperhead is far in excess of its book value:

	Market Value
Common stock (8 million shares at $2)	$16,000,000
Short-term loans	$ 2,000,000

Ms. Kraft owns .625% of the firm, which proposes to increase common stock to $17 million and cut short-term debt. Ms. Kraft can offset this by (a) borrowing .00625 × 1,000,000 = $6,250, and (b) buying that much more Copperhead stock.

2. a. $.5r_E + .5 \times 5 \ .5r_E + .5 \times 5\%$ = 12.5%; r_E = 20%

    b. 12.5%

    c. E/P = 20%; P/E = 5

    d. $50

    e. $.5 \times \beta_E + .5 \times 0 = 1.0$; β_E = 2.0.

3. Expected return on assets is $r_A = .08 \times 30/80 + .16 \times 50/80 = .13$. The new return on equity will be $r_E = .13 + (20/60)(.13 - .08) = .147$.

4. a.

Operating income ($)	500	1,000	1,500	2,000
Interest ($)	250	250	250	250
Equity earnings ($)	250	750	1,250	1,750
Earnings per share	.33	1.00	1.67	2.33
Return on shares (%)	3.3	10	16.7	23.3

    b. $\beta_A = \left(\dfrac{D}{D+E} \times \beta_D \right) + \left(\dfrac{E}{D+E} \times \beta_E \right)$

$$.8 = (.25 \times 0) + (.75 \times \beta_E)$$
$$\beta_E = 1.07$$

5.   a.   True

         b.   True (as long as the return earned by the company is greater than the interest payment, earnings per share increase, but the PyE falls to reflect the higher risk).

         c.   False (the cost of equity increases with the ratio D/E).

         d.   False (the formula $r_E = r_A + (D/E)(r_A - r_D)$ does not require r_D to be constant).

         e.   False (debt amplifies variations in equity income).

         f.   False (value increases only if clientele is not satisfied).

6.   a. $r_A = .15$, $r_E = .175$

         b. $\beta_A = .6$ (unchanged), $\beta_D = .3$, $\beta_E = .9$.

7.   See Figure 17.3.

8.   Currently $r_A = r_E = .14$, or 14%. From proposition 2 the leverage causes r_E to increase to $r_E = r_A + (r_A - r_D)(D/E) = .14 + (.14 - .095) \times (45/55) = .1768$, or 17.68% After-tax WACC = $.095 \times (1 - .40) \times .45 + .1768 \times .55 = .1229$, or 12.29%.

9.   a.   The two firms have equal value; let V represent the total value of the firm. Rosencrantz could buy one percent of Company B's equity and borrow an amount equal to:

$$0.01 \times (D_A - D_B) = 0.002V$$

              This investment requires a net cash outlay of (0.007V) and provides a net cash return of:

$$(0.01 \times Profits) - (0.003 \times r_f \times V)$$

              where r_f is the risk-free rate of interest on debt. Thus, the two investments are identical.

b. Guildenstern could buy two percent of Company A's equity and lend an amount equal to:

$$0.02 \times (D_A - D_B) = 0.004V$$

This investment requires a net cash outlay of (0.018V) and provides a net cash return of:

$$(0.02 \times \text{Profits}) - (0.002 \times r_f \times V)$$

Thus the two investments are identical.

c. The expected dollar return to Rosencrantz' original investment in A is:

$$(0.01 \times C) - (0.003 \times r_f \times V_A)$$

where C is the expected profit (cash flow) generated by the firm's assets. Since the firms are the same except for capital structure, C must also be the expected cash flow for Firm B. The dollar return to Rosencrantz' alternative strategy is:

$$(0.01 \times C) - (0.003 \times r_f \times V_B)$$

Also, the cost of the original strategy is (0.007V_A) while the cost of the alternative strategy is (0.007V_B).

If V_A is less than V_B, then the original strategy of investing in Company A would provide a larger dollar return at the same time that it would cost less than the alternative. Thus, no rational investor would invest in Company B if the value of Company A were less than that of Company B.

10. When a firm issues debt, it shifts its cash flow into two streams. MM's Proposition I states that this does not affect firm value if the investor can reconstitute a firm's cash flow stream by creating personal leverage or by undoing the effect of the firm's leverage by investing in both debt and equity.

It is similar with Carruther's cows. If the cream and skim milk go into the same pail, the cows have no special value. (If an investor holds both the debt and equity, the firm does not add value by splitting the cash flows into the two streams.) In the same vein, the cows have no special value if a dairy can costlessly split up whole milk into cream and skim milk. (Firm borrowing does not add value if investors can borrow on their own account.) Carruther's cows will have extra value if consumers want cream and skim milk and if the dairy cannot split up whole milk, or if it is costly to do so.

11. a. The market price of the stock is not affected by the announcement.

b. Since the market price of the shares is $10, the company can buy back:

$$\$160 \text{ million}/\$10 = 16 \text{ million shares}$$

c. After the change in capital structure, the market value of the firm is unchanged:

$$\text{Equity + Debt} = (9 \text{ million} \times \$10) + \$160 \text{ million} = \$250 \text{ million}$$

d. After the change in structure, the debt ratio is:

$$\text{Debt/(Debt + Equity)} = \$160 \text{ million/\$250 million} = 0.64$$

e. No one gains or loses. (See the answer to the next question.)

12. a. The market value of the firm's equity increases by $30 million, the amount of the decrease in the market value of the firm's existing debt. Therefore, the price of the stock increases to:

$$(\$150 \text{ million} + \$30 \text{ million})/15 \text{ million shares} = \$12$$

b. Since the market price of the shares is $12, the company can buy back:

$$\$60 \text{ million/\$12} = 5 \text{ million shares}$$

c. After the change in capital structure, the market value of the firm is unchanged:

$$\text{Equity + Debt} = (10 \text{ million} \times \$12) + \$130 \text{ million} = \$250 \text{ million}$$

d. After the change in structure, the debt ratio is:

$$\text{Debt/(Debt + Equity)} = \$130 \text{ million/\$250 million} = 0.52$$

e. The investors in the existing debt lose $30 million while the shareholders gain this $30 million. The value of each share increases by:

$$\$30 \text{ million/15 million shares} = \$2$$

13. The company cost of capital is:

$$r_A = (0.8 \times 0.12) + (0.2 \times 0.06) = 0.108 = 10.8\%$$

Under Proposition I, this is unaffected by capital structure changes. With the bonds remaining at the 6% default-risk free rate, we have:

Debt-Equity Ratio	r_E	r_A
0.00	0.108	0.108
0.10	0.113	0.108
0.50	0.132	0.108
1.00	0.156	0.108
2.00	0.204	0.108
3.00	0.252	0.108

See figure on next page.

14.   This is not a valid objection. MM's Proposition II explicitly allows for the rates of return for both debt and equity to increase as the proportion of debt in the capital structure increases. The rate for debt increases because the debt-holders are taking on more of the risk of the firm; the rate for common stock increases because of increasing financial leverage. See Figure 17.2 and the accompanying discussion.

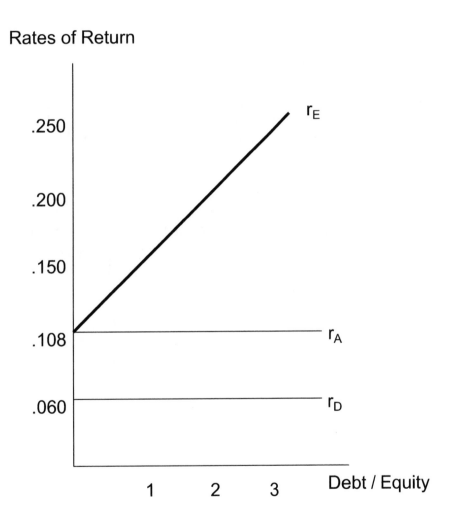

15.   a.   Under Proposition I, the firm's cost of capital (r_A) is not affected by the choice of capital structure. The reason the quoted statement seems to be true is that it does not account for the changing proportions of the firm financed by debt and equity. As the debt-equity ratio increases, it is true that both the cost of equity and the cost of debt increase, but a smaller proportion of the firm is financed by equity. The overall effect is to leave the firm's cost of capital unchanged.

b.   Moderate borrowing does not significantly affect the probability of financial distress, but it does increase the variability (and market risk) borne by stockholders. This additional risk must be offset by a higher average return to stockholders.

16. a.   If the opportunity were the firm's only asset, this would be a good deal. Stockholders would put up no money and, therefore, would have nothing to lose. However, rational lenders will not advance 100% of the asset's value for an 8% promised return unless other assets are put up as collateral.

Sometimes firms find it convenient to borrow all the cash required for a particular investment. Such investments do not support all of the additional debt; lenders are protected by the firm's other assets too.

In any case, if firm value is independent of leverage, then any asset's contribution to firm value must be independent of how it is financed. Note also that the statement ignores the effect on the stockholders of an increase in financial leverage.

b.   This is not an important reason for conservative debt levels. So long as MM's Proposition I holds, the company's overall cost of capital is unchanged despite increasing interest rates paid as the firm borrows more. (However, the increasing interest rates may signal an increasing probability of financial distress—and that can be important.)

17. Examples of such securities are given in the text and include unbundled stock units, preferred equity redemption cumulative stock and floating-rate notes. Note that, in order to succeed, such securities must both meet regulatory requirements and appeal to an unsatisfied clientele.

18. a.   As leverage is increased, the cost of equity capital rises. This is the same as saying that, as leverage is increased, the ratio of the income after interest (which is the cash flow stockholders are entitled to) to the value of equity increases. Thus, as leverage increases, the ratio of the market value of the equity to income after interest decreases.

b.   (i) Assume MM are correct. The market value of the firm is determined by the income of the firm, not how it is divided among the firm's security holders. Also, the firm's income before interest is independent of the firm's financing. Thus, both the value of the firm and the value of the firm's income before interest remain constant as leverage is increased. Hence, the ratio is a constant.

(ii) Assume the traditionalists are correct. The firm's income before interest is independent of leverage. As leverage increases, the firm's cost of capital first decreases and then increases; as a result, the market value of the firm first increases and then decreases. Thus, the ratio of the market value of the firm to firm income before interest first increases and then decreases, as leverage increases.

19. We begin with r_E and the capital asset pricing model:

$$r_E = r_f + \beta_E \, (r_m - r_f) = 0.10 + 1.5 \, (0.18 - 0.10) = 0.22 = 22.0\%$$

Similarly for debt:

$$r_D = r_f + \beta_D \, (r_m - r_f)$$

$$0.12 = 0.10 + \beta_D \, (0.18 - 0.10)$$

$$\beta_D = 0.25$$

Also, we know that:

$$r_A = \left(\frac{D}{D+E} \times r_D \right) + \left(\frac{E}{D+E} \times r_E \right) = (0.5 \times 0.12) + (0.5 \times 0.22) = 0.17 = 17.0\%$$

To solve for β_A, use the following:

$$\beta_A = \left(\frac{D}{D+E} \times \beta_D \right) + \left(\frac{E}{D+E} \times \beta_E \right) = (0.5 \times 0.25) + (0.5 \times 1.5) = 0.875$$

20. We know from Proposition I that the value of the firm will not change. Also, because the expected operating income is unaffected by changes in leverage, the firm's overall cost of capital will not change. In other words, r_A remains equal to 17% and β_A remains equal to 0.875. However, risk and, hence, the expected return for equity and for debt, will change. We know that r_D is 11%, so that, for debt:

$$r_D = r_f + \beta_D \, (r_m - r_f)$$

$$0.11 = 0.10 + \beta_D \, (0.18 - 0.10)$$

$$\beta_D = 0.125$$

For equity:

$$r_A = \left(\frac{D}{D+E} \times r_D \right) + \left(\frac{E}{D+E} \times r_E \right)$$

$$0.17 = (0.3 \times 0.11) + (0.7 \times r_E)$$

$$r_E = 0.196 = 19.6\%$$

Also:

$$r_E = r_f + \beta_E (r_m - r_f)$$
$$0.196 = 0.10 + \beta_E (0.18 - 0.10)$$
$$\beta_E = 1.20$$

21. [Note: In the following solution, we have assumed that $200 million of long-term bonds have been issued.]

a. E = $55 × 10 million = $550 million

V = D + E = $200 million + $550 million = $750 million

$$\frac{D}{V} = \frac{\$200 \text{million}}{\$750 \text{million}} = 0.267$$

$$\frac{E}{V} = \frac{\$550 \text{million}}{\$750 \text{million}} = 0.733$$

After-tax WACC = $r_D (1 - T_c)\dfrac{D}{V} + r_E \dfrac{E}{V}$

$$= 0.07 \times (1 - 0.35) \times 0.267 + (0.12 \times 0.733) = 0.1001 = 10.01\%$$

b. The after-tax WACC would increase to the extent of the loss of the tax deductibility of the interest on debt. Therefore, the after-tax WACC would equal the opportunity cost of capital, computed from the WACC formula without the tax-deductibility of interest:

$$\text{WACC} = r_D \frac{D}{V} + r_E \frac{E}{V} = (0.07 \times 0.267) + (0.12 \times 0.733) = 0.1067 = 10.67\%$$

22. We make use of the basic relationship:

$$r_A = \left(r_D (1 - T_c)\frac{D}{V} \right) + \left(r_E \times \frac{E}{V} \right)$$

Since overall beta (β_A) is not affected by capital structure or taxes, then:

$$r_A = r_f + \beta_A (r_m - r_f) = 0.06 + (1.5 \times 0.08) = 0.18$$

The following table shows the value of r_E for various values of D/E (and the corresponding values of D/V), derived from the above formula. The graph is on the next page.

D/E	D/V	r_A	r_D	r_E
0.00	0.00000	0.18	0.0600	0.1800
0.05	0.04762	0.18	0.0600	0.1871
0.10	0.09091	0.18	0.0600	0.1941
0.15	0.13043	0.18	0.0600	0.2012
0.20	0.16667	0.18	0.0600	0.2082
0.25	0.20000	0.18	0.0600	0.2153
0.30	0.23077	0.18	0.0610	0.2221
0.35	0.25926	0.18	0.0620	0.2289
0.40	0.28571	0.18	0.0630	0.2356
0.45	0.31034	0.18	0.0640	0.2423
0.50	0.33333	0.18	0.0650	0.2489
0.55	0.35484	0.18	0.0660	0.2554
0.60	0.37500	0.18	0.0670	0.2619
0.65	0.39394	0.18	0.0680	0.2683
0.70	0.41176	0.18	0.0690	0.2746
0.75	0.42857	0.18	0.0690	0.2814
0.80	0.44444	0.18	0.0700	0.2876
0.85	0.45946	0.18	0.0725	0.2929
0.90	0.47368	0.18	0.0750	0.2981
0.95	0.48718	0.18	0.0775	0.3031
1.00	0.50000	0.18	0.0800	0.3080

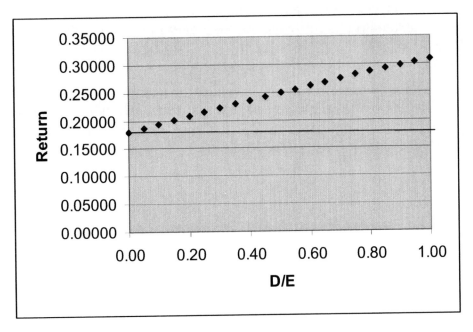

23. Assume the election is near so that we can safely ignore the time value of money.

Because one, and only one, of three events will occur, the guaranteed payoff from holding all three tickets is $10. Thus, the three tickets, taken together, could never sell for less than $10. This is true whether they are bundled into one composite security or unbundled into three separate securities.

However, unbundled they may sell for more than $10. This will occur if the separate tickets fill a need for some currently unsatisfied clientele. If this is indeed the case, then Proposition I fails. The sum of the parts is worth more than the whole.

24. Some shoppers may want only the chicken drumstick. They could buy a whole chicken, cut it up, and sell off the other parts in the supermarket parking lot. This is costly. It is far more efficient for the store to cut up the chicken and sell the pieces separately. But this also has some cost, hence the observation that supermarkets charge more for chickens after they have been cut.

    The same considerations affect financial products, but:
    a.   The proportionate costs to companies of repackaging the cash flow stream are generally small.
    b.   Investors can also repackage cash flows cheaply for themselves. In fact, specialist financial institutions can often do so more cheaply than the companies can do it themselves.

25. Firms that are able to identify an 'unsatisfied' clientele and then design a financial service or instrument that satisfies the demands of this clientele can, in violation of MM's capital-structure irrelevance theory, enhance firm value. However, if this is done successfully by one financial innovator, others will follow, eventually restoring the validity of the MM irrelevance theory.

    If the financial innovation can be patented, the creator of the innovation can restrict the use of the innovation by other financial managers and thereby continue to use the innovation to create value. Consequently, MM's capital-structure irrelevance theory would potentially be violated during the life of the patent.

CHAPTER 18
How Much Should a Corporation Borrow?

Answers to Problem Sets

1. The calculation assumes that the tax rate is fixed, that debt is fixed and perpetual, and that investors' personal tax rates on interest and equity income are the same.

2. a. PV tax shield = $T_c D$ = $16.

    b. $T_c \times 20$ = $8.

3.

Relative advantage of debt = $\dfrac{1-T_p}{\left(1-T_{pE}\right)\left(1-T_c\right)}$

$$= \frac{.65}{(1)(.65)} = 1.00$$

Relative advantage $\quad = \dfrac{.65}{(.85)(.65)} = 1.18$

4. A firm with no taxable income saves no taxes by borrowing and paying interest. The interest payments would simply add to its tax-loss carry-forwards. Such a firm would have little tax incentive to borrow.

5. a. Direct costs of financial distress are the legal and administrative costs of bankruptcy. Indirect costs include possible delays in liquidation (Eastern Airlines) or poor investment or operating decisions while bankruptcy is being resolved. Also the threat of bankruptcy can lead to costs.

    b. If financial distress increases odds of default, managers' and shareholders' incentives change. This can lead to poor investment or financing decisions.

    c. See the answer to 5(b). Examples are the "games" described in Section 18-3.

6.	Not necessarily. Announcement of bankruptcy can send a message of poor profits and prospects. Part of the share price drop can be attributed to anticipated bankruptcy costs, however.

7.	More profitable firms have more taxable income to shield and are less likely to incur the costs of distress. Therefore the trade-off theory predicts high (book) debt ratios. In practice the more profitable companies borrow least.

8.	Debt ratios tend to be higher for larger firms with more tangible assets. Debt ratios tend to be lower for more profitable firms with higher market-to-book ratios.

9.	When a company issues securities, outside investors worry that management may have unfavorable information. If so the securities can be overpriced. This worry is much less with debt than equity. Debt securities are safer than equity, and their price is less affected if unfavorable news comes out later.

	A company that can borrow (without incurring substantial costs of financial distress) usually does so. An issue of equity would be read as "bad news" by investors, and the new stock could be sold only at a discount to the previous market price.

10.	a.	The cumulative requirement for external financing.

	b.	More profitable firms can rely more on internal cash flow and need less external financing.

11.	Financial slack is most valuable to growth companies with good but uncertain investment opportunities. Slack means that financing can be raised quickly for positive-NPV investments. But too much financial slack can tempt -mature companies to overinvest. Increased borrowing can force such firms to pay out cash to investors.

12.	a.	$\text{PV(tax shield)} = \dfrac{T_C(r_D D)}{1 + r_D} = \dfrac{0.35(0.08 \times \$1,000)}{1.08} = \$25.93$

	b.	$\text{PV(tax shield)} = \displaystyle\sum_{t=1}^{5} \dfrac{0.35(0.08 \times \$1,000)}{(1.08)^t} = \$111.80$

	c.	$\text{PV(tax shield)} = T_C D = \$350$

13.   For $1 of debt income:

Corporate tax = $0
Personal tax = $0.35 × $1 = $0.350
      Total   = $0.350

For $1 of equity income, with all capital gains realized immediately:

Corporate tax = 0.35 × $1 = $0.350
Personal tax = 0.35 × 0.5 × [$1 − (0.35×$1)] + 0.15 × 0.5 × [$1 − (0.35×$1)]
              = $0.163
      Total   = $0.513

For $1 of equity income, with all capital gains deferred forever:

Corporate tax = 0.35 × $1 = $0.350
Personal tax = 0.35 × 0.5 × [$1 − (0.35×$1)] = $0.114
      Total   = $0.464

14.   Consider a firm that is levered, has perpetual expected cash flow X, and has an interest rate for debt of r_D. The personal and corporate tax rates are T_p and T_c, respectively. The cash flow to stockholders each year is:

$$(X - r_D D)(1 - T_c)(1 - T_p)$$

Therefore, the value of the stockholders' position is:

$$V_L = \frac{(X)(1 - T_c)(1 - T_p)}{(r)(1 - T_p)} - \frac{(r_D)(D)(1 - T_c)(1 - T_p)}{(r_D)(1 - T_p)}$$

$$V_L = \frac{(X)(1 - T_c)(1 - T_p)}{(r)(1 - T_p)} - [(D)(1 - T_c)]$$

where r is the opportunity cost of capital for an all-equity-financed firm. If the stockholders borrow D at the same rate r_D, and invest in the unlevered firm, their cash flow each year is:

$$[(X)(1 - T_c)(1 - T_p)] - [(r_D)(D)(1 - T_p)]$$

The value of the stockholders' position is then:

$$V_U = \frac{(X)(1 - T_c)(1 - T_p)}{(r)(1 - T_p)} - \frac{(r_D)(D)(1 - T_p)}{(r_D)(1 - T_p)}$$

$$V_U = \frac{(X)(1 - T_c)(1 - T_p)}{(r)(1 - T_p)} - D$$

18-3

The difference in stockholder wealth, for investment in the same assets, is:

$$V_L - V_U = DT_c$$

This is the change in stockholder wealth predicted by MM.

If individuals could not deduct interest for personal tax purposes, then:

$$V_U = \frac{(X)(1-T_c)(1-T_p)}{(r)(1-T_p)} - \frac{(r_D)(D)}{(r_D)(1-T_p)}$$

Then:

$$V_L - V_U = \frac{(r_D)(D) - [(r_D)(D)(1-T_c)(1-T_p)]}{(r_D)(1-T_p)}$$

$$V_L - V_U = (D\,T_c) + \left(D\,\frac{T_p}{(1-T_p)} \right)$$

So the value of the shareholders' position in the levered firm is relatively greater when no personal interest deduction is allowed.

15. Long-term debt increases by: $10,000 − $4,943 = $5,057 million

The corporate tax rate is 35%, so firm value increases by:

$0.35 \times \$3,874 = \$1,770$ million

The market value of the firm is now: $79,397 + $1,770 = $81,167 million

The market value balance sheet is:

Net working capital	$4986	$10,000	Long-term debt
PV interest tax shield	3500	10,175	Other long-term liabilities
Long-term assets	72,681	60,992	Equity
Total Assets	$81,167	$81,167	Total value

16. Assume the following facts for Circular File:

Book Values

Net working capital	$20	$50	Bonds outstanding
Fixed assets	80	50	Common stock
Total assets	$100	$100	Total value

Market Values

Net working capital	$20	$25	Bonds outstanding
Fixed assets	10	5	Common stock
Total assets	$30	$30	Total value

a. Playing for Time

Suppose Circular File foregoes replacement of $10 of capital equipment, so that the new balance sheet may appear as follows:

	Market Values		
Net working capital	$30	$29	Bonds outstanding
Fixed assets	8	9	Common stock
Total assets	$38	$38	Total value

Here the shareholder is better off but has obviously diminished the firm's competitive ability.

b. Cash In and Run

Suppose the firm pays a $5 dividend:

	Market Values		
Net working capital	$15	$23	Bonds outstanding
Fixed assets	10	2	Common stock
Total assets	$25	$25	Total value

Here the value of common stock should have fallen to zero, but the bondholders bear part of the burden.

c. Bait and Switch

	Market Values		
Net working capital	$30	$20	New Bonds outstanding
		20	Old Bonds outstanding
Fixed assets	20	10	Common stock
Total assets	$50	$50	Total value

17. Answers here will vary according to the companies chosen; however, the important considerations are given in the text, Section 19.3.

18. a. Stockholders win. Bond value falls since the value of assets securing the bond has fallen.

b. Bondholder wins if we assume the cash is left invested in Treasury bills. The bondholder is sure to get $26 plus interest. Stock value is zero because there is no chance that the firm value can rise above $50.

c. The bondholders lose. The firm adds assets worth $10 and debt worth $10. This would increase Circular's debt ratio, leaving the old bondholders more exposed. The old bondholders' loss is the stockholders' gain.

d. Both bondholders and stockholders win. They share the (net) increase in firm value. The bondholders' position is not eroded by the issue of a junior security. (We assume that the preferred does not lead to still more game playing and that the new investment does not make the firm's assets safer or riskier.)

e. Bondholders lose because they are at risk for a longer time. Stockholders win.

19. a. SOS stockholders could lose if they invest in the positive NPV project and then SOS becomes bankrupt. Under these conditions, the benefits of the project accrue to the bondholders.

b. If the new project is sufficiently risky, then, even though it has a negative NPV, it might increase stockholder wealth by more than the money invested. This is a result of the fact that, for a very risky investment, undertaken by a firm with a significant risk of default, stockholders benefit if a more favorable outcome is actually realized, while the cost of unfavorable outcomes is borne by bondholders.

c. Again, think of the extreme case: Suppose SOS pays out all of its assets as one lump-sum dividend. Stockholders get all of the assets, and the bondholders are left with nothing. (Note: fraudulent conveyance laws may prevent this outcome)

20. a. The bondholders may benefit. The fine print limits actions that transfer wealth from the bondholders to the stockholders.

b. The stockholders may benefit. In the absence of fine print, bondholders charge a higher rate of interest to ensure that they receive a fair deal. The firm would probably issue the bond with standard restrictions. It is likely that the restrictions would be less costly than the higher interest rate.

21. Other things equal, the announcement of a new stock issue to fund an investment project with an NPV of $40 million should increase equity value by $40 million (less issue costs). But, based on past evidence, management expects equity value to fall by $30 million. There may be several reasons for the discrepancy:

(i) Investors may have already discounted the proposed investment. (However, this alone would not explain a fall in equity value.)
(ii) Investors may not be aware of the project at all, but they may believe instead that cash is required because of, say, low levels of operating cash flow.
(iii) Investors may believe that the firm's decision to issue equity rather than debt signals management's belief that the stock is overvalued.

If the stock is indeed overvalued, the stock issue merely brings forward a stock price decline that will occur eventually anyway. Therefore, the fall in value is not an issue cost in the same sense as the underwriter's spread. If the stock is not overvalued, management needs to consider whether it could release some information to convince investors that its stock is correctly valued, or whether it could finance the project by an issue of debt.

22. a. Masulis' results are consistent with the view that debt is always preferable because of its tax advantage, but are not consistent with the 'tradeoff' theory, which holds that management strikes a balance between the tax advantage of debt and the costs of possible financial distress. In the tradeoff theory, exchange offers would be undertaken to move the firm's debt level toward the optimum. That ought to be good news, if anything, regardless of whether leverage is increased or decreased.

    b. The results are consistent with the evidence regarding the announcement effects on security issues and repurchases.

    c. One explanation is that the exchange offers signal management's assessment of the firm's prospects. Management would only be willing to take on more debt if they were quite confident about future cash flow, for example, and would want to decrease debt if they were concerned about the firm's ability to meet debt payments in the future.

23. a.

	Expected Payoff to Bank	Expected Payoff to Ms. Ketchup
Project 1	+10.0	+5
Project 2	$(0.4 \times 10) + (0.6 \times 0) = +4.0$	$(0.4 \times 14) + (0.6 \times 0) = +5.6$

Ms. Ketchup would undertake Project 2.

    b. Break even will occur when Ms. Ketchup's expected payoff from Project 2 is equal to her expected payoff from Project 1. If $\times$ is Ms. Ketchup's payment on the loan, then her payoff from Project 2 is:

$$0.4(24 - X)$$

Setting this expression equal to 5 (Ms. Ketchup's payoff from Project 1), and solving, we find that: $\times = 11.5$

Therefore, Ms. Ketchup will borrow less than the present value of this payment.

24. One advantage of setting debt-equity targets based on bond ratings is that firms may minimize borrowing costs. This is especially true of bond covenants establish lower ratings as a condition of default. One disadvantage is that firms may not take full advantage of tax benefits from debt financing if they refuse to borrow amounts they could finance with relative safety.

25. The right measure in principle is the ratio derived from market-value balance sheets. Book balance sheets represent historical values for debt and equity which can be significantly different from market values. Any changes in capital structure are made at current market values.

   The trade-off theory proposes to explain market leverage. Increases or decreases in debt levels take place at market values. For example, a decision to reduce the likelihood of financial distress by retirement of debt means that existing debt is acquired at market value, and that the resulting decrease in interest tax shields is based on the market value of the retired debt. Similarly, a decision to increase interest tax shields by increasing debt requires that new debt be issued at current market prices.

   Similarly, the pecking-order theory is based on market values of debt and equity. Internal financing from reinvested earnings is equity financing based on current market values; the alternative to increased internal financing is a distribution of earnings to shareholders. Debt capacity is measured by the current market value of debt because the financial markets view the amount of existing debt as the payment required to pay off that debt.

26. If it was always possible to issue stock quickly and use the additional proceeds to repurchase debt, then firms may indeed avoid financial distress. But potential equity investors may be reluctant to buy stock in a firm if adverse market events are likely to place the bonds in default: they would effectively be putting money into a sinking ship, and those proceeds would go to repay the senior bond claims in bankruptcy. This is especially true if the bonds quickly move into default (or if there are cross-default provisions where one bond series default triggers other defaults).

   In some cases, bondholders may recognize that the firm has greater value as a going concern and agree to take a haircut on interest payments in exchange for an equity infusion. Under these circumstances, a firm may indeed be able to raise additional equity—but the negotiations and gamesmanship of these workout situations can get tricky.

CHAPTER 19
Financing and Valuation

Answers to Problem Sets

1. Market values of debt and equity are $D = .9 \times 75 = \$67.5$ million and $E = 42 \times 2.5 = \$105$ million.
    $D/V = .39$.
    $WACC = .09(1 - .35).39 + .18(.61) = .1325$, or 13.25%.

2. Step 1: $r = .09(.39) + .18(.61) = .145$.
    Step 2: $r_D = .086$, $r_E = .145 + (.145 - .086)(15/85) = .155$.
    Step 3: $WACC = .086(1 - .35).15 + .155(.85) = .14$.

3. a. False

    b. True

    c. True

4. The method values the equity of a company by discounting cash flows to stockholders at the cost of equity. See Section 19.2 for more details. The method assumes that the debt-to-equity ratio will remain constant.

5. a. True

    b. False, if interest tax shields are valued separately

    c. True

6. APV 5 base-case NPV ± PV financing side effects

    a. APV $= 0 - .15(500,000) = -75,000$

    b. APV $= 0 + 76,000 = +76,000$

7. a. 12%, of course.

    b. $r_E = .12 + (.12 - .075)(30/70) = .139$, WACC $= .075(1 - .35)(.30) + .139(.70) = .112$, or 11.2%.

8. a. Base-case NPV $= -1,000 + 1200/1.20 = 0$

    b. PV tax shield $= (.35 \times .1 \times .3(1000))/1.1 = 9.55$. APV $= 0 + 9.55 = \$9.55$

9. No. The more debt you use, the higher rate of -return equity investors will require. (Lenders may demand more also.) Thus there is a hidden cost of the "cheap" debt: It makes equity more expensive.

10. Patagonia does not have 90% debt capacity. KCS is borrowing $45 million partly on the strength of its existing assets. Also the decision to raise bank finance for the purchase does not mean that KCS has changed its target debt ratio. An APV valuation of Patagonia would probably assume a 50% debt ratio.

11. If the bank debt is treated as permanent financing, the capital structure proportions are:

Bank debt ($r_D = 10$ percent)	$280	9.4%
Long-term debt ($r_D = 9$ percent)	1800	60.4
Equity ($r_E = 18$ percent, 90×10 million shares)	900	30.2
	$2980	100.0%

    WACC* $= [0.10 \times (1 - 0.35) \times 0.094] + [0.09 \times (1 - 0.35) \times 0.604] + [0.18 \times 0.302]$
    $= 0.096 = 9.6\%$

12. Forecast after-tax incremental cash flows as explained in Section 6.1. Interest is not included; the forecasts assume an all-equity financed firm.

13. Calculate APV by subtracting $4 million from base-case NPV.

14. We make three adjustments to the balance sheet:
    - Ignore deferred taxes; this is an accounting entry and represents neither a liability nor a source of funds
    - 'Net out' accounts payable against current assets
    - Use the market value of equity (7.46 million × $46)

Now the right-hand side of the balance sheet (in thousands) is:

Short-term debt	$ 75,600
Long-term debt	208,600
Shareholders' equity	343,160
Total	$627,360

The after-tax weighted-average cost of capital formula, with one element for each source of funding, is:

$$WACC = [r_{D\text{-}ST} \times (1 - T_c) \times (D\text{-}ST/V)] + [r_{D\text{-}LT} \times (1 - T_c) \times (D\text{-}LT/V)] + [r_E \times (E/V)]$$

$$WACC = [0.06 \times (1 - 0.35) \times (75,600/627,360)] + [0.08 \times (1 - 0.35) \times (208,600/627,360)]$$

$$+ [0.15 \times (343,160/627,360)]$$

$$= 0.004700 + 0.017290 + 0.082049 = 0.1040 = 10.40\%$$

15. Assume that short-term debt is temporary. From Problem 14:

Long-term debt	$208,600
Share holder equity	343,160
Total	$551,760

Therefore:

$$D/V = \$208,600/\$551,760 = 0.378$$

$$E/V = \$343,160/\$551,760 = 0.622$$

Step 1:

$$r = r_D\,(D/V) + r_E\,(E/V) = (0.08 \times 0.378) + (0.15 \times 0.622) = 0.1235$$

Step 2:

$$r_E = r + (r - r_D)\,(D/E) = 0.1235 + (0.1235 - 0.08) \times 0.403 = 0.1410$$

Step 3:

$$WACC = [r_D \times (1 - T_C) \times (D/V)] + [r_E \times (E/V)]$$

$$= (0.08 \times 0.65 \times 0.287) + (0.1410 \times 0.713) = 0.1155 = 11.55\%$$

16. Base case NPV = $-\$1,000 + (\$600/1.12) + (\$700/1.12^2) = \$93.75$ or $93,750

Year	Debt Outstanding at Start Of Year	Interest	Interest Tax Shield	PV (Tax Shield)
1	300	24	7.20	6.67
2	150	12	3.60	3.09

APV = $93.75 + $6.67 + $3.09 = 103.5 or $103,500

17. a. Base-case NPV = –$1,000,000 + ($95,000/0.10) = –$50,000

PV(tax shields) = 0.35 × $400,000 = $140,000

APV = –$50,000 + $140,000 = $90,000

b. PV(tax shields, approximate) = (0.35 × 0.07 × $400,000)/0.10 = $98,000

APV = –$50,000 + $98,000 = $48,000

The present value of the tax shield is higher when the debt is fixed and therefore the tax shield is certain. When borrowing a constant proportion of the market value of the project, the interest tax shields are as uncertain as the value of the project, and therefore must be discounted at the project's opportunity cost of capital.

18. The immediate source of funds (i.e., both the proportion borrowed and the expected return on the stocks sold) is irrelevant. The project would not be any more valuable if the university sold stocks offering a lower return. If borrowing is a zero-NPV activity for a tax-exempt university, then base-case NPV equals APV, and the adjusted cost of capital r* equals the opportunity cost of capital with all-equity financing. Here, base-case NPV is negative; the university should not invest.

19. a. Base-case NPV $= -\$10 + \sum_{t=1}^{10} \frac{\$1.75}{1.12^t} = -\$0.11$ or $-\$110,000$

APV = Base-case NPV + PV(tax shield)

PV(tax shield) is computed from the following table:

Year	Debt Outstanding at Start of Year	Interest	Interest Tax Shield	Present Value of Tax Shield
1	$5,000	$400	$140	$129.63
2	4,500	360	126	108.02
3	4,000	320	112	88.91
4	3,500	280	98	72.03
5	3,000	240	84	57.17
6	2,500	200	70	44.11
7	2,000	160	56	32.68
8	1,500	120	42	22.69
9	1,000	80	28	14.01
10	500	40	14	6.48
			Total	575.74

APV = –$110,000 + $575,740 = $465,740

b. APV = Base-case NPV + PV(tax shield) − equity issue costs

$$= -\$110{,}000 + \$575{,}740 - \$400{,}000 = \$65{,}740$$

20. Spreadsheet exercise; answers will vary.

21. Note the following:
- The costs of debt and equity are not 8.5% and 19%, respectively. These figures assume the issue costs are paid every year, not just at issue.
- The fact that Bunsen can finance the entire cost of the project with debt is irrelevant. The cost of capital does not depend on the immediate source of funds; what matters is the project's contribution to the firm's overall borrowing power.
- The project is expected to support debt in perpetuity. The fact that the first debt issue is for only 20 years is irrelevant.

Assume the project has the same business risk as the firm's other assets. Because it is a perpetuity, we can use the firm's weighted-average cost of capital. If we ignore issue costs:

$$WACC = [r_D \times (1 - T_C) \times (D/V)] + [r_E \times (E/V)]$$

$$WACC = [0.07 \times (1 - 0.35) \times 0.4] + [0.14 \times 0.6] = 0.1022 = 10.22\%$$

Using this discount rate:

$$NPV = -\$1{,}000{,}000 + \frac{\$130{,}000}{0.1022} = \$272{,}016$$

The issue costs are:

Stock issue: $0.050 \times \$1{,}000{,}000 = \$50{,}000$
Bond issue: $0.015 \times \$1{,}000{,}000 = \$15{,}000$

Debt is clearly less expensive. Project NPV net of issue costs is reduced to: ($272,016 − $15,000) = $257,016. However, if debt is used, the firm's debt ratio will be above the target ratio, and more equity will have to be raised later. If debt financing can be obtained using retaining earnings, then there are no other issue costs to consider. If stock will be issued to regain the target debt ratio, an additional issue cost is incurred.

A careful estimate of the issue costs attributable to this project would require a comparison of Bunsen's financial plan 'with' as compared to 'without' this project.

22. Disagree. The Goldensacks calculations are based on the assumption that the cost of debt will remain constant, and that the cost of equity capital will not change even though the firm's financial structure has changed. The former assumption is appropriate while the latter is not.

23.

		Latest year	Forecast				
		0	1	2	3	4	5
1.	Sales	40,123.0	36,351.0	30,155.0	28,345.0	29,982.0	30,450.0
2.	Cost of Goods Sold	22,879.0	21,678.0	17,560.0	16,459.0	15,631.0	14,987.0
3.	Other Costs	8,025.0	6,797.0	5,078.0	4,678.0	4,987.0	5,134.0
4.	EBITDA (1 – 2 – 3)	9,219.0	7,876.0	7,517.0	7,208.0	9,364.0	10,329.0
5.	Depreciation and Amortization	5,678.0	5,890.0	5,670.0	5,908.0	6,107.0	5,908.0
6.	EBIT (Pretax profit) (4 – 5)	3,541.0	1,986.0	1,847.0	1,300.0	3,257.0	4,421.0
7.	Tax at 35%	1,239.4	695.1	646.5	455.0	1,140.0	1,547.4
8.	Profit after tax (6 – 7)	2,301.7	1,290.9	1,200.6	845.0	2,117.1	2,873.7
9.	Change in working capital	784.0	–54.0	–342.0	–245.0	127.0	235.0
10.	Investment (change in Gross PP&E)	6,547.0	7,345.0	5,398.0	5,470.0	6,420.0	6,598.0
11.	Free Cash Flow (8 + 5 – 9 – 10)	648.7	–110.1	1,814.6	1,528.0	1,677.1	1,948.7

PV Free cash flow, years 1-4	3,501.6
PV Horizon value	15,480.0
PV of company	18,981.7

Horizon value in year 4
24,358.1

The total value of the equity is: $18,981.7 – $5,000 = $13,981.7

Value per share = $13,981.7/865 = $16.16

24.   **a.**   For a one-period project to have zero APV:

$$APV = C_0 + \frac{C_1}{1 + r_A} + \frac{(T_C \times r_D \times D)}{1 + r_D} = 0$$

Rearranging gives:

$$\frac{C_1}{-C_0} - 1 = r - (T_C \times r_D)\left(\frac{D}{-C_0}\right)\left(\frac{1 + r_A}{1 + r_D}\right)$$

For a one-period project, the left-hand side of this equation is the project IRR. Also, $(D/-C_0)$ is the project's debt capacity. Therefore, the minimum acceptable return is:

$$r^* = r_A - (T_C \times r_D \times L)\left(\frac{1 + r_A}{1 + r_D}\right)$$

b. $r^* = 0.0984 - (0.35 \times 0.06 \times 0.20)\left(\dfrac{1.0984}{1.06}\right) = .09405$

25.   Fixed debt levels, without rebalancing, are not necessarily better for stockholders. Note that, when the debt is rebalanced, next year's interest tax shields are fixed and, thus, discounted at a lower rate. The following year's interest is not known with certainty for one year and, hence, is discounted for one year at the higher risky rate and for one year at the lower rate. This is much more realistic since it recognizes the uncertainty of future events.

26. The table below is a modification of Table 19.1 based on the assumption that, after year 7:

- Sales remain constant (that is, growth = 0%);
- Costs remain at 76.0% of sales;
- Depreciation remains at 14.0% of net fixed assets;
- Net fixed assets remain constant at 93.8;
- Working capital remains at 13.0% of sales.

TABLE 20.1 Free cash flow projections and company value for Rio Corporation ($ millions)

	Latest year	Forecast							
	0	**1**	**2**	**3**	**4**	**5**	**6**	**7**	**8**
1. Sales	83.6	89.5	95.8	102.5	106.6	110.8	115.2	118.7	118.7
2. Cost of goods sold	63.1	66.2	71.3	76.3	79.9	83.1	87.0	90.2	90.2
3. EBITDA (1 − 2)	20.5	23.3	24.4	26.1	26.6	27.7	28.2	28.5	28.5
4. Depreciation	3.3	9.9	10.6	11.3	11.8	12.3	12.7	13.1	13.1
5. Profit before tax (EBIT) (3 − 4)	17.2	13.4	13.8	14.8	14.9	15.4	15.5	15.4	15.4
6. Tax	6.0	4.7	4.8	5.2	5.2	5.4	5.4	5.4	5.4
7. Profit after tax (5 − 6)	11.2	8.7	9.0	9.6	9.7	10.0	10.1	10.0	10.0
8. Investment in fixed assets	11.0	14.6	15.5	16.6	15.0	15.6	16.2	15.9	13.1
9. Investment in working capital	1.0	0.5	0.8	0.9	0.5	0.6	0.6	0.4	0.0
10. Free cash flow (7 + 4 − 8 − 9)	2.5	3.5	3.2	3.4	5.9	6.1	6.0	6.8	10.0

		(Horizon value in year 7)
PV Free cash flow, years 1-7	24.0	
PV Horizon value	60.7	110.9
PV of company	84.7	

Assumptions:

	0	1	2	3	4	5	6	7	8
Sales growth (percent)	6.7	7.0	7.0	7.0	4.0	4.0	4.0	3.0	0.0
Costs (percent of sales)	75.5	74.0	74.5	74.5	75.0	75.0	75.5	76.0	76.0
Working capital(% of sales)	13.3	13.0	13.0	13.0	13.0	13.0	13.0	13.0	13.0
Net fixed assets (% of sales)	79.2	79.0	79.0	79.0	79.0	79.0	79.0	79.0	79.0
Depreciation (% net fixed assets)	5.0	14.0	14.0	14.0	14.0	14.0	14.0	14.0	14.0

Tax rate, %	35.0
Cost of debt, % (r_D)	6.0
Cost of equity, % (r_E)	12.4
Debt ratio (D/V)	0.4
WACC, %	9.0
Long-term growth forecast, %	0.0

Fixed assets and working capital

	0	1	2	3	4	5	6	7	8
Gross fixed assets	95.0	109.6	125.1	141.8	156.8	172.4	188.6	204.5	217.6
Less accumulated depreciation	29.0	38.9	49.5	60.8	72.6	84.9	97.6	110.7	123.9
Net fixed assets	66.0	70.7	75.6	80.9	84.2	87.5	91.0	93.8	93.8
Net working capital	11.1	11.6	12.4	13.3	13.9	14.4	15.0	15.4	15.4

Appendix Problems

1. The award is risk-free because it is owed by the U.S. government. The after-tax amount of the award is: $0.65 \times \$16$ million = $\$10.40$ million

   The after-tax discount rate is: $0.65 \times 0.055 = 0.03575 = 3.575\%$

   The present value of the award is: $\$10.4$ million/$1.03575 = \$10.04$ million

2. The after-tax cash flows are: $0.65 \times \$100,000 = \$65,000$ per year

   The after-tax discount rate is: $0.65 \times 0.09 = 0.0585 = 5.85\%$

   The present value of the lease is equal to the present value of a five-year annuity of $\$65,000$ per year plus the immediate $\$65,000$ payment:

   $\$65,000 \times$ [annuity factor, 5.85%, 5 years] + $\$65,000 =$

   $(\$65,000 \times 4.2296) + \$65,000 = \$339,924$

CHAPTER 20
Understanding Options

Answers to Problem Sets

1. Call; exercise; put; European.

2. Figure 20.13a represents a call seller; Figure 20.13b represents a call buyer.

3. a. The exercise price of the put option (i.e., you'd sell stock for the exercise price).

   b. The value of the stock (i.e., you would throw away the put and keep the stock).

4. Value of call + PV(exercise price) = value of put + value of asset (e.g., share). *See table below.*

At Maturity:	Share Price Exceeds Exercise Price		Share Price below Exercise Price	
	Action	Value	Action	Value
Call + PV(EX)	Exercise call	Stock price	Don't exercise call	Exercise price
Put + share	Don't exercise put	Stock price	Exercise put	Exercise price

   Relationship holds only for European options with same exercise price.

5. Buy a call and lend the present value of the exercise price.

6. a. Keep gold stocks and buy 6-month puts with an exercise price equal to 83.3% of the current price.

   b. Sell gold stocks, invest £485,000 for 6 months at 6%. The remaining £115,000 can be used to buy calls on the gold stocks with the same exercise price.

7. a. See Figure 4, on next page.

   b. Stock price – PV(EX) = 100 – 100/1.1 = $9.09.

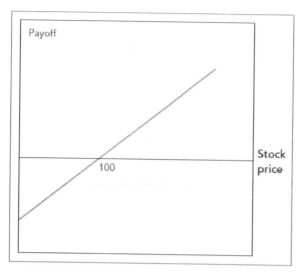

FIGURE 4
Chapter 20, Question 7.

8. Figure 20.13(b) doesn't show the cost of purchasing the call. The profit from call purchase would be negative for all stock prices less than exercise price plus cost of call. Figure 20.13(a) doesn't record the proceeds from selling the call.

9. a. Zero

    b. Stock price less the present value of the exercise price.

10. The call price (a) increases; (b) decreases; (c) increases; (d) increases; (e) decreases; (f) decreases.

11. a. All investors, however risk-averse, should value more highly an option on a volatile stock. For both ExxonMobil and Google the option is valueless if final stock price is below the exercise price, but the option on Google has more upside potential.

    b. Other things equal, stockholders lose and debtholders gain if the company shifts to safer assets. When the assets are risky, the option to default is more valuable. Debtholders bear much of the losses if asset value declines, but shareholders get the gains if asset value increases.

12. a. The put places a floor on value of investment, i.e., less risky than buying stock. The risk reduction comes at the cost of the option premium.

    b. Benefit from upside, but also lose on the downside.

c. A naked option position is riskier than the underlying asset. Investor gains from increase in stock price, but loses entire investment if stock price is less than exercise price at expiration.

d. Investor exchanges uncertain upside changes in stock price for the known up-front income from the option premium.

e. Safe investment if the debt is risk free.

f. From put-call parity, this is equivalent (for European options) to 'buy bond.' Therefore, this is a safe investment.

g. Another naked, high-risk position with known up-front income but exposure to down movements in stock price.

13. While it is true that both the buyer of a call and the seller of a put hope the price will rise, the two positions are not identical. The buyer of a call will find her profit changing from zero and increasing as the stock price rises [see text Figure 20.1(a)], while the seller of a put will find his loss decreasing and then remaining at zero as the stock price rises [see text Figure 20.2(b)].

14. You would buy the American call for $75, exercise the call immediately in order to purchase a share of Pintail stock for $50, and then sell the share of Pintail stock for $200. The net gain is: $200 – ($75 + $50) = $75.

If the call is a European call, you should buy the call, deposit in the bank an amount equal to the present value of the exercise price, and sell the stock short. This produces a current cash flow equal to: $200 – $75 – ($50/1 + r)
At the maturity of the call, the action depends on whether the stock price is greater than or less than the exercise price. If the stock price is greater than $50, then you would exercise the call (using the cash from the bank deposit) and buy back the stock. If the stock price is less than $50, then you would let the call expire and buy back the stock. The cash flow at maturity is the greater of zero (if the stock price is greater than $50) or [$50 – stock price] (if the stock price is less than $50). Therefore, the cash flows are positive now and zero or positive one year from now.

15. Let P_3 = the value of the three month put, C_3 = the value of the three month call, S = the market value of a share of stock, and EX = the exercise price of the options. Then, from put-call parity:

$$C_3 + [EX/(1 + r)^{0.25}] = P_3 + S$$

Since both options have an exercise price of $60 and both are worth $10, then:

$$S = EX/(1 + r)^{0.25} = \$60/(1.05)^{0.25} = \$59.27$$

16. From put-call parity:

$$C + [EX/(1 + r)^{(1/3)}] = P + S$$

$$P = -S + C + [EX/(1 + r)^{(1/3)}] = -55 + 19.55 + [45/(1.025^{(1/3)})] = \$9.18$$

17. The $100 million threshold can be viewed as an exercise price. Since she gains 20% of all profits in excess of this level, it is comparable to a call option. Whether this provides an adequate incentive depends on how achievable the $100 million threshold is and how Ms. Cable evaluates her prospects of generating income greater than this amount.

18. a. The payoffs at expiration for the two options are shown in the following position diagram:

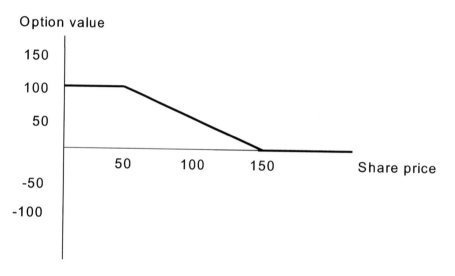

Taking into account the $100 that must be repaid at expiration, the net payoffs are:

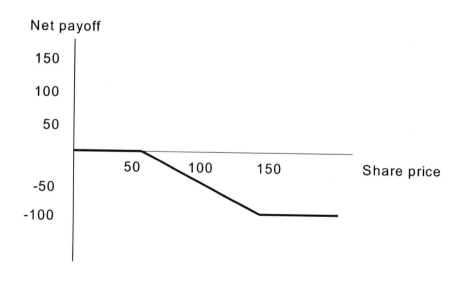

b. Here we can use the put-call parity relationship:

Value of call + Present value of exercise price = Value of put + Share price

The value of Mr. Colleoni's position is:

Value of put (EX = 150) – Value of put (EX = 50) – PV (150 – 50)

Using the put-call parity relationship, we find that this is equal to:

Value of call (EX = 150) – Value of call (EX = 50)

Thus, one combination that gives Mr. Colleoni the same payoffs is:

- Buy a call with an exercise price of $150
- Sell a call with an exercise price of $50

Similarly, another combination with the same set of payoffs is:

- Buy a put with an exercise price of $150
- Buy a share of stock
- Borrow the present value of $150
- Sell a call with an exercise price of $50

19. Statement (b) is correct. The appropriate diagrams are in Figure 20.6 in the text. The first row of diagrams in Figure 20.6 shows the payoffs for the strategy:

Buy a share of stock and buy a put.

The second row of Figure 20.6 shows the payoffs for the strategy:

Buy a call and lend an amount equal to the exercise price.

20. Answers here will vary depending on the options chosen, but the formulas will work very well; discrepancies should be on the order of 5 percent or so, at most.

21. We make use of the put-call parity relationship:

Value of call + Present value of exercise price = Value of put + Share price

a. Rearranging the put-call parity relationship to show a short sale of a share of stock, we have:

(– Share price) = Value of put – Value of call – PV(EX)

This implies that, in order to replicate a short sale of a share of stock, you would purchase a put, sell a call, and borrow the present value of the exercise price.

b. Again we rearrange the put-call parity relationship:

PV(EX) = Value of put – Value of call + Share price

This implies that, in order to replicate the payoffs of a bond, you buy a put, sell a call, and buy the stock.

22.   a.   Use the put-call parity relationship for European options:

Value of call + Present value of exercise price = Value of put + Share price

Solve for the value of the put:

Value of put = Value of call + PV(EX) – Share price

Thus, to replicate the payoffs for the put, you would buy a 26-week call with an exercise price of $100, invest the present value of the exercise price in a 26-week risk-free security, and sell the stock short.

     b.   Using the put-call parity relationship, the European put will sell for:

$$\$8 + (\$100/1.05) – \$90 = \$13.24$$

23.   a.

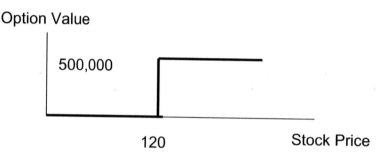

     b.   This incentive scheme is a combination of the following options:

- Buy 4,000,000 call options with an exercise price of $119.875.
- Sell 4,000,000 call options with an exercise price of $120.

24.   Straddle

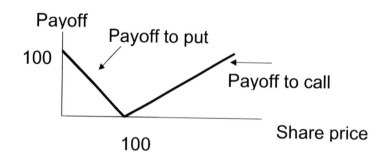

Butterfly

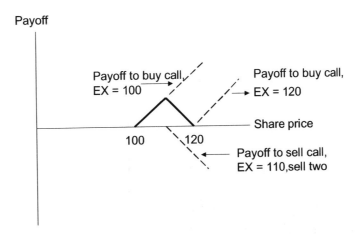

The buyer of the straddle profits if the stock price moves substantially in either direction; hence, the straddle is a bet on high variability. The buyer of the butterfly profits if the stock price doesn't move very much, and hence, this is a bet on low variability.

25. Answers here will vary according to the stock and the specific options selected, but all should exhibit properties very close to those predicted by the theory described in the chapter.

26. Imagine two stocks, each with a market price of $100. For each stock, you have an at-the-money call option with an exercise price of $100. Stock A's price now falls to $50 and Stock B's rises to $150. The value of your portfolio of call options is now:

	Value
Call on A	0
Call on B	50
Total	$50

Now compare this with the value of an at-the-money call to buy a portfolio with equal holdings of A and B. Since the average change in the prices of the two stocks is zero, the call expires worthless.

This is an example of a general rule: An option on a portfolio is less valuable than a portfolio of options on the individual stocks because, in the latter case, you can choose which options to exercise.

27. Consider each company in turn, making use of the put-call parity relationship:

Value of call + Present value of exercise price = Value of put + Share price

Drongo Corp. Here, the left-hand side [$52 + ($50/1.05) = $99.62] is less than the right-hand side [$20 + $80 = $100]. Therefore, there is a slight mispricing. To take advantage of this situation, one should buy the call, invest $47.62 at the risk-free rate, sell the put, and sell the stock short.

Ragwort, Inc. Here, the left-hand side [$15 + ($100/1.05) = $110.24) is greater than the right-hand side [$10 + $80 = $90]. Therefore, there is a significant mispricing. To take advantage of this situation, one should sell the call, borrow $95.24 at the risk-free rate, buy the put, and buy the stock.

Wombat Corp. For the three-month option, the left-hand side [$18 + ($40/1.025) = $57.02] and the right-hand side [$7 + $50 = $57] are essentially equal, so there is no mispricing.

For the first six-month option, the left-hand side [$17 + ($40/1.05) = $55.10] is slightly greater than the right-hand side [$5 + $50 = $55], so there is a slight mispricing.

For the second six-month option, the left-hand side [$10 + ($50/1.05) = $57.62] is slightly less than the right-hand side [$8 + $50 = $58], and so there is a slight mispricing.

28. One strategy might be to buy a straddle, that is, buy a call and a put with exercise price equal to the asset's current price. If the asset price does not change, both options become worthless. However, if the price falls, the put will be valuable and, if price rises, the call will be valuable. The larger the price movement in either direction, the greater the profit.

    If investors have underestimated volatility, the option prices will be too low. Thus, an alternative strategy is to buy a call (or a put) and hedge against changes in the asset price by simultaneously selling (or, in the case of the put, buying) delta shares of stock.

29. a. Purchase a call with a given exercise price and sell a call with a higher exercise price; borrow the difference necessary. (This is known as a 'Bull Spread.')

     b. Sell a put and sell a call with the same exercise price. (This is known as a 'Short Straddle.')

     c. Borrow money and use this money to buy a put and buy the stock.

     d. Buy one call with a given exercise price, sell two calls with a higher exercise price, and buy one call with a still higher exercise price. (This is known as a 'Butterfly Spread.')

30.   a.   If the land is worth more than $110 million, Bond will exercise its call option. If the land is worth less than $110 million, the buyer will exercise its put option.

      b.   Bond has: (1) sold a share; (2) sold a put; and (3) purchased a call. Therefore:

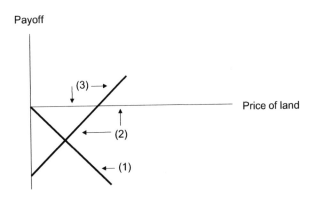

         This is equivalent to:

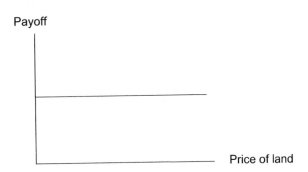

      c.   The interest rate can be deduced using the put-call parity relationship. We know that the call is worth $20, the exercise price is $110, and the combination [sell share and sell put option] is worth $110. Therefore:

Value of call + Present value of exercise price = Value of put + Share price

Value of call + PV(EX) = Value of put + Share price

$20 + [110/(1 + r)] = 110$

$r = 0.222 = 22.2\%$

      d.   From the answer to Part (a), we know that Bond will end up owning the land after the expiration of the options. Thus, in an economic sense, the land has not really been sold, and it seems misleading to declare a profit on a sale that did not really take place. In effect, Bond has borrowed money, not sold an asset.

31.   One way to profit from Hogswill options is to purchase the call options with exercise prices of $90 and $110, respectively, and sell two call options with an exercise price of $100. The immediate benefit is a cash inflow of:

$$(2 \times \$11) - (\$5 + \$15) = \$2$$

Immediately prior to maturity, the value of this position and the net profit (at various possible stock prices) is:

Stock Price	Position Value	Net Profit
85	0	0 + 2 = 2
90	0	0 + 2 = 2
95	5	5 + 2 = 7
100	10	10 + 2 = 12
105	5	5 + 2 = 7
110	0	0 + 2 = 2
115	0	0 + 2 = 2

Thus, no matter what the final stock price, we can make a profit trading in these Hogswill options.

It is very unlikely that you can identify such opportunities from data published in the newspaper. Someone else has most likely already noticed (even before the paper was printed, much less distributed to you) and traded on the information; such trading tends to eliminate these profit opportunities.

32.   a.   From the put-call parity relationship:

Value of call + Present value of exercise price = Value of put + Share price

Equity + PV(Debt, at risk-free rate) = Default option + Assets

$250 + $350 = $70 + $530

       b.   Value of default put = $350 – $280 = $70

CHAPTER 21
Valuing Options

Answers to Problem Sets

1. a. Using risk-neutral method, $(p \times 20) + (1 - p)(-16.7) = 1$, $p = .48$.

Value of call = $\dfrac{(.48 \times 8) + (.52 \times 0)}{1.01} = 3.8$

b. Delta = $\dfrac{\text{spread of option prices}}{\text{spread of stock prices}} = \dfrac{8}{14.7} = .544$

c.

	Current Cash Flow	Possible Future Cash Flows	
Buy call	−3.8	0	+8.0
equals			
Buy .544 shares	−21.8	−18.2	+26.2
Borrow 18.0	+18.0	−18.2	−18.2
	−3.8	0	+8.0

d. Possible stock prices with call option prices in parentheses:

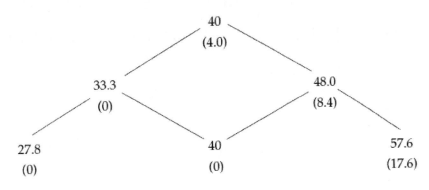

Option prices were calculated as follows:

Month 1: (i) $\dfrac{(.48 \times 0) + (.52 \times 0)}{1.01} = 0$, (ii) $\dfrac{(.48 \times 17.6) + (.52 \times 0)}{1.01} = 8.4$.

Month 0: $= \dfrac{(.48 \times 8.4) + (.52 \times 0)}{1.01} = 4.0$

e. Delta = $\dfrac{\text{spread of option prices}}{\text{spread of stock prices}} = \dfrac{8}{14.7} = .544$

2. a. No. The maximum delta is 1.0 when the ratio of stock price to exercise price is very high. (b) No. (c) Delta increases. (d) Delta increases.

3. Using the replicating-portfolio method:

    a. If month 3 stock price = 350.85, delta = $(30 – 0)/(430 – 286.27)$ = .209
        To replicate call, buy .209 shares, and borrow PV(59.752)
        Option value = $.209 \times 350.85 – 59.752/1.0075$ = 13.93

    b. If month 3 stock price = 527, delta = $(245.90 – 30)/(645.90 – 430)$ = 1
        To replicate call, buy 1 share, and borrow PV(527)
        Option value = $1 \times 527 – 400/1.0075$ = 129.98

    c. At month 0 delta = $(129.98 – 13.93)/(527 – 350.85)$ = .659
        To replicate call, buy .659 shares, and borrow PV(217.29)
        Option value = $.659 \times 430 – 217.29/1.0075$ = 67.7

Using the risk-neutral method:
$p \times .2269 + (1 – p) \times .184 = 0.0075$: p = .4671

    a. If month 3 stock price = 350.85
        Option value = $(.4671 \times 30 + .5329 \times 0)/1.0075$ = 13.93

    b. If month 3 stock price = 527
        Option value = $(.4671 \times 245.90 + .5329 \times 30)/ 1.0075$ = 129.99

    c. At month 0 option value = $(.4671 \times 129.99 + .5329 \times 13.93)/1.0075$ = 67.7

The put option can be valued using put-call parity:
Value of put = $67.7 + 400/1.0075 – 430$ = 34.72

4. Stock price is either 430*0.80 = 344, with an option value of 0,
Or 430*1.25 = 537.5 with an option value of 107.5

Replication portfolio:
Option delta = $(107.5-0)/(537.5-344)$ = 0.556 or 5/9
Value of call = $430*5/9 – ((5/9*344-0)/1.015)$ = 50.6021

Risk neutral:
P = $(0.015 – (–0.2))/(0.25-(–0.2))$ = 0.477778
Expected value of call option = $(0.477778*107.5) + (1 – 0.477778)*0$ = 51.36114
Value of Call = $51.36114/1.015$ = 50.6021

The value falls because now there is less upside for the call option.

5. a. Delta = $100/(200 – 50)$ = .667.

b.

	Current Cash Flow	Possible Future Cash Flows	
Buy call	−36.36	0	+100
equals			
Buy .667 shares	−66.67	+33.33	+133.33
Borrow 30.30	+30.30	−33.33	−33.33
	−36.36	0	+100

c. $(p \times 100) + (1-p)(-50) = 10$, $p = .4$

d. Value of call = $\dfrac{(.4 \times 100) + (.6 \times 0)}{1.10} = 36.36$

e. No. The true probability of a price rise is -almost certainly higher than the risk neutral probability, but it does not help to value the option.

6. a. Call value = $3.44.
    b. Put value = call value + PV(exercise price) − stock price = $1.67.

7. True; as the stock price rises, the risk of the option falls.

8. a. You would exercise early if the stock price was sufficiently low. There may be little opportunity for further gains in the option value and it would be better to invest the exercise price to earn interest.

    b. Don't exercise early. The interest savings from delaying payment of the exercise price is larger than the dividend foregone.

    c. If the stock price and dividend are sufficiently high, it may pay to exercise early to capture the dividend.

9. a. $u = e^{0.24 \sqrt{0.5}} = 1.185$; $d = 1/u = 0.844$

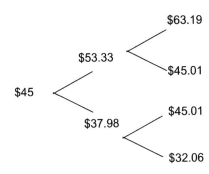

$u = e^{0.24 \sqrt{0.25}} = 1.127$; $d = 1/u = 0.887$

$u = e^{0.3 \sqrt{0.5}} = 1.236$, $d = 1/u = 0.809$

21-3

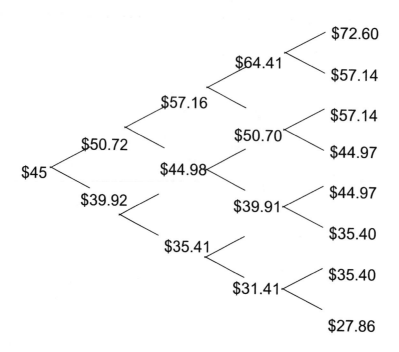

b. $u = e^{0.3 \sqrt{0.25}} = 1.162$; $d = 1/u = 0.861$

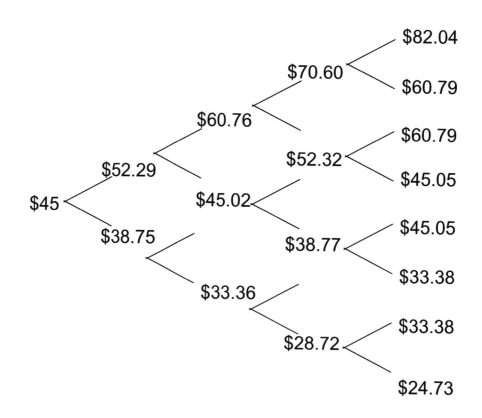

10.　a.　Let p equal the probability of a rise in the stock price. Then, if investors are risk-neutral:

$$(p \times 0.15) + (1 - p) \times (-0.13) = 0.10$$

$$p = 0.821$$

The possible stock prices next period are:

$$\$60 \times 1.15 = \$69.00$$

$$\$60 \times 0.87 = \$52.20$$

Let X equal the break-even exercise price. Then the following must be true:

$$X - 60 = [(p)(\$0) + (1 - p)(X - 52.20)]/1.10$$

That is, the value of the put if exercised immediately equals the value of the put if it is held to next period. Solving for X, we find that the break-even exercise price is $61.52.

　　b.　If the interest rate is increased, the value of the put option decreases.

11.　a.　The future stock prices of Moria Mining are:

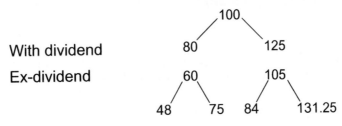

With dividend

Ex-dividend

Let p equal the probability of a rise in the stock price. Then, if investors are risk-neutral:

$$(p \times 0.25) + (1 - p) \times (-0.20) = 0.10$$

$$p = 0.67$$

Now, calculate the expected value of the call in month 6.

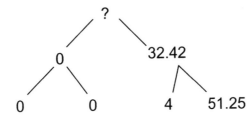

21-5

If stock price decreases to $80 in month 6, then the call is worthless. If stock price increases to $125, then, if it is exercised at that time, it has a value of ($125 − $80) = $45. If the call is not exercised, then its value is:

$$\frac{(0.67 \times \$51.25) + (0.33 \times \$4)}{1.10} = \$32.42$$

Therefore, it is preferable to exercise the call.

The value of the call in month 0 is:

$$\frac{(0.67 \times \$45) + (0.33 \times \$0)}{1.10} = \$27.41$$

b.   The future stock prices of Moria Mining are:

With dividend

Ex-dividend

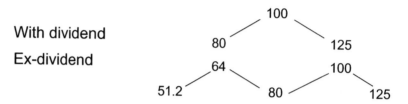

Let p equal the probability of a rise in the price of the stock. Then, if investors are risk-neutral:

$$(p \times 0.25) + (1 − p) \times (−0.20) = 0.10$$
$$p = 0.67$$

Now, calculate the expected value of the call in month 6.

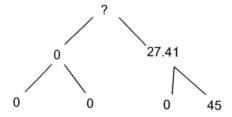

If stock price decreases to $80 in month 6, then the call is worthless. If stock price increases to $125, then, if it is exercised at that time, it has a value of ($125 − $80) = $45. If the call is not exercised, then its value is:

$$\frac{(0.67 \times \$45) + (0.33 \times \$0)}{1.10} = \$27.41$$

Therefore, it is preferable to exercise the call.

The value of the call in month 0 is:

$$\frac{(0.67 \times \$45) + (0.33 \times \$0)}{1.10} = \$27.41$$

12. a. The possible prices of Buffelhead stock and the associated call option values (shown in parentheses) are:

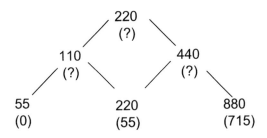

Let p equal the probability of a rise in the stock price. Then, if investors are risk-neutral:

$$p(1.00) + (1-p) \times (-0.50) = 0.10$$

$$p = 0.4$$

If the stock price in month 6 is $110, then the option will not be exercised so that it will be worth:

$$[(0.4 \times \$55) + (0.6 \times \$0)]/1.10 = \$20$$

Similarly, if the stock price is $440 in month 6, then, if it is exercised, it will be worth ($440 – $165) = $275. If the option is not exercised, it will be worth:

$$[(0.4 \times \$715) + (0.6 \times \$55)]/1.10 = \$290$$

Therefore, the call option will not be exercised, so that its value today is:

$$[(0.4 \times \$290) + (0.6 \times \$20)]/1.10 = \$116.36$$

b. (i) If the price rises to $440:

$$\text{Delta} = \frac{715-55}{880-220} = 1.0$$

(ii) If the price falls to $110:

$$\text{Delta} = \frac{55-0}{220-55} = 0.33$$

c. The option delta is 1.0 when the call is certain to be exercised and is zero when it is certain not to be exercised. If the call is certain to be exercised, it is equivalent to buying the stock with a partly deferred payment. So a one-dollar change in the stock price must be matched by a one-dollar change in the option price. At the other extreme, when the call is certain not to be exercised, it is valueless, regardless of the change in the stock price.

d. If the stock price is $110 at 6 months, the option delta is 0.33. Therefore, in order to replicate the stock, we buy three calls and lend, as follows:

	Initial Outlay	Stock Price = 55	Stock Price = 220
Buy 3 calls	–60	0	165
Lend PV(55)	–50	+55	+55
	–110	+55	+220
This strategy Is equivalent to:			
Buy stock	–110	+55	+220

13. a. Yes, it is rational to consider the early exercise of an American put option.

b. The possible prices of Buffelhead stock and the associated American put option values (shown in parentheses) are:

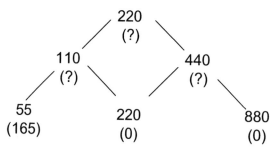

Let p equal the probability of a rise in the stock price. Then, if investors are risk-neutral:

p (1.00) + (1 – p) × (–0.50) = 0.10

p = 0.4

If the stock price in month 6 is $110, and if the American put option is not exercised, it will be worth:

[(0.4 × $0) + (0.6 × $165)]/1.10 = $90

On the other hand, if it is exercised after 6 months, it is worth $110. Thus, the investor should exercise the put early.

Similarly, if the stock price in month 6 is $440, and if the American put option is not exercised, it will be worth:

[(0.4 × $0) + (0.6 × $0)]/1.10 = $0

On the other hand, if it is exercised after 6 months, it will cost the investor $220. The investor should not exercise early.

Finally, the value today of the American put option is:

[(0.4 × $0) + (0.6 × $110)]/1.10 = $60

c.   Unlike the American put in part (b), the European put can not be exercised prior to expiration. We noted in part (b) that, If the stock price in month 6 is $110, the American put would be exercised because its value if exercised (i.e., $110) is greater than its value if not exercised (i.e., $90). For the European put, however, the value at that point is $90 because the European put can not be exercised early. Therefore, the value of the European put is:

[(0.4 × $0) + (0.6 × $90)]/1.10 = $49.09

14.   a.   The following tree shows stock prices, with option values in parentheses:

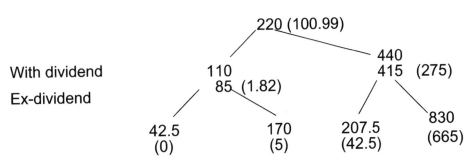

We calculate the option value as follows:

1.   The option values in month 6, if the option is not exercised, are computed as follows:

$$\frac{(0.4 \times \$5) + (0.6 \times \$0)}{1.10} = \$1.82$$

$$\frac{(0.4 \times \$665) + (0.6 \times \$42.5)}{1.10} = \$265$$

If the stock price in month 6 is $110, then it would not pay to exercise the option. If the stock price in month 6 is $440, then the call is worth: ($440 − $165) = $275. Therefore, the option would be exercised at that time.

2.   Working back to month 0, we find the option value as follows:

$$\text{Option value} = \frac{(0.4 \times \$275) + (0.6 \times \$1.82)}{1.10} = \$100.99$$

b. If the option were European, it would not be possible to exercise early. Therefore, if the price rises to $440 at month 6, the value of the option is $265, not $275 as is the case for the American option. Therefore, in this case, the value of the European option is less than the value of the American option. The value of the European option is computed as follows:

$$\text{Option value} = \frac{(0.4 \times \$265) + (0.6 \times \$1.82)}{1.10} = \$97.36$$

15. The following tree (see Problem 12) shows stock prices, with the values for the option in parentheses:

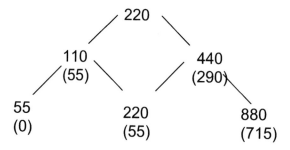

The put option is worth $55 in month 6 if the stock price falls and $0 if the stock price rises. Thus, with a 6-month stock price of $110, it pays to exercise the put (value = $55). With a price in month 6 of $440, the investor would not exercise the put since it would cost $275 to exercise. The value of the option in month 6, if it is not exercised, is determined as follows:

$$\frac{(0.4 \times \$715) + (0.6 \times \$55)}{1.10} = \$290$$

Therefore, the month 0 value of the option is:

$$\text{Option value} = \frac{(0.4 \times \$290) + (0.6 \times \$55)}{1.10} = \$135.45$$

16. a.   The following tree shows stock prices (with put option values in parentheses):

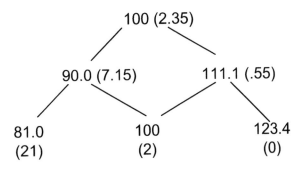

100 (2.35)

90.0 (7.15)   111.1 (.55)

81.0   100   123.4
(21)   (2)   (0)

Let p equal the probability that the stock price will rise. Then, for a risk-neutral investor:

$(p \times 0.111) + (1 - p) \times (-0.10) = 0.05$

$p = 0.71$

If the stock price in month 6 is C$111.1, then the value of the European put is:

$$\frac{(0.71 \times C\$0) + (0.29 \times C\$2)}{1.05} = C\$0.55$$

If the stock price in month 6 is C$90.0, then the value of the put is:

$$\frac{(0.71 \times C\$2) + (0.29 \times C\$21)}{1.05} = C\$7.15$$

Since this is a European put, it can not be exercised at month 6.

The value of the put at month 0 is:

$$\frac{(0.71 \times C\$0.55) + (0.29 \times C\$7.15)}{1.05} = C\$2.35$$

b.   Since the American put can be exercised at month 6, then, if the stock price is C$90.0, the put is worth (C$102 – C$90) = C$12 if exercised, compared to C$7.15 if not exercised. Thus, the value of the American put in month 0 is:

$$\frac{(0.71 \times C\$0.55) + (0.29 \times C\$12)}{1.05} = C\$3.69$$

17.   a. $P = 200$ $EX = 180$ $\sigma = 0.223$ $t = 1.0 \; r_f = 0.21$

$$d_1 = \log[P/PV(EX)]/\sigma\sqrt{t} + \sigma\sqrt{t}/2$$
$$= \log[200/(180/1.21)]/(0.223 \times \sqrt{1.0}) + (0.223 \times \sqrt{1.0})/2 = 1.4388$$
$$d_2 = d_1 - \sigma\sqrt{t} = 1.4388 - (0.223 \times \sqrt{1.0}) = 1.2158$$

$N(d_1) = N(1.4388) = 0.9249$

$N(d_2) = N(1.2158) = 0.8880$

Call value $= [N(d_1) \times P] - [N(d_2) \times PV(EX)]$

         $= [0.9249 \times 200] - [0.8880 \times (180/1.21)] = \$52.88$

  b.

$1 + \text{upside change} = u = e^{\sigma\sqrt{h}} = e^{0.223 \sqrt{1.0}} = 1.2498$

$1 + \text{downside change} = d = 1/u = 1/1.2498 = 0.8001$

Let p equal the probability that the stock price will rise. Then, for a risk-neutral investor:

     $(p \times 0.25) + (1 - p) \times (-0.20) = 0.21$

     $p = 0.91$

In one year, the stock price will be either $250 or $160, and the option values will be $70 or $0, respectively. Therefore, the value of the option is:

$$\frac{(0.91 \times 70) + (0.09 \times 0)}{1.21} = \$52.64$$

  c.

$1 + \text{upside change} = u = e^{\sigma\sqrt{h}} = e^{0.223 \sqrt{0.5}} = 1.1708$

$1 + \text{downside change} = d = 1/u = 1/1.1708 = 0.8541$

Let p equal the probability that the stock price will rise. Then, for a risk-neutral investor:

     $(p \times 0.171) + (1 - p) \times (-0.146) = 0.10$

     $p = 0.776$

The following tree gives stock prices, with option values in parentheses:

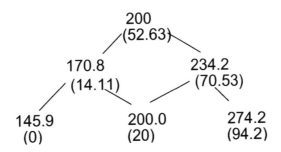

Option values are calculated as follows:

1. $\dfrac{(0.776 \times \$20) + (0.224 \times \$0)}{1.10} = \$14.11$

2. $\dfrac{(0.224 \times \$20) + (0.776 \times \$94.2)}{1.10} = \$70.53$

3. $\dfrac{(0.224 \times \$14.11) + (0.776 \times \$70.53)}{1.10} = \$52.63$

d.   (i)   Option delta $= \dfrac{\text{spread of possible option prices}}{\text{spread of possible stock prices}}$

$$\text{Option delta} = \frac{70.53 - 14.11}{234.2 - 170.8} = 0.89$$

To replicate a call, buy 0.89 shares and borrow:
[(0.89 × $170.8) − $14.11]/1.10 = $125.37

(ii)   Option delta $= \dfrac{94.2 - 20}{274.2 - 200} = 1.00$

To replicate a call, buy one share and borrow:
[(1.0 × $274.2) − $94.2]/1.10 = $163.64

(iii)   Option delta $= \dfrac{20 - 0}{200 - 145.9} = 0.37$

To replicate a call, buy 0.37 shares and borrow:
[(0.37 × $200) − $20]/1.10 = $49.09

18. To hold time to expiration constant, we will look at a simple one-period binomial problem with different starting stock prices. Here are the possible stock prices:

	100	
50		200

	110	
55		220

Now consider the effect on option delta:

Option Deltas		Current Stock Price	
		100	110
In-the-money	(EX = 60)	140/150 = 0.93	160/165 = 0.97
At-the-money	(EX = 100)	100/150 = 0.67	120/165 = 0.73
Out-of-the-money	(EX = 140)	60/150 = 0.40	80/165 = 0.48

Note that, for a given difference in stock price, out-of-the-money options result in a larger change in the option delta. If you want to minimize the number of times you rebalance an option hedge, use in-the-money options.

19. a.

$$P = 430 \qquad EX = 400 \qquad \sigma = 0.4068 \qquad t = 0.5 \qquad r_f = 0.03 \text{ (annually)}$$

$$d_1 = \log[P/PV(EX)]/\sigma\sqrt{t} + \sigma\sqrt{t}/2$$

$$= \log[430/(400/1.015)]/(0.4068 \times \sqrt{0.5}) + (0.4068 \times \sqrt{0.5})/2 = 0.447$$

$$d_2 = d_1 - \sigma\sqrt{t} = 0.447 - (0.4068 \times \sqrt{0.5}) = 0.159$$

$$N(d_1) = 0.6726$$

$$N(d_2) = 0.5633$$

Call value = $[N(d_1) \times P] - [N(d_2) \times PV(EX)]$

$$= [0.6726 \times 430] - [0.5633 \times (400/1.015)]$$
$$= \$289.2 - 222.0$$
$$= \$67.2$$

The call value has increased since we are more in the money. Since we are borrowing 222 (beta = 0) and investing 289.2 in the stock (beta = 1.27), the risk of this call option can be calculated as:

$$= (-220 \times 0 + 289.2 \times 1.27) / (-220 + 289.2)$$
$$= 5.46$$

So risk falls as the exercise price is reduced.

b.

$$P = 430 \qquad EX = 430 \qquad \sigma = 0.4068 \qquad t = 1.0 \qquad r_f = 0.03 \text{ (annually)}$$

$$d_1 = \log[P/PV(EX)]/\sigma\sqrt{t} + \sigma\sqrt{t}/2$$

$$= \log[430/(430/1.03)]/(0.4068 \times \sqrt{1}) + (0.4068 \times \sqrt{1})/2 = 0.276$$

$$d_2 = d_1 - \sigma\sqrt{t} = 0.447 - (0.4068 \times \sqrt{1}) = -0.1307$$

$N(d_1) = 0.6088$

$N(d_2) = 0.4480$

Call value = $[N(d_1) \times P] - [N(d_2) \times PV(EX)]$

$$= [0.6726 \times 430] - [0.5633 \times (430/1.003)]$$
$$= \$261.7 - 187.0$$
$$= \$74.7$$

The call value has increased with the longer time period. Since we are borrowing 187 (beta = 0) and investing 261.7 in the stock (beta = 1.27), the risk of this call option can be calculated as:

$$= (-187 \times 0 + 261.7 \times 1.27) / (-187 + 261.7)$$
$$= 4.45$$

So risk falls even further as the maturity is extended.

20. a. The call option. (You would delay the exercise of the put until after the dividend has been paid and the stock price has dropped.)

   b. The put option. (You never exercise a call if the stock price is below exercise price.)

   c. The put when the interest rate is high. (You can invest the exercise price.)

21. a. When you exercise a call, you purchase the stock for the exercise price. Naturally, you want to maximize what you receive for this price, and so you would exercise on the with-dividend date in order to capture the dividend.

   b. When you exercise a put, your gain is the difference between the price of the stock and the amount you receive upon exercise, i.e., the exercise price. Therefore, in order to maximize your profit, you want to minimize the price of the stock and so you would exercise on the ex-dividend date.

22. $P = 30$ $EX = 45.25$ $\sigma = 0.41$ $t = 7.0$ $r_f = 0.05$

$$d_1 = \log[P/PV(EX)]/\sigma\sqrt{t} + \sigma\sqrt{t}/2$$

$$= \log[30/(45.25/1.05^{\wedge}7)]/(0.41 \times \sqrt{7.0}) + (0.41 \times \sqrt{7.0})/2 = 0.4783$$

$$d_2 = d_1 - \sigma\sqrt{t} = 0.4783 - (0.41 \times \sqrt{7.0}) = -0.6064$$

$N(d_1) = 0.6838$

$N(d_2) = 0.2721$

Call value = $[N(d_1) \times P] - [N(d_2) \times PV(EX)]$

$$= [0.6838 \times 30] - [0.2721 \times (45.25/1.05^{\wedge}7] = \$11.76$$

23. Individual exercise; answers will vary.

24. For the one-period binomial model, assume that the exercise price of the options (EX) is between u and d. Then, the spread of possible option prices is:

For the call: $[(u - EX) - 0]$

For the put: $[(d - EX) - 0]$

The option deltas are:

Option delta(call) = $[(u - EX) - 0]/(u - d) = (u - EX)/(u - d)$

Option delta(put) = $[(d - EX) - 0]/(u - d) = (d - EX)/(u - d)$

Therefore:

[Option delta(call) − 1] = $[(u - EX)/(u - d)] - 1$

$= [(u - EX)/(u - d)] - [(u - d)/(u - d)]$

$= [(u - EX) - (u - d)]/(u - d)$

$= [d - EX]/(u - d) =$ Option delta(put)

25. If the exercise price of a call is zero, then the option is equivalent to the stock, so that, in order to replicate the stock, you would buy one call option. Therefore, if the exercise price is zero, the option delta is one. If the exercise price of a call is indefinitely large, then the option value remains low even if there is a large percentage change in the price of the stock. Therefore, the dollar change in the value of the option will be much smaller than the dollar change in the price of the stock, so that the option delta is close to zero. Between these two extreme cases, the option delta varies between zero and one.

26.   Both of these announcements may convey information about company prospects, and thereby affect the price of the stock. But, when the dividend is paid, stock price decreases by an amount approximately equal to the amount of the dividend. This price decrease reduces the value of the option. On the other hand, a stock repurchase at the market price does not affect the price of the stock. Therefore, you should hope that the board will decide to announce a stock repurchase program.

27.   a.   Using the figures in Section 21-3, beta = 1.27

       b.

$$P = 430 \qquad EX = 430 \qquad \sigma = 0.4068 \qquad t = 1.0 \qquad r_f = 0.03 \text{ (annually)}$$

$$d_1 = \log[P/PV(EX)]/\sigma\sqrt{t} + \sigma\sqrt{t}/2$$

$$\quad = \log[430/(430/1.03)]/(0.4068 \times \sqrt{1}) + (0.4068 \times \sqrt{1})/2 = 0.276$$

$$d_2 = d_1 - \sigma\sqrt{t} = 0.447 - (0.4068 \times \sqrt{1}) = -0.1307$$

$$N(d_1) = 0.6088$$

$$N(d_2) = 0.4480$$

$$\text{Call value} = [N(d_1) \times P] - [N(d_2) \times PV(EX)]$$

$$\qquad = [0.6726 \times 430] - [0.5633 \times (430/1.003)]$$
$$\qquad = \$261.7 - 187.0$$
$$\qquad = \$74.7$$

Since we are borrowing 187 (beta = 0) and investing 261.7 in the stock (beta = 1.27), the risk of this call option can be calculated as:

$$= (-187 \times 0 + 261.7 \times 1.27) / (-187 + 261.7)$$
$$= 4.45$$

       c.   From the put-call parity relationship:

Value of call + Present value of exercise price = Value of put + Share price

Value of put = Value of call + PV(EX) – Share price

Thus, to replicate the payoffs for the put, you would buy a call with an exercise price of $430, invest the present value of the exercise price, and sell the stock short.

The risk of this position can thus be calculated as:

$$= [(74.7 \times 4.45) + (430/1.03 \times 0) - 430 \times 1.27] / (74.7 + 417.5 - 430)$$
$$= 4.46$$

Note that this is the same as the call position

d.   One share stock plus one put option

This is the same as the previous problem except the stock positions cancel out leaving us with a call at an exercise price of $430 and our investment in the present value of the exercise price.

The risk of this position can thus be calculated as:

$$= [(74.7 \times 4.45) + (430/1.03 \times 0) / (74.7 + 417.5)$$
$$= 0.675$$

We have partially hedged our position.

e.   One share stock plus one put option minus one call option

This is the same as the previous problem except the call positions cancel out leaving us with our investment in the present value of the exercise price.

The risk of this position can thus be calculated as:

$$= (430/1.03 \times 0) / (417.5)$$
$$= 0.00$$

We have reduced our position to a risk free loan.

28.   a.   As the life of the call option increases, the present value of the exercise price becomes infinitesimal. Thus the only difference between the call option and the stock is that the option holder misses out on any dividends. If dividends are negligible, the value of the option approaches its upper bound, i.e., the stock price.

b.   While it is true that the value of an option approaches the upper bound as maturity increases and dividend payments on the stock decrease, a stock that never pays dividends is valueless.

1. a. The value of the alternative share = (V/N) where V is the total value of equity (common stock plus warrants) and N is the number of shares outstanding. For Electric Bassoon:

$$\frac{V}{N} = \frac{20{,}000 + 5{,}000}{2{,}000} = \$12.50$$

When valuing the warrant, we use the standard deviation of this alternative 'share.' This can be obtained from the following relationship:

The proportion of the firm financed by equity (calculated before the issue of the warrant) *times* the standard deviation of stock returns (calculated before the issue of the warrant)
        is equal to
the proportion of the firm financed by equity (calculated after the issue of the warrant) *times* the standard deviation of the alternative share.

   b.   The value of the warrant is equal to the value of [1/(1 + q)] call options on the alternative share, where q is the number of warrants issued per share outstanding. For Electric Bassoon:

q = 1,000/2,000 = 0.5

Therefore:

1/(1 + q) = 1/1.5 = 0.67

The value of the warrant is: (0.67 × $6) = $4
At the current price of $5 the warrants are overvalued.

Answers to Problem Sets

1. a. Increase value (unless the cash flows from the Mark II needed to be discounted at a higher rate).

    b. Increase value.

    c. Reduce value.

2. The company can buy furniture and resell (abandon) if the start-up fails, but the abandonment value of used furniture is not great. It's often better to retain flexibility by renting.

3. The life of a project is not fixed ahead of time. IM&C has the option to abandon the guano project after 2 or 3 years if performance is poor. If performance is great, exercise of the abandonment option could be delayed well beyond the estimated 7-year life.

4. a. You learn more about land prices and best use of the land.

    b. By developing immediately, you capture rents immediately.

5. Gas turbines can be started up on short notice when spark spreads are high. The turbines' value comes from flexibility in production.

6. Real options can be complex. Many real-options problems are not well structured, and it can be difficult to lay out a roadmap of future events and decisions. Competitive interactions can generate further complications.

7. a. True

    b. True

    c. True

    d. True

    e. True—the series of smaller plants generates real options, but the large plant may nevertheless be more efficient.

8. Designing the initial investment project to create inexpensive options for later expansion. Investing in a series of modular production facilities rather than committing to a single large plant. Using standardized equipment with good salvage values. Waiting and gathering information before investing (the timing option).

9. a. A five-year American call option on oil. The initial exercise price is C$70 a barrel, but the exercise price rises by 5% per year.

   b. An American put option to abandon the restaurant at an exercise price of $5 million. The restaurant's current value is ($700,000/r). The annual standard deviation of the changes in the value of the restaurant as a going concern is 15%.

   c. A put option, as in (b), except that the exercise price should be interpreted as $5 million in real estate value plus the present value of the future fixed costs avoided by closing down the restaurant. Thus, the exercise price is: $5,000,000 + ($300,000/0.10) = $8,000,000. Note: The underlying asset is now PV(revenue − variable cost), with annual standard deviation of 10.5%.

   d. A complex option that allows the company to abandon temporarily (an American put) and (if the put is exercised) to subsequently restart (an American call).

   e. An in-the-money American option to choose between two assets; that is, the developer can defer exercise and then determine whether it is more profitable to build a hotel or an apartment building. By waiting, however, the developer loses the cash flows from immediate development.

   f. A call option that allows Air France to fix the delivery date and price.

10. a. $P = 467$ $EX = 800$ $\sigma = 0.35$ $t = 3.0$ $r_f = 0.10$

$$d_1 = \log[P/PV(EX)]/\sigma\sqrt{t} + \sigma\sqrt{t}/2$$
$$= \log[467/(800/1.10^3)]/(0.35 \times \sqrt{3.0}) + (0.35 \times \sqrt{3.0})/2 = -0.1132$$
$$d_2 = d_1 - \sigma\sqrt{t} = -0.1132 - (0.35 \times \sqrt{3.0}) = -0.7194$$

$N(d_1) = N(-0.1132) = 0.4550$

$N(d_2) = N(-0.7194) = 0.2360$

Call value $= [N(d_1) \times P] - [N(d_2) \times PV(EX)]$
$$= [0.4550 \times 467] - [0.2360 \times (800/1.10^3)] = \$70.64$$

b. $P = 500$ $EX = 900$ $\sigma = 0.35$ $t = 3.0$ $r_f = 0.10$

$d_1 = \log[P/PV(EX)]/\sigma\sqrt{t} + \sigma\sqrt{t}/2$

$\quad = \log[500/(900/1.10^3)]/(0.35 \times \sqrt{3.0}) + (0.35 \times \sqrt{3.0})/2 = -0.1948$

$d_2 = d_1 - \sigma\sqrt{t} = -0.1948 - (0.35 \times \sqrt{3.0}) = -0.8010$

$N(d_1) = N(-0.1948) = 0.4228$

$N(d_2) = N(-0.8010) = 0.2116$

Call value $= [N(d_1) \times P] - [N(d_2) \times PV(EX)]$

$\quad\quad = [0.4228 \times 500] - [0.2116 \times (900/1.10^3)] = \$68.33$

c. $P = 467$ $EX = 900$ $\sigma = 0.20$ $t = 3.0$ $r_f = 0.10$

$d_1 = \log[P/PV(EX)]/\sigma\sqrt{t} + \sigma\sqrt{t}/2$

$\quad = \log[467/(900/1.10^3)]/(0.20 \times \sqrt{3.0}) + (0.20 \times \sqrt{3.0})/2 = -0.8953$

$d_2 = d_1 - \sigma\sqrt{t} = -0.8953 - (0.20 \times \sqrt{3.0}) = -1.2417$

$N(d_1) = N(-0.8953) = 0.1853$

$N(d_2) = N(-1.2417) = 0.1072$

Call value $= [N(d_1) \times P] - [N(d_2) \times PV(EX)]$

$\quad\quad = [0.1853 \times 467] - [0.1072 \times (900/1.10^3)] = \$14.07$

11. $P = 1.7$ $EX = 2$ $\sigma = 0.15$ $t = 1.0$ $r_f = 0.12$

$d_1 = \log[P/PV(EX)]/\sigma\sqrt{t} + \sigma\sqrt{t}/2$

$\quad = \log[1.7/(2/1.12^1)]/(0.15 \times \sqrt{1.0}) + (0.15 \times \sqrt{1.0})/2 = -0.2529$

$d_2 = d_1 - \sigma\sqrt{t} = -0.2529 - (0.15 \times \sqrt{1.0}) = -0.4029$

$N(d_1) = N(-0.2529) = 0.4002$

$N(d_2) = N(-0.4029) = 0.3435$

Call value $= [N(d_1) \times P] - [N(d_2) \times PV(EX)]$

$\quad = [0.4002 \times 1.7] - [0.3435 \times (2/1.12^1)] = \$0.0669$ million or $\$66,900$

12. The asset value from Practice Question 11 is now reduced by the present value of the rents:

PV(rents) = 0.15/1.12 = 0.134

Therefore, the asset value is now (1.7 − 0.134) = 1.566

P = 1.566   EX = 2   σ = 0.15   t = 1.0 r_f = 0.12

$d_1 = \log[P/PV(EX)]/\sigma\sqrt{t} + \sigma\sqrt{t}/2$

$= \log[1.566/(2/1.12^1)]/(0.15 \times \sqrt{1.0}) + (0.15 \times \sqrt{1.0})/2 = -0.8003$

$d_2 = d_1 - \sigma\sqrt{t} = -0.8003 - (0.15 \times \sqrt{1.0}) = -0.9503$

$N(d_1) = N(-0.8003) = 0.2118$

$N(d_2) = N(-0.9503) = 0.1710$

Call value = $[N(d_1) \times P] - [N(d_2) \times PV(EX)]$

$= [0.2118 \times 1.566] - [0.1710 \times (2/1.12^1)] = \$0.0263$ million or $26,300

13. a. The values in the binomial tree below are the ex-dividend values, with the option values shown in parentheses.

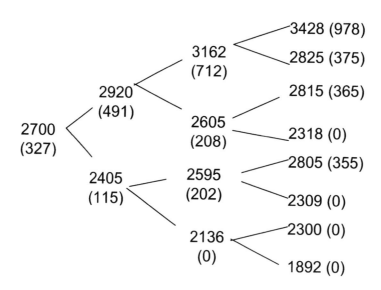

b. The option values in the binomial tree above are computed using the risk neutral method. Let p equal the probability of a rise in asset value. Then, if investors are risk-neutral:

p (0.10) + (1 − p) × (−0.0909) = 0.02

p = 0.581

If, for example, asset value at month 6 is $3,162 (this is the value after the $50 cash flow is paid to the current owners), then the option value will be:

$$[(0.419 \times 375) + (0.581 \times 978)]/1.02 = \$711$$

If the option is exercised at month 6 when asset value is $3,212 then the option value is: $3,212 – $2,500 = $712
Therefore, the option value is $712.

At each asset value in month 3 and in month 6, the option value if the option is not exercised is greater than or equal to the option value if the option is exercised. (The one minor exception here is the calculation above where we show that the value is $712 if the option is exercised and $711 if it is not exercised. Due to rounding, this difference does not affect any of our results and conclusions.) Therefore, under the condition specified in part (b), you should not exercise the option now because its value if not exercised ($327) is greater than its value if exercised ($200).

c.   If you exercise the option early, it is worth the with-dividend value less $2,500. For example, if you exercise in month 3 when the with-dividend value is $2,970, the option would be worth: ($2,970 – $2,500) = $470. Since the option is worth $491 if not exercised, you are better off keeping the option open. At each point before month 9, the option is worth more unexercised than exercised. (As noted above in part (b) there is one minor exception to this conclusion.) Therefore, you should wait rather than exercise today. The value of the option today is $327, as shown in the binomial tree above.

14.   a.   Technology B is equivalent to Technology A multiplied by a certain ratio of 0.9375. Since PV(A) = $18 million then, ignoring abandonment value:

$$PV(B) = PV(A) * 0.9375$$

$$= \$16.875 \text{ million}$$

b.   Assume that, if you abandon Technology B, you receive the $17 million salvage value plus cash flow of $1.5 million for a total of $18.5 million. Then, if demand is sluggish, you should exercise the put option and receive $18.5 million. If demand is buoyant, you should continue with the project and receive $22.5 million. So, in year 1, the put would be worth: ($18.5 million – $15 million) = $3 million if demand is sluggish and $0 if demand is buoyant.

We can value the put using the risk-neutral method. If demand is buoyant, then the gain in value is: ($22.5 million/$16.875 million) −1 = 33.3%

If demand is sluggish, the loss is: ($15 million/$16.875 million) − 1 = −11.1%

Let p equal the probability of a rise in asset value. Then, if investors are risk-neutral:

$$p (0.333) + (1 - p) \times (-0.111) = 0.07$$

$$p = 0.408$$

Therefore, the value of the option to abandon is:

$$[(0.592 \times 0) + (0.408 \times 3)]/1.07 = \$1.14 \text{ million}$$

15. a. You can't use any one discount rate for the option payoffs. The risk of an option changes as asset price changes and time passes.

b. The risky asset may be worth less as a consequence of its riskiness, but the option on the risky asset is more valuable because the option owner can capitalize from up moves while not losing due to down moves.

c. The value of an option depends on the value of the underlying asset. DCF valuation of investment projects is necessary in order to determine the value of the underlying asset.

16. If oil and natural gas prices are highly positively correlated, then the value of the option is low. For example, if both prices simultaneously increase to a relatively high level (or decrease to a relatively low level), then there is little or no benefit in switching from one fuel to the other. On the other hand, if the prices are negatively correlated (which is, or course, highly unlikely), then the value of the option is high. In this scenario, an increase in the price of oil, for example, will likely be associated with a decrease in the price of natural gas, and therefore the option to switch from high-priced oil to relatively lower-priced natural gas is a valuable option. If the prices are uncorrelated, then the option has moderate value, since an increase in the price of one fuel may (or may not) be associated with a decrease in the price of the other. In general, the more highly positively correlated the prices are, the lower the value of the option.

17. The valuation approach proposed by Josh Kidding will not give the right answer because it ignores the fact that the discount rate within the tree changes as time passes and the value of the project changes.

18. Excel problem; approaches will vary. However, answers should demonstrate the relationships identified in Table 20.2.

19. The value of an option to acquire an asset (i.e., a call option) decreases with the difference between the risk-free rate of interest (r_f) and the weighted average cost of capital (WACC) of the asset. That is, as (WACC – r_f) increases, the value of the call option decreases. Suppose that the increase in (WACC – r_f) results from an increase in WACC, or a decrease in r_f, or both. Each of these changes decreases the value of a call. An increase in WACC reduces the present value of the underlying asset, which reduces the value of the call. Also, a decrease in r_f reduces the value of the call. An increase in (WACC – r_f) can also result from changes in both WACC and r_f in the same direction but by different amounts (e.g., both rates increase, but the percentage point increase in WACC is greater than the percentage point increase in r_f). While an increase in r_f increases the value of the call, this increase would typically be much smaller than the decrease in the value of the call resulting from an even larger percentage point increase in WACC. The impact of an increase r_f would arise from the effect of discounting over the life of the option, typically a relatively short period of time. An increase in WACC could have a substantial impact (due to the effect of discounting cash flows over long periods of time) on the present value of the underlying asset if cash flows occur several years in to the future.

20. You don't take delivery of the new plant until month 36. Think of the situation one month before completion. You have a call option to get the plant by paying the final month's construction costs to the contractors. One month before that, you have an option on the option to buy the plant. The exercise price of this second call option is the construction cost in the next to last month. And so on.

   Alternatively, you can think of the firm as agreeing to construction and putting the present value of the construction cost in an escrow account. Each month, the firm has the option to abandon the project and receive the unspent balance in the escrow account. Thus, in month 1, you have a put option on the project with an exercise price equal to the amount in the escrow account. If you do not exercise the put in month 1, you get another option to abandon it in month 2. The exercise price of this option is the amount in the escrow account in month 2. And so on.

21. a. An increase in PVGO increases the stock's risk. Since PVGO is a portfolio of expansion options, it has higher risk than the risk of the assets currently in place.

    b. The cost of capital derived from the CAPM is not the correct hurdle rate for investments to expand the firm's plant and equipment, or to introduce new products. The expected return will reflect the expected return on the real options as well as the assets in place. Consequently, the rate will be too high.

Study Guide

for

Principles of
Corporate Finance

Tenth Edition

Contents

1
Goals and Governance of the Firm

INTRODUCTION

This chapter introduces the topic of the book - corporate finance, which is about making financial decisions for corporations. The chapter also discusses the key role played by the financial manager who makes these decisions with the help and advice of other managers. The chapter introduces three broad themes that recur repeatedly throughout the book:

- Maximizing value of the firm
- The opportunity cost of capital
- Corporate governance, the incentives that make governance effective and the critical importance of these incentives and the governance structure.

KEY CONCEPTS IN THE CHAPTER

Corporate Investment and Financing Decisions: Financial decisions fall into two broad categories: *Investment decisions* and *Financing decisions*. A typical business needs *assets* – plant and machinery, buildings, computers and information systems, warehouses, etc. – to produce whatever goods and services that the business sells to its customers. These assets are bought by the firm as a result of the firm's financial manager making a decision to invest in these assets. Firms invest in *real assets* – physical assets like machinery or computer systems – and *intangible assets* through research and development. The investment decisions are typically known as *capital budgeting (*or CAPEX - short for capital expenditure) decisions. Investment decisions are among the most important decisions made a firm's managers as they determine the success or failure of the firm. Please note that the financial manager does not make investment decisions all by herself; she gets help and advice from by her colleagues who have the appropriate technical, marketing, or other expertise. Investment decisions may involve, depending on the business of the firm, a manufacturing plant, opening new stores or buying locomotives. Examples of some major investment decisions made by a few well known corporations are given Table 1.1 of the Brealey, Myers, and Allen (BMA) text.

While investing decisions focus on which assets to buy, the funds needed for the purchase of these assets come from the *financing decisions*. Financial managers sell *financial securities* or claims to investors. These claims may be in the form of *bonds*, which are debt securities sold in the capital markets. Alternately, the financial manager may decide to sell ownership claims or *stock* in the form of shares of the corporation. Another way of using equity financing is to reinvest the profits. The financial manger of a profitable firm has the option of reinvesting some or all of the profits back in the firm. If he decides to pay out part of the profits to the firm's shareholders as *dividends*, it reduces the amount available for reinvestment. Decision to pay dividends can be considered part of the financing decision. Dividend payout decisions are covered in chapter 16. The mix of financing sources used by a firm is labeled *capital structure.*

Examples of some typical financing decisions are also shown in Table 1.1 of BMA text. The financing choices available to a firm are many and vary in all kinds of details. A firm can borrow for 5 years or 10 years or even 30 years. Of course, the interest rate paid and other conditions such as the restraints imposed by the lender will differ as well.

A **corporation** is a legal entity that is owned a number of stockholders. Most businesses evolve from small *privately held* corporations to large *public* corporations. The corporate form enjoys the advantages of limited liability for the owners (stockholders) and the ability to attract large amounts of capital. Professional managers are hired to manage today's typical corporations. This separation of ownership and management gives the firm permanence and a firm, unlike a partnership or proprietorship, is not affected by the demise of its owners (shareholders). The different organizational forms of business are discussed in chapter 14. Corporations are governed by the *articles of incorporation*. Corporations enjoy considerable flexibility of operation. The disadvantages of the corporate form include costly legal and accounting set-up and double taxation of earnings.

Financial Manager's Role: Throughout the book, the term financial manager is used in a broad sense meaning anyone who deals with investment and/or financing decisions for a business. The financial management function becomes more complex as the firm gets larger and is headed by a *chief financial officer (CFO*. The CFO oversees the *treasurer* and the *controller* and generally holds additional responsibility for financial policy and corporate planning. The treasurer deals with cash management, raising capital and managing relations with investors and financial institutions. The controller is entrusted with responsibility for managing the firm's internal accounting, preparation of financial statements, and tax obligations. While small firms typically have a treasurer as the only financial manager, larger firms will have a controller also. The CFO is part of the top management team for the firm and often is a member of the board of directors. Important financial decisions are often referred to the board of directors and are subject to their approval.

As stated earlier, corporations use different real assets such as buildings and machinery to run their businesses and finance the acquisition of these assets partly by raising finances through the issue of financial securities, which are traded in the *financial markets* (see figure 1.1 in the text). The financial manager plays the key role of deciding which assets to invest in and how to finance them. Most firms will have other managers in charge of marketing, production, and other functions. These managers work with the financial manager(s) in managing a corporation's operations. A typical corporation operates in a global market place with offices and factories located in many countries. Financial markets are also global and companies often raise financing from investors located in many different countries.

Opportunity Cost of Capital: Corporations are owned by shareholders and ideally financial manager has to make all her decisions keeping in mind the best interests of the shareholders. Since shareholders can invest their money outside the firm as well, the rate of return earned by an investment by the firm should be at least as high as what the shareholders can earn outside the firm on investments of comparable risk. This rate is the *opportunity cost of capital* and determined as the rate of return expected to be received from alternate investments of identical risk. The opportunity cost is a function of the risk characteristics of the investment. In simple terms, it is the rate of return on investments of comparable risk. One typically looks to the financial markets to identify an investment of comparable risk. We deal with explicit models for measurement of risk and estimation of rates of returns in later chapters. The terms discount rate, opportunity cost, and *hurdle rate* are often used synonymously. While financial markets generally function well and provide good information to help the financial manager determine the appropriate opportunity cost, there may be times when the reliability of market prices can be questioned.

Goals of Corporation: Shareholders own the corporation and would like to maximize their wealth. Individual shareholders will have different preferences with respect to consumption and saving. However, they would all like to be wealthier rather than be poorer. Financial markets enable efficient exchange of capital between individuals. Lenders save and postpone consumption and borrowers can consume now based on expected future income. Thus, the existence of well-functioning financial markets enables us to separate the individual stockholders consumption preferences from the corporate management decisions. Since individual shareholders can use the financial markets to achieve their consumption choices, managers can concentrate on maximizing the value of the firms by investing in projects that earn a return higher than the opportunity cost of capital. This will maximize the stockholders' wealth and this wealth can be traded in the financial market freely to manage ones own preferred consumption level. Individual investors can choose their patterns of consumption preferences by appropriate lending or borrowing choices. Managers need not worry about individual stockholders' preferences as long as the financial markets are well-functioning. Managers should act to maximize the stockholders' wealth and can do this by investing in projects that earn returns higher than the opportunity cost.

It is sometimes suggested that firms should maximize profits. However, profit maximization is not a satisfactory goal as the definition or timing of profits can be vague and ambiguous. Further, profit by itself does not capture the risk involved in the investment.

The term *stakeholders* is used to describe broadly all those involved in a firm – shareholders, employees, customers, suppliers, the community in which the firm is operating, etc. Stakeholders such as employees, customers, suppliers, etc. are important for the success of the firm. Given this, is the focus on shareholder wealth fair to the other stakeholders? Note that each of the stakeholders interacts with the firm through competitive markets and can demand fair rewards or compensation for their transactions with the firm. It is very unlikely that managers can maximize shareholder wealth at the expense of other stakeholders. Customer satisfaction and employees' loyalty are essential for the success of the firm. Managers would do well to follow and obey the rule of law, both in letter and spirit. They should also be seen as acting in moral and ethical ways. Trust and reputation are very valuable for firms' success in dealing with all their stakeholders. Assuming that the firm operates in competitive markets using fair, moral and ethical means, a manager maximizing stockholders' wealth also maximizes the society's wealth because the increased wealth comes from value created by the business and not at the expense of other stakeholders.

The emphasis of the focus on shareholders seems to differ by countries. Managers in countries like Germany and Japan seem to take a broader view of their role compared to the managers in the US and the UK. This may reflect the historic differences in the evolution of the markets across the different countries. As markets and business have become more global, there appears to be some convergence towards greater emphasis on shareholder value.

Agency problems and Corporate Governance: Most large corporations have tens of thousands of shareholders and it will be impossible to have the "owners" manage the business directly. Therefore, separation of ownership and management becomes a necessity. This paves the way for hiring of professional managers to manage the business and allows continuity in management un-affected by changes in ownership. The disadvantage of this separation of ownership and management is that it causes potential *principal-agent problems*. The managers are the agents of the stockholders, who are the principals. The managers may not always act in the best interest of the stockholders. Agency costs are the costs incurred when managers do not act in the interests of the stockholders and their actions need to be monitored. Obviously, owner-managers do not incur any agency costs, as there are no conflicts of interest. Other principal-agent situations in corporate finance include the relationships between the senior managers and the junior managers and that between the lenders and stockholders. The problems of agency costs receive detailed coverage in later chapters.

Costs of agency problems can be significantly mitigated by good *corporate governance*. Key elements of good governance include the following:

Legal and Regulatory requirements: The Securities and Exchange Commission *(SEC)* has strict information and disclosure requirements for public corporations. These include accounting and reporting standards and disclosures of important events related to the corporation. Trading in the firm's securities by the firm's insiders (senior managers and directors for example) based on information not publicly available is prohibited.

Compensations Plans: One of the best ways to align managers' interests with that of the shareholders is to design compensation plans which give incentives to managers to maximize the firm's stock value. Stock options are the most common examples of this type of compensation.

Board of Directors: The board of directors of a firm is elected by the shareholders. The board appoints and monitors the senior management of the firm who, in turn, manages the operations of the firm as the means to maximizing shareholders wealth. An active and independent board ensures that managers act in the interest of stockholders. The Sarbanes-Oxley Act requires more independent directors.

Monitoring: Managers are watched and monitored by, besides the board of directors, lenders, and security analysts.

Takeovers: Poorly performing managers are likely to lose their jobs when the companies run by them get taken over. The threat of takeovers can be a strong motivator.

Shareholder Pressure: Shareholders of under-performing corporations can put pressure on the management by attempting to elect more independent directors. In some cases, there are also large individual and activist shareholders or institutional (mutual funds or hedge funds) shareholders who can effectively put pressure on managers to shape up. Another tool available to any shareholder is the "Wall Street Walk" or sale of shares of a poorly managed and underperforming firm. This can lead to lower stock price and increased threat of takeover.

CHAPTER SUMMARY

This chapter provides an introduction to the topic of corporate finance and describes the role of the financial manager in managing a business. The chapter discusses briefly the corporate form of ownership. Most large corporations are organized as public corporations and are usually owned by thousands of stockholders. A corporation has a legal distinct identity. The stockholders have limited liability, and owners are usually not associated with managing the company directly. This separation of ownership and management enables businesses to hire professional managers to run the business and allows the business to operate independent of changes in ownership.

The financial manager plays an important role in the management of the company and is concerned with decisions relating to investment and financing. Depending on the size of the company, the finance function may be organized in different ways. Small companies have a treasurer while larger firms may have a treasurer and a controller. While the treasurer is in charge of cash management and obtaining finances for the business, the controller's job is to see that money is used efficiently and well. Very large corporations have a chief financial officer, who oversees the treasurer and the controller and is part of the senior management team of the company.

Shareholders of corporations want corporate manager to maximize its value and the current stock price. This goal will satisfy all shareholders regardless of their consumption preferences as long as there are well functioning financial markets. These markets enable individual shareholders to manage their consumption at their preferred level. Financial managers can maximize the firm's value by ensuring good investment and financing decisions.

Shareholders would want the managers to maximize their wealth by maximizing the value of the company's stock. Managers might be interested in objectives other than stockholders' interests. This conflict is one of the several different types of agency problems affecting the management of large corporations. The agency problems and the related costs can be mitigated by good corporate governance. Key elements of good governance include: legal requirements, outside monitoring by security analysts, a strong and independent board of directors, threat of takeovers and shareholder pressures.

LIST OF TERMS

Agency problem
Agent
Bond
Capital budgeting
Chief financial officer
Controller
Corporate governance
Corporation
Financial assets
Financial market
Financing
Hurdle rate
Intangible asset

Investment
Limited liability
Opportunity cost
Principals
Rate of return
Real asset
Share
Securities
Stakeholders
Stock
Tangible asset
Treasurer

EXERCISES

Fill-in Questions

1. Most large businesses are organized as _____.

2. The financial manager is concerned with _____ and _____ decisions.

3. A _____ is responsible for managing cash and raising finances for the business.

4. The _____ oversees the treasurer and the _____ and is part of the senior management team.

5. A company's _____ include machinery, buildings, and patents.

6. Trademarks, patents, and technical expertise are examples of _____assets.

7. Stocks and bonds are examples of _____ assets.

8. Shareholders of a corporation have _____.

9. Debt securities issued by corporations are called _____.

10. Managers are _____ of shareholders, who are the _____.

11. _____ is the process of investment decision making.

12. Corporations issue _____ in capital markets to raise money.

13. Employees, suppliers, shareholders, and customers are often referred to as _____.

14. Managers should invest in projects with rates of return _____ than the opportunity cost of capital.

15. The expected return from comparable investments in the securities markets gives the _____ _____ for the project.

16. Opportunity cost of capital for a project is _____ _ _____ on alternate investments of comparable risk.

17. A good system of _____ _____ is required to ensure that the managers act in the best interests of the shareholders.

Problems

1. Identify the investment and financing decisions from the following list:
   a. Buying new machinery
   b. Issuing bonds
   c. Acquiring a company
   d. Borrowing from the local bank
   e. Receiving credit from a supplier
   f. Buying new computers to replace the old machines affected by the year 2000 problem
   g. Building a new warehouse

2. Separate the real assets from the financial assets:
   a. Shares of IBM
   b. Patents for a new process to manufacture microprocessors
   c. Roads
   d. Brand names
   e. Treasury bonds
   f. An IOU from Warren Buffett

Essay Questions

1. Why are most large businesses organized as corporations?

2. "Separation of ownership and management is necessary and desirable." Discuss.

3. Describe the differences between each of the following:
   a. A tangible asset and intangible asset
   b. Investment and financing
   c. The treasurer and the controller

4. "Corporate managers will generally act in the interests of their stockholders." Discuss.

5. Explain why corporate managers need not be concerned with the stockholders' individual consumption preferences, even though they are managing the firm on behalf of the stockholders.

ANSWERS TO EXERCISES

Fill-in Questions

1. Corporations
2. Investment, financing
3. Treasurer
4. Chief financial officer, controller
5. Real assets
6. Intangible
7. Financial
8. Limited liability
9. Bonds
10. Agents, principals
11. Capital budgeting
12. Securities

13. Stakeholders
14. Greater
15. Opportunity cost

16. Rate of return
17. Corporate governance

Problems

1. a. Investment
   b. Financing
   c. Investment
   d. Financing
   e. Financing
   f. Investment
   g. Investment

2. a. Financial assets
   b. Real assets
   c. Real assets
   d. Real assets
   e. Financial assets
   f. Financial assets

2
How to Calculate Present Values

INTRODUCTION

This is the first of three chapters dealing directly with valuation of assets. The chapter introduces the most basic and fundamental concept of finance - *time value of money*. This concept forms the basis for most valuation models. It is often expressed as follows: a dollar today is worth more than a dollar received tomorrow. This is because the dollar you have today can be invested at some rate of return (*opportunity cost*) so that the value (*future value*) is higher than the dollar you invested. *Present value* gives the current value of a cash flow received at a future point in time. Application of this concept enables you to value different kinds of assets, especially those, which are not commonly traded in well-functioning markets. The concept has application in making investment decisions. *Net present value (*NPV) is simply the sum of the present values of all cash flows from an investment minus the cost of the investment. NPV is the effective net benefit or value of the investment. Opportunity cost, as discussed in the last chapter, represents the rate of return on investments of comparable risk. You are also briefly introduced to another basic lesson: a riskier cash flow is worth less than an equal amount of a less risky cash flow.

The chapter helps you build expertise in calculating present values and future values of different cash flow streams by presenting a number of useful short cuts for some commonly occurring cash flow patterns. These are:

- Perpetuity: a fixed payment each year (period) forever
- Annuity: a fixed payment each year (period) for a limited number of years (periods)
- Growing perpetuity: cash flows or payments growing at a constant rate each year forever
- Growing annuity: an annuity with the cash flow that growing at a constant rate

The chapter concludes with a discussion of interest rates as they are quoted, the difference between compound interest and simple interest, and the effect of different compounding intervals on effective annual cost.

Present value calculations can be done in several ways: using the basic formulas, using tables of discounting or compounding factors, using business calculators or using computer spreadsheet software like Excel. We provide solutions using both the tables and a popular business calculator (BA II Plus).

KEY CONCEPTS IN THE CHAPTER

Future Value and Present Value: If you have one dollar today and you can invest it at an interest rate of r, this investment will be worth $\$1(1+r)$ next year. We can write:

Future value (FV) = $C_0 (1 + r)$. In general: $FV_t = C_0 (1 + r)^t$

How much is $1 to be received next year worth today? This value is its *present value* (PV) and you can see that it will be $1/ (1 + r).

PV of any cash flow (C_1) received next year = $\dfrac{C_1}{1+r} = C_1(\dfrac{1}{1+r}) = C_1DF_1;$

Where, DF_1 = Discount factor = $\dfrac{1}{1+r}$

The present value of any future cash flow is its current equivalent. This process of computing present value is called *discounting* and can be extended to future cash flows beyond next year. The rate of interest or return used in computing the PV is called the *discount rate.* Other terms like hurdle rate or *opportunity cost* are also used to denote this.

Net Present Value: NPV of an asset or investment is the present value of the cash flows produced by the asset less the cost of acquiring the asset. Smart investors will only acquire assets that have positive NPVs and will attempt to maximize the NPV of their investments. The *rate of return* received from an investment is the profit divided by the cost of the investment. Positive NPV investments will have rates of return higher than the opportunity cost. This gives an alternate investment decision rule: Good investments are those that have rates of return higher than the opportunity cost.

$$NPV = C_0 + \frac{1}{1+r} \times C_1$$

$$\text{Rate of return} = \frac{\text{Profit}}{\text{Investment}}$$

Two equivalent investment decision rules can be summarized as follows:
  i. Accept positive NPV investments.
  ii. Accept investments with rates of return higher than the opportunity cost or the hurdle rate.

Opportunity Cost: What rate should be used to discount a future cash flow generated by an asset? This rate is the *opportunity cost of capital* was briefly discussed in the last chapter. This is the rate of return expected to be received from alternate investments forgone. The opportunity cost is a function of the risk characteristics of the investment and should reflect the investment's risk. In simple terms, it is the rate of return on investments of comparable risk. One typically looks to the capital market to identify an investment of comparable risk. Higher risk cash flows are worth less than less risky ones. We deal with explicit models for measurement of risk and estimation of rates of returns in later chapters. The terms discount rate, opportunity cost, and hurdle rate are often used synonymously.

Present Value of a Stream of Cash Flows: The present value (PV) of a cash flow received one year from now is:

$$PV = \frac{C_1}{1+r} \text{; where } C_1 \text{ is the cash flow and r is the discount rate.}$$

Alternately, $PV = DF_1 \times C$, where DF_1 is known as the discount factor and $= \dfrac{1}{1+r}$

We can extend this approach and calculate the PV of any future cash flow.

PV of C_2 received two years from now	$= C_2/(1+r)^2 = DF_2 \times C_2$
PV of a cash flow received t years from now	$= C_t/(1+r)^t = DF_t \times C_t;$
Where, $DF_t = 1/(1+r)^t$.	

For a stream of cash flows C_1, C_2, ...C_t received at 1, 2, ... t years from now, the present value is the sum of present values of the individual cash flows.

$$PV = \frac{C_1}{(1+r)} + \frac{C_2}{(1+r)^2} + \ldots + \frac{C_t}{(1+r)^t} = DF_1 \times C_1 + DF_2 \times C_2 + \ldots + DF_t \times C_t$$

The general formula for the present value of a stream of cash flows, known as the discounted cash flow formula, is given below:

$$PV = \sum_{t=1}^{n} \frac{C_t}{(1+r)^t}$$

Here is an example of a present value problem. Jim Lander just signed up with a professional basketball team and has been offered a contract, which pays him $3 million next year, $4 million the year after and $5 million in three years. If the discount rate is 12%, what is the present value of the total payments to James?

Present value = $3/1.12 + 4/ (1.12)^2 + 5/ (1.12)^3 = 2.679 + 3.189 + 3.559 = \$9.427$ million

Alternately we can use the discount factors as below:

Year	Cash flow (Column 2)	Discount factor (12%) (Column 3)	Present value (Col.2 × Col. 3)
1	$3 million	0.893	3×0.893 = 2.679
2	$4 million	0.797	4×0.797 = 3.188
3	$5 million	0.712	5×0.712 = 3.560
Total			$9.427 million

We can also use a business calculator to directly calculate the present values. This is shown in the worked examples given later in this chapter.

11

Special Streams of Cash Flows: There are four special types of cash flow streams commonly encountered in business and everyday life. Short cuts are available to compute the present values (and future values, where relevant) of these special cases. The special cases are discussed next.

<u>Perpetuity</u>: A perpetuity is an unending stream of equal payments received or paid at equal intervals of time. Imagine you have $5,000 invested in a bank account and the bank promises to pay you $250 every year as long as you have the money with the bank. The rate of return on this investment is $250/$5,000 = 5%. This can go on forever as long as you keep the deposit with the bank.

The rate of return on a perpetuity = Payment/Present value.

Or, $r = \dfrac{C}{PV}$, or $PV = \dfrac{C}{r}$

It follows that the present value of a stream of equal payments received each year forever will simply be the payment divided by the rate of return.

Alternately, you might prefer to remember that the annual payment is just the principal value times the interest rate ($250 = $5,000 × 0.05, or C = PV × r). Now you can rearrange the expression to get PV = C/r.

Example: John Moore wants to endow a Chair in the Finance Department at Central State University. The University suggests an endowment with an annual income of $250,000. If the endowment investments can earn 5% annually, how much should Mr. Moore donate now?

Donation = Annual Payment/Rate of return = $250,000/0.05 = $5,000,000

<u>Annuity</u>: Annuities are "truncated" perpetuities. The present value of an annuity for 10 years is the difference in the present values of a perpetuity now (first payment at the end of this year) and the present value of another perpetuity with first payment at the end of 11 years. You can generalize this approach and get the present value for a t-year annuity as PV (perpetuity A) – PV (Perpetuity B), where the payments for A starts next year and payments for B starts at the end of t+1 years.

$$PV(\text{Perpetu ity A}) = \frac{C}{r}$$

$$PV(\text{Perpetu ity B}) = \frac{C}{r} \times \frac{1}{(1+r)^t}$$

PV(Annuity for t years) = PV(Perpetuity A) − PV(Perpetuity B)

$$= C\left(\frac{1}{r} - \frac{1}{r(1+r)^t}\right)$$

$$= C\,(\text{Annuity Factor}).$$

The present value annuity factor formula can be written in different forms as follows:

$$\text{Present value annuity factor} = \frac{1}{r} - \frac{1}{r(1+r)^t} = \frac{1}{r} - \frac{1}{(1+r)^t} = \frac{(1+r)^t - 1}{r(1+r)^t}$$

This annuity assumes that payments will come at the end of each year and is called *ordinary annuity*. A stream of cash flows with payments at the beginning of each year is called an *annuity due*. Since each payment in the annuity due begins one year earlier, the present value of the annuity due will be higher than the present value of an ordinary annuity by a factor of $(1+r)$ or:

PV (Annuity due) = PV (Ordinary annuity) $\times$ $(1+r)$.

Typical examples of annuities include mortgage loans and car loans. Please note that these loans are usually structured as monthly annuities.

Example: Jon Masters bought a car for $21,000 and financed 90% of the purchase price with a loan at an annual interest of 6%. Jon will repay the loan with 48 monthly payments starting next month. What is his monthly payment?

The loan amount = $21,000 $\times$ 0.9 = $18,900 = PV (Annuity) = PV = C $\times$ (Annuity factor), where C is the monthly payment.
C = Loan amount/Annuity factor

$$\text{Present value annuity factor} = \frac{1}{r} - \frac{1}{r(1+r)^t}$$

r = monthly interest rate = 6/12 = 0.5%
Annuity factor = $(1/0.005) - [1/(0.005 \times 1.005^{48})]$ = 42.580
Payment = $18,900/42.580 = $443.87

The car loan of the above example is an *amortizing* loan. Each loan payment includes an interest component and principal component. One can construct an amortization table showing how much of each payment is interest and how much the principal. See worked example below.

For some problems, computation of future value may be of more interest. For example, if you are planning to save for your retirement by investing $1,000 in a mutual fund every year for the next 35 years and the rate of return expected is 8%, how much would you accumulate at the end of 35 years? The answer is the future value of the annuity. The formula for the future value can be easily derived from the present value formula.

Future value annuity factor = Present value annuity factor $\times$ $(1+r)^t$

$$\text{Future value annuity factor} = \frac{(1+r)^t - 1}{r}$$

The future value annuity factor for the example above $= \dfrac{(1.08)^{35} - 1}{0.08} = 172.317$

The accumulated future value = $1,000 $\times$ 172.317 = $172,317.

<u>Growing perpetuity:</u> The present value of a perpetuity that has a stream of cash flows growing at a constant rate, g, is given by the following formula:

$$PV \quad \frac{C_1}{r-g} =, \text{ where } C_1 \text{ is the cash flow to be received one year from now.}$$

The formula works as long as r is greater than g.

Example: Central State University (refer to the example above) suggests that the endowment income should be annually adjusted for expected salary growth of 4%. How much should the initial endowment be if the first year's income is $250,000 and the estimated rate of return on the investments is 5%?

$$\text{Donation} = \$250,000/ (0.05-0.04) = \$25,000,000$$

<u>Growing annuity:</u> We can also get short cut formulas for the present value of an annuity that has a growing cash flow stream. Remember that an annuity is simply a truncated perpetuity and its present value is simply the difference between the present values of two perpetuities. Thus, present value of a growing annuity with cash flow of C and growth rate of g, can be written as:

$$PV \text{ of growing annuity} = \frac{C}{r-g}\left(1 - \frac{(1+g)^t}{(1+r)^t}\right)$$

APR and effective interest rates: Banks and other lending institutions are required to inform borrowers the *annual percentage rate (*APR) they are charging on loans. APR, however, does not reflect the effective cost of a loan if the bank charges interest rate more frequently than once a year. This is typically the case for most consumer loans. For example, when a bank charges 6 percent APR on a car loan, it will actually charge 0.5 percent interest (6%/12 = 0.5%) monthly. Computation of interest requires specifying the frequency of accounting for interest. A 6% annual rate of interest can mean different things depending on how frequently the interest is credited (or debited) to the account. If the interest is debited (or, credited if it is a deposit) monthly, you have compounding twelve a year. This gives you an effective interest rate of $(1 + r/12)^{12} - 1$. Thus for a 6% APR loan with monthly compounded interest, the effective rate = $1.005^{12} - 1 = 0.0617 = 6.17\%$. On the other hand, a 6% APR loan with interest debited semi-annually will have an effective rate of: $1.03^2 - 1 = 6.09\%$. Note that as the compounding frequency increases, the effective rate will be higher. The APR, however, is not affected by the compounding frequency.

In general, compounding m times a year gives $(1 + r/m)^m$ after 1 year. As *m* approaches infinity, $(1 + r/m)^m$ approaches $(2.71828)^r$, which is e^r. This is called continuous compounding. $1 invested at a continuously compounded rate of *r* grows to $\$e^r$ in 1 year and to $\$e^{rt}$ in t years.

Explanation of Formulas and Mathematical Expressions

Notations: C_0 = Investment (or Cost of) in the project = Cash flow at time 0
C_1 = Cash flow at time 1, r = Discount rate or opportunity cost of capital

Formulas:
$$PV = \frac{1}{1+r} \times C_1 = \text{Discount factor} \times \text{Cash flow}$$

$$\text{Discount Factor} = \frac{1}{1+r}$$

$$FV = C_0(1+r)$$

$$NPV = C_0 + \frac{1}{1+r} \times C_1$$

$$\text{Rate of return} = \frac{\text{Profit}}{\text{Investment}}$$

Investment Decision Rules:
   i.   Accept positive NPV investments.
   ii. Accept investments with rates of return higher than the opportunity cost or the hurdle rate.

Points to keep in mind:
   i. C_0 is the initial investment and is usually negative.
   ii.   Discount factor will be less than 1.
   iii. The discount rate should be a function of the riskiness of the cash flow.
   iv.   The higher the discount rate, lower the discount factor and lower the PV.

Formulas:
$$PV = \frac{1}{(1+r)^t} \times C_t = \text{Discount factor} \times \text{Cash flow}$$

$$\text{Discount Factor} = \frac{1}{(1+r)^t}$$

$$\text{Future value} = C_0(1+r)^t$$

Present value of a stream of cash flows:

$$PV = \sum_{t=1}^{n} \frac{C_t}{(1+r)^t}$$

PV of special types of cash flows:

$$\text{PV of a perpetuity} = \frac{C}{r};$$

$$\text{PV of an annuity} = C\left(\frac{1}{r} - \frac{1}{r(1+r)^t}\right)$$
$$= C(\text{Annuity Factor})$$

$$\text{Annuity factor} = \frac{1}{r} - \frac{1}{r(1+r)^t}$$

$$\text{PV of a growing perpetuity} = C_1/(r - g)$$

$$\text{Future value of an annuity} = C\left(\frac{(1+r)^t - 1}{r}\right)$$

$$\text{Present value of a growing annuity} = \frac{C}{r-g}\left(1 - \frac{(1+g)^t}{(1+r)^t}\right)$$

Using a Business Calculator: The business calculator has become a common tool of the business student and is very useful for solving all types of present value problems. While the details of operations differ for the different models, all business calculators share common features, which enable you to solve for the different parameters in typical TVM problems. In this guide, we provide calculator solutions using Texas Instruments' BA II Plus model in addition to solutions using formulas or the present value tables given in the text.

Most business calculators are designed to solve TVM problems in one of two formats: i) The annuity and a single future value format and ii) net present value of uneven cash flows format. The annuity format allows you to calculate any one of five parameters given the other four. The parameters are: present value (PV), future value (FV), payment (PMT), the number of years (periods), and the rate of return or interest rate (I). The NPV format allows direct calculation of NPV or the internal rate of return (IRR) for any stream of cash flows.

Example: What is the future value of $1,600 invested for 5 years in an account earning 6% annually?

Before you start work on the problem, please note that this is an annual compounding problem and therefore you have to set your calculator for annual compounding. This can be done as follows: Press 2nd, and P/Y. Enter 1 and hit the Enter key. Your calculator should now read P/Y = 1. Use the down arrow key (second key from the right on the top row) to see C/Y = 1. You have now set the calculator to do discounting and compounding for annual cash flows for which interest is compounded at annual intervals.

Solution: PV = $1,600, FV = Solve, PMT = 0, N = 5, I = 6; Answer: FV = −$2,141.16.

The calculator shows the answer as a negative number to indicate that the direction of cash flow will be the opposite of the initial flow; i.e. you deposit $1,600 now and you receive $2,141.16 five years later. In order to avoid any confusion, from now on, we will follow the convention of using positive numbers for cash inflows and negative numbers for outflows.

Example: What is the annual payment, which will repay a 3-year, $21,000 loan at an interest rate of 9%? Assume equal payments.

Solution: This is an annuity problem.
PV = $21,000, FV = 0, N = 3, I = 9; PMT = Solve = −$8,296.15

Example: You have invested $72,000 in a mutual fund earning 8% annual return. What will be the accumulated value of your account at the end of 12 years?

Solution: PV = −$72,000, PMT = 0, N = 12, I = 8, FV = Solve = +$181,308.25

Example: You have invested $72,000 in a mutual fund earning 8% annual return. How many years will it take to accumulate $500,000?

Solution: PV = −$72,000, FV = +500,000, PMT = 0, I = 8, N = Solve = 25.18 years.

Example: You have invested $72,000 in a mutual fund. If you want to accumulate $500,000 in 20 years, what annual rate of return should you earn?

Solution: PV = −$72,000, FV = +500,000, PMT = 0, N = 20, I = solve = 10.17%

Example: Simi Smith is saving for retirement by investing $2000 every year in a mutual fund that is expected to earn a return of 9% annually. If she invests this way for the next 25 years, how much would she have in the fund at the end of 25 years?

Solution: N = 25, I = 9%, PV = 0, PMT = −$2000, FV = solve = $169,401.79

WORKED EXAMPLES

1. Caroline Yang, a software engineer has the opportunity to invest in two projects. Details are given in the table below.

Project	Description	Investment	Payback
A	Developing a simple software package for a local bank.	$120,000	$144,000
B	Developing a complex software package for an online travel services company. The payment for the project will be received in the form of stocks in the company.	$120,000	$200,000

a. Calculate the rate of return on each investment.
b. If the opportunity cost or the hurdle rate for the projects is 15%, calculate the NPV for the projects.
c. Calculate the NPV if the opportunity cost is 25%.
d. Do you think it is correct to discount the two project cash flows with the same hurdle rate?
e. How would you determine the right hurdle rate or opportunity cost for each project?
f. Ms. Yang does not have all the money needed to buy the resources needed for the projects. Does that change her decision on the projects?

SOLUTION

a. Rate of Return on Project A = ($144,000 − $120,000)/$120,000 = 20%
   Rate of Return on Project B = ($200,000 − $120,000)/$120,000 = 66.7%

b. NPV of project A = −$120,000 + ($144,400/1.15) = $5,217.39
   NPV of project B = −$120,000 + ($200,000/1.15) = $53,913.04

c. NPV of project A = −$120,000 + ($144,000/1.25) = − $4,800
   NPV of project B = −$120,000 + ($200,000/1.25) = $40,000

d. The two projects have very different risk characteristics. Project B is more risky and should have a higher hurdle rate.

e. For project A, the risk is nearly identical to the local bank's debt. For project B, the risk is similar to that of investing in the stocks of companies in online travel services business.

f. Yang should be able to raise the money needed to invest in the project through the capital market.

2. Rose Perez invests $6,500 in a mutual fund that is expected to earn an annual return of 9%. How much will Rose have in the account at the end of 5 years?

SOLUTION: PV = −$6,500, PMT = 0, N = 5, I = 9, FV = solve = +$10,001.06

3. Jane Duck wants to create an endowment income of $12,000 a year for her alma mater, but proposes that the first payment be made 3 years from now. If she can earn a return of 6% on her investments, how much should she invest now?

SOLUTION

The present value of the perpetuity will be $12,000/0.06 = $200,000. This amount has to be invested by the end of 2 years so that the first payment of $12,000 will be received at the end of 3 years. FV = +$200,000, PMT = 0, N = 2, I = 6, PV = solve = $177,999.29

4. Josh Hyman borrows $125,000 to buy his home. The loan carries an annual interest of 9% and requires 180 equal monthly payments. Calculate the monthly payment. Construct an amortization table showing the first and the last two payments.

SOLUTION

PV = Loan amount = +$125,000; FV = 0, N = 180, I = 9/12 = 0.75, PMT = Solve = −$1,267.83

Amortization Table

Month	Beginning balance	Interest paid	Principal paid	Ending balance
1	$125,000.00	$937.50	$330.33	$124,669.67
2	$124,669.67	$935.02	$332.81	$124,336.86
...	.....	.....	.....	.....
179	$2,507.43	$18.80	$1,249.03	$1,258.40
180	$1,258.40	$9.43	$1,258.40	$0.00

Note that the interest + principal paid = monthly payment of $1,267.83. The BA II Plus calculator has an Amortization worksheet, which will help you complete the amortization table. Once you compute the payment using the TVM worksheet, hit 2nd, Amort; then enter for P1 = 1, P2 = 1. Use the arrow key to go down the worksheet to read values for ending balance, principal paid, and interest paid. Repeat the steps to complete the table. You should not change any of the values in the TVM worksheet while using the Amort worksheet.

Note that the interest rate was set the monthly rate. Alternately, you can do monthly compounding and monthly payment problems by setting the P/Y = 12, C/Y = 12 and entering the annual interest value for I. The calculator set-up would be as follows:
2nd, P/Y; P/Y = 12, 2nd, QUIT; PV = +$125,000; FV = 0, N = 180, I = 9, PMT = Solve = −$1,267.83.

CHAPTER SUMMARY

The chapter introduces the basic concepts relating to time value of money and valuation of assets. Many corporate assets are typically not traded in markets, and therefore need to be valued using present values of cash flows generated by these assets. Value of an asset is the present value of the cash flows produced by the asset. The chapter also introduces two equivalent rules for investment decisions: the NPV rule and the rate of return rule. NPV rule requires that you invest in projects that have positive NPV. The rate of return rule requires investment in projects, which have rate of return higher than the opportunity cost of capital. The chapter further describes several techniques for calculation of present values of different streams of cash flows. Shortcuts and formulas are developed for special streams of cash flows such as perpetuity, annuity, growing perpetuity and growing annuity. These have wide applications in personal and corporate finance. The chapter also discusses the annual percentage rate or APR and the impact of compounding frequencies on the effective rate paid.

LIST OF TERMS

Amortization
Annual percentage rate (APR)
Annuity

Continuously compounded rate of interest
Discount factor
Discount rate
Effective annual rate
Hurdle rate
Net present value
Opportunity cost
Perpetuity
Present value
Rate of return

EXERCISES

Fill-in Questions

1. Present value of a cash flow to be received one year from now will _____ when the discount rate increases.

2. If the discount rate is 12%, the discount factor for a cash flow received one year from now will be _____.

3. The NPV rule for investment requires managers to invest only in projects that have _____ NPV.

4. Managers should invest in projects with rates of return _____ than the opportunity cost of capital.

5. A future cash flow is multiplied by the _____ to give its present value.

6. The _____ of an asset is the difference between the PV of its cash flows and its cost.

7. The expected return from comparable investments in the securities markets gives the _____ _____ for the project.

8. Higher risk projects will have _____ opportunity cost of capital.

9. The present value of a future cash flow is calculated by discounting it at the appropriate _____.

10. A constant stream of cash flows for a limited number of years coming at regular intervals is called a (an) _____.

11. A constant stream of cash flows that go on forever is called a _____.

Problems

1. You can buy a 1-year T-bill for $989 now. The bill will pay $1,000 one year from now. What is your rate of return on this investment?

2. Vinita Mercer, a professional beach volleyball player will be paid $15,000,000 by her major league team. She will be paid $5,000,000 now and $10,000,000 1 year from now. Using a discount rate of 12%, calculate the PV of Mercer's pay.

3. Calculate the discount factors for the following discount rates: (a) 20%, (b) 30%, and (c) 100%.

4. June Wayne is planning to buy an old apartment building and modernize it into a new condo complex of six condominiums. She can buy the building for $400,000 and the cost of modernizing is estimated to be $350,000. The project will be completed in one year and each condominium is expected to sell for $200,000. Calculate: (a) the expected rate of return on the project, (b) PV of the cash flows from the sale of the condos, and (c) the NPV of the project. Assume the opportunity cost for the project to be 20%.

5. John Miser has $20,000 to invest. He is considering two projects. Project A requires an investment of $10,000 and will pay $11,000 after one year. Project B also requires $10,000 but will pay only $10,700 after one year. What should Mr. Miser do if his opportunity cost of capital is: (a) 6%, (b) 9%, or (c) 12%?

6. Imagine an economy in which there are just three individuals: A, B, and C. Each has some money to invest and a number of possible investment projects, each of which would require $1,000. A has $2,000 to invest and two projects, each with 11% return. B has $1,000 to invest and has projects yielding 11% and 7%. C has $1,000 to invest and projects offering 15% and 12% returns. (a) What projects will be undertaken if there is no lending or borrowing? (b) If they do borrow from and lend to each other, what projects will be undertaken and what will the interest rates be?

7. ABC Corp. has opportunities to invest in three projects with potential payoffs next year linked to the state of the economy. Each project requires an investment of $3 million. The payoffs for different states of the economy are given below:

Project	State of the Economy and Project Payoffs			Hurdle Rate
	Recession	Normal	Boom	
A	$2 million	$4 million	$6 million	20%
B	$3 million	$3.5 million	$4 million	10%
C	$1.5 million	$4 million	$6.5 million	35%

Assume that each state of the economy has equal chances of occurring. Calculate the expected cash flows next year, the rate of return, and the NPV for each project. Which project(s) should be accepted by the company?

8. a. Calculate the NPV and rate of return for each of the investments given in the table below. Assume that the opportunity cost of capital to be 15% for all the investments.

   b. It is learned that all four projects require the use of a team of engineers who are very busy and will be available to work on only one of the four projects. In other words, you can choose only one of the four projects. Which one will you choose?

Table for problem 8

Project	Initial Cash Flow	Cash Flow in Year 1
A	−$6,000	$12,000
B	−$8,000	$12,000
C	−$16,000	$24,000
D	−$21,000	$30,000

9. Here are some investments earning different interest rates and invested for different periods. Calculate the accumulated values at the investment period for each one.
   a. $1,000 invested for 4 years at 8% interest.
   b. $1,000 invested for 8 years at 9%.
   c. $250 invested for 5 years at 7%
   d. $250 invested for 10 years at 7%.

10. How long will it take to double $1,000 invested at (a) 3%, (b) 5%, (c) 10%, (d) 12%, or (e) 15%?

11. An investment of $10,000 will produce income of $2,500 a year for 5 years. Calculate its NPV if the discount rate is 9%.

12. An investment costing $4,000 will produce cash flows of $1,500 in year 1, $1,200 in year 2, and $2,000 in year 3. Calculate its net present value at (a) 0%, (b) 6%, and (c) 12%.

13. Mary Jane has already saved $10,000 in a mutual fund account and expects to save an additional $9,000 for each of the next 2 years. She expects to pay $12,000 each at the end of 2 years and 3 years for her son's college education. How much can she afford to spend now on a vacation if she expects to earn (a) 7% and (b) 10%?

14. I will receive $4,000 in 1 year's time and annually thereafter in perpetuity from my late uncle's estate. What is the value of this perpetuity at an interest rate of (a) 8% and (b) 10%?

15. How much is the previous perpetuity worth if it begins in 5 years' time instead of one year? Assume an interest rate of 8%.

16. I now discover that my uncle's will provides that I receive $4,000 in 1 year's time and that this amount is to be increased annually at a rate of 6%. What is the present value of this growing stream of income at an interest rate of (a) 8% and (b) 10%?

17. Bollywood Inc. is expected to pay a dividend of $4 next year. The dividends are expected to grow at a constant rate of 8%. If the shareholders require a return of 12%, what will be the likely price of the stock?

18. I took a car loan of $20,000 from my credit union. The loan carries an annual interest rate of 6% and is to be repaid in 30 equal monthly payments. Calculate the monthly payment.

19. I am saving for the down payment needed to buy a house. I just invested $1,000 and I expect to save a further $1,000 at the end of each of the next six years. If I invest my savings at 12% interest, how much will I have at the end of 6 years?

20. A store offers the following credit terms on a color television set priced at $320: only $20 down and 18 monthly payments of $20. (a) Is this an attractive proposition if I can borrow at 1% per month? (b) What monthly interest rate is being charged? (c) What annual rate is being charged?

21. How much does $1,000 grow to at continuously compounded interest when invested for (a) 9 years at 6% and (b) 6 years at 9%?

22. Can you derive the formula for the future value of growing annuity whose initial payment of C is growing at the rate of g; interest rate is r. Assume t periods.

23. John wants to save for his 6-year-old daughter's college education. He believes he has 12 years to accumulate the needed $200,000. What is the annual amount he needs to invest in a mutual fund that would give her an annual return of 8%?

24. Refer to problem 23. If John decides to increase his annual investment by 5% each year, what would be his initial investment?

25. What annually compounded rate is equivalent to an interest rate of 12% compounded: (a) semi-annually, (b) quarterly, (c) monthly, (d) weekly (or 52 times a year), (e) daily (365 times a year), and (f) continuously?

Essay Questions

1. Explain the NPV and rate of return rules for investment decisions.

ANSWERS TO EXERCISES

Fill-in Questions

1. Decrease
2. $1/1.12 = 0.893$
3. Positive
4. Greater
5. Discount factor
6. NPV
7. Opportunity cost
8. Higher
9. Discount rate
10. Annuity
11. Perpetuity

Problems

1. ($1,000 − $989)/$989 = 1.11%

2. $5,000,000 + PV of $10,000,000 received 1 year from now =
   $5,000,000 + $10,000,000/1.12 = $13,928,571.43

3. (a) $1/1.2 = 0.833$ (b) $1/1.3 = 0.769$ (c) $1/2 = 0.5$

4. a. Revenue from the sale of condos = 6 × $200,000 = $1,200,000
       Rate of return = Profit/Cost; Profit = $1,200,000 − $750,000 = $450,000
       Cost = $750,000; Rate of return = $450,000/$750,000 = 60%

   b. PV of cash flows = $1,200,000/1.20 = $1,000,000

   c. NPV = $1,000,000 − $750,000 = $250,000

5. Calculate the NPVs at each cost of capital for both projects.
   a. NPV of project A at 6%   = ($11,000/1.06) − $10,000 = $377.36
      NPV of project B at 6%   = ($10,700/1.06) − $10,000 = $94.34
      Accept both projects.

   b. NPV of project A at 9%   = ($11,000/1.09) − $10,000 = $91.74
      NPV of project B at 9%   = ($10,700/1.09) − $10,000 = −$183.49
      Accept A, reject B.

   c. NPV of project A at 12%   = ($11,000/1.12) − $10,000 = −$178.57
      NPV of project B at 12%   = ($10,700/1.12) − $10,000 = −$446.43
      Reject both projects.

6. a. In the absence of lending and borrowing, A will undertake the two projects with 11% return, B will undertake the project with 11% return and C will undertake the 15% project.

    b. C will borrow from either A or B to undertake the 12% project in addition to the 15% project. One of the 11% projects will be dropped. The rate of interest will be 11%.

7. Project A: Expected cash flow next year = ($2 m + $4 m + $6 m)/3 = $4 m
              Rate of return = ($4 m − $3 m)/$3 m = 33.33%
              PV of cash flow = $4 m/1.20 = $3.333; NPV = $0.333 m

    Project B: Expected cash flow next year = ($3 m + $3.5 m + $4 m)/3 = $3.5 m
              Rate of return = ($3.5 m − $3 m)/$3 m = 16.67%
              PV of cash flow = $3.5 m/1.10 = $3.182; NPV = $0.182 m

    Project C: Expected cash flow next year = ($1.5 m + $4 m + $6.5 m)/3 = $4 m
              Rate of return = ($4 m − $3 m)/$3 m = 33.33%
              PV of cash flow = $4 m/1.35 = $2.963; NPV = −$0.037 m

    Accept projects A and B. Reject C.

8. a. Project A:
        NPV = $12,000/1.15 − $6,000 = $4,434.78,
        Rate of return = ($12,000−$6,000)/$6,000 = 100%

        Project B:
        NPV = $12,000/1.15 − $8,000 = $2,434.78,
        Rate of return = ($12,000−$8,000)/$8,000 = 50%

        Project C:
        NPV = $24,000/1.15 − $16,000 = $4,869.57
        Rate of return = ($24,000−$16,000)/$16,000 = 50%

        Project D:
        NPV = $30,000/1.15 − $21,000 = $5,086.96
        Rate of return = ($30,000−$21,000)/$21,000 = 42.9%

        All four projects are good investments.

    b. Since only one of the four projects can be chosen, the right decision will be to choose the project with the highest NPV. Choose Project D. This is an example where the NPV rule and the rate of return rule give different decisions.

9.

	N	I	PV	PMT	FV = Solve
			Calculator solutions		
A	4 years	8%	−1000	0	1360.49
B	8 years	9%	−1000	0	1992.56
C	5 years	7%	−250	0	350.64
D	10 years	7%	−250	0	491.79

10. $PV = \$1,000$, $FV = -\$2,000$, $PMT = 0$, (a) $I = 3$, $N =$ solve $= 23.45$ years; (b) $I = 5$, $N =$ solve $= 14.21$ years; (c) $I = 10$, $N =$ solve $= 7.27$ years; (d) $I = 12$, $N =$ solve $= 6.12$ years; and (e) $I = 15$, $N =$ solve $= 4.96$ years.

11. You can find the present value of the cash inflows, which are in the form of an annuity. Then, subtract the initial investment of $10,000.
$N = 5$, $I = 9$, $PMT = -\$2,500$, $FV = 0$, $PV =$ solve $= \$9,724.13$
$NPV = -\$10,000 + \$9,724.13 = -\$275.87$

12. This problem can be most easily solved using the calculator's cash flow work sheet and the NPV function. Enter the cash flows as follows:
    $CF_0 = -\$4,000$ (Initial cash flow),
    $CO_1 = \$1,500$, $FO_1 = 1$ (This indicates that this cash flow occurs only once)
    $CO_2 = \$1,200$, $FO_2 = 1$;
    $CO_3 = \$2,000$, $FO_3 = 1$
Once the cash flow data are entered, you proceed to the NPV function work sheet by pressing the NPV key. Entering the appropriate values for I (discount rate), and going down the work sheet using the down arrow key, you can compute the NPVs.
(a) $I = 0$, $NPV = \$700$; (b) $I = 6$, $NPV = \$162.33$; and (c) $I = 12$, $NPV = -\$280.52$

13. The amount she can afford to spend on her vacation is the difference between the present values of her savings and the college education costs. First calculate the present value of Mary Jane's savings for the next two years (an annuity with two payments) and add this to her current savings of $10,000.

   a. PV of the 2 year annuity; $N = 2$, $I = 7$, $PMT = -\$9,000$, $FV = 0$, $PV =$ Solve $= \$16,272.16$
   Total PV of savings $= \$16,272.16 + \$10,000 = \$26,272.16$.
   PV of education costs:
   $12,000 at the end of 2 years: $N = 2$, $I = 7$, $PMT = 0$, $FV = -\$12,000$, $PV =$ Solve $= \$10,481.26$

   $12,000 at the end of 3 years: $N = 3$, $I = 7$, $PMT = 0$, $FV = -\$12,000$, $PV =$ Solve $= \$9,795.57$
   Total PV of education costs $= \$10,481.26 + \$9,795.57 = \$20,276.83$
   Amount she can spend on vacation $= \$26,272.16 - \$20,276.83 = \$5,995.33$

b. PV of the 2 year annuity; N = 2, I = 10, PMT = −$9,000, FV = 0, PV = Solve = $15,619.83

Total PV of savings = $15,619.83 + $10,000 = $25,619.83

PV of education costs:

$12,000 at the end of 2 years − N = 2, I = 10, PMT = 0, FV = −$12,000, PV = Solve = $9,917.36

$12,000 at the end of 3 years − N = 3, I = 10, PMT = 0, FV = −$12,000, PV = Solve = $9,015.78. Total PV of education costs = $9,917.36 + $9,015.78 = $18,933.13

Amount she can spend on vacation = $25,619.83 − $18,933.13 = $6,686.70

14. a. PV of perpetuity = C/r = $4,000/0.08 = $50,000
    b. PV of perpetuity = $4,000/0.10 = $40,000

15. N = 5, I = 8%, PV = Solve, PMT = 0, FV = $50,000; PV = $34,029.16

16. a. This is a growing perpetuity. PC = C/(r − g) = $4,000/(0.08 − 0.06) = $200,000
    b. If r = 10%, PV = $4,000/(0.1−0.06) = $100,000

17. The stock can be valued as a growing perpetuity. Price = $4/(0.12 − 0.08) = $100

18. N = 30, I = 0.5, PV = $20,000, FV = 0, PMT = solve = −$719.58.

19. See this as a six-year annuity plus an initial $1,000.
    N = 6, I = 12, PV = −$1,000, PMT = −$1,000, FV = solve = $10,089.01

20. a. You are taking a loan of $320−$20 = $300.
    Your interest rate is 1% per month, your payment will be:
    N = 18, I = 1%, PV = $300, PMT = Solve = $18.29. Since you are required to pay more than this amount, this is not an attractive proposition.

    b. For payment of $20/month, the interest is:
    N = 18, I = Solve, PV = $300, PMT = $20; I = 1.99%.
    So the effective interest being charged is 1.99%/month.
    Effective annual rate = $(1.0199)^{12} - 1 = 26.67\%$.

21. a. and b. The answers for both parts are the same because the product of interest rate (r) and number of years (t) is the same and the future value factor for continuous compounding is given by the formula e^{rt}. $= 2.7183^{0.54} = 1.716$; FV = $1,000 × 1.716 = $1,716.

22. $$FV = \frac{C}{r - g} \left((1 + r)^t - (1 + g)^t \right)$$

23. This can be solved easily with the calculator as follows:
    N = 12, I = 8, PV = 0, FV = $200,000, PMT = solve = −$10,539

24. Future value factor for a growing annuity (see solution to problem 22 above) is:

$$((1 + r)^t - (1 + g)^t)/(r - g) = ((1.08)^{12} - (1.05)^{12})/(0.08 - 0.05) = 24.0771$$

The initial investment would be = $200,000/24.0771 = $8,306.64

25. The equivalent annually compounded rate or the effective annual rate (EAR) is given by the formula $(1 + i/m)^m - 1$, where i is the nominal annual rate or the annual percentage rate (APR) and m is the frequency of compounding. The EAR for the different compounding frequencies is:

   a. $m = 2$, EAR = 12.36%
   b. $m = 4$, EAR = 12.5509%
   c. $m = 12$, EAR = 12.6825%
   d. $m = 52$, EAR = 12.7341%
   e. $m = 365$, EAR = 12.7475%
   f. EAR = $e^{0.12} - 1 = 0.127497 = 12.7497\%$.

3

Valuing Bonds

INTRODUCTION

This chapter applies the lessons learned from the last chapter to the valuation of bonds. The value of a bond, like that of any financial asset, is simply the present value of the cash flows produced by the bond discounted at the appropriate required rate of return. The chapter then proceeds to analyze the relationship between bond prices and interest rate changes and explain the concepts of duration and modified duration, which can be used to understand the changes in bond prices caused by changes in interest rate. The chapter also explains the term structure and the relationship between nominal rates and real interest rates. Most of the discussions in the chapter are carried out using government bonds, which are assumed to be free of default risk. The last section introduces corporate bonds, which yield higher returns because of the risk of default and also because they are less liquid than government debt.

While the chapter is unlikely to make an expert bond trader, it provides answers to some vexing questions on interest rates, debt values and their changes from time to time. Financial managers have to deal with the valuation of debt at some point or other and it is essential that they understand the basic theoretical principles, which explain the relationship among term structure, risk structure, and debt values.

KEY CONCEPTS IN THE CHAPTER

Valuation of Bonds: Bonds are debt instruments issued by corporations and governments. They usually carry regular interest payments, called coupons, and have a stated term or maturity. When you invest in a bond, you receive yearly (or more commonly half-yearly in the US) coupon payments. At the end of the term of the bond, you will receive the principal or face value of the bond. If we know the required rate of return for the investment in the bond, we can calculate the present value of these payments. The price of the bond should equal the total present value of all the coupon payments and the face value payment. For example, if 5% return is required on a 3-year 4% coupon bond with a face value of $1000, the price will equal:

$$PV = \frac{40}{1.05} + \frac{40}{1.05^2} + \frac{1040}{1.05^3} = \$972.77$$

Conversely, if we know the price, we can compute the return earned on the bond investment. This return is the *yield to maturity* for the bond or the internal rate of return (discussed in Chapter 5) for the investment in the bond. Note that while most bonds in Europe have annual coupon payments, the bonds issued in the U.S, typically have semi-annual coupons and the yield and price calculations will have to be adjusted to reflect this fact.

Interest Rates, Bond Prices, Duration and Volatility: Bond prices and interest rates are inversely related. When interest rates go up, bond prices go down. The prices of long-term bonds vary more than short-term bonds. In other words, long-term bonds are more sensitive to interest rate changes than the short-term bonds. *Duration* and *modified duration* (also known as *volatility)* are two useful measures, which enable us to formalize the relationship between bond prices and changes in interest rates. Duration is the average time for the total cash flow to be realized from an asset, such as a bond. It is actually a weighted average, where the time to each cash flow is weighted by the ratio of its present value to the total value of the bond. The other statistic, modified duration (volatility) is easily obtained from duration. In fact, it is just duration discounted by one time period. Volatility measures the sensitivity of the asset price (in percent) to a (unit) change in its yield. Both of these measures are extremely important for understanding the riskiness of bonds and portfolios containing bonds.

$$\text{Duration} = \frac{1 \times PV(C_1)}{V} + \frac{2 \times PV(C_2)}{V} + \ldots + \frac{i \times PV(C_i)}{V} + \ldots.$$

Where, V is the total value of the bond.

$$\text{Modified duration} = \frac{\text{Duration}}{1 + \text{yield}}$$

Modified duration and duration are useful practical measures, which help in managing interest rate risk. The risk management techniques use the properties of duration and try to match the duration of their asset and liability portfolios. Note that the changes in bond prices are given by the following relationship:

$$\text{Change in bond price} = \text{Modified duration} \times \text{change in interest rates}$$

Thus, if modified duration is 3.5 and interest rate fall by 0.5 percent, the bond price will rise by 3.5×0.5, or 1.75 percent. This relationship is very useful in understanding changes in bond values. It should be mentioned that the relationship holds across different maturities only when the yield curve makes parallel shift. That is, interest rate changes are same at all maturities. In practice, changes in short-term interest rates and long-term rates are not always same and therefore the one-factor model may explain only part of the changes in bond values.

Spot Rates, Term Structure, and Yield to Maturity: The spot rate is the rate of interest obtainable on a bond at the present time period. The series of spot rates for bonds of different maturities results in a term structure of interest rates. Typically, the term structure is upward sloping, with long-term rates higher than short-term rates. The term structure is a series of spot rates $r_1, r_2, \ldots r_i, \ldots$ for different maturities. If $C_1, C_2, \ldots C_i$ are the cash flows received from a bond investment, the value of the bond is:

$$PV = \frac{C_1}{(1 + r_1)} + \frac{C_2}{(1 + r_2)^2} + \ldots \frac{C_i}{(1 + r_i)^i} + \ldots,$$

Where, r_i is the spot rate for the "*i*th" year.

This is how each bond is valued in the market. However, we use the yield to maturity as a summary measure. The PV of a bond can be expressed by the following equation:

$$PV = \frac{C_1}{(1+y)} + \frac{C_2}{(1+y)^2} + \ldots \frac{C_i}{(1+y)^i} + \ldots$$

Where, y = yield to maturity. The yield to maturity is an internal rate of return and unambiguous and easy to calculate. It is, however, an oversimplification of the reality in that it assumes that yield to maturity does not change across different terms (i.e. $r_1 = r_2 = r_3$) and a constant reinvestment rate of return. It is important to note that yield to maturity does not determine price; it is vice versa.

The term structure of government bonds can be estimated using a series of zero coupon "strips". This is the yield curve you see in the Wall Street Journal every day. This provides the spot rates for different maturities.

Explaining the Term Structure: The term structure is not constant. While most of the times, the yield curve is up-ward sloping, occasionally; you find short-term rates to be higher than long-term rates. The term structure shows not only the spot rates for different maturities ($r_1, r_2, r_3, \ldots$), it also implies one-period rates of returns or *forward* interest rates for different points in time. For example, if r_1 and r_2 are the spot rates for 1-year and 2-year maturity, then the implied forward rate for year 2, $f_2 = (1+r_2)^2/(1+r_1) - 1$. One theory that attempts to explain the term structure is the *expectations* theory, which postulates that the forward rate must equal expected future spot rate. In other words, an investor interested in a two-year investment can get the same return investing either in a two-year bond or a one-year debt now and followed by another one-year debt next year. Expectations theory suggests that an upward sloping yield curve is the result of expected higher interest rates in the future. Empirical support for the expectations theory is limited and the historic returns on long-term Treasury bonds have been consistently higher than the returns on short-term T-bills. Expectations theory implies risk neutral investors, who would treat short-term and long-term investments same.

It appears, though, that investors want higher returns or a premium for holding long-term bonds. This premium is the difference between forward rates and expected future spot rates. The explanations for these premiums are based on either the uncertainty associated with holding long-term debt or the presence of inflation. Investors might consider long-term bonds more risky because of the term itself. Alternately, they may feel that the presence of inflation adds extra uncertainty about the real returns from long-term bonds and thus making long-term bonds more risky compared to short-term investments. Note that none of these explanations is totally satisfactory. Term structure analysis is static; it catches a slice of time and fixes interest rates of like kind and quality bonds.

Real and Nominal Interest Rates: Nominal interest rates and cash flows measure what happens in ordinary or current dollar units. Real rates and cash flows measure what happens in units of purchasing power. The nominal or the *money* rate of interest is what you see given in the business pages and quoted for your mortgage or car loans. Most debt securities promise a fixed nominal interest rate. The exception is the US government issues Treasury Inflation Protected Securities (TIPS), which promise real returns. Historically, while nominal rates have varied a lot the real rates are more stable and have averaged between 1 and 2% for the last 50 years. This is true for the US as well as most other industrialized countries.

The relationship between real and nominal cash flows is given by the equation:

$$\text{Real cash flow} = \text{Nominal cash flow}/(1+\text{inflation rate})$$

The relationship between real rate and nominal rate is captured by the following equation known as the Fisher equation:

$$1 + r_{nominal} = (1 + r_{real})(1 + \text{inflation rate})$$

An approximate form of this relationship is written as $r_{nominal} = r_{real} + \text{inflation rate}$

For example, if the nominal interest rate is 5% and inflation rate is 3%, the real rate is $(1.05/1.03) - 1 = 1.94\%$. Using the approximate relationship, the answer is 2%.

It follows that a change in the expected inflation rate will cause the same change in the money rate or *nominal interest rate.* Critics of Fisher's theory argue that real rates are affected by inflation rates. Historically, real rates have changed over time. Part of the problem is Fisher's theory is in terms of expected inflation. Unfortunately, expected inflation and hence, real rates are not observable. What is observed is the difference between nominal rates and actual inflation. Empirical studies indicate that inflation expectations have been the principal causes of nominal interest rate changes. Fisher's theory appears to hold in broad approximation. Remember that the real rate is an expected rate. The actual realized real rates may be different from what you expected to get when you bought a T-bill or some other investment. Also, the real rates have varied over time.

Corporate Bonds and Risk of Default: Borrowers other than the US Federal government (or the respective governments in other countries) also issue debt in the form of bonds. The issuers include corporations as well as state and local authorities. These bonds differ from the treasury bonds in one fundamental aspect – they have some risk of default. Therefore, interest rates differ not only across maturities, but also across borrowers. Bonds have market-related risks and firm-specific default risks. When the value of bonds and the term structure of interest rates are determined, default risk must also be considered. The threat of default adds uncertainty to the payments expected from the bond investment. The *expected cash flow* from a risky bond is less than the *promised cash flow* and the *expected yield* will be less than the *promised yield.* In practical terms, investors would demand higher returns on a bond that has the risk of default. Note that the yield to maturity of a risky bond does not represent its *expected yield* but only the promised yield. The expected yield will be less because of the default risk. It should be mentioned that the spread between treasury bonds and corporate bonds of same maturity is also affected by the lower liquidity of the latter. In general, higher the default risk, lower the liquidity.

Bond Ratings: Bond ratings attempt to measure the risk of default. Bond ratings are assigned by the rating agencies based on their analysis and judgment of the firm's financial and business prospects and probable default. Moody's, Standard and Poor, and Fitch are the well-known rating agencies. The ratings range from the highest rated AAA (Aaa by Moody's) to the lowly C for bonds with high probability of default. Bond ratings generally reflect the probability of default quite well and can be seen as a proxy for the default risk. Investment grade bonds are bonds rated BBB by Standard and Poor or Baa by Moody's. Bonds rated less than these are termed high-yield or *junk bonds*. Since the 1980s there is a wider acceptance of bond issues with ratings lower than investment grade and this has helped many young, growing and risky companies raise debt capital to finance their growth or acquisitions.

Floating rate and Convertible Bonds: Corporate bonds, unlike treasury bonds, have a lot more variety in the details of the terms of issue. While most corporate bonds come with specified terms to maturity and coupon rates they also often offer special features. The two special types of bonds discussed in this chapter are *floating rate bonds* and *convertible bonds*. Floating rate bonds have their coupon payments reset periodically (say, annually) to reflect changes in market interest rates. For example, the coupon rate might be specified as treasury rate plus fixed margin, say, 2%. Convertible bonds offer the bond holders an option to receive common shares of the firm in exchange for the face value of the bond. The lenders would be willing to take a lower coupon payment in exchange for this valuable option. Chapters 23 and 24 describe these and other types of corporate bonds in detail.

WORKED EXAMPLES

1. What is the price of a 10-year, 5.5% coupon bond with a $1,000 face value if investors require a 4.5% return? What is its yield to maturity if its price is $960? Assume annual coupon payments.

SOLUTION

PMT = Coupon payment = $55, FV = Face value = $1,000, N = 10, I = 4.5,
PV = Price = Solve = −$1,079.13

Yield to maturity for a price of $960: PV = −$960, FV = +$1,000, PMT = +$55, N = 10,
I = Yield to maturity = solve = 6.04%

2. Calculate the yield to maturity on a 14-year bond carrying a coupon rate of 5%. Assume par value of $1,000, the interest is payable annually and the bond is selling at 97.

SOLUTION

Here is the BA-II Plus calculator solution:
N = Number of coupons = 14, I = yield to maturity = solve, PV = price of the bond = −$970,
PMT = coupon payments = $50, FV = principal paid at maturity = $1,000,
I = yield to maturity = 5.31%

3. Calculate the duration and modified duration of an 8%, 5-year Treasury bond whose yield to maturity is 4%.

SOLUTION

Duration = $[1 \times PV(C_1)/V] + [2 \times PV(C_2)/V] + [3 \times PV(C_3)/V] + \ldots\ldots$
Yield = 4%, Coupon = 8.00%

Year	C_t	PV(C_t) at 4%	Proportion of Total Value = PV(C_t)/V	Proportion of Value × Time = t × PV(C_t)/V
1	80	76.92	0.0653	0.0653
2	80	73.96	0.0628	0.1256
3	80	71.12	0.0604	0.1812
4	80	63.38	0.0580	0.2320
5	1080	887.68	0.7535	3.7675
Total	1,400	1178.06	1.000	4.3716

Duration = 4.3716 years, Modified duration = 4.3716/1.04 = 4.2035%

4. What is the impact of a 0.5 percentage point increase and decrease in interest rates on the present value of the bond in problem 3 above? Compute their volatility and compare with what you would have estimated from their duration.

SOLUTION

The yields are now 3.5% or 4.5%. The results of the computations are as follows:

	New Price	% Change
Yield falls to 3.5	1,203.17	2.13
Yield rises to 4.5	1,153.65	−2.08
Difference	49.52	4.21

The volatility calculated from the duration = 4.3716/1.04 = 4.2035%

5. Determine the better financial strategy when confronted with a 2-year spot rate of 4.5%, a 1-year spot rate of 4%, and an expected spot rate on 1-year bonds 1 year from now of 5%. Assume you do not need your money for 2 years and are not bothered by risk.

SOLUTION

To find the answer, you want to know the expected return of each strategy. The setup is:

$$\$1,000(1 + r_1)[1 + E(_1r_2)] \text{ compared with } \$1,000(1 + r_2)^2$$

where:

r_1 = 1-year spot rate

$E(_1r_2)$ = expected spot rate on 1-year bonds 1 year from now

r_2 = 2-year spot rate

Substituting the values above, we obtain:

$\$1,000(1 + 0.04)(1 + 0.05)$	compared with	$\$1,000(1 + 0.045)^2$
$\$1,000(1.04)(1.05)$	compared with	$\$1,000(1.045)^2$
$\$1,000(1.092)$	compared with	$\$1,000(1.092025)$
$\$1,092.00$	compared with	$\$1,092.25$

For all practical purposes, there is no difference between the two outcomes; therefore, you would be indifferent about this investment.

If you wish to lock in the final outcome of $1,092, say, because of your queasiness about the expected 1-year spot rate, choose the 4.5%, 2-year spot rate. You should also note that the implied forward rate is:

$$(1 + r_2)^2 = (1 + r_i)(1 + f_2)$$

where f_2 is the implied forward rate. Substituting the above values, we obtain:

$$(1 + 0.045)^2 = (1 + 0.04)(1 + f_2)$$
$$(1.045)^2 = (1.04)(1 + f_2)$$
$$1.09025 = 1.04(1 + f_2)$$
$$f_2 = 1.09025/1.04 = 5.0024\%$$

As expected, the implicit forward rate is almost exactly equal to the expected future spot rate, again indicating a condition of relative indifference.

2. Find the real rate of interest, given that the nominal rate is 5% and the inflation rate is 2.5%.

SOLUTION

The solution is obtained by using the formula:

$$1 + r_{money} = (1 + r_{real})(1 + i)$$

where

r_{money} = nominal or money rate of interest

r_{real} = real rate of interest

i = inflation rate

Substituting in the equation, we obtain: $1 + 0.05 = (1 + r_{real})(1 + 0.025)$

We then solve for r_{real}:

$$1 + r_{real} = (1 + r_{money})/(1 + i) = 1.05/1.025 = 1.0388$$
$$r_{real} = 0.0244 = 2.44\%$$

One can also use the approximate relationship: Nominal rate = real rate + inflation rate. This would give a value for real rate of: $5\% - 2.5\% = 2.5\%$.

CHAPTER SUMMARY

This chapter applies the principles of discounted cash flow to value bonds. Valuation of bonds is a straight-forward exercise of finding the present value of its coupon payments and the principal received at the maturity. Bond values reflect present values of the cash flows discounted by the series of spot rates over the bond's maturity. For convenience, the yield to maturity is used as a summary measure of the rate of return. It is important to understand that the yield to maturity is derived from the price of the bond and not the other way around. Duration and modified duration (volatility) are useful measures of the sensitivity of a bond's value to changes in interest rates.

The chapter also attempts to explain the term structure using the expectations theory as the starting point. The expectations theory ignores the possibility of risk and lacks convincing empirical support. There appears to be a risk premium in the term structure and the forward interest rates are, on average, higher than future spot rates. This risk premium can be on account of inflation or general risk based on future uncertainty.

The chapter also looks at the relationship between nominal and real interest rates. Irving Fisher's theory still forms the basis for the widely accepted rule of thumb:

Real interest rate = Nominal interest rate − inflation.

Keep in mind that only the nominal rate is observed and the other two are expectations. Fisher's theory should be seen as a broad approximation.

The final section looks at corporate bonds. Yield on corporate bonds will be higher than that of treasury bonds of same maturity because of their default risk and lower liquidity. Corporate bonds have more variety in some of the details. These include floating coupon rate and conversion option. Corporate default risk is captured by bond ratings.

LIST OF TERMS

Coupon rate	Nominal interest rate
Convertible bonds	Real interest rate
Duration	Spot rate
Expectations theory	Strips
Face value	Term structure of interest rates
Floating rate bonds	Volatility
Forward rate	Yield to maturity
Maturity date	

EXERCISES

Fill-in Questions

1. The amount of money repaid at the maturity of a bond is the _____.

2. Most bonds usually pay regular interest payments called the _____.

3. The principal amount owed on a bond is repaid on its _____.

4. The rate of return on a bond investment when it is held to maturity is called its _____.

5. The term structure of interest rates consists of a series of _____ on bonds of comparable risk.

6. A bond's internal rate of return is called _____.

7. When government bonds are repackaged into mini-bonds, each of which makes only one payment; they are known as _____.

8. _____ measures the average time that the total cash flow from an asset is realized over the life of that asset.

9. _____ measures the percentage change in the price of a bond or other asset corresponding to a unit change in its yield.

10. The _____ rate between two dates is the interest rate we can lock into between buying them today and by selling discount bonds for those two dates.

11. The _____ of the term structure of interest rates says the only reason for an upward-sloping term structure is that investors expect future spot rates to be higher than current spot rates.

12. Under Fisher's scheme of interest rates, if the forecasted inflation rate is 3% and the real interest rate is 2%, the nominal interest rate is _____.

13. The interest rate, which is the stated rate in loan and other transactions, is the _____ interest rate.

14. Nominal interest rate less the rate of inflation is the approximate _____ interest rate.

15. _____ include a premium for anticipated inflation.

16. A corporate bond, which has its coupon payment reset periodically is known as a _____ bond.

17. A corporate bond that offers the bondholder an option to exchange the bond for a specified number of common shares of the borrower at a specified price is known as _____ bond.

Problems

1. Value a bond which pays 4.75% coupon has a face value of $1,000, 20 years till maturity, and the investors require a rate of return of 5%. Assume annual coupon payments.

2. If the above bond is selling at a price of $1,035, what is the yield to maturity?

3. An U.S. Treasury bond of 12 years maturity and 4% coupon is quoted at a yield to maturity of 3.7%. (a) Calculate its correct price, given that it makes semi-annual coupon payments and the quoted yield is semi-annually compounded. (b) Calculate the (incorrect) price that would have been obtained by assuming annual payments and compounding.

4. Calculate the yield to maturity on a 15-year bond carrying a coupon rate of 4.5%. Assume that the interest is payable annually and the bond is selling at 92.

5. As the financial manager of Fab Corp. you estimate the following spot interest rates on Treasury securities: $r_1 = 4.00$, $r_2 = 5.00$, $r_3 = 5.60$, $r_4 = 7.20$, $r_5 = 6.50$. Your company's bonds have an 11% coupon rate, interest is payable annually, and they mature in exactly 5 years.
   a. Assuming the bond to be risk-free, estimate the present value of the bond?
   b. Calculate the present values of the following Treasury issues: (1) 5%, 3-year bond and (2) 8%, 3-year bond.
   c. Determine the yield to maturity of each of the bonds.
   d. Explain the differences between the yields to maturity you observe.

6. Calculate the duration and modified duration of 9% and 13% coupon 5-year corporate bonds which yield 8.00%.

7. Find the impact of a 0.5 percentage point increase and decrease in interest rates on the present value of each of the two bonds in problem 6. Use this to compute their volatilities and compare with your answer from problem 6.

8. Find the real interest rate, given that the nominal rate is 5% and the inflation rate is 2%.

9. If the money rate of interest is 4% and the real rate is expected to be 2.5%, what is the implied inflation rate? How realistic is it to assume that the real rate will be 2.5%?

10. How different is your inflation estimate in Problem 9 if you use the approximate formula, subtracting one rate from the other?

Essay Questions

1. Explain the relationship between the price of a bond and the yield to maturity. Does the yield determine the price or is it the other way around? What really determines the price of a bond in the market?

2. Explain the term structure of interest rates and the theories that attempt to explain the term structure.

3. How are nominal rates of interest adjusted for the effects of inflation? Explain fully, using whatever equations you feel necessary.

4. Why do corporate bonds have higher yields compared to treasury bonds of same maturity?

ANSWERS TO EXERCISES

Fill-in Questions

1. Face Value
2. Coupons
3. Maturity date
4. Yield to maturity
5. Spot rates
6. Yield to maturity
7. Strip
8. Duration
9. Expectations Theory
10. Modified duration (Volatility)
11. Forward
12. Expectation Theory
13. 5% approximate, 5.06% exact
14. Nominal
15. Real
16. Nominal interest rates
17. Floating rate
18. Convertible

Problems

1. Calculator solution: N = 20, I = 5, PMT = $47.5, FV = $1,000, PV = solve = −$968.84

2. Calculator solution: N = 20, PV = −$1,035, PMT = $47.5, FV = $1,000, I = YTM = 4.48%.

3. a. Calculator solution: N = 2 × 12 = 24, I = 3.7/2 = 1.85, PMT = $20, FV = $1,000, PV = solve = −$1,028.86;
   b. Incorrect price: N = 12, I = 3.7, PMT = $20, FV = $1,000, PV = solve = −$1,028.65

4. 5.28% [N = 15, PV = −$920, PMT = $45, FV = $1,000, I = SOLVE = YTM = 5.28%]

5. a.

PERIOD	INTEREST RATE	CASH FLOW	PRESENT VALUE
1	4.00	110	105.77
2	5.00	110	99.77
3	5.60	110	93.41
4	7.20	110	83.29
5	6.50	1,110	810.17
			1,192.41

b.

	PERIOD	INTEREST RATE	CASH FLOW	PRESENT VALUE
(1)	1	4.00	50	48.08
	2	5.00	50	45.35
	3	5.60	1,050	891.66
				985.09
(2)	1	4.00	80	76.92
	2	5.00	80	72.56
	3	5.60	1,080	917.13
				1,066.61

c. Using the values the different bonds above the yield to maturity can be calculated as below:

Fab Corp Bond	6.38%
T-Bond 1	5.55%
T-Bond 2	5.53%

d. The yields to maturity are different because of the differences in coupon rates and the timing of cash flows for the different bonds.

6. Yield = 8.00%, Coupon = 9.00%

Year	C_t	PV(C_t) at 8.00%	Proportion of Total Value [PV(C_t)/V]	Proportion of Value × Time
1	90	83.33	0.0801	0.0801
2	90	77.16	0.0742	0.1484
3	90	71.44	0.0687	0.2061
4	90	66.15	0.0636	0.2544
5	1,090	741.84	0.7134	3.5670
Total	1,450	1,039.92	1.00	4.2560

40

Yield = 8.00%, Coupon = 13.00%

Year	Ct	PV(C$_t$) at 8.00%	Proportion of Total Value [PV(C$_t$)/V]	Proportion of Value × Time
1	130	120.37	0.1003	0.1003
2	130	111.45	0.0929	0.1858
3	130	103.20	0.0860	0.2581
4	130	95.55	0.0797	0.3186
5	1,130	760.06	0.6411	3.2054
Totals	1,650	1,190.63	1.00	4.0682

Discounting by their yields, we find that the modified duration of the two bonds are:
9.00% bond: 3.941, 13% bond: 3.767.

7. The yields are now 7.50 or 8.50%. We obtain:

	9% Bonds		13% Bonds	
	New Price	% Change	New Price	% Change
Yield falls to 7.50	1,060.69	1.997	1,222.51	2.678
Yield rises to 8.50	1,019.70	−1.944	1,177.33	−1.117
Difference	40.99	3.941	45.18	3.767

The volatility results for the two bonds are as follows:

Bond	Volatility (direct)	Volatility (from problem 6)
9%	3.941	3.941
13%	3.767	3.767

8. $1 + r_{real} = (1 + r_n)/(1 + i) = 1.05/1.02$, $r_{real} = 2.94\%$.

9. $1 + I = (1 + r_n/(1 + r_{real}) = 1.04/1.025$; $I = 1.46\%$.
   Assumption of a real rate of 2.5 % is realistic, because it is close to the historical average.

10. Note that: $i = r_n − r_{real} = 4\% − 2.5\% = 1.5$; 4 basis points different from 9 above.

4

The Value of Common Stocks

INTRODUCTION

This chapter applies the lessons learned from the last two chapters to valuing stocks and businesses. The chapter begins with a description of stock trading activities and follows this with an explanation of stock valuation. Unlike bonds, stocks do not have specified cash flows; however, the value of a share can be seen as the present value of all the future dividends paid by the stock. This principle of stock valuation, with some modifications, can be applied to valuing businesses in general. The value of any asset is the present value of the free cash flows generated by the asset. The discount rate for computation of the present value should be the required rate of return demanded by the investors for investing in the asset. This required rate of return will be a function of the risk of the investment.

One of the simplest approaches to valuing stocks is to use metrics based on the value of similar stocks and the accounting book value or earnings per share numbers. This method does not take into account characteristics unique to a firm such as risk or growth opportunities. There are three methods of valuing a stock that take into account the risk and growth opportunities and based on the cash flows produced by the firm. These estimate the value of a stock as: i) as the present value of future dividends, ii) as the present value of free cash flow, or iii) as present value of current earnings plus the present value of growth opportunities.

The current market price of a stock can be used to estimate the *market capitalization rate* (cost of equity capital) or the investors' expected rate of return on the stock. This rate has practical applications in setting rates for regulated utilities and other industries.

KEY CONCEPTS IN THE CHAPTER

How Stocks are traded: Corporations issue new shares in the *primary market*, which is essentially a distribution network of investment bankers, and brokerage firms, who sell these initial issues to individual investors, mutual funds, and other buyers. Once issued, the stocks trade in the *secondary markets*. Well-known secondary markets include the New York Stock Exchange (NYSE), the "over-the-counter market" which is a network of dealers displaying prices through the National Association of Security Dealers' Automated Quotation system (NASDAQ). NYSE and many other exchanges are *auction markets*, where buyers and sellers are matched by *market makers* or by computers. Stocks are also trade through *electronic communication networks* (ECN), which connect traders with each other. The <u>Wall Street Journal</u> and other newspapers publish price, dividend, P/E ratio, and other information on stock market transactions. The securities traded in the secondary markets include stocks, bonds, warrants, and portfolios of stocks known as *exchange traded funds (ETF)*. ETFs tracking many popular market indexes such as the Standard and Poor (S&P) 500 and the Dow Jones Industrial Average as well as many country indices are available.

Valuation of Common Stocks: The simplest approach to valuing stocks is *valuation by comparables.* This method uses metrics such as market-to-book value ratio or price-earnings (PE) ratio of firms that are similar to the one that is being valued. Book value is the total value of shareholders' equity in the balance sheet of the firm. This can be expressed as total book value or book value per share. One calculates the stock value by multiplying the firm's book value per share by the market-to-book ratio of similar firms in the industry or the firm's earnings per share by the PE ratio of comparable firms in the same industry. While the method is simple, the approach does not take into account individual firm characteristics such as risk and growth opportunities. We revisit PE ratio a little later in the chapter.

A more fundamental and basic approach to valuation uses the cash flows generated by the investment in a firm's stock. If the stock is expected to pay a dividend of DIV_1 at the end of the year and the expected price of the stock at the end of the year is P_1, then for an investor requiring a return of r, the price of a stock today is:

$$P_0 = \frac{DIV_1 + P_1}{(1+r)}$$

This can be extended to future years, so that the price next year can be written as:

$$P_1 = \frac{DIV_2 + P_2}{(1+r)}$$

Substituting this into the previous equation for P_0 gives:

$$P_0 = \frac{DIV_1}{(1+r)} + \frac{DIV_2 + P_2}{(1+r)^2}$$

You can substitute the value for P_2 in terms of D_3 and P_3 and so on. This gives you the value of P_0 as the present value of dividends expected to be paid on that stock.

$$P_0 = \sum_{t=1}^{\infty} \frac{DIV_t}{(1+r)^t}$$

The value of a firm will be the present value of all future dividends paid on its current outstanding shares. Future dividends on new stocks issued in later years should not be included.

Estimation of Market Capitalization Rate: The expected return, r is often called the *market capitalization rate.* All securities in the same risk class are priced to offer the same expected return. If one stock offered a higher return, everyone would rush to buy it, pushing its price up and the expected return down. We can use the valuation of a growing perpetuity learned in Chapter 2 to value a stock for which the dividend is expected to grow at a constant rate. If the expected dividend growth rate is g, then

$$P_0 = \frac{D_1}{r - g}$$

Note that this formula requires that $r > g$.

For a stock with constant growth dividends, the market capitalization rate r is given by:

$$r = \frac{D_1}{P_0} + g$$

This is a useful formula to estimate the capitalization rate or the required rate of return on a company's stock. This is the *cost of equity* for the company. Care has to be taken to ensure that the estimated growth rate is realistic and closely approximates the market expectations for the stock. Regulators use the above model to estimate the fair rate of return on gas and electric utilities. For companies which have a regular pay out of dividends and reinvestment of remaining earnings, the growth rate can be approximated as: g = return on equity x plow back ratio, where the plow back (or retention) ratio is the fraction of earnings reinvested in the business.

Some cautionary notes on the estimation of the capitalization rate are in order. Estimates for a single stock may be unreliable and it is better to look at the average of estimates for a number of companies. Remember that the estimated growth rate should reflect long-term average growth rate rather that the current high or low rate.

The Relationship between Price and Earnings: The valuation model derived earlier shows the relationship between dividends and stock price. Investors often classify stocks as *growth* or *income* stocks depending on the relative growth of earnings and the earnings-price ratio. A growth stock typically has low earnings price ratio (or high PE ratio) and provides most of the return to investors in the form of capital gains. It is important to note that growth, per se, does not add value; only growth opportunities which have positive net present value are valuable and worth pursuing. Depending on the type of growth opportunities, we consider three cases.

a. Zero growth case: In this case, all earnings will be distributed as dividends, therefore $DIV_1 = EPS_1$, where EPS_1 is the earnings per share. $r = DIV_1 / P_0 = EPS_1 / P_0$ or the expected return equals dividend yield and earnings price ratio.

b. Growth rate is positive but the projects have zero NPV: A part of the earnings is reinvested and $(EPS_1 / P_0) > (DIV_1 / P_0)$. The investors exchange reduction in current dividends for gain in long-term dividends; however, the return earned is exactly equal to the opportunity cost of capital and there is no gain in value. Again, $EPS_1 / P_0 = r$.

c. A company with positive NPV growth opportunities: In this case, the company's growth adds value. The price of the stock is increased by the investment in the growth opportunities. A dollar of current dividend is traded off for more than one dollar equivalent in future dividends. This growth adds to the value of the company. The relationship among the stock price, earnings and the present value of growth opportunities (PVGO) can be expressed by the following equations:

$$P_0 = \frac{EPS_1}{r} + PVGO$$

$$\frac{EPS_1}{P_0} = r(1 - \frac{PVGO}{P_0})$$

The earnings price ratio will be less than the capitalization rate if the PVGO is positive. The larger the PVGO as a percentage of the stock price, the more the earnings price ratio will understate the capitalization rate. PVGO is rarely negative, as firms are not required to invest in projects with negative NPVs. Typically, growth stocks will have a higher percentage of their value represented by PVGO and will thus have low earnings price ratios (or high PE ratios).

PE ratios are the inverse of earnings price ratios and are published along with stock price quotations in the newspaper. They may be based on the most recent earnings announcements or the next year's earnings. As stated earlier, stocks of companies with high PVGO will show high P/E ratios. This implies higher expected future earnings. Of course, stocks whose current earnings are low may also show high P/E ratios. It should be remembered that high PE ratios do not mean low cost of capital. It should also be remembered that earnings numbers are influenced by the company's choice of accounting procedures and are unlikely to reflect the amount of money, which could be paid out without affecting its capital value. The PE ratio can therefore be very misleading even for comparisons of similar companies.

Valuation of a Business Using Discounted Cash Flow: Valuing a business is similar to valuing a stock. Instead of looking at dividends, one has to look at the *free cash flow* produced by the business. The free cash flow is the cash flow that can be withdrawn from the business each year after meeting all its investment needs. Growing firms typically invest more than the depreciation amount and investments made might exceed their earnings. During these years their free cash flow will be negative. When the investment needs are less than their earnings, the business generates free cash flow, which is similar to dividends. The value of the business is the present value of the free cash flows generated by the business. The procedure for valuation includes estimating free cash flows to a time *horizon* from which point the cash flows follow a constant growth pattern. The steps involved in valuation of a business are given below:

1. Estimate the free cash flows generated by the business. The free cash flows will be negative for the years when the investment needs of the business exceed its earnings.

2. Choose the horizon date. Free cash flows are estimated to the horizon date from which point the cash flows follow a simple growth pattern. The horizon value can be estimated using one of the short cut valuation formulas.

3. Estimate the horizon value. This will require knowledge of the required rate of return, r. The value of the business can be written as:

$$V = \frac{FCF_1}{1+r} + \frac{FCF_2}{(1+r)^2} + ... \frac{FCF_H + PV_H}{(1+r)^H}$$

The value of the business and the horizon value, PV_H, will be very sensitive to the assumptions used. Therefore, it is always prudent to cross check the value using other valuation measures or benchmarks such as PE ratios, market to book ratios of other similar companies.

WORKED EXAMPLES

1. Estimation of PVGO: WMR Corp. is expected to earn $3 per share next year. The company is expected to distribute dividends of $2 and reinvest the remaining earnings on projects with an average ROE of 12%. Its capitalization rate is estimated to be 8%. Calculate the stock price, the PE ratio, and the PVGO. What percentage of the stock price is represented by the PVGO?

SOLUTION

Dividends next year = DIV_1 = $2; Plowback ratio = ($3 − $2)/$3 = 0.33
Growth rate = Plow back ratio × ROE = 0.33 × 0.12 = 0.04
Price = $2/(0.08 − 0.04) = $50; PE ratio = $50/$3 = 16.67
PVGO = P − (EPS_1/r) = $50 − ($3/0.08) = $12.5. PVGO reflect 25% of the value of the stock.

An alternate way of estimating the PVGO is to look at the investment made in the first year and its NPV. The $1 invested in the first year earns $1 × 0.12 = $0.12 in perpetuity. PV of this cash flow is $0.12/0.08 = $1.5, NPV = $1.5 − $1 = $0.5. Each year the company is making similar investments, which are growing at 4%. Thus, the PVGO is a growing perpetuity = $0.5/(0.08 − 0.04) = $12.50.

2. Valentine Corp. is an established movie producer that specializes in cartoons and animation movies. The projected earnings and cash flow for the company are given below. Simran Jesani wants to buy the business and requires a rate of return of 20% on her investment. Estimate the value of the business.

Dollars million

Years	1	2	3	4	5	6
Assets	50	75	100	125	140	151.2
Earnings	12	18	24	30	33.6	36.29
Net Investment	25	25	25	15	11.2	12.10
Free cash flow	−13	−7	−1	15	22.4	24.19
Earnings growth from previous period (%)		50	33.3	25	12	8

SOLUTION

The cash flows start growing at a constant rate of 8% from the end of 5 years. At this stage, the business is reinvesting one-third of each year's earnings and is earning a ROE of 24%. Therefore, the growth rate = 24 × 1/3 = 8%. We can choose 5 years as the horizon. The value of the business at this point is that of a growing perpetuity growing at 8%.

Horizon Value = Value at the end of five years = 22.4 × 1.08/(0.20 − 0.08) = $201.6 million

Value of the business = Present value of free cash flows

$$\text{PV(Free cash flows)} = \frac{-13}{1.2} + \frac{-7}{(1.2)^2} + \frac{-1}{(1.2)^3} + \frac{15}{(1.2)^4} + \frac{22.4 + 201.6}{(1.2)^5} = \$80.98 \text{ million}$$

Note: Present value computations like the above can be easily solved using the Cash Flow and NPV worksheets in the BA II Plus calculator. The calculator entries are as follows:
$CF_0 = 0$, $CO1 = -13$, $FO1 = 1$, $CO_2 = -7$, $FO2 = 1$, $CO_3 = -1$, $FO3 = 1$, $CO_4 = 15$, $FO4 = 1$, $CO_5 = -224$, $FO5 = 1$. Once you complete the cash flow worksheet, use the NPV worksheet: $I = 20$, NPV (CPT) = $80.98 million.

CHAPTER SUMMARY

This chapter applies the principles of discounted cash flow to valuing stocks and businesses. The cash flows generated by a stock are the dividends and therefore the value of a stock will be the present value of all future dividends paid by it. This does not imply that the return on a stock investment is only in the form of dividends. The value of stock held for one year is the present value of the dividends expected to be received and the expected price at the end of the year. Thus, the return received on a stock investment is the dividend yield and the expected capital gain from the price appreciation. Extending this logic for longer periods will lead to the result that the current price is the present value of all future dividends.

Using the simplifying assumption of constant dividend growth, current price of a stock can be derived as the value of a growing perpetuity: $P_0 = D_1/(r - g)$. The assumption of constant growth should be seen as an approximation rather than an exact condition. The formula also provides one with a simple approach to estimating market capitalization rate or cost of equity capital from current market price of the stock: $r = (D_1/P_0) + g$.

The stock valuation model can be used to derive the relationship between earnings, growth opportunities, and the current stock price. The current price of a stock is the sum of the present value of the current earnings in perpetuity and the present value of growth opportunities or PVGO. This relationship also leads to the result that the earnings price ratio will understate the capitalization rate for companies with significant growth opportunities.

The approach used to value stocks is extended to value businesses. In general, the value of a business will be the present value of the free cash flows generated by the business. Free cash flows are similar to dividends and are the earnings less net investments needed to be made in the business to generate the earnings.

LIST OF TERMS

Cost of equity capital
Dividend yield
Free cash flow
Growth stock
Income stock
Market capitalization rate

Payout ratio
Plowback ratio (Retention ratio)
Price-earnings ratio (PE ratio)
Primary market
Return on equity (ROE)
Secondary market

EXERCISES

Fill-in Questions

1. New York Stock Exchange is an example of a _____.

2. The market capitalization rate for a firm's common stock is also known as its _____.

3. The _____ is the return that investors require from investment in a stock or bond.

4. Annual dividend per share/share price = _____.

5. The proportion of earnings retained in the business is called _____.

6. New issues of stocks are issued through the _____, which is a network of investment bankers and brokerage firms.

7. The proportion of earnings paid out as dividends is called _____.

8. A firm with significant opportunities to invest in positive net present value projects will have a high _____ ratio.

9. Stocks, which give a high proportion of their return in the form of dividends, are usually called _____.

10. Stocks, which are expected to have high price appreciation, are known as _____.

11. The cash generated by a company net of its investment needs is the _____.

12. The ratio of the net profit earned by a company to the book value of stockholders' equity is _____.

Problems

1. Nimbus Corp. is expected to pay dividends of $2, $3, and $5 for the next three years. Thereafter, the dividends are expected to grow at a constant rate of 8%. If the required rate of return is 16%, what will be the current stock price? What will be the stock price next year and at the end of three years?

2. Blue Heron Corp. is expected to pay a dividend of $2.5 a share next year. The dividends are expected to grow at the rate of 6% annually. If the current stock price is $60, what is the implied market capitalization rate?

3. You forecast that ITT will pay a dividend of $2.40 next year and that dividends will grow at a rate of 9% a year. What price would you expect to see for ITT stock if the market capitalization rate is 15%?

4. Refer to problem 3 above. If the price of ITT is $30, what market capitalization rate is implied by your forecasts of problem 3?

5. Great Leaps Corp. stock is currently selling at $45. Next year's earnings are expected to be $3. Assuming that the current level of earnings can be maintained without any new investment, calculate the PVGO if the investors require a return of: (a) 10% (b) 15%.

6. Roshan Corp. retains 60% of its earnings and invests them at an average return on equity (ROE) of 15%. Kiran, Inc. retains only 30% of its earnings but invests them at an average ROE of 25%. Which company has the higher P/E ratio?

7. Bear Corp. shares are expected to pay a dividend of $4 next year. The dividends are expected to decrease (because the company's sales are declining on account of an industry wide decline) at the rate of 15% annually. If the market capitalization rate is 15%, what will be the current stock price?

8. The current earnings of M & M Corp. are $5 a share, and it has just paid an annual dividend of $2. The company is expected to continue to retain 60% of its earnings for the next 3 years and that both earnings and dividends will grow at 20% a year over that period. From year 4 on, the payout ratio is expected to increase to 70% and the growth rate to fall to 10%. If the capitalization rate for this stock is 15%, calculate (a) its price, (b) its price-earnings ratio, and (c) the present value of its growth opportunities.

9. Big Enchilada Corp. (BEC) has the following estimated earnings and net investments.

Dollar millions

Years	1	2	3	4	5	6
Assets	24.00	40.00	52.00	60.00	68.00	73.44
Earnings	4.80	8.00	10.40	10.80	10.88	11.75
Investments	16	12.00	8.00	8.00	5.44	5.88

The company will continue a payout ratio of 50% beyond year 6 and earn 16% on the assets. If the market capitalization rate is 15%, estimate the value of the business as the present value of free cash flows.

10. Refer to problem 9. What is the horizon value at the end of year 5? If the industry values for mature companies similar to BEC in year 5 are: P/E ratio = 16 and Market-to-book ratio = 1.5. Compare alternate valuation methods to the horizon value estimated using the constant growth model.

11. Big Bull Corp. is expected to pay dividends of $3, $5, and $7 for the next three years. Thereafter, the dividend is expected to grow at the rate 8%. If the market capitalization rate is 16%, calculate the current stock price and the stock price for each of the next three years.

12. Calculate the dividend yield and capital gains for each of the next three years for the Big Bull Corp. of problem 11.

Essay Questions

1. "High P/E ratios imply high growth." Discuss.

2. What is the relationship between earnings price ratio and market capitalization rate?

3. A company's earnings figure represents money, which in principle may be distributed to shareholders. Explain why the stock price represents the present value of dividends rather than earnings.

4. Some companies have a policy of retaining all earnings and never paying a dividend. Does this invalidate the principle that the stock price equals the present value of future dividends?

ANSWERS TO EXERCISES

Fill-in Questions

1. Secondary market
2. Cost of equity
3. Market capitalization rate
4. Dividend yield
5. Plowback (retention) ratio
6. Primary market
7. Payout ratio
8. P/E ratio
9. Income stocks
10. Growth stocks
11. Free cash flow
12. Return on equity

Problems

1. $P_0 = DIV_1/(1 + r) + DIV_2/(1 + r)^2 + DIV_3/(1 + r)^3 + P_3/(1 + r)^3$;
    where $P_3 = DIV_4/(r - g) = 5 \times 1.08/(0.16 - 0.08) = \$67.50$;
    $P_0 = (2/1.16) + (3/1.16^2) + (5 + 67.5)/1.16^3 = 50.40$; $P_1 = (3/1.16) + (5 + 67.5)/1.16^2$
    $= \$56.47$

2. $r = DIV_1/P + g = \$2.5/\$60 + 0.06 = 0.1017 = 10.17\%$

3. $P_0 = DIV_1/(r - g) = \$2.4/(0.15 - 0.09) = \$40$

4. $r = DIV_1/P + g = \$2.40/\$30 + 0.09 = 0.17 = 17\%$

5. (a) $PVGO = P - EPS_1/r = \$45 - \$3/0.10 = \$15$; (b) $PVGO = \$45 - \$3/0.15 = \$25$

6. $P_0 = EPS_0(1 + g)(payout)/(r - g)$; $g = ROE \times plowback$; PE ratio $= (1 + g)(payout)/(r - g)$
    For Roshan Corp., P/E ratio $= 1.09 \times 0.4/(r - 0.09)$.
    For Kiran Inc., P/E ratio $= 1.075 \times 0.7/(r - 0.075)$.
    P/E ratios for Roshan Corp. and Kiran Inc. are shown for different values of r:

R	10%	12%	14%
Roshan Corp.	43.6	14.5	8.72
Kiran Inc.	30.1	16.72	11.58

    We can solve for the value of r at which the P/E will be same for both companies. The value turns out to be 11.06% and the P/E is 21.1.

7. $P_0 = \$4/[0.15 - (-0.15)] = \$13.33$

8. $DIV_0 = \$2$, $DIV_1 = \$2 \times 1.2 = \$2.40$, $DIV_2 = \$2.40 \times 1.2 = \$2.88$, $DIV_3 = \$2.88 \times 1.2 = 3.46$,
    $EPS_4 = \$5 \times 1.2^3 \times 1.1 = \$9.50$, $DIV_4 = \$9.50 \times 0.7 = \$6.65$, $P_3 = \$6.65/(0.15 - 0.1) = \$133$,
    $P_0 = (2.4/1.15) + (\$2.88/1.15^3) + [(\$3.46 + \$133)/1.15^3] = \$93.99$, P/E $= \$93.99/2 = 47$,
    $PVGO = P_0 - (EPS_1/r) = \$93.99 - (\$6/0.15) = \$53.99$.

9. The earnings, investments, and free cash flows (in \$ millions) for the first 5 years are given in the table below. From year six, the free cash flows are growing at 8%. We can calculate the horizon value at the end of year 5 and then discount all cash flows and the horizon value to the present at the market capitalization rate of 15%.

Years	1	2	3	4	5
Earnings	4.80	8.00	10.40	10.80	10.88
Investments	16.00	12.00	8.00	8.00	5.44
Free cash flow	−11.20	−4.00	2.40	2.80	5.44

Value of cash flows from year 6 onwards = Free cash flow$_6$)/(r − g)
$$= (5.44 \times 1.08)/(0.15 - 0.08) = 5.88/0.07 = \$84 \text{ million}$$
Value of the business = PV(Free cash flows)

$$= \frac{-11.20}{1.15} + \frac{-4}{(1.15)^2} + \frac{2.40}{(1.15)^3} + \frac{2.80}{(1.15)^4} + \frac{5.44 + 84}{(1.15)^5}$$

$$= \$34.88 \text{ million}$$

10. Horizon value using free cash flow approach = \$84 million
    Horizon value using the PE ratio = 16 × \$5.44 = \$87.04 million.
    Using market-to-book = 1.5 × 68 = \$102 million.

11. DIV$_4$ = \$7 × 1.08 = \$7.56, P$_3$ = \$7.56/(0.16 − 0.08) = \$94.50, P$_0$ = \$3/1.16 + (\$5/1.16^2) + [(\$7 + \$94.50)/1.16^3] = \$71.33, P$_1$ = \$5/1.16 + (\$101.5/1.16^2) = \$79.74, P$_2$ = \$101.5/1.16 = \$87.50.

12. Dividend yield for year 1 = \$3/71.33 = 4.21%, Capital gains = (P$_2$ − P$_1$)/P$_1$ = 11.79%. Dividend yield for year 2 = \$5/79.74 = 6.27%, Capital gains = 9.73%. From year 3 onwards, the dividend yield will be 8% and the capital gains will also be 8%. The capital gains for a stock with constant growth dividends will equal the growth rate in dividends.

5

Net Present Value and Other Investment Criteria

INTRODUCTION

We have already learnt the concept of net present value (NPV) and its application for making investment or capital budgeting decisions. Shareholders like to have more wealth and companies can help them do this by investing positive NPV projects. This chapter provides a more detailed discussion of the NPV approach and compares it with three other widely used, but flawed, measures. These are:

- Book (or accounting) rate of return,
- Payback period, and
- Internal rate of return (IRR).

The chapter describes these methods and their major drawbacks. The measures are inferior to the NPV and should not, with the qualified exception of the IRR, normally be relied upon to provide sound corporate investment decisions. IRR can provide correct and sound decisions if used properly. The primary reason why a chapter is devoted to these measures is that these are commonly used in corporate practice and are often popular. A widely acclaimed survey of corporate financial managers shows that more three-fourth of the managers use IRR and fifty-seven% use the payback. Therefore, it is essential that you should understand the different decision tools and the pitfalls in their use.

The chapter also discusses the capital rationing problem, which implies that the firm is constrained by paucity of funds available and may not be in a position to invest in all good projects. The *profitability index* is a decision tool tailored for this situation.

KEY CONCEPTS IN THE CHAPTER

NPV Basics: The first section gives a review of the net present value method. NPV represents the value added to the business by the project or the investment. It represents the increase in the market value of the stockholders' wealth. Accepting a project with positive NPV will make the stockholders better off by the amount of its NPV. NPV is the theoretically correct method to use in most situations. Other measures are inferior because they often give decisions different from those given by following the NPV rule. They will not serve the best interests of the stockholders.

Here is a review of the steps involved in calculating NPV, the decision rule for using NPV, and the advantages of NPV. This is followed by similar review of each of the other measures.

Calculating NPV:
Forecast the incremental cash flows generated by the project. Determine the appropriate discount rate, which should be the opportunity cost of capital. Calculate the sum of the present values (PV) of all the cash flows generated by the investment.
NPV = PV of cash inflows − initial investment.

Decision rule and interpretation:
Accept projects with NPV greater than zero. For mutually exclusive projects, accept the project with the highest NPV, if the NPV is positive. NPV represents the value added to the by the project stockholders' wealth. The discount rate should reflect the opportunity cost of capital or what the stockholders can expect to earn from other investments of equivalent risk.

Advantages:
The NPV approach correctly accounts for the time value of money and adjusts for the project's risk by using the opportunity cost of capital as the discount rate. Thus, it clearly measures the increase in market value or wealth created by the project. The NPV of a project is not affected by "packaging" it with another project. In other words, NPV (A+B) = NPV (A) + NPV (B). NPV is the only measure that provides the theoretically correct measure of a project's value.

Book Rate of Return (BRR): This is a rate of return measure based on accounting earnings and is defined as the ratio of book income to book assets.

Decision rule and interpretation:
Accept projects with returns greater than the average return on the book value of the firm, or some benchmark return. The book rate of return depends on the accounting rules followed by the company and not on the cash flows generated by the project.

Advantages and disadvantages:
Accounting earnings are reported by firms to the stockholders and the book return measure fits in with the reported earnings and the accounting procedures used by firms. However, the measure suffers from the serious drawback that it does not measure the cash flows or economic profitability of the project. It does not consider the time value of money and gives too much weight to distant earnings. The measure depends on the choice of depreciation method and other accounting conventions used by the firm. The BRR can give inconsistent ranking of projects and rankings may be altered by packaging. There is no consistent relationship between the book return and the IRR. We revisit BRR in chapter 12 and 28 and discuss some of the problems of using book returns.

Payback Period: The payback period is simply the time taken by the project to return the initial investment in the project. The measure is very popular and is widely used; it is also a flawed and an unreliable measure.

Calculation:
The cash flows from each year are added to find out the point in time at which the cumulative cash flows equal the initial investment.

Decision rule and interpretation:

Accept projects with payback less than some specified period. E.g. accept projects with payback of 4 years or less. Payback represents the number of years required for the original cash investment to be returned, but the time value of money is ignored. Therefore, it will be misleading to think that all cash flows after payback represent profit.

Advantages and disadvantages:

It is simple to calculate and easy to comprehend. However, payback period has very limited economic meaning because it ignores the time value of money and the cash flows after the payback period. It can be inconsistent and the ranking of projects may be changed by packaging with other projects.

Discounted payback is a modified version of the payback measure and uses the discounted cash flows to compute payback. This is an improvement over the traditional payback in that the time value of money is recognized. A project, which has a measurable discounted payback, will have a positive NPV. However, the other disadvantages of payback still apply. It is also not simple anymore.

Internal (or Discounted-Cash-Flow) Rate of Return (IRR): IRR is defined as the discount rate at which the NPV equals zero. Note that the yield to maturity computed for a bond is the IRR for one's investment in the bond.

Calculation:

Follow the steps for calculating the NPV and calculate the NPV for several discount rates. Start with a low discount rate and then calculate the NPV at progressively higher rates till the NPV calculated has a negative value. In general, the NPV will decrease as the discount rate is increased. Plot the NPVs (y-axis) against the discount rate (x-axis). The IRR is that discount rate at which the line crosses the X-axis (NPV = 0). Most business calculators are programmed to compute IRR directly.

Decision rule and Interpretation:

Accept projects that have IRR greater than the opportunity cost of capital. IRR is often interpreted as the effective rate of return for the investment made in the project. Strictly, this interpretation is true only for a one-period project.

Advantages and Disadvantages:

Used properly, the IRR will give the same result as the NPV for independent projects and for projects with normal cash flows.[1] As long as the cost of capital is less than the IRR, the NPV for the project will be positive. IRR can rank projects incorrectly, and the rankings may be changed by the packaging of the projects. For mutually exclusive projects, IRR can give incorrect decisions and should not be used to rank projects. If one must use IRR for selection between two mutually exclusive projects, it should be done by calculating the IRR of the differences between the cash flows of the projects. This will work only if the two projects have the risk required rate of return.

---

1. Normal projects are projects with an initial investment (negative cash flow) followed by a number of positive cash flows.

IRR can also be misleading in cases where the project cash flow patterns are the opposite of the normal project. These projects give cash inflows first, followed by outflows. Thus, it is like borrowing and in such cases, the IRR decision rule should be reversed. The project should be accepted only if the IRR is *less than* the hurdle rate.

Another problem with IRR is that projects whose cash flows change sign more than once may have more than one IRR. In such cases, it may not be obvious whether a high IRR is good or bad. One will need to look at the *NPV profile* (the NPV-discount rate graph) to identify the discount rate range for which the NPV is positive. *Modified IRR* is an improvement over the IRR and is used to overcome the problem of multiple IRRs. The cash flows that change signs during the project's life are discounted using the opportunity cost of capital and added to the cash flows of other years. This removes the multiple changes of sign. IRR does not allow different discount rates to be used for different time periods', i.e., one cannot consider the term structure of interest rates.

Capital Rationing and the Profitability Index: Occasionally, companies face resource constraint or capital rationing. The amount available for investment is limited so that all positive NPV projects cannot be accepted. In such cases, stockholder wealth is maximized by taking up projects with the highest NPV per dollar of initial investment. This approach is facilitated by the *profitability index* (PI) measure. The profitability index is defined as: NPV/Investment[2]. The decision rule for profitability index is to accept all projects with a PI greater than zero. This rule is equivalent to the NPV rule. The modified rule applied in the case of capital rationing is to accept projects with the highest profitability index first, followed by the one with next highest, and so on till the investment dollars are exhausted. This rule will maximize the NPV and stockholder wealth. If the resource constraint is on some other resources, the profitability index needs to be modified to measure the NPV per unit of the resource that is rationed. When more than one resource is rationed, a more complicated (linear programming) analysis is needed. The profitability index cannot cope with mutually exclusive projects or where one project is contingent on another.

Capital constraints are often imposed by top management of companies to force divisions to focus on priorities and to weed out projects that stem from over-optimism. Such cases are termed *soft rationing*. The more serious case of capital rationing is when a firm cannot raise capital to finance all its positive NPV projects. This implies capital market imperfections and is termed *hard rationing*. The use of NPV is still justified in such cases as long as the firm's stockholders have opportunities to invest in capital markets in projects comparable to the ones taken up by the firm.

NPV and Other Criteria: NPV is superior to other criteria because: i) it is the only measure which considers the time value of money, properly adjusting for the opportunity cost of capital, ii) gives consistent measures of the project's value (i.e. not affected by packaging with other projects), and iii) it clearly measures the value added to the stockholders' wealth. However, the other three criteria for the evaluation of projects are found to be popular among some corporate financial managers. If you have to use them, make sure that you understand their limitations and only use them in the best possible way. Remember that it is the cash flows that determine the

---

2. Some textbooks define profitability index as PV(Cash inflows)/PV(Investment). This is also known as the benefits/cost ratio. The decision rule with is definition would be: accept if PI is > 1.

value of a project. Inadequate forecast of the cash flows can be far more disastrous than using the wrong appraisal technique. Cash flow forecasts are difficult to make and can be expensive. It does not make sense to waste the forecasts by using an inferior method of evaluation.

WORKED EXAMPLE

Joy Rides, Inc. is considering an expansion project with an estimated investment of $1,500,000. The equipment will be depreciated to zero salvage value on a straight-line basis over 5 years. The expansion will produce incremental operating revenue of $600,000 and incremental operating costs, excluding depreciation, of $200,000 annually for 5 years. The company's opportunity cost of capital is 12%. Ignore taxes. Calculate: (a) payback period, (b) book rate of return, (c) NPV, (d) IRR, and (e) profitability index.

SOLUTION

First calculate the annual earnings and cash flows:

Operating revenues	= $600,000
Less:	
Operating costs	= $200,000
Depreciation	= $300,000
Book Income	= $100,000
Add back:	
Depreciation	= $300,000
Cash flow	= $400,000

a. Payback = $1,500,000/$400,000 = 3.75 years

b. Average book income = $100,000,
   Average book value of investment = ($1,500,000 + 0)/2 = $750,000
   Book rate of return = $100,000/$750,000 = 13.33%

c. NPV calculation:

	Amount	Discount factor	Present value
Year 0 Initial investment	−$1,500,000	1	−$ 1,500,00
Years 1 through 5 Cash flow	$ 400,000	3.605	$1,442,000
Net Present Value			−$ 58,000

d. IRR is calculated by trial and error. Calculate the NPV at different discount rates:
   NPV at 10% = $400,000(discount factor for 10%, 5 years) − $1,500,000
       = $400,000 × 3.791 − $1,500,000 = $16,400
   NPV at 11% = $400,000 × 3.696 − $1,500,000 = −$21,600
   IRR lies between 10% and 11%. IRR = 10 + [16,400/(16,400 + 21,600)] = 10.43%
   Note: You can obtain the solution directly by using the calculator.
   PV = −$1,500,000, FV = 0, PMT = $400,000, N = 5, I = IRR = solve = 10.42%

e. Profitability Index = NPV/Investment = −$58,000/$1,500,000 = −0.04

SUMMARY

This chapter reviews the different decision tools used to evaluate projects. The chapter begins with a review of NPV, which was introduced in chapter 2. This is followed by a detailed discussion of three other commonly used, but inferior, tools for evaluation of capital budgeting projects. The book rate of return is an accounting measure and suffers from all the weaknesses inherent in accounting earnings being subject to the relatively arbitrary nature of accounting assumptions. The book return computation does not use cash flows and can lead to poor investment decisions. The payback period is simply the number of years required to recoup the project's initial investment. Aside from its simplicity, there is not much to be said for the payback; it ignores the time value of money, ignores all cash flows after the payback period, and leads to inconsistent ranking of projects.

The internal rate of return or IRR is based on discounted cash flows and can give correct decisions for independent projects with normal cash flow patterns. The decision rule is to accept projects with an IRR greater than the cost of capital or required rate of return. Any project that satisfies this rule will have a positive NPV. However, the measure should not be used for selection of the best among mutually exclusive projects. A modified approach is needed to get the correct decision using IRR when selecting among mutually exclusive projects. The approach involves calculating the IRR for the differences in cash flows of the two mutually exclusive projects.

NPV is superior to the other decision tools because it gives the correct decision and is a direct measure of the value added to the stockholders' wealth. The only exception occurs when a firm is constrained by capital rationing. This implies that the firm cannot finance all positive NPV projects and should therefore choose projects that give the highest NPV for each dollar of investment. The profitability index can be used to make the correct choice for this situation.

LIST OF TERMS

Book rate of return
Capital rationing
Discounted-cash-flow rate of return
Discounted payback
Internal rate of return

Linear programming
Mutually exclusive projects
Payback period
Profitability index

EXERCISES

Fill-in Questions

1. The _____ is the time it takes an investment to repay its initial investment.

2. The _____ is the time beyond which cash flows could disappear and still leave the project with a positive net present value.

3. The _____ is defined as the book income/book investment.

4. The _____ is the discount rate for which the NPV equals zero.

5. _____ is needed to deal with capital rationing or resource constraint problem spread over more than one year.

6. _____ are competing projects among which only one can be selected.

7. The NPV of the project divided by the initial investment is called _____.

8. _____ is another name for the IRR.

9. _____ exists when a firm is constrained by limited availability of funds to invest.

Multiple Choice Questions

Choose from among the five criteria to which the statement applies. Net present value (NPV), payback (P), book rate of return (BRR), internal rate of return (IRR), or profitability index (PI):

	NPV	P	BRR	IRR	PI	None
1. Could be misleading if the project cash flow patterns are reversed.						
2. Affected by the depreciation method used.						
3. Puts too much weight on distant cash flows.						
4. May have several values.						
5. Gives the same accept-reject decisions as NPV on single projects with normal cash flows.						
6. Works well for single period capital rationing.						
7. Ignores cash flows beyond some point.						
8. Can use multiple discount rates.						
9. Gives consistent rankings even if the projects are packaged together differently.						
10. Gives the same decisions as the NPV for independent projects with normal cash flows.						

Problems

1. Black and Company is considering an investment in a new plant, which will entail an immediate capital expenditure of $4,000,000. The plant is to be depreciated on a straight-line basis over 10 years to zero salvage value. Operating income (before depreciation and taxes) is expected to be $800,000 per year over the 10-year life of the plant. The opportunity cost of capital is 14%. Calculate (a) the book rate of return, (b) the payback and discounted payback periods, (c) NPV, (d) IRR, and (e) the profitability index. There are no taxes.

2. Benita Frank owns a computer reselling business and is expanding her business. The estimated investment for the expansion project is $85,000 and it is expected to produce cash

flows after taxes of $25,000 for each of the next 6 years. An alternate proposal involves an investment of $32,000 and after-tax cash flows of $10,000 for each of the next 6 years. The opportunity cost of capital is 13%. Calculate (a) payback, (b) book rate of return, (c) IRR, and (d) NPV and advise Benita.

3. Refer to problem 2. Is there an opportunity cost of capital that would make Benita indifferent between the two projects?

4. For each of the following projects, calculate the IRR, NPV, and the profitability index. Assume the cost of capital to be 10%. Rank the projects using each criterion.

Projects	Cash flow in $ (1,000)			
	Year 0	Year 1	Year 2	Year 3
Project A	−100			145
Project B	−100	115		
Project C	−100	230	−120	
Project D	−45	20	20	20

5. An investment of $100 will produce a level stream of cash flows for T years. Find what level of cash flows will give an IRR of: (a) 12% and (b) 14% for T = 6 years and T = 10 years.

6. Rocks, Inc. is considering the following mutually exclusive investments. Calculate the payback, IRR, and the NPV for the two projects. Assume a cost of capital of 13%. Which project would you choose? Why do the ranking by the different methods differ?

Projects	Project cash flows – ($1,000s)			
	Year 0	Year 1	Year 2	Year 3
Project A	−400	220	310	0
Project B	−400	130	190	260

7. Ruckhouser Corp. has an opportunity cost of capital of 10% and the following projects. Assuming theses to be independent projects, select the best project(s) for the company. Explain why all the projects will not be selected.

Projects	Cash flow in $ (1,000)				
	Year 0	Year 1	Year 2	Year 3	IRR - %
Project A	−112	40	50	60	15
Project B	45	60	−70	−70	16
Project C	−100	−26	80	80	11
Project D	146	−70	−60	−50	12
Project E	−100	450	−550	175	29

8. Refer to question 7. How would your decision change if the projects were not independent projects?

9. Fingerhaus, Inc. is considering a project with an investment of $300,000. The project is expected to generate annual cash flows of $85,000 in the first two years and $100,000 from years 3 to 7. At the end of year 8, the company will have to incur a cash flow of $250,00 to clean up the plant facility. Calculate the NPV and IRR for the project. Assume a cost of capital of 12%.

10. M & M Corp. has existing operations that will generate cash flows of $150,000 in year 1 and $200,000 in year 2. If the company makes an investment of $40,000 now, it can expect to receive $230,000 in year 1 and $170,000 in year 2. M & M's cost of capital is 12%. Calculate the NPV and IRR of the project. Why is the IRR a poor measure of the project's profitability in this case?

11. Please refer to problem 10 above. M & M Corp. finds that the investment needed for the project is $50,000 instead of $40,000. Evaluate the project.

12. Mickey Minn Corp. is considering the following projects. The company is facing resource constraints and can invest only $800,000 this year. Advice the company.

Projects	Investment ($1,000s)	NPV ($1,000s)	IRR (%)
A	100	8	13.9
B	400	43	14.4
C	300	25	16.0
D	200	23	14.1
E	200	21	16.1
F	200	19	15.7

Essay Questions

1. IRR should never be used to evaluate mutually exclusive projects. Discuss.

2. Why is NPV superior to the other measures of project profitability?

3. IRR, used properly, will give correct decisions. Discuss.

4. How can the problem of capital rationing be handled? Discuss the role and limitations of profitability index as the criterion to be used for projects under capital rationing.

5. Why are the measures payback and book rate of return used in capital budgeting?

ANSWERS TO EXERCISES

Fill-in Questions

1. Payback period
2. Discounted payback
3. Book rate of return
4. Internal rate of return
5. Linear programming
6. Mutually exclusive projects

7. Profitability index
8. Discounted-cash-flow rate of return

9. Capital rationing

Multiple Choice Questions

1. IRR
2. None
3. BRR
4. IRR
5. IRR

6. PI
7. P
8. NPV
9. NPV
10. IRR

Problems

1. a. Operating revenues = $800,000
   Less depreciation   = $400,000
   Book Income   = $400,000
   Cash flow   = $800,000

   Average book income = $400,000
   Average book value of investment = ($4,000,000+0)/2 = $2,000,000
   Book rate of return = $400,000/$2,000,000 = 20%

   b. Payback period = $4,000,000/$800,000 = 5 years
   Discounted payback is the number of years needed to get the PV of the cash flows to equal the initial investment.
   Using the calculator: PV = −$4,000,000, PMT = $800,000, FV = 0,
   I = 14%, N = solve = Discounted payback = 9.2 years.

   c. NPV: Present value of cash flows = $800,000 × 5.216 = $4,172,800
   NPV = $4,172,800 − $4,000,000 = $172,800
   Alternately, using the calculator you can find the present value of the cash flows to equal
   $4,172,892. NPV = $172,892
   (N = 10, I = 14, FV = 0, PMT = $800,000, PV = solve = $4,172,892)

   d. IRR can be directly obtained by using the calculator:
   PV = −$4,000,000, PMT = $800,000, FV = 0, N = 10, I = solve =
   IRR = 15.1%

2. Proposal 1: Payback = $85,000/$25,000 = 3.4 years
   Book income = $25,000 − Depreciation = $25,000 − ($85,000/6) = $10,833
   Book rate of return = $10,833/$42,500 = 25.5%
   IRR = 19.1% (PV = −$85,000, FV = 0, PMT = $25,000, N = 6, I = IRR)
   NPV = present value of cash flows − $85,000 = $99,939 − $85,000 = $14,939
   (PMT = $25,000, FV =0, N = 6, I = 13, PV = solve = $99,939)

Proposal 2: Payback = $32,000/$10,000 = 3.2 years
Book rate of return = $4,667/$16,000 = 29.2%
IRR = 21.6%
NPV = $7,975
Benita should choose proposal 1 as it has a higher NPV. IRR, BRR, or the payback should not be used to choose among mutually exclusive projects.

3. The cost of capital at which the two projects will produce the same NPV can be found by calculating the IRR of the difference in cash flows between the two projects. Proposal 1 requires an additional investment of $53,000 and generates extra cash flows of $15,000 for six years. The IRR for this set of cash flows is 17.6% (PV = −53,000, PMT = 15,000, N = 6, I = IRR). This also means that for any cost of capital below 17.6%, proposal 1 will have a higher NPV.

4. Project A:
    IRR = 13.2% (PV = −100, FV = 145, PMT = 0, N = 3, I = IRR)
    NPV = $8,940 (PV of $145 received 3 years from now is $108.94)
    Profitability index = 8.94/100 = 0.0894

    Project B:
    IRR = 15%; NPV = $4,545; Profitability index = 0.0455

    Project C:
    IRR = −20% and 50%. The project has two IRRs because of the pattern of cash flows (two sign changes).
    NPV = −100 + (230/1.1) − (120/1.21) = 9.917 = $9,917
    Profitability index = 0.0992

    Project D:
    IRR = 15.9%; NPV = $4,737; Profitability index = 4.737/45 = 0.1053

    Ranking of projects:

IRR:	1. C	2. D	3. B	4. A (also C)
NPV:	1. C	2. A	3. D	4. B
PI:	1. D	2. C	3. A	4. B

5. a. PV = −100, FV = 0, I = 12%, N = 6 years,
        PMT = solve = $24.32. For 10 years, N = 10, PMT = $17.70

    b. PV = −100, FV = 0, I = 14%, N = 6 years,
        PMT = solve = $25.72. For 10 years, N = 10, PMT = $19.17

6. Payback for A = 1 + 180/310 = 1.58 years.
    Payback for B = 2 + 80/260 = 2.31
    NPV for A = $37,466; NPV for B = $44,035
    IRR for A = 19.7%; IRR for B = 18.7%

Based on NPV, the company should choose project B. Payback and IRR rank project A better because of the difference in cash flow patterns. Project A has more of its cash flow in the earlier years.

7. The NPVs for the projects are as follows:

Project A = $10,765
Project B = -$10,898
Project C = $2,585
Project D = -$4,789
Project E = -$13,974

Only projects A and C have positive NPVs. The others are really "borrowing" projects and should not be selected as the cost of borrowing (IRR) is higher than the opportunity cost of capital.

8. If the projects were mutually exclusive, one would select project A as it has the highest NPV.

9. Using the calculator:
$CF_0 = -300,000$, $CO_1 = 85,000$, $FO_1 = 2$, $CO_2 = 100,000$, $FO_2 = 5$
$CO_3 = -250,000$, $FO_3 = 1$, IRR = solve = 16.6%; NPV: I = 12%,
NPV = 30,054

10. Incremental cash flows are: $CF_0 = -40,000$, $CO_1 = 80,000$,
$CO_2 = -30,000$; NPV: I = 12, NPV = $7,512; IRR = 50%

11. With an increase of $10,000 in the initial investment, the project's NPV will become negative. NPV = -$2,488; IRR = 0.

12. The profitability index and ranking based on PI for the different projects are:

Project	Investment	PI	Ranking
Project A	$100,000	0.080	6
Project B	$400,000	0.108	2
Project C	$300,000	0.083	5
Project D	$200,000	0.115	1
Project E	$200,000	0.105	3
Project F	$200,000	0.095	4

Projects D, B, and E should be selected to invest the $800,000.

6

Making Investment Decisions with the Net Present Value Rule

INTRODUCTION

This chapter provides a detailed account of the nuts and bolts issues of making investment decisions and applying the NPV rule in practice. The focus is on three tasks faced by the financial manager involved in practical capital budgeting. The first task is to determine what should be discounted to compute the NPV. The answer, of course, is the cash flows relevant to the project. This principle is conceptually simple, but needs elaboration and examples. The second task is the actual compilation of the "bottom-line" cash flow forecasts. The chapter describes the items to be included and also excluded and gives a detailed example.

The third problem in the application of the NPV rule arises when one has to modify the NPV rule to suit special situations relating to mutually exclusive project choices. This often requires converting the NPV into equivalent annual costs or benefits for the project choice. A typical example might involve alternative proposals, with different project lives, for the replacement of existing machinery. The proper evaluation in this case will be to compare the alternatives in terms of the equivalent annual costs rather than the total costs for each alternative. This technique finds extensive application in a number of different situations. The chapter also presents situations where the NPV rule has to be modified because of the interactions between investment projects and other activities or decisions of the firm. These project interactions have to be carefully sorted out and included in the project analysis and decision. Investment timing, treatment of inflation, and cash flows in different currencies are some of the topics discussed in the chapter.

KEY CONCEPTS IN THE CHAPTER

Focus on Cash Flow: Investment decisions should be based on the analysis of cash flows and not accounting earnings. It is important to understand that accounting earnings can differ from cash flows because of the set of rules followed by accountants in classifying income and expenditures. Care has to be taken to ensure that cash flows are counted at the point of time they are received or paid out. This might require more than a simple manipulation of accounting numbers.

Incremental, After-tax Cash Flow: Project evaluation should be based on after-tax cash flows caused by or incidental to the project. All the cash flows that are caused by or are due to the project or are changed by the acceptance of the project should be considered. The following are some useful pointers in identifying the relevant cash flows:

Incremental, not average: It is easy to confuse between the average cost and incremental cost. What is relevant to the project analysis is the portion of the cost or revenue in cash flow terms that will change because of the project. Expenses incurred regardless of what happens to the project should not be considered, as they are not affected by the project.

All incidental effects: All cash flows flowing out of the decision on the project should be included in the project analysis. If the project causes a sales increase in another division's business or an increase in administrative expenses, these should be included in project evaluation. In some cases benefits from the project might include increased future sales of services and supplies. If these increases will not occur without the project, then they are incremental cash flows due to the project and should be included in the project evaluation.

Working capital changes: Changes in working capital needs caused by the project are part of the cash flows that should be included. It is easy to miss these and one has to be careful to account for the changes in inventory, receivables, and accounts payables.

$$\text{Change in net working capital} = \text{Increase in accounts receivable} + \text{Increase in inventory} - \text{Increase in accounts payable}$$

Please note that working capital needs can change during the life of the project. The investment in working capital is usually recovered at the end of the project.

Sunk costs: Sunk costs are costs that have already been incurred and will not be affected by the decision on the project. These should be ignored, as they are not incremental to the project.

Opportunity costs: Opportunity costs of all resources, including managers and other personnel working on the project, should be included even if there may not be an explicit cash flow relating to that item. When a project uses a resource already owned by the company, it might appear that there is no cash flow involved. However, note that the resource is not available for any alternate use. Thus, the execution of the project precludes alternate use of the resource and the project should be charged for the use of the resource.

Allocated overheads: Accounting rules followed by companies often include allocated overhead charges for use of services. These are typically based on the company's historic averages that often do not bear any direct relationship to the project's actual usage of services or other resources. Thus allocated overheads should be ignored and be counted only to the extent they are actual incremental costs.

Financing charges: Interest payments and other financing charges are normally not included in project cash flows. Throughout this chapter, we assume that the project is financed through all equity funds. This enables us to separate investment and financing decisions. The effect of financing mix will be built into project evaluation through appropriate adjustments to the cost of capital. We discuss this in detail in later chapters.

Depreciation: Depreciation is not a cash flow but has cash flow consequences because it is a deductible expense for tax purposes. Most corporations keep, quite legally, two sets of books– one for reporting earnings to stockholders and another for tax returns filed with the Internal Revenue Service (IRS). The U.S. tax laws permit accelerated depreciation for most assets used in business. These are based on notional lives assigned to classes of assets. Table 6.4 in the text gives the depreciation schedules for different classes of assets. The effect of depreciation is to provide a *tax shield or* reduction in taxes equal to the dollar amount of depreciation multiplied by the marginal tax rate of the company.

Salvage Value: Typically, cash flow forecasts for project evaluation assume that the project runs for a certain number of years. When project ends, the plant and equipment can be sold for their salvage value. This should be considered as part of the project cash flows. If the salvage value is different from the depreciated book value of the assets, there is tax implication as well. Cash flow from salvage would generally be positive unless the project has shut-down or clean-up costs.

Consistent Treatment of Inflation: Inflation affects both the project cash flows and the opportunity cost of capital that is used to discount the cash flow. One has to be careful to treat inflation effects consistently and correctly. The opportunity cost of capital estimated from current market costs are *nominal* costs with inflation effects already built into them. Thus, it is easy to discount *nominal* (money) cash flows at a *nominal* discount rate. Some companies prefer to project cash flows in *real* terms and discount them at a real rate of interest. The relationship between nominal rates, real rates, and inflation is given by the equation:

$$1 + r_{nomial} = (1 + r_{real})(1 + \text{inflation rate}).$$

It is important to be consistent in the treatment of inflation. Discount nominal cash flows with a nominal rate or discount real cash flows with a real rate; do not mix them.

NPV in Other Currencies: The general principles of finance you learn in this book have universal relevance and applicability. Thus, while an American company will compute its cash flows and NPVs in US dollars, a Japanese firm will do the same using the same principles we discuss in this and other chapters, but in Japanese yen. A German or French firm will have its cash flows in the Euro. Some details will differ, though. For example, nominal interest rates, inflation rates, and the opportunity cost of capital may be different from country to country. The tax rates and depreciation rules are decided by the local governments in each country and can also be substantially different.

Investment Timing: Many projects can be started now or some time in the future. The fact that the project has a positive net present value does not necessarily imply that now is the best time to initiate the project. Valuing the timing option is simple when there is no uncertainty. One can calculate the project's NPV at various dates of project commencement and pick the one date with the highest NPV. Of course, this will not work when there is uncertainty. The timing option exists, if the project's commencement can be delayed.

The optimal choice of timing is the one that maximizes the NPV. Imagine you have some vintage whiskey for which you can get $1,000 now or $2,000 if you sell it five years from now. If the present value of $2,000 received 5 years from now is higher than $1,000, it makes sense to wait. It is quite likely that you will get even more than $2,000 if you sell it six years later or seven years later. The optimal choice will be the one that gives the highest present value.

Equivalent Annual Cash Flows: The NPV is the current equivalent of cash flows during the life of a project. For certain situations, the NPV will have to be converted to equivalent annual cash flows or benefit. Converting the present value (or NPV) into equivalent annual cash flows is easy; you simply divide the net present value by the appropriate annuity factor. The approach is particularly useful for deciding among similar facilities (such as machines) with different lives and for deciding on when an existing facility should be replaced. Some typical cases where this approach is appropriate are discussed below.

Projects with different lives: The basic NPV rule will not provide correct decisions in the evaluation of mutually exclusive projects with different lives. We can convert the project's costs or benefits into annual equivalents and choose the better alternative.

The replacement decision: The capital cost of a new machine can be restated in terms of the equivalent annual cost (EAC). Its optimal life is the one that minimizes its EAC. We can decide whether to replace an existing machine by comparing its cost for the next year (including the loss of salvage value over the year) against the EAC of the new machine.

In a world of certainty, EAC is simple to compute and use. Inflation can be factored in or we can do the analysis in real terms. However, situations involving technological changes or other uncertainties could complicate the problem.

The cost of excess capacity: Currently available excess capacity of any resource (plant, computers, or a warehouse) may not be free as increased utilization of the resource (such as a computer) may bring forward the date of future replacement of the facility. It is, therefore, essential to consider the cost (the opportunity cost) of the use of this excess capacity and factor that into the project's cash flows.

WORKED EXAMPLES

1. Gino's Trattoria is considering a new project, which requires an investment of $2 million. The project is expected to generate sales revenue of $1 million in the first year, $2 million in the second year and $3 million each for years 3, 4, and 5. The cost of goods sold is expected to be 75% of sales revenue. Other costs are expected to be 7% of sales in the first year and 5% of sales thereafter. The project will need working capital investment of $200,000 in the first year and an additional $100,000 in the second year. The investment in plant ($2 million) will be depreciated using the MACRS schedule for the 5-year class. If the company's opportunity cost of capital is 10%, calculate the NPV for the project. Assume that the plant will operate for 6 years, and at the end of 6 years, the plant can be sold for a salvage value of $300,000. The tax rate for the company is 36%.

SOLUTION

Cash flows ($1000s)

Years	0	1	2	3	4	5	6
1. Investment and salvage	−2,000						192[1]
2. Sales		1,000	2,000	3,000	3,000	3,000	3,000
3. Cost of goods sold		750	1,500	2,250	2,250	2,250	2,250
4. Other costs		70	100	150	150	150	150
5. Depreciation		400	640	384	230	230	116
6. Pre-tax profit [2−3−4−5]		−220	−240	216	370	370	484
7. Tax at 36% of 6		−79	−86	78	133	133	174
8. Profit after tax [6−7]		−141	−154	138	237	237	310
9. Operating cash flow [8+5]		259	486	522	467	467	426
10. Change in working capital		−200	−100				300
11. Total cash flows [1+9+10]	−2,000	59	386	522	467	467	918
12. Present value at 10%	−2,000	54	319	392	319	290	518
13. Net present value	−2,000+54+319+392+319+290+518 = −108						

Notes: 1. Salvage value $300,000 less tax of $108,000 = $192,000

2. Marie's Nuts is considering replacing their roaster oven with a new one. They have received two offers. Oven A has an initial cost of $34,000, annual operating costs of $6,000, and an operating life of 4 years. Oven B has an initial cost of $24,000, annual operating costs of $8,000, and operating life of 3 years. Which oven is the better choice? Assume an opportunity cost of capital of 12%.

SOLUTION

Since the two ovens have different "project lives," we will have to calculate the EACs of the PV of costs.

Present value of costs for oven A: Using the Cash flow and NPV worksheets of BA II Plus:
CF_0 = $34,000, CO_1 = $6,000, FO_1 = 4; NPV: I = 12, NPV = $52,224
EAC: N = 4, I = 12, PV = $52,224, PMT = EAC = Solve = $17,194

Present value of costs for oven B: Using the Cash flow and NPV worksheets of BA II Plus:
CF_0 = $24,000, CO_1 = $8,000, FO_1 = 3; NPV: I = 12, NPV = $43,215
EAC: N = 3, I = 12, PV = $43,215, PMT = EAC = Solve = $17,992

A is the better choice as it has lower EAC.

71

SUMMARY

This chapter describes the application of the NPV rule to practical project evaluation. The focus is on three key tasks faced by financial managers engaged in capital budgeting decisions: i) what to discount, ii) how to compile the overall cash flow forecast from the various details relating to the project, and iii) how to deal with special situations where the simple NPV rule would have to be modified to give the value maximizing decision. Project evaluation should use incremental after-tax cash flows. Specifically, the evaluator should consider all cash flows incidental to and caused by the project. Care has to be taken to ensure that items like working capital increases are considered and sunk costs are ignored.

The treatment of inflation in project evaluation should be consistent. One should avoid the confusion between real and nominal cash flows. If nominal cash flows are used, they should be discounted with a nominal cost of capital. By the same token, real cash flows should be discounted by a real cost of capital.

The NPV rule has to be modified in some cases involving projects with unequal lives, replacement decision for old machinery with some useful life, and the cost of excess capacity. These problems can be evaluated using the technique of EAC. It is also necessary, in the case of excess capacity, to explicitly recognize the opportunity cost of using the capacity, the cost being early replacement of the resource being used.

LIST OF TERMS

Accelerated depreciation
Equivalent annual cost
Net working capital
Nominal interest rate
Opportunity costs
Real interest rate

Recovery period class
Straight-line depreciation
Sunk costs
Tax depreciation
Tax shield

EXERCISES

Fill-in Questions

1. Costs that occurred in the past and are irrecoverable are called _____.

2. The cost of a resource for its best alternative use is its _____.

3. Current assets minus current liabilities equal _____.

4. An interest rate adjusted for inflation, so that it represents an increase in purchasing power, is called the _____ rate.

5. The stated interest rate in most transactions has no adjustment for inflation and is the _____ rate.

6. Under_____, the amount of depreciation is the same each year.

7. _____ is the general term for any depreciation method that provides larger deductions in the early years of the asset's life.

8. To work out the after-tax cash flows from an investment, we need to know what_____ is allowed, rather than how it is depreciated for accounting purposes.

9. The tax depreciation allowed for a particular asset depends on which_____it belongs to.

10. The tax depreciation amount multiplied by the tax rate is called the depreciation _____.

11. The _____of equipment is the constant annual charge, which, over the life of the equipment, has the same present-value cost as the equipment.

Problems

1. Ohno Hardware Inc. (OHI) is considering an investment of $5 million in plant and machinery. This is expected to produce sales of $2 million in year 1, $4 million in year 2, and $6 million in year 3. Subsequent sales will increase at the expected inflation rate of 10%. The plant is expected to be scrapped after 6 years with a salvage value of $1 million. It is depreciated for tax purposes on a straight-line basis of $1 million per year. Costs of goods sold are expected to be 70% of the sales. Working capital requirements are negligible. OHI pays tax at 35%. Calculate the expected cash flows in each year and the NPV of the investment when the required rate of return is 16%.

2. Repeat the calculation of problem 1, doing the analysis in *real* instead of nominal terms. Discount the cash flows using the approximate real rate of 5.45%.

3. How does your analysis of problem 1 change if the new plant qualifies for tax depreciation under the 5-year recovery period class?

4. Kats Corp. is evaluating an investment project, which will cost $40 million and generate taxable revenues of $11 million per year for 7 years. There will be no salvage value at the end of this period. Kats is currently unsure whether the investment will belong to the 3-year, 5-year, or 7-year recovery period class. Calculate the NPV of the project for each of these three possibilities. Kats' tax rate is 35% and its required return is 15%.

5. Teal Corp. must choose between machines A and B, which perform exactly the same operations but have different lives of 2 and 3 years, respectively. Machine A costs $30,000 initially and has annual costs of $5,000. Machine B has an initial cost of $40,000 and annual costs of $7,000. If Bluebird's cost of capital is 10%, which machine should it choose?

6. A machine costs $100,000. At the end of the first year, $5,000 must be spent on maintenance. Each year, the cost of maintenance rises by 15%. How long should the machine be kept before it is scrapped if the opportunity cost of capital is 10%? (Assume the machine has a zero salvage value.)

7. CME Company is considering whether to replace an existing machine or to spend money on overhauling it. The replacement machine would cost $18,000 and would require maintenance of $1,500 at the end of every year. At the end of 10 years, it would have a scrap value of $2,000 and would not be maintained. The existing machine requires increasing amounts of maintenance each year, and its salvage value is falling as shown below:

Year	Maintenance Cost	Salvage Value
0	$2,000	$2,500
1	$3,000	$2,000
2	$4,000	$1,500
3	$5,000	$1,000
4	$5,000	0

If CME faces an opportunity cost of capital of 15%, when should it replace the machine?

8. The acceptance of a particular capital budgeting proposal will mean that a new computer costing $200,000 will be purchased in 1 year's time instead of in 3 years' time. This also implies that an extra computer programmer costing $30,000 a year must be hired in year 1 instead of year 3. Work out the present-value cost of these two items when the opportunity cost of capital is 14%.

Essay Questions

1. Project evaluation should consider only incremental after-tax cash flows. What are incremental, after-tax cash flows?

2. Depreciation is not a cash flow and therefore should not be considered in project evaluation. Discuss.

3. "We always allocate a proportion of company overhead to a new project in relation to its payroll requirements. After all, in the long run, there's no difference between average and marginal cost." Discuss.

4. Describe how to work out the economic life of a piece of machinery and how to decide when to replace an existing machine, which performs the same function.

ANSWERS TO EXERCISES

Fill-in Questions

1. Sunk costs
2. Opportunity cost
3. Net working capital
4. Real interest
5. Nominal interest
6. Straight line depreciation
7. Accelerated depreciation
8. Tax depreciation
9. Recovery period class
10. Tax shield
11. Equivalent annual cost

Problems

1. The cash flows and the present values are given in the table below.

Cash flows ($1000s)

Years	0	1	2	3	4	5	6
1. Investment and salvage	−5,000						650[1]
2. Sales		2,000	4,000	6,000	6,600	7,260	7,986
3. Cost of goods sold		1,400	2,800	4,200	4,620	5,082	5,590
4. Depreciation		1,000	1,000	1,000	1,000	1,000	0
5. Pre-tax profit [2−3−4]		−400	200	800	980	1,178	2,396
6. Tax at 35% of 5		−140	70	280	343	412	839
7. Profit after tax [5−6]		−260	130	520	637	766	1,557
8. Operating cash flow [7+4]		740	1,130	1,520	1,637	1,766	1,557
9. Total cash flows [1+8]	−5,000	740	1,130	1,520	1,637	1,766	2,207
10. Present value at 16%	−5,000	638	840	974	904	841	906
11. Net present value	−5,000 + 638 + 840 + 974 + 904 + 841 + 906 = 103						

Notes: 1. Salvage value $1,000,000 less tax of $35,000 = $650,000

2. The real cash flows and the present values are given in the table below.

Cash flows ($1000s)

Years	0	1	2	3	4	5	6
1. Nomianl cash flows (same as in problem 1)	−5,000	740	1,130	1,520	1,637	1,766	2,207
2. Real cash flows[1]	−5,000	673	934	1,142	1,118	1,097	1,246
3. Present value at 5.45%	−5,000	638	840	974	904	841	906
4. Net present value	−5,000 + 638 + 840 + 974 + 904 + 841+906 = 103						

Notes: 1. The real cash flows are calculated by the following formula = $C_t/1.1^t$

3. See the table below.

Years	0	1	2	3	4	5	6
1. Investment and salvage	−5,000						650[1]
2. Sales		2,000	4,000	6,000	6,600	7,260	7,986
3. Cost of goods sold		1,400	2,800	4,200	4,620	5,082	5,590
4. Depreciation		1,000	1,600	960	576	576	288
5. Pre-tax profit [2−3−4]		−400	−400	840	1,404	1,602	2,108
6. Tax at 35% of 5		−140	−140	294	491	561	738
7. Profit after tax [5−6]		−260	−260	546	913	1,041	1,370
8. Operating cash flow [7+4]		740	1,340	1,506	1,489	1,617	1,658
9. Total cash flows [1+8]	−5,000	740	1,340	1,506	1,489	1,617	2,308
10. Present value at 16%	−5,000	638	996	965	822	770	947
11. Net present value	−5,000 + 638 + 996 + 965 + 822 + 770 + 947 = 138						

4. The tables below give the cash flows and the NPV for the 3 different scenarios.

Cash flows ($millions)

	3 Year class	5 year class	7 year class
Investment	−40.00	−40.00	−40.00
PV of depreciation tax shield	10.72	9.66	8.78
PV of Net revenues	29.75	29.75	29.75
Net present value	0.47	−0.59	−1.47

PV of depreciation tax shield for the 3-year class computation:
Tax shield = $40 m × depreciation rate × tax rate. (See table 6.4 for the depreciation rates.)
$CF_0 = 0$, $CO_1 = \$40.0$ m × 0.3333 × 0.35 = $4.667 m, $FO_1 = 1$
$CO_2 = \$40.0$ m × 0.4445 × 0.35 = $4.667 m, $FO_2 = 1$
$CO_3 = \$40.0$ m × 0.1481 × 0.35 = $2.073 m, $FO_3 = 1$
$CO_4 = \$40.0$ m × 0.0741 × 0.35 = $1.037 m, $FO_4 = 1$
NPV: I = 15, NPV = 10.720 million

PV of net revenues: N = 7, I = 15, PV = SOLVE, PMT = $11 M × (1−0.35) = $7.15 m
PV = $29.75 million

5. Present value of costs for A = $38,678, EAC = $22,286
   Present value of costs for B = $57,408, EAC = $23,085
   A is cheaper.

6. The maintenance cost at the end of year 1 is $5,000, year 2 is $5,000 × 1.15 = $5,750, and so on. You can calculate the PV of the maintenance costs and the initial investment of $100,000 and convert them into EACs for 5 years, 10 years, and so on. The lowest EAC is for 12 years as shown in the table below.

Years kept	PV of cost	Annuity factor	EAC (PV/Ann. Factor)
5	119,459	3.791	$31,512
10	149,192	6.145	$24,279
11	155,974	6.495	$24,014
12	163,063	6.814	$23,931
13	170,475	7.103	$24,000

Note that when you keep the machine for 5 years, you spend the maintenance cost for only 4 years.

7. The present value of total costs of the new machine is $24,663. This converts to an EAC of $4914.20. The costs of each year's operation of the old machine (adjusted to the end of each year) are given below.

Years	Cost of operation	How calculated
1	$3,175	$(2000 + 2500) \times 1.15 - 2000$
2	$4,250	$(3000 + 2000) \times 1.15 - 1500$
3	$5,325	$(4000 + 1500) \times 1.15 - 1000$
4	$6,900	$(5000 + 1000) \times 1.15$

The old machine should be replaced after 2 years.

8. Present-value cost of change in computer timing:
Cost of spending $200,000 in 3 years: N = 3, I = 14, FV = −$200,000, PV = $134,994
Cost of spending $200,000 in 1 year: N = 1, I = 14, FV = −$200,000, PV = $175,438
Difference = $40,444

Present-value cost of extra programmer: N = 2, I = 14, PMT = $30,000, PV = solve = −$49,400.

7

Introduction to Risk, Return, and the Opportunity Cost of Capital

INTRODUCTION

This chapter is the first of three chapters dealing with the risk and return trade-off, and its implications to corporate finance. The chapter provides a historic overview of the capital market performance of treasury bills, treasury bonds, and stocks. This is followed by an introduction to risk and measuring risk. Investing in a portfolio of stocks helps one to reduce risk considerably. Investors generally dislike uncertainty or risk and agree that a safe dollar is worth more than a risky one. Investors will have to be persuaded to take higher risk by the offer of higher returns. The next two chapters will connect all this to the opportunity cost of capital for corporations.

The chapter starts with a detailed description of the historic performance of different securities in the U. S. capital markets. This lesson is used to provide basic benchmarks for risk and return. The statistical measures of variance and standard deviation are used to measure the risk of individual securities and portfolios. Individual stocks are more risky than portfolios. As the number of stocks in a portfolio increases, the risk of the portfolio is reduced. The reduction in risk however levels off once the number of stocks in the portfolio reaches a certain number. Thus, there is a certain level of risk that you can never diversify away. This undiversifiable risk stems from economy-wide perils that affect all businesses; it is called market risk. The risk a security adds to a well-diversified portfolio depends on its market risk. This risk is called beta and finds extensive applications in later chapters.

Statistics: This chapter uses some basic statistical concepts and will be easy to follow if you already know some elementary statistics. The text gives all the necessary definitions, but you may want to refresh your memory from a statistics textbook. It will help if you are familiar with the terms such as variance, standard deviation, and covariance, and normal distribution.

KEY CONCEPTS IN THE CHAPTER

Capital Market History: The chapter begins with a description of the market performance of three different classes of securities over the 109-year period from 1900 to 2008. The three portfolios are: the U. S. treasury bills, the long-term U. S. government bonds, and a portfolio of U. S. common stocks. Treasury bills are considered risk-less and the benchmark for the safest investment possible. The treasury bonds have higher risk and the stocks the most risky portfolio of the three. The historic returns for the Treasury bill portfolio averaged 4.0% in nominal terms compared to the 5.5% for the treasury bonds, and 11.1% for the stock portfolio. These numbers show that the risk premium provided by the stocks amount to 7.1%. The real returns on the portfolios were 1.1%, 2.6% and 8.5% respectively.

<u>Use of historic returns:</u> The historic data are often used for valuation or cost of capital estimation. Two types of average measures are calculated from the historic data: the arithmetic average and the geometric mean. The arithmetic average will be higher than the geometric mean and is the appropriate yardstick to use for valuation or cost of capital estimation.

Interest rates change frequently, and the expected return on the market will change with them. However, the risk premium on the market (the difference between the market return and the return on the risk-free investment (T-bill) is fairly stable. Therefore, when we wish to estimate today's expected return on the market portfolio, we should take the current treasury-bill yield and add to it the normal risk premium (the long-term average) equities have earned above treasury bills. As an example, the current T-bill yield (as of October 2009) is about 0.1% (an unusually low rate, thanks to the current financial crisis and the monetary policy pursued by the Federal Reserve). The long-term average risk premium is 7.1%. Therefore, the expected market return can be estimated as 0.1 + 7.1 = 7.2%. Note that not everyone agrees that the long-term average from the historic data is the right risk premium for the market. It is possible that for a number of reasons, the long-term average may be overestimating the expected risk premium. These include the higher than international average risk premium enjoyed the U.S. market and the possibility that some of the high actual returns of the second half of the last century might actually have been unexpected. We learnt in chapter 4 that the market capitalization rate can be computed as the sum of dividend yield and the expected growth in dividends. If we use this approach to estimate the market return we get an estimate of 9.6%. Of course, dividend yields have also fluctuated a lot over time. All of this tells you that it is not easy to forecast expected return.

Risk: The idea of risk is a familiar one and implies uncertain outcomes. It also means that there are a number of possible outcomes and some of the outcomes are not desirable. The return from an investment in a stock or a portfolio of common stocks cannot be predicted with any accuracy because it is risky. The use of statistics helps us to analyze this type of risk in a precise way. The spread of past returns gives a good indication of the range of uncertainty about future returns. The spread, or the uncertainty of outcomes, is measured by the standard deviation or the variance.

The standard deviation of the annual returns on the stock portfolio over the last 109-year period is 20.2% compared to only 2.8% for the portfolios of treasury bills. The higher risk of the stock portfolio explains its high return. Note that the standard deviation of the stock returns decreased significantly from a recent high of 70% during October and November of 2008 to about 31% in May 2009.

Diversification and Risk: Diversification is an important concept with powerful implications. When stocks are combined into portfolios, it is observed that the risk of the portfolio decreases as the number of stocks in the portfolio increases. The risk in a diversified portfolio is lower than for a single security because the returns of different stocks do not move perfectly together. Statistically, individual stock returns are less than perfectly correlated. When we hold many stocks, the risks, which are unique to each one, tend to cancel, as they are largely unconnected. Some risks, though, stem from uncertainty about factors, which affect the whole of the market. This market risk cannot be eliminated by diversification and must be borne by investors, and investors can expect to earn a higher return for bearing higher market risk.

Calculation of Portfolio Returns and Risk Measures: The chapter describes how the expected return and standard deviation of a portfolio may be calculated from the characteristics of the individual stocks. It also describes how we can calculate the risk that a particular stock adds to an incompletely diversified portfolio. The section on formulas and computations describe the methods. If these seem too complicated to you, the chapter also gives the following useful rule of thumb to the benefits of diversification. The variance of a portfolio consisting of equal holdings of N stocks is equal to:

Average covariance + (1/N) (average variance − average covariance)

As N becomes larger, 1/N becomes very small and the significance of the individual variances becomes less and less.

Beta: The contribution each security makes to the risk of a well-diversified portfolio depends on the security's covariance with other securities in the portfolio. This will depend on how sensitive it is to the changes in the market portfolio. Beta measures this sensitivity. The average stock return will tend to move up and down nearly in tandem with the market. It will move up 5% when the market moves up 5%. Of course, sometimes it will go up (or down) more or less than the market. However, on average, it moves one for one with the market. This means that its beta is 1. A stock that is more sensitive to market movements might tend to move twice as far (10%) in response to a market rise of 5%. Conversely, it would tend to fall 10% if the market fell 5%. This stock is twice as sensitive as the average, and its beta is 2.

The beta of a portfolio is the weighted average of the betas of the stocks included in it. In other words, if a portfolio consists of 30% of stocks with betas of 1.5 and 70% of stocks with betas of 0.8, the beta of the portfolio is $(0.3 \times 1.5) + (0.7 \times 0.8) = 1.01$. When a portfolio is well diversified, the amount of unique risk (or company-specific risk) it contains is negligible. In this case, the standard deviation of the portfolio will be its beta multiplied by the standard deviation of the return on the market portfolio. This makes beta an important number. Beta measures how much a stock contributes to the risk of a well-diversified portfolio.

Diversification and Value Additivity: Diversification is good for individual investors. Since it would be relatively easy for investors to diversify directly by holding a variety of stocks, they have no reason to pay more for the stocks of companies, which are already diversified. This has implications for corporate attempts at diversification for the purpose of risk reduction. The implication is that the value of a project does not depend on how its returns mesh with the returns from other activities of the company, which undertakes it. If the capital market establishes a value of PV (A) for asset A and PV (B) for asset B, the market value of a firm that holds only these two assets is:

PV (AB) = PV (A) + PV (B)

This is known as the value additivity principle.

Explanation of Formulas and Mathematical Expressions: The chapter describes a number of formulas for calculating expected returns, standard deviations, variances, and betas of securities and portfolios.

<u>Expected return of portfolios:</u> The expected return of a portfolio of stocks is the weighted average of the expected returns on the individual stocks. Expected portfolio return, r_p, i.e. given by:

$$r_p = x_1 r_1 + x_2 r_2 + \ldots\ldots + x_n r_n$$

where x_1 = proportion of portfolio in stock 1, r_1 = expected return on stock 1, etc.

Example: Stocks A, B and C have returns of 12%, 16%, and 11% respectively. What is the expected return of a portfolio, which includes 40% of its value invested in A, 40% in B, and 20% in C?

$$\text{Expected return} = (0.4 \times 12) + (0.4 \times 16) + (0.2 \times 11) = 13.4\%$$

<u>Portfolio variance:</u> Portfolio variance is not the simple weighted average of the individual standard deviations (unless they are perfectly correlated). The portfolio variance is a function of the individual variances of the different stocks and the covariance of all the pairs of stocks in the portfolio.

$$
\begin{aligned}
\text{Portfolio variance} \;=\; & x_1^2 \sigma_1^2 + x_1 x_2 \sigma_{12} + \cdots + x_1 x_N \sigma_{1N} \\
& + x_2 x_1 \sigma_{21} + x_2^2 \sigma_2^2 + \cdots + x_2 x_N \sigma_{2N} \\
& + \cdots + \cdots + \cdots \\
& + x_N x_1 \sigma_{N1} + x_N x_2 \sigma_{N2} + \cdots + x_N^2 \sigma_N^2
\end{aligned}
$$

where, σ_1^2 = variance of stock 1 (σ_1 is its standard deviation)

$\quad\sigma_{12}$ = covariance between stock 1 and stock 2, = $\sigma_1 \sigma_2 \rho_{12}$, where ρ_{12} is the correlation between stock 1 and stock 2.

If there are N equal-size holdings (i.e. $x_i = 1/N$),

portfolio variance = $(1/N)^2 [N \times \text{average variance} + (N^2 - N) \times \text{average covariance}]$
$\qquad\qquad = \text{average covariance} + (1/N) \times (\text{average variance} - \text{covariance})$

<u>A security's contribution to portfolio risk:</u> From the top row of the portfolio variance calculation:

Stock l's contribution to risk = $x_1 (x_1 \sigma_1^2 + x_2 \sigma_{12} + \cdots + x_N \sigma_{1N})$
Proportionate contribution to risk = $x_1 \sigma_{1P}/\sigma_P^2$
where σ_{1P} is its covariance with the portfolio and σ_P^2 is the variance of the portfolio.

Here σ_{1P}/σ_P^2 is the sensitivity of stock 1 to changes in portfolio value.
Since σ_{1M}/σ_M^2 = beta, beta measures a stock's contribution to the risk of the market portfolio.

$$\text{Beta of stock i} = \frac{\sigma_{im}}{\sigma_m^2} = \frac{\rho_{im}\sigma_i}{\sigma_m}$$

<u>The effect of individual stocks on portfolio risk</u>: The risk of a well-diversified portfolio depends on the market risk of the securities included in the portfolio. Beta (β) measures the market risk of a stock as its sensitivity to market movements. Stocks with betas greater than one are usually more sensitive (than the average stock) to market movements. Stocks with betas less than one are less sensitive to market movements. The beta of a portfolio is the weighted average of the beta of the securities included in it. That is,

$$\beta_P = x_1\beta_1 + x_2\beta_2 + \text{·········} + x_N\beta_N$$

The standard deviation of a well-diversified portfolio is its beta times the standard deviation of the market portfolio. A diversified portfolio of high-beta stocks is therefore more risky than a diversified portfolio of low-beta stocks. Beta is important because it measures how much a stock contributes to the risk of a well-diversified portfolio.

WORKED EXAMPLES

1. Calculate the standard deviation and expected return for the portfolio given below, and work out how each stock contributes to the portfolio's risk.

Stock	Percentage held	Expected return	Standard deviation	Correlation among stocks		
				Stock 1	Stock 2	Stock 3
Stock 1	40	15	18	1	0.1	0.4
Stock 2	30	16	24	0.1	1	0.5
Stock 3	30	20	36	0.4	0.5	1

SOLUTION

To work out the standard deviation of a portfolio, we need to first calculate the covariance between stocks. Covariance $\sigma_{ij} = \sigma_i\sigma_j\rho_{ij}$
Given below is a table of all the covariances. All values are rounded off to whole numbers.

Stocks	Stock 1	Stock 2	Stock 3
Stock 1	$18 \times 18 \times 1 = 324$	$18 \times 24 \times 0.1 = 43$	$18 \times 36 \times 0.4 = 259$
Stock 2	$24 \times 18 \times 0.1 = 43$	$24 \times 24 \times 1 = 576$	$24 \times 36 \times 0.5 = 432$
Stock 3	$36 \times 18 \times 0.4 = 259$	$36 \times 24 \times 0.5 = 432$	$36 \times 36 \times 1 = 1296$

Notice that this table is symmetric about the diagonal (that is, $\sigma_{12} = \sigma_{21}, \sigma_{13} = \sigma_{31}$, etc.). To get the portfolio covariance, each covariance (σ_{ij}) is multiplied by the percentages held in each of the stocks (x_ix_j). The table below gives the values for covariance multiplied by the corresponding x_ix_j.

Stocks	Stock 1	Stock 2	Stock 3
Stock 1	$0.4 \times 0.4 \times 324 = 51.8$	$0.4 \times 0.3 \times 43 = 5.2$	$0.4 \times 0.3 \times 259 = 31.1$
Stock 2	$0.3 \times 0.4 \times 43 = 5.2$	$0.3 \times 0.3 \times 576 = 51.8$	$0.3 \times 0.3 \times 432 = 38.9$
Stock 3	$0.3 \times 0.4 \times 259 = 31.1$	$0.3 \times 0.3 \times 432 = 38.9$	$0.3 \times 0.3 \times 1296 = 116.6$

The portfolio variance is the sum of the values all the cells.

Portfolio variance = $51.8 + 51.8 + 116.6 + 2(5.2 + 31.1 + 38.9) = 370.6$

Portfolio standard deviation = $\sqrt{370.6} = 19.25\%$

Portfolio return = $(0.4 \times 15) + (0.3 \times 16) + (0.3 \times 20) = 16.8\%$

The sum of each row in the variance calculation shows how much each stock contributes to the total variance.

Contribution by stock 1 = $\sigma_{1P}/\sigma_P^2 = (51.8 + 5.2 + 31.1)/370.6 = 0.24$
Contribution by stock 2 = $\sigma_{2P}/\sigma_P^2 = (5.2 + 51.8 + 38.9)/370.6 = 0.26$
Contribution by stock 3 = $\sigma_{3P}/\sigma_P^2 = (31.1 + 38.9 + 116.6)/370.6 = 0.50$

To get the sensitivity of each stock to changes in the portfolio value or beta of the stock with respect to this portfolio, we need to divide the proportionate contribution by the percentage of each stock in the portfolio.

$$\beta_1 = 0.24/0.4 = 0.6, \; \beta_2 = 0.26/0.3 = 0.87, \; \beta_1 = 0.50/0.3 = 1.67$$
(Note that these are betas with respect to this portfolio and not the market.)

2. Marquis Fund has four stocks in its portfolio. The percentage of each stock held and the beta for each stock are: Stock A – 15%, beta = 1.2; Stock B – 25%, beta = 0.9; Stock C – 30%, beta = 1.8; and Stock D – 30%, beta = 0.6. Calculate the portfolio beta.

SOLUTION

Portfolio beta = $(0.15 \times 1.2) + (0.25 \times 0.9) + (0.3 \times 1.8) + (0.3 \times 0.6) = 1.13$

SUMMARY

This chapter provides the first formal introduction to risk and the measurement of risk. The chapter begins with a detailed description of the history of the U. S. capital market from 1900 to 2008. This history lesson is a useful way to understand the risk-return trade off faced by an investor in the capital market. The market performance provides useful benchmarks of risk and return with the U. S. Treasury bills as the risk-free investment and the market portfolio of common stocks as the risky investment with significantly higher expected return.

The chapter also introduces you to the effects of diversification. Shareholders can, and do, reduce their risk very significantly by diversification. The risk that matters to them is, therefore, the market risk that each security adds to a diversified portfolio. This leads to the risk measure, beta, which is the sensitivity of a security's return to the return on the market portfolio. It is the beta of a security that determines how much risk that security contributes to a diversified portfolio. We will revisit beta in later chapters and it will be a very useful tool in estimating the opportunity cost of capital for investment projects.

The value of diversification does not imply that corporations can create shareholder value by diversifying their business assets. The value of a project depends only on its cash flows and its market risk and not on how well its returns relate to the other activities of the company. This implies value additivity: the value of project A and the value of project B combined is simply the sum of value of A and the value of B.

LIST OF TERMS

Beta (β)	Market risk
Correlation	Market risk premium ($r_m - r_f$)
Covariance	Risk-free rate of return (r_f)
Diversification	Standard deviation (σ)
Expected market return (r_m)	Unique risk
Expected return	Value additivity
Market portfolio	Variability
Market return	Variance (σ^2)

EXERCISES

Fill-in Questions

1. Combining stocks into a portfolio provides an investor _____ and risk reduction.

2. The difference between the risk free rate and the _____ is called the _____.

3. Diversification cannot eliminate all risk because all stocks are subject to _____.

4. The average annual _____ between 1900 and 2008 was 11.1%.

5. Diversification reduces _____.

6. The principle of _____ means that PV (AB) = PV (A) + PV (B).

7. The _____ of the market as a whole is one.

8. The _____ of the U. S common stock portfolio has averaged about 20% over the 109 year period of 1900 to 2008.

9. Projects, which have the same risk as the market portfolio, can be evaluated by a discount rate equal to the _____ plus the normal risk premium for the market portfolio.

10. The contribution a stock makes to the portfolio risk is measured by its _____.

11. _____ is the square of standard deviation.

12. The covariance between two stocks is the product of their standard deviations and the _____ coefficient between them.

13. The variability of a well-diversified portfolio depends almost entirely on the average _____between individual stocks.

Problems

1. Fall Specials Company is considering investing in a project, which has risk similar to the market risk. The current risk free rate as measured by the rate on treasury bills is 0.2% and the average for the last three years was 3.8%. The returns on the S&P 500 portfolio for the last three years were 7%, 21%, and −32%. Suggest an appropriate discount rate for the project.

2. Stock A has an expected return of 16% and standard deviation of 28%. Stock B has an expected return of 21% and standard deviation of 36%. Calculate the expected return and standard deviation of a portfolio which is invested equally in the two stocks if the correlation coefficient between the stock returns is: (a) 1, (b) 0.5, and (c) −0.5.

3. Refer to the problem 2 above. If the correlation coefficients of stock returns of A and B to the market portfolio were 0.7 and 0.3 respectively and the standard deviation of market returns is 14%, what will be the betas for A and B?

4. A portfolio of stocks has risk similar to a portfolio consisting of 40% of Treasury bills and 60% of Standard & Poor's index. The Treasury bill rate is 0.2%, and you expect a normal risk premium of 7.1% on the market portfolio. What return would you expect from the portfolio of stocks?

5. Refer to problem 4. What will be the beta of the portfolio?

6. Your investment will give a return of either −10 or +30%. (a) Calculate the expected return and the standard deviation of return if these outcomes are equally likely. (b) Calculate the expected return and the standard deviation of return if there is a 0.6 probability of the −10% return and a 0.4 probability of the +30% return.

7. A portfolio consists of the three stocks with betas of 0.8, 1.4, and 1.6. If the portfolio is equally invested in each stock, what is the portfolio beta?

8. The diagram below shows the effect of diversification. Label the diagram with appropriate words for the different letters.

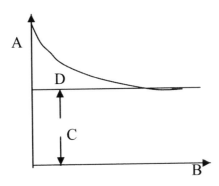

9. Details of the stocks held in a portfolio are given below.

Stocks	Beta	Expected return	Percentage held
Stock A	1.1	14	25
Stock B	0.8	10	18
Stock C	1.4	17	23
Stock D	1.5	19	34

   Calculate the expected return and the beta of this portfolio.

10. Calculate the betas of the following stocks if the standard deviation of the market returns is 14%.

Stocks	Standard deviation	Correlation coefficient with the market portfolio
Stock P	18%	0.7
Stock Q	24%	0.3
Stock R	38%	0.5
Stock S	42%	0.2

11. The average variance of the annual returns from a typical stock is about 1,500, and its average covariance with other stocks is about 400. Work out what this implies for the standard deviation of returns from: (a) a fully diversified portfolio, (b) a portfolio of 64 stocks, (c) a portfolio of 16 stocks, and (d) a portfolio of 4 stocks. Assume equal-size holdings of each stock.

12. You hold a portfolio of 16 Stocks, each of which has a variance of 1,500 and a covariance of 400 with the other stocks. One stock comprises 25% of your portfolio, and the other stocks are held in equal amounts of 5% each. (a) What is the standard deviation of your portfolio? (b) How many stocks held in equal amounts would give approximately the same standard deviation?

Essay Questions

1. Why diversification cannot eliminate all the risk?

2. Describe what is meant by the beta of a stock. Why is a stock's beta more important than its standard deviation?

3. Is it possible for a company's stocks to have a high standard deviation but a low beta? What kind of industries will this stock belong to?

4. Stockholders of publicly quoted companies do not benefit from corporate diversification since they can diversify for themselves. Discuss under what conditions (if any) this principle extends to the case of a privately held company, which is 100%, owned by a single individual.

ANSWERS TO EXERCISES

Fill-in Questions

1. Diversification
2. Expected market return, market risk premium
3. Market risk
4. Market return
5. Unique risk
6. Value additivity
7. Beta
8. Standard deviation
9. Risk free rate
10. Beta
11. Variance
12. Correlation
13. Covariance

Problems

1. Use the current risk-free rate and the long-term average risk premium.
   Discount rate = risk-free rate + risk premium
   $$= 0.2\% + 7.1\% = 7.3\%$$

2. Expected return = $(0.5 \times 16) + (0.5 \times 21) = 18.5\%$

   a. Variance of the portfolio = $0.5 \times 0.5 \times 28^2 + 2 \times 0.5 \times 0.5 \times 28 \times 36 \times 1 + 0.5 \times 0.5 \times 36^2 = 1024$, standard deviation = 32 [Since the correlation coefficient is 1, the standard deviation will be the weighted average of the standard deviations of the two stocks.]
   b. Variance = 772, Standard deviation = 27.8%.
   c. Variance = 268, Standard deviation = 16.4%.

3. $\beta_A = (28/14) \times 0.7 = 1.4$, $\beta_B = (36/14) \times 0.3 = 0.8$

4. Expected return = $(0.4 \times 0.2) + 0.6 \times (0.2 + 7.1) = 4.46\%$

5. Beta of the portfolio = $(0.4 \times 0) + (0.6 \times 1) = 0.6$ (T-bill being risk-free will have beta of zero.)

6. a. Expected return = 10%, Standard deviation = 20%.
   b. Expected return = 6%, Standard deviation = 19.6%.

7. Portfolio beta = $(0.8 + 1.4 + 1.6)/3 = 1.27$

8. A = Portfolio standard deviation, B = Number of stocks, C = Market risk, D = Unique risk

9. Expected return = $(0.25 \times 14) + (0.18 \times 10) + (0.23 \times 17) + (0.34 \times 19) = 15.67\%$
   Portfolio beta = $(0.25 \times 1.1) + (0.18 \times 0.8) + (0.23 \times 1.4) + (0.34 \times 1.5) = 1.25$

10. $\beta_P = (18/14) \times 0.7 = 0.9$, $\beta_Q = 0.51$, $\beta_R = 1.36$, $\beta_S = 0.6$

11. Portfolio variance = Average covariance + (1/N) (Average variance – Average covariance).
    For fully diversified portfolio, N is very large and Portfolio variance = Average covariance.
    For others substitute the value of N = 64, 16, and 4 to get the answers.
    (a) Standard deviation = Square root of 400 = 20%; (b) 20.43%;
    (c) 21.65%; d. 25.98

12. a. Variance = 510, Standard deviation = 22.58%.
    b. Variance = 400 + (1/N)(1500 – 400) = 510, Solving for N, N = 10

8

Portfolio Theory and the Capital Asset Pricing Model

INTRODUCTION

Chapter 7 introduced risk and risk measurement and showed us how diversification leads to risk reduction. There is a limit to risk reduction as only risk unique to individual securities can be diversified away. The risk that a security bears as part of the overall economic system remains in the portfolio and is termed market risk. A fully diversified portfolio will have only market risk. This chapter builds on the lessons of chapter 7 and presents formal models linking risk and expected return. The chapter begins with a discussion of the portfolio theory pioneered by Harry Markowitz. This theory formed the basis for the most popular and widely used model of risk-return relationship known as the Capital Asset Pricing Model or CAPM. The CAPM has some empirical evidence to support the basic conclusions derived from the model. It has also been challenged by other theories that rely on assumptions less restrictive than the ones used by CAPM. The chapter presents some alternative theories to CAPM. While CAPM is far from perfect, it remains the most widely accepted model, primarily because of its relative simplicity and ease of application.

KEY CONCEPTS IN THE CHAPTER

Portfolio Theory: Stock market returns of individual stocks measured over relatively short periods closely approximate the normal distribution. Given this, one can describe the entire distribution of the returns in terms of two parameters- the mean and standard deviation. The standard deviation of returns measures risk. Individual investors are assumed to be risk-averse and they would like to be compensated for bearing more risk. This also means that they like higher returns and lower risk.

The portfolio theory gives the basic principles of selecting the optimal portfolio in terms of risk and return. We learned in the last chapter that when two stocks are combined into a portfolio, the risk (standard deviation of the portfolio) is less than the average of the two individual standard deviations. Of course, when combining securities into a portfolio, an infinite number of combinations are possible. But investors would choose only those that are *efficient portfolios*. Portfolios are considered efficient if, for a given standard deviation, they give the highest return, or for a given return they have the lowest standard deviation. Investors need only consider efficient portfolios, for all other portfolios give them a poorer deal.

Investors have more than two stocks to choose from and we can extend the idea of efficient portfolio to the universe of available securities. All the efficient portfolios can be identified and depending on one's own risk-return preference, an investor can choose the best portfolio of his liking. The technique of *quadratic programming* can be used to choose the efficient portfolio of one's preference. If one were to graph the set of all efficient portfolios selected from all the stocks available it will look like the curve shown in Figure 1. The part BC of the curve represents all the available efficient portfolios. Any choice not on the efficient set will be dominated by a portfolio on the efficient set. Every investor will only choose a portfolio on this curve.

Figure 1

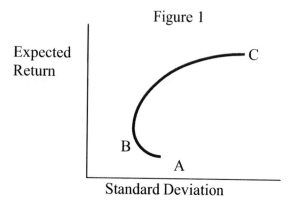

Investors' choices can be expanded by introducing the possibility of lending or borrowing at the risk-free rate. This will allow the investors to combine investing in the stock portfolios given by the efficient set with lending or borrowing (borrowing can be seen as negative lending). The possibilities are shown in Figure 2.

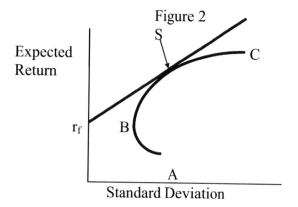

Investors can choose along the line starting from the risk-free rate to the portfolio S. The portfolio at S has the highest ratio of risk premium to standard deviation. The ratio of risk premium to standard deviation is called the Sharpe ratio.

$$\text{Sharpe ratio} = \frac{r_p - r_f}{\sigma_p}$$

If the investor chooses to invest all her money in risk-free lending, she will have the risk-free rate at zero standard deviation. Any point between r_f and S will mean that part of the money is invested in the stock portfolio S and the remaining lent at the risk-free rate. An investor is also free to choose points to the right of S. This would mean that the investor is borrowing money at the risk free rate and investing that along with his own money in portfolio S. You can clearly see that regardless of where the investor wants to be, the stock portfolio will be the same, namely the portfolio S. In other words, S is the best of all the efficient portfolios and every investor will be invested in this portfolio. This will also mean that every stock will be held as part of this portfolio.

An investor's task can be separated into two parts: first, to choose the best (risky) portfolio of stocks S and, second, to combine it with the right amount of lending or borrowing to adjust to the preferred level of risk. This is known as the separation theorem: the job of selecting individual stocks in one's portfolio can be independently of one's risk preference. In a competitive market, there is no reason to concentrate portfolios in any particular stock, and we can identify S as the market portfolio. Everyone holds S. Risk preference only decides what fraction of one's investment goes to S.

Capital Asset Pricing Model: Capital Asset Pricing Model (CAPM) is an extension of what we saw in Figure 2. Investing in risky assets such as the market portfolio S should carry a premium compared to the risk-free rate. Otherwise, investors will not take the risk. The market portfolio is the basic benchmark of risk in the CAPM. The risk premium on the market portfolio, measured as the difference between the market return and the risk-free rate is called the market risk premium. The beta for the market portfolio is 1. The CAPM postulates a linear relationship between risk and return as shown in Figure 3. Figure 3 shows the *security market line* (SML).

Figure 3

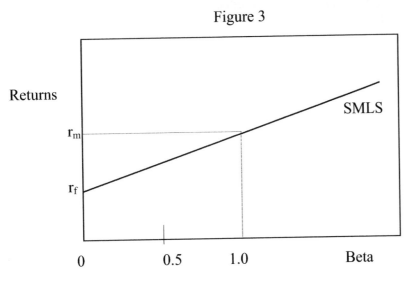

The risk of each stock is measured by its beta and the risk premium varies in direct proportion to beta. All stocks will lie along the SML and the expected return on a stock can be calculated by adding the risk premium to the risk-free rate.

Expected risk premium $= r - r_f = \beta(r_m - r_f)$

A key implication of the CAPM is that the risk of a stock that matters is its contribution to portfolio risk. This is what is measured by beta and depends on the stock's sensitivity to changes in the value of the market portfolio.

<u>Validity of CAPM:</u> Over the years, a lot of research has been done to test the validity of CAPM. The CAPM is a theory about expected returns. We can only measure actual returns. This makes it difficult to test the theory as it is conceived. Another problem in testing CAPM is that the market portfolio should include all assets, not just stocks traded in stock exchanges. In practice, most of the tests use stock market indexes such as the S & P 500 as proxies for the market portfolio.

A test (one of many) of the validity of CAPM was performed using portfolio returns over the period 1931 to 2008. The study grouped all New York Stock Exchange stocks into 10 portfolios selected according to the ranking of the betas of their stocks. Every year these portfolios were readjusted, using monthly data from the previous 5 years, so that portfolio 1 always contained the 10% of stocks with the lowest betas, portfolio 2 the next 10%, and so on up to portfolio 10 with the highest beta stocks. The performance of these portfolios was assessed over the 78-year period. The results showed a strong positive relationship between beta and returns and thus broad support for the CAPM. However, it was found that the security market line was flatter than the theory predicted and it was above the risk-free rate.

The above noted study also showed that the CAPM relationship held a lot better during the period 1931 to 1965 than during 1966 t0 2008. The relationship between beta and the risk premium was particularly flat during the more recent period. It has been argued that some of these results could be attributed to sampling errors (the realized average returns are not the same as the previously expected ones). There is also evidence that suggests that beta is not the only factor that affects expected returns. Firms, which are small, and ones, which have low market-to-book ratios, seem to provide higher average returns irrespective of their betas. It is difficult to judge the economic significance of these results. The small-firm effect is found to be less in more recent studies. It is also possible that some of the results that cast doubts on the validity of the CAPM can be produced by statistical strategies (known as "data mining"). The supporters of the CAPM believe that the broad conclusions of the theory are valid.

Arbitrage Pricing Theory: The arbitrage pricing theory (APT) was the first serious challenger to CAPM. It does not involve many of the restrictive assumptions of CAPM. It postulates that each stock's return depends on several pervasive macroeconomic factors and the risk premium depends on the factor weights. The general model can be written as:

$$\text{Return} = a + b_1 (\text{factor } 1) + b_2 (\text{factor } 2) + \cdots\cdots$$

Alternately, the risk premium: $r - r_f = b_1 (\text{premium}_1) + b_2 (\text{premium}_2) + \cdots\cdots$

The APT is general and has appealing features. The model is general and is dependent on the absence of arbitrage opportunities. The model does not specify either the number of factors or identity of these factors. The major problem is that there is little agreement on what the factors are. There have been many empirical attempts at identifying the factors. These have been met with limited success. The APT is still a long way from replacing the CAPM as the primary theory for risk-return relationship.

The Three-Factor Model: Eugene Fama and Kenneth French incorporate the small-firm effect and the book-to-market ratio effect seen in empirical studies into a formal risk-return relationship model. The model can be represented as:

$$r - r_f = b_{market} \left(r_{1market\text{-}factor} \right) + b_{size} \left(r_{size\ factor} \right) + b_{book\text{-}to\text{-}market} \left(r_{book\text{-}to\text{-}market} \right)$$

The model is a practical extension of CAPM.

WORKED EXAMPLES

1. Daisy Chang wants to invest $100,000. She has the choice of a risky portfolio of stocks, M, with an expected return of 10% and a standard deviation of 16%. She can also lend and borrow at the risk-free rate of 4%. Show how Daisy can construct a portfolio with standard deviations of (a) 8%, (b) 24%, and (c) 32%. Calculate the expected return for each of these portfolios.

SOLUTION

Since the standard deviation of lending or borrowing at the risk free rate is zero, the portfolio standard deviation is the fraction invested in M multiplied by its standard deviation. If she invests half of her money ($50,000) in M, the portfolio standard deviation will be: $0.5 \times 16 = 8\%$. If she borrows $50,000 and invests $150,000 ($100,000 of her own plus the borrowed $50,000) in M, the standard deviation of her investment portfolio will be $1.5 \times 16 = 24\%$. Similarly, to get a portfolio with standard deviation of 32%, she will have to borrow $100,000 and invest $200,000 in M. The expected return for each portfolio will be:

   a. $(0.5 \times 4) + (0.5 \times 10) = 7\%$
   b. $(1.5 \times 10) - (0.5 \times 4) = 13\%$
   c. $(2 \times 10) - (1 \times 4) = 16\%$

2. The Treasury bill rate is 1% and the market portfolio return is expected to be 8%.
   a. What is the market risk premium?
   b. What is required rate of return on an investment, which has a beta of 1.8?
   c. If the expected return on Grey Puppet Corp. stock is 12%, what is its beta?
   d. If an investment with a beta of 1.4 were expected to give a return of 10%, would you accept it?

SOLUTION

   a. Market risk premium = $8 - 1 = 7\%$
   b. Expected rate of return for an investment of beta of $1.8 = 1 + 1.8(7) = 13.6\%$
   c. Return $= 1 + \beta\ (7) = 12$, $\beta = \dfrac{12 - 1}{7} = 1.57$
   d. Expected rate of return as per CAPM $= 1 + 1.4(7) = 10.8\%$. The investment return is less than the expected rate of return as per CAPM. Hence, it is not an acceptable investment.

95

3. Gemini Inc. wishes to use the Fama-French 3-factor model to estimate its cost of equity capital. The company has estimated the following factor sensitivities and factor risk premiums:

Factors	Factor Sensitivity	Factor risk premium
Market factor	1.2	6.2%
Size factor	−0.5	2.6
Book-to-market factor	0.2	5.2

If the risk free rate is 1.5%, estimate the cost of equity capital for the firm.

SOLUTION

Risk premium = $1.2 \times 6.2 - 0.5 \times 2.6 + 0.2 \times 5.2 = 7.18\%$
Cost of equity capital = $1.5 + 7.18 = 8.68\%$.

SUMMARY

The chapter describes the basic principles of portfolio selection and the theories, which provide formal models of the relationship between risk and return. Risk averse investors choose portfolios based on risk and return. It makes sense to choose only efficient portfolios–portfolios, which provide the highest return for a given level of risk. In the presence of the possibility of risk-free lending and borrowing, investors will end up choosing the one portfolio that, in combination with risk-free lending/borrowing, gives the best choices regardless of one's own risk preferences. This forms the basis for the widely accepted theory, Capital Asset Pricing Model. The CAPM uses the market portfolio as the basic benchmark for risky investments and the risk of any stock or investment is measured relative to the market portfolio. The risk measure is beta and it reflects the stock's sensitivity to changes in the value of the market portfolio. The risk-return relationship is captured by the security market line and the risk premium on any stock is proportional to its beta.

The CAPM theory finds some empirical support, though questions have been raised about the strict validity of the security market line. Alternative theories of risk-return relationship include the arbitrage pricing theory and the three-factor model. Each of these theories has some intellectual appeal and might someday prove to be a replacement to the CAPM; however for the present the CAPM still rules. The primary attraction of the CAPM is its relative simplicity and ease of practical application. The CAPM should be seen as an approximate and partial explanation of the risk-return trade off faced by the investor.

LIST OF TERMS

Arbitrage pricing theory
Capital Asset Pricing Model
Efficient portfolios
Expected risk premium
Market risk premium

Normal distribution
Quadratic programming
Security market line
Three-factor model

EXERCISES

Fill-in Questions

1. The _____ uses less restrictive assumptions than the CAPM does and postulates that returns are dependent on pervasive macroeconomic factors.

2. The distribution of stock returns when measured over fairly short periods, closely follow _____.

3. A(n) _____ is a portfolio that gives the highest expected return for a given standard deviation or the lowest standard deviation for a given return.

4. Fama and French proposed the _____.

5. Optimal portfolio selection can be done using the_____ technique.

6. The _____ relates the risk premium to sensitivity of the asset's returns to changes in the value of the market portfolio.

7. The expected return on a stock investment, according to CAPM, equals the risk free rate plus _____.

8. The difference between the expected market return and the risk-free rate is _____.

9. According to the CAPM, the expected returns from all investments must plot along the _____.

Problems

1. Pick the better investment from each of the following pairs of portfolios.
   a. Portfolio A: expected return 14%, variance 400.
      Portfolio B: expected return 13%, variance 441.
   b. Portfolio J: expected return 20%, variance 529.
      Portfolio K: expected return 20%, variance 400.
   c. Portfolio R: expected return 8%, variance 225.
      Portfolio S: expected return 9%, variance 225.
   d. Portfolio X: expected return 12%, variance 380.
      Portfolio Y: expected return 15%, variance 460.

2. Calculate the expected return for the following portfolios:
   a. beta = 1.2
   b. beta = 1.5
   c. beta = 0.5
   d. beta = 0
   Assume the risk free rate to be 2.5% and the expected market risk premium to equal 8%.

3. Your broker is urging you to invest in one of three portfolios on which the returns are expected to be as follows: portfolio A - 12%; portfolio B - 16%; portfolio C - 20%. You believe these estimates, but you also have sufficient data to calculate the betas of the portfolios with confidence. You find the betas are 0.5 for A, 1.1 for B, and 2.0 for C. Which portfolio is best and why? (Hint: See if you can duplicate portfolio B by some combination of A and C.)

4. Stock J has a beta of 1.2 and an expected return of 12%, and stock K has a beta of 0.8 and an expected return of 9.4%. What must be (a) the expected return on the market and (b) the risk-free rate of return, to be consistent with the capital asset pricing model?

5. Stock A has an expected return of 14% and a beta of 1.1. Stock B has an expected return of 18. The risk free rate is 5.2%. Assume that stock A is correctly priced (i.e. it is on the security market line). If stock B has a beta of 1.4, is it correctly priced?

6. An alternate form of the CAPM is written as: $r = \alpha + \beta r_m$. Write a general expression for α and find the value for α for each of the following cases: (a) beta = 1, (b) beta = 2 and (c) beta = 0. What is the value of beta if α = zero?

7. The return on a proposed investment is expected to be 24%. The standard deviation is estimated at 30%. The risk free rate is 4%. Assume the expected market risk premium to be 9%. Assume that the standard deviation of market returns to be 15%. If the project correlates fairly highly with the economy, comment on the attractiveness of the project.

8. You are told that Rice Corp. stock has a beta of 1.2. Estimate its cost of equity capital.

9. A three factor APT model has the following factors and risk premiums:

Factors	Risk premiums
Change in GNP	4%
Change in dollar exchange rates	−2
Change in energy prices	−1

Calculate the expected rates of return on the following stocks, assuming the risk-free rate to be 4.5%.
a. Company A: $b_1 = 0.5$, $b_2 = -1.5$, $b_3 = 0.3$
b. Company B: $b_1 = 1.2$, $b_2 = 0$, $b_3 = -0.5$
c. Company C: $b_1 = 2$, $b_2 = 0.5$, $b_3 = -2$

10. Use the information on factor risk premiums from the worked example three-factor model problem to calculate the required rate of return on the following stocks with factor sensitivities to market, size, and book-to-market as follows:
a. Factor sensitivities: 1.2, 2, and 0
b. Factor sensitivities: 1.5, 0.3, and 1

Essay Questions

1. Explain the basic principles of portfolio theory. What is an efficient portfolio?

2. Explain the separation theorem and how it leads to all investors choosing the same portfolio of common stocks.

3. Compare and contrast the CAPM, consumption CAPM, and the APT.

4. The CAPM can be considered a special case of the APT. Discuss.

ANSWERS TO EXERCISES

Fill-in Questions

1. Arbitrage pricing theory
2. Normal distribution
3. Efficient portfolio
4. The three-factor model
5. Quadratic programming
6. Capital asset pricing model
7. Risk premium
8. Market risk premium
9. Security market line

Problems

1. The efficient portfolios are:
   a. Portfolio A - higher return, lower variance
   b. Portfolio K - same return, lower variance
   c. Portfolio S - higher return, same variance
   d. Cannot decide between the two without knowing the investor's risk preference

2. The expected returns can be calculated by the formula: $r = r_f + \beta (r_m - r_f)$
   a. $r = 2.5 + 1.2(8) = 12.1\%$
   b. $r = 14.5\%$
   c. $r = 6.5\%$
   d. $r = 2.5\%$

3. A portfolio containing 60% A and 40% C will have the same beta as that of B but has lower return (15.2%) than that of B. Thus, B is a better choice.

4. $r_f + 1.2(r_m - r_f) = 12$, $r_f + 0.8(r_m - r_f) = 9.4$ Solving for r_f and r_m, gives you: $r_f = 4.2\%$, $r_m = 10.72\%$.

5. Stock A return $= 5.2 + 1.1(r_m - 5.2) = 14$, $r_m = 13.2\%$.
   Expected return for B, as per CAPM $= 5.2 + 1.4(13.2 - 5.2) = 16.4\%$.
   This is lower than the expected return given. Stock B will not be on the SML.

6. $\alpha = (1 - \beta)$ rf
   a. If $\beta = 1$, $\alpha = 0$.
   b. If $\beta = 2$, $\alpha = -r_f$
   c. If $\beta = 0$, $\alpha = r_f$
   If $\alpha = 0$, $\beta = 1$

7. Beta for the project = $(\rho_{mp} \times \sigma_p)/\sigma_m$, where ρ_{mp} is the correlation coefficient for the project returns with the market returns and σ_p and σ_m the standard deviation of the project returns and the market returns respectively. If the correlation coefficient is positive 1 (the highest possible value), the beta for the project will be = 30/15 = 2. Substituting the values in the CAPM formula for required rate of return, you get required return = 4 + 2(9) = 22%. The project's return is higher than this and it appears to be a good project.

8. Based on historic market risk premium of about 7.6%, the risk premium for this stock will be 1.2 × 7.6 = 9.12%. Add this to the current risk-free rate to get an estimate of the cost of equity capital.

9. The returns for the different stocks are:
   a. r = 4.5 + 0.5(4) − 1.5(−2) + 0.3 (−1) = 9.2%
   b. r = 4.5 + 1.2(4) + 0 −0.5(−1) = 9.8%
   c. r = 4.5 + 2.0(4) + 0.5(−2) −2(−1) = 13.5%

10. The returns are:
    a. r = 4.5 + 1.2(6.2) + 2(2.6) + 0 = 17.14%
    b. r = 4.5 + 1.5(6.2) + 0.3(2.6) + 1(5.2) = 19.78%

9

Risk and the Cost of Capital

INTRODUCTION

Investment decisions require evaluation of cash flows produced by the proposed projects using appropriate, risk-adjusted discount rates. This takes us to one of the most common and important applications of the CAPM. This chapter describes this application and explains how to estimate the required rate of return or discount rate for projects using the CAPM. It is important to remember that the required rate of return on a project is a function of the risk of the project and does not depend on which company undertakes it. The relevant risk of the project is, of course, its market risk or beta and not the total risk. A company's stock beta and its cost of capital reflect the nature of all its assets as well as the financial leverage or the debt it carries in its balance sheet. Using the company cost of capital as the discount rate for all its new projects would be a serious error. We would still want to know what return is expected from the securities of a company and the cost of capital for the company as a whole, because this provides us with a benchmark return. From this, we can work out what return is required from projects whose risks are similar to those of the company's existing business. Riskier projects should have a higher hurdle rate and safer projects a lower rate.

The chapter describes how one can estimate betas for companies using market information. We can estimate the beta of a stock by comparing the stock's returns over time against the market returns. Individual company beta estimates tend to be unstable and it is often better to calculate the beta for the industry group to which the company belongs. The chapter also discusses the common, but often erroneous, practice of using arbitrary risk premiums (fudge factors) to adjust for projects considered risky. Other related topics covered include the relationship between beta and operating leverage, the basic determinants of beta and the concept of certainty equivalent. The certainty equivalent is an alternate approach to adjust for the risk of cash flows. Most of the discussions on risk-adjusted returns in the chapter use the CAPM as the theoretical risk-return model. The basic principles covered in the chapter can be extended to other risk-return models like the APT or the three-factor model as well.

KEY CONCEPTS IN THE CHAPTER

Company and Project Cost of Capital: *Cost of capital* for a company is the required rate of return demanded by the investors on the securities issued by the company. In practice, this is the weighted average of the return on the company's securities, typically debt and equity. Companies estimate their cost of capital using market data and use this company cost of capital as the discount rate for evaluating new projects. This cost of capital is appropriate and correct only if the project under consideration is exactly like the existing operations of the company, which is unlikely to be the case for any company with more than one type of business. Please remember that required rate of return demanded by investors depends on the use to which the capital is put.

Each project has to be evaluated as a mini-firm and the required rate of return for the project should be a function of only its market risk or beta. It should not make any difference as to which company undertakes the project. This follows directly from the CAPM and the value additivity principle. Thus, the discount rate used to evaluate a project should be estimated using the project's beta.

This does not mean that company cost of capital estimates have no practical value. In fact, they are extremely useful in estimating market's assessment of the required rate of return on the typical mix of the company's assets. Thus, for any project, which is of comparable risk, the company cost of capital might be a very good measure. For projects, which have higher risk, a higher discount rate will need to be used and projects, which have lower risk, should be evaluated with lower rate of return.

Debt and Cost of Capital: Companies generally use a financing mix comprising debt and equity. The cost of capital for a company will reflect the mix of financing used. The following relationships have to be kept in mind when using the cost of capital is to value a company's assets.

If D = Debt, E = Equity, then the value of the firm $V = D + E$

$$\text{Company cost of capital} = r_{assets} = r_{portfolio} = \frac{D}{V} \times r_D + \frac{E}{V} \times r_E$$

The company cost of capital is the expected return on a portfolio of the debt and equity of the firm. This reflects the average cost for the funds used by the firm and is often referred to as the *weighted average cost of capital* (WACC). The computation of the WACC is complicated by the impact of corporate taxes. The after-tax WACC will be:

$$r_D \frac{D}{V}(1 - T_c) + r_E \frac{E}{V},$$

Where, T_C is the corporate tax rate. We will return to this topic in Chapters 17 and 19.

Cost of Equity and Beta: The beta of a company's stock measures how its price responds to market movements and is estimated by plotting or regressing the returns on the stock against the returns on the market index. Monthly returns are commonly used and the slope of the fitted line through the scatter of points is the beta of the stock. Typically the estimated beta is used to compute the cost of equity capital using the CAPM formula: $r = r_f + \beta (r_m - r_f)$. It is important to note that estimates of individual company betas are highly unstable and it is better to use industry betas with any adjustment for financial leverage as discussed later. A beta, calculated for an industry group, would generally provide a more accurate measure of the beta of a project than that of the estimate for a single company.

One can also use published betas produced by a number of brokerage and advisory services. A number of financial news web sites also publish information on betas. The *R-squared* (R^2)

gives the proportion of the variance of the stock returns explained by market movements. One can also interpret this as the percentage of market risk in the stock's total risk. If a stock's return shows an R^2 of 30%, it implies that 30% of its risk is market risk. The remaining 70% is unique or company specific risk. Note that the betas calculated from regression are estimates and are subject to high degrees of error. The *standard error* of beta estimate measures the probable accuracy of the estimate.

As stated before, the required rate of return for a project depends on its systematic risk and is measured by its beta. The problem of choosing a suitable discount rate for a project therefore amounts to working out what sort of beta it has. We cannot do this directly because individual investment projects are not traded in the New York Stock Exchange. The best approximation is obtained by estimating the betas of companies, which are in the same business as the project. If one can estimate the betas for a number of companies in an industry and then estimate an average beta for the industry, this will be a reliable estimate for the industry represented by the companies.

Cyclicality, Operating Leverage, and Beta: High standard deviation of earnings does not necessarily mean high beta. What matters are the earnings variability and its relationship to the market returns. Cyclical firms, whose earnings are strongly dependent on the state of the business cycle, tend to have high betas. Variability of earnings can be due to unique risk. A strong relationship between a firm's earnings and aggregate market earnings means high market risk. The *accounting beta* or the *cash-flow beta* can be used to measure this. These betas are estimated using the accounting earnings or cash flows instead of security returns.

Beta is also a function of the operating cost structure. Other things equal, higher fixed costs will mean higher beta. The high level of fixed cost produces a leverage effect, which makes profits particularly vulnerable: a small percentage change in revenues will produce a much larger percentage change in profits. Companies with high fixed costs (often called high *operating leverage*) tend to have high betas. The relationship can be expressed as follows:

$$\beta_{\text{asset}} = \beta_{\text{revenue}} \left\{ 1 + \frac{PV(\text{fixed cost})}{PV(\text{asset})} \right\}$$

Arbitrary Discount Rates: Corporate managers often face the task of setting discount rates for projects, which are different from the typical project handled by them. These projects may be considered riskier than normal and are often evaluated with an arbitrary and higher discount rate than normal. The higher discount rate is often obtained by adding a *fudge factor* or an arbitrary premium to the normal project rate and is supposed to cover for an imprecise cash flow estimate and/or for the perceived higher uncertainty surrounding the project. This is not a good practice and one needs to think through the nature of the risk involved and distinguish between systematic and unique risk. The question is not simply what makes an asset's future earnings uncertain.

What matters is the extent to which abnormally low earnings are likely to coincide with low earnings in the economy as a whole. It is also better to sort out the cash flow estimation problems by correcting the estimates rather than add an arbitrary risk premium for a vaguely defined risk. High discount rates heavily penalize projects with cash flows in later years of the project's life.

Betas and Discount Rates for International Projects: The conventional wisdom on overseas investments is that they are generally riskier than investments in one's own country. This perception is based on the general feeling that things get more uncertain when one leaves one's home country. However, this ignores the fact that the risk that matters should be the non-diversifiable risk that is measured by beta and that beta is a function of not only the standard deviation of the project's cash flows but also the correlation of the project's cash flows to the domestic market returns. While the standard deviation for foreign projects can be higher than their domestic counterparts, it is also generally true that the correlation of such projects are a lot less than a comparable domestic project will have to the domestic market return. Thus, it does not automatically follow that foreign projects will have higher betas and should be evaluated at higher discount rates. One should analyze both the standard deviation and the correlation of the project to the home market returns. This will apply to a foreign company undertaking a project in the U.S. as well.

Certainty-Equivalent Cash Flows: The standard approach for calculating present value of a stream of uncertain cash flows is to discount the cash flows using a *risk-adjusted rate* derived from the CAPM or some other risk-return model. That is:

$$NPV = \sum_{t=0}^{n} \frac{C_t}{(1+r)^t}$$

Where, $r = r_f + \beta(r_m - r_f)$. This procedure would be inappropriate for a project whose beta is expected to vary through time. In such cases, it is better to use the certainty equivalent cash flows (CEQ), which are cash flows fully, adjusted for the risk involved so that they can be discounted using the risk-free rate. Thus, the NPV can be written as:

$$NPV = \sum_{t=0}^{n} \frac{CEQ_t}{(1+r_f)^t}$$

The certainty equivalent CEQ_t is some fraction of the expected cash flow C_t. The two methods must give the same present value, so

$$NPV = \sum_{t=0}^{n} \frac{CEQ_t}{(1+r_f)^t} = \sum_{t=0}^{n} \frac{C_t}{(1+r)^t} = \sum_{t=0}^{n} \frac{C_t}{(1+r_f)^t} \times \frac{(1+r_f)^t}{(1+r)^t}$$

$$CEQ_t = a_t C_t, \text{ where } a_t = \frac{(1+r_f)^t}{(1+r)^t}$$

The certainty equivalent approach is suited for projects where cash flows have uneven risk through the life of the project, so that using one constant discount rate will lead to incorrect decisions.

WORKED EXAMPLES

1. Mesa Buttons, Inc. (MBI) is interested in finding the appropriate discount rate for two new projects it is considering in foreign countries. The table below gives some of the relevant details for the projects along with the details for a nearly identical project MBI just completed in its plant near Midland, TX.

Particulars	Project Midland	Project Brazil	Project China
Cost of capital	16%	To be decided	To be decided
Standard deviation	28%	64%	82%
Correlation to US market	0.8	0.3	0.4
Beta	1.6	Not known	Not known

MBI assumed a risk-free rate of 4% and market risk premium of 7.5%. Use the information to compute the betas for the foreign projects and advice the firm

SOLUTION

Beta for the project = $\dfrac{\rho_{P,M}\sigma_P}{\sigma_M}$ where is the $\rho_{P,M}$ is the correlation coefficient between the project and the market returns and σ_P and σ_M are the standard deviations for the project and the market returns respectively. Beta for the project = $1.6 = \dfrac{0.8 \times 28}{\sigma_M}$, $\sigma_M = 14\%$.

Beta for the Brazilian project = $\dfrac{0.3 \times 64}{14} = 1.37$, Beta for the Chinese project = $\dfrac{0.4 \times 82}{14} = 2.34$

Cost of capital of the Brazilian project = $4 + 1.37(7.5) = 14.3\%$
Cost of capital of the Chinese project = $4 + 2.34(8) = 21.7\%$

2. Optitech Labs, Inc. (OLI) is considering a project, which requires an investment of $200,000 now to buy the exclusive rights to a new high tech airport security system using eye scanning technology. The security system is still under trial. The results of the trial will be known next year. The experts associated with the project feel that there is a 50% chance that the trials will be successful. If found successful, OLI will invest $2,000,000 and install the system in airports around the country. The project will generate a cash flow of $400,000 forever, starting from year 2. The project has a beta of 1.1. The risk free rate is 4% and the market risk premium is 8%. The cost of capital for the typical project is thus estimated at 12.8%. Ms. Lila Mani, the CEO of the company, feels that the project has very high risk and therefore wants to discount the cash flows from the project using a rate of 26% (approximately double the normal rate). Calculate the NPV of the project using the 26% discount rate. Is there a more appropriate way to evaluate the project?

SOLUTION

NPV using 26% discount rate $= -200{,}000 - \dfrac{2{,}000{,}000}{1.26} + \dfrac{400{,}000\,/\,0.26}{1.26} = -\$566{,}300$

A more appropriate approach will be to evaluate the project in steps. The cash flows from the $2,000,000 investment made next year have the same risk as any other airport security system projects or the discount rate for this should be: $r = r_f + \beta(r_m - r_f) = 3 + (1.1 \times 9) = 12.9\%$. The NPV of the investment of $2,000,000 will then be:

$$NPV = -2{,}000{,}000 + \dfrac{400{,}000}{0.129} = \$1{,}100{,}775$$

There is a 50% chance of this happening. That is, for the initial investment of $200,000, the company will get either zero (the trial fails) or $1,100,775 (trial succeeds). Thus, the overall project NPV for the initial investment of $200,000 is:

$$NPV = -200{,}000 + \dfrac{0.5 \times 1{,}100{,}775}{1.129} = \$287{,}500$$

SUMMARY

This chapter deals with the application of CAPM to practical capital budgeting problems. These problems include estimation of required rates of returns for projects and cost of capital. The chapter stresses the essential element of the CAPM – the risk that matters is the non-diversifiable risk. Thus, the required return on any investment should be related to this risk component and not the total risk. The chapter also points out the fact that the required rate of return on a project will depend on its market risk and not who undertakes the project. It is a mistake to use the company cost of capital to evaluate all the projects undertaken by a company. The company cost of capital reflects the mix of assets the company has and the only project to which one can apply the company cost of capital are those, which are mirror images of the company's existing operations.

Estimation of a company's stock beta involves determining the relationship between the stock's returns and the market returns. This is easily accomplished by plotting the two sets of returns on a graph and calculating the slope of the fitted line.

The chapter also discusses the common but erroneous practice of adding fudge factors to account for perceived risks. The fudge factors are arbitrary risk premiums and in many cases reflect non-systematic or diversifiable risk. They are also often used for the correction of cash flow estimation problems. One should look at the factors causing the risk and try to identify the effect they will have on the project's beta. Remember that beta is a function of not only the project cash flows' variance, but also the correlation of these cash flows to market returns. Other things equal, a non-cyclical project will have a lower beta compared to a cyclical project.

The standard approach to project evaluation uses a risk-adjusted discount rate for discounting all cash flows. This assumes that the project's cumulative risk increases at a constant rate. There may be projects that have cash flows whose risk does not increase steadily. For such projects, the certainty equivalent approach might be preferable. This allows separate risk adjustment for cash flows of different periods.

LIST OF TERMS

Accounting beta   Industry beta
Business risk   Operating leverage
Cash-flow beta   Project beta
Certainty equivalent   Risk-adjusted rate
Company cost of capital   Weighted average cost of capital
Cyclical

EXERCISES

Fill-in Questions

1. The use of the _____ as a discount rate ignores differences in the risk of projects.

2. The discount rate for evaluating a capital budgeting proposal should be derived from the _____.

3. _____ measures the return on the portfolio of the company's stocks and debt.

4. The cost of capital depends on the _____ of the firm's investments.

5. Companies with high fixed costs have high _____.

6. A firm whose revenues and earnings are strongly dependent on the state of the business cycle is said to be a _____ firm.

7. We can measure the strength of the relationship between a firm's earnings and the aggregate earnings on real assets by estimating either its _____ beta or its _____.

8. Instead of discounting the expected value of a cash flow by its _____, we may discount its _____ at the risk-free rate.

9. The beta of a portfolio of stocks drawn from a single industry is called a (n) _____.

Problems

1. A firm is considering the following projects:

PROJECT	BETA	EXPECTED RETURN,%
A	0.7	11
B	1.4	15
C	1.8	18
D	0.9	12

The firm's cost of capital is 13%. The risk-free rate is 3% and the expected market risk premium is 9%.
   a. Which projects will be accepted if the firm's cost of capital is used?
   b. Which projects should be accepted?

2. Hill Corp. is considering investing in two new projects. Project A is estimated to give a return of about 14%. The estimated standard deviation for the cash flows from the project is 30% and the correlation coefficient of the cash flows to market returns is 0.4. The standard deviation for the market returns is 15%. The expected market return is 14% and the risk free rate is 5%. The CEO of the company has decided that the project is not a good investment because of its "high risk" as measured by the standard deviation. The CEO does like Project B, which is expected to give a return of 20% with the same standard deviation of cash flows as Project A. The correlation coefficient for this project's cash flow with that of the market is estimated at about 0.9. Is the CEO right? Is Project B a better investment than project A? Explain your answer to the CEO.

3. Other things being equal, which company (from each of the following pairs) do you think should be using the higher discount rate in its capital budgeting?
   a. (i) A steel company, (ii) a brewing company
   b. (i) a manufacturer of recreational vehicles, (ii) a mining company
   c. (i) a company with high operating leverage, (ii) a company with high financial leverage
   d. (i) a manufacturer of office equipment, (ii) an electric utility company.

4. A project is expected to generate net cash flows of $1,000 in each of years 1 and 2. Its beta will be 1.5 throughout its life. The risk-free interest rate is 3%, and the expected return on the market is 9%. Calculate:
   a. the present value of the cash flows
   b. the certainty equivalents of the cash flows
   c. the ratios of the certainty equivalents to the expected cash flow (that is, a_1 and a_2).

5. MBA Inc. is expanding its business in Europe. It is evaluating projects in 4 countries with details as follows:

Country	Project standard deviation	Correlation of project returns to US market returns
Country A	36%	0.4
Country B	28%	0.6
Country C	42%	0.2
Country D	22%	0.8
US project	18%	0.9

The standard deviation of U.S. market returns is 14%. Calculate the beta for evaluation of the projects in each country.

Essay Questions

1. Write a short memorandum describing how you will set discount rates for projects with different risks.

2. Your company uses the DCF rate of return to appraise new investment projects in the following way:
   a. Projects with paybacks less than 3 years are accepted if their DCF rate of return exceeds 12%.
   b. Projects with paybacks longer than 3 years are accepted if their DCF rate of return exceeds 16%.

   Discuss the advantages and disadvantages of this rule.

3. Describe how you would calculate the cost of capital of a company using the CAPM.

4. Explain why foreign projects need not necessarily have a higher discount rate than their domestic counterparts.

5. Explain the difference between the use of risk-adjusted discount rates and certainty-equivalent cash flows. Give an example of a situation where you think the certainty-equivalent method is preferable.

ANSWER TO EXERCISES

Fill-in Questions

1. Company cost of capital
2. Project beta
3. Weighted average cost of capital
4. Business risk
5. Operating leverage

6. Cyclical
7. Accounting, cash-flow beta
8. Risk-adjusted rate, certainty equivalent
9. Industry beta

Problems

1. a. Only B and C will be accepted. A and D will be rejected.

   b. The company should use risk-adjusted rates based on project betas. The risk-adjusted rates based betas for the different projects are: A = 9.3%, B = 15.6%, C = 19.2% and D = 11.1%. B and C have returns less than their required rates of return; so they should be rejected. A and D have returns higher than the required rates and should be accepted.

2. Beta for Project A $= \dfrac{0.4 \times 30}{15} = 0.8$; Beta for Project B $= \dfrac{0.9 \times 30}{15} = 1.8$

   Based on the betas, the required rates of returns for the projects will be 12.2% and 21.2%. This shows that project A gives a return higher than its required rate of return, while project B does not clear its hurdle rate.

3. a. i   b. i   c. i   d. i

4. a. Using $r = 3 + 1.5(12 - 3) = 16.5\%$, PV = $1,595.17

   b. Certainty-equivalent cash flows are:
      Year 1 = 1000 × (1.03/1.165) = $884.12
      Year 2 = 1000 × (1.03/1.165)^2 = $781.67.

   c. a_1 = 1.03/1.165 = 0.884 and a_2 = (1.03/1.165)^2 = 0.782

5. The betas for the different country projects are:

   Country A = (0.4 × 36/14) = 1.03;
   Country B = (0.6 × 28/14) = 1.2
   Country C = (0.2 × 42/14) = 0.6
   Country D = (0.8 × 22/14) = 1.26
   U.S.   = (0.9 × 18/14) = 1.16

10
Project Analysis

INTRODUCTION

The chapters covered so far gave us the basic tools and techniques needed to evaluate projects. Chapters 2 to 6 showed us how to calculate net present values and how to use them to make capital budgeting decisions. Chapters 7 to 9 explained how the risk of a project affects the discount rate that should be used to evaluate it. However, investment decisions require a lot more than the knowledge of tools and techniques. There are a number of practical issues to be considered. A manager should be able to understand what is going on inside a project. Detailed project analysis enables a manager to understand the vulnerabilities, strengths and weaknesses of a project. Chapters 10, 11, and 12 deal with these issues. This chapter addresses specific questions such as how to analyze capital investment projects, how to ensure that cash-flow forecasts are realistic, and how to organize and control capital expenditures.

The chapter begins with a description of the investment process adopted by firms. The chapter then describes the following five commonly used techniques of project analysis: *sensitivity analysis, scenario analysis, break-even analysis, the Monte Carlo simulation*, and *decision trees*. These techniques can help the financial manager understand the project's structural strengths and weaknesses, its dependence on one or more key inputs, and interrelationships the project might have with future decisions. A financial manager should not simply accept a set of cash-flow forecasts, choose a discount rate, and crank out a net present value. She must understand the internal workings of the project and think about where those cash flows came from and what can go wrong with them.

The chapter also provides an overview of *real options* associated with projects. Managers and companies are not passive investors in the investment projects undertaken by the company. Managers have the ability, intention and resources to continually monitor projects as they proceed and will modify the projects to adapt to the changing conditions in the market. This ability to modify projects creates real options linked to projects. These options add value to the project and have to be evaluated as part of the project evaluation process.

KEY CONCEPTS IN THE CHAPTER

The Investment Process: A structured and formal process of generating project proposals and passing them through a rigorous evaluation process is essential to ensure that good projects are approved and the not-so-good ones rejected. The investment (capital budgeting) process typically involves the following four stages.

Preparation of capital budget: This is a broad list of projects to be taken up during the year. The list has summary details and is typically generated through a *bottom-up* process with different departments, plants, or divisions coming up with their list of proposed projects. The budgeting process should begin with key macroeconomic forecasts and forecasts related to the firm's business that are consistent across all the projects being considered. Assumptions built into project estimates should also be checked to ensure consistency across the different projects.

Project authorization: This step involves formal vetting of the projects by the top management through appropriate analyses and screening. The step ensures that the projects included reflect the firm's strategic direction. It is quite common and natural for the project sponsors to be strongly biased in favor of the projects they propose and the senior management approving the projects should be on guard against this bias. Before expenditure on individual projects is committed through *appropriation requests,* project details are prepared and analyses using NPV or other measures of project acceptability are conducted. Typically, managers are delegated authority to approve expenditures up to set ceilings with the projects requiring large investment requiring approval at the highest level or the board of directors.

Implementation and control: Project details are monitored during construction with appropriate information feed back to top management for control and necessary corrective actions. Project cost, time schedule, and any change in key inputs or factors affecting the project viability are among the elements monitored regularly.

Post-audit: Firms do post-audits of completed projects shortly after the project is completed. This enables the management to identify the errors and omissions with respect to project details. The step is part of a continuous learning process for everyone involved in project management and enables the firm to avoid the errors in the future.

Note that there are important and often sizable investments made by firms, which are not part of the capital budgeting process. These include R and D, marketing campaigns, training and development expenditures, and investment in information technology. The control systems and screening procedures in place should take into account the existence of these projects and ensure that proposals for these expenses are evaluated properly.

Sensitivity Analysis: Sensitivity analysis is a very useful and important project analysis tool. It is simple to apply and understand and can be particularly effective in identifying the need for additional information. Sensitivity analysis captures the effect of key inputs or variables on the project, one variable at a time. It answers questions such as: what happens to the NPV of the project if the cost of goods sold turns out to be at its pessimistic worst?

The NPV of a project is arrived at by combining a number of different forecasts to estimate the after-tax cash flows and then discounting these cash flows. The forecasts include the size of the total market for the product, the company's share of that total market, the price of the product, etc. All the numbers that go into the analysis are the best estimates or expected values. We cannot, however, be sure what the actual outcome will be for any of these variables. Sensitivity analysis identifies the difference made by the variation from the forecast for any key input. The method for accomplishing this is to identify the key variables that determine the success of the project, such as sales volume, fixed cost, unit variable cost, and selling price. For each variable, the expected value is replaced by both an optimistic and a pessimistic estimate, and the cash flows and NPVs are recalculated. This is done by taking one variable at a time. In this way financial managers can identify those variables, which affect NPV most. Additional information or research to reduce the uncertainty of those variables, as well as other, overlooked factors, may then be in order.

The results of the sensitivity analysis is typically set out in tables such as the one below which represents part of Table 10-2 of the Brealey, Myers and Allen text.

NET PRESENT VALUE (Billions of yen)			
Variable	Pessimistic	Expected	Optimistic
Market size	1.1	3.4	5.7
Market share	−10.4	3.4	17.3
Unit price	−4.2	3.4	5.0
Unit variable cost	−15.0	3.4	11.1
Fixed cost	0.4	3.4	6.5

The table clearly shows that the impact of variations in the unit variable cost or the market share is far more significant than the impact of variations in the total market size or of the project's fixed costs. The manager can now consider actions that might reduce or eliminate the uncertainty with respect to these key components. For example, it may be worth investing in a market survey, which will reduce the uncertainty about market share. A survey, which indicates poor prospects for the company, would allow the project to be abandoned before any major expenditure is incurred. Alternately, expenditure on a different advertising campaign might bolster market share and improve the prospects for the project. Thus, sensitivity analysis alerts the management to the importance of keeping a sharp eye on what happens to components key to the success of the project. In the above example, the analysis brings out the crucial nature of the variable costs and market share. Steps could be taken to remove uncertainty with respect to these key project elements. These could include hedging in commodity futures markets, negotiating long-term supplier contracts, or commission an additional design study on material efficiency.

The strength of sensitivity analysis lies in its ability to highlight key variable and key assumptions, to expose inconsistencies, and to identify where additional information is worthwhile. Sensitivity analysis, however, is limited in its scope because of the subjectivity of the optimistic and pessimistic forecasts and because it ignores interrelationships among variables.

Scenario Analysis: Scenario analysis can be seen as the logical extension of sensitivity analysis. Altering the variables one at a time, as is done for sensitivity analysis, ignores the fact that the variables are usually interrelated. One way around this problem is to look at how the project would fare under a number of different plausible scenarios of the future. Forecasts are made for all variables so as to be consistent with a particular view of the world. In the text, for example, the forecasters are asked to consider the effects of an immediate 20% rise in the price of oil, and the NPV of the project is recalculated on the resulting assumptions.

Scenario analysis can be very useful to evaluate the project's exposure to a combination of changes in key variables. The manager can specify the scenarios he would like to have the project analyzed under.

Break-even Analysis and Operating Leverage: Break-even analysis calculates the sales level that will give zero NPV for the project. Knowing the break-even level, one can assess the chances of the project's success. The break-even point can be computed by working out the NPV or the present values of cash inflows and outflows at different sales level. Many companies (and textbooks) use the break-even level known as the accounting break-even level. This is computed on a different basis and is the level of sales that gives a zero accounting profit. Zero accounting profit could mean a big economic loss or negative NPV because the accounting profit measure ignores cost of capital.

Break-even analysis enables managers to analyze the impact of *operating leverage* or fixed costs on the project's NPV. A project with high fixed costs will have a NPV, which is more sensitive to the level of sales. At higher sales levels, the project would do very well, but if the sales levels happen to be lower than expected, the project would fare worse than one with lower operating leverage. This technique can be useful to evaluate alternate production technologies that have different fixed-variable cost mix.

Degree of operating leverage (DOL) measures the sensitivity of profits to changes in sales.

$$DOL = \frac{\text{Percentage change in profits}}{\text{Percentage change in sales}} = 1 + \frac{\text{Fixed costs}}{\text{Profits}}$$

A high degree of operating leverage implies high sensitivity of profits to changes in sales. Note that DOL is measured in terms of accounting profits and not in terms of cash flows.

Monte Carlo Simulation: Monte Carlo simulation (or simulation, for short) may be regarded as the ultimate extension of the idea of scenario analysis. In scenario analysis, we look at a small number of specially chosen scenarios. In simulation, the analysis is extended to include a very large number of possible combinations of changes in key variables. Simulation analysis uses complex computer programs to generate possible values for all key inputs to the project. The project analyst specifies probability distributions for all these variables and the computer generates random values for the key variables and the project is simulated. The process is repeated a number of times to produce a distribution of project cash flows. This provides you with a picture of the variability of the project's cash flows. All interrelationships among the variables can be taken into account in the simulation model.

Simulation involves four stages:

- Establish equations to model the cash flows of the project. These must reflect any interdependencies among variables.
- Specify the probabilities of forecast errors of different magnitudes for each variable
- Simulate the cash flows. The computer picks random values for the various inputs from the respective probability distributions and calculates the cash flows. This is repeated a large number of times until an accurate picture of the distribution of cash flows for each year is obtained.
- Calculate the present values of the cash flows. The simulation runs give the expected cash flows for the project.

Monte Carlo simulation has its good and bad points. On the positive side, simulation forces explicit specification of interdependencies. It can be used also to explore possible modifications to a project. On the negative side, simulation can be time-consuming and expensive. Realism means complexity; building the model may have to be delegated and this can diminish its credibility to the decision maker. It may replace one "black box" with another.

Real Options: The simple discounted cash flow (DCF) analysis used to compute NPV and evaluate projects does not work very well for all projects. The DCF analysis is designed for analyzing those investments, which do not change their nature during the life of the project. It is ideally suited for evaluating passive investments like bonds and stocks. Corporate assets are, on the other hand, actively managed by the manager and the projects can very often change their nature in terms of expansion and abandonment possibilities, timing of the investment and flexibility of input and output. Projects, which can be modified or adapted to varying market conditions, have *real options* in them. These options add value to the project and thus have to be included in the evaluation of the projects with real options. The options are generally worth more when the project faces higher uncertainty. The real options associated with projects can be classified one of the following four types. Real options are discussed again in Chapter 22.

The Option to Expand: Capital budgeting projects are rarely finite, clean-cut one of a kind investment with no connections to the future. Many projects have expansion opportunities attached to them. These follow-on investment opportunities add value to the original project. Typical examples include R & D projects and investments in new markets, foreign countries, and new technology. Remember that the uncertainties associated with the project actually make the value of options even more attractive. The value of all the options to expand is included in the present value of growth opportunities (PVGO) discussed in Chapter 4.

The Option to Abandon: The option to abandon a project, when things are not going as well as one expected, is a very valuable option that can enhance the value of the project. The abandonment option can be analyzed in terms of the possible project outcomes. For simplicity and convenience, we can assume that two mutually exclusive outcomes are possible: one is a success route; the other is a failure route. The option to bail out is worth something, especially if the bail out value exceeds the value of the project at that time. An abandonment option can be seen as an insurance policy.

The Timing Option: This was briefly discussed in chapter 6. Valuing a timing option is simple when there is no uncertainty. One can calculate the project's NPV at various dates of project commencement and pick the one date with the highest NPV. Of course, this will not work when there is uncertainty. The timing option exists, if the project's commencement can be delayed.

Production Option: The ability to switch production facilities to manufacture different types of products or use different types of raw materials is a very valuable option for manufacturing companies. In general, flexibility is very useful in manufacturing especially, when the nature of the demand for the company's products can change very quickly. The flexibility can be to switch machine set ups, sources of raw material or utility, or location of manufacturing from one country to another.

Decision Trees: Decision trees are very useful for analyzing a sequence of different possible uncertain events and decisions through time. Decision trees can show linkages among decisions spread over different periods and dependent on possible and uncertain future outcomes. Moreover, they force implicit assumptions to be expressed. In particular, they enable us to analyze such things as the option to expand, and the option to abandon a failing project.

To draw a decision tree, branches from points marked with squares are used to denote different possible decisions. Branches from points marked with circles denote different possible outcomes (with their probabilities often indicated in brackets) and the decisions and outcomes are linked in the logical sequence. Present values are calculated starting from the end the most distant branches first. "Roll back" to the immediate decision by accepting the best decision at each of the later stages. (See problem 2 of the worked examples.)

While the basic technique is simple, the usefulness of decision trees is limited, however, because they become unmanageably complex very quickly. They also fail to tell us how to adjust our discount rates to reflect the differences in risk among alternatives.

WORKED EXAMPLES

1. The following forecasts have been prepared for a new investment of $20 million with an 8-year life:

	PESSIMISTIC	EXPECTED	OITIMISTIC
Market size (Units)	60,000	90,000	140,000
Market share,%	25	30	35
Unit price	$750	$800	$875
Unit variable cost	$500	$400	$350
Fixed cost, millions	$7	$4	$3.5

Use straight-line depreciation and assume a tax rate of 35%, and an opportunity cost of capital of 14%. Calculate the NPV of this project and conduct a sensitivity analysis. What are the principal uncertainties of the project?

SOLUTION

The first step is to calculate the annual cash flows from the project for the base case (the expected values). These may be calculated as shown:

DESCRIPTION	HOW CALCULATED	VALUE ($ in millions)
1. Revenues	90,000 × 0.30 × $800	21.600
2. Variable cost	90,000 × 0.30 × $400	10.800
3. Fixed cost	$4,000,000	4.000
4. Depreciation	$20,000,000/8	2.500
5. Pretax profit	Item 1 − (items 2 + 3 + 4)	4.300
6. Tax	Item 5 × 0.35	1.505
7. Net profit	Item 5 − item 6	2.795
8. Net cash flow	1tem 7 + item 4	5.295

This level of cash flow occurs for each of the 8 years of the project. The present value is computed using the BA II Plus calculator:

$CF_0 = -\$20.00$ million, $CO_1 = -\$5.295$ million, $FO_1 = 8$, NPV: $I = 14\%$, NPV $= \$4.563$ million

Now that the base case has been completed, the next step is to alter the forecasts one at a time to their optimistic and pessimistic values. The easiest way to do this is to work out how much each change affects the net cash flow and then use the annuity factor as before to work out the NPV. For example, the optimistic value of the market size increases the pretax revenues by $50,000 \times 0.30 \times (\$800 - \$400) = \$6$ million; so it increases the (after-tax) net cash flow by $\$6$ million $\times 0.65 = 3.90$ million, to $\$9.195$ million. The NPV now becomes

$CF_0 = -\$20.00$ million, $CO_1 = -\$9.195$ million, $FO_1 = 8$, NPV: $I = 14\%$, NPV $= \$22.654$ million

The following table shows the net cash flows and NPVs corresponding to the pessimistic and optimistic forecasts for each variable.

| | Net Cash Flow ($m) | | NPV ($m) | |
	Pessimistic	Optimistic	Pessimistic	Optimistic
Market size	2.96	9.20	−6.27	22.67
Market share, %	4.13	6.47	−0.84	10.01
Unit price	4.42	6.61	0.50	10.66
Unit variable cost	3.54	6.17	−3.58	8.63
Fixed cost	3.35	5.62	−4.46	6.07

The table clearly shows that the most crucial variable is the total market size. Both the fixed and variable costs also need watching, while market share and unit price seems less likely to cause serious problems.

2. Merry-Go-Round is evaluating a possible investment in a new plant costing $2,000. By the end of a year, it will know whether cash flows will be $300 a year in perpetuity or only $140 a year in perpetuity. In either case, the first cash flow will not occur until year 2. Alternately, the company would be able to sell their plant in year 1 for $1,800 if the demand is low and for $2,000 if the demand is high. There is a 65% chance that the project will turn out well and a 35% chance it will turn out badly. The opportunity cost of funds is 10%. What should the company do?

Year 0   Year 1

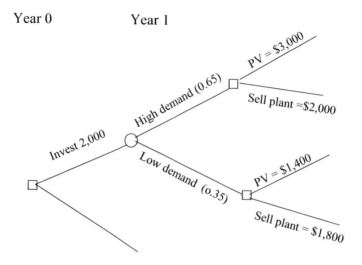

SOLUTION

The problem can best be analyzed by the decision tree shown above. If things go well, the cash flows of $300 in perpetuity starting in year 2 will be worth $300/0.1 = $3,000 in year 1. If things go badly, the cash flows will be worth $140/0.1 = 1,400 in year 1. To analyze the decision tree, we work backwards from the most distant branches of the tree. At the decision branch points, marked with squares, we make decisions. At the uncertainty ones, marked with circles, we calculate expected values. So, if things go well (high demand), we will decide to continue with the plant at a value of $3,000 in year 1. However, if things go badly (low demand), we will prefer to sell it for $1,800 rather than wait for cash flows worth only $1,400. We can now take the expected value at the uncertainty branch point by weighting each possible outcome by its probability. Expected value in year 1 = $3,000 × 0.65 + $1,800 × 0.35 = $2,580
Net present value of the investment = $2,580/1.1 − $2,000 = $345.45

The project is worth pursuing.

CHAPTER SUMMARY

Investment decision making involves a lot more than simply cranking out cash flow estimates, discounted cash flows, and NPVs based on these estimates. This chapter is the first of three chapters that analyze the issues and the challenges involved in making investment decisions and ensuring that projects taken up are really positive NPV projects. This chapter begins with a description of the capital budgeting process, which includes the four stages of *budget preparation, project authorization,* procedures for *control of projects,* and *post-audits* conducted soon after project completion. Ideally, the capital budgeting process should combine bottom-up projects generation and top down strategic planning.

Investments are always fraught with uncertainties and a project can be vulnerable to a number of factors external and beyond the manager's control. Project analysis enables the manager to identify the project's vulnerabilities and the major threats faced by the project. The chapter describes three approaches to identifying these vulnerabilities and threats – sensitivity analysis, scenario analysis, and the Monte Carlo simulation. Sensitivity analysis is the simplest of these and evaluates the impact on the project's NPV caused by changes in key variables, one variable at a time. This type of analysis enables the manager to identify variables crucial to the project's financial health. The manager might find it prudent to spend resources on getting additional information to reduce the uncertainties related to these crucial variables. An extension of sensitivity analysis is the scenario approach where the impact on the project's NPV under different scenarios, where more than one variable might change, is examined.

One can look at all possible combinations of variables and get a complete distribution of possible cash flows from the project by using the Monte Carlo simulation approach. This approach uses a complete model of the project cash flows and assigns probability distributions for the all variables to obtain random values for different variables. Simulation runs produces distribution of cash flows for each year of the project. Simulation can be very useful in understanding the risk and complexities of the project. It forces the project analyst to raise questions that otherwise might not be asked. The process has its limits, though, and can easily be abused. Simulation produces a vast array of data and, in some cases, manager could conceivably get lost in the process.

Very few projects are simple, one time "accept or reject" cases. Projects often involve linkages of decisions over time and can include options to expand, abandon, timing of the investment or otherwise modify the project. These options add value to the project and it is important that they are evaluated properly. Decision tree analysis is ideally suited to evaluate these cases where one is faced with a sequence of possible decisions.

It is important to remember that none of the techniques discussed in this chapter replaces the NPV analysis; they only facilitate better decision making by enabling more accurate computation of the NPV. These techniques help the manager understand the project better and learn what could go wrong with the project.

LIST OF TERMS

Abandonment value
Appropriation request
Break-even analysis
Capital budget
Decision tree
Monte Carlo simulation
Post-audit

Probability
Production options
Project analysis
Real options
Scenario analysis
Sensitivity analysis

EXERCISES

Fill-in-Questions

1. The initial step in the investment process is the preparation of the list of projects proposed to be undertaken during the year called _____.

2. Most companies require that a formal _____ be prepared before funds are released for a project.

3. _____ of projects is usually undertaken soon after the projects are completed.

4. Sensitivity analysis, simulation, and decision trees are three different forms of _____.

5. _____ shows the effect of changes in key variables such as sales, costs, etc., on the value of an investment project.

6. The analysis of a project under different _____ gives us a way to do a kind of sensitivity analysis that takes the interrelationships among variables into account.

7. _____ identifies the level of sales for which the project gives zero NPV.

8. _____ uses a complete model of the project and distribution of all key variables to simulate thousands of project runs and produces a complete distribution of project cash flows.

9. Sequential decisions can be analyzed by constructing a (n) _____.

10. One of the difficulties of using a decision tree or simulation is that it becomes necessary to specify the _____ of different future outcomes.

11. The problem of whether to terminate a project before the end of its normal economic life is called the _____ problem.

12. Many projects can be modified and adapted to meet changing market conditions. These options to modify projects are known as _____ _____.

13. Manufacturing plants included as part of investment projects can be designed to include _____ to meet flexible market and production needs.

Problems

1. Horizontal Drillers Inc. is evaluating a project to produce a high tech deep-sea oil exploration device. The investment required is $80 million for a plant with a capacity of 15,000 units a year. Sales are expected to average 80% of capacity. The plant is expected to operate for 5 years. The device will be sold for a price of $12,000 per unit. The variable cost is $7,000/unit and fixed costs, excluding depreciation, are $25 million per year. Use straight-line depreciation and a tax rate of 36%. The required rate of return is 12%.

    a. Calculate the NPV of the project
    b. Do a sensitivity analysis for the following pessimistic and optimistic assumptions:
       Pessimistic: Sales – 15% lower, Unit price – 10% lower, Fixed costs – 10% higher.
       Optimistic: Sales – 15% higher, Unit price – 10% higher, Fixed costs – 10% lower.

2. Caramel, Custard and Confections Corporation (CCCC) is considering an investment of $500,000 in a new plant for producing a new line of confections. The plant, which has an expected life of 4 years, has a maximum capacity of 700,000 units per year, and sales are expected to be 85% of this in each of the 4 successive years of production. Fixed costs are $200,000 per year and variable costs are $1.20 per unit produced. The product will be sold at a unit price of $2. The plant will be depreciated straight-line over 4 years, and it is expected to have a zero salvage value. The required rate of return on the project is 15% and the corporation tax rate is 35%.

    a. Calculate the NPV of this project under the assumptions given above.
    b. Calculate how sensitive the NPV of the project is to variation in the level of sales, the unit price, the unit variable coot, and the level of fixed costs.
    c. CCCC is uncertain how to price its new product. What price would give a zero NPV?

3. In the investment project of problem 2, calculate what level of sales would give break-even in terms of (a) zero NPV and (b) zero accounting profit.

4. In problem 2, CCCC estimated that the annual sales would be 595,000 units, but there is some chance that the sales level will be inadequate to justify the capital expenditure. By commissioning a market survey, CCCC can hope to reduce this risk. CCCC's marketing department has some experience with such surveys. They estimate that there is a 20% chance that the survey will revise the forecast sales to 500,000 or less, in which case the project would not be worth undertaking. If this does not occur (the remaining 80% of the time), they would expect the sales forecast to be revised upward to 640,000 units. What is the maximum amount that CCCC should be prepared to pay for a survey of this kind?

5. Emerald and Blue has an investment project with the following characteristics:
    Cost of investment: $800,000
    Expected sales volume: 21,000 units per year for 7 years
    Unit price: $150
    Unit variable cost: $120
    Annual fixed costs: $400,000

Life of investment: 7 years (zero salvage value)
Tax rate: 35%
Required rate of return: 12%

Calculate the NPV of this investment and perform a sensitivity analysis (use straight-line depreciation).

6. Analyze the project of problem 2 under the following two scenarios:

	Pessimistic scenario	Optimistic scenario
Sales volume	Expected value − 20%	Expected value + 10%
Unit price	Expected value − 10%	Expected value + 20%
Variable cost	Expected value + 10%	Expected value − 5%
Fixed cost	Expected value + 10%	Expected value − 5%

7. In problem 4, the first year of operation would give CCCC the same information as their market survey. After that year, if things go badly (with expected sales of 415,000 units), they can abandon the project to obtain a salvage value of $400,000 (less $8,500 tax) by selling the plant to another company. What value does the market survey have in the light of this option to abandon the project after it has been started?

Essay Questions

1. Describe the various stages of the capital budgeting process.

2. Describe the technique of sensitivity analysis as applied to the appraisal of capital investment projects. What reservations do you have about its usefulness?

3. Describe how to calculate the break-even point for a capital investment project. Why is it misleading to calculate the break-even point in terms of accounting profit?

4. Work out and describe in detail how you would produce and use a Monte Carlo simulation model to represent the purely financial aspects of pursuing an MBA degree in one of the top ten schools. Assume you will be in a business related career for the next 15 years. Some of the things to keep in mind include: the investment in time and money, possible benefits of the MBA, and the pitfalls (things which could go wrong). Make sure to build appropriate interrelationships between variables into the model where necessary.

5. What are the typical real options associated with capital budgeting projects? Do these options always add value to the project?

6. A decision must be made whether to launch a new product immediately or subject it to further market research or abandon the idea altogether. Your boss has heard that decision trees can help with this kind of problem. Write a report on how a decision tree might be used in this situation. Describe what sort of information you would need to apply this in practice and how it would be used.

ANSWERS TO EXERCISES

Fill-in Questions

1. Capital budget
2. Appropriation request
3. Post audit
4. Project analysis
5. Sensitivity analysis
6. Scenarios
7. Break-even analysis

8. Monte Carlo simulation
9. Decision tree
10. Probabilities
11. Abandonment value
12. Real options
13. Production options

Problems

1. a. The following table derives the cash flows and NPV for the base case:

Item	Dollars in Thousands	
	Year 0	Years 1 to 5
Investment	−80,000	
Revenue		144,000
Variable cost		84,000
Fixed cost		25,000
Depreciation		16,000
Pre-tax profit		19,000
Tax @ 36%		6,840
Net profit		12,160
Net cash flow		28,160
NPV @ 12%		21,510

b. The sensitivity analysis is presented in the table below: ($1,000)

Sensitivity to change of	Effect on annual cash flow	Effect on NPV
Pessimistic:		
15% lower sales	−5,760	−20,764
10% lower price	−9,216	−33,222
10% Higher fixed cost	−1,600	−5,768
Optimistic		
15% higher sales	5,760	20,764
10% higher price	9,216	33,222
10% lower fixed cost	1,600	5,768

2. a. The following table derives the cash flows and NPV for the base case and for the pessimistic and optimistic scenarios of problem 6. (All cash flows in $1000s)

Item	Year 0	Years 1 to 4 Expected	Pessimistic	Optimistic
Investment	−500			
Revenue		1190.0	856.8	1570.8
Variable cost		714.0	628.3	746.1
Fixed cost		200.0	220.0	190.0
Depreciation		125.0	125.0	125.0
Pretax profit		151.0	−116.5	509.7
Tax		52.9	−40.8	178.4
Net Profit		98.1	−75.7	331.3
Net cash flow		223.1	49.3	456.3
NPV at 15%		137.0	−359.3	802.7

b. The next table shows how given changes in sales, variable cost, unit price, and fixed cost affect the net cash flows and the NPV. The final column also shows the levels that give break-even points (i.e., zero NPV):

Sensitivity to change of:	Effect on cash flow	Effect on NPV	Break-even level
100,000 sales (units)	52.00	148.46	502,660 units
10-cent variable cost	−38.68	−110.42	$1.32
10-cent unit price	38.68	110.42	$1.88
$10,000 fixed cost	6.50	−18.56	$273,875

c. The final column indicates that a price of $1.88 gives a zero NPV.

3. a. The final column of the previous table also shows that the level of sales required for the break-even point in terms of zero NPV is 502,660 units per year.

b. The base case gave a pretax profit of $151,000 at sales of 595,000. Each unit reduction in sales reduces pretax profits by $0.80, so sales will have to fall by 151,000/0.80 = 188,750 to eliminate profits entirely. That is, break-even sales are 406,250.

4. Without the extra information, the value of the project is its base-case NPV of $137,000. With the information, there is a 20% chance of a zero NPV and an 80% chance of $203,807 (= $137,000 + 148,460 × 45/100). The new NPV is equal to $163,046 (= $203,807 × 0.80) less the cost of the information. The information must be worth $26,046 (= $163,046 − $137,000).

5. Cash flows and NPV for the base case are given below ($ 1,000s):

Item	Year 0	Expected cash flow Years 1 to 7
Investment	−800	
Revenue		3150.0
Variable cost		2520.0
Fixed cost		400.0
Depreciation		114.3
Profit before tax		115.7
Tax		40.5
Profit after tax		75.2
Cash flow		189.5
Base case NPV at 12%		64.8

The sensitivity analysis is given for increase in the value of key inputs.

$1,000s

Sensitivity to	Effect on cash flow	Change in NPV
Sales increase by 1000 units	19.50	+89.0
Variable cost increase by $1	−13.65	−62.3
Unit price increase by $1	13.65	+62.3
Fixed costs increase by $10,000	−6.50	−29.7

6. See the answer to problem 2.

7. Without the abandonment option, we found in problem 4 that the project had an NPV of $163,046 less the cost of the survey, or $137,000 without the survey. This gave the survey a value of $26,046.

With the abandonment option, there is now a 20% chance of abandoning at an NPV of −$46,913. This is calculated as follows: the expected first year sales of 415,000 will give a cash flow of $129,550, and there will be $400,000 less $8,500 tax from selling the plant. This makes an expected $521,050/1.15 − $500,000 = −$46,913. There is also an 80% chance of $203,807. Combining the two figures, we find that the abandonment option increases the NPV of the project to $153,663 (= −$46,913 × 0.2 + $203,807 × 0.8). This reduces the value of the survey information to $16,663 (= $153,663 − $137,000).

11

Investment, Strategy, and Economic Rents

INTRODUCTION

This chapter explains the link between strategy and finance and provides some very valuable lessons in the economics of competition. Modern market economies have intense competition in nearly all industries. Very few firms can expect to earn economic profits or have positive NPV investments unless they have a sustainable competitive advantage in the businesses they are engaged in. A project looks good either because it is really good or simply because the cash flow projections are too good and erroneously make the project look good. Regardless of our expertise in the theory of making capital budgeting decisions, we will end up making bad decisions if our forecasts of cash flows turn out badly. This chapter shows you how you can ensure that these forecasts are as good as possible.

The first section of the chapter describes how some difficult forecasting problems may be avoided by making full use of available market information. The second section gives a very brief overview of important concepts from the field of business strategy and then discusses the basis for economic rent. A positive NPV can arise only if the firm has valuable resources, skills or capabilities, which are superior to those of the competitors in the industry. In other words, the firm has to have *competitive advantage*, which can be exploited by it to earn economic rent. It is important to understand the nature of such an advantage. What is it that enables one firm and not another to exploit the opportunity provided by the project? If you can answer this question satisfactorily, you probably have understood the project and the source of the positive NPV. By the same token, when one cannot explain the source of positive NPV through real competitive advantage enjoyed by the firm, the project's positive NPV should be seriously questioned. These ideas are elaborated in the third section of the chapter using the Marvin Enterprises example.

Note that competition in most industries will be relentless and dynamic. It is unlikely that a firm's competitive advantage will allow it to gain economic rent forever because other firms are not going to be idle and will whittle away the advantage over time. In other words, competitive advantage is never permanent, so it is reasonable to expect that the source of the positive NPV will disappear over time. You want to keep this in mind when you prepare your cash flow estimates.

KEY CONCEPTS IN THE CHAPTER

Market Values as Source of Price Information: Market prices provide extremely useful information about the value of commodities, goods and services, which are traded in the markets. Since investments in commodities do not provide annual dividends, today's price of a commodity is the present value of the future price of the same. The CEO of a gold mine can look to the current gold price for the present value of future sales of gold because this is consistent with the equilibrium expected return to investors in gold. You can use market prices to reduce the chance of forecasting errors swamping genuine information. Information that is not generally known can be analyzed separately and added to (or subtracted from) the market value.

Refer to the department store example used in the text. A department store investment involves at least two distinct bets: one on real estate prices and another on whether the real estate is best suited to running a department store. It is helpful to imagine the business as divided into two parts: a real estate subsidiary that buys the building and rents it out and a retailing one that rents and operates it. This forces you to consider whether the department store is the best current use for the real estate, and whether it is likely to remain so. It would be foolish to make a lousy department store investment because of optimism about real estate prices. Instead, it would be better to buy the real estate and rent it out, though a real estate company would have more expertise in this area. Conversely, it would be silly to be deterred from going ahead with a profitable department store because of pessimism about real estate prices. Instead, it is better to sell the real estate and then rent it back for the department store.

Economic Rents and Competitive Advantage: Economic rents are profits in excess of cost of capital. Companies can extract economic rents from its customers only if they have an edge over the competition. This edge may be in the superiority of the firm's resources and skills relative to those possessed by the competitors in the industry. Possession of key strategic assets, which cannot be easily copied or acquired by competitors, can lead to a firm's superiority. The competitive advantage enjoyed by the firm is a function of both the industry in which the firm competes and the unique strategy employed the firm to compete in the industry. The competitive dynamics of an industry can be analyzed through Michael Porter's *five forces model.* The five forces are:

- The intensity of rivalry among existing competitors.
- The threat of entry by new competitors.
- The threat of substitute products.
- The relative bargaining power of the suppliers.
- The relative bargaining power of the buyers.

A firm's unique competitive strategy may take one of three forms: *cost leadership, differentiation,* or *focus* on a market niche. The really successful firm is the one, which is able to take advantage of the opportunities available in the industry using its unique skills and resources. In other words, the firm has a competitive advantage.

In competitive markets, all that a firm can expect to get is a fair price covering all its costs. Competition will drive the price down to the point where the price will equal the cost of producing the product or service (cost includes the cost of capital). Whenever you have a positive NPV project, remember that the positive NPV is simply the present value of future economic rents. Look for the source of the economic rent. Economic rent may exist in the short-term when the industry is not in long-run equilibrium. Over the long-term, a company can expect to have economic rents only if it has some kind of monopoly or market power. You should be able to identify the source. Remember the following three points:

- When an industry is in a long-run competitive equilibrium, all assets earn just their opportunity cost of capital, their NPVs are zero, and economic rents are zero.

– Firms can earn temporary (or permanent) economic rents if there is temporary dis-equilibrium, or if they have some degree of monopoly or market power.
– Never accept that a project has a positive NPV unless you understand why your firm has a competitive advantage in doing it.

Technology, Competition, and Economic Rents: *Marvin Enterprises* is an extended and useful illustration of what happens in an industry when a firm has a technological break-through and is poised to exploit it. While the example is fictitious, the issues it poses are very real and have many parallels in today's world.

The example is about a company that has developed a new technology, but there are other firms hot on its heels and its relative advantage is expected to last for only 5 years. After 5 years, new investments will come in and drive the price of the product down to its equilibrium level. The company will therefore earn abnormally high profits or economic rents only over the first 5 years.

The main argument of the case runs as follows: The price of a product depends on the total quantity produced. The producers compete with each other and will expand their capacity until the new investment has a zero net present value. From this, it follows that any single producer can expect to find positive NPV projects only if the firm has some kind of relative advantage over the competition. Such advantages certainly exist: a company may have built up a good reputation for its brand name in the marketplace. You can see that these advantages are hard-won and must be protected tenaciously.

The case raises two other important issues. The first is the effect of Marvin Enterprises' new investment on its existing business. Its proposed expansion is sufficiently large to affect the price of the product it is selling. Marvin must worry about the loss of revenue on its existing operations and include this in its calculation of the NPV of the new project. In more extreme situations, this could lead to situations where a company is willing to suppress its new technology completely.

Second, the less efficient producers play an extremely important role. As the capacity of the industry is increased, the price of the product falls, and it becomes increasingly difficult for these producers to stay in business. If the price falls far enough, some producers may withdraw from the market, and other marginal producers may be on the point of doing so. In this situation, the price of the product will be at the point where it just pays the least efficient remaining producer to stay in business. The size of the economic rent obtained by a more efficient producer will simply reflect the difference between its costs (including the opportunity cost of the capital employed) and that of the least efficient producer.

Beware of the misleading argument that a fully depreciated plant is cheaper to run than an otherwise identical un-depreciated one. This argument is often made, but it is falsely based on interpreting accounting income as if it were cash flow. Remember, only cash flows matter, not accounting numbers. Since, in this example, there are no taxes; there is absolutely no difference between cash flows of a depreciated plant and those of an un-depreciated one.

Here is a summary of the key points made in the discussion of the Marvin Enterprises case:

- Anticipated and prolonged economic rents are uncommon.
- High economic rents usually attract competitors; try to estimate the timing and extent of new entry that will reduce or eliminate the economic rent.
- Identify your firm's competitive advantages, and try to protect and capitalize on them.
- New generations of technology will tend to reduce the value of earlier generation assets. A growth industry has no mercy on laggards.
- The NPV of a project may be reduced by the impact it has on the firm's existing business. This can provide an incentive to slow down the speed of innovation.
- A *marginal producer* is one who will quit if the price goes any lower, i.e., for whom price equals manufacturing cost plus opportunity cost of not selling out. The economic rent to a more efficient producer is simply the difference between its costs and those of a marginal producer.
- A high salvage value increases economic rents. The book value of the old plant is irrelevant.

WORKED EXAMPLE

The Greystone Tire & Rubber Company is considering a new investment in a fully automated tire plant. Its existing plant produces 1 million tires a year. It cost $80 million 5 years ago, and it could be scrapped for $30 million at any time. The production costs per tire of the old and new plants can be broken down as follows:

	Old Plant	New Plant
Raw Materials and energy	$15	$17
Labor	10	3
Other direct costs	5	5
Total direct costs	$30	$25

The new plant will be able to produce 500,000 tires a year, and it will cost $35 million. The current price of tires is $38 each. Greystone's new investment is not expected to affect this, but the price may fall when other companies complete their modernization programs in 2 years' time. Greystone's cost of capital is 10%, and there are no corporate taxes.

a. What is the NPV of the new plant?
b. When will the old plant be scrapped, and what is its value today?
c. The costs of raw materials and energy suddenly double. The price of tires changes to $50. What are the answers to (a) and (b) now?

SOLUTION

a. The capital outlay required on the new plant is $70 per annual tire capacity. The break-even price to give a zero NPV is therefore (10% × $70) + $25 (direct costs) = $32. This is the price that we should expect to see in 2 years' time. With the price now at $38, Greystone can expect economic rents of $6 per tire per year for the first two years. The NPV of the new plant is therefore:

$$500{,}000 \times \left(\frac{\$6}{1.1} + \frac{\$6}{1.1^2} \right) = \$5{,}206{,}611$$

b. The old plant should be scrapped when it can no longer earn the opportunity cost of its salvage value, that is, 10% × $30 million, or $3 on each tire produced. It will be scrapped when the price falls below $33, that is, in 2 years' time. Meanwhile, it will produce cash flows of $8 million for 2 years. Its value today is therefore:

$$\frac{\$8{,}000{,}000}{1.1} + \frac{\$8{,}000{,}000 + \$30{,}000{,}00}{1.1^2} = \$38{,}677{,}686$$

c. The change in energy and materials costs modifies the direct costs to $45 and $42 for the old and new plants, respectively. This increases the breakeven price on the new plant to $49, just $1 below the current price of $50. The economic rent is now only $1 per tire produced (for 2 years), so the NPV of the new plant is:

$$500{,}000 \times [(\$1/1.1) + (\$1/1.1^2)] = \$867{,}769$$

The old plant will now be scrapped only if the price of tires falls below $45 + $3 = $48. It is now sensible for manufacturers to build only sufficient new plants to push the price down to $49. The old plant is no longer expected to be scrapped but will earn $5 per tire for 2 years and $4 per tire after that. In year 2, it will be worth 4/0.1 = $40 million; so today it is worth:

$$\frac{\$5{,}000{,}000}{1.1} + \frac{\$5{,}000{,}000 + \$40{,}000{,}000}{1.1^2} = \$41{,}735{,}537$$

CHAPTER SUMMARY

Project evaluations can show positive NPVs either because the cash flow projections are too good (and wrong) or the project is really good and the company can extract economic rents on account of competitive advantage over its rivals. Managers should ensure that when they accept positive NPV projects, they belong to the latter group. The biggest practical difficulty in applying the NPV criterion is in establishing reliable cash flow forecasts. The chapter illustrates the most important dangers and difficulties in forecasting cash flows, and it provides advice on how best to combat them. Although it is hard to provide rules, which would cover all situations, it is common sense to look for the source of the positive NPV. The key idea is that you can expect a positive NPV only if you have some kind of competitive advantage relative to your rivals in the industry.

Market prices provide very useful information on the value of many assets and commodities. Unless you have reason to believe that you know better than the market, you would be well advised to accept the markets values. This applies to real estate or gold or oil, any of the well-traded assets or commodities. If you think an asset is worth more in your possession than its market value, you should be able to explain why.

Technological breakthroughs can give companies tremendous advantage and significant economic rents. However, this advantage does not last forever; competitors catch up soon. This economic rent will be a direct function of the cost difference between the technology leader and the surviving marginal producer. Marginal producers will survive as long as the price in the market is above their cost. It should also be noted that technological breakthroughs might not be an unmixed blessing as they affect existing operations of the company negatively just as much as they harm the competitors' business. The impact of new investments on existing operations should be analyzed carefully as part of the new project evaluation.

LIST OF TERMS

Competitive advantage
Differentiation strategy
Five forces
Marginal producer

Cost leadership strategy
Economic Rent
Focus strategy

EXERCISES

Fill-in Questions

1. A firm needs to have _____ over its rivals in the same business in order to economic profits.

2. The key aspects of the industry structure that determine the opportunities for economic rent available an industry can be understood by analyzing the _____ of industry competition.

3. A _____ is a producer who will cease production if there is any fall in the price at which the product is sold.

4. _____ is the term used to describe profits, which are in excess of the cost of capital.

5. The competitive strategies used by firms include _____, _____ and _____.

Problems

1. Which of the following are true and which are false?

   a. A monopoly can obtain permanent economic rents unless it is regulated in some way.
   b. The average forecasting error for the cash flow of a project is zero.
   c. New capacity decisions must take account of the effect on sunk costs, such as investments in existing plants.
   d. No firm can earn economic rents if it has to buy inputs at a price that reflects their value to the firm.
   e. Marginal producers have assets with zero market value.
   f. Fully depreciated assets always have a present value of zero.
   g. Stock prices reflect the value of growth opportunities only after the firm has announced its plans to invest in new capacity.

2. Nevada Mining Company is considering opening a second gold mine. This mine will cost $25 million to develop, and it will produce 30,000 ounces of refined gold a year for 5 years at a cost of $320 an ounce. The current gold price is $450 an ounce, and the opportunity cost of funds is 10%.

   a. What is the NPV of this project if you assume that the gold price will grow at 5% per year?
   b. What is the NPV if you assume that the gold price is expected to grow at the cost of funds?

3. Blue Mobile Corp. (BMC) makes mobile phones that sell for $80 each and cost $50 each to manufacture. The existing plant produces 30 million units per year, which represents a significant part of the total market. The company is considering investing in a new plant that will increase capacity by 20 million units per year. When the increased volume of production hits the market, the market price of mobile phones is expected to fall to $65 per unit. BMC is currently negotiating contracts for the construction of its new plant, which will reduce production costs to $30 per unit. The cost of capital for this project is 15%.

   a. What is the maximum price that BMC should be prepared to pay for its new plant, assuming that it can expect to retain a monopoly of the more efficient production technology indefinitely?
   b. What would the plant be worth to another company that did not already mobile phones?

133

4. The manufacture and sale of Holy Moos is highly competitive. The industry is composed of three firms with the following capacities and manufacturing costs:

Firms	Sales (million units)	Unit cost
A	8	8
B	6	9
C	4	10
Total	18	

The demand curve for Holy Moos is given by:

Price (in dollars) = $24 - 0.5 \times$ (quantity in millions)

The industry opportunity cost of capital is 10%, and new plant costs $70 per unit of capacity. All the plants have indefinitely long lives but could be scrapped at salvage values of $30 per unit of capacity. Firm C discovers a way of reducing unit-manufacturing costs to $7, keeping capital costs unchanged. It manages to secure monopoly rights to the technique for an extremely long period, and it decides to challenge firm A's market leadership by immediately adding 5 million units of the new capacity.

a. What is the present value of firm C's existing plant after the new capacity is added?
b. What is the maximum addition to capacity before it is worthwhile to scrap firm C's original plant?
c. What is the NPV of firm C's new investment project?
d. Can firm C make any profitable investment without first disposing of its old plant?

5. Bay Corp. and Valley Inc. have identical plants that can each manufacture 100,000 chips a year, at a unit cost of $6. These plants could be scrapped at any time with a scrap value of $1.5 million. Bay Corp. plant has been fully depreciated for tax purposes, whereas Valley Inc. plant has been depreciated only to a book value of $1 million and will give rise to annual $500,000 depreciation allowances for the next 2 years. Since both companies pay tax at 50%, Bay Corp. would realize only a net of $750,000 from scrapping its plant immediately; while Valley Inc. would realize $1.25 million net. At what prices for chips will each company find it economical to cease production immediately and scrap its plant? (Assume the opportunity cost of capital is 10 %.)

6. The market for shipping crude oil can be represented in terms of a number of types of tanker serving a number of different routes. One very simplified representation is given in the table below. It shows, in millions, the available tonnage of each class of tanker, the total tonnage required on each route, and the operating costs of each tanker on each route. All tankers are available for charter in a competitive market, and the price mechanism will allocate them to routes so as to minimize the total costs of transporting crude. All tankers have a useful life of 15 years and can be sold for scrap at any time for $150 per ton. Assume the cost of capital is 10%.

Tanker Type	Tonnage	Annual Operating Costs per Ton		
		Route 1	Route 2	Route 3
VLCC	500	$30	$34	Too large
MLCC	400	$35	$37	$38
Other	300	$40	$40	$40
Total tonnage required		300	500	250

a. What type or types of tanker will be used on each route?
b. What will be the annual rental (per ton) for chartering each type of tanker?
c. What will be the market price per ton) for purchasing each type of tanker?
d. What could happen to the usage and the prices of each type of tanker if the tonnage of VLCCs increased to 700?
e. What would happen if (with no increase in the tonnage of VLCCs) an environmental lobby succeeded in banning VLCCs from 50% of the required tonnage of route 1?

Essay Questions

1. Describe the different kinds of biases in forecasts that can affect capital budgeting decisions. Give some guidelines for minimizing their effects.

2. Explain the link between strategy and finance. Why is it necessary to understand the source of NPV?

3. Discuss the relationship among competitive advantage, economic rent, and positive NPV projects.

4. Explain clearly why a company may have an economic incentive to suppress an improvement in technology.

5. Explain clearly what is meant by the statement, "The level of economic rents is determined by the costs of the marginal producer."

6. In the Marvin Enterprises example, users of the earlier and more expensive technologies were prepared to continue to produce even at prices that gave negative profits after depreciation. Explain what factors determine their willingness to do so.

7. Describe an industry that has experienced the type of situation and decisions described in Marvin Enterprises. What are the most important similarities and differences between your example and the imaginary gargle blaster industry?

8. Discuss whether a company can still have an incentive to suppress an improvement in technology if all its shareholders hold the market portfolio.

ANSWERS TO EXERCISES

Fill-in Questions

1. Competitive advantage
2. Five forces
3. Marginal producer

4 Economic rent
5. Cost leadership, differentiation and focus

Problems

1. a. True
    b. False
    c. True
    d. True

    e. False
    f. False
    g. False

2. a. For each ounce of gold mined per year, the present value of the gross revenue stream is:
        $450 \times$ (annuity factor: $t = 5$, $r = 1.1/1.05 = 4.76\%$; 4.358) = \$1,961
        PV of costs = \$320 $\times$ (annuity factor: $t = 5$, $r = 10\%$; 3.791) = \$1,213
        NPV = $-25,000,000 + 30,000\ [1,961 - 1,213] = -\$2,560,000$

    b. NPV = $-25,000,000 + 30,000\ [(5 \times 450) - (\$1,213)] = \$6,110,000$

3. a. BMC will gain net revenues of \$35 on each of its 20 million new units a year, and it will lose \$15 each of its existing 30 million units of output. This gives an incremental cash flow of:

    $$(20,000,000 \times \$35) - (30,000,000 \times \$15) = \$250 \text{ million}$$

    At a 15% discount rate, the present value is \$1,667 million, and this is the maximum price BMC should be prepared to pay.

    b. Another company would not stand to lose revenues on the existing plant. The new plant would be worth \$700 million/0.15 = \$4,667 million to such a company.

4. a. The extra capacity will drive the price down to \$12.50 [\$24 $- (0.5 \times 23)$], but it is best to scrap C's old plant at any price below \$13 [\$10 $+ (\$30 \times 0.1)$]. The existing plant is therefore worth only its salvage value of \$120 million ($4 \times \$30$).

    b. 4 million units, because at a price of \$13 the unit will have to be scrapped. A total capacity of 22 million units will cause the price to fall to \$13 = \$24 $- (0.5 \times 22)$.

    c. Assuming the equilibrium price is \$13, the NPV of firm C's project is given as

    $$\begin{aligned} \text{NPV} &= [5,000,000 \times (\$6/0.1 - \$70)] - [\$4,000,000 \times (\$5/0.1 - \$30)] \\ &= -\$50,000,000 - \$80,000,000 \\ &= -\$130,000,000 \end{aligned}$$

If firm C scraps all its old plant and the price goes to $14.50, the NPV is still negative (−$55 million).

d. It is not possible. When the price is $15, each unit of investment has a NPV of −$70 + $8/0.1 = $10, but unless the old investment has been scrapped, we also reduce the present value of the old plant by

$$4 \times \$0.5/0.1 = \$20$$

5. The incremental cash flows from Bay Corp. decision to maintain production are as follows:

	YEAR 0	YEAR 1
Net revenues after tax		$0.5 \times (P - 6) \times 0.1$
Proceeds on disposal	−0.75	0.75

Where P is the unit price in dollars and the cash flows are expressed in millions of dollars. These cash flows will have a positive NPV if the price is greater than $7.50.

Similarly, the incremental cash flows from Valley Inc.'s decision to maintain production are:

	YEAR 0	YEAR 1
Net revenues after tax		$0.5 \times (P - 6) \times 0.1$
Depreciation tax shield		0.25
Proceeds on disposal	−1.25	1.00

These cash flows will have a positive NPV if the price is greater than $8.50.

6. a. We can figure out from the structure of operating costs that the total costs of transporting crude are minimized when the demands of each route are satisfied as follows:

    Route 1: 300 VLCC
    Route 2: 200 VLCC, 300 MLCC
    Route 3: 100 MLCC, 150 other

   b. Since 150 "other" tankers are in use and the remaining 150 are idle, this category of tanker represents a marginal producer, and its rent must equal the opportunity cost of salvage. Since the cost of capital is 10% and the salvage value is $150 per ton, the rental must be $15 per ton.

   MLCCs and "other" tankers are both used on route 3, but the MLCCs are cheaper to operate by $2 per ton. They can therefore command a $2 higher rental of $17 per ton.

   VLCCs and MLCCs are both used on route 2, with a $3 cost advantage to the VLCCs. This gives them a $3 rental advantage, and the VLCC rental is $20 per ton.

c. Capitalizing the rentals of $20, $17, and $15, we find that the market prices of the VLCC, MLCC, and "other" tankers are $200, $170, and $150.

d. Route 2: 400 VLCC, 100 MLCC; route 3: 250 MLCC. All "other" would be scrapped, MLCC would drop to salvage value of $150 per ton, and VLCC to $180 per ton.

e. Compared with (a), the 150 tons of route 1 VLCCs would switch with 150 tons of route 2 MLCCs. There is no change in tanker prices. Price for shipping oil on route 1 increases by $5 per ton.

12

Agency Problems, Compensation, and Performance Measurement

INTRODUCTION

Decisions on long-term investments or capital budgeting are among the most important made by corporate managers. The right decisions lead to value creation but the wrong ones cause poor performance and a decrease in shareholder value. Managers are agents of shareholders and are susceptible to temptations, which give rise to agency problems. These agency problems can be mitigated only by monitoring of the managers as well as well-designed compensation plans, which align the managers' interests to those of the shareholders. This chapter focuses on two main topics: *Incentives* that are required to ensure that the managers make optimal investment decisions in the best interests of the shareholders, and *performance measurement* of the firm that is accurate and appropriate for the incentives to work. The concept of residual income or economic value added (EVA) is presented. EVA can serve as a very useful performance measure and an alternative to the traditional accounting measure, the return on investment.

KEY CONCEPTS IN THE CHAPTER

Incentives and Compensation: The senior management of the firm depends on lower level managers and employees for a number of important decisions relating to all aspects of capital budgeting decisions. Many of these decisions are carried out at the lower levels. A number of investments, again carried out at lower levels, do not even appear in the capital budget. These include research and development, employee training, and marketing outlays. Small decisions add up and eventually can have significant impact on the firm's value. For all these reasons, the top management has to ensure that employees at all levels have the right incentives to identify and invest in positive NPV projects. Please note that the senior management may also be subject to the typical temptations that affect lower level managers.

Agency Problems: The stockholders are the principals and the managers are their agents entrusted with the responsibility of running the firm on behalf of the stockholders. Very few corporate managers own any significant amounts of the stock of the firm they are managing. Therefore, they may not necessarily share the stockholders' enthusiasm for maximizing NPV or taking up risky, but worthwhile projects. This is the essence of the agency problems, which cause sub-optimal behavior on the part of the managers. Some examples of this behavior include – *reduced efforts* (or shirking), use of *perks, empire building* or expanding the business for its own sake, taking up *entrenching investments* which ensures the manager's position, and a tendency to avoid *risk* even when it is in the interest of the stockholder. The empire-building propensity is caused by the fact that the manager's relative importance, authority, and position are a function of the size of the operation she or he commands rather than the value added by it. The reduction in value of the firm caused by the agency problems is the agency cost.

Mitigating Agency Costs: While the agency cost cannot be totally eliminated, the organization of the capital budgeting process and the rewards system for managers should be structured such that the agency cost is reduced to the minimum possible. This is achieved through a mix of *monitoring* of managers' behavior and by designing the managers' rewards and incentives in a way to align the managers' interests with that of the stockholders. Monitoring is done at different levels and is delegated by the stockholders to the board of directors who monitor the top management. The top management in turn takes care of monitoring the managers at lower levels. Accounting firms who perform regular audits of companies' books of accounts and financial statements perform an important role in the overall monitoring of corporations. In general, small stockholders leave it to the larger stockholders to closely watch corporate performance on a regular basis. This might actually lead to the *free-rider problem*, where everyone assumes that someone else will do the job and nobody does it.

Management Compensation: Monitoring has its limits and to be effective has to be used in combination with well-designed *compensation plans* for managers. The ideal compensation plans will succeed in aligning the managers' interest with that of the stockholders. A fixed salary will never work, as this does not give any incentive to the manager to do the best she or he can. Part of the problem in rewarding managers is the fact that managerial inputs cannot be measured effectively and the output depends on not only managerial efforts and competence but also on external factors on which the manager has no control. In practice, more and more firms are designing managerial compensation packages such that they include a fixed component and bonuses or rewards for improved corporate performance. Rewards for the top management can be based on the overall corporate performance or price of the firm's shares. However, compensating managers at divisional and plant levels on the basis of the company's share performance is not fair and will not produce the best efforts from these managers. Here one has to use other measures of performance.

In general, the compensation structure used by American firms is unique compared to those of the other industrialized countries and different, particularly in two respects. Typically, the total compensation received by American CEOs and others in top management is considerably higher compared to the compensation enjoyed by top management in other countries. However, the American CEO receives a much smaller part of the compensation through base pay and more of the compensation through bonuses and incentive pays including stock options. Compensation plans based on stock options have become more common and have the advantage of aligning managers' interests to those of the stockholders. Some recent examples, however, suggest that stock option based compensation plans can also lead to accounting and other short-term manipulations causing serious damage to the firm.

The perceived high levels of compensations received by the top managers have always attracted debate and some controversy. This is especially true of some major financial institutions that were the recipients of large US federal government bail out financing in 2008. Governments in the US as well as Europe have imposed some restrictive regulations on compensation as a result of this.

More and more corporations in many countries are adopting compensation plans where most of the bonus is awarded based on the performance of the firm's stock. These plans typically use one of three approaches: stock options, restrictive stocks that have to be held for a certain number of years, or performance shares. Stock options were the most popular approach in the US in the 1990s perhaps because of the accounting rules that permitted award of options to employees without having to account for the cost of the award. The accounting rules were changed in 2006. This, as well as the potential for abuse, has caused some changes and other stock based approaches are becoming more popular. Please no approach is perfect and the agency costs of non-owner managers can never be totally eliminated.

Measuring Performance: If performance based compensation plans for managers are to be effective, the measures of performance have to reflect the performance accurately. The traditional tool used in the past is the accounting measure, *return on investment (*ROI). The ROI and accounting earnings (net income) have two major advantages: i) it measures performance on absolute basis and ii) this can be used to measure performance of managers of departments and divisions. However, the accounting measures also suffer from some major drawbacks: i) it is subject to manager's control, ii) they are often biased and are subject to the type of accounting rules used, and iii) the typical accounting profit does not include any provision for the cost of funds used in the business. This means that positive earnings and earnings growth by themselves do not reflect superior performance. Accounting earnings are also biased against new investments in that they understate a project's profitability in the early years of the project and overstate the same in the later years. Comparison of accounting earnings across firms in different industries can be very misleading. Unless firms earn more than their cost of capital, they are not adding value to the firm or its stockholders. Please note that ROI is sometimes referred to return on capital (ROC). Another accounting performance measure that is similar is return on assets (ROA). The definitions of these ratios sometimes differ and one has to be careful before comparing these measures.

Residual *income* or the *economic value added* (EVA) is an alternative performance measure, which overcomes most of the drawbacks of the accounting earnings. EVA, a copyrighted term registered by the consulting firm, Stern and Stewart, measures the value added after covering the cost of capital for the investment used in the business. It equals the income earned less the cost of funds used. A similar measure is the *economic profit* (EP) used by McKinsey and Company. This is measured as the capital used in the business multiplied by the difference between the return on investment and the cost of capital. EVA explicitly recognizes the cost of capital and focuses on profits earned after meeting the cost of capital. It has become quite popular in recent years and firms use EVA to measure and reward divisional performance. While EVA is a great improvement over the accounting earnings, it retains some of the biases of the accounting profits. Thus for new projects or investments carrying long-term benefits and short-term costs, EVA will understate the value added in the early years. The problem here is that EVA, like accounting earnings, understates economic income. This is often because of overstatement of depreciation or inclusion of elements, which are investments rather than current expenses (e.g. R & D). Effective implementation of EVA as a measurement and compensation tool requires changing some of the accounting rules or adjusting them so that EVA is an accurate reflection of the value added.

Economic depreciation measures the real decline in the value of the asset and thus is measured by the change in the present value of cash flows generated by the asset. Unlike accounting or book depreciation, economic depreciation can be negative (i.e. the value of the asset increases).

Use of accounting profit measures are widespread and is perhaps unavoidable. One should be careful and be aware of the limitations of the accounting measures and try to use EVA or a similar economic profit measure that accounts for the cost of capital. A recent academic study suggests that many senior managers believe that accounting earnings are the most important numbers reported to the investors. They also manage the earnings, possibly at the cost of long-term value of the firm.

Explanation of Formulas and Mathematical Expressions

Notations: C_1 = Cash receipts during the period;
P_0, P_1 = Price of the asset at the beginning and the end of the period
BV_0, BV_1 = Book value at the beginning and the end of the period
r = Cost of capital; ROI = Return on investment

$$\text{Rate of return} = \frac{C_1 + (P_1 - P_0)}{P_0}$$

EVA = Income earned − Cost of capital × Investment
Economic Income = Cash receipts − Economic depreciation
Economic depreciation = $P_0 - P_1$
EP = (ROI − r) Capital employed
Book income = Cash receipts − Book depreciation = $C_1 + (BV_1 - BV_0)$

$$\text{Book ROI} = \frac{C_1 + (BV_1 - BV_0)}{BV_0}$$

Points to keep in mind:
  i.   EVA = EP.
  ii. Book depreciation will always be positive or zero.
  iii. Economic depreciation may be negative or the asset value may increase.

WORKED EXAMPLE

Bugsy Inc. is considering an investment of $120 million on a project with the following expected cash flows. The project generates cash flows for 5 years and will be closed down after that. Assume cost of capital of 15% and straight-line depreciation for book income calculations.

Year	0	1	2	3	4	5
Cash flows (millions)	−120	20	30	46.3	46.3	46.3

Calculate the NPV for the project and forecast the book income, the ROI, the economic income and EVA for the project.

SOLUTION

$$NPV = -120 + \frac{20}{1.15} + \frac{30}{(1.15)^2} + \frac{46.3}{(1.15)^3} + \frac{46.3}{(1.15)^4} + \frac{46.3}{1.15^5} = 0$$

Forecast of book income and ROI:

Cash flow in millions

Years	1	2	3	4	5
Cash flow	20	30	46.3	46.3	46.3
Beginning book value	120	96	72	48	24
Ending book value	96	72	48	24	0
Change in book value	−24	−24	−24	−24	−24
Book income	−4	6	22.3	22.3	22.3
Book ROI	−0.033	0.063	0.310	0.465	0.929
Book depreciation	24	24	24	24	24

Book income = cash flow + change in book value
Book ROI = Book Income/Beginning book value

Forecast of economic income, economic rate of return, and EVA:
Note the following relationships:
Economic income = cash flow + change in present value
Economic return = Economic income/Beginning present value
Economic value added = Economic income − cost of capital × beginning value

Cash flow in millions

Years	1	2	3	4	5
Cash flow	20	30	46.3	46.3	46.3
Beginning present value	120	118	105.7	75.3	40.3
Ending present value	118	105.7	75.3	40.3	0
Change in value	−2	−12.3	−30.4	−35	−40.3
Economic income	18	17.7	15.9	11.3	6
Economic rate of return	0.15	0.15	0.15	0.15	0.15
Economic depreciation	2	12.3	30.4	35	40
Economic value added	0	0	0	0	0

CHAPTER SUMMARY

This chapter describes the challenges posed by the agency problems in designing the right monitoring and compensation plans, which will ensure that the managers will maximize NPV. Structuring rewards and incentives for managers require accurate measurement of performance. The chapter analyzes the drawbacks of the widely used accounting measures of performance. The accounting earnings and ROI understate the profitability of new projects and overstate the earnings and ROI of older projects. Alternate measures like EVA based on economic income and economic depreciation are better in measuring performance.

LIST OF TERMS

Agency problems   Economic profit
Economic depreciation   Economic value added
Economic income   Return on investment

EXERCISES

Fill-in Questions

1. The accounting _____ generally understates the profitability of new projects.

2. Economic income is measured by the cash flow plus the change in the _____ of the assets.

3. Senior management can be considered as the _____ of the _____.

4. Senior managers are monitored by _____.

5. Auditing firms also provide _____ of the firm's performance.

6. Managers sometimes sponsor projects, which have a _____ for their skills.

Problems

1. True or False?

   a. Fixed salaries rarely provide the right incentives for managers.
   b. Accounting ROI provides an absolute measure of performance.
   c. Inflation has little effect on the ROI as it affects both the revenues and costs.
   d. All important expenditures pass through the capital budgeting process.
   e. Economic value added as usually calculated reflects the NPV of the project.
   f. Book depreciation cannot be negative.
   g. Economic depreciation can be negative.
   h. Changing project hurdle rates has little effect on the number of projects proposed.

2. Web Café is considering an expansion project, which requires an investment of $200,000 and is expected to produce after-tax annual cash flows of $60,000 for each of the next five years. The cash flows beyond five years are ignored. Calculate the NPV, IRR, pay back, and the average accounting ROI for the project. Assume a cost of capital of 15% and straight-line depreciation.

3. A project has the following cash flows: $C_0 = -168$, $C_1 = 60$, $C_2 = 75$, $C_3 = 90$.

   a. Calculate the IRR.
   b. Find the accounting rate of return for each year using straight-line depreciation.
   c. Calculate the weighted average accounting rate of return using the beginning period book value discounted at the IRR as the weight for each year.

4. An asset costs $740,000 and is expected to produce a cash flow of $180,000 each year for the next 6 years. The cost of capital is 12%.

   a. Calculate the accounting income using straight-line depreciation.
   b. Calculate the economic income for each year.
   c. What are the cash flows required to make the economic depreciation straight-line and provide the same present value?

5. Division X of ABC Inc. has an accounting income of $145,000. The division uses assets of $800,000 and has a cost of capital of 15%. Calculate the ROI and the EVA.

6. Given below are the income and asset values for three divisions of Patel Corp. Calculate the ROI and the EVA. Between accounting income and EVA, which measures the performance of the divisions better?

	Division 1	Division 2	Division 3
Net Income	$215 million	$400 million	$125 million
Assets employed	$2,100 million	$2,600 million	$750 million
Cost of capital	14%	11%	12%

Essay Questions

1. Discuss the relative merits of using EVA and ROI for measuring the operating performance of divisions and departments.

2. Explain the importance of timely and accurate information in the capital budgeting process.

3. "It is not possible or even desirable to eliminate all agency costs." Discuss.

4. Describe some of the problems involved in managing and controlling the capital budgeting process and ensuring that managers maximize the shareholders' wealth.

5. Compare and contrast economic and book income. Do you agree with the view that accountants should not try to measure economic income?

ANSWERS TO EXERCISES

Fill-in-Questions

1. Return on investment
2. Value
3. Agents, shareholders
4. Board of directors
5. Monitoring
6. Need

Problems

1. True or False?
   a. True c. False e. False g. True
   b. True d. False f. True h. True

2. NPV = $1,129   IRR = 15.24%   Pay back period = 3.33 years

$$\text{Average accounting ROI} = \frac{\text{Average Accounting Income}}{\text{Average Investment}}$$
$$= \$20,000/\$100,000 = 20\%$$

Average accounting income = cash flow − book depreciation = $60,000 − $40,000 = $20,000

3. a. IRR = 15 %
   b. Accounting rates of return are given in the table below:

	Year 1	Year 2	Year 3
Cash flow	60	75	90
Beginning book value	168	112	56
Depreciation	56	56	56
Book income	4	19	34
Accounting ROI (%)	2.38	16.96	60.71

c. Weighted average accounting ROI:

Year	Discounted book value	Weight	Accounting ROI	Weighted ROI
1	168/1 = 168	168/307.73 = 0.5459	2.38	1.30
2	112/1.15 = 97.39	97.39/307.73 = 0.3165	16.96	5.37
3	$56/(1.15)^2 = 42.34$	42.34/307.73 = 0.1376	60.71	8.35
Total	307.73	1.00		15.02

The weighted average ROI is the same (except for rounding error) as the IRR.

4. a. Accounting income = cash flow − depreciation = $180,000 − ($740,000/6) = $56,667

   b.

Year	0	1	2	3	4	5	6
Cash flow		180	180	180	180	180	180
Present value	740	649	547	432	304	161	0
Economic depreciation		91	102	115	128	143	161
Economic income		89	78	65	52	37	19

   c. Each year the present value should decrease by (740,000/6) = $123,333. Each year's cash flow will be the depreciation amount + 12% of the previous year's present value. The present value and cash flows are given in the table below:

Year	Present value	Cash flow
0	$740,000	
1	$616,667	$212,133
2	$493,333	$197,333
3	$370,000	$182,533
4	$246,667	$167,733
5	$123,333	$152,933
6	0	$138,133

5. ROI = \$145,000/\$800,000 = 18.13%
EVA = \$145,000 − 0.15×\$800,000 = \$25,000

6.

	Division 1	Division 2	Division 3
Net income	\$215 million	\$400 million	\$125 million
ROI	215/2100 = 10.24%	400/2,600 = 15.38%	125/750 = 16.67%
EVA	$215 − 0.14 \times 2100 =$ −\$79 million	$400 − 0.11 \times 2600 =$ \$114 million	$125 − 0.12 \times 750 =$ \$35 million

The EVA is a better measure of performance as it adjusts for the capital employed and the business risk through the cost of capital. Division 1 has not earned enough income to cover its cost of capital.

13

Efficient Markets and Behavioral Finance

INTRODUCTION

This chapter is the first of several chapters dealing with corporate financing decisions. The chapters covered so far have focused on the asset side of the balance sheet. The focus now shifts to raising funds to finance corporate investments. While both financing and investment decisions can add or destroy value, it is much harder to find positive NPV financing decisions. Financial markets are generally very efficient and fiercely competitive. It is very difficult to make easy gains through financing decisions. While analyzing investment decisions, we have assumed away the financing question or taken the financing as given. The same approach, in reverse, is used for evaluating the financing decisions. With the investment decisions as given, what will be the best financing decision? The primary goal of maximizing the NPV remains the same.

Understanding market efficiency and its implications is the key to understanding all financing decisions. The chapter explains the concept of market efficiency in detail and reviews the evidence supporting and contradicting market efficiency. The chapter also provides an overview of behavioral finance, which offers plausible explanations for the occasional inefficiencies or anomalies of the market. The chapter concludes with the six lessons and the key implications of market efficiency for the corporate finance manager. The fundamental point made in this chapter is that owing to the extremely competitive nature of the financial markets, it will be very hard to find positive NPV financing opportunities.

KEY CONCEPTS IN THE CHAPTER

NPV of Financing Decisions: When corporations raise money in the capital market through a bond or stock issue, they receive funds in exchange for explicit or implied promise of future payments to the investors who buy these bonds or stocks. The NPV for a financing decision can be calculated just like it was done for the investment decisions, though the pattern of cash flows will be somewhat different, with cash inflows at the beginning and outflows in later years. The discount rate used for computing present values should reflect the normal cost of the type of financing used. In general, financing decisions differ from investment decisions in the following ways: i) financing decisions are more complex because of the variety of financing forms used – debt, preferred stock, common stock, long-term and short term debt, convertible debt, debt with adjustable interest rates, to name some typical forms used, ii) it is harder to find positive NPV financing decisions because of intense competition in the capital market, and iii) financing decisions can often be reversed more easily than most investment decisions. Another important difference between financing and investment is that firms rarely have a competitive advantage in financing unlike in real product markets where they have often built up competitive advantage in terms of brand loyalty, reputation for quality and service, lower cost, etc. It is also true that financial markets are far less segmented than some might imagine. Capital flows freely across borders and different types of markets.

Market Efficiency: A market is considered efficient when prices in the market fully reflect the information about the securities. Since new information about securities, by definition, will be random, price changes also must be random. In other words, day-to-day price changes cannot be predicted and will be totally random. Way back in 1953, Maurice Kendall, a British statistician found that actual price changes were as random as the results of a serial coin tossing game with a slightly higher pay-off for heads. A direct implication of market efficiency is that it will not be easy to find positive NPV financing or investment opportunities because it is very difficult to find under-priced or overpriced securities. Economists have classified market efficiency into three forms based on the type of information that is reflected in security prices. These are briefly described below.

Weak form efficiency: The market is said to be weak form efficient if prices fully reflect all information about past prices. In other words, market prices will not follow any predictable patterns. Any forecast based on past price patterns will be useless as investment tools and will not help an investor make superior returns. Competition for profits will destroy any useful patterns or cycles.

Semi-strong form efficiency: The market is said to be semi-strong form efficient if security prices fully reflect all publicly available information such as news media stories, announcement of earnings, issues of stocks or bonds, stock splits, mergers, etc. A semi-strong form efficient market will react quickly and instantaneously to new information and it will be impossible to trade on the news and make money.

Strong form efficiency: The most rigorous form of efficiency implies that security prices will fully reflect all information including that, which is not publicly available. It implies that even information, which is unearthed by careful and expensive research by analysts and investment managers, will not give you superior returns because the prices would already reflect even this information.

Semi-strong form efficiency implies weak form efficiency and strong form efficiency implies weak and semi-strong form efficiencies. Market efficiency is the result of competition among investment analysts, portfolio managers, and professional traders who attempt to exploit any mis-pricing observed in the market. The analysts and portfolio managers spend enormous amounts of resources to uncover the latest and most useful information about any stock they are interested in. The market competition among these professionals will ensure that market prices reflect all available information.

Empirical Evidence: Market efficiency is one of the most researched topics in financial economics and empirical evidence generally finds market to be efficient. Different types of tests were used to test the different forms of market efficiency. Weak form efficiency was tested by using trading rules suggested by technical analysts who claimed to have discovered patterns in price movements. It was invariably found that these trading rules did not generate superior profits. Other tests for weak form efficiency included tests for significant relationships between successive daily or weekly returns. Tests have found little serial correlation in daily or weekly returns for markets in many different countries.

The tests for semi-strong form efficiency have included analyzing market reactions to earnings announcements; stock splits, accounting changes, and mergers or other significant corporate events. In general, these tests attempt to isolate the effect of the news or event on the stock price. The tests estimate the *abnormal stock return* as the measure of the impact of the news or event. The abnormal return is defined as actual return − *expected return*. The expected return is estimated using the simple market model: $\alpha + \beta$ (actual market return). The abnormal return computed this way excludes the effect of market-wide influences. These tests for semi-strong efficiency have generally shown that market reaction to events and news items of significance is swift and nearly instantaneous leaving very little time to make profitable trades once the news is announced.

Performance of mutual fund managers and stock analysts has been used to test the strong form efficiency. If these professionals show superior performance, it can be interpreted as market inefficiency. While some fund managers appear to have shown consistently better performance, most studies have failed to find superior performance by fund managers and analysts. In general, few mutual funds consistently do better than the market averages or comparable benchmarks. When the mutual fund performance is adjusted for expenses, the returns on average are lower than comparable market benchmarks. This is fairly strong evidence in support of the efficient market hypothesis.

Evidence against Market Efficiency: While the evidence for market efficiency is very convincing, researchers have also discovered a number of *anomalies* or *puzzles*, which seem to indicate some market inefficiencies. These anomalies include: significantly higher returns for smaller stocks, persistent patterns of higher returns for the month of January compared to other months, lower returns for Mondays compared to Fridays, and patterns indicating differing returns for different times of the trading day. Researchers have offered different explanations for these puzzles and anomalies. The small firm effect, for example, may be explained as one of three possible cases: i) higher risk premium required by investors that is not fully captured by the CAPM, ii) result of the specific time period used for the study – the effect would disappear if one looked at the returns for the nineties, and iii) a possible exception to the efficient market theory. Recent years seem to show somewhat of a reversal in the small firm performance, as large firms appear to have done better.

Two other anomalies appear to have persisted. The *earnings announcement* puzzle shows that market under-reacts to earnings announcements such that firms with best earnings news outperform those with worst earnings news implying investor under-reaction to earnings announcements. The *new issue puzzle* is the sharp price rise for new stock issues immediately following their issue and the below market long-term (five-year) performance for these stocks. For the period 1970-2003 portfolio of new issue stocks, bought right after the issue, showed returns 4.1% lower than comparable portfolios.

Efficient markets are not easy to reconcile with asset bubbles, which seem to recur in history. The examples include the Japanese real estate and stock market bubble, the US dot-com bubble between 1995 and early 2000, and the more recent real-estate bubble in the US that led to the sub-prime crisis and a sharp stock market fall. It is possible that wrong incentives and agency problems fed these bubbles and caused them to expand before bursting, most professional investors and analysts failed to see what was coming.

Relative vs. Absolute Efficiency: An implication of market efficiency is that securities are fairly priced and the prices reflect the intrinsic value of the securities. The dot-com bubble raises serious doubts about the market's ability to value securities correctly. It is hard to argue that the prices were fair both at the peak of the boom and after the bubble had burst. While one can justify large price changes as the result of changes in expectations of earnings growth, it will be hard to argue that the market or the investors can always correctly price securities on an absolute basis. The pricing or valuation can be correct only in a relative sense. It is impossible to test absolute intrinsic valuation and thus absolute efficiency. We can price the stock of Pfizer and be reasonably sure about its valuation, only if we assume that Merck or some other pharmaceutical company comparable to Pfizer is priced correctly. In the absence of such a benchmark for comparison, we cannot be sure of our valuation. Thus, while we are reasonably certain about the market being relatively efficient, one cannot make any claim about absolute market efficiency. Note that the above explanation can be applied to the dot-com bubble also.

Market anomalies may lead to under-pricing or overpricing of the firm's stock. It is important to note that overpricing of your firm's stock does not mean that it is good to issue stocks and invest in negative NPV projects; you are better off in investing in the capital markets in other securities. Under-pricing of your stock precludes you from issuing stocks.

Behavioral Finance: Behavioral finance, with its foundations on human psychology, attempts to explain market anomalies and investor behavior. Essentially, the behavioralists suggest that investor behavior is less than perfectly rational. Investors often overreact or under-react based on short-term memory. These behavioral traits manifest in the investors' *attitude to risk;* they become are more risk-averse than justified. Most investors are also prone to make systematic errors in assessing probable likelihood of different events and seem to be guided more by their recent experience than by the totality of lessons covering all the information from the past. Investors also seem to suffer from overconfidence. These behavioral inadequacies and less than rational behavior on the part of many investors are offered as explanation for market inefficiencies and anomalies.

Further, there are limits to arbitrage that makes it difficult for all anomalies and mispricing to arbitraged away. In theory, it is expected that *arbitrage* by smart and resourceful traders will force market to *converge* to efficiency. Such trades by the arbitrageurs are called *convergence trading.* While arbitrage is technically defined risk-free profit opportunity; the trades are rarely risk free and in practice there are limits to arbitrage. The arbitrageur might end up suffering huge losses before seeing convergence converting the losses to profits. The Long Term Capital Management story is a cautionary tale for anyone out to make a quick profit on some perceived market inefficiency.

The Six Lessons of Market Efficiency: While the anomalies and puzzles raise serious questions about market efficiency, the finance manager will do well to heed some basic lessons about market behavior. These are summarized below.

Lesson 1 - Markets have no memory: This stresses weak form efficiency and clearly implies that attempts at timing the market for bond or stock issue are unlikely to result in value maximizing decisions. Historic prices and recent trends are not much help in forecasting the market trend.

Unfortunately, it is often true that some managers try to time the market by picking the best time to issue securities.

Lesson 2 - Trust market prices: It is not possible for most investors to consistently find bargains or under-priced securities in the market. Market prices reflect the collective wisdom of all the investors and analysts and therefore will be the best estimates of the value of the securities. In other words, it is unreasonable and unwise to assume that one can predict security prices better than the market itself.

Lesson 3 - Read the entrails: Market prices tell us a lot about the future. Security prices typically reflect what investors expect to happen in the future. For example, the difference between short-term and long-term interest indicates the expected changes in interest rates. The return offered by a company's bonds and the variability of its common stock prices are good indicators of the probability of its going bankrupt. Market reactions to corporate announcements such as mergers, acquisitions, and restructuring give managers fair indication of the valuation effect of these actions.

Lesson 4 - There are no financial illusions: Investors are concerned with the firm's cash flows and are unlikely to be impressed by accounting gimmicks or other cosmetic changes, which do not enhance the cash flows. Therefore, a firm cannot expect to increase its value by merely cosmetic changes such as stock splits or by manipulating the earnings reported to shareholders.

Lesson 5 - The do-it-yourself alternative: Investors will not pay others for anything that they can create or do themselves at a lower cost. An implication of this lesson is that corporate combinations pursuing diversification for risk reduction is unlikely to be valued highly in the market as investors can duplicate this strategy at lower costs by buying shares of companies in different industries.

Lesson 6 - Seen one stock, seen all: Unlike branded products, stocks do not have unique qualities; investors buy a stock if the expected return it offers is fair compensation for the risk it entails. This means that stocks, which offer similar return-risk trade off, are near perfect substitutes for each other and the demand for any given stock is highly elastic. The implication is that large blocks of a stock can be sold at close to the market price as long as the market is convinced that you have no private information.

Explanation of Terms and Mathematical Expressions

NPV of financing = Present value of amount raised − Present value of all future payments

NPV of a loan (or bond issue) = Amount borrowed − PV (interest payments) − PV (principal payments)

Abnormal return = Actual return − Expected return

Expected return = $\alpha + \beta r_m$, where α is the return on the stock when the market return is zero and β is the beta of the stock.

Abnormal return measures the extra return on a stock as a reaction to a specific announcement by the company and is used to measure the impact of an action taken by the company using the event study method.

WORKED EXAMPLE

a. Merkur GmbH, a German machine tool manufacturer, is planning to expand its manufacturing base in the US and has been offered a special loan of $25 million by the state of Alabama. The loan is for a term of 5 years and carries an interest of 4% to be paid annually. Mekur's normal borrowing rate for 5 year borrowing is 6%. What is the value of this special loan to Merkur?

b. Myro Labs, a biotech firm, is trying to decide on an issue of new shares. The company already has 6 million shares outstanding and it is authorized to issue up to an additional 2 million shares. The company's shares are currently selling at $50.

    i. What proportion of the firm will have to be sold in order to raise $15 million if shares can be sold: at $50 each and at $30 each?

    ii. What is the loss to the existing shareholders if the shares are actually sold to new investors at $30?

    iii. If the market is efficient, what is the likely price at which the company can sell the shares?

SOLUTION

a. The special loan offer is obviously a good one and the value of the special loan can be calculated by computing the NPV of the loan using Merkur's normal borrowing rate of 6%.
NPV = + 25 − PV (interest payments) − PV (principal) = 25 − 4.212 − 18.682 = $2.106 m

b. i. Number of shares to be issued to raise $15 m:
@ $50/share = 15,000,000/50 = 300,000; total shares after the issue = 6,300,000
Proportion sold to new investors = 300,000/6,300,000 = 4.76%
@ $30/share = 15,000,000/30 = 500,000; total shares after the issue = 6,500,000
Proportion sold to new investors = 500,000/6,500,000 = 7.69%

    ii. Value of the firm before the new issue = $50 × 6,000,000 = $300 m

New capital raised	= $30 × 500,000 = $15 m
Total value of the firm after issue	= $315 m
Value per share	= $315/6.5 = $48.46/share
Loss to existing stockholders	= 6,000,000 ($50−$48.46) = $9.24 m

    iii. If the market is efficient, the stocks could be sold at a price closer to $50 than at $30.

CHAPTER SUMMARY

This chapter covered one of the most important ideas of modern financial economics – the efficient market hypothesis. The financial markets are characterized by intense competition among investors trying to exploit all the information they have and thus causing prices to be fair and competitive. It is not easy to make money in the financial markets; one can only get fair returns for the risk born. Market prices fully reflect information available about the securities. Market efficiency is termed weak form, semi-strong form, or strong form depending on the type of information, which is reflected in the security prices (historic prices for weak form, public information for semi-strong form, and all information for strong form). The three forms are nested; strong form efficiency implies the other two forms and semi-strong form implies weak form efficiency.

Empirical evidence strongly supports weak form and semi-strong form and offers qualified support for the strong form. Researchers have discovered several anomalies and puzzles. This has led to some serious challenges to the efficient market hypothesis. Market efficiency implies fair valuation of assets; however, valuation can only be relative. There is no way we can be sure about intrinsic valuation of assets in an absolute sense. We can only be certain of market efficiency in a relative sense. Behavioral finance attempts to provide explanations for market inefficiencies. However, this approach falls short of providing predictive tools that will help one make money in the market. Efficient market provides six important lessons to the finance manager. A smart manager will heed these lessons, as ignoring them is unlikely to lead to value enhancing decisions.

LIST OF TERMS

Arbitrage
Abnormal return
Convergence trading
Efficient market
Elasticity of demand

Random walk
Semi-strong form efficiency
Strong-form efficiency
Weak form efficiency

EXERCISES

Fill-in Questions

1. In an efficient market, security prices fully reflect _____ about the securities.

2. The three forms of market efficiency are _____, _____, and _____.

3. A strong form efficient market implies _____ and _____ also.

4. The prices of securities appear to follow a _____ in which each successive price change is independent of all previous price changes.

5. A strong form efficient market implies that investors can only earn a _____ return on their investment.

6. If prices reflect all published information, the market satisfies the conditions for _____.

7. If prices fully reflect historic information on prices, the market is said to be _____.

8. The _____ of an article is the percentage change in the quantity demanded for one- percent change in its price.

9. The abnormal return on a firm's stock is the difference between its actual return and its _____ return.

10. _____ involves convergence trading by arbitrageurs.

Problems

1. True or False?

    a. A market which is weak form efficient will also be semi-strong form efficient.
    b. A strong form efficient market will also be weak form efficient.
    c. In an efficient market, investors can only earn the risk free rate of return.
    d. The demand elasticity for stocks is fairly low.
    e. If short-term interest rates were lower than long-term rates, it would be better to borrow short-term.
    f. In an efficient market investors cannot expect to earn high abnormal returns.

2. Paradise Electronics Corp. (PEC) is planning to invest in a new microprocessor plant in Ireland and the Irish government has offered them a low interest loan for $15 million. The loan has a term of 3 years and an interest rate of 3%. The cost of a comparable bank loan for PEC is 5%. What is the value of the special loan to PEC?

3. Hick Bill Inc. has 72 million shares outstanding and the stock is currently selling at $96. The company announced a 2 for 1 stock split. What will be the stock price after the split becomes effective? How many outstanding shares will there be after the split?

4. Krytech believes that its stock is currently overvalued by the market. Its shares are selling at $60 although management believes they are worth only $40. There are currently 10 million shares outstanding, and the company plans to raise $50 million by issuing 1 million shares at $50 each. The existing shareholders can sell their rights to subscribe to this issue for $9,090,900. Assume that the existing stockholders sell their rights and all the new shares are taken up by new investors. How much will the original shareholders have gained if: (a) the shares were worth only $40 before and (b) they were worth $60?

5. You can buy a 12% coupon, 15-year bond at $1,000 (face value). It is expected that one year from now, the bond will yield 10%. (a) If this forecast is correct, what will be your return on this investment? (b) What implications does this have for forecasting interest rates in terms of (i) its usefulness and (ii) its difficulty? Assume interest is paid annually.

6. The highly respected economic forecasting department of a major United States bank announces that its latest forecast predicts a significant upturn in economic activity and corporate profits starting in 2 years and lasting for 3 or 4 years. What effect on share prices do you expect this to have (a) immediately, (b) in 2 years, and (c) in 6 years?

7. Identify for which two of the following items demand is least elastic with respect to price and for which two it is most elastic: (a) steak, (b) tobacco, (c) a financial security, (d) gasoline, (e) tuxedos, and (f) shortening.

8. Davy Technology Inc. has a market value of $724 million. Pampaq Inc. has a market value of $376 million. A proposed merger between them seems likely to reduce the standard deviation of their equity returns from 40% individually to 25% combined. What would you expect the market value of the combined company to be after the merger, if risk reduction is the only benefit from the merger?

9. Which of the following is most likely to result in an increase in the value of a company's shares? (a) It announces that its long-awaited contract with the federal government has now been finalized, and production will begin as soon as a satisfactory specification can be agreed upon. (b) As a result of a change in its depreciation policy, the earnings figure in its newly released annual report is almost double the figure for the previous year. (c) It announces a 50% increase in its dividend. (d) Its main competitor announces a price cut.

10. In 1998, Daimler Benz, the German automobile manufacturer, and Chrysler Corporation agreed to merge. Each Chrysler share was to be exchanged for 0.625 shares of Daimler. Shortly after the announcement, Chrysler shares were selling for $52 and the Daimler shares were selling at $96. (The basic share traded in German marks, but its equivalent American Depository Receipts (ADR) traded in the New York stock exchange.). Some saw this as an opportunity to make money with no risk and an example of market inefficiency. What do you think?

Essay Questions

1. "Financing decisions are easier to make, but it is harder to increase shareholder value through financing decisions." Discuss.

2. "There are so many anomalies and puzzles that efficient market is an exception rather than the rule." Discuss.

3. Double-Bull mutual fund has earned high annual returns for each of the last three years beating the market handily. Can this be seen as clear evidence against the strong form efficiency?

4. "Performance of some very successful mutual funds is proof that the market is inefficient." Discuss.

ANSWERS TO EXERCISES

Fill-in Questions

1. Information
2. Weak form, semi-strong form, strong form
3. Semi-strong form and weak form
4. Random walk
5. Fair
6. Semi-strong form
7. Weak form
8. Demand elasticity
9. Expected
10. Arbitrage

Problems

1. a. False   d. False
    b. True   e. False
    c. False   f. True

2. Value of the special loan to PEC = NPV of the loan financing at 5%
    $$= +15 - \text{PV (interest payments)} - \text{PV (principal)}$$
    $$= +15 - (2.7232 \times 0.45) - (0.8638 \times 15)$$
    $$= \$0.817 \text{ million}$$

3. Stock price after the split = $96 \times 1/2 = \$48$
    Number of shares after the split $= 72 \times 2/1 = 144$ million shares

4. a. If the shares were worth $40:
        Value before issue = $40 \times 10 = \$400$ million
        After the issue, the existing stockholders receive $9.0909 million and $10/11^{th}$ of the value of the firm before the issue plus the $50 million raised by the issue.

        Value after the issue = $9.0909 + 10/11(400+50) = \$418.182$ million
        The existing shareholders have benefited by $18.182 million.

    b. If the shares were worth $60:
        Value before issue = $60 \times 10 = \$600$ million
        After the issue, the existing stockholders receive $9.0909 million and $10/11^{th}$ of the value of the firm before the issue plus the $50 million raised by the issue.
        Value after the issue = $9.0909 + 10/11(600+50) = \$600$ million

5. a. The value of the value of the bond one-year from now will rise to $1,147.33 [N = 14, I = 10, PV = solve, PMT = $120, FV = $1,000]. An investor buying the bond today will receive the coupon of $120 plus $1,147.33 earning a total return of 26.73 per cent.

    b. Any one who can forecast interest rates accurately can make a lot of money. It will be extremely difficult to make accurate forecasts.

6. There will be an immediate effect on the stock price to the extent that the forecast represents an improvement for the company's prospects. There will be no effect in later years.

7. The tobacco and tuxedos will have the lowest elasticity and the financial security and shortening will have the highest.

8. There will be no gain from the merger and value of the combined company will be about $1,100 million. The market price for each company already reflects its market risk as measured by its beta and the merged firm's beta will be the weighted average of the two betas.

9. The award of the contract is likely to result in an increase in its stock price to the extent this is not already expected and reflected in the price. Announcements c and d may affect the stock price to the extent they were unexpected.

10. If Chrysler shares were to fully reflect the value of the impending merger, they should be selling at $96 × 0.625 = $60. Thus, it appears that they are undervalued. However, an arbitrage transaction involving buying Chrysler shares and selling Daimler shares in equivalent quantities is unlikely to be risk free. Two factors to be considered are:
(i) potential foreign exchange risk (Daimler shares are priced in German marks), and
(ii) possible breakdown in the merger talks. Thus, the market price is probably a reflection of the risks involved rather than an opportunity to make money in a risk free transaction.

14

An Overview of Corporate Financing

INTRODUCTION

This chapter provides a descriptive overview of corporate financing and the three main types of securities that corporations issue: common stock, preferred stock, and debt. The chapter also includes a broad introduction to financial markets and institutions. While companies finance a large part of their new investments from internally generated funds, they also use large amounts of externally raised money. Most of this external funding comes from the issuance of either debt or equity.

The first section of the chapter provides a description of the changing patterns of corporate financing in the U.S. The section also includes a very interesting comparison of debt ratios across countries. It is important to realize that comparisons of this type have to take into account the differences in accounting rules and conventions followed in different countries. Each of the next three sections covers common stock, debt, and a short introduction to financial markets and institutions and their role in the economy.

The simple classification of external financing sources as debt and equity takes away all the details in which these can be different. The debt securities issued by a company can differ in so many little details, with some important consequences for the firm. Even equity issues can have different classifications based on voting rights. All these have given rise to a number of technical terms used in the world of corporate finance. The chapter explains these terms and the context of the use for them. Students of finance are expected to have at least a passing familiarity with this language of investment banking. The list of the main new terms and the set of fill-in questions should prove very useful in learning these terms.

KEY CONCEPTS IN THE CHAPTER

There are few new concepts in this chapter. The chapter essentially provides a descriptive overview of corporate financing. Here is a summary of the substantive material included in the text.

Patterns of Corporate Financing: The pattern of financing used by American companies during the last fifteen years has been fairly consistent and shows heavy reliance on internally generated funds. It appears that firms find internal financing to be more convenient. Some critics of this approach have suggested that corporate managers may be more risk-averse than warranted and may be putting their own interests ahead of that of the shareholders. One could also point out the advantages of internal funds. Use of internal funding saves issue expenses and avoids sending bad-news signals to the market. Another interesting fact revealed by the recent financing pattern is the net negative stock issue for most years. For thirteen of the last fifteen years, companies bought back stock or there was net negative stock issue.

Companies have to make two basic financing decisions: what percentage of profits to be paid out as dividends (the remaining to be reinvested in business) and what mix of debt and external equity should be used to finance the deficit. These questions take you directly to dividend and debt policies and are discussed in chapters 16, 17, and 18. Overall, financing decisions can be regarded as the marketing of a package of securities with rights to the company profits and cash flows.

In general, during the last five decades, companies' balance sheets have shown a marked increase in the proportion of debt to total assets. At least part of the reason is the progressive inflation that increased the market values of assets relative to their book values. It is also observed that debt ratios of the nineties are similar to the ratios of the 1920s and 1930s. The proportion of debt in U.S. balance sheets does not seem too out of line when international comparisons are made. One has to be careful to correct for accounting differences before drawing conclusions about differences across countries. The U.S. companies are roughly in the middle of the international pack compared.

Common Stock: Common stock represents ownership of the company and common stockholders, as owners of the company, have general preemptive right to anything of value that the company may wish to distribute after satisfying claims of lenders and preferred stockholders. They receive distribution of profits usually in the form of dividends. While most companies have only one form of common stock, some companies have issued stocks of different classes with different voting rights.

A company is allowed to issue shares up to the amount specified by its *authorized* share capital, which can only be increased with the permission of the shareholders. *Outstanding shares* are those held by investors. Shares that have been issued but subsequently repurchased and held by the company are called *treasury shares*. They are said to be issued but not outstanding. All issued shares are entered in the company's accounts at their par value. Because some states do not allow companies to sell shares below par value, par value is generally set at a low figure, which has no economic significance.

The stockholders, as owners of the company, have the ultimate control of the company. Their control over the company's affairs is manifested by their right to vote on appointments to the board of directors and on some other issues such as a merger of the company with another. The stockholders have to approve any major change in the articles of incorporation of the company. Voting may be on a *majority* basis or on a *cumulative* basis. Cumulative voting makes it more likely for minority groups to obtain representation on the board. Under this system shareholders may, if they wish, allot all their votes to one candidate. For example, if six directors are to be elected, a shareholder can allocate all six votes from each share to a single candidate and does not have to choose six candidates to vote for. Where there are different classes of stocks with different voting rights, the classes with more voting rights will generally command a premium in the market. The premium will be a function of the extra benefits the stockholders can get because of their superior voting rights. A recent study found that the premium is significantly higher in certain foreign countries (Mexico, Italy) compared to the premium in the US.

Ownership interests in businesses may be held in forms other than common stock. While common stocks are issued by corporations, comparable ownership securities for other organization forms of business are called different names such as units in *master limited partnerships* and *real estate investment trusts*.

Preferred Stock: Preferred stock is legally considered as equity but generally has only limited voting rights. Unlike common stock, though, most preferred stock is issued with a stipulated dividend and this dividend has to be paid before any dividend to common stockholders can be paid. Preferred stockholders' claims take precedence over that of the common stockholders if the company ever goes out of business. In general, only a small portion of corporate financing needs is met through the issue of preferred stock. It can be very useful means of financing in certain special situations.

There are some interesting tax implications with preferred stock dividends. Preferred stock dividends are not tax-deductible expenses for the company paying them. However, corporations receiving preferred stock dividends have to pay tax only on 30% of the dividends. Most of the preferred stocks is held by corporations (favorable treatment of dividend income), and most is issued by regulated utility companies (who would be made to lower their rates if they used subsidized debt instead).

Corporate Debt: There are a great variety of ways in which companies can borrow money. The common feature is that the company promises to make regular interest payments and to repay the principal amount according to an agreed schedule. The shareholders' liability is limited, so lenders can only look to the earnings and assets of the company for their payment. Lenders cannot look beyond those assets to the shareholders for repayment. Some of the more common choices available to firms considering debt issue are summarized below.

- *Maturity or the term of debt:* Companies can borrow short-term or long-term. Short-term debt is typically used for seasonal needs related to working capital, while long-term debt is usually chosen for financing long-term assets. Debt issued may have provisions for repayment on a steady basis or at the end of maturity. The borrower may have a right to prepay the debt and occasionally the lender may demand prepayment.
- *Fixed rate or floating rate:* The interest rate may be *fixed* for the whole term of the loan when the debt is issued. Alternatively, it may be a *floating rate*, determined from time to time during the term according to an agreed formula such as "1% above *prime*" or "1/2% above *LIBOR*." Floating rate debt may be issued using a number of different benchmark interest rates.
- *Country and currency:* Although most borrowing by United States corporations is done in the United States and in United States dollars, firms may also borrow in foreign countries or in foreign currencies. When a company issues debt in a currency outside the currency's home country (e.g. yen bonds outside Japan), these are called *eurobonds*. Note that the new European currency is also called Euro and one could now talk of a Euro eurobond.
- *Seniority:* Debt may be junior or senior. If the company goes bankrupt, its junior (or *subordinated*) debt is not eligible to receive payment until all senior debt has been paid in full.
- *Security:* Debt may be secured by some or all of the assets of the company. A lot of corporate debt is issued as unsecured debt without explicit collateral. Secured debt has first claim, in the event of default, on the assets specified as collateral. A *mortgage* is an example of this, while long-term bonds, which are unsecured, are called debentures.

- *Public versus privately placed debt:* Bonds sold as a public issue are offered to anyone who wants to buy them and can be freely traded afterwards. Bonds sold in a private placement are sold directly to a small number of qualified institutional investors, and subsequently can only be resold among these investors.
- *Warrants:* companies often issue warrants as part of a package to sell other securities. Most commonly they are used to sell bonds. Warrants give their owner the right to purchase one share of common stock at a specified price on or before a specified future date. Thus, they are essentially call options issued by the company.
- *Convertible Bonds:* These are bonds issued by the company that can be exchanged for (or converted to) a specified number of shares on specific future dates if the holder wishes. The holder will, of course, wish to convert if the stock price goes up well above the level when conversion makes sense. If the stock price does not go up, the holder has no obligation to convert. Essentially, a convertible bond is like a package of a bond plus a warrant. One difference is that when the convertible bondholder converts, she exchanges the bond for a certain number of shares, but pays no cash. The warrant holder has to pay cash to get his shares.

Please note that accounts payable and leases are also debt or debt-like obligations.

Financial Markets: Financial markets and intuitions are essential and very important parts of the market economy. Financial markets facilitate exchange of capital between savers or surplus units and borrowers or deficit units. Corporations and other borrowers sell financial assets such as stocks and bonds in the *primary market* to raise cash for the business. The stocks and bonds issued in the primary market are then traded in the *secondary markets* (e.g. the New York Stock Exchange), which provide liquidity and convenience for the stockholders and bondholders. The secondary markets include not only the organized exchanges such as the NYSE, but also the *over-the-counter* (OTC) markets, which are essentially network of dealers and traders brought together often through the electronic medium. Foreign exchange markets and the NASDAQ are examples of OTC markets.

The Financial Crisis of 2007-2009: The US economy in general and financial markets in particular have been badly shaken by one of the worst economic crisis brought about by some troubles for some major financial institutions and a recession that is considered the worst since the Great Depression of the 1930s. The crisis was precipitated by a number of related and chain of events. The Federal Reserve's easy money policy since 2000 coupled with flow of foreign capital from Asian economies contributed to low interest rates and easy credit of dubious quality. This caused a bubble in residential real estate. Much of the mortgages that financed the real estate bubble were securitized and were owned by financial institutions in the US and around the world. The real estate bubble was not limited to the US; countries like UK and Spain also experienced similar bubbles. When the bubble burst, real estate prices fell sharply and the mortgage backed securities prices fell sharply as well. A number of financial institutions were in trouble and were bailed out or merged with relatively stronger institutions. The one exception was Lehman Brothers, which went into bankruptcy in 2008 causing a panic in the markets and sharp decline in stock prices. Many institutions were affected. The Federal Reserve and the US treasury stepped in and averted further collapse by providing funds and guarantees to many of the troubled institutions (AIG, Citigroup to name just two). The crisis was global in nature and economies around the world were affected.

Financial Institutions: Financial institutions are key players in financial markets and own large proportion of securities issued by corporations. Commercial banks, saving and loan companies, mutual funds and insurance companies are among the major institutions. These institutions act as *financial intermediaries* between lenders or savers and borrowers. Commercial banks collect deposits from individuals and corporations and provide loans, mostly short-term, to commercial and other borrowers. Insurance companies provide long-term financing and own both long-term debt and common stock.

Financial institutions differ from manufacturing corporations in both the assets they own and the ways they raise financing. While most of the assets owned by manufacturing corporations would be real assets, the assets owned by financial institutions comprise mostly financial assets such as bonds, stocks and various kinds of loans to individuals and businesses. Similarly, the sources of funds available to financial institutions are unique to the nature of their business and include deposits of various kinds, insurance policies, and other investments. Essentially, these institutions sell one kind of claims and then repackage them into a different type of financial assets. They add value by providing risk and term intermediation as well as savings in transaction costs.

Financial institutions play a very important role in the smooth functioning of the economic system. They provide *payment mechanism* for most of the commercial and personal transactions in the economy. This is facilitated through a variety of means including checking accounts, credit and debit cards, and electronic and other means of transfer of funds. Financial institutions also facilitate transfer of funds between saving units (those who want to invest) and deficit units (those who want to borrow). Different institutions do these in many different ways. Banks provide opportunities for investing simple deposit instruments, while mutual funds offer virtually unlimited ways of investing money for different terms and at different risk levels. Financial institutions also provide *risk pooling* and risk management services. Again, insurance companies and mutual funds have a number of products to meet the needs of individuals and businesses.

While financial markets and institutions serve the same basic functions around the world and since the dawn of market economy, market forces and changing regulatory structure have caused the role of the institutions to change over time. Two trends are note worthy. First, there has been a significant shift and change in the role of commercial banks as providers of commercial credit. Larger corporations depend a lot less on commercial banks for their financing needs as they find it cheaper and more convenient to borrow from the market directly or from other institutions like insurance companies and mutual funds. The second trend is *globalization* of markets. This has resulted in extensive cross-border lending and borrowing on the part of companies from different countries and investors.

CHAPTER SUMMARY

This chapter provided an overview of the different types of securities issued and used by corporations. The chapter offered a historic perspective on the changing patterns of corporate financing in the U.S. and provided international comparisons with other industrialized countries. The primary objective of the chapter is to familiarize you with the broad features of corporate securities and the terminology used in corporate finance.

Corporations use three types of securities to raise the financing they need. The simplest of these is common stock. Common stockholders are owners of the corporation and are entitled to profits, vote on the composition of the company's board of directors, and other important matters. Companies occasionally use preferred stock, though its use is far less common than debt and is used in special situations. Preferred stock has features of both debt and common stock – it has a fixed payment, but it is legally considered equity, and payments to preferred stockholders are not tax-deductible.

Debt is widely used by companies to meet part of their external funding needs. Debt comes in many different varieties and the chapter lists the many features taken on modern day corporate debt. Debt can be classified in terms of its maturity, repayment provisions, seniority of the debt, security, interest payment, issue procedures, and currency of the debt.

The chapter also gave you a glimpse of financial markets and institutions and their role in the economy. Financial institutions are key players in the markets and hold many of financial securities issued by corporations.

LIST OF TERMS

Authorized share capital
Convertible bond
Cumulative voting
Eurobond
Eurodollar
Floating rate
Line of credit
Majority voting

Outstanding shares
Par value
Preferred stock
Secured
Senior
Subordinated
Treasury shares
Warrant

EXERCISES

Fill-in Questions

1. The maximum number of shares that a company can issue is known as its
   _____.

2. Shares that have already been issued and are held by investors are called
   _____.

3. _____ are shares that have been repurchased by the company.

4. The _____ of a security is the value at which it is entered in the company's books.

5. _____ is the name for the voting system under which each director is voted on separately.

6. The voting system under which a stockholder may cast all of her or his votes for one candidate is known as _____.

7. In the event of bankruptcy, _____ debt must be repaid before subordinated debt receives any payment.

8. _____ debt represents a junior claim, which, in the event of default, is paid only after all senior creditors are satisfied.

9. In the event of default, _____ debt has first claim on specified assets.

10. The interest on a (n) _____ loan varies with the short-term interest rate.

11. A (n) _____ is a dollar that has been deposited with a bank outside the United States.

12. A (n) _____ is an issue of debt that is sold simultaneously in several countries.

13. _____ stock is an equity security, which offers a fixed dividend that must be paid before any dividend can be paid on the common stock.

14. A (n) _____ is a long-term security issued by a company, which gives the holder the right to purchase one share of common stock at a set price on or before a set date.

15. A bond that may be converted to the company's common stock at the discretion of the holder is called a (n) _____.

Problems

1. The authorized share capital of Grayson Corp. is 8 million. The equity is currently shown in the company's accounts as follows:

	Dollars
Common stock ($0.10 par value)	500,000
Additional paid-in capital	4,500,000
Retained earnings	23,000,000
Common equity	28,000,000
Treasury stock (1,000,000 shares)	4,000,000
Net common equity	24,000,000

   a. How many shares are issued?
   b. How many are outstanding?
   c. How many more shares can be issued without the approval of the shareholders?
   d. What is the share price if it is twice its book value?

2. Grayson Corp. of problem 1 issues a further 1 million shares at an issue price of $4 a share. How will the equity be shown in the company's books after the issue?

3. There are nine directors to be elected, and I own a round lot of 100 shares. What is the maximum number of votes I can cast for my favorite candidate under: (a) majority voting and (b) cumulative voting?

4. The shareholders of Bounty Corp. need to elect five directors. There are 4 million shares outstanding. How many shares do you need to own to ensure that you can elect at least one director (a) under majority voting and (b) under cumulative voting?

5. The Clear Mustard Company has the following income for the year:

Taxable income from operations	$253,000
Interest income	42,000
Dividends from preferred stock	20,000
Dividends from common stock	10,000
Total income	$325,000

It has paid interest charges amounting to $59,000 and dividends on its preferred and common stock of $35,000 and $50,000 respectively. If it pays tax at 35%, what is its tax bill for the year?

6. The Clear Mustard Company of the last problem had the following income and payments in the previous year:

Income from:
Operations	$224,000
Interest	32,000
Preferred dividends	40,000
Common dividends	40,000
	$336,000

Payments:
Interest	$44,000
Preferred dividends	$35,000
Common dividends	$45,000

How much tax should it have paid?

7. Which of the following are true and which are false?

   a. Commercial banks provide over 50% of all corporate financing needs.
   b. The assets owned by financial institutions differ significantly from those owned by manufacturing corporations.
   c. All partners in a master limited partnership have unlimited liability.
   d. U.S. leverage ratios have risen steadily over the last 40 years.

Essay Questions

1. Explain how issued share capital is shown in a company's accounts, and describe what rights and privileges shareholders enjoy.

2. Describe the variety of different types of debt that a company can issue.

3. What is preferred stock, who issues it, who buys it, and why?

4. Describe the main sources and uses of companies' funds.

5. Describe the role and functions of financial markets and institutions in the economic system.

ANSWERS TO EXERCISES

Fill-in Questions

1. Authorized share capital
2. Outstanding shares
3. Treasury shares
4. Par value
5. Majority voting

6. Cumulative voting
7. Senior
8. Subordinated
9. Secured
10. Floating-rate
11. Eurodollar
12. Eurobond
13. Preferred
14. Warrant
15. Convertible bond

Problems

1. a. 5 million shares   b. 4 million shares   c. 3 million shares
   d. The book value = $24,000,000/4,000,000 = 6; Market price $= 2 \times \$6 = \$12$

2. The books will show the equity account as follows:

	Dollars
Common stock ($0.10 par value)	600,000
Additional paid-in capital	8,400,000
Retained earnings	23,000,000
Common equity	32,000,000
Treasury stock (1,000,000 shares)	4,000,000
Net common equity	28,000,000

3. a. 100 votes   b. 900 votes

4. a. More than half the outstanding shares are needed, that is, 2,000,001 shares.
   b. As long as your candidate comes out in the top of a field of six or more candidates she will get elected. This means that she needs one more than one-sixth, that is, 666,667 are sufficient.

5. The taxable income is calculated as follows:

Income from operations	$253,000
Interest income	42,000
30% of dividends	9,000
	$304,000
Less interest expense	59,000
	$245,000

Its tax bill is 35% of $245,000, which is $85,750.

6. Taxable income is given by:

Income from operations	$224,000
Interest income	32,000
30% of dividends	24,000
	$280,000
Less interest expense	44,000
Taxable income	$236,000

Tax is 35% of $236,000, which is $82,600.

7. a. False
    b. True
    c. False
    d. True

15

How Corporations Issue Securities

INTRODUCTION

This chapter describes the procedures used by corporations for raising long-term funds in the capital market and provides a wealth of institutional details and guidance to managers on decisions about long-term capital. It describes the *venture capital* financing of a young company and then takes you through to the company's *initial public offering* (IPO). The subsequent sections describe the *general cash offer* used for most public issues of debt or equity securities in the United States. Equity issues made directly to existing shareholders are called *privileged subscription issues* or *rights issues*. The chapter also discusses the role of the *underwriter* and the costs of different types of issues. An overview of *private* placements is also included in the chapter.

Financial managers concerned with raising finance need to decide the method of issue, the size of the issue, the pricing of the security, the use of an underwriter, and the type of underwriting arrangement. The manager should also be concerned with the effect the issue will have on the firm's market value. All these are closely related to market efficiency. The manager will do well to remember the lessons of market efficiency learned in Chapter 13. Here are some important implications of market efficiency relevant to this chapter.

Financing Decisions and Stockholder Wealth: In general, it is very unlikely that financing decisions will enhance the market value of the firm as a whole. It is reasonable to assume that most financing decisions have a net present value of zero. This is because a positive NPV financing decision is one where the money raised exceeds the value of the liability created. In the highly competitive capital market, it is not possible for any firm to consistently fool investors in this way.

Financing Decisions and the Distribution of Wealth: Financing decisions can, however, affect the distribution of wealth between security holders and that there may be wealth transfer between one group of security holders and another. If new securities are underpriced, new holders will obtain a bargain at the expense of existing holders. This is not a problem, however, in the case of rights issues, where existing holders are given the rights to subscribe in proportion to the size of their holdings.

The Importance of Market Prices: When a company is deciding on the issue price for new securities, the best guide to what a company can hope to obtain is the price of closely comparable securities, which are already traded.

KEY CONCEPTS IN THE CHAPTER

Venture Capital: Equity investment in the early stages of a business can be very risky and is often called venture capital. Venture capital is key to the success of any growing new business as the original investors and founders of the business are unlikely to have the needed capital. The investment is risky, but is rewarded by the high returns of the successful ventures. Specialist investors who are often organized as partnerships typically provide this type of financing. Wealthy individuals and financial institutions are also important players in the venture capital business. In order to monitor the progress of the business and to limit the risk of the investment, venture capital financing is provided in stages with each additional stage of funding contingent on successful completion of set targets or milestones. *First-stage financing* generally is based on a *business plan*. The business plan describes the exact nature of the proposed business: the product, the market, the resources it will use, and the income it will generate. In obtaining an injection of equity capital, the *after-the-money valuation* is important in putting an implicit valuation on the entrepreneurs' existing equity. Successful completion of the first stage will lead to the *second-stage financing* and possibly further stages before the company is ready to go public with an initial public offering.

Venture capital market: The United States has a well-developed venture capital market. Most of venture capital funding is provided by specialist partnerships, which pool funds from a variety of investors and seek out fledgling companies to invest in. Some large technology companies are also active in providing venture capital to firms in the areas of their interest. Occasionally, start-up firms obtain funding from wealthy individuals or *angel investors*. Venture capital firms provide more than capital and often help the young start-up companies with advice and management expertise. Venture capital firms get their returns either from the sale of the funded firm or when a successful start-up decides to go public. Note that venture capital investments are very risky. Generally, for every ten first-stage venture capital investments, only two or three may survive as successful businesses. However, if one funded firm becomes very successful, it will make up for all the others.

Venture capital funding is usually provided through limited private partnerships set up with fixed life of about 10 years. The fund's management company will be the general partner and will be responsible for making all the investment decisions. The management company is compensated through a fixed fee plus a percentage of profits, called *carried interest*. The term *private equity investing* is used to describe the activities of not only venture capital funds but also other partnerships which provide financing for corporations in financial trouble, for acquisitions, and for going-private transactions.

The Initial Public Offering: The initial public offering or IPO is the first issue of shares a corporation to the general public. Generally, IPOs are done when the business has made considerable progress and is on its way to successfully establishing itself in the market. The IPO establishes a market value of the investment made by the founding entrepreneurs and the venture capitalists. A *primary offering* is one where shares are sold to raise additional cash for the company. Often a primary offering is combined with a *secondary offering* where existing shareholders (the venture capitalists and sometimes the founding entrepreneurs) sell some of their shares.

The Underwriters: An *underwriter* is used to sell the offered shares to the general investor. The underwriters provide valuable advice on all matters related to the stock issue. They also buy the stock from the company and then resell it to investors. The underwriters establish the price of the stock set for IPO and gauge the demand for the issue through discussions and survey of potential investors such as mutual fund managers and other clients. This process of compiling a list of potential orders is known as *bookbuilding*. The underwriters are compensated through the spread between the *issue price* (or *offering price*) and the price at which they buy the securities from the company. Where a new issue of common stock is unusually risky, the underwriter may handle the issue on a *best-efforts* basis (not guaranteeing to sell the entire issue) or on an *all-or-none* basis (where the deal is called off completely if the entire issue is not sold).

A syndicate of underwriters usually handles large issues. In this case, the syndicate manager keeps about 20% of the spread, a further 20 to 30% goes to pay the members of the group who buy the issue, and the remainder goes to the firms who actually sell the issue. Members of the underwriting syndicate are not allowed to sell securities at below the issue price, although they may be allowed to "support" the market by buying them at the market price. This helps stabilize the market for the stock in its early trading days. Underwriters often get an option (called *greenshoe option)* to buy additional shares from the company. This provision enables them to sell more than the committed number of shares in case they find that the demand for the stock is high. It also nets them extra profit if the stock offering has high demand and the stock price rises on trading on the opening day.

Issue Procedures: The formal procedures for an IPO start with the appointment of the managing and co-managing underwriters. The managing underwriter maintains the *book* for the issue which tracks the potential demand for the issue and helps in estimating the likely issue price. The bookbuilding approach to gauging demand and arriving at the issue price is popular in the US. An alternate approach to selling the securities uses auctions. The auctions can be *discriminatory auctions* or *uniform price auctions*. In the former method, each successful bidder pays the price he or she has bid, whereas in the uniform price auction everyone pays the same price, namely the lowest winning bid price.

The company enters into a formal agreement with the underwriters specifying details of the underwriting commitment, the spread and any greenshoe option agreed. Following these steps a *registration statement* is prepared for submission to the Securities and Exchange Commission (SEC). This statement presents information about the proposed financing, the firm's history, existing business, and plans for the future. The first part of the registration statement is usually distributed as a preliminary *prospectus*, also called a *red herring*. It contains a statement printed in red ink, which draws attention to its preliminary status and that securities are not permitted to be sold until the registration becomes effective. A marketing campaign for the issue is launched through road shows arranged by the underwriters. Meanwhile, the SEC studies the documentation and sometimes requests changes to it. Finally, an amended statement is filed with the SEC. After registration, the final prospectus is issued, giving the issue price, which is fixed at this stage. A *registrar* is appointed to record any issues of stock and to prevent unauthorized issues' taking place. A *transfer agent* is also appointed to look after the transfer of the newly issued securities. These steps are followed by the formal issue, allotment of stock by the underwriters and trading of the stock in the secondary market. Typically, the lead underwriter makes market in the stock providing liquidity and also initiates research coverage on the stock.

<u>Costs of new issue:</u> Public issue can be expensive. The costs include the administrative and transaction costs as well as the cost due to underpricing of the shares. The administrative costs include preparation of all the documentation by management, legal counsel, and accountants, besides other fees, printing and mailing costs. Underpricing of the issue is the hidden cost and can be very high in many cases. The company and its underwriters discuss and agree on the issue price. The company would, of course, like to secure the highest possible price. But if the price is set too high and the issue fails, the underwriter could suffer heavy financial losses and a loss of reputation. If the stock is underpriced the existing stockholders have given away part of the firm. A study of nearly 16,000 new issues from 1960 to 2008 indicated average under-pricing of 17.3%. It is sometimes argued that underpricing of an issue leads to successful IPO, because it pushes up the demand for the shares and leads to higher stock prices after the stock has started trading in the market. This helps the firm in raising capital in the future. One can also see the incentive the underwriter has for underpricing because that lowers the risk of loss from the issue.

Winners curse may be part of the explanation for underpricing found in many IPOs. This means that a successful bidder in an auction is likely to have overvalued the asset. Thus, investors, being unaware of other investors' valuation of the stock, can end up paying a high price.

Sale of Security by Public Companies: Public issue of securities can be either *general cash offers* or *rights issues*. General cash offers are made to the public. This is the most commonly used mode for all debt and most equity issues in the United States. In some other countries it is common to find rights issues (also known as *privileged subscription issues)* where the issue is offered to the existing shareholders as a right. The shareholders can sell their rights to subscribe to the issue in the market.

Corporations can file a single *shelf registration* statement covering financing plans for up to 2 years into the future. This provides prior approval to issue a stated amount of securities during this period and without being tied to particular underwriters. The company is then able to issue securities at its convenience and it can do it at very short notice. Large, well-established corporations often issue securities in more than one country and these are known as *International issues*. Both debt and equity securities are issued in international markets and the regulatory procedures depend on the countries included. SEC approval is not required if the securities are not issued to investors in the United States.

There is considerable economy of scale in issue costs. The percentage cost is smaller for large issues than for small ones. We also have to consider the effects of under-pricing and price pressure. The announcement of new issues of common stock on average results in a decline in the stock price of about 3% for industrial issues in the United States. This is probably an information effect: managers are more likely to issue stock when they think it is overvalued.

Rights Issue (The Privileged Subscription): A rights issue can be a very effective and inexpensive way of raising additional funding. The issue is offered to the firm's existing stockholders in proportion to their current holding in the company. The stockholders can transfer or sell their rights in the market. Rights issue effectively avoids wealth transfer between existing stockholders and new stockholders, since they are one and the same. Therefore, the actual pricing of the issue is of little consequence.

Private Placements: A private placement is an alternative to public issue and has certain advantages compared to a public offering. Private placements do not involve registration and is limited to a few buyers. Transaction costs will be lower. The placement can be made very quickly. There are disadvantages too. The securities issued in this way are very illiquid and are held for long-term investment rather than resale. This is a greater disadvantage for issues of common stock than for debt issues, so private placements of common stock (called *letter stock*) are rare. Bond issues, particularly of small- and medium-sized firms, account for the bulk of private placements. Since 1990, large financial institutions (known as *qualified institutional buyers*) have been allowed by the SEC to trade unregistered securities among themselves, and this has provided a further boost to this market.

WORKED EXAMPLES

1. Cory Leone and Maurice Greenberg are biotechnologists who pioneered new applications of DNA. They founded LeoGreen Biotech Corp (LBC) to commercialize these applications. The entrepreneurs' original investment in LBC amounted to $30,000. Six months after the launch of LBC, the friends were able to obtain first-stage financing of $500,000 and the after-the-money valuation on the firm was placed at $1 million. A year later at the next stage of financing LBC the enterprise was valued at $5 million before financing.

    a. What (paper) return and increase in value did the entrepreneurs get in each of these two stages?

    b. How would your answer to the previous question change if they had agreed on a first-stage after-the-money valuation of $800,000 million instead of $1 million and a second stage valuation of $4 million?

SOLUTION

   a. Cory and Maurice have a paper value of $500,000 for their stock at the first stage. With the additional $500,000 external financing, they now have 50% of the firm's stock. At the second stage, when the company is valued at $5 million their stocks are worth $2.5 million. These valuations represent 16.67 fold and 5-fold increases in the two stages, representing returns of 1567% and 400% respectively.

   b. At $800,000 firm valuation, Cory and Maurice have a paper value to their stock of $300,000 at the first stage. This gives them 37.5% of the stock in the firm ($300,000/$800,000). This is worth $1.5 million at the second stage ($4 m × 0.375). These valuations represent 10-fold and 5-fold increases in the two stages giving returns of 900% and 400% respectively.

2. Jackrabbits Corporation is making a rights issue to raise $6 million. Baby Rabbit owns 20,000 shares. Just before the issue, Jackrabbits' stock price was $20, and the terms of the issue are 1 new share for every 4 shares held at a subscription price of $15. Calculate (a) the expected price of the stock after the rights issue, (b) the value of the right to buy one

new share and (c) the rights Baby will have to sell to maintain the same ($400,000) investment in the company?

SOLUTION

a. For every 4 shares worth $20 before the issue, there will be 5 shares worth $20 × 4 + $15 (= $95) after the issue. Each share will, therefore, be worth $95/5, so the ex-rights price is $19.

b. The value of right to buy one new share = $19 − $15 = $4.

c. Baby Rabbit will get 5,000 rights and if he were to keep all his rights, he would end up with 25,000 shares valued at a total of 25,000 × $19 = $475,000. In order to retain his original investment, he should have $400,000/$19 = 21,053 shares. Therefore, he needs to keep only 1,053 rights and sell the remaining 3,947 rights. This will give him $3,947.

CHAPTER SUMMARY

This chapter provided a summary description of the procedures used by corporations for raising long-term finance through the issue of securities. Corporations raise finances through a variety of ways. Young start-up companies get much of their early funding through venture capital financing. Established and mature companies are able to raise money through seasoned issues. The chapter highlighted some very important implications for the financial manager. These can be summarized as below:

- Larger is cheaper. This suggests that there is economy of scale in raising money and the manager can take advantage of this by avoiding small issues.

- Beware of under-pricing. Perhaps the most significant of the hidden costs of financing is under-pricing of the security. This is especially true for the IPOs. Underwriters may be tempted to go too far to reduce the fear of winners' curse make an impression on the investor, but this comes at the expense of the issuing firm's existing stockholders.

- Winners' curse may need to be addressed in IPOs and careful design of issue procedures is needed.

- New stock issues cause lowering of stock price. This may be due to information the market might be reading into the company's actions. Managers would do well to keep the market fully informed.

- Take advantage of shelf-registration, which is particularly useful for debt issues of established, financially strong firms.

LIST OF TERMS

After-the-money valuation
All-or-none
Best efforts
Bookbuilding
Business plan
Carried interest
Discriminatory auction
First-stage financing
General cash offer
Initial public offering
Issue price
Offering price
Preemptive rights
Primary offering
Private equity investing
Private placement
Privileged subscription

Prospectus
Red herring
Registrar
Registration statement
Rights issue
Road show
Seasoned stock issue
Secondary offering
Shelf registration
Spread
Transfer agent
Underpricing
Underwriting
Uniform price auction
Unseasoned issue
Venture capital

EXERCISES

Fill-in Questions

1. Equity investment in young private companies is generally known as
   _____.

2. In order to obtain capital, the young company must first prepare a detailed
   _____.

3. The first injection of equity capital from the venture capital market is known as
   _____.

4. The proportion of the company, which the original owners will have to give up, depends on the _____ of the company.

5. The first issue of a security by a company is known as a(n) _____ or a(n) _____.

6. Before a general cash offer or a large public issue, corporations often put on a _____ to familiarize the investors with the company.

7. When new shares are sold to raise additional cash for the company, it is called _____.

8. When shares of existing shareholders are offered to the public, it is called _____.

179

9. An issue of securities that is offered to the general public or investors is called a(n) _____.

10. An issue of securities that is offered to current stockholders is usually called a(n) _____.

11. Rights issues are also known as _____ issues.

12. For most public issues, a(n) _____ must be submitted to the Securities and Exchange Commission.

13. Information about an issue is provided in its _____, which must be sent to all purchasers and to all those who are offered securities through the mail.

14. The preliminary prospectus is called a(n) _____.

15. The share of profits received by the management company of a venture capital fund is usually called _____.

16. _____ is the process through which the managing underwriter collects information, gauges the demand for the issue and compiles a list of potential orders for the IPO.

17. A financial institution is usually appointed as _____ to record the issue and ownership of the company's securities.

18. A(n) _____ may be appointed to look after the transfer of newly issued securities.

19. The sale of a public issue is normally handled by a(n) _____, who provides financial and procedural advice and usually buys the security for less than the offering price and accepts the risk of not being able to resell it.

20. The underwriter's _____ is the difference between the price at which the underwriter buys an issue from a company and the _____ or _____.

21. Occasionally, the underwriter does not guarantee the sale of an entire issue but handles the issue on a(n) _____ basis, promising only to sell as much of the issue as possible.

22. _____ underwriting is where the entire issue is cancelled if the underwriter is unable to resell it all at the offer price.

23. _____ occurs in a general cash offer when securities are sold at an offer price, which is below their market price.

24. When _____ is used to sell securities, each winner is required to pay the price he or she has bid for the issue.

25. Stock for which there is an existing market goes by the spicy name of _____ stock.

26. The _____ rights of common stockholders (to anything of value distributed by the firm) include the right to subscribe to new offerings.

27. The _____ provides an alternative to making a public offering.

28. When _____ is used to sell securities, everyone pays the same price.

29. _____ allows large corporations to obtain prior approval for their financing plans for up to 2 years into the future.

30. The term _____ is used to describe the activities of venture capital funds and other partnerships, which provide financing to companies in distress, for acquisitions and for going-private transactions.

Problems

1. Windsors is a young company started by two sisters, Ann and Wendy, with their savings amounting to $200,000. The firm received venture capital financing two years after its start-up. The venture capitalists provided first-stage financing of $2.5 million and valued the firm after-the-money at $5 million. Two years later, the firm received second-stage financing from the same venture capital company. Windsors received $6 million and was valued at $20 million after-the-money. A year later, Windsors was ready for its IPO and the underwriters valued the company (before the IPO) at $60 million. Calculate the returns for the sisters and the venture capital firm at each stage of financing.

2. The entrepreneurs' original investment in Marvin Enterprises amounted to $100,000. First-stage financing raised $1 million and placed a $2 million after-the-money valuation on the firm. At the next stage, the enterprise was valued at $10 million.

   a. What (paper) return and increase in value had the entrepreneurs enjoyed by each of these two stages?
   b. How would your answer to the previous question change if they had agreed on a first-stage after-the-money valuation of $1.50 million instead of $2 million and a second stage valuation of $9 million?

3. AZB Corp. decides to issue the stock via a general cash offer. The board believes it can raise the $18 million the company requires by issuing shares at $36. The company has 5 million shares outstanding and the current stock price is $40. Ignoring the underwriter's spread, calculate the following:

   a. The number of new shares that AZB will have to offer.
   b. The expected price of the shares after the issue.
   c. The loss per share to existing holders.
   d. The percentage reduction in value of an existing stockholder's investment in the company
   e. The net present value of purchasing 100 shares via the general cash offer.

4. AZB is considering the alternative of a privileged subscription stock issue to raise $18 million. The terms of the issue are 1 for 10 at $36, and the corporation's current stock price is $40. Calculate the following:

   a. The market value of the corporation's equity prior to the issue.
   b. The percentage increase in market value due to the issue.
   c. The expected price of the stock after the issue.
   d. The expected price of the right to buy one share.

5. Vanessa's Attic is issuing a 20-year bond to raise $10 million. The corporation can choose one of the following alternatives:

   a. Issue the bond publicly, in which case it will be sold at par and will carry a 9% coupon. The underwriter's spread would be 0.5%, and there are no other issue costs.
   b. Issue the bond through a private placement, in which case it will be sold at par and carry a 9 1/8% coupon. The total cost of the private placement will be $20,000.

   Assume annual coupon payments. Which option should the firm choose?

Essay Questions

1. Discuss the following statement: Venture capital is essential for a young, growing company, but it is also an expensive way of raising money.

2. Describe the main features of the process by which a young company might raise venture capital.

3. Discuss the following statement: Rights issue is the best way to raise new equity for an established company, as one does not have to worry about underpricing.

4. Discuss the relative merits of a public issue versus a private placement for a company wishing to raise new debt finance. What factors should be taken into account in pricing the bond issue?

5. Compare and contrast the role of the investment banker (or underwriter) in (a) general cash offers of either stock or bonds and (b) private placements of bonds

6. Describe how the costs of raising new capital depend on the type and amount of financing raised.

ANSWERS TO EXERCISES

Fill-in Questions

1. Venture capital
2. Business plan
3. First-stage financing
4. After-the-money valuation
5. Initial public offering, unseasoned issue
6. Road show
7. Primary offering
8. Secondary offering
9. General cash offer
10. Rights issue
11. Privileged subscription
12. Registration statement
13. Prospectus
14. Red herring
15. Carried interest
16. Bookbuilding
17. Registrar
18. Transfer agent
19. Underwriter
20. Spread; issue price; offering price
21. Best efforts
22. All-or-none
23. Under-pricing
24. Discriminatory auction
25. Seasoned
26. Preemptive
27. Private placement
28. Uniform price auction
29. Shelf registration
30. Private equity investing

Problems

1. The sisters' initial investment of $200,000 became $2.5 million in the first stage financing providing 12.5 fold increase or 1,150% return. During the next phase, the $2.5 million became $7 million (half of $20 million − $6 million). This is now 35% of the value of the firm. The return during this phase is 180%. At the time of IPO, the sisters' stake is valued at $21 million ($60 million × 0.35) and the return during this phase is 200%. The venture capitalists' initial investment of $2.5 million became $7 million at the time of second financing providing a return of 180%. During the next phase their investment of $13 million became $39 million to give a return of 200%.

2. The original stockholders' investment in the firm has a paper value of $1 million at the first stage. With an additional $1 million raised, they own 50% of the firm. At the second stage, when the company is value at $10 million, their stake is worth $5 million. These valuations represent 10-fold and 5-fold increases in the two stages, representing returns of 900% and 400% respectively.

   a. At a $1.5 million firm valuation, the original stockholders' investment would have a paper value of $0.5 million at the first stage. With an additional $1 million raised, they have only one-third of the company's stock. At the second stage, when company is

183

valued at $9 million their stake is worth $3 million. These valuations represent 5-fold and 6-fold increases in the two stages (returns of 400% and 500% respectively).

3. a. Number of new shares = $18,000,000/$36 = 500,000 shares
    b. Value of company after issue = $200,000,000 + $18,000,000 = $218,000,000
       Share price after issue $218,000,000/5,500,000 = $39.64
    c. Loss per share to existing holders = $40 − $39.64 = $0.36
    d. Percentage reduction in value = ($0.36/$40) × 100% = 0.90%
    e. NPV of purchasing 100 shares via offer = 100× ($39.64 − $36) = $364

4. a. Value of equity before issue = 5,000,000 × $40 = $200,000,000.
    b. Increase in value = $18 m/$200 m × 100% = 9%.
    c. Share price after issue = $218 m/5.5 = $39.64.
    d. Value of the right to buy one share = $39.64 − $36.00 = $3.64

5. a. Cost of public issue = $10,000,000 × 0.5% = $50,000
    b. Cost of private placement = $20,000 + additional interest cost
       Additional interest = $10,000,000 × 1/8% = $12,500 per year for 20 years
       If we discount these interest payments at 9%, i.e., the market rate for identical cash flows which are traded in the capital market, we obtain, PV = $114,107
       [N = 20, I = 9%, (P/Y = 1), PV = SOLVE, PMT = $12,500, FV = 0]
       Total cost of private placement = $20,000 + $114,107 = $134,107

That is, shareholders will be better off if the firm chooses the public issue alternative.

16
Payout Policy

INTRODUCTION

This chapter addresses the issue of dividends or payout policy. Corporations can return cash to their stockholders either by paying them dividends or buying back (repurchasing) shares. Firms face the choice of the amount of payout as well as the form, dividends or buybacks. Payout policy is a controversial issue and the controversy surrounds the question - do dividends increase the value of a firm? Part of the controversy and confusion about dividends arises from the way the issue is framed. In order to decide whether dividends add value to the firm, one has to keep other variables like investment policy and debt policy constant. One has to isolate the dividend policy effects from those of capital budgeting and borrowing decisions. This means that the dividend policy trade-off is between retaining earnings for reinvestment on the one hand and paying dividends and financing the investments with newly issued stocks on the other. In other words, dividend policy issue is not about paying off any excess funds the company has; but whether a company should pay out earnings as dividends when it can profitably reinvest the same.

Three broad and divergent – the right, the left and the centrist – views have emerged in response to this question. The rightist view reflected the prevailing wisdom before the seminal work by Modigliani and Miller (MM) and held that increased dividend payouts increase firm value. MM argued that a firm's value is decided by the success of its investments and not by how it pays dividends. This could be seen as the centrist or middle of the road view. A more radical – the leftist – view suggests that in view of the differential taxation of dividends and capital gains, dividends will reduce the firm's value as they are taxed at a higher rate. This view has less force in the U.S. now that the tax rate on both dividends and capital gains is same.

The dividend irrelevancy argument of MM assumes a world of perfect capital markets where there are no taxes or transactions costs. In this world, shareholders will find no difference between capital gains and dividend income. MM's position was a direct challenge to the traditional view, which held that high payout ratios tend to increase the value of the firm. While there is still debate on the issue, it appears that there is more acceptance of the general wisdom of the centrists' view that the payout policy by itself cannot affect firm value. Payout should be seen as a function of the life cycle of the firm and the investment opportunities that the firm has. A young firm that is still in the growth phase and with plenty of opportunities to invest in profitable projects will have little cash left over for dividends. An older, mature firm, on the other hand, will have fewer investment opportunities and more cash for dividends.

The chapter begins with some descriptive material on dividends and stock repurchases. This is followed by a section on the corporate practice and the information content of dividends and stock repurchase. The central question of payout policy and value of the firm is addressed next with detailed critiques of the three different views. The chapter also includes a description of alternative tax systems and their implications for dividends.

KEY CONCEPTS IN THE CHAPTER

The Choice of Payout Policy: Corporations return cash to the investors through dividends or by buying back shares. While dividends still account for a larger percentage pf earnings returned to shareholders, stock repurchases are becoming more common and popular. A change in the SEC regulation in 1983 is cited as the primary reason for the more widespread practice of stock repurchases. The practice of regular cash dividends is less common than it used to be. The percentage of American corporations paying regular cash dividends has declined from about 64% in 1980 to 52% now. Many growth companies have never paid dividends.

Dividends and Stock Repurchases: Dividends have been around for a long time. In order to familiarize yourself with the way dividends are paid out and handled by corporations, you should know terms and phrases commonly used by corporations. Here is a summary description of the mechanics and an explanation of the terms used.

The mechanics: The board of directors decides the amount of dividends and how they are to be paid, on the recommendation of the management of the company. Corporations in the U.S. generally pay their dividends quarterly, although any other schedule is possible. There are legal restrictions in most states on what can be paid out as dividends. Generally, dividends cannot be paid out of legal capital, usually defined as the par value of all outstanding shares. When there is no par value, the legal capital is usually defined as the receipts from the stock issue. Some exceptions to this rule may be permitted for mining companies.

The company makes an announcement of the dividend decision on the *announcement date*. The announcement gives the details of when the dividend will be paid to shareholders who are registered in the company's books.

Dividend reinvestment plans (DRIP) have become popular with stockholders and many corporations have instituted these plans. This allows the shareholder to automatically reinvest the dividends in the company's shares often at a discount from the current market price.

Terminology: A number of terms are commonly used to describe the various dates and events associated with dividend payments. Here is a list:

Announcement date: This is the date on which the dividend is formally announced by the company and starts the dividend process for that specific dividend. The announcement carries details of different dates important for the payment of the announced dividend.

Ex-dividend date: This is the first day on which the stock trades without the right to receive the announced dividend. This will be a few days before the record date. A person who sells the stock before the ex-dividend date will still receive the dividend when it is paid out, even though he will not be holding the stock on that date.

Record date: This is the date on which the list of shareholders eligible to receive the dividend is made. This follows the ex-dividend date.

Payment date: This is the date on which checks are sent to shareholders of record. Normally, it takes about 2 weeks after the record date.

With-dividend: This denotes that shares are selling with the cash dividend attached. All the stocks traded before the ex-dividend date will carry the right of dividends.

Corporations, which do pay dividends, typically have regular quarterly dividends. Occasionally companies pay an extra dividend when further cash is available. A stock dividend affects the stock price as the number of shares increases without any change in the value of the company's assets. Share (stock) repurchase is another way of returning cash to the stockholders. Stock repurchases permit the investors to choose whether to receive the cash or not. It also enjoys favorable tax treatment.

Share repurchase: Share repurchase can be an attractive alternative to cash dividends. It is attractive for two reasons: i) it lets the stockholder choose whether to receive the cash or retain his level of ownership and ii) gains from stocks sold are treated as capital gains (assuming the stockholder has held the stock for more than one year). Corporations use four different ways to repurchase stocks: open market purchase, tender offer, *Dutch auction*, and negotiated repurchase. Open market repurchases are the most common. A tender offer is an offer to buy back a certain number of shares, often at a premium. For a Dutch auction the firm sets a series of prices at which it will buy back shares and shareholders submit offers at these different prices. The firm then selects the lowest price at which the desired number of shares can be bought. Negotiated purchases are common when one or a few shareholders are involved in the repurchase transaction. *Greenmail* transactions, in which shares from a hostile bidder are repurchased by the target firm is an example of negotiated repurchase.

Corporate Practice: A survey of corporate managers conducted in 2004 provided very useful information on how corporations decide on dividend payments. The findings can be summarized by the following stylized facts:

- Managers are reluctant to make any major changes in dividends unless they are sure that the changes will not be reversed.
- Managers practice short-term smoothing of dividends to avoid the risk of a reduction in payout. Dividends follow changes in the long run, sustainable earnings. In other words, major changes are not made unless the managers are sure that changes in earnings are long-term and not transient.
- The changes in dividends are considered more important than the level of dividends.

Share repurchases are generally not seen as a substitute for cash dividends; many companies do both repurchases and have cash dividends. Repurchases are used to return extra cash back to investors and are more volatile than cash dividends. Many countries did not permit corporations to buy back their own shares. Now many of these countries have changed the laws to allow stock repurchases.

Information Content of Dividends and Stock Repurchases: Dividends and stock repurchases may signal important information to shareholders because they may indicate management's assessment of future sustainable earnings. Dividend increases are viewed as a signal of increased future earnings. Dividend cuts signal bad news about the future. Empirical evidence on this is mixed and there has been some research that found that dividend increases do not predict growth.

Share repurchases are different from dividends in that they are, usually, one-time events. A company may resort to share repurchase when it has more cash than it can profitably invest. Alternately, a share repurchase may be financed by additional borrowing. In either case, the manager is clearly indicating that stockholders' money is not being retained for making unprofitable investments. Yet, another reason for share repurchase may be the manager's confidence in the future prospects of the company and feeling that the stock is currently undervalued. Empirical evidence shows that share repurchases in general are greeted positively by the investors. The positive reaction is even greater when the stock repurchase is at a significant premium to the current price.

The Payout Controversy: The essence of the controversy centers on the extent to which dividend policy affects the value of the enterprise. There is little dispute as to the relevance and importance of dividends as signals of future prospects of the company. What is to be settled is whether the dividend decision itself contributes to a change in the value of the company. MM initiated the whole debate with their irrelevance view. We discuss this and the three main views in this controversy.

The MM irrelevance view: MM started the whole controversy by challenging the prevailing view on dividend policy. They showed that under perfect market conditions, a firm's value is decided by its investments and not its dividends. MM's argument begins with these assumptions:

- No taxes, transactions costs, or other market imperfections.
- A fixed investment policy or capital budgeting program.
- A financing policy in which borrowing is set.
- Remaining needed funds come from retained earnings, and extra cash is paid as dividends.
- Capital markets are efficient and transactions take place at fair prices.

Given the assumptions, it is very hard to reject MM's basic conclusion that dividend policy is irrelevant. Essentially, a firm's original shareholders can raise cash in two ways. They can collect dividends or they can sell a part of their holdings in the market to receive the same amount of cash (see figure 16-5). In each case, the cash received is offset by a decline in the value of the old stockholders' claim on the firm. If the firm pays a dividend, each share is worth less because more shares have to be issued against the firm's assets. If the old stockholders sell some of their shares, each share is worth the same but the old stockholders have fewer shares. It follows that:

- If dividends are increased, the firm must issue more shares (because investments and borrowing are fixed).
- No one will buy the shares at more or less than their true value.

- The total market value of the firm is unchanged, and the sale of new shares only results in a transfer of part ownership of the firm from the old shareholders to the new.
- The new purchasers receive shares at a price less than that on the old shares, and it is less by the amount of the dividend paid.
- In efficient capital markets, shareholders that need cash can either sell shares or receive cash dividends and the path they choose will not make any difference to the value of the firm.

Thus, dividend policy is irrelevant and depends on the firm's investment and financing decisions. Note that share repurchases are the reverse of the above process: Dividend reductions are accompanied by an equivalent reduction in shares, and total wealth of shareholders is unaffected.

The MM position can be challenged using evidence of market imperfections or inefficiencies. Taxes and transaction costs, however, might drive one to the conclusion that dividends may actually decrease value (See the "leftists" view below). Other imperfections such as the existence of a special clientele who prefer high-payout stocks or dividends as purveyor of valuable information about future prospects do make a case for the relevance of dividends. We will come back to this after summarizing the other views on dividend policy.

The MM irrelevance proposition applies to share repurchases decisions also. That is, keeping investment and debt policy constant, a firm's value is unaffected by any decisions to repurchase stock. Again, this assumes away any signaling effect from share repurchases.

The Rightists: The traditional finance literature before MM favored liberal dividends. This belief was supported by many in business and investment communities because they believed increased dividends made shareholders better off. The main arguments made in support of dividends centered on: i) dividends are less risky than capital gains and ii) capital market imperfections give rise to investors who prefer high dividends for personal and institutional reasons. Analysis of these arguments shows that they have limited validity in refuting MM's irrelevance conclusions. While it is true that dividends are more stable than capital gains, it is also true that the risk of the cash flows of the firm is determined by the firm's investment and debt policies. The dividend payout should not have any effect. As for the clientele argument, it is conceded that there are groups of investors who like regular and high dividends and therefore high payout firms. However, the demand for high payout firms by this clientele would be fully satisfied by now and it is very hard to imagine that a company can gain value by simply changing its payout policies.

The empirical evidence supporting the traditional view is limited. A better argument could be that investors lack complete trust in managers to spend retained earnings wisely. The dividend decision forces the managers to raise additional finances from capital markets to finance any new investment. This keeps them on a tight leash and possibly more efficient in spending shareholders' money.

<u>Taxes and the Radical Left:</u> The radical left position in the dividend controversy focuses primarily on the tax effects, which influence the preference for cash dividends. When dividends are taxed more heavily than capital gains, paying higher dividends will actually lead to a loss in value. The firm is better off paying any excess cash through stock repurchases rather than dividends. Thus, radical left view is that dividends are bad for the stockholders as they cause avoidable taxes. Of course, this extreme view will run afoul of the IRS and therefore few managers ever declare a policy on the lines suggested by the leftists' view.

Empirical studies give some support to the leftists' view in that investors in low marginal tax brackets appear to prefer high-payout stocks, and vice versa. However, note that there are serious measurement and other problems in some of these studies. It is very hard to measure expected return and tax effects caused by dividends. Further, tax effects on dividends are not uniform across different investors.

The tax law changes affect the relative advantage of capital gains over dividends. The current tax rate on both capital gains and dividends is same and thus weakens the case for the leftists' view. Of course, there is always a tax advantage for capital gains in that the tax is to be paid only when the gain is realized. In other words, one can choose to defer the taxes indefinitely.

Alternative Tax Systems: The chapter includes a brief discussion of alternative tax systems employed in different countries. These can be summarized as below:

- *The two-tier system:* Dividends are taxed at both corporate and individual levels. This is the approach followed in the U.S.
- *Split-rate system:* Investors are taxed at higher rates on dividends than on capital gains, but the firm is taxed more heavily on retained profits than on distributed profits. This is the system followed in Germany.
- *Imputation system:* Dividends are taxed at the individual level, but the corporate share of taxes is deductible from their tax bill. This approach is used in Australia.

The Middle-of-the-Roaders: This position essentially holds that a company's value is not affected by its dividend policy. While conceding the effect of market imperfections on MM's theoretical arguments, this group views that the impact of market imperfections is not significant. If low or high payouts increased the value of the firm, financial managers would do so. The fact that we do not see a rush to change dividend policies one way or the other suggests that it is not terribly important.

Payout Policy and the Life Cycle of the Firm: The essence of MM's view on dividends is this: Dividend policy should be seen as a residual decision after the firm has made its investment and financing decisions. A firm should pay dividends (or use stock repurchases) when it has cash left over after meeting all its investment funding needs. This fits well with the life cycle view of dividend payout policy. A young firm with plenty of growth opportunities will not have any cash left over dividends. As the firm ages, the investment opportunities tend to decrease and the firm can start paying dividends or stock buy backs. A mature and profitable is likely to have few investment opportunities and more cash for dividends.

WORKED EXAMPLES

1. Match the following dates from the left and the right columns.

    (A) Friday, November 2   (a) record date
    (B) Tuesday, November 13   (b) announcement date
    (C) Friday, November 16   (c) ex-dividend date
    (D) Tuesday, December 8   (d) payment date

SOLUTION

    (A) Friday, November 2   (b) Announcement date
    (B) Tuesday, November 13   (c) Ex-dividend date
    (C) Friday, November 16   (a) Record date
    (D) Tuesday, December 8   (d) Payment date

2. Creigh Corporation paid $0.75 per quarter in 2008. Calculate the stock's dividend yield based on its recent market price of $40.00.

SOLUTION

Dividend yield = yearly cash dividends/current market price per share
$$= (4 \times \$0.75)/40.00 = \$3.00/\$40.00 = 7.5\%$$

3. If Creigh Corporation's 2008 earnings per share were $5.50 and per share and the annual cash dividends were $3, what was the company's dividend payout?

SOLUTION

Payout ratio = estimated cash dividends per share/estimated earnings per share
$$= \$3.00/\$5.80 = 51.72\%$$

4. Creigh Corporation declared a stock dividend of 25% and its market price was $40. Assuming nothing else changed what would you expect the price of the shares to be after the stock dividends are distributed?

SOLUTION

The stock dividend, by itself, has no expected effect on the value of the firm.
Thus, 1.25 × Price per share after stock dividend = $40
Price per share after stock dividend = $40/1.25 = $32

5. Lentle Corporation's financial numbers are as follows:

Net income	$45 million
Earnings per share	$3
Number of shares outstanding	15 million
Price-earnings ratio	10

The management plans to repurchase 5% of the company's outstanding shares at the going market price. What effect does the stock repurchase have on the above numbers? What effect does it have on the value of the firm? Explain.

SOLUTION

The earnings per share is $3 and with a P/E of 10, the stock price will be $30. The company's market value is $450 million ($30 × 15 million). The company needs $22.5 million in cash to buy 0.75 million shares at $30 each. If it does not have the cash, it must sell assets. If it sells assets, its net income will shrink to $42.75 million. Second, the number of shares outstanding decreases to 14.25 million. Third, earnings per share remain at $3 ($42.75 million/14.25 million shares). And fourth, because the price-earnings ratio stays the same, the value of the shares also stays at $30 each.

Prior to the repurchase the value per share was $30 with 15 million shares outstanding and the firm's value at $450 million. After the repurchase, the value of the shares remains at $30 each, which, when multiplied by the 14.25 million then outstanding, results in a total value of $427.5 million, which equals, not coincidentally, the value before repurchase less the value of assets used to repurchase the shares. The size of the firm decreases with no gain or loss to its shareholders.

LIST OF TERMS

Announcement date	Regular cash dividend
Ex-dividend	Repurchase
Legal capital	Special dividend
Payment date	Stock dividend
Payout policy	Target payout ratio
Payout ratio	With-dividend
Record date	

EXERCISES

Fill-in Questions

1. The date on which dividend checks are actually mailed out is the _____.

2. _____ is concerned with the trade-off between retaining earnings on the one hand and paying out cash and issuing new shares on the other.

3. The _____ is the date on which the list of registered shareholders that are to receive cash dividends is made.

4. Shares bought and sold before the record date are said to be transacted _____ whereas those bought and sold after the record date are said to be transacted _____.

5. A firm's _____ consists of the par value of all its outstanding shares.

6. The date on which the company makes a formal announcement of its dividends is the
   _____.

7. _____ are cash dividends, which a company usually expects to be able to maintain in the future.

8. _____ are cash dividends paid irregularly and are not necessarily expected to be maintained in the future.

9. _____ are similar to stock splits in that no cash is paid to stockholders.

10. The percentage ratio of cash dividends to earnings is called the _____.

11. A recent empirical study showed that corporations tend to adjust their payout ratios towards a _____.

12. Corporations sometimes buy back or _____ their own shares.

13. The United States has a (n) _____ system in which dividends are taxed at both corporate and investor levels.

Problems

1. Arrange the following dates into order of occurrence: Payment date, announcement date, ex-dividend date, and record date.

2. On June 1, 2007 Dundee Corporation split its stock 2 for 1. The cash dividend is $0.125 a quarter. The closing stock price on the record date was $29.875.

   a. What would you expect the price of the stock to be before the split, assuming nothing else changed?
   b. Could the adjustments in per share price and cash dividends have been accomplished by a stock dividend?
   c. If so, what size would the stock dividend have to be to accomplish this goal?
   d. What was the annual dividend yield before and after the split?
   e. What was the payout ratio, given expected annual 2007 earnings of $1.95 a share?
   f. During the past 10 years the company's payout ratio averaged about 16%. Are you willing to say that this particular payout contained valuable information? Why or why not?

3. On Friday, August 8, 2008, Rise Corp. announced a quarterly dividend of 12.5 cents and a stock dividend of 10% payable on Monday, September 8, 2008 to shareholders of record on Friday, August 22, 2008.

   a. If the August 11 market price of $16.50 remains the same, at what price would you expect the stock to sell for after the cash and stock dividends?
   b. When would you expect the stock to go ex-dividend?

c. Assuming that the quarterly cash dividend of 12.5 cents per share will continue after the stock dividend, what is the effective percentage increase in the cash dividend?

d. What is the expected annual dividend yield, using your estimate of the ex-dividend price and the 12.5 cents quarterly cash dividend?

e. If expected annual earnings per share are $3, what is the annual expected dividend payout?

4. On Thursday, July 15, 2004, City First Bank declared a 20% common stock dividend payable on August 16 to stockholders of record on July 26. It was also announced that the cash dividend payment of $0.25 a share per quarter, payable on September 6 to stockholders of record on August 19, would remain the same.

a. By how much did the quarterly dividend increase?

b. What would you expect the price of shares to be after the stock dividend, given that on the date of the announcement they were selling at 24 ¼?

c. Are the shareholders necessarily any better off? That is, does their wealth increase as a result of the stock dividend?

5. On May 18, 2007 Murray Corp. announced a 1-for-10 reverse split, the event to occur on June 11, subject to shareholder approval. The stock's closing price on May 18 was 1 3/8. If nothing changes, at what price would you expect the stock to sell after the stock split is made effective on June 8?

Essay Questions

1. Explain the mechanics of paying dividends.

2. "Stock repurchases can add value to the firm, even though dividends do not." Discuss.

3. Compare and contrast the middle-of-the-roaders' view and the MM irrelevance proposition.

4. How can it be said that cash dividends are financially equivalent to stock issues, once investment and financing policies are fixed? Explain fully.

ANSWERS TO EXERCISES

Fill-in Questions

1. Payment date
2. Payout policy
3. Record date
4. With dividend; ex-dividend
5. Legal capital
6. Announcement date
7. Regular cash dividends
8. Special dividends
9. Stock dividends
10. Payout ratio
11. Target payout ratio
12. Repurchase
13. Two-tier system

Problems

1. Announcement date, ex-dividend date, record date, and payment date.

2. a. $30.00 \times 2 = \$60.00$.
   b. Yes.
   c. 100%, so that two additional shares are outstanding for every old share.
   d. Before: $[(\$0.125 \times 4)/\$59.75] \times 100 = 0.84\%$;
      After: $[(\$0.125 \times 4)/\$29.875] \times 100 = 1.67\%$.
   e. $[(\$0.125 \times 4)/\$1.95] \times 100 = 25.6\%$.
   f. No, this is not an unusual event. Invariably, large deviations from the usual contain valuable information.

3. a. $(\$16.50 - \$.125)/1.10 = \$14.89$, or $\$14.875$ to the nearest eighth of a dollar.
   b. Tuesday, August 19, 2008.
   c. 10%.
   d. $(\$0.125 \times 4)/\$14.875 = 3.36\%$.
   e. $\$0.50/\$3.00 = 16.7\%$.

4. a. The cash dividend increase was also 20%. Think of it this way: if you had one share before the split, you received $1.00 a year in cash dividends; afterward, you have 1.2 shares, on which you receive $0.25 a share for a total of $1.2 \times \$0.25 \times 4 = \$1.20$; an increase of 20%.
   b. One would expect the stock to decline to: $\$24.25/1.2 = \$20.21$.
   c. The shareholders, all else the same, are not necessarily better off. If the dividend increase were expected, that would be built into the dividend discount model and reflected in share prices. If the dividend increase were unexpected, there might well be positive wealth effects for shareholders because the unexpected increase in dividends may signal from management sustainable earning power to cover not only the increase in dividends but also all other corporate needs. The share price closed down one-eighth on the day of the announcement, suggesting that the dividend increase was expected.

5. $10 \times \$1.375 = \$13.75$.

17

Does Debt Policy Matter?

INTRODUCTION

This chapter is the first of three chapters, which analyze the effects of financing mix on the value of the firm. The term *capital structure* is used to describe the financing mix used by the firm. The financing mix available to a firm is not limited to debt and equity and includes other sources like preferred stock as well as several different types of debt. The theoretical analysis here is confined to the choice between debt and equity. This chapter describes the classic Modigliani and Miller (MM) propositions concerning the capital structure of business firms. The MM propositions are derived assuming perfect market conditions where there are no taxes, transaction costs or information asymmetry between managers and investors. Chapter 18 reviews the effects of these deviations on the choice of the financing mix. Chapter 19 analyzes the valuation implications and describes two alternate approaches of incorporating the financing effects on valuation.

MM's proposition 1 states that under perfect market conditions the value of a firm is unaffected by the financing mix of debt and equity used by the firm. Proposition 2, which is the corollary of the first proposition, states that the required rate of return on the equity increases with an increase in proportion to debt such that the weighted-average cost of capital does not change. The implication of these two propositions is that the choice of debt-equity mix or capital structure is irrelevant and has no effect on the value of the firm. Debt policy does not matter and investment and financing decisions can be separated.

The propositions are clearly difficult to challenge, once the perfect market conditions are accepted. The primary logic of the MM propositions is that a firm's value is based only on the stream of cash flows produced by its assets. The claims to this cash flow can be packaged in different ways, but unless there are market imperfections, arbitrage across these claims will ensure that the value of the firm is unaffected by the capital structure changes.

In practice, capital structure matters because deviations from perfect market conditions are present in the real world. The significance of the MM propositions is not that they depict a realistic picture of the world, but a clear understanding of the propositions enables you to understand why capital structure decisions are important and why one capital structure may be better than another.

KEY CONCEPTS IN THE CHAPTER

The Effects of Financial Leverage in Perfect Markets: Under perfect market conditions, financial leverage has no effect on the value of the firm. MM presents simple arguments to prove this point. Imagine two firms, U (unleveraged) and L (for leveraged), with identical operating cash flows but with different capital structures. Owning one percent of firm U will be equivalent in terms of claims to cash flows to owning one percent of both the debt and equity of firm, L. Ownership of one percent of each firm gives claims to identical cash flows. Therefore, the values of these claims should be identical. Hence, $V_U = V_L$. An alternate approach is to compare ownership of one percent of the equity of the leveraged firm to ownership of one percent of the unleveraged firm and finance it by borrowing an amount equal to one percent of the leveraged firm's debt. Again, the claims are identical and it leads to the result, $V_U = V_L$. It follows that under these conditions, debt policy is irrelevant. This is proposition 1.

Proposition 1 is essentially a restatement of the *value additivity principle* (see chapter 7): PV (A+B) = PV (A) + PV (B). Proposition 1 applies this in reverse. It can be called the *law of conservation of value*. These concepts can be extended to include other financing choices such as preferred stock or different forms of debt. The value of an asset is based on the cash flows produced by the asset and is not affected by the nature of claims against it.

MM's arguments supporting proposition 1 assume that both firms and individuals can borrow at the same interest rate. This assumption is not crucial to the proposition. A fact, which might appear to give corporate debt some advantage, is that corporate stockholders have limited liability and thus can borrow with limited liability. Individuals by themselves cannot have limited liability. Thus, corporate debt might have some advantage over personal debt. However, the advantage is unlikely to be of any significant value now since there are any number of corporations that can and have issued limited liability debt. In other words, any demand for limited liability debt would have been fully met by now.

Financial Risk and Expected Returns: Proposition 1 leads to proposition 2, which gives the relationship of returns on the debt, equity, and the asset return. If proposition 1 is to hold, the asset return, r_A is unaffected by leverage. This means that when the firm borrows, the required rate of return demanded by the shareholders increases as their risk increases. Proposition 2 states that the expected return on equity increases in proportion to the debt-equity ratio, expressed in market value. The rate of increase in return depends on the difference between the return on assets and the return on debt. The relationship can be expressed as follows:

$$r_A = \frac{D}{D+E} r_D + \frac{E}{D+E} r_E$$

We have seen this before in chapter 9 as the *weighted average cost of capital.*

Rearranging, r_E is given by:

$$r_E = r_A + (r_A - r_D)\frac{D}{E}$$

The essential implication of proposition 2 is that the increased return given by the equity in a leveraged firm reflects the increased risk. Therefore, the shareholders will demand a higher *required* rate of return. Or, the higher expected rate of return for the equity is simply the reflection of the higher risk involved and will be exactly matched by the higher required rate of return by the stockholders. Thus, the higher return is not going to result in a higher value of the stock.

Capital Structure and Beta: The effect of leverage on beta is similar to the effect on expected return. The relationship can be stated as follows:

Beta of the firm's assets:

$$\beta_A = \beta_D \frac{D}{V} + \beta_E \frac{E}{V}$$

Note that asset beta does not change. We can rearrange the above expression to obtain beta equity of a leveraged firm.

$$\beta_E = \beta_A + D/E(\beta_A - \beta_D)$$

The Weighted Average Cost of Capital: Prior to MM's work, the traditional wisdom was that some leverage was beneficial and by leveraging, a firm increased the return on equity. The traditional position used the *weighted-average cost of capital,* which is the expected return on the portfolio of all the company's securities. Weighted-average cost of capital is used to compute net present values of project cash flows when the project being evaluated does not differ from the firm's business risk. If leverage lowers the weighted-average cost of capital, then (assuming that the leverage *does not lower* cash flows correspondingly) the value of the firm will increase.

The traditional position held that increasing leverage resulted in lower weighted-average cost of capital because an increase in the cost of equity, if at all, is not proportionate to the increase in leverage. The traditional view, if correct, has the following implications:

- Proposition 2 does not hold or the expected return on equity does not increase as a firm borrows more.
- The weighted-average cost of capital declines at first as the debt-equity ratio increases and then rises.
- There is an optimal D/E ratio for which the cost of capital is lowest.

A word of caution is in order. The firm should try to *maximize* the value of the firm. This is not always equivalent to having the *lowest cost of capital.* The two goals will be equivalent *only* if the operating income is not affected by the change in leverage.

Beware of the managers who make the simplistic argument that they can enhance the firm's value by lowering the cost of capital, by borrowing more, as the cost of debt is lower than the cost of equity. This argument ignores proposition 2.

The traditional view made two arguments to support its claim. The first one essentially said that the shareholders did not increase their *required* rate of return in exact proportion to the rise in leverage. This argument implied some irrationality on the part of the shareholders. If some debt is good, more debt must be even better, and the optimal leverage would be one hundred percent debt. The second argument used possible imperfections in the market and the advantage for corporate debt over personal debt suggesting that individuals could not borrow at the same rate as corporations. It is true that some individuals face higher borrowing cost on account of transaction costs (lack of economies of scale). Such individuals might find it advantageous to borrow through a corporation. However, any such demand for corporate debt must be fully satisfied now. In other words, trying to make money by leveraging now is like trying to make money selling automobiles or personal computers. You are late by a few decades.

Essentially, borrowing costs should be a function of the risk of the borrower or more specifically, the use to which the borrowed money is put (or to be more exact, how the loan is backed or secured). Most individuals can get mortgage loans or margin loans from their broker at very competitive rates.

To sum up, the traditional view lacks support and it is not backed by valid arguments. One has to look elsewhere for weaknesses in MM's position. If you can find deviations from the perfect market framework used by MM, you can find situations where their propositions will not hold. Many of these deviations are created by government regulations. Chapter 18 focuses on the practical implications of the market imperfections for corporate debt policy.

It is possible that there may be unsatisfied clienteles demanding specially designed securities with unique features. If a firm can design and structure a package of securities that exploits these needs, it can profit from it and you will find an exception to MM's proposition 1. Of course, investment bankers are trying to do this all the time and it is very unlikely that there is any unsatisfied demand for the garden-variety or plain vanilla debt security. The next several chapters describe different type of securities invented by investment bankers and companies. It is however, hard to see that a firm's value can be increased greatly by these innovations in the absence of some government created imperfection.

After-Tax Weighted Average Cost of Capital

The MM propositions would need to be modified significantly to include the impact of real-world deviations from the perfect market framework used in their analysis. We do this in the next chapter, but can take a peek at one of the tools widely used in corporate finance practice. The weighted average cost of capital we saw in the previous section is not the one firms use to evaluate projects which have the same risk as that of the firm as a whole. The cost of capital used reflects the tax deduction allowed for interest payments and is the *after-tax weighted average cost of capital,* which was introduced in Chapter 9.

After-tax weighted average cost of capital $= r_D (1 - T_C) \dfrac{D}{V} + r_E \dfrac{E}{V}$

WORKED EXAMPLES

1. Black Bird Corp. operates in perfect capital markets with no corporate or personal taxes. The company has 30% debt and 70% equity in its capital structure. The expected return on debt is 10% and the rate of return on equity is 14%. Calculate its expected return on assets.

SOLUTION

$$r_A = \frac{\text{Expected Operating Income}}{\text{Market Value of all securities}}$$

$$= (\text{proportion in debt} \times \text{expected return on debt}) + (\text{proportion in equity} \times \text{expected return on equity})$$

$$= (\text{weight of debt} \times \text{cost of debt}) + (\text{weight of equity} \times \text{cost of equity})$$

$$= W_D r_D + W_E r_E = [D/(D + E) \times r_D] + [E/(D + E) \times r_E]$$

$$= (0.30 \times 0.10) + (0.70 \times 0.14) = 12.8\%$$

2. Wise Aaron Corp. has an operating income is $12,000, and the market value of all its all-equity-financed securities is $60,000. If the company decides to sell $20,000 of debt and retire an equal amount of equity, how will the rate of return for equity change? Assume that it operates in perfect capital markets with no corporate or personal taxes, and that the expected return on debt is 12%.

SOLUTION

$$r_A = \text{expected operating income/market value of all securities}$$
$$= \$12,000/\$60,000 = 20\%$$

In an all-equity-financed firm, the return on equity r_E is equal to the return on assets; so

$$r_E = r_A = 20\%$$

While borrowing changes the return on equity, it will not change the return on assets. This will remain the same because the value of the firm does not change and the expected operating income does not change. Therefore, the return on equity is:

$$r_E = r_A + (D/E)(r_A - r_D)$$
$$= 0.20 + (\$20,000/\$40,000)(0.20 - 0.12) = 0.20 + 0.5(0.08) = 24\%$$

3. Use the information given in problem 2 and assume that the beta of the firm is 1.2 before the debt financing and the beta of the debt is 0.5. What is the beta of the equity with the debt financing given in problem 2? What will the beta of the equity be if the debt-equity ratio were 30, 60, and 70%?

SOLUTION

The beta of the equity without any debt financing is the same as the beta of the assets because no other securities are outstanding. After the financing, the beta of the equity changes as follows:

$$\beta_E = \beta_A + (D/E)(\beta_A - \beta_D) = 1.2 + 0.5(1.2 - 0.5) = 1.55$$

For the other debt proportions, β_E is given in the table below.

D/E (%)	β_E
30	1.41
60	1.62
70	1.69

4. Beta of equity with no debt is 1.2. Calculate the equity betas for different debt levels for the following values of beta for debt: 0, 1.2 and 0.5. Compare these results with those of problem 3.

SOLUTION

The values for β_E for different debt/equity ratios and different β_D are given in the table below.

D/E (%)	β_E for different value of β_D		
	$\beta_D = 0$	$\beta_D = 1.2$	$\beta_D = 0.5$
0	1.20	1.20	1.20
5	1.26	1.20	1.24
10	1.32	1.20	1.27
20	1.44	1.20	1.34
40	1.68	1.20	1.48
60	1.92	1.20	1.62
80	2.16	1.20	1.76
100	2.40	1.20	1.90

While the data above are somewhat contrived, several interesting results emerge. You can clearly see that the increase in the risk or beta of the equity with increased debt levels is a function of the beta or risk of the debt itself. First, when the beta of the debt is equal to the beta of the firm, when it is all-equity-financed, for all practical purposes, the company has issued another dose of equity and not debt. Consequently, the beta of the equity does not change. If the company were able to issue debt at the zero-beta level, the risk-free rate, the betas of the equity would tend to increase substantially with additional debt. In practice and in most cases, the beta of corporate debt is greater than zero but less than the beta of the all-equity-financed firm.

5. May Burke, the financial manager of Leverage Unlimited, thinks she can increase shareholder value by increasing the leverage of the company. The company is currently all equity financed and is earning 20%. The company can borrow at 10% and the beta of the debt is at 0.4. The beta of equity before borrowing is 1.2. There are 10,000 shares outstanding and the price-earnings ratio of the common shares is 5 on an operating income of $25,000. The company can be expected to continue to generate that amount of operating income after the debt financing. Ms. Burke feels that the leverage will substantially raise the value of the firm and wants to buy back half the shares of the company. Formulate a response to Ms. Burke assuming operation in perfect capital markets with no corporate or personal taxes.

SOLUTION

Value of the firm before the debt financing = $25,000/0.20 = $125,000
Value per share is = $125,000/10,000 = $12.50
Earnings per share = $25,000/10,000 = $2.50
Price-earnings ratio = $12.50/$2.50 = 5

Next, determine the earnings per share after the debt financing. The company must sell $62,500 of debt at the going market rate of 10% in order to repurchase an equivalent amount of equity ($125,000 × 0.5).

Operating income	$25,000
less interest	6,250
Equity earnings	$18,750

With 5,000 shares now outstanding, earnings per share increase to $3.75 ($18,750/5000 shares). Ms. Burke assumes that she can still get the same price-earnings ratio of 5. Then, the shares have a market price of $18.75 (5 × $3.75). But going into debt entails additional risk to the shareholders. The beta will increase substantially. Using the formula:

$$\beta_E = \beta_A + D/E(\beta_A - \beta_D)$$

Before borrowing:

$$\beta = 1.2 + 0.0(1.2 - 0) = 1.2$$

After borrowing:

$$\beta = 1.2 + 1.0(1.2 - 0.4) = 1.2 + 0.8 = 2.0$$

Risk increases by two-thirds. With increased risk, the required rate of return on equity increases too. Assuming that the return on asset stays same, we can calculate the required return as follows:

$$r_E = r_A + (D/E)(r_A - r_D)$$
$$= 0.20 + 1.0(0.20 - 0.10) = 0.20 + 0.10 = 30\%$$

Value per shares = $3.75/0.30 = $12.50

Thus, there is no change in the value of the stock and leverage does not increase the value of the stock. Any increase in earnings is fully neutralized by the corresponding increase in risk and required rate of return. The price-earnings ratio will go down and the market price of the shares will remain the same.

6. GBK Inc. has 40% debt and 60% in its capital structure. Cost of debt (before tax) is 11%. Currently, GBK stock is selling at a price of $40. GBK paid a dividend of $3 on its stock last year. The dividends are expected to grow at a constant rate of 8%. Calculate the cost of equity and weighted average cost of capital. Assume Tax rate = 36%.

SOLUTION

First calculate the cost of equity using the DCF method.

$$r_E = \frac{D_1}{P_0} + g = \frac{3 \times 1.08}{40} + 0.08 = 0.161 = 16.1\%$$

After-tax weighted average cost of capital = 0.11(0.4)(0.64) + 0.161(0.6) = 0.128 = 12.8%

SUMMARY

This chapter presents the well-known Modigliani-Miller propositions on debt policy under perfect market conditions. Proposition 1 states that a firm's value is unaffected by changes in leverage. Proposition 2 states that the risk of equity and therefore the required return increase in proportion to the debt-equity ratio. Thus, under perfect market conditions, debt policy is irrelevant and the firm's value is not affected by changes in financial leverage. The value of a firm depends only on the cash flows produced by its assets. While financial leverage tends to magnify returns to common stockholders, their risk is increased too. Therefore, they require higher returns on their shares; thus, the value of a share remains unchanged.

Proposition 1 is very general and applies to all types of securities (short-term debt vs. long term debt, equity vs. preferred stock, etc.) and one can say that no combination of securities is better than any other. The MM propositions have replaced the traditional view that the cost of capital will tend to decrease initially as debt is added to the capital structure but that it will increase only after a market-determined intolerable-threshold level of risk is passed. At that point, the cost of equity and the cost of debt increase significantly. The traditional view cannot be supported unless one is willing to accept irrational behavior on the part of investors or the presence of market imperfections.

MM's propositions cannot be refuted once the perfect market conditions are accepted. Any violation of MM's propositions can only be caused by market imperfections. These market imperfections are often created by government regulations (differential tax treatment of income streams, for example) and can create profitable opportunities for firms. It is also possible that there are clienteles for specific types of securities such as money market mutual funds and floating-rate notes. However, demand for by any such security is often quickly met by an adequate supply of the security in demand and a firm getting into these markets now is unlikely to benefit.

LIST OF TERMS

After-tax weighted average cost of capital
Capital structure
Financial leverage
Gearing
Law of conservation of value

Proposition 1
Proposition 2
Separation of investment and financing
Value additivity
Weighted-average cost of capital

EXERCISES

Fill-in Questions

1. _____ is another term used to describe financial leverage.

2. _____ is the term used to describe the mix of debt and equity used by a firm.

3. MM's _____ states that the value of the firm is not changed by the mix of debt and equity.

4. A firm that borrows is said to engage in _____.

5. The _____ states that the value of an asset is preserved regardless of the nature of the claim on it.

6. The _____ is the sum of the returns on debt and equity each weighted by its percentage in the capital structure.

7. _____ states that the expected return on the common stock of a financially leveraged firm increases in proportion to the debt ratio.

8. Proposition 1 of MM permits _____ decisions.

9. Proposition 1 is a restatement of the _____ principle learned in Chapter 7.

10. Firms use the _____ for discounting the cash flows from projects, which have the same risk as that of the firm as a whole.

Problems

1. Pier Morganty Corp. is operating in perfect market conditions with no corporate or personal taxes. The company's debt has an expected return of 11% and the return on equity is 16%. The debt to assets ratio is 40%. Calculate the return on assets.

2. Use the information given in problem 1. How will the return on equity change if the debt is increased to 60%?

3. What is the expected return on assets for a firm that is 60% debt-financed and pays an expected return on debt of 9% and has a required return on equity of 20%? Assume the firm operates in perfect capital markets with no corporate or personal income taxes.

4. Your firm's expected operating income is $5,000, and the market value of its outstanding securities is $25,000 when it is all-equity-financed. Assuming that the firm operates in perfect capital markets with no corporate or personal taxes, calculate the required return on equity when the firm sells enough debt to repurchase half of the outstanding equity for each of the following rates of return on debt: (a) 8%, (b) 10%, and (c) 12%.

5. Using the data in problem 4 above, beta for the firm at 1.5, and the beta for the debt of 0.6, what is the beta of the equity after the financing?

6. The financial manager of Moon Bucks, Inc. estimates that she will increase the earnings per share of her presently all-equity-financed firm if she borrows at the going market rate of 8%. She estimates the debt's beta to be 0.3 and the beta of the all-equity firm is 0.8. A return of 12.5% is expected on the all-equity firm, the price-earnings ratio of 8 is expected to persist, expected operating income is $300,000, and 100,000 shares are outstanding. She plans to replace 40% of her equity with debt. How will the values of the shares change?

7. Please refer to problem 1. If the firm is operating in the real world with marginal corporate tax rate of 40%, what would be the cost of capital used for evaluating the projects with the same risk as that of the firm as a whole?

Essay Questions

1. Explain the Modigliani and Miller's propositions 1 and 2 and their implications for financial managers.

2. Discuss the following argument often heard in defense of leverage. "Cost of debt is definitely less than the cost of equity. By using the cheaper source of funds, a firm can increase the return available to its equity holders and thereby increase their value."

3. "Modigliani and Miller propositions 1 and 2 have very little practical appeal as they assume the so called perfect market conditions, which do not exist." Give a detailed response to that statement.

4. How may individual investors augment or undo the debt policy of firms in which they wish to invest? Explain fully. Also explain why this concept is important to the Modigliani-Miller position regarding debt policy.

5. Demonstrate how the beta of a firm's stock is dependent on the beta of the capital structure components.

ANSWERS TO EXERCISES

Fill-in Questions

1. Gearing
2. Capital structure
3. Proposition 1
4. Financial leverage
5. Law of conservation of value

6. Weighted-average cost of capital
7. Proposition 2
8. Separation of financing and investment
9. Value additivity
10. After-tax weighted average cost of capital

Problems

1. $(0.4 \times 0.11) + (0.6 \times 0.16) = 14\%$

2. $r_E = r_A + D/E\ (r_A - r_D) = 0.14 + 1.5(0.14 - 0.11) = 18.5\%$

3. $(0.6 \times 0.09) + (0.4 \times 0.2) = 13.4\%$

4. $r_A = \$5,000/\$25,000 = 20\%$. $r_E = r_A + D/E(r_A - r_D)$.
   a. When $r_D = 8\%$, $r_E = 0.20 + [(0.5/0.5)(0.20 - 0.08)] = 32$
   b. When $r_D = 10\%$, $r_E = 30\%$
   c. When $r_D = 12\%$, $r_E = 28\%$.

5. $\beta_E = \beta_A + D/E(\beta_A - \beta_D) = 1.5 + 1.0(1.5 - 0.6) = 2.40$

6. The analysis is the same as that for problem 5 of the Worked Examples.

   First, calculate the value of the all-equity firm:

   > Value = \$300,000/12.5% = \$2,400,000
   > Value per share = \$2,400,000/100,000 shares = \$24
   > Earnings per share = \$300,000/100,000 = \$3

   Then, compute the effect of debt financing on earnings per share:

   > Amount of required debt: 0.4(\$2,400,000) = \$960,000

Operating income	= \$300,000
less interest (0.08 × \$960,000)	= 76,800
Equity earnings	= \$223,200

   > Earnings per share: \$223,200/60,000= \$3.72

207

Now, calculate the beta of equity after debt financing:
Before-debt financing: 0.8; after:

$$\beta_E = \beta_A + D/E(\beta_A - \beta_D)$$
$$= 0.8 + 0.4/0.6(0.8 - 0.3)$$
$$= 1.133$$

Now, we can calculate the return on equity, after debt financing:

$$r_E = r_A + (D/E)(r_A - r_D)$$
$$= 0.125 + (0.4/0.6)(0.125 - 0.08)$$
$$= 15.5\%$$

Market price of equity after debt financing can be calculated as below:

Market price per share = $3.72/0.155 = $24

Value of equity = market price per share × number of shares
= $24 × 60,000 = $1,440,000

Value of firm after debt financing = Debt + Equity
= $960,000 + 1,440,000
= $2,400,000

The value of the firm is unaffected by the leverage.

7. The firm will use the after-tax weighted average cost of capital.

The after-tax weighted average cost of capital = 0.11(0.6) (0.4) + (0.6 × 0.16) = 12.24%.

18
How Much Should a Corporation Borrow?

INTRODUCTION

The last chapter presented the MM propositions and the view that debt policy did not matter under perfect market conditions. We know, however, that in the real world debt policy matters because there are a number of deviations from the perfect market conditions assumed in MM's theoretical framework. This chapter considers the impact of these deviations from the perfect market assumptions used by MM and provides the practical world's view of debt policy. While capital markets work reasonably well, there are the following factors to consider: corporate and personal income taxes, the probability of bankruptcy and the costs associated with it, costs of other forms of financial distress, and differing goals and conflicts of interests among lenders and shareholders. These factors cause the debt policy to assume practical relevance and importance. The MM analysis enables us to understand the significance of these deviations from the perfect market conditions and their impact on corporate debt policy.

The chapter presents two broad theories to explain capital structures of corporations. The first theory, known as the *trade-off theory*, suggests that corporations can arrive at an optimal debt ratio by comparing the positive and negative aspects of borrowing. The primary positive side or benefit of borrowing is that interest payments to lenders are tax-deductible. Thus, the government subsidizes part of the payments to the lenders. The negative side of borrowing comes from the costs associated with bankruptcy and financial distress.

The second theory is known as the *pecking order theory* and is based on the observed behavior of financial managers. Financial managers appear to prefer a hierarchy of financing sources and their order of preference runs as follows: first choice is internal funds (retained earnings), followed by external debt financing, and external equity being the last choice. This behavior can be explained by the *information asymmetry* between managers and investors.

KEY CONCEPTS IN THE CHAPTER

Corporate Taxes and Debt Policy: One of the most important deviations from the classic MM framework is the presence of corporate income taxes and the differential treatment meted out to interest payments on debt. Firms are allowed to deduct interest payments from their income subject to taxation. This creates a subsidy for borrowing and effectively expands the corporate pie available for distribution to investors (stockholders and bondholders). If a firm borrows D dollars at an interest rate of r_D the firm reduces its annual tax bill by $T_c r_D D$, where T_c is the corporate tax rate. If the debt is permanent, then the present value of this tax shield is:

$$T_c r_D D / r_D = T_c D$$

Thus, the firm's value can be increased by borrowing and the increase in value will equal $T_c D$.

We can modify the MM proposition 1 to the following expression:

$$\text{Value of firm} = \text{Value of all-equity-financed firm} + T_cD$$

While the model is simple, it is less than satisfactory. The basic problem with this is that it leads to an optimal debt ratio of one hundred percent. This, of course, does not make any sense. In fact we find many successful companies with very little borrowing in their balance sheet.

Debt Policy and Corporate and Personal Taxes: The issue of taxes gets complicated when personal taxes are also considered. In a world where both corporations and individuals are taxed on their income, the firm does well by its investors when it minimizes not just the corporate taxes but the total taxes paid by the firm and its investors. Consider a firm with both debt and equity. Each dollar of operating income (income before taxes and interests) can be paid out either as equity income or as interest income. Let the tax rates on interest income and equity income be T_p and T_{pE} respectively. There are two ways you can pay the operating income to the investor – either as interest to the bondholder or as dividend to the stockholder. If it is paid out as dividends, the effective cash flow to the stockholder will be as follows:

Operating income	=	$1
less corporate taxes	=	$1 - T_c$
Personal tax on equity income	=	$T_{pE}(1 - T_c)$
Net of all taxes	=	$(1 - T_{pE})(1 - T_c)$

When a dollar of operating income is paid out to the bondholder, the firm saves corporate taxes and the bondholder gets $(1 - T_p)$. Under these conditions, the debt policy will be irrelevant, if:

$$1 - T_p = (1 - T_{pE})(1 - T_c)$$

This can happen only if the corporate tax rate, T_c, is less than T_p and T_{pE} is very small. This is what Merton Miller used to suggest that debt policy could very well be irrelevant. Miller suggested that the effective tax on equity income is very low as most of the income could be in the form of capital gains. Miller's arguments were formulated in the 1970s, when tax rates were very different from what they are now. The current tax laws have reduced the personal tax rates on dividend income and on capital gains to 15% at the highest income level. Further, since the investor can defer the tax on capital gain till the security is sold, the effective tax rate on capital gain would be a lot less.

A practical rule on debt policy would be to structure debt and equity such that the total tax bill paid by the firm and the investors is minimized. In order to figure out the relative tax advantage of debt and equity funding, the text uses the following values for the different tax rates: $T_p = 35\%$, $T_{pE} = 12.4\%$ and $T_c = 35\%$. The value for T_{pE} is computed assuming an effective tax rate of 7.5% on capital gains to reflect the benefit of deferred realization of gains and 15% on dividend income. It is also assumed that 35% of the stock returns are received in the form of capital gains. Thus, $T_{pE} = 0.35 \times 7.5 + 0.65 \times 15 = 12.4\%$. With these assumptions, a dollar of pre-tax income paid out as interest would mean net receipts of 65 cents for the investor. A dollar of pre-tax income routed through equity will end up as 57 cents $((1 - 0.35)(1 - 0.124))$ of after-tax income for the stockholder. Thus there is a moderate tax advantage of about 8 cents in favor of debt financing.

Note that these numbers are crude estimates and different assumptions can lead to different values for the comparative advantage to borrowing. In general, companies, which are unsure that the corporate tax shield will be used to its full advantage, have less incentive to borrow. Many firms have non-interest tax shields available, which will help them reduce their tax bills without resorting to debt financing.

Financial Distress and Debt Policy: The prospect of *financial distress* concerns investors and reduces the present value of the firm. Financial distress occurs when the firm cannot meet its obligations to the creditors. The ultimate in financial distress is *bankruptcy* and liquidation of the business. The risk and cost of financial distress increase as borrowing increases. Financial distress can be costly and leads to a loss in the value of the business. The fear of the prospect of financial distress affects the market value of the levered firm's stocks and bonds. The value of the firm can be written as:

Value of firm = value if all-equity-financed + PV (tax shield) – PV(costs of financial distress)

Financial distress costs include *bankruptcy costs*, costs of operating under the cloud of bankruptcy, and *agency costs* arising from the perverse incentive problems faced by the stockholder of a leveraged firm. Bankruptcy is the legal mechanism allowing creditors to take over the assets of the firm and control the business. Bankruptcy costs are the costs of using the system. These direct costs include the legal and accounting costs. These costs can be large and reduce the total payoff to shareholders and creditors. Evidence suggests that bankruptcy costs can be large both in an absolute sense and significant even relative to firm value. Smaller firms can have a much higher percentage of costs relative to their size.

Other financial distress costs vary with asset types and the nature of the firm. These costs arise from the difficulties of operating a firm in financial distress. For example, an airline facing potential bankruptcy will find it very difficult to hire able pilots. Similarly, any firm selling a durable product like a computer or a car will find it difficult to attract customers if the customers are suspicious of the long term viability of the firm. These are part of the indirect costs of bankruptcy.

Agency costs are incurred on account of the incentive problems created by the conflicts of interest between creditors and shareholders of non-bankrupt but financially troubled firms. The stockholders have an incentive to behave in ways that would be less than optimal. There are different variations of the non-optimal behavior or games and all of them can be costly to the lenders. These games include:

- Risk shifting or investing in risky but negative NPV projects,
- Refusing to contribute equity capital,
- Cash in and run or paying themselves cash dividends,
- Playing for time, and
- Bait and switch or issuing progressively more and riskier debt.

The lenders anticipate these sub-optimal behaviors on the part of the stockholders and attempt to rein-in the behavior by incorporating strict conditions in debt contracts. These, in turn, restrict stockholder flexibility and add to the costs of doing business.

The costs of financial distress vary with the type of assets. In general, tangible assets like real estate and buildings lose less value when the firm faces financial distress. These assets tend to be less firm-specific. On the other hand, intangible assets such as know-how, growth opportunities, and employees' human and organizational capital would lose much of their value when the firm faces financial distress. These assets have most of their value as part of the firm and in the hands of another owner; they tend to be worth a lot less.

The Trade-off Theory: The trade-off theory postulates that firms balance the benefits (tax-shield) and costs (financial distress costs) and arrive at an optimal debt ratio. Thus, the optimal debt ratio reflects a trade-off between tax shields and the costs of financial distress. The trade-off theory suggests that firms may have different target debt ratios. The optimal debt ratio will be a function of the type of assets and the ability of the firm to use the tax-shield provided by debt. Firms with assets, which are tangible and easily transferable to others, can be expected to borrow more. Examples of this type of firms include airlines, retailers, and banks. On the other hand, firms with high levels of intangible assets, which can lose value in financial distress, will not use much debt. Pharmaceutical companies, high tech firms, and software companies are typical examples of this kind.

Empirical studies find broad support for the trade-off theory. Companies with more tangible and easily transferable assets (e.g. airlines) tend to borrow more and firms with more intangible assets (e.g. high tech companies) borrow less. It is also seen that companies, which go private through leveraged buy-outs, are generally mature companies with cash-cow businesses. However, many profitable companies – those that would tend to benefit the most from tax shields – borrow very little and appear to ignore the potential benefits from debt financing. This phenomenon remains a puzzle and is not easily explained by the trade-off theory. The fact that corporate debt ratios are not much higher than now than what they were about a century ago does not fit well with the predictions of the trade-off theory. Debt ratios across countries also cannot be explained by tax differences.

The Pecking Order Theory of Financing Choices: The pecking order theory of capital structure is fashioned from the observed practice of companies. Firms appear to have a preferred order of financing choices—internal equity (retained earnings) being the most preferred and external equity being the least preferred. A formal framework for the theory uses *asymmetric information* between the manager and the investor as the basis for the theory. Given asymmetric information, it is rational for the manager to prefer the use of retained earnings first. The manager would also prefer to issue debt rather than common stock, as the common stock would be potentially under-priced. According to the pecking order theory, there is no well-defined target debt-equity ratio because the firm looks at internal equity differently from external equity. The theory explains why profitable firms tend to borrow less.
A recent empirical study of firms across seven industrialized countries shows that debt ratio depend on the following main factors:

Size: Larger firms tend to have higher debt ratios.
Tangible assets: Higher debt ratios for firms with higher fixed assets.
Profitability: More profitable firms borrow less.
Market to book ratio: Firms with higher market to book ratios have lower debt ratios.

The above evidence can be interpreted as supporting both theories to some extent. The trade-off theory explains inter-industry differences very well and also appears to have some additional explanatory power after the pecking order theory variables are accounted for. It appears that larger firm behavior tend to be in line with the pecking order view and smaller firms capital structure differences are better explained by the trade-off theory. A recent study also found evidence that corporate debt ratios incorporate the cumulative effects of *market timing*. This suggests that firms might actually prefer to issue equity when stock prices are high.

The pecking order theory suggests that managers would like to maintain a *financial slack*, which would provide flexibility of means for meeting future financing needs. Thus, they would hold reserves of marketable securities and have spare borrowing capacity. Firms also adapt their target dividend ratios to their investment opportunities while trying to avoid sudden changes in dividends. Note, however, that the availability of slack is not an un-mixed blessing and can tend to make the manager-shareholder agency problems worse.

Summary Comments on Capital Structure Theory: No one theory can explain all the complexities found in actual capital structures used by the many corporations across different industries. Each of the theories discussed above has some merits and can explain some of the corporate practice. Financing choices made by each corporation are driven by a number of factors specific to that firm. Young firms with high growth opportunities and firm-specific assets could find potential financial distress costs associated with debt prohibitive and hence use very little debt. Some firms may find that the tax deduction provided by debt to be very important. On the other hand, profitable firms may find the use of debt unnecessary and may be following the pecking order theory. It is possible that as these firms mature and find fewer growth opportunities, they may increase their use of debt and buy back stock or pay large dividends. There are no easy formulas that determine a firm's optimal debt ratio.

WORKED EXAMPLES

1. Two firms are identical in all respects except that one firm is 100% financed by common stock and the other is 50% equity-financed and 50% debt-financed at 8% a year. The balance sheets of the two firms are as follows:

ALL EQUITY FIRM				EQUITY AND DEBT FIRM			
Assets	$10,000	Equity	$10,000	Assets	$10,000	Debt (8%)	$ 5,000
						Equity	5,000
Total	$10,000	Total	$10,000	Total	$10,000	Total	$10,000

Assume that the company has an operating income of $1,500. Show that the interest paid on debt is a tax shield.

SOLUTION

The income statements for the two firms can be shown as below:

	ALL EQUITY FIRM	EQUITY AND DEBT FIRM
Earnings before interest and taxes	1,500	$1,500
Interest expenses		400
Pretax income	1,500	1,100
Tax at 35%	525	385
Net income to stockholders	$ 975	$ 715
Total income to bond and stockholders	$ 975	$400 + $715 = $1,115
Interest tax shield (0.35 × interest)	$ 0	0.35 × $400 = $140

The interest tax shield is the difference between the streams of payments received by the investors of the two firms.

2. What is the present value of the tax shield as calculated in problem 1?

SOLUTION

Assume that the risk of the investment in the tax shield requires a rate of return equal to that paid on the debt, namely, 8%. If the financing is considered permanent, the problem is one of solving for the present value of perpetuity.

$$\text{Present value of tax shield} = \$140/0.08 = \$1,750$$

Because the total amount of the debt is $5,000, the present value of the tax shield is the amount of the total debt that the government underwrites when it allows interest to be deducted as an expense. The difference between the total debt and the federal subsidy, $3,250 ($5,000 − $1750), is the amount the company underwrites. Also, note that the present value of the tax shield is independent of the return on the debt. The cash difference between taxes paid, $140 ($525 − $385), makes going into debt a profitable investment, worth $1,750. Restated,

$$\text{Present value of tax shield} = \frac{\text{corporate tax rate} \times \text{expected interest payment}}{\text{expected return on debt}}$$

$$= T_c(r_D D)/r_D = T_c D = 0.35 \times (0.08 \times \$5,000)/0.08$$
$$= 0.35 \times \$5,000 = \$1,750$$

3. The balance sheet for Henry Coes Corp. is given below. The company has no long-term debt now and its balance sheet is shown below. Ignoring personal taxes, work out how much shareholders would benefit if the company borrowed $1,000 million of long-term debt and used it to repurchase stock.

214

Balance Sheet for Henry Coes Corp. ($ in millions)

Balance Sheet – Book Values			
Net working capital	500	Long-term debt	0
Long-term assets	2,100	Equity	2,600
Total assets	$ 2,600	Total liabilities and equity	2,600
Balance Sheet – Market Values			
Net working capital	500	Long-term debt	0
Long-term assets	6,500	Equity	7,000
Total assets	7,000	Total liabilities and equity	7,000

SOLUTION

Increase in value = $1,000 × 0.35 = $350 million.
This increase in value will accrue to the shareholders. Thus, while the book value of equity will decrease by the amount of repurchase ($1,000 million), the market value will decrease by only $650 million only. This is the net advantage to shareholders for going into debt. The book and market value balance sheets after the debt issue and stock repurchase are given below.

Balance Sheets for Henry Coes Corp. – After borrowing $1,000 m ($ in millions)

Balance Sheet – Book Values			
Net working capital	500	Long-term debt	1,000
Long-term assets	2,100	Equity	1,600
Total assets	$ 2,600	Total liabilities and equity	2,600
Balance Sheet – Market Values			
Net working capital	500	Long-term debt	1,000
Long-term assets	6,850	Equity	6,350
Total assets	7,350	Total liabilities and equity	7,350

SUMMARY

This chapter's main point is that *debt policy does matter,* once taxes, the probability of bankruptcy, financial distress, and potential conflicts of interest among the firm's security holders are factored in. The chapter considers, one by one, the main deviations from the MM perfect market framework and arrives at practical implications for corporate debt policy. We end up with two theories of capital structure – the trade-off theory and the pecking order theory. It should be kept in mind that the two theories are not mutually exclusive and corporate practice reflects both theories.

Corporate taxes combined with the tax-deductibility of interest are compelling reasons why debt policy counts. Interest on debt is deductible before corporate taxes are paid and that creates a tax shield, which enhances the after-tax value of the firm. Tax shields are valuable assets; their value being the present value of reduced taxes. Personal taxes introduce additional complications. Miller's analysis reflects these and suggests that the advantage to debt may not be that significant.

While tax shield encourages borrowing, non-trivial costs of financial distress are the costs paid for the benefit of debt. Because promises made to creditors may be broken or honored only with substantial difficulty, a firm is not able to borrow as much as it may choose. The prospective cost of financial distress reduces the value of the firm. These costs include the cost of bankruptcy, as well as, the indirect costs of time and effort to resolve a financially distressed condition. Further, whenever financial distress arises, there are a variety of tactics, which stockholders may resort to in order to minimize their risk exposure and gain at the cost of the lenders. These tactics or "games" represent the agency costs of borrowing and include risk shifting, refusing to contribute equity capital, taking cash out of the enterprise, and making decisions, which defer the day of reckoning. To forestall the possibility of such maneuvers, restrictive provisions are often incorporated into bond contracts, which in effect offset some of the benefits of debt financing.

The trade-off theory of capital structure suggests that a firm's debt-equity decision is really one of trading off interest tax shields against the cost of financial distress. This helps to explain, at least partially, why different companies have different debt-equity ratios. The pecking-order theory says that financial managers have a preferred, ordered set of financing options, and they go down that list in order of preference. The first choice is internal funds or retained earnings. This is followed by the safest external source of financing, usually debt. External equity is the least preferred source. In order to accommodate the choice of financing preferences, companies typically maintain somewhat sticky dividend policies and some financial slack. The hierarchy of preferences seems to reflect the information asymmetry between the mangers and the stockholders or investors. Empirical evidence lends support to both theories to an extent.

Debt may or may not be a good alternative to equity financing. Factors to consider are the total tax liability to shareholders, a firm's business risk, the types of assets that produce operating income, and the need for financial slack and these factors vary a lot across firms and industries. No one theory can explain capital structures of all firms and there is no easy formula that determines the optimal debt ratio.

LIST OF TERMS

Agency costs
Bankruptcy
Bankruptcy costs
Capital gains
Financial distress
Financial distress costs
Financial slack

Information asymmetry
Pecking order
Tax-deductible
Tax shield
Trade-off theory
Value of all-equity firm

EXERCISES

Fill-in Questions

1. The main benefit of corporate debt is that the interest is a(n) _____ expense.

2. An investor willing to lend at a before-tax return of 10% must be willing to lend at an after-tax return of _____ if her marginal income tax rate is 36%.

3. _____ between managers and investors forms the basis for the pecking order theory.

4. The direct costs of _____ consist of the present value of administrative, court, and legal fees, which reduce the total payoff to shareholders and bondholders.

5. The indirect costs of financial distress, which arise out of conflicts of interest between the shareholders and the lenders and the incentives for sub-optimal behavior on the part of the shareholders, are called _____ .

6. In a financially distressed firm, a project whose net present value is $200 will add (exactly, less than, more than) _____ $200 to the value of shareholders.

7. The bondholders of a financially distressed firm have (more, less) _____ to gain from investments, which increase firm value, the greater, the probability of default.

8. The effective rate of tax on _____ is often lower than the statutory rate since gains remain untaxed until they are realized.

9. Firms should strive to maximize the (after-tax, before-tax) _____ income of shareholders.

10. If $1 - T_p$ is greater than $(1 - T_{pE})(1 - T_c)$, corporate borrowing is (better, worse) _____ than personal borrowing.

11. It pays companies to issue more debt as long as the corporate tax shield (exceeds, is less than) _____ the personal tax cost to the marginal lender.

12. The _____ of capital structure says that firms attempt to find an optimal debt ratio by comparing the benefits and costs of leverage.

13. Firms whose assets are risky and mostly intangible tend to borrow (less, more) _____ than firms whose assets are tangible and relatively safe.

14. A preferred hierarchy of financing choices is called the _____ theory of capital structure.

15. _____ refers to the extent to which a firm has flexible opportunities for meeting its future financing needs.

Problems

1. Compute the present value of interest tax shields resulting from each of the following debt issues. Consider only corporate taxes, the marginal rate of which is 35%.

   a. A $1,000, 1-year loan at 9%.
   b. A 7-year loan of $1,000 at 9%. Assume principal is repaid at maturity.
   c. A $1,000 perpetuity at 8%.

217

2. The book and market value balance sheets of Bonnie Walker, Inc. are given below. Assume that: (1) the MM theory holds except for taxes, (2) no growth, (3) the debt is permanent, (4) 35% corporate tax rate, and (5) the interest rate on debt is 8%.

   a. How can the market value of the firm be greater than its book value?
   b. Demonstrate the extent to which the stockholders would be better off if the company were to sell additional debt at 8%, using the proceeds to purchase $40 of stock.
   c. Demonstrate the effects of replacing $40 of permanent, 8% debt with equity.

Balance Sheets for Bonnie Walker ($ in millions)

Balance Sheet – Book Values				Balance Sheet – Market Values			
Net working capital	$ 40	Long-term debt	$ 70	Net working capital	$ 40	Long-term debt	$ 70
Long-term assets	70	Equity	$ 40	Long-term assets	$110	Equity	$ 80
Total Assets	$110	Total liabilities and equity	$110	Total assets	$150	Total liabilities and equity	$150

3. Moonshines, Inc. has serious problems and is facing bankruptcy. Its market value balance sheet is as follows:

Net working capital	$500	Bonds	$650
Long-term assets	200	Equity	50
	$700		$700

Evaluate the following actions the financial manager is contemplating. Present an objective evaluation of each action. Assume each action is independent of all other actions.

a. The company pays a cash dividend of $75.
b. The company sells its long-term assets for $100, collects $450 from its net working capital, closes its doors, and invests the cash of $550 in U.S. Treasury bills at the going rate of 8%.
c. The company is confronted with an investment opportunity, which has a net present value of $200 but decides not to undertake it.
d. The company is confronted with an investment project whose net present value is $200 and sells new equity to undertake it.
e. The company is confronted with an investment opportunity whose net present value is $200 and borrows $200 to undertake it.
f. The lenders agree to extend the due date of its debt from 1 year to 2 years. Or from 1 year to 5 years.
g. The lenders agree to extend the due date of its debt from 1 year to 2 years, provided the lenders control all working capital and investment decisions, as well as prohibiting the issuance of any further debt.

4. Compute the total corporate and personal taxes paid on debt and equity income for each of the following cases. Assume a corporate income tax rate of 35%; realized capital gains are taxed at 20% and all cash dividends are taxed as ordinary income; the interest rate on debt is 10%; earnings before interest and taxes are $1,000; the levered firm borrows $1,000; and, where the condition calls for it, all earnings for shareholders are paid to them.

CASE	BONDHOLDERS' TAX BRACKET	STOCKHOLDERS' TAX BRACKET	FORM OF EQUITY INCOME
1	0	0	All dividends
2	0.15	0.15	All dividends
3	0.15	0.15	All unrealized capital gains
4	0.28	0.28	All dividends
5	0.28	0.28	All unrealized capital gains
6	0.36	0.36	All dividends
7	0.36	0.36	All unrealized capital gains

For each case, identify whether the levered or unlevered firm has the tax advantage? What implications do the differences you observe have for making financial decisions of the firm? For individual investors?

5. You are the financial manager of a Fortune 500 company. You are asked to demonstrate how interest tax shields may contribute to the value of the stockholders' equity. Assume that the company has a market value of about $30 billion, has about $2 billion of short-term debt, and very little long-term debt. Assume that debt can be issued at a rate equal to about 8% and that the corporation's income tax rate is 35%.

Essay Questions

1. Explain the trade-off theory of capital structure.

2. Explain MM's proposition 1, as corrected for the presence of corporate income taxes.

3. Describe the pecking-order theory of capital structure. Compare the theory with the trade-off theory. Does it make sense for a company to follow the pecking order theory?

4. Select five Fortune 500 firms and describe their capital structure in terms of the two theories discussed in the chapter.

5. How can it be said that it may not be in the stockholders' self-interest to contribute fresh equity capital, even if that means foregoing positive net present value investment opportunities?

ANSWERS TO EXERCISES

Fill-in Questions

1. Tax-deductible
2. 6.4%
3. Information asymmetry
4. Financial distress
5. Agency costs
6. Less than
7. More
8. Capital gains

9. After-tax
10. Better
11. Exceeds
12. Trade-off theory
13. Less
14. Pecking order
15. Financial slack

Problems

1. a. Interest tax shield: $0.35(\$1,000 \times 0.09) = \$31.5$; PV(tax shield) $= \$31.5/1.09 = \$28.90$.

   b. Present value of tax shield: $N = 7$, $I = 9$, PMT $= \$31.5$, FV $= 0$; PV $=$ solve $= \$158.54$.

   c. PV(tax shield) $= (0.35 \times \$1000 \times .08)/0.08 = \$350$. Or, $T_c \times D = 0.35 \times \$1,000 = \$350$.

2. a. Book values are based largely on historical costs, whereas market values are based on expected profitability. Companies earning profits higher than their cost of capital will typically have market values higher than book value.

   b. PV of tax shield $= T_cD = 0.35 \times \$40 = \$14.00$. The value of total assets will increase by this amount. $40 m of shares are repurchased. This amount less the tax shield will be the net change in the value of equity. The new market value balance sheet is shown below.

Net working capital	$ 40.00	Debt	$110.00
Long-term assets	124.00	Equity	54.00
	$164.00		$164.00

   c. This is the reverse of b above. Assets now decline by $14.00 and equity increases by only $26.00.

   Market value valance sheet after the equity issue:

Net working capital	$ 40.00	Debt	$ 30.00
Long-term assets	96.00	Equity	106.00
	$136.00		$136.00

3. a. Bond value falls, stockholders gain.
   b. Bondholders will get $550; stockholders will get nothing.
   c. Everyone loses.
   d. Bondholders gain because the debt ratio improves; stockholders also gain.

e. Bondholders could gain or lose, depending on the risk of the project.
f. Bondholders lose in both instances.
g. Bondholders may gain in this case.

4. The details for case 5 are shown below. The results for all cases are summarized in the table below.

INCOME STATEMENTS

	TAX RATE	UNLEVERED FIRM	LEVERED FIRM
Earnings before interest and taxes		1,000	1,000
Interest		0	100
Pretax income		1,000	900
Corporate tax at	35%	350	315
Net income to stockholders		650	585
Total income to stockholders and bondholders (before tax)		650	685
Tax on firm		350	315
Tax on bondholders at	28%	0	28
Tax on stockholders	0%	0	0
Total income to stockholders and bondholders (after tax)		650	657
Total taxes paid:		350	343

Advantage to debt = $7 (on $1,000 debt at 10% interest)

The tax advantage to debt for the different cases is given in the table below.

You can also calculate the effective advantage to debt as the difference between $1 - T_p$ and $(1 - T_{pE}) \times (1 - T_C)$, where T_p is the personal tax rate on interest income and T_{pE} is the personal tax rate on equity income and T_C is the corporate tax rate.

				Total Taxes Paid		
Cases	Corporate Tax rate	Tax on bondholders	Tax on stockholders	Unlevered Firm	Levered Firm	Advantage to Debt
1	0.35	0	0	$350	$315	$35
2	0.35	0.15	0.15	$447.5	$417.75	$29.75
3	0.35	0.15	0	$350	$330	$20
4	0.35	0.28	0.28	$532	$506.8	$25.2
5	0.35	0.28	0	$350	$343	$7
6	0.35	0.36	0.36	$584	$561.6	$22.4
7	0.35	0.36	0	$350	$351	−$1.0

5. One billion dollars of debt, at an interest rate of 8%, enables the firm to reduce it annual tax bill by $28 million ($1,000 × 0.08 × 0.35). If the debt is permanent, the present value of this debt will be $350 million ($28/0.08). Assuming the effect of financial distress costs to be negligible, the firm value will increase by about $350 million. This increase in value will go the shareholders.

19

Financing and Valuation

INTRODUCTION

So far, we have treated investment and financing to be separate and have not considered any interaction between the two. This assumed the MM perfect market world where the investment decisions could be made without any reference to how the investments are financed. This chapter provides you with tools required to make investment decisions when they are affected by financing decisions. The chapter gives useful and practical pointers to deal with capital budgeting situations where investment and financing decisions interact. The chapter also explains how to handle the cash flows which are very safe or of low risk.

The chapter describes two equivalent approaches to incorporating the effects of financing interactions. The first approach uses the popular and widely used tool of the after-tax weighted-average cost of capital (WACC). WACC incorporates the effect of tax shields into the discount rate used to value the cash flows produced by a project. WACC is typically calculated using actual market data and balance sheets for companies or industries. Usually, WACC works quite well, if you know its limitations and potential pitfalls.

The second approach adds the present value of the financing effects to the base-case net present value and calculates the *adjusted present value or APV* of the project. The modified MM proposition 1 described in Chapter 18 is an example of the APV approach. The approach is very general and can be useful in cases where WACC does not work very well because the assumptions for the correct use of WACC are violated. The APV approach is also useful in cases where the project or the investment decision involves special or subsidized financing or costs of issuing securities needed to finance the project.

The chapter also provides a primer on valuing businesses. The WACC can be used as the discount rate for valuing businesses just as it is used for evaluation of investment projects. The value of a business is simply the present value of all *free cash flows* generated by the business.

Before we begin the lessons of this chapter, it might be useful to have a quick review of the investment decision making process we have used so far. The following steps are involved in evaluating investment opportunities:

- Forecast the project's incremental after-tax cash flows.
- Assess the project's risk.
- Estimate the opportunity cost of capital.
- Calculate NPV, using the discounted-cash-flow formula.

Remember that the opportunity cost of capital reflects the projects business risk and does not include any effect of financial leverage. This chapter tells you how to incorporate the effect of borrowing.

KEY CONCEPTS IN THE CHAPTER

The After-tax Weighted-Average Cost of Capital: We had a glimpse of the after-tax weighted average cost of capital (WACC) in chapters 9 and 17. The WACC incorporates the tax deductibility of borrowing into the discount rate used to evaluate project cash flows. Thus, WACC is the adjusted discount rate or cost of capital. The formula for WACC is:

$$WACC = r_D(1 - T_c)D/V + r_E(E/V)$$

where, r_D = Before-tax cost of debt,
$\qquad r_E$ = Cost of equity
$\qquad T_c$ = Marginal tax rate for the firm
$\qquad D/V$ = Debt to assets ratio
$\qquad E/V$ = Equity ratio

It is simply the cost of the source of funds weighted by the percentage of each source in the balance sheet. The formula is general and can easily be adapted to include preferred stock or even separate costs for short-term and long-term debts. For example, if a firm uses preferred stock in its financial mix, the WACC can be written as:

$$WACC = r_d(1 - T_c)D/V + r_P(P/V) + r_E(E/V),$$

where r_P is the cost of preferred stock and P/V is the ratio of preferred stock to assets.

In practice, WACC is typically calculated using actual balance sheet data for firms and all the variables used in the formula refer to the whole firm. Therefore, when it is directly used to evaluate projects, the following points should be kept in mind:

- WACC calculated from actual company data should be used for project evaluation only when the project is a carbon copy of the firm or represents the same average risk as the firm.
- The project supports the same debt ratio as the firm.
- WACC assumes that the debt ratio (D/V) is maintained by regular re-balancing.
- The debt ratio and equity ratio should be based on market values, rather than book values.
- When computing WACC from actual numbers, care has to be taken for properly adjusting or accounting for current liabilities, short-term debt, and deferred taxes. The usual approach is to net these out of the balance sheet. However, if the short-term debt is part of the permanent financing mix used by the firm, it should probably be included in the WACC.
- Industry WACCs might be better than individual firms' cost when used for project analysis, especially by firms outside the industry.
- Immediate source of funds for the project is of no relevance for computing the WACC.

Valuation of Businesses: Valuation of businesses is similar to project evaluation and investment analysis. We had our first look at valuation in Chapter 4. It is an extension of valuation of stock and instead of looking at dividends; one has to look at the *free cash flow* produced by the business. The important point to note is that the cash flows should be estimated just as one would do for investment projects. In other words, the cash flows are forecast assuming all-equity financing and by discounting with the WACC, we are able to include the value of the interest tax shields. The free cash flow is the cash flow that can be withdrawn from the business each year after meeting all its investment needs. Note that the cash flow estimates should exclude interest payments as well as non-cash elements. Growing firms typically invest more than the depreciation amount and investments made might exceed their earnings. During these years their free cash flow will be negative. When the investment needs are less than their earnings, the business generates free cash flow, which is similar to dividends. The value of the business is the present value of the free cash flows generated by the business. The procedure for valuation includes estimating free cash flows to a time *horizon* at which point the cash flows follow (or assumed to follow a constant growth pattern. The steps involved in valuation of a business are given below:

1. Estimate the free cash flows generated by the business. The free cash flows will be negative for the years when the investment needs of the business exceed its operating cash flows. Note that the increase in working capital should be included in the investment needs. Free cash flow can be estimated using the following simple formula:

   Free cash flow = Profit after tax + Depreciation + Investment in fixed assets + Investment in working capital

   Note that usually, the investment in fixed assets and working capital would be cash outflows and therefore negative.

2. Choose the horizon date. Free cash flows are estimated to the horizon date at which point the cash flows are assumed to follow a simple growth pattern. The horizon value can be estimated using one of the short cut valuation formulas.

3. Estimate the horizon value. This will require knowledge of the WACC. The value of the business can be written as:

$$V = \frac{FCF_1}{1 + WACC} + \frac{FCF_2}{(1 + WACC)^2} + \dots \frac{FCF_H + PV_H}{(1 + WACC)^H}$$

   The value of the business and the horizon value, PV_H, will be very sensitive to the assumptions used. Therefore, it is always prudent to cross check the value using other valuation measures or benchmarks such as P/E ratios, market to book ratios of other similar companies.

Adjusting WACC for changes in Debt ratio and Business Risk: WACC is very useful when it is properly used. It can be adjusted for changes in debt ratios or business risk changes by applying the equations from MM's propositions 1 and 2. (See worked example 3.)

Step 1: Calculate the opportunity cost of capital: $r = r_D D/V + r_E E/V$

Step 2: Estimate the cost of debt at the new debt ratio and calculate the new cost of equity:

$$r_D = r + (r - r_D)/D/E$$

Step 3: Recalculate the WACC at the new financing weights.

The adjustments can be used for betas also using the following equations from Chapter 9:

$$\beta_{asset} = \beta_{debt} (D/V) + \beta_{equity} (E/V)$$
$$\beta_{equity} = \beta_{asset} + (\beta_{asset} - \beta_{debt})D/E$$

Valuation using Flow-to-Equity Method: The valuation approach described above values the business as a whole and one simply deducts the value of debt to find the value of equity. Alternate approach for finding equity value would be to discount the cash flows available to equity holders using the cost of equity capital. Both methods would give the same value, if the debt ratio is constant over time. The flow to equity method may seem simpler to use when the debt ratios change; however one should note that the cost of equity changes with the changes in debt ratio. Thus, one has to change the discount rate with each change in debt ratio.

Adjusted Present Value: Adjusted present value (APV) is an alternative to using the WACC. Technically, the APV is more general and can be used in cases where the WACC may not be able to capture all the side effects of financing decisions. The general expression for APV can be written as below:

$$APV = \text{base-case NPV} + \text{sum of present values of all financing side-effects}$$

The base-case NPV is the NPV of the project cash flows using the opportunity cost of capital. You are assuming that the project is an all equity-financed mini-firm. Here are the steps involved in computing the APV.

- First, calculate the base-case NPV, i.e. without financing side effects.
- Identify the financing side effects. The effects can be from: issue costs, tax shields, special interest loans, etc.
- Compute the present values of all the side effects using the appropriate discount rates.
- Add the present values of the side effects to the base-case NPV to get the APV.

Generally, issue costs reduce the project's NPV, while tax shields or special financing deals add to the NPV. Care has to be taken when computing the present value of tax shields. The amount supported by the debt has to be estimated. The tax shield also depends on whether the debt is fixed in dollar terms or is assumed to be constantly re-balanced. The WACC approach follows the latter assumption. Following rule 1 generally gives a higher value for the present value of the tax shield and therefore a higher APV.

Discounting Safe, Nominal Cash Flows: This topic is discussed in the appendix to the chapter. Safe, nominal cash flows are comparable to debt-service like cash flows. This is because the firm is committed to making the stipulated dollar cash flows. The correct discount rate to use, in such cases, is the after-tax unsubsidized borrowing rate.

This rule is useful in the evaluation of special or subsidized financing deals. Such deals could be evaluated using the concept of *equivalent loans*.

Equivalent loan = Present value of the cash flows needed to service the debt.

Again, this present value is calculated using the firm's after-tax borrowing rate. Thus, any subsidized loan at interest rates below the market rate will be like signing up for an equivalent loan at your normal borrowing rate. The equivalent loan will be lower than the subsidized loan amount. The difference between the actual amount borrowed and the equivalent loan is the NPV of the special financing deal. The examples of safe, nominal cash flows include fixed payment contracts like leases and depreciation tax shields.

WORKED EXAMPLES

1. Valentine Corp. (VC) has a total market value of $524 million. The market value of equity is $300 million and the company carries debt valued at $224 million. The before-tax cost of debt is 9% and the cost of equity is estimated at 14%. The marginal tax rate is 35%. Estimate the weighted-average cost of capital for the company.

SOLUTION

The weighted average cost of capital = $r_D(1 - T_C)D/V + r_E E/V$
D = $224 million, E = $300 million, V = D + E = $524 million
D/E = 0.4275, V/E = 0.5725

Substituting these and other values into the equation for WACC,

WACC = 0.09(0.65)0.4275 + 0.14 (0.5725) = 10.52%

2. VC (see example 1 above) is considering a project, which is expected to produce $12.5 million in annual after-tax cash flows for the next 5 years. The project has the same risk as the company's existing operations and is expected to support the same debt capacity. What is the NPV of the project if the estimated investment required for the project is $45 million?

SOLUTION

NPV of the project = −45 + PV of cash inflows. Using a calculator, PV of $12.5 million for 5 years: N = 5, I = 10.52, PMT = $12.5, FV = 0, PV = solve = $46.762 million.
NPV = −45 + 46.762 = $1.762 million.

3. VC is planning to spend large amounts of money on R & D over the next few years and feels that it may not be able to use all the tax shields generated by a 42.75% debt ratio. The company considers lowering the debt ratio to 20%. How will this change its WACC and cost of equity? Assume that the lower debt ratio will reduce the before-tax cost of debt to 8%.

SOLUTION

Note that the change in debt ratio will lower the cost of equity. The problem can be solved by using the "three step" process of unlevering and relevering the WACC.

Step 1: Unlever the WACC to calculate the opportunity cost of capital, r.
$$r = r_D D/V + r_E E/V = 0.09(0.4275) + 0.14(0.5725) = 0.1186 = 11.86\%$$

Step 2: Calculate the cost of equity at debt ratio of 20%.
$$r_E = r + (r_A - r_D)D/E = 0.1186 + (0.11.86 - 0.08)0.2/0.8 = 0.1283 = 12.83\%$$

Step 3: Calculate the new WACC.
$$WACC = 0.08(1 - 0.35)0.2 + 0.1283(0.8) = 11.30\%$$

4. Gary Teeker is the financial manager of Wosley Corp., a family owned firm. Mr. Teeker has been asked by the family members to value the firm. The business generates an after-tax cash flow of $1.5 million a year. This is expected to continue indefinitely at this level. The firm's marginal tax rate is 36%. The industry average data for comparable companies are as follows:

Cost of debt = 12%, Average beta for comparable companies = 1.5.
Risk free rate = 4.5%, Market risk premium = 9%.

The company's debt ratio at 40% is very close to the industry average. Help Mr. Teeker value the firm. Explain the steps used in valuation.

SOLUTION

We need to compute the cost of equity and then the weighted average cost of capital.
Using the CAPM, $r_E = 4.5 + 1.5 (9) = 18\%$.

$$WACC = r_D(1 - T_c)D/V + r_E(E/V)$$
where, r_D = the firm's current borrowing rate
T_c = the marginal corporate income tax
r_E = the expected rate of return on the firm's stock (a function of the firm's business risk and its debt ratio)
D,E = the market values of currently outstanding debt and equity
$V = D + E$ = the total market value of the firm

The weighted-average cost of capital for the firm is therefore:

$$WACC = 0.12(1 - 0.36)0.4 + 0.18(0.6) = 13.87\%$$

The value of the firm = $1.5 million/0.1387 = $10.8147 million

5. Rummy Corp. is considering an investment project, which will generate a level after-tax cash flow of $500,000 a year in the next 5 years. Returns on comparable risk investment opportunities are 14%. The investment requires a cash outlay of $1.5 million. Compute the net present value of this project.

SOLUTION

This straightforward capital budgeting problem requires you to find the present value of $500,000 a year for each of 5 years, using the discount rate of 14%. The cash outlay is then deducted from the present value of that stream of cash to obtain NPV. The calculations are:

$$NPV = -1,500,000 + \sum_{t=1}^{5} \frac{\$500,000}{(1.14)^t}$$

[Use the calculator for the PV computation: N = 5, I = 14, pmt = $500,000, FV = 0, PV = SOLVE, PV = $1,716,541]

$$NPV = -\$1,500,000 + \$1,716,541 = \$216,541$$

6. Rummy Corp. of problem 5 above does not have the cash available to undertake the project. Therefore, it is investigating the possibility of selling stock. The financial manager discovered that for issues of that size, the effective cost to the firm would be 16% of the gross proceeds to the company. How much must the company raise in order to net $1.5 million, and what impact does the cost of issuing common stock have on the project's NPV?

SOLUTION

This is a problem of determining the adjusted present value (APV) of the investment, taking into account the costs incurred when external financing is needed. First, find the amount of money that must be raised so that the company obtains the needed $1.5 million. The company will receive only 84% of the amount raised. Thus, the amount of money (gross proceeds) to be raised equals:

Gross proceeds of the issue = $1,500,000/0.84 = $1,785,714

Issue costs = $1,785,714 - $1,500,000 = $285,714

Because this is an additional cash outlay prompted by this project, it must be included in the analysis. The APV will be:

$$APV = \text{base-case NPV} - \text{issue cost}$$
$$= \$216,541 - \$285,714$$
$$= -\$69,173$$

The issue cost makes the project unacceptable.

7. Rummy is comfortable with a 65% target debt ratio. It borrows at the rate of 12%, pays the principal in equal yearly installments, and pays interest based on the unpaid balance. Debt issue costs are 5% of the gross proceeds, and equity issue costs are those of problem 6. The tax on the corporation, bondholders, and shareholders is 30%. What does this do to APV?

SOLUTION

This extension of the basic problem requires you to incorporate the present value of the interest tax shield to make it complete. Let's go through it in steps.

Step 1: We already know the value of the base case is $216,541.

Step 2: Determine the issue cost. To calculate the issue cost of debt, determine how much will be needed. It is $975,000(0.65 × $1,500,000). Next, determine how much should be raised to obtain that amount: It is $1,026,316($975,000/0.95). The issue cost is determined by taking the difference between the amount that must be raised and the amount that is actually used: It is $51,316($1,026,316 − $975,000). The issue costs of equity are similarly determined. The amount needed is $525,000 ($1, 500,000 × 0.35). The amount to be raised is $625,000 ($525,000/0.84). The issue cost is $100,000($625,000 − $525,000).

Step 3: Determine the present value of the interest tax shield. Before you can do that, however, you must determine the annual installment payments, the annual interest payable in each year, the annual tax shelter, and the present value of the annual tax shelter. The annual installments are $205,263($1,026,316/5 years) plus interest on the remaining balance. The table is as follows. (Because the debt is not subsidized, it is evaluated at the 12% borrowing rate.)

YEAR	DEBT OUTSTANDING AT START OF YEAR	INTEREST	INTEREST TAX SHIELD	PRESENT VALUE TAX SHIELD
1	$1,026,316	$123,158	$36,947	$32,989
2	821,053	98,526	29,558	23,563
3	615,790	73,895	22,168	15,779
4	410,527	49,263	14,779	9,392
5	205,264	24,632	7,390	4,193
				$85,916

Combine all the PVs to obtain APV.

$$APV = \text{base-case PV} - \text{PV of issue cost} + \text{PV of tax shield}$$
$$= \$216,541 - (\$51,316 + \$100,000) + \$85,916$$
$$= \$151,141$$

Accept the project.

8. Lee Morgan Company is considering an investment project that costs \$2 million and is expected to generate savings of \$295,000 a year forever. The business risk of this project warrants a rate of return of 15%. Calculate the net present value of the project, assuming no tax shields. Then, calculate the project's NPV, assuming tax shields that arise because additional 12% debt may be issued in amounts equal to 30% of the cost of the project. The overall tax rate is 30%. Finally, determine the minimum acceptable base-case NPV, as well as, the minimum internal rate of return.

SOLUTION

The solution to this problem is straightforward. The base-case NPV is:

$$\text{Base-case NPV} = \text{cash outlay} + \text{present value of a perpetuity}$$
$$= -\$2,000,000 + (\$295,000/0.15)$$
$$= -\$2,000,000 + \$1,966,667$$
$$= -\$33,333$$

The project cannot be accepted as it is.

$$\text{Present value of tax shield} = (\$600,000 \times 0.12 \times 0.30)/0.12 = \$180,000$$

Now, the project is acceptable. It has a positive APV.

$$APV = \text{base-case NPV} + \text{PV tax shield} = -\$33,333 + \$180,000 = \$146,667$$

To find the minimum level of income *net* of the tax effects (of −\$180,000):

$$-\$180,000 = -\$2,000,000 + (\text{annual income}/0.15)$$

Solving for annual income, we obtain:

$$\text{Annual income} = (\$2,000,000 - \$180,000) \times 0.15 = \$273,000$$

This is the minimum annual income this project must generate in order to make it acceptable. The minimum acceptable rate of return is:

$$\$273,000/\$2,000,000 = 0.1365 = 13.65\%$$

9. Euro-American Corp (EAC). is planning an investment in a European country. The local government has offered EAC a subsidized loan of $12 million for a term of 3 years. The loan will carry an interest rate of 3% annually. EAC's current borrowing rate is 8%. The company's marginal tax rate is 30%. EAC will pay interest only during the three years and the entire principal amount is repaid at the end of 3 years. The investment project has a base NPV of negative $600,000. Should EAC invest in the project?

SOLUTION

The after-tax unsubsidized borrowing rate is 5.6%. [0.08(1 − 0.30)]. This is the rate at which the loan cash flows are to be discounted. The table below gives the cash flows and their discounted values.

Period	0	1	2	3
Cash flow (in thousands)	12,000	−360	−360	−12,360
Tax shield		108	108	108
After-tax cash flow	12,000	−252	−252	−12,252
Marginal tax rate	30%			
Present value of outlays		−239	−226	−10,404
Sum of present values	−10,869			
NPV of loan financing	1,131			

APV of the project = −$600,000 + $1,131,000 = $531,000.

Accept the project.

10. Bunny Corp. is an established movie producer that specializes in cartoons and animation movies. The projected earnings and cash flow for the company are given below. Jake Candy wants to buy the business and requires a rate of return of 20% on his investment. Estimate the value of the business.

Dollars million

Years	1	2	3	4	5	6
Assets	50	75	100	125	140	151.2
Earnings	12	18	24	30	33.6	36.29
Net Investment	25	25	25	15	11.2	12.10
Free cash flow	−13	−7	−1	15	22.4	24.19
Earnings growth from previous period (%)		50	33.3	25	12	8

SOLUTION

The cash flows start growing at a constant rate of 8% from the end of 5 years. At this stage, the business is reinvesting one-third of each year's earnings and is earning a ROE of 24%. Therefore, the growth rate = 24 × 1/3 = 8%. We can choose 5 years as the horizon. The value of the business at this point is that of a growing perpetuity growing at 8%.

Horizon Value = Value at the end of five years = $22.4 \times 1.08/(0.20 - 0.08) = \$201.6$ million

Value of the business = Present value of free cash flows

$$PV(FreeCashflows) = \frac{-13}{1.2} + \frac{-7}{(1.2)^2} + \frac{-1}{(1.2)^3} + \frac{15}{(1.2)^4} + \frac{22.4 + 201.6}{(1.2)^5} = \$80.98 \; million$$

Note: Present value computations like the above can be easily solved using the Cash Flow and NPV worksheets in the BA II Plus calculator. The calculator entries are as follows:

$CF_0 = 0$, $CO1 = -13$, $FO1 = 1$, $CO2 = -7$, $FO2 = 1$, $CO3 = -1$, $FO3 = 1$, $CO4 = 15$, $FO4 = 1$, $CO5 = -224$, $FO5 = 1$. Once you complete the cash flow worksheet, use the NPV worksheet: $I = 20$, NPV (CPT) = \$80.98 million.

SUMMARY

This chapter enables us to deal with the all too common cases of investment and financing interactions. We discussed investment decisions in many previous chapters assuming that investment and financing could be clearly separated. However, when financing decisions give rise to side effects such as tax shields, they have to be accounted for. The chapter describes two basic approaches to deal with this problem. The first approach is to adjust the discount rate used to evaluate the cash flows. The second approach evaluates the financing effects and adds the present values of these effects to the all-equity financed project NPV.

The chapter also describes an approach to valuation of businesses by discounting the free cash flows by the WACC. In general, the value of a business will be the present value of the free cash flows generated by the business. Free cash flows are similar to dividends and are the earnings less net investments needed to be made in the business to generate the earnings. The value of equity can be obtained by subtracting the value of debt from the business value.

The weighted-average cost of capital represents the first and the most popular approach of combining investment and financing decisions. It is typically calculated using company balance sheets valued at market values of debt and equity. The weighted-average cost of capital approach to adjusting discount rates says the proper discount rate used to evaluate projects of risk identical to that of the firm is the market value weighted cost of capital. As long its limitations are understood, WACC is very useful. Care has to be taken to use it right. Remember, that WACC computed from actual company balance sheets should be used only for projects that resemble the company as a whole pretty closely. WACC also assumes that the debt is maintained by regular re-balancing of the sources of funds.

WACC is flexible and versatile and can be adjusted for changes in leverage and business risk. WACC is an adjusted cost of capital, which captures the tax shield benefit of debt. The CAPM can be used to adjust or compute the cost of equity for changes in business risk or leverage.

The adjusted present value approach is an alternative to using the WACC. The APV is simply the base-case NPV of the project, which is assumed to be all-equity financed plus the present value of all financing side effects. APV can be adapted to deal with different types of side effects such as issue costs, tax shields, special financing deals, etc. While computing APV, care has to be taken to ensure the proper assumptions about financing. In general, the true value of the tax shield is invariably less than that implied by the corporate marginal tax rate.

The chapter also presents (in the appendix) the rules for evaluating safe, nominal cash flows. The proper discount rate to use in such cases is the after-tax borrowing rate. The cash flows may be viewed as the amount of money needed to service an equivalent amount of debt. Two common examples of this type of cash flows are depreciation tax shields and payouts that are fixed by contract. The procedure of treating cash flows as debt-equivalent loans is consistent with adjusted-discount-rate approaches. The approach can be very useful in evaluating subsidies and special financing deals which go with some projects.

LIST OF TERMS

After-tax weighted average cost of capital	Opportunity cost of capital
Adjusted net present value	Subsidized financing
Base-case NPV	Target debt ratios
Business risk	Value additivity
Corporate debt capacity	Weighted-average cost of capital

EXERCISES

Fill-in Questions

1. The adjusted net present value is equal to _____ plus the present value of the effects of financing decisions.

2. The _____ is the discount rate, which reflects only the business risk of the project and is used to calculate the base-case NPV.

3. The opportunity cost of capital depends on the _____ of the investment project to be undertaken.

4. The adjusted net present value analysis of a project has to take into account the change in _____ of the firm brought about by the project.

5. _____ is normally computed using the firm's market value balance sheets or the firm's _____.

6. The use of APV assumes that _____ holds.

7. The APV approach can be used to evaluate the value of _____.

Problems

1. The balance sheet of Barry Moore Corp. shows a debt ratio (debt to assets) of 35%. The company's cost of debt (before tax) is 8% and the beta of the company stock is 1.5. The risk free rate is 5% and the expected market risk premium is 8.5%. The marginal tax rate is 30%. Calculate the weighted-average cost of capital for the firm.

2. Ms. Moore, the CEO of the firm, suggests the company needs to increase debt to 45% of assets. The cost of debt will increase to 9%. What will be the effect this will have on the WACC?

3. Texas Incinerator Corp. (TIC) is evaluating a $1 million investment project, which is expected to generate level, after-tax cash flows of $300,000 a year in each of the next 6 years. Rates of return obtainable on investments of comparable risk are 12%. Compute the net present value of this project.

4. TIC will finance the project in problem 3 entirely by the sale of stock. The cost of floating the stock is 12% of the gross proceeds. How much must the company raise, and what impact does the flotation costs have on the net present value of the project?

5. The Perpetual Motion Company is evaluating a $6 million plant expansion, which it estimates will generate $750,000 in after-tax cash perpetually. The return obtainable on investments of comparable risk is 13%.

    a. Calculate the net present value of the project, assuming no tax shields.
    b. Calculate the project's net present value, assuming tax shields produced by the issuance of 9% debt in amounts equal to 40% of the project's cost. The company's marginal tax rate is 34%.
    c. Determine the minimum acceptable base-case NPV.
    d. Determine the minimum acceptable internal rate of return.

6. Using the data in problem 5, calculate the weighted-average cost of capital.

7. You are considering a project in an East European country. The project has an investment of $4 million. The government of the country offers a special incentive package for investments in the country, which includes tax rebates amounting to 10% of the initial investment for each of the first two years. The project is expected to generate enough taxable income during the first two years to fully use the tax rebate. Your company's borrowing rate is 10% and its tax rate is 30%. What is the value of the tax rebate?

8. Big Enchilada Corp. (BEC) has the following estimated earnings and net investments.

Years	1	2	3	4	5	6
Assets	24.00	40.00	52.00	60.00	68.00	73.44
Earnings	4.80	8.00	10.40	10.80	10.88	11.75
Investments	16	12.00	8.00	8.00	5.44	5.88

Dollar millions

The company will continue a payout ratio of 50% beyond year 6 and earn 16% on the assets. If the weighted average cost of capital is 15%, estimate the value of the business as the present value of free cash flows.

Essay Questions

1. Describe the differences between opportunity cost of capital and weighted average cost of capital. What are the primary assumptions you make when you use the weighted-average cost of capital based on actual values from a corporate balance sheet?

2. You are asked to help a friend value his family business. The business is a Tex-Mex restaurant and has had growing revenues for the last five years. The growth rate in the recent past has been of the order of 15% annually. Explain to your friend how you would go about valuing the restaurant business. What are some of the information you would need to do the valuation? What models would you use?

3. Explain the APV approach to evaluating the financing effects. Are there cases where the financing side effects can be negative?

4. Your company has been offered a special loan by a state government to induce your company to invest in their state. Describe how you will calculate the value of this offer.

5. Discuss the following statement – "Any safe or low risk cash flow should be evaluated using the risk-free rate, as these cash flows are certain and have no risk."

6. Why it is often better to use industry weighted average cost of capital than individual firm's cost of capital?

ANSWERS TO EXERCISES

Fill-in Questions

1. Base-case net present
2. Opportunity cost of capital
3. Business Risk
4. debt capacity
5. After-tax weighted average cost of capital, target debt ratio
6. Value additivity
7. Subsidized financing

Problems

1. Cost of equity $= r_E = r_f + \beta(r_m - r_f) = 5 + 1.5(8.5) = 17.75\%$
   Cost debt $= r_D = 8\%$
   WACC $= 0.08(1 - 0.30)0.35 + 0.1775(0.65)$
   $ = 0.0196 + 0.1154$
   $ = 13.50\%$

2. Use the three-step process to unlever and relever the WACC.

   Step 1: Unlever the WACC to calculate the opportunity cost of capital, r.
   $ r = r_D D/V + r_E E/V = 0.08(0.35) + 0.1775(0.65) = 0.1434 = 14.34\%$

   Step 2: Calculate the cost of equity at the 45% debt ratio.
   $ r_E = r + (r_A - r_D)D/E = 0.1434 + (0.1434 - 0.09)0.45/0.55 = 0.1871 = 18.71\%$

   Step 3: Calculate the new WACC.
    WACC $= 0.09(1 - 0.3)0.45 + 0.1871(0.55) = 0.1313 = 13.13\%$

3. Use the Cash flow and NPV worksheet: $CF_0 = -\$1,000,000$, $CO_1 = \$300,000$, $FO_1 = 6$;
   NPV: $I = 12$, NPV $= \$233,422$

4. Proceeds needed: $\$1,000,000/(1 - 0.12) = \$1,136,364$
   Issue cost: $\$1,136,364 - \$1,000,000 = \$136,364$
   APV $=$ base-case NPV $-$ issue cost
   $ = \$233,422 - \$136,364 = \$97,058$

5. a. Base-case NPV $= -\$6,000,000 + \$750,000/0.13 = -\$6,000,000 + \$5,769,231$
   $ = -\$230,769$

   b. Amount borrowed: $\$6,000,000 \times 0.4 = \$2,400,000$
   Tax shield $= \$2,400,000 \times 0.09 \times 0.34 = \$73,440$
   APV $=$ base-case NPV $+$ PV of tax shield
   $ = -\$230,769 + (\$73,440/0.09)$
   $ = -\$230,769 + \$816,000$
   $ = \$585,231$

   c. Acceptable minimum base-case NPV $= -\$816,000$
   Minimum annual income $=$ (cash outlay $+$ minimum base case NPV) $\times$ required return
   $ = (\$6,000,000 - \$816,000) \times 0.13 = \$673,920$

   d. Minimum return $= \$673,920/\$6,000,000 = 11.23\%$

6. Before we can calculate the weighted-average costs of capital, we need to first calculate the r_E using the equation:

$$r_E = r + (r - r_D)D/E = 0.13 + (0.13 - 0.09)0.4/0.6 = 0.13 + 2.67 = 0.1367 = 15.67\%$$

$$
\begin{aligned}
WACC &= r_D(1 - T_c)D/V + r_E(E/V) \\
&= 0.09(1 - 0.34)0.4 + 0.1567\,(0.6) \\
&= 11.78\%.
\end{aligned}
$$

7. The value of the incentive package can be calculated by discounting the resulting cash flows by your after-tax borrowing cost. Your after-tax borrowing rate r^* is:

$$r^* = r_D(1 - T_C) = 0.10(1 - 0.3) = 0.07 = 7\%.$$

The cash flows from the package will be $1 million for each of the first two years. Present value: N = 2, I = 7, PV = solve, PMT = $0.4 million, FV = 0, PV = $0.7232 million.

8. The earnings, investments, and free cash flows (in $ millions) for the first 5 years are given in the table below. From year six, the free cash flows are growing at 8%. We can calculate the horizon value at the end of year 5 and then discount all cash flows and the horizon value to the present at the market capitalization rate of 15%.

Years	1	2	3	4	5
Earnings	4.80	8.00	10.40	10.80	10.88
Investments	16.00	12.00	8.00	8.00	5.44
Free cash flow	−11.20	−4.00	2.40	2.80	5.44

Value of cash flows from year 6 onwards = Free cash flow$_6$/(r − g) = (5.44 × 1.08)/(0.15 − 0.08) = 5.88/0.07 = $84 million

Value of the business = PV(Free cash flows)

$$= \frac{-11.20}{1.15} + \frac{-4}{(1.15)^2} + \frac{2.40}{(1.15)^3} + \frac{2.80}{(1.15)^4} + \frac{5.44 + 84}{(1.15)^5}$$

$$= \$34.88 \text{ million}$$

20

Understanding Options

INTRODUCTION

Options are important innovations of modern finance and an understanding of the theory and practice of option valuation and applications will help the financial manager do his or her job better. This chapter is the first of three dealing with options. The chapter gives you a detailed introduction to the two basic options, *calls* and *puts* and helps you understand the working of options through *position diagrams* which shows the pay-off of different positions in calls, puts, or shares held by an investor. Although the chapter focuses primarily on exchange-traded options on stocks the concepts and valuation principles are general and can be extended to options on different assets and liabilities. While formal valuation of options is left to the next chapter, this chapter gives you an intuitive understanding of what determines an option's value. Chapter 22 deals with the applications of option theory to real options. Later chapters describe warrants, convertible bonds and other types of securities, which are examples of options commonly used in corporate financing.

Most stock options are traded in exchanges and are not controlled by the corporations on whose stocks these options are based. These options do not directly affect the corporations or their balance sheets. However, a financial manager needs to understand options and their valuation, as these are very useful in managing and understanding risk associated with many management decisions. Nearly all corporate securities are options themselves or have some kind of options embedded in them. Financial managers will also have to deal with options related to commodities, exchange rates, and interest rates. Corporate bonds often have call features and other options attached to them. Options are also part of many capital budgeting decisions, which involve *embedded* options to expand, abandon, or, in other ways, modify the project cash flows. A clear understanding of the principles of option valuation will help the manager understand the trade-off involved and arrive at the optimal decision.

KEY CONCEPTS IN THE CHAPTER

Calls and Puts: There are two basic options: *calls* and *puts*. A call option gives its owner the right to buy an asset at a specified *exercise price*, or *strike price*, during a specified period. A put option gives its owner the right to sell an asset at a specified exercise price during a specified period. A *European* option is exercisable only at maturity while an *American* option is exercisable any time up to its expiration date. Here are some terms associated with options.

- *Underlying asset* – e.g. an option on one share of IBM.
- *Type of option* – call or put.
- *Exercise price* or *strike price* – the price at which the buyer of the option gets the right to buy (call) or sell (put) the asset to the seller of the option. The seller of the option is often called the *writer* of the option.

- *Maturity* or *expiration date* – the date till (American) or on (European) which the option can be exercised.
- *Option premium* – This is the price paid to buy the option.
- *Asset price* – The price of the underlying asset.
- *In-the-money* or *out-of-the-money* – An option is said to be in-the-money if the exercise of the option makes money for you at that moment. A call option will be in-the-money if the share price is above the exercise price and a put option will be in-the-money if the share price is below the exercise price.

Calls, Puts, Shares, and Combinations: Position diagrams show the pay-off from an option, or for that matter, holding any asset. These are very useful in understanding the value of owning derivative securities based on an asset and the exposure the owner has relative to the changes in value of the asset. Learn to draw the position diagrams for the simple options and assets first and then graduate to the different combinations of options and assets. Given below are pay-off diagrams for holding a share, a put and a call. Your pay-off is on the vertical axis and the stock price is on the horizontal axis.

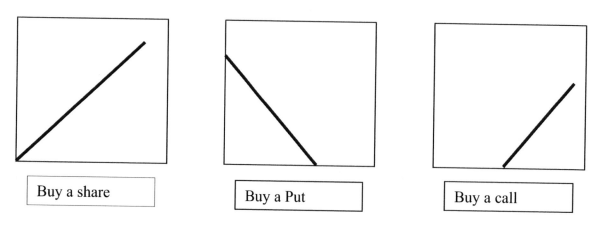

| Buy a share | Buy a Put | Buy a call |

Note that the position diagrams are not profit diagrams, as they do not include the original cost or price paid for the options or the asset. Studying different combinations of options and positions in shares enables us to understand options and their pay-offs better. Figure 20.6 in the text gives some interesting combinations. Consider the following four positions: buying a call, buying a put, buying a share and depositing an amount equal to the present value of the exercise price. Note that the combination of buying a call and investing the present value of the exercise price in a safe asset gives you a pay-off identical to buying a put and buying the share. Thus, of the four positions, only three can have independent values. In other words, you can always create the fourth asset or security by a combination of the other three. This helps in the valuation of options. The relationship among these four assets is called the *put-call parity*. This can be expressed as:

Value of a call + present value of exercise price = value of put + share price

We can rearrange this in several different ways to express the value of a call or a put in terms of the other three.

Value of call = value of put + share price − present value of exercise price
Value of put = value of call − value of share + present value of exercise price

The relationship can be stated in words in different ways:

- Buying a call and selling a put is identical in pay-off to buying a share and borrowing the present value of the exercise price.
- Buying a put is identical in pay-off to buying a call, selling a share, and investing the present value of the exercise price.

Identifying Options: Options are not always easy to identify. Warrants and conversion features are obvious options. As long as there is a pay-off, which is contingent on the value of another asset, an option is present. You come across a number of options in everyday life some of which may not be obvious. Some examples include:

- The right to drop a course within the first two or three weeks for a full refund of fees paid.
- A money-back guarantee on articles purchased.
- The right to get a ticket for your university's homecoming football game.
- A fully refundable air ticket.

Try identifying the options in the above (see worked example 4 for answers).

Determinants of Option Value: Formal valuation of options is discussed in Chapter 21. This chapter gives you a clear understanding of the basic determinants of the value of an option. The value of a call at expiration is simply the difference between the stock price and the exercise price, with a minimum value of zero. For example, an IBM option with an exercise price of $105 will be worth $5 if the stock price is $110. If the stock price is less than $105 the option is worth nothing. At anytime before expiration, the option will be worth more than the difference between the exercise price and the asset price. Review figure 20-10, which shows the value of a call option at different values of the stock price. Note that the figure applies to an option that has some time to expiration, so that the option has a "time premium." As long as there is time left to maturity and potential volatility in the stock value, an option will have value above the expiration value. An option will never be worth more than the price of the stock, which is an upper bound for the value of a call option. The lower bound for an option's value is zero or the difference between the stock price and the exercise price, whichever is higher. An option value equals zero when the value of the underlying asset is equal to or less than the exercise price. Option values tend to increase as the value of the underlying asset exceeds the exercise price. Here are some additional facts on a call option value:

- For a given exercise price, the value of an option increases as the stock price increases.
- When the stock price becomes high relative to the exercise price, the option value approaches the stock price less the present value of the exercise price. As the stock price increases the probability of exercise also increases and when the stock price is sufficiently higher than the exercise price, exercise is almost certain.
- The value of an option increases with the rate of interest (r_f). This is because holding an option is equivalent to getting an interest free loan equal to the exercise price. Higher the interest rate, higher is the value of this loan.
- The value of an option increases with the time to expiration (t).

- The value of an option increases with the variability of the share prices. Higher the probability of large stock price changes, higher the value of the option. In other words, an option on a stock with high standard deviation of returns (σ) will be worth more than an option on a stock with lower variability of returns.

The table below summarizes the effect of changes in the key variables on the value of a call option.

Variables	Change in the value of a call option when the variable increases
Stock price (P)	Positive
Exercise Price (EX)	Negative
Interest rate (r_f)	Positive
Time to expiration (t)	Positive
Volatility (σ)	Positive

WORKED EXAMPLES

1. Find the value of a call option, given that the present value of the exercise price is $35, the value of the put is $10, and the share price is $33.

SOLUTION

Use the put-call parity:

$$\text{Value of call} + \text{present value of exercise price} = \text{value of put} + \text{share price,}$$

$$\begin{aligned}\text{Value of call} &= \text{value of put} + \text{share price} - \text{present value of exercise price} \\ &= \$10 + \$33 - \$35 \\ &= \$8\end{aligned}$$

2. Find the implied present value of the exercise price of a 13-week call, given that the value of the call option is $8, the value of the put option is $5, and the market price is $20.

SOLUTION

$$\begin{aligned}\text{Present value of exercise price} &= \text{value of put} + \text{share price} - \text{value of call} \\ &= \$5 + \$20 - \$8 = \$17\end{aligned}$$

3. Given below are recent quotations for options on IBM shares. IBM stock was selling at 106.50 and the call money rate (the rate charged by banks on loans to brokers with stocks as collateral) was 3.25%.

Strike Price	Call Price	Put Price
$105	$5.30	$3.60
110	3.00	6.40

a. Which options are in-the-money and which is out-of-the-money?
b. Assume that there is exactly 40 days to expiry. What values would put-call parity imply for European puts? What reasons might account for the traded ones being worth slightly more?

SOLUTION

a. The $105 call and the $110 put are in-the-money. The other options are out-of-the-money.
b. The 40 day discount factor for the 3.25% call money rate = $1/(1.0325^{40/365}) = 0.9965$. The values of European puts are given by:

Value of put = PV (exercise price) + V (call) – share price
V ($105 put) = $105 × 0.9965 + 5.30 – $106.5 = $3.43
V ($110 put) = $110 × 0.9965 + 3.00 – $106.5 = $6.12

The traded options are American options. The early exercise feature of these puts is valuable, and more so if the option is in-the-money.

4. Can you identify the options included in the following situations:

   a. The right to drop a course within the first two or three weeks for a full refund of fees paid.
   b. A money-back guarantee on articles purchased.
   c. The right to get a ticket for your university's homecoming football game.
   d. A fully refundable air ticket.

SOLUTION

   a. The right to drop a course is a put option. You are "selling" the course back to the university.
   b. A money-back guarantee is also a put option as you are selling the article back to the shop.
   c. This would be a call option.
   d. Another put option.

5. Here are prices quoted for a series of call options on Money Machine.com (all with the same expiration date):

Exercise Price	Option price
$50	$ 4
$60	$ 8
$70	$13

Can you suggest a trading strategy, which will make money for you?

SOLUTION

The prices do not seem to be real. If they are, you can easily make money by buying the $50 option and selling the other two contracts. In the real world, higher exercise price call options would sell at lower prices.

6. Mary Stiller, the new CEO of World Grossing Corp, a global trading firm, was offered the following bonus package based on World Grossing stock price at the end of the year. Ms. Stiller will get $10,000 for every dollar of price increase above a base stock price of $50 with a maximum bonus of $100,000. Can you identify the combination of options, which will give the same pay-off as the bonus package?

SOLUTION

The bonus package is equivalent to a combination of the following: Buying 10,000 call options with exercise price of $50 and selling 10,000 call options with exercise price of $60. Check this out for different stock prices:

Stock price	$50	$55	$60	$65	$70
A. Value of $50 options	$0	$50,000	$100,000	$150,000	$200,000
B. Value of $60 options	$0	0	0	$ 50,000	$100,000
Net value = A − B	$0	$50,000	$100,000	$100,000	$100,000

SUMMARY

This chapter is the first of three covering options and describes the two basic types of options – calls and puts. The use of position diagrams helps us understand the pay-off for calls, puts and various combinations of owning stocks, and the options. These help you identify options embedded in many real life situations and construct packages for different pay-off situations. The chapter explains the various characteristics of options and the effects of the changes in the different variables affecting the value of an option. The value of a call option is a function of the exercise price, the stock price, the risk-free rate of interest, time to expiration, and the volatility of returns measured by the standard deviation of returns. While a higher exercise price would mean a lower call option value, all the other variables have a positive relationship with the value of a call. Note that the value of the option is not affected by the expected return on the stock. Most corporate securities have features of options or have options embedded in them.
The financial manager will have a number of uses for options. Some of these include capital budgeting decisions, financing decisions, and risk management. A good understanding of the way options work and the knowledge of how to value them will be very useful for a corporate financial manager.

LIST OF TERMS

American option
Call option
European option
Exercise price
In-the-money
Out of the money

Position diagram
Put option
Put-call parity
Strike price
Volatility

EXERCISES

Fill-in Questions

1. A(n) _____ gives its owner the right (without the obligation) to buy an asset at a specified exercise price, or _____ price.

2. A(n) _____ gives its owner the right to sell stock at a specified price.

3. _____ call options may be exercised only on the expiration day, whereas _____ call options may be exercised on or before the expiration day.

4. For European options, the value of a call option plus the present value of the _____ equals the value of the _____ plus the share price.

5. The best way to show the effect of using combinations of options is to draw a _____.

6. When a firm borrows, (shareholders, creditors) _____ acquire the company and (shareholders, creditors) _____ obtain an option to buy it back.

7. The value of limited liability lies in the option to default and is the value of a (put, call) _____ option on the firm's assets with an exercise price equal to the promised payment to (creditors, owners) _____.

8. If the following variables decrease, the changes in the call option prices are (positive, negative):

   Stock price   _____
   Exercise price   _____
   Interest rate   _____
   Time to expiration   _____
   Stock price volatility   _____

9. When an asset's value exceeds the strike price, then the call option on it is said to be (in, out of) _____ the money and the put option is said to be (in, out of) _____ the money.

10. This relationship, value of call + present value of exercise price = value of put + share price, is called _____.

11. In the language of option pricing, the annualized standard deviation of the return on the underlying asset is called its _____.

Problems

1. Find the value of a call option, given that the present value of the exercise price is $26, the value of the put is $2, and the share price is $30.

2. Find the implied present value of the exercise price of a 26-week call, given the value of the call option is $1, the value of the put option is $7, and the market price is $35.

3. Identify the options involved in the following:

   a. The CEO of Crazy Fox gets 10,000 shares when he is hired. He can sell the shares back to the company at a price of $40 if he is fired within the next two years.

   b. A cereal manufacturer has a long-term contract with an agricultural trading company for the supply of corn and wheat. The transactions would normally be at market prices. However, the contract stipulates a minimum price the cereal company will pay if the market price falls below that price. The contract also stipulates a ceiling price, if the market price goes above that price.

4. The following are recent quotes for call options on General Electric shares expiring in 35 days.

Exercise Price	Call price
$37.50	$3.40
$40.00	$1.75
$45.00	$0.15

Assume an interest rate of 3.25%. The stock price was $40.41. Use the put-call parity to estimate the prices for the put options. Do you expect these prices to be different from the prices quoted in the market?

5. Mary Stiller, the new CEO of World Grossing Corp. is offered the following bonus package (instead of the one in worked example 6): She will get $75,000 if the share price closes at $50 or higher in six months time. Can you identify the combination of options or other securities that will give this pay-off?

6. Given below are the pay-off diagrams for certain combinations of options or securities. Can you identify the combinations?

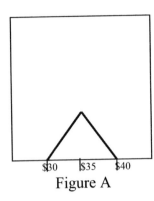

Figure A

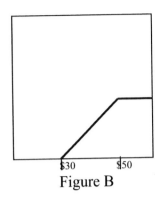

Figure B

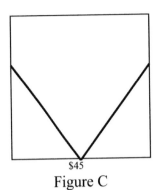

Figure C

Essay Questions

1. Explain the following statement – "The riskier the stock, the more valuable the option."

2. Explain why financial managers should be interested in options.

3. List and explain the key elements, which determine the value of options.

4. Describe the typical corporation's debt and stockholders' equity as options.

ANSWERS TO EXERCISES

Fill-in Questions

1. Call options; strike
2. Put option
3. European, American
4. Exercise price; put option
5. Position diagram
6. Creditors; shareholders

7. Put; creditors
8. Negative, positive, negative, negative, negative
9. In; out of
10. Put-call parity
11. Volatility

Problems

1. Value of call = value of put + share price − PV of exercise price
   = $2 + $30 − $26 = $6

2. PV of exercise price = value of put + share price − value of call
   = $7 + $35 − $1 = $41

3. a. A put options with exercise price of $40.

    b. The two parties have sold each other a call option and a put option. The cereal manufacturer has bought a call option (sold by the trading firm) with the exercise price equal to the ceiling price. The agricultural trading firm has bought a put option (sold by the cereal manufacturer) with the exercise price equal to the minimum price.

4. The 35 day discount factor for the 3.25% call money rate = $1/(1.0325^{35/365}) = 0.9969$. The values of European puts are given by:

    Value of put = PV (exercise price) + V(call) – share price

    $$V(\$37.5 \text{ put}) = \$37.5 \times 0.9969 + 3.40 - \$40.41 = \$0.38$$

    $$V(\$40 \text{ put}) = \$40 \times 0.9969 + 1.75 - \$40.41 = \$1.22$$

    $$V(\$45 \text{ put}) = \$45 \times 0.9969 + 0.15 - \$40.41 = \$4.60$$

These are the values for European options. Quoted prices available in the market are for American puts and these are likely to be somewhat higher.

5. If you buy 75,000 calls with exercise price of $49 and sell 75,000 calls with exercise price of $50, you will almost always get the payoff stipulated in the bonus package. The payoff will be different if the stock price ends up between $49 and $50. You could narrow the difference between the option combinations and the bonus by fine tuning the option exercise prices in the combination as follows: 150,000 contracts each with exercise prices of $49.50 and $50; 300,000 contracts each with exercise prices of $49.75 and $50; or 750,000 contracts each with exercise prices of $49.90 and $50.

6. Figure A pay-off is for the following combination: Buy one call with exercise price of $30, sell two calls with exercise price of $35 and buy one call with exercise price of $40. Figure B involves a combination of buying a call with exercise price of $30 and selling a call with exercise price of $50. Figure C is the payoff you get when you buy both a call and put with the same exercise price of $45.

21

Valuing Options

INTRODUCTION

This chapter explains the valuation of options from the first principles. We start with the simplified version of the binomial method for valuing options. This approach uses option-equivalent portfolios using ownership in stock and borrowing. Alternately, one could use the risk-neutral method, which involves computing the probability of stock price changes under the assumption of risk-neutral investors. The two methods are equivalent and give the same valuation. The general binomial method and its applications are presented later. This is followed by the Black and Scholes formula, which is easier and more accurate than the binomial method. The formula is illustrated with a worked out example. The chapter also reviews the application of the binomial option-pricing model to American options. Remember that the Black-Scholes model was derived for the European call option. Valuation of American options as well as European options on stocks paying dividends need to be adapted or modified to the specific situation. In some cases, the step-by-step binomial method may the only right approach. The appendix to the chapter discusses the dilution effect of company issued calls and warrants. The Black-Scholes formula, with some modifications, can be used to value the warrants.

KEY CONCEPTS IN THE CHAPTER

A Simple Option Valuation Model: We learned in Chapter 20 the basic properties of options and the key determinants of the value of an option. We now approach the important problem of computing the value of an option. So far, the discounted cash flow approach has been the basic procedure we used for valuation. However, discounted cash flows will not work for options, because:

- Difficulty in forecasting cash flows from an option, though it is possible to do.
- Impossible to find the correct opportunity cost of capital because an option's risk changes every time its price changes. An in-the-money option is safer than one out-of-the-money and a stock price increase raises option prices and reduces risk, and vice versa, each time stock prices change.
- Options are always riskier than the underlying stock because they have higher betas and higher standard deviations of return.

The problem of option valuation is solved by creating an option equivalent portfolio by combining the stock and borrowing. Initially, we simplify the problem by assuming that the stock can take only two possible values when the option expires. A portfolio of the stock and a loan is constructed such that it gives the same pay-off as the option at the time of expiration. Thus, the value of the option can be written as:

Value of call = value of the number of shares in the equivalent portfolio – borrowed amount.

The number of shares needed to replicate one call is the *hedge ratio* or *option delta*. This ratio is computed as follows:

$$\text{Option delta} = \frac{\text{spread of possible option prices}}{\text{spread of possible share prices}}$$

An equivalent, but alternative, approach is to assume that the investors are *risk-neutral*. With this assumption, we can get the investors to be satisfied with the risk-free rate of return on their stock investment. We can now estimate the *probability of stock price* going up or down and thereby calculate the value of the option.

$$\text{Probability of rise in stock value} = \frac{\text{interest rate} - \text{downside change}}{\text{upside change} - \text{downside change}}$$

This value is the probability of the price change in the risk-neutral world. Note that this is not the real probability, but a synthetic construct, which enables us to value the option.

The Binomial Method: The above approaches to valuation are somewhat simplistic and assume that the stock will have just two possible values (one up and one down) in the next period. The approach is general and is a simplified version of the *binomial* method. Essentially, we assume the possible changes over the next period to be just two - an "up" value and a "down" value. We can extend the binomial method by assuming shorter time intervals and then replicate the process. That is, we can break down a one-month option into a series of 30 one-day options and ultimately into shorter and shorter intervals so that you end up with continuous changes. While doing this type of option valuation manually will be cumbersome, one can find computer programs that will make the computations less time consuming.

<u>The General Binomial Method:</u> The basic approach in the binomial method involves specifying two (and only two) possible asset value changes per unit of time under consideration. We then assume that the investors will be risk-neutral and will be satisfied with a rate of return equal to the risk-free interest rate. Given these conditions, it is easy to calculate the implied probability (p) that the asset will rise (the probability of a fall in value will be, of course, 1−p). We can find the pay-off for the option for the two asset values and calculate the expected value of the option. There are generalized formulas to determine asset value changes based on the standard deviation of asset returns.

$1 + \text{upside change} = u = e^{\sigma\sqrt{h}}$

$\text{Upside change} = e^{\sigma\sqrt{h}} - 1$

$1 + \text{downside change} = d = 1/u$

$\text{Downside change} = (1/u) - 1$

Where,

e = base for natural logs = 2.718
σ = standard deviation of (continuously compounded) annual returns on asset
h = interval as a fraction of a year

As the number of intervals is increased, the values you obtain from the binomial method should get closer and closer to the Black-Scholes value.

The Binomial Method and Decision Trees: The application of the binomial method looks and feels a lot like the decision trees we have seen in the capital budgeting chapters. However, the binomial method is not another application of decision trees. Option pricing theory is needed to solve the problems described in this chapter. Discounted cash flows will not work because there is no single discount rate, which will capture the changing risk involved. The option theory is more powerful and will provide simpler solutions where decision trees cannot or become too complex.

The Black-Scholes Formula: Extension of the binomial approach to larger and larger number of sub-periods comprising smaller and smaller intervals will ultimately result in a smooth continuous distribution of stock price changes. Black and Scholes achieved this theoretically and derived a formula for the value of an option. The formula can be written as:

$$\text{Value of option} = [\text{delta} \times \text{share price}] - [\text{bank loan}]$$
$$= [N(d_1) \times P] - [N(d_2) \times PV(EX)]$$

Where:

$$d_1 = \frac{\log[P/PV(EX)]}{\sigma\sqrt{t}} + \frac{\sigma\sqrt{t}}{2}$$

$$d_2 = d_1 - \sigma\sqrt{t}$$

N(d) = cumulative normal probability density function
EX = exercise price of option
PV(EX) is calculated by discounting at risk-free interest rate for t-periods in the usual way.
t = number of periods to exercise date
P = price of stock now
σ = standard deviation per period of (continuously compounded) rate of return on stock
Notice that the Black-Scholes formula has all the properties we expected. It increases with P, σ, and t, and decreases with PV(EX). It also increases smoothly as a function of P from C = 0 for small P up to P – PV(EX) for large P.

Using Black-Scholes Model: Using Black-Scholes model is not particularly difficult, once the values of the variables are known. See the worked examples and the problems at the end. $N(d_1)$ and $N(d_2)$ can be calculated from the tables for the probability tables for normal distribution (Appendix A - Table 6 in the textbook). Alternately, you can use the NORMDIST function in the Excel spreadsheet program. For example, if you want to find the value for $N(d_1)$ where $d_1 = 0.501$, type in "= NORMDIST(0.501, 0,1, TRUE)" in the EXCEL spreadsheet, you will get the value $N(d_1) = 0.308$. Once you get the values of $N(d_1)$ and $N(d_2)$, you can substitute these in the Black-Scholes formula and get the option value. See the worked examples below. The values for $N(d_1)$ and $N(d_2)$ for all the solutions were calculated using the EXCEL spreadsheet program.

The Black-Scholes formula is more accurate, easier to use and realistic than the binomial method. The model has found extensive practical applications in business and finance. These include, among others, valuation of executive stock options, warrants and convertible bonds, and valuing portfolio insurance products. Note that from given market prices for options and other parameters, one can estimate the variability of stock returns using the Black-Scholes formula.

Options are more risky than the underlying assets. Given that a long position in a call option is equivalent to buying $N(d_1)$ shares and borrowing $N(d_2) \times$ present value of the exercise price at the risk free rate, one can calculate the beta of the call. See worked example 3.

Option Values at a Glance: The Black-Scholes formula applies to the European call on stocks, which do not pay any dividends. In order to apply this for the valuation of American calls as well as dividend paying stocks, you will have to modify the model or apply the general binomial method. Here is a summary of these situations.

American call - no dividends: In the absence of dividends, the value of a call option increases with the time to maturity. An American call should not be exercised before maturity. Therefore, the value of the American call will be same as that given by the Black-Scholes model for the European call.

European Puts - no dividends: Using the put-call parity, you can derive the value of a European put.

Value of put = Value of call – Value of stock + PV(Exercise price)

American put - no dividends: It sometimes pays to exercise an American put before maturity in order to reinvest the exercise price. An American put is always more valuable than a European put. The Black-Scholes formula does not allow for early exercise and thus, cannot be used to value an American put exactly. We can use the step-by-step binomial method by checking at each point whether the option is worth exercising the option ahead of its maturity.

European Calls on Dividend - paying stocks: For European calls on dividend-paying stocks, the value obtained by the Black-Scholes model will overstate the value of the option as part of the share value is composed of the present value of dividends, which the option holder does not receive. Therefore, the share price will need to be reduced to reflect the present value of the lost dividends.

American calls on dividend - paying stocks: The fact that a stock pays dividends does not necessarily imply that the option should be exercised early. The dividend gain is to be compared with the interest lost by the early exercise. Again, the best approach to valuing the option is to use the step-by-step binomial method and check at each stage whether the option is more valuable if exercised just before the ex-dividend date or held for at least one more period.

Dilution Effects and Valuation of Warrants: This topic is discussed in the appendix to the chapter. Exchange traded options are traded among investors who are usually not associated with the firm on whose stock the option value is based on. The exercise of these options does not have any impact on the firm's balance sheet or its value. Occasionally, firms issue call options and warrants. When these options and warrants are exercised the outstanding number of shares increases and there is a dilution effect, which affects the value of the options. The most common warrant is a long-term call option that is attached to a bond or a stock issue. It usually gives its holder an option to *buy for cash* another security of the company, usually its common stock. Warrants are usually detachable, meaning that they may be sold and exercised apart from the security with which they were offered. Warrant holders are not entitled to vote, nor do they receive cash dividends. Their interest in the company is usually protected against stock splits and stock dividends. The Black-Scholes options valuation formula may be used to value on a warrant provided it contains no unusual features and does not pay cash dividends. Cash dividends and dilution arising from the additional shares from the exercise of the warrants, however, present difficulties in using the Black-Scholes model. Consequently, adjustments for dilution are required. The binomial method is needed to value stocks with cash dividends.

Valuation of Warrants: Warrants are American call options and can be valued using the Black-Scholes model. Like any other American option, the value depends on the share price, exercise price, the volatility, the interest rate, and the time to maturity. Warrant valuation needs to be adjusted for the fact that the exercise of the warrant results in an increase in the number of shares outstanding. This causes dilution and needs to be adjusted for.

The value of a warrant at maturity can be written as:

$$\text{Value at maturity} = \frac{1}{(1+q)}\text{maximum}(\frac{V}{N} - EX, 0),$$

Where, q = number of warrants issued per share outstanding
    N = number of shares outstanding
    EX = exercise price of the warrant
    V = value of the equity of the firm *after the issue* of the warrant

In effect, the warrant is worth $1/(1+q)$ times the value of a call option written on the stock of an alternate firm with the same equity V and outstanding shares N, but with no warrants. This would require calculating the value of the share price of this notional firm and also adjust the volatility (standard deviation) of its equity to reflect the balance sheet of the notional firm. Problem 6 of the worked examples shows the calculations involved.

Some exotic options: The last section of the chapters lists some fancier and exotic options. Here is a listing with brief definitions:

Asian option – Exercise price of this option is the average of the asset price during the life of the option. This is also called average option.

Barrier option – This option's payoff depends on the asset price reaching a specified level.

Bermuda option – This is an option which is exercisable on discrete dates before maturity.

Caput option – This is a call on a put option.

Chooser option – The option holder has to decide before maturity whether the option is a call or put.

Compound option – This is an option on an option.

Digital option – Also called binary option, this has payoff of zero or a fixed amount.

Lookback option – This allows the option holder to choose the exercise price as any of the asset price values that occurred before a given date.

WORKED EXAMPLES

1. MBM Corp shares are currently trading at $105. You are required to value a six-month call option on MBM shares. The exercise price is given as $105. You are also told to assume that the stock can take only one of two possible values: $84 or $131.25. Assume an interest rate of 3.5%. Value the option using the option equivalent portfolio and the risk-neutral method.

SOLUTION

We can represent the situation six months from now as follows:

This pay-off for the options can be replicated by a portfolio of stock and loan.

Number of shares in the portfolio = Option delta or hedge ratio = $\dfrac{\$26.25 - 0}{\$131.25 - \$84} = 0.5556$

A portfolio of 0.5556 shares and a loan $45.87 will give the same payoff as the option as shown below. Note that the interest rate for six months = 3.5%/2 = 1.75%

	Low stock price = $84	High stock price = $131.25
Value of 1 call option	0	$26.25
0.5556 shares	0.5556 × $84 = $46.67	0.5556 × $131.25 = $72.92
Loan + Interest on a loan of $45.87	$45.87 × 1.0175 = $46.67	$45.87 × 1.0175 = $46.67
Total pay-off	0	$26.25

Note: The loan amount is set such that the portfolio will have the same payoff as the option.

Value of call = 0.5556 shares − $45.87 = $58.34 − $45.87 = $12.47

Risk-neutral method: The upside change in the stock price is 0.25 and the downside change is −0.20. Therefore, if the investors were risk-neutral, they would expect to get a return of 1.75% for the six-month period. We can compute the probability from the following equation:

$$p(0.25) + (1 − p)(−0.2) = 0.0175;$$

$$p = \frac{0.0175 + 0.20}{0.25 + 0.2} = 0.4833$$

The value of the option in six months is $26.25.
Current value = $26.25 × 0.4833/1.0175 = $12.47

2. Data for an option valuation problem are given below. Explain the Black-Scholes option valuation formula and compute the value of a European call option with exercise price of $120. Also, value a European put with the same exercise price. Show all steps.

Time	3 years
Standard deviation of continuously compounded return on asset	0.635
Current asset price	$100
Option exercise price	$120
Interest rate	8%

SOLUTION

Basic Black-Scholes formula can be written as below:

$$\text{Value of option} = [\text{delta} \times \text{share price}] − [\text{bank loan}]$$
$$= [N(d_1) \times P] − [N(d_2) \times PV(EX)]$$

where:

$$d_1 = \frac{\log[P/PV(EX)]}{\sigma\sqrt{t}} + \frac{\sigma\sqrt{t}}{2}$$

$$d_2 = d_1 - \sigma\sqrt{t}$$

$N(d)$ = cumulative normal probability density function
EX = Exercise price of option = \$120, PV(EX) = \$120/(1.08^3) = \$95.26
t = number of periods to exercise date = 3 years
P = price of stock now = \$100
σ = standard deviation per period = 0.635

$d_1 = 0.5941,$ $N(d_1) = 0.7238$
$d_2 = -0.5058,$ $N(d_2) = 0.3065$

Value of call = 0.7238 × \$100 − 0.3065 × \$95.26 = \$72.38 − \$29.20 = \$43.18
Value of put = Value of call + PV(EX) − stock price
= \$43.18 + \$95.26 − \$100 = \$38.44

3. If the beta for the shares given in example 2 above is 1.4, how risky is the call option?

SOLUTION

Call = A Portfolio of [$N(d_1)$ × Share − $N(d_2)$ × PV (Exercise price) loan at risk free rate]

$$\text{Beta of call} = \frac{0.7238 \times 100 \times 1.4 - 0.3065 \times 95.26 \times 0}{0.7238 \times 100 - 0.3065 \times 95.26} = \frac{101.33}{72.38 - 29.20} = 2.35$$

4. Karl Cahn Partners (KCP), a private take-over specialist firm, has embarked on an acquisition strategy to buy several other privately held companies. It presently has an opportunity to buy RRK Inc., but needs another six months to complete its analysis. It has instructed the CFO to negotiate an option to buy RRK. What price should the CFO be willing to pay for the option? The estimated standard deviation of RRK is 0.60, the value of its shares is \$50 apiece, and the estimated equivalent to an exercise price is \$70. Assume the interest rate is 7%.

SOLUTION

Summary of data:

Price of stock = \$50
Exercise price = \$70
PV (EX) = \$70/(1.07$^{0.5}$) = \$67.67
Standard deviation = 60%
Years to maturity = 0.5 years
Interest rate = 7%

$d_1 = -0.5012, N(d_1) = 0.3081$

$d_2 = -0.9255, N(d_2) = 0.1774$

$V \text{ (call)} = N(d_1)P - N(d_2) \times PV(EX)$

$\qquad = 0.3081 \times \$50 - 0.1774 \times \$67.67$

$\qquad = \$15.40 - \$12.00$

$\qquad = \$3.40$

5. Refer to problem 4 above. If RRK has been issued a put option by KCP with the same exercise price, how much is it worth?

SOLUTION

Use the put-call parity:

$$\text{Present value of exercise price} = \text{value of put} + \text{share price} - \text{value of call}$$

$$\text{Value of put} = \text{present value of exercise price} - \text{share price} + \text{value of call}$$
$$= \$67.67 - 50.00 + 3.40$$
$$= \$21.07$$

6. Suppose you are offered a 1-year option to buy the Euro at the exchange rate of $0.90 = 1$ Euro. You have the following additional information:

Maturity of option	$t = 1$
Exercise price	$E = \$0.90$
Current exchange rate (price) of Euro	$P = \$0.90$
Standard deviation of exchange-rate changes	$\sigma = .15$
Dollar interest rate	$r_\$ = .05$
Euro	$r_E = 0.06$

SOLUTION

To value the call option, you must first reduce the current price of the Euro by the amount of the lost interest.

$\text{Adjusted price of Euro, } P^* = \text{current price}/(1 + r_E) = 0.90/1.06 = \$0.85$

$\text{Price/PV(exercise price)} = P^*/[E/(1 + r_\$)] = 0.85/(0.90/1.05) = 0.9906$

$d_1 = \log[P/PV(EX)]/\sigma \sqrt{t} + \sigma\sqrt{t}/2; \ d_2 = d_1 - \sigma\sqrt{t}$

$\sigma = 0.15, t = 1 \text{ year}, \quad \sigma\sqrt{t} = 0.15, d_1 = -0.0118, d_2 = -0.1382$

$N(d_1) = 0.5047 \quad N(d_2) = 0.4450$

$\text{Value of the call option} = N(d_1)P - N(d_2) \times PV(EX)$

$\qquad\qquad = 0.5047 \times \$0.85 - 0.4450 \times 0.86$

$\qquad\qquad = \$0.0471 = 4.71 \text{ cents/Euro}$

7. The table below contains information about Mory Corp.'s recently issued subordinated bonds with detachable warrants.

   a. Calculate the cost of the warrants.
   b. Calculate the call option value without the dilution effects.
   c. Calculate the call option value with the dilution effects. (Assume the alternative firm's standard deviation of stock price changes is 39%.)

Details of Warrants Issued by Mory Corp.

Item	Value
Amount of loan	$120,000,000
Debt value without warrants	$105,000,000
Number of shares outstanding (N)	12,000,000
Current stock price	$40.00
Value of firm before debt issue	$540,000,000
Existing loans	$60,000,000
Number of warrants issued/share outstanding (q)	0.10
Total number of warrants issued	1,200,000
Exercise price of warrants (EX)	$52.00
Years to expiration of warrants (t)	5
Annual standard deviation of stock price changes	0.36
Rate of interest	6.00%

SOLUTION

a. Cost of warrants = total amount of loan − value of loan without warrants
   = $120 million − $105 million = $15 million
   Cost per warrant = 15/1.2 = $12.50 per warrant

b. Since we are not concerned about the dilution effect, we calculate the value of the option as if it were a regular call option on the stock.

$$\sigma\sqrt{t} = 0.36\sqrt{5} = 0.8050, \quad PV(EX) = \frac{\$52}{(1.06)^5} = \$38.86$$

Share price/PV(EX) = $40/$38.36 = 1.0294

$d_1 = \log[P/PV(EX)]/\sigma\sqrt{t} + \sigma\sqrt{t}/2$
   $= \log 1.0294/0.8050 + 0.8050/2 = 0.4385$
$d_2 = d_1 - \sigma\sqrt{t} = -0.3665$
$N(d_1) = 0.6695; \quad N(d_2) = 0.3570$ (Values obtained using Excel spread-sheet.)

Value of call option value = $N(d_1) \times P - N(d_2) \times PV(EX)$
   $= 0.6695 \times \$40 - 0.3570 \times \$38.86 = \$12.91$

c. To calculate the value of the warrant with the dilution effect, we use the value of the stock of the alternate firm where the stock price = V/N. The value of the warrant is 1/1+q times this option value.

Equity (V) of the alternate firm = original firm's total assets − value of loans

= $660 million − $165 million = $495 million

Current share of alternative firm = V/N
= $495 million/12 million shares
= $41.25 per share

$\sigma \sqrt{t} = 0.39\sqrt{5} = 0.8721$

Share price/PV(EX) = $41.25/$38.86 = 1.0616

$d_1 = \log 1.0616/0.8721 + 0.8721/2 = 0.50465$
$d_2 = d_1 - \sigma\sqrt{t} = -0.3675$
$N(d_1) = 0.6931; N(d_2) = 0.3566$

Value of call option value = $N(d_1) \times P - N(d_2) \times PV(EX)$
= $0.6931 \times \$40 - 0.3566 \times \$38.86$
= $14.73

Dilution factor = 1/1+q = 1/1.1
Warrant value of original firm with dilution = $[1/(1 + q)] \times$ value of call on alternative firm
= $(1/1.1) \times \$14.73$
= $13.39

SUMMARY

This chapter is an extension of Chapter 20 and applies the lessons learned in the last chapter to valuation of options. First, a simplified version of the binomial method is presented. The chapter also reviews the general binomial method, which is a very versatile tool in option valuation. By applying it over shorter and shorter periods, the binomial method approaches the Black-Scholes method in terms of accuracy. The chapter also presents the more rigorous Black-Scholes model. The model is not too difficult to apply, once you learn how to calculate the normal probability distribution values required in the formula.

The Black-Scholes formula is easier to use and more accurate than the binomial method. However, the model strictly applies only to European call options on to non-dividend paying stocks. European puts on non-dividend paying stocks can be valued using the Black-Scholes formula for the call option and then the put-call parity learned in the last chapter. American calls on non-dividend paying stocks can be valued using the Black-Scholes formula, as the value of both types of options would be same in this case. For options on dividend paying stocks, the Black-Scholes formula need to be applied with some modification or the step-by-step binomial method should be used. The Black-Scholes model can be adapted to value warrants and other options, which may be affected by dilution on exercise.

LIST OF TERMS

American Option
Binomial method
Black-Scholes
Currency Option

European Option
Hedge ratio
Option delta
Warrants

EXERCISES

Fill-in Questions

1. The number of shares needed to create the option equivalents from buying and selling common stocks and borrowing is called the _____ or _____.

2. The _____ method shows how to replicate the outcomes from an option for the evolution of the stock price.

3. The _____ formula assumes lognormal distribution of stock price changes. The formula is derived for the European call options.

4. An option to buy British pounds at a stipulated exchange rate is a(n) _____ option.

5. As the number of intervals for analyzing options is increased from 1 to 52, the _____ method produces results that are very close to the _____ model.

6. An American call option on a stock, which pays no dividends should not be exercised before maturity; therefore, its value is the same as a _____ call.

7. A(n) _____ put is always more valuable than a(n) _____ put.

8. A(n) _____ gives its owner the right to (buy, exchange) _____ stock for cash, whereas a convertible security gives its owner the right to (buy, exchange) _____ the bond for stock.

Problems

1. XYZ, Inc., has a 3-month option to acquire a publicly traded company, ABC Corp. Here are the assumptions the CFO made to analyze how to construct option equivalents.

Exercise price	$70
Current price of ABC stock	$70
Price may move only up or down:	
Estimated low price	$59.50
Estimated high price	$82.40
1-year interest rate	6%

   Demonstrate how to replicate the pay-off from a call option.

260

2. Use the Black-Scholes model to evaluate the $105 IBM call option expiring in 40 days. IBM stock is selling at 106.50 and the call money rate (charged to brokers on stock exchange collateral) was 3.25%. Assume a standard deviation of 26%.

3. Use the Black-Scholes model to evaluate the following IMK Corp option: Exercise price = $135, Stock price $130, Volatility = 26%, time to expiration = 3 months, and the risk-free interest rate = 6.25%.

4. Private, Inc. (PI) has an opportunity to buy Family Corp. (FC) another privately held company. PI needs more time to evaluate the deal and has negotiated a 60-day option to buy the company. The exercise price is set at $75. How much is the option worth to PI given that the estimated standard deviation of FC is 40% and the estimated value of each share of FC is $60. Assume the risk-free rate is 4.5%.

5. Refer to problem 4 above. FC persuades PI to write a put option with the same exercise price. How much is this option worth to FC?

6. You are offered a 1-year option to buy Mambian Crusados at $0.50/Crusado. The current exchange rate is $0.55/Crusado. You have the following information:

Maturity of option	$t = 1$
Standard deviation of exchange-rate changes	$\sigma = 0.16$
Dollar interest rate	$r_\$ = 0.05$
Crusado interest rate	$r_M = 0.08$

What is the value of this currency option?

7. The table below contains information about Brady Corp.'s recently issued bonds with detachable warrants.

   a. Calculate the cost of the warrants.
   b. Calculate the call option value without the dilution effects.
   c. Calculate the call option value with the dilution effects. (Assume the alternative firm's standard deviation of stock price changes is 34%.)

Brady Corp. – Details of Warrants

Item	Value
Amount of loan	$30,000,000
Debt value without warrants	$25,000,000
Number of shares outstanding	3,000,000
Current stock price	$36.00
Value of firm before debt issue	$128,000,000
Existing loans	$20,000,000
Number of warrants issued per share outstanding	0.12
Total number of warrants issued	360,000
Exercise price of warrants	$42
Years to expiration of warrants	6
Annual standard deviation of stock price changes	0.32
Rate of interest	6%

Essay Questions

1. Explain the technique of creating option-equivalent combinations using stocks and bank loans.

2. Describe the general binomial method. How does this method compare with the Black-Scholes model?

3. Explain the approach you would take to value an American call on a dividend paying stock.

4. "An American call option should never be exercised before its maturity." Discuss this statement.

5. "The Black-Scholes formula applies only to European calls on on-dividend paying stocks." Discuss this statement.

ANSWERS TO EXERCISES

Fill-in Questions

1. Hedge ratio; option delta
2. Binomial
3. Black-Scholes
4. Currency
5. Binomial; Black-Scholes
6. European
7. American, European
8. Warrant; buy; exchange

Problems

1. The pay-off for the call option for the high and low values of the stock and for a portfolio of equivalent stock + loan combination are given in the table below. The number of stocks required to duplicate the option pay-off is calculated using the hedge ratio or option delta formula.

$$\text{Hedge ratio} = \text{option delta} = \frac{\text{spread of possible option values}}{\text{spread of possible share values}}$$
$$= \$12.50/\$22.90 = 0.5415$$

Thus, if you buy 0.5415 shares and borrow \$31.74, the pay-off for the option is duplicated. See the table below.

	Low stock price = \$59.5	High stock price = \$82.40
Value of 1 call option	0	\$12.40
0.5415 shares	\$32.22	\$44.62
Loan + Interest on a loan of \$31.74	\$32.22	\$32.22
Total pay-off	0	\$12.40

Value of one call option = $0.5415 \times \$70 - \$31.74 = \$37.91 - \$31.74 = \$6.17$

2. Summary of data needed:

Price of stock = \$106.4
Exercise price = \$105
Standard deviation = 26%
Years to maturity = 40/365 = 0.1096 years
Interest rate = 3.25%
PV (EX) = $\$105/(1.035^{0.1096}) = \$104.60$

Black-Scholes formula: $V \text{ (call)} = N(d_1) \times P - N(d_2) \times PV \text{ (EX)}$

$$d_1 = \frac{\log[P/PV(EX)]}{\sigma\sqrt{t}} + \frac{\sigma\sqrt{t}}{2}$$

$$d_2 = d_1 - \sigma\sqrt{t}$$

$$d_1 = \frac{\log(\$106.5/\$104.63)}{0.26\sqrt{0.1096}} + \frac{0.26\sqrt{0.1096}}{2}$$

$d_1 = 0.2516$, $d_2 = 0.1656$, $N(d_1) = 0.5993$, $N(d_2) = 0.5658$
Value of call = $0.5993 \times \$106.5 - 0.5658 \times \$104.60 = \$4.65$

3. $d_1 = \log[P/PV(EX)]/\sigma\sqrt{t} + (\sigma\sqrt{t})/2$
     $= -0.1087$
    $d_2 = d_1 - \sigma\sqrt{t} = -0.2387$

    $N(d_1) = 0.4567, N(d_2) = 0.4057$
    Value of call $= N(d_1) \times P - N(d_2) \times PV(EX)$
    $\qquad = 0.4567 \times \$130 - 0.4057 \times 132.97 = \$5.43$

4. $d_1 = -1.2502, d_2 = -1.4124$
    $N(d_1) = 0.1056, N(d_2) = 0.0789$
    Value of call $= 0.1056 \times \$60 - 0.0789 \times \$74.46 = \$0.46$

5. Using the put-call parity:
    $V(put) = V(call) + PV(EX) -$ share price
    $\qquad = \$0.46 + \$74.46 - \$60 = \$14.92$

6. To value the call option, you must first reduce the current price of the Crusado by the amount of the lost interest.

    Adjusted price of Crusado, $P^* =$ current price$/(1 + r_M) = 0.55/1.08 = \$0.5093$
    Price/PV(exercise price) $= P^*/[E/(1 + r_S)] = 0.5093/(0.50/1.05) = 1.0695$
    $d_1 = \log[P/PV(EX)]/\sigma\sqrt{t} + \sigma\sqrt{t}/2; \quad d_2 = d_1 - \sigma\sqrt{t}$
    $\sigma = 0.15, \quad t = 1$ year, $\quad \sigma\sqrt{t} = 0.15$
    $d_1 = 0.4999 \qquad d_2 = 0.3399$
    $N(d_1) = 0.6914 \quad N(d_2) = 0.6330$

    Value of the call option $= N(d_1)P - N(d_2) \times PV(EX)$
    $\qquad = 0.6914 \times \$0.5093 - 0.6333 \times 0.4762$
    $\qquad = \$0.051$ or 5.1 cents/Mark

7. a. Cost of warrants $= \$30$ million $- \$25$ million $= \$5$ million
        Cost per warrant $= \%5$ million$/0.36 = \$13.89$ per warrant

    b. $\sigma\sqrt{t} = 0.32\sqrt{6} = 0.7838$
        $PV(EX) = \$42/(1.06)^6 = \$29.61$

        Share price/PV(EX) $= \$36/\$29.61 = 1.2159$

        $d_1 = \log 1.2159/0.7838 + 0.7838/2 = 0.6413$
        $d_2 = d_1 - \sigma\sqrt{t} = -0.1426$
        $N(d_1) = 0.7393; \quad N(d_2) = 0.4433$

        Value of call option $= N(d_1) \times P - N(d_2) \times PV(EX)$
        $= 0.7393 \times \$36 - 0.4433 \times \$29.61 = \$13.49$

c. Dilution factor = $1/(1 + q) = 1/1.12$
Current equity value V = \$158 million − \$45 million = \$113 million
Current share price of alternative firm = \$113 million/3 million = \$37.67 per share

$\sigma\sqrt{t} = 0.34\sqrt{6} = 0.8328$

Share price/PV(EX) = \$37.67/\$29.61 = 1.2723

$d_1 = \log 1.2723/0.8328 + 0.8328/2 = 0.7056$
$d_2 = d_1 - \sigma\sqrt{t} = -0.1273$; $N(d_1) = 0.7598$; $N(d_2) = 0.4494$

Value of call option = $N(d_1) \times P - N(d_2) \times PV(EX)$
$\qquad\qquad\qquad = 0.7598 \times \$37.67 - 0.4494 \times \$29.61$
$\qquad\qquad\qquad = \$15.31$

Warrant value of original firm with dilution = $(1/1.12) \times \$15.31 = \$13.67$

22

Real Options

INTRODUCTION

This chapter uses and extends the lessons learned in Chapters 20 and 21 to evaluate the real options of different types, which are often encountered by the corporate financial manager. Real options can be very valuable and can add value to the firm, if they are understood correctly and acted upon. Chapter 10 provided a brief introduction to the four common real options typically found in many capital investment projects. These are:

- The option to expand and make follow-on investments.
- The option to abandon or shrink a project.
- The option to wait and learn before investing.
- The option to change the input, the output or the production methods.

These options need to be considered as part of the capital investment project and included in the value of the project. The chapter provides a number of examples of valuing these options using the Black-Scholes or the binomial method. The options approach to valuation of these special situations associated with capital budgeting decisions is necessitated by the fact that simple discounted cash flow (DCF) analysis does not work very well in these cases. The DCF analysis is designed for analyzing investments, which do not change their nature during the life of the project. It is ideally suited for evaluating passive investments like bonds and stocks. Most corporate assets or investment projects are, on the other hand, actively managed by the manager. Projects can very often change their nature in terms of risk, cost structure, and expansion or abandonment possibilities. A smart manager will respond appropriately to these changes. These situations are best valued as options, which permit multiple decision points. The additional rounds of decisions give the manager more choices and enable the firm to capitalize on good fortune or to mitigate losses. The choices create uncertainty, which often makes the option more valuable.

KEY CONCEPTS IN THE CHAPTER

The Value of Follow-on Investment Opportunities: Many capital budgeting projects have expansion or follow-on investment opportunities attached to them. These expansion or follow-on projects are real options and should be considered while evaluating the original project. A pure DCF analysis of the follow-on project will not do justice to it. Even when the follow-on project is a negative NPV project, it can add value to the original project. It can be seen as an out-of-the-money call option. Note that such an option will have higher value if the uncertainty is higher and time to expiration is longer. These properties are somewhat counter-intuitive and the opposite of what one would find in the DCF analysis. Typical investments with follow-on projects include R & D projects and investments in new markets, foreign countries, and new technology. Remember that the uncertainties associated with the follow-on project actually make the value of options even more attractive.

As mentioned before, DCF analysis cannot do justice to the follow-on projects. This is because managers are actively involved in the management of both the initial project and the follow-on projects. The company will take up the follow-on projects only if they are found attractive or become in-the-money at the time the investment is called for.

The follow-on projects can be evaluated as call options. The investment required in the project is the exercise price and the present value of cash flows from the project is the asset price. The volatility of the project cash flows is to be measured as the standard deviation of the return on a stock with characteristics similar to that of the project. It may not be easy to find a stock with these characteristics, but the company's experience from the past might be of some help.

The Timing Option: Most investment projects have built-in timing option in that the firm can make the investment now or some time in the future. A project with a positive net present value with a timing option is in effect a mutually exclusive project with itself with a later starting date. The cost of delaying the investment is the lost cash flow during the delay; but the important benefit is that you can learn a lot more about the prospects of the project and uncertainties surrounding the project might be cleared up. Delaying the investment might be the right choice if the value of the option is significant.

Valuing the timing option is simple when there is no uncertainty. One can calculate the project's NPV at various dates of project commencement and pick the one date with the highest NPV. When there is uncertainty involved, as is in most cases, the option is best valued as a call option. The option associated with the timing of the project can be valued using the binomial method and the risk-neutral technique. The present value of the cash flows from the project will be the asset value and the investment required for the project is the exercise price. Cash flows from the project are similar to dividends on a stock. By delaying the exercise of the option, you are loosing the current cash flows, but gaining the time premium of the option. This premium will be a function of the volatility and time. These options can be valued using the step-by-step binomial method.

The Option to Abandon: This is the opposite of the option to expand. The option to reduce the size of the project or scrap it altogether, when things do not turn out as expected, is very valuable and enhances the project's value. The abandonment option can be seen as a put option and can be analyzed in terms of the possible project outcomes. The valuation of the abandonment option can be done using the binomial method. You start by estimating the present value of the project without the option to abandon. This is done by using the standard DCF approach. The steps to create a binomial tree giving the values for various possible project outcomes follow this. The "up" and the "down" values are computed for the different nodes on the tree. You then compute the risk-neutral probability for the upside change and the downside change. Using these probabilities and working back-wards from the end point of the project one can complete the tree by estimating the value of project for different nodes of the tree. Given the salvage value for the assets of the project at the various points in the project life, you can compute the value of the abandonment option for the different nodes. For each node you have two values for the project – one is the present value of the future cash flows and the other the salvage or abandonment value. The higher of the two is the effective value of the project at each node. We can work backwards to compute the effective value of the project incorporating the abandonment value. The difference between this value and the simple DCF present value of the project is the value of the abandonment put option.

Abandonment value and project life: For most projects, the effective project life is not known at the time the project is being evaluated. One makes specific assumptions about project life based on past experience with similar projects. This assumption is needed when one uses the standard DCF procedure for evaluation of capital budgeting projects. A real options approach will enable the project analyst to go beyond the one project life assumption. Essentially, one has to build a binomial tree extending to a point well beyond the usually assumed project life and then follow the procedure described above to find the optimal life for the project.

Temporary Abandonment: Often businesses face situations when it makes sense to abandon assets temporarily for possible use in future. Plants are shutdown when demand falls to a point where it does not make sense to operate them. The plants are mothballed with the expectation of being restarted when the demand picks up again and operations are profitable. In general mothballing of assets and reactivating these later costs money. It will pay to mothball an asset if the value of the mothballed asset is more than the value of the asset in operation plus the cost of mothballing it. Similarly, a mothballed asset will be put back in service when the value of the asset in operation exceeds the value of the mothballed asset plus the cost of reactivating it.

Flexible Production: Flexibility in manufacturing, procurement or other operating activities can have significant option value. Flexibility in production or manufacturing can be designed and built into a plant or manufacturing system. While such a plant or system can cost more than a plant or system without the flexibility, the former is more valuable because of the flexibility option. The flexibility may be with respect to any of the following: switching machine set ups to produce different products, switching from one source (or type) of raw material, or even switching the location of manufacturing from one country to another. These options are somewhat more complicated than the abandonment or follow-on options, but the principles learned in the chapter can be used to evaluate them. The options are more valuable if the uncertainty relating to the inputs of the system is high. For example an option to switch feedstock from natural gas to a liquid fuel is very valuable if the ratio of the prices of the two is very volatile.

Aircraft Purchase Option: An option that can be very valuable is the option relating to the procurement of key inputs to the business. An interesting example is the one discussed in the text, which describes an option on the purchase of airplanes by airlines. Most long-term procurement decisions involve three possible choices – a firm commitment now, a contract with a variable procurement option, or a commitment later. Again the value of the option will be a positive function of the uncertainty surrounding the component to be procured and the variability in the benefits and costs relating to it.

A Conceptual Issue: Option pricing models assume creation of option-equivalent portfolios constructed from the asset and a loan. This is valid for stocks and other financial assets, which are widely traded in the market. The real options discussed in this chapter involve real assets, which are seldom widely traded in the market. This raises the question of the validity of using the option pricing models for the valuation of the real options. However, this should not be a serious problem as long as there are traded assets or portfolios of risk characteristics identical to that of the assets included in the real option. The assumption is similar to what is made in the standard capital budgeting evaluation procedures used.

The conceptual challenges in applying real options analysis to problems in corporate finance and business are far more easily tackled than the practical issues. These practical issues include the fact that the real options involved can be very, very complex and might require enormous computational power. In such cases, an approximate answer might just as well serve the purpose. A second issue could be that the problem may lack a clearly definable structure and you may find it difficult to specify the quantitative values needed to conduct an option analysis. Last, but definitely not the least, the fact that in many cases competitors are also likely to have similar real options and it is nearly impossible to model their actions and reactions to your proposed actions. In short, competitors are never passive and you reach the limits of real options analysis.

WORKED EXAMPLES

1. Conner Canary Corp. (CCC) is considering a new technology for an ultra-electronic combination internal combustion electric engine. The technology is expected to revolutionize automobile industry and could lead to the ultimate zero emission cars. The net present value of the initial project is negative and is estimated at −$15 million. However, the company's chief technologist is keen on the project because the project will open up opportunities for the next generation of combination engines, which are expected to produce zero emission vehicles (ZEV). The estimated NPV of the ZEV project is −$25 million. Investment decision in the ZEV project must be made in 2010 (3 years from now). The other details of the ZEV project are given below:

Investment required in 2010	= $360 million
PV of cash flows expected (in 2010)	= $335 million
Standard deviation for comparable projects	= 35%
Required rate of return for the typical combination engine projects	= 16%
Interest rate	= 6%

CCC's CEO, Jose Mendez needs to make a decision on the initial project. Evaluate the project.

SOLUTION

The problem is an example of a project with a follow-on investment. The fact that the follow-on project has a negative NPV does not necessarily mean that it should be rejected. The follow-on project is a call option and has to be evaluated as such. We can use the Black-Scholes model to evaluate the value of the option.

Value of the call option = $N(d_1)P - N(d_2) \times PV(EX)$;
where $d_1 = \log[P/PV(EX)]/\sigma\sqrt{t} + \sigma\sqrt{t}/2$, $d2 = d_1 - \sigma\sqrt{t}$

$P = \$335/(1.16)^3 = \$214.623$ million

This is the value of the cash flow from the project. This should be discounted using the required rate of return for the project.

$PV (EX) = \$360/(1.05)^3 = \$302.26$ million

This is part of the option pricing process and the rate used to find the PV should be the interest rate.

$\sigma = 0.35$, t = 3 years, $\sigma\sqrt{t} = 0.6062$, $d_1 = -0.2617$; d2 = -0.8680
$N(d_1) = 0.3968$, $N(d_2) = 0.1927$

Value of the call option = $N(d_1)P - N(d_2) \times PV(EX) = 0.3968 \times \$214.623 - 0.1927 \times \$302.26$
$= \$26.92$ million

The value of the option when added to the NPV of the project, gives a positive value for the project: −$20 million + $26.92 million = $6.92 million.

2. Figure 22-1 summarizes the possible payoffs from the new project being considered by ABC Inc. The project is worth $30 million based on the cash flows projected. If things go well, the project will be worth $45 million by the end of the first year. If things do not go well, the business will be worth only $20 million. The company can get $25 million for the plant and machinery in the worse case scenario. Calculate the value of the abandonment option. Assume an interest rate of 10%.

Value = $30 million

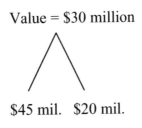

$45 mil. $20 mil.

Figure 22-1

SOLUTION

Using the risk-neutral approach, we can calculate the probability of a rise in the asset value. (Note: This is the notional probability in a risk-neutral world for option valuation; not the real probability. This value should not be used to calculate present value of the cash flows.)

The probability of a rise is:

p = (r – down side change)/(upside change – down side change);
where r = the interest rate = 0.10
upside change = (45/30) – 1 = 0.50
downside change = (20/30) – 1 = −0.33
p = 0.43/0.83 = 0.52

The value of the put option is zero for the upside change and $5 million for the downside change ($25 – $20). The expected future value of the put = 0.52 × 0 + 0.48 × $5 = $2.40 million
Current value = $2.40/1.10 = $2.182 million

3. Rainbow Rivet Company has a project, which requires a cash outlay of $75 million. The company has the option to delay the project for up to 2 years. The project's current cash flow is $15 million, and the cost of capital is 15%. The company estimates that the project's cash flows may decrease by 20% or increase by 25%. Assume that the investment cannot be postponed beyond the end of the second year. The risk-neutral rate is 5%. Value the option.

SOLUTION

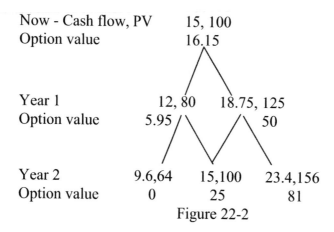

Now - Cash flow, PV   15, 100
Option value   16.15

Year 1   12, 80   18.75, 125
Option value 5.95   50

Year 2   9.6,64   15,100   23.4,156
Option value   0   25   81

Figure 22-2

Cash flows, end-of-year values and option values are all in million dollars.

Figure 22-2 shows the project's possible cash flows, end-of-year values and the option values at the different points in time. With a cash flow of $15 million, the value of the project is $100 million, when discounted at the market-required rate of 15%. If demand turns out to be low in year 1, the cash flow is only $12 million, and the remaining value of the project falls to 12/0.15 = $80 million. If demand is high in year 1, the cash flow is $18.75 and the value rises to 18.75/0.15 = $125 million. A second year of low demand would cause the cash flows to fall to $9.6 and the project value to fall to $64, and so on.

Notice that if you undertake the investment right away, you capture the first year's cash flow ($12 or $18.75). If you delay, you miss out on this cash flow, but you now have more information on how the project is likely to work out. In addition, that information has value.

If demand is high in the first year, the company has a cash flow of $18.75 million and a value of $125 million at the end of the first year. The total return is $(18.75 + 125)/100 - 1 = 0.4375$, or 44%. If demand is low, the cash flow is $12 and the year-end value is $80. Total return is $(12 + 80)/100 - 1 = -0.08$, or $- 8\%$.

The probability of a rise is:

$$p = [0.05 - (- 0.08)]/[0.44 - (-0.08)]$$
$$= 0.25$$

The probability of a decline = $1 - p = 1 - 0.25 = 0.75$

To find the call option value on the project with an exercise price of $75, begin at the end and work backwards. If the project value is $64, the option to invest is worthless. (Asset price is less than the exercise price.) At the other two points, the option is worth $25 million ($100 − $75), and $81 million ($156 − $75).

At the end of year 1, we need to calculate the option value as the higher of the following: i) value if the investment option is exercised ($5 million on the left branch ($80 − $75), and $50 on the right branch ($125 − $75) and ii) the expected value of the options from the end of year 2. The values are given in Figure 22-2. The value for the left branch for the options = $5.95 = ($25 × 0.25)/1.05. For the right branch, the value of the options from the next year will work out to $37.14 million [($25 × 0.75 + $81 × 0.25)/1.05]. This is lower than the value of the option if exercised at that point ($50 million = $125 − $75).

The value of option now = ($5.95 × 0.75 + $50 × 0.25)/1.05 = $16.15 million.

This, however, is less than the value if the option is exercised now: $25 million = $100 − $75 million. Thus, the company should go ahead and invest in the project right now.

SUMMARY

This chapter is an extension of Chapter 21 and applies the lessons learned in the last two chapters to the analysis and valuation of real options faced by corporate financial managers. These real options are: the option for follow-on investment, the abandonment option, the timing option, and the option to vary production or other resources to achieve flexibility in production or procurement or other operating activities. These options can be valued using the Black-Scholes or binomial method with the risk-neutral approach as appropriate. These options are extremely valuable and a manager's ability to understand and correctly value these options will enable him (her) to manage the corporate resources better. Note that the real options compliment the DCF analysis of many capital budgeting situations rather than replace it. Also, real options are more valuable when the uncertainty involved is higher and the time to expiration of the option is longer. Care and judgment will have to be used in obtaining the parameters required for valuation of these options. One should also keep in mind the practical challenges arising out of the complexity of the problem, the lack of a well defined structure, and the responses of competitors in possession of similar real options.

LIST OF TERMS

Abandonment option
Call option
Flexible production facilities

Put option
Real options
Timing option

EXERCISES

Fill-in Questions

1. Capital budgeting decisions often involve _____ options.

2. A(n) _____ option is an insurance policy that pays off when the value of the asset is less than the option's exercise price.

3. An abandonment option is a(n) _____ option with an exercise price equal to the sales value of the assets.

4. Decisions concerning the timing of investments and the value of follow-on investments are examples of _____ options.

5. The _____ option is essentially one of choosing the optimal point for investment.

6. Real options may be provided by _____ where inputs or outputs may easily be varied.

Problems

1. Burgers & Burgers Corp. (BBC) is considering a new technology for a new hybrid burger with high protein and very low fat content. The net present value of the project is negative and is estimated at −$10 million. However, the company's chief food-technologist is keen on the project because the project will open up opportunities for the next generation of burgers, which are expected to be of zero fat content. The estimated NPV of the ZB (for Zero fat content burger) project is −$65 million. Investment decision must be made in 2012 (two years from now). The other details of the ZB project are given below:

Investment required in 2012	= $250 million
PV of cash flows expected (in 2012)	= $185 million
Standard deviation for comparable projects	= 45%
Required rate of return for the typical high-tech burger projects	= 18%
Interest rate	= 8%

BBC's CEO, Ms. Marie Hunt has asked you, the CFO, to help her decide on the investment. What would you do?

2. TVS Corp. has a project with the following estimated values: $10 million by the end of the first year, if the things work out well; and $2.7 million if things do not turn out well. In the latter case, the company can sell the assets for $3 million. There is a 50% chance that the business will succeed. Assets of comparable risk carry a required return of 23%.

a. Based only on the above information, calculate the present value of the project. Round up as you go through the steps.

b. Does this analysis incorporate the option embedded in the project? Should it? Why? If so, what is the option worth? That is, what is the present value of the firm with the embedded option?

3. Refer to problem 2. Suppose now that in each 6-month period the firm may either rise in value by 40% or fall by 30%. Assume further that the company has the option to sell the project at the end of the year for $3 million. What option values emerge?

4. The percentage change for upside and downside changes in problem 2 work out to 92 and −48%. What is the implied volatility? How will the upside and downside value change if the period of analysis is six months and the implied volatility is the same.

Essay Questions

1. What are real options? Describe two types of real options and tell how you would value them.

2. Describe the step-by-step approach of evaluating abandonment option associated with a project.

3. Rocky D. Feller, the CEO of a large American automobile company and is convinced that the long-term prospects of automobile industry in China and India are very good. However, the projects proposed for these two countries turn out to be negative NPV projects. He feels that the project analysis does not do justice to future expansion possibilities in the two countries. Identify the real options involved in the projects and suggest an evaluation approach, which will take into account future prospects available in foreign markets.

4. Discuss the following statement. "All capital budgeting projects include options of various kinds. Therefore, it is better to evaluate them using option valuation techniques rather the DCF approach."

ANSWERS TO EXERCISES

Fill-in Questions

1. Real
2. Abandonment
3. Put
4. Call
5. Timing
6. Flexible production facilities

Problems

1. The problem is an example of a project with a follow-on investment similar to the worked example 1. The follow-on project is a call option and has to be evaluated as such. We can use the Black-Scholes model to evaluate the value of the option.

    Value of the call option $= N(d_1)P - N(d_2) \times PV(EX)$

    $d_1 = \log[P/PV(EX)]/\sigma \sqrt{t} + /\sigma\sqrt{t}/2$, $d_2 = d_1 - \sigma\sqrt{t}$
    $P = \$185/(1.18)^2 = 132.86$; $PV(EX) = \$250/(1.08)^2 = \$214.33$

    $\sigma = 0.45$, $t = 2$ years, $\sigma\sqrt{t} = 0.6364$
    $d_1 = -0.4332$; $d_2 = -1.0696$
    $N(d_1) = 0.3325$; $N(d_2) = 0.1424$

    Value of the call option $= N(d_1)P - N(d_2) \times PV(EX)$
    $= 0.3325 \times \$132.86 - 0.1424 \times 214.33$
    $= \$13.66$ million

The value of the option when added to the NPV of the project, gives a positive value for the project: $-\$10$ million $+ \$13.66$ million $= \$3.66$ million.

2. a. With a 50% chance that the business will succeed, the expected value in year 1 is $(0.50 \times 10) + (0.5 \times 2.7) = \$6.4$ million. At a discount rate of 23%, the present value is $6.4/1.23 = \$5.2$ million. The rest of the problem deals with valuing a put option. Begin with a diagram such as Figure 22-3 and the following information.

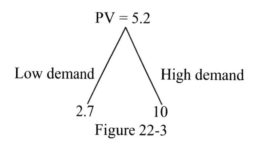

PV = 5.2

Low demand / \ High demand

2.7   10

Figure 22-3

Expected cash flow $=$ [(probability of high demand $\times$ 10) + (probability of low demand $\times$ 2.7)]
$= (0.5 \times 10) + (0.5 \times 2.7) = 6.4$ million
Present value $= 6.4/1.23 = 5.2$ million

b. | | |
    |---|---|
    | Present value of business without option to abandon | $5.2 million |
    | Exercise price | $3.0 million |
    | Maturity | 1 year |
    | Interest rate | 5% |
    | Better-case scenario: Future value with high demand | $10.0 million |
    | Worse-case scenario: Future value with low demand | $2.7 million |

Percentage change in the value of the business:

Upside = (10.0/5.2) − 1 = 0.92 = 92%; Downside = (2.7/5.2) − 1 = 0.46 = − 48%

Next, calculate the probability that value will rise:

$$p = (r − \text{downside change})/(\text{upside change} − \text{downside change})$$
$$= [0.05 − (− 0.48)]/[0.92 − (−0.48)]$$
$$= 0.53/1.48 = 0.38; 1 − p = 0.62$$

If the project is successful, the option to abandon = 0. If it is unsuccessful, the company can sell the assets and net 3.0−2.7 = 0.3 million.

The expected value of the option one period from now is:

$$(\text{probability of rise} × 0) + [(1 − \text{probability of rise}) × 0.3]$$
$$= (0.38 × 0) + (0.62 × 0.3) = \$186,000$$

The current value of the option to abandon is:

$$(\text{expected future value})/(1 + \text{interest rate}) = 186,000/1.05 = \$177,143$$

Value of business with abandonment option = value of business without abandonment
option + value of option
= 5.2 + 0.177 = 5.38 million

3. Figure 22-4 shows the possible firm values by the year-end. When the firm is worth 2.548 million, the option is worth:

Exercise price − firm value = 3 − 2.548 = 452,000

$$p = (r − \text{downside change})/(\text{upside change} − \text{downside change})$$
$$= [0.05 − (− 0.30)]/[0.40 − (−0.30]$$
$$= .35/.70 = 0.5$$
$$1 − p = 0.5$$

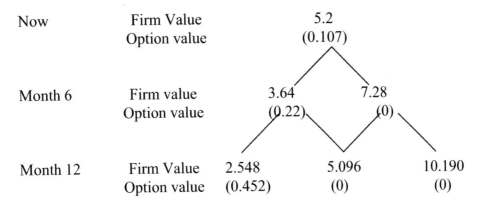

Now	Firm Value	5.2
	Option value	(0.107)
Month 6	Firm value	3.64 7.28
	Option value	(0.22) (0)
Month 12	Firm Value	2.548 5.096 10.190
	Option value	(0.452) (0) (0)

Figure 22-4

Figures in parentheses show the values of an option to sell the firm's assets for $3 million.

In month 6, firm value is 3.64 million, and there is a 50-50 chance that, at the end of the year, the option will be worthless or worth $0.452 million.

Expected value of option at end of year = $(0.5 \times 0) + (0.5 \times 0.452) = \$0.226$ million

Value at month 6 = $0.226/1.025 = \$0.220$ million

Option Value Now: Figure 22-4 contains values in parentheses for each step.
The expected value of the option

in month 6 = [(Probability of rise) × 0] + [(1 − probability of rise) × 0.220]
= $(0.5 \times 0) + (0.5 \times 0.220) = \$0.110$ million

Value today = (expected value of option at month 6)/(1 + interest rate)
= $0.110/1.025 = \$0.107$ million

4. Upside change $= u = 0.92; 1 + u = 1.92 = e^{\sigma\sqrt{h}}$

   $h = 1$; Taking Log of both sides; $\log(1.92) = \sigma\sqrt{h} = 0.652$; $\sigma = 0.652 = 65.2\%$.

   The implied volatility or standard deviation of the annual returns is 65.2%.

   The upside and downside changes for 6-month intervals are:
   Upside change (6-month interval) = $e^{0.652\sqrt{0.5}} - 1 = 1.586 - 1 = 0.59$
   Downside change = $(1/u) - 1 = 1/1.586 - 1 = 0.631 - 1 = -0.37$